BUILDING MODELS FOR MARKETIN

BUILDING MODELS FOR MARKETING DECISIONS

by

Peter S.H. Leeflang
University of Groningen, The Netherlands

Dick R. Wittink
Yale School of Management, U.S.A. and
University of Groningen, The Netherlands

Michel Wedel
University of Groningen, The Netherlands

and

Philippe A. Naert
Tilburg University, The Netherlands

KLUWER ACADEMIC PUBLISHERS
BOSTON / DORDRECHT / LONDON

Library of Congress Cataloging-in-Publication Data

ISBN 0-7923-7772-9 (HB)
ISBN 0-7923-7813-X (PB)

Published by Kluwer Academic Publishers,
P.O. Box 17, 3300 AA Dordrecht, The Netherlands.

Sold and distributed in North, Central and South America
by Kluwer Academic Publishers,
101 Philip Drive, Norwell, MA 02061, U.S.A.

In all other countries, sold and distributed
by Kluwer Academic Publishers,
P.O. Box 322, 3300 AH Dordrecht, The Netherlands.

Printed on acid-free paper

Printed in the Netherlands.

To our spouses:

Hanneke
Marian
Hennie
Magda

Contents

Preface

This book is about marketing models and the process of model building. Our primary focus is on models that can be used by managers to support marketing decisions. It has long been known that simple models usually outperform judgments in predicting outcomes in a wide variety of contexts. For example, models of judgments tend to provide better forecasts of the outcomes than the judgments themselves (because the model eliminates the noise in judgments). And since judgments never fully reflect the complexities of the many forces that influence outcomes, it is easy to see why models of actual outcomes should be very attractive to (marketing) decision makers. Thus, appropriately constructed models can provide insights about structural relations between marketing variables. Since models explicate the relations, both the process of model building and the model that ultimately results can improve the quality of marketing decisions.

Managers often use rules of thumb for decisions. For example, a brand manager will have defined a specific set of alternative brands as the competitive set within a product category. Usually this set is based on perceived similarities in brand characteristics, advertising messages, etc. If a new marketing initiative occurs for one of the other brands, the brand manager will have a strong inclination to react. The reaction is partly based on the manager's desire to maintain some competitive parity in the marketing variables. An economic perspective, however, would suggest that the need for a reaction depends on the impact of the marketing activity for the other brand on the demand for the manager's brand. The models we present and discuss in this book are designed to provide managers with such information.

Compared with only a few decades ago, marketing models have become important tools for managers in many industries. Prior to the introduction of scanner equipment in retail outlets, brand managers depended upon ACNielsen for bimonthly audit data about sales, market shares, prices, etc. for the brands in a given product category. Those data were rarely good enough for the estimation of demand functions. Indeed, Art Nielsen used to say that Nielsen was in the business of reporting the score and was not in the business of explaining or predicting the score. With technological advances (e.g. the availability of scanner data, improved hardware and software), the opportunity to obtain meaningful estimates of demand functions vastly improved.

We use a simplified example to illustrate the possible impact of models on marketing decisions. When the scanner data from supermarkets became available for the first time in the late 1970's, graphs of store sales, prices and promotions over time (weeks) showed that temporary price cuts often produced extremely high increases in sales of the promoted brand. A manager for whom the brand's market share is an important performance measure would be inclined to seize the apparent opportunity to boost sales. Thus, weekly scanner data, offered insights into short-term effects to managers that were unavailable from the bimontly audit data. These new insights formed one of the reasons why promotional expenditures in the US grew dramatically in the 1970's and the 1980's. The modeling of promotional effects was initiated quickly by IRI after scanner data became available. Yet it has taken many years of model building and testing by ACNielsen, IRI and many academic researchers, before a reasonably comprehensive understanding of the effects of promotional activities resulted. The results suggest that the sales increases that are attributed to brand switching are typically negated by competitive reactions. Another part of the sales increase is due to purchase acceleration most of which does not result in consumption increases. In addition, increases in promotional expenditures (relative to, say, television advertising) appear to increase consumers' price sensitivities and to reduce brand loyalties. The extensive amount of modeling that has been done commercially and academically suggests that promotions are rarely profitable. Not coincidentally the insights from models are partly responsible for the apparent decline in promotional expenditures in the US, both in an absolute sense and relative to television advertising in the late 1990's.

Scanner data offer an opportunity for managers to obtain a detailed understanding of the complexities of the marketplace. At the same time the explosion of these data makes it inescapable for the manager to use tools for analysis. Indeed, managers will be more effective decisions makers if they use models for relatively routine decisions so that they have more time for decisions that require creativity and for other elements outside the purview of model building. However, models differ greatly in their quality and usability for marketing decisions. Indeed, many managers have had bad experiences, perhaps because a model builder oversold the model's potential. Alternatively, inappropriate requirements such as: "only a model with a R^2 value of at least 90 percent is acceptable", may have influenced the model-building process in an undesirable manner.

In this revised edition of *Building Implementable Marketing Models* (Naert, Leeflang, 1978) we provide a detailed discussion of the following steps in the model-building process: specification, estimation, validation, and use of the model. The managerial usefulness of a given model will be greatly enhanced if the model-building exercise follows carefully designed procedures. This book is our attempt to provide a structure for model building. The content of the book should be of interest to researchers, analysts, managers and students who want to develop, evaluate and/or use models of marketing phenomena.

Managers will particularly benefit from models of marketing phenomena if they understand what the models do and do not capture. With this understanding they can, for example, augment model-based conclusions with their own expertise about complexities that fall outside the modelers' purview. Importantly, the systematic analysis of purchase (and other) data can provide competitive advantages to managers. Model benefits include cost savings resulting from improvements in resource allocations as we discuss in various applications. And the leaders or first movers in the modeling of marketing phenomena can pursue strategies not available nor transparent to managers lagging in the use of data.

The book is suitable for student use in courses such as "Models in Marketing", "Marketing Science" and "Quantitative Analysis in Marketing" at the graduate and advanced undergraduate level. The material can be supplemented by articles from journals such as the *Journal of Marketing Research, Marketing Science, Management Science and The International Journal of Research in Marketing.*

It consists of four parts. Part I provides an introduction to marketing models. It covers the first four chapters and deals with the definition of a model, the benefits to be derived from model building, and a typology of marketing models.

In part II, which covers 10 chapters, we give guidelines for model specification and we discuss examples of models that were developed in the past thirty years. We start with some elementary notions of model specification. Then we discuss the modeling of marketing dynamics and implementation criteria with respect to model structure. This is followed by a presentation of descriptive, predictive and normative models, models to diagnose competition, etc. We discuss many specification issues such as aggregation, pooling, asymmetry in competition and the modeling of interdependencies between products. The primary focus is on models parameterized with aggregate data. In Chapter 12 we introduce models that describe individual (choice) behavior.

Part III (4 chapters) covers topics such as data collection, parameterization and validation. We present estimation methods for both objective and subjective data.

Aspects of implementation are the topics of Part IV, which covers (three) chapters on determinants of model implementation, cost-benefit considerations and the future of marketing models.

Chapters 2-10 in this book correspond with chapters 2-9 of Naert and Leeflang (1978). These chapters have been updated and rewritten. Chapters 11-18 are new and/or are completely rewritten. Chapters 19 and 20 are partly based on Chapters 13 and 14 from Naert, Leeflang. The discussion about the future of marketing models (Chapter 21) is new.

Several colleagues have contributed with their comments on various drafts. We thank Albert van Dijk, Harald van Heerde, Martijn Juurlink, Marcel Kornelis and Tom Wansbeek (all from the Department of Economics, University of Groningen) for their comments. Harald's input deserves special attention because he is the author of

Section 16.7. We are also indebted to our students whose suggestions improved the readability of the text. Four of them should be mentioned explicitly: Hans Mommer and Martijn van Geelen, who gave important inputs to Section 16.9, Martijn Juurlink and Brian Lokhorst. We are much indebted to Albert van Dijk, Martijn Juurlink and Suwarni Bambang Oetomo for deciphering many barely readable scribbles and for creating a carefully typed form. We would like to thank Siep Kroonenberg for her technical assistance with LaTeX. Albert also showed that he is very adept at managing the manuscript through the various stages until its completion.

Peter Leeflang, Groningen
Dick Wittink, New Haven/Groningen
Michel Wedel, Groningen
Philippe Naert, Tilburg

October, 1999

PART ONE

Introduction to marketing models

CHAPTER 1

Introduction

Model building in marketing started in the fifties. It is now a well-developed area with important contributions by academics and practitioners. Models have been developed to advance marketing knowledge and to aid management decision making. Several state-of-the-art textbooks review and discuss many of the models.[1] This book is a revised version of *Building Implementable Marketing Models* (BIMM).[2] BIMM was not positioned as a "state-of-the-art book". Instead, it elaborated on the following steps in the model-building process: specification, estimation, validation, and use of the model. In the current book we maintain the focus on these steps, with the aim to contribute to the increased implementation of marketing models.

In the past two decades, the use of information in marketing decision making has undergone revolutionary change.[3] There are important developments in the availability of new data sources, new tools, new methods and new models. These developments provide rich opportunities for researchers to provide new insights into the effects of marketing variables, and at the same time force managers to reconsider modus operandi.

Closely related to the process and the activity of model building in marketing is the field of *marketing science*. One interpretation of marketing science is that it represents the scientific approach to the study of marketing phenomena. In its broadest sense this perspective should include the many disciplines relevant to marketing. However, the term marketing science has been appropriated in the early 1980's by researchers who favor quantitative and analytical approaches.

We describe the purpose of the current book in more detail in Section 1.1. In Section 1.2 we present the outline, and in Section 1.3 we define and discuss the concept of a model.

---

1. Some examples are King (1967), Montgomery, Urban (1969), Simon, Freimer (1970), Kotler (1971), Leeflang (1974), Fitzroy (1976), Parsons, Schultz (1976), Lilien, Kotler (1983), Schultz, Zoltners (1981), Hanssens, Parsons, Schultz (1990), Lilien, Kotler, Moorthy (1992) and Eliashberg, Lilien (1993).
2. Naert, Leeflang (1978).
3. Bucklin, Lehmann, Little (1998).

1.1 Purpose

Operations research (OR) and management science (MS) largely emerged during and after World War II with algorithms and processes applicable to production and logistics. Successes in those areas encouraged researchers to solve problems in other areas such as finance and marketing in the early 1960's. Initially, the emphasis was on the application of existing OR/MS methods for the solution of marketing problems. And econometric methods were introduced into marketing to estimate demand relationships. These econometric applications were hampered by the limited availability of relevant data. Thus, the early publications of applied econometrics in marketing have to be seen more as treatises on the possible use of methods than as papers providing useful substantive results. Now, at the end of this millennium it is predicted that in the coming decades, a growing proportion of marketing decisions will be automated by ever-more-powerful combinations of data, models, and computers and

"... *the age of marketing decision* support ... *will usher in the era of marketing decision* automation"

(Bucklin et al., 1998, p. 235).

We distinguish five eras of model building in marketing.[4]

1. The first era is defined primarily by the transposition of OR/MS methods into a marketing framework. These OR/MS tools include mathematical programming, computer simulations, stochastic models (of consumer choice behavior), game theory, and dynamic modeling. Difference and differential equations, usually of the first order, were used to model dynamics.[5] The methods were typically not realistic, and the use of these methods in marketing applications was therefore very limited.

2. The second era can be characterized by models adapted to fit the marketing problems, because it was felt that lack of realism was the principal reason for the lack of implementation of the early marketing models. These more complex models were more representative of reality, but they lacked simplicity and usability. In this era, which ended in the late sixties/early seventies, descriptive models of marketing decision making and early econometric models attracted research attention. In a critical evaluation of the literature, Leeflang (1974) argued that many of those models failed to represent reality. For example, the models typically did not consider the effects of competition, were static and only considered one marketing instrument. Specific models were created to deal with specific marketing problems such as models for product decisions, for pricing decisions, for sales force management decisions, etc. See Montgomery and Urban (1969) and Kotler (1971) for illustrative state-of the-art books in this respect.

3. The third era starts in the early 1970's. There is increased emphasis on models that are good representations of reality, and at the same time are easy to use. Thus the focus

---

4. The definitions of the first three eras are due to Montgomery (1973).
5. See also Eliashberg, Lilien (1993).

shifts from "isolated" decision problems to implementation and implementability.

Pioneering work on the implementation issue is provided by Little (1970) on the concept of a decision calculus. He first examines the question of why models are not used, and he suggests the following possible answers:

- good models are hard to find;
- good parameterization is even harder;
- managers do not understand models;
- most models are incomplete.

Little also prescribes remedial action. He states that a manager needs a decision calculus, i.e. a model-based set of procedures by which the manager can bring data and judgments to bear on the decisions. He proposes criteria which a model must satisfy in order for it to be labeled a decision calculus model. Little (1970, p. B470) argues that a model should be:

- simple;
- robust;
- easy to control;
- adaptive;
- complete on important issues;
- easy to communicate with.

This list includes criteria related to model structure or model specification and criteria related to ease of use. In later publications Little (1975a, 1975b) adds a seventh criterion viz. that a model should be evolutionary. This addition is based on the argument that the user should often start with a simple structure, to which detail is added later. This criterion relates to implementation strategy.

In this era we also see the introduction of models parameterized with subjective (and objective) data. The argument for the use of subjective data is the following. If there is a lack of data or a lack of data with sufficient quality, a model that captures a decision maker's judgment about outcomes under a variety of conditions can provide the basis for superior decisions in future time periods relative to the decision maker's judgments made in those future time periods. The arguments include consistency in model-based judgments and the systematic consideration of variation in multiple variables.[6] Other developments include strategic marketing (planning) models and Marketing Decision Support Systems (MDSS). In addition, some research focuses on the relations between marketing models and organizational design, and between marketing decisions and issues in production and logistics. Importantly, due to Little, this is an era in which researchers attempt to specify implementable marketing models.

4. The fourth era, starting in the mid 1980's, is an era in which many models are actually *implemented*. An important force that drives implementation is the increased

---

6. For more detail see Section 16.9.

availability of marketing data. The data include standard survey and panel data, often collected by computer-aided personal and telephone interviewing, and customer transaction databases.[7] Of particular relevance to the focus of this book is the increasing use by retailers of scanning equipment to capture store- and household-level purchases.[8] This "scanning revolution", combined with developments in the availability of other data services, also stimulates the application of new methods. Thus although marketing problems were initially forced into existing OR/MS frameworks and methods, a subfield in marketing now exists in which quantitative approaches are developed and adapted.[9] The modeling developments focus on questions in product design, on models of consumers' choice processes, on the optimal selection of addresses for direct mail, on models that account for consumer behavior heterogeneity, on marketing channel operations, on optimal competitive strategies and on the estimation of competitive reactions. These developments result in models that increasingly:

- satisfy Little's implementation criteria;
- are parameterized based on a large number of observations;
- account for errors in the data, etc.

The models also tend to be complete on important issues and more frequently consider, for example, all relevant marketing instruments and the effects of competition.[10] Of course, the increased availability of data also offers opportunities for researchers to build models that can advance our marketing knowledge and that can produce generalizable phenomena.

This development has been stimulated by an organized "stream of research" known as "marketing science". Briefly, in 1979 Montgomery and Wittink organized a *Market Measurement and Analysis* conference at Stanford University (Montgomery, Wittink, 1980), sponsored by the Institute of Management Sciences (TIMS) and the Operations Research Society of America (ORSA). The success of this conference led not only to the organization of a similar conference every subsequent year, but also to the renaming of it as the *Marketing Science Conference* a few years later. The net proceeds of the conference are a critical resource for the journal *Marketing Science* first issued in 1982. Both the conference and the journal favor quantitative, analytical treatments of marketing problems. The empirical research tradition, closely aligned with the quantitative, analytical approach, has generated a plethora of published empirical results pertaining to a wide variety of marketing issues. As has occurred in many social sciences, this gave cause to researchers to conduct meta analyses that advance our marketing knowledge (Section 3.3).

---

7. Wansbeek, Wedel (1999).
8. See, for example, Bucklin, Gupta (2000) who report the findings from an exploratory investigation of the use of UPC scanner data in the consumer packaged goods industry in the U.S.
9. Wansbeek, Wedel (1999, p.2).
10. Illustrative in this respect is the statement made by Hanssens (1980b, p. 471) "that the explicit modeling of competitive behavior is fairly rare in market model building, primarily because data on competitive marketing expenditures are very difficult to obtain".

The "fourth era"[11] is also characterized by a latent demand for models by firms. In earlier eras the model builder - model user interface was probably dominated by the supply side. Thus, analysts still had to sell their models and convince the user of potential benefits.

This era can also be characterized as an age of marketing decision support.[12] In the 1980's (and 1990's) there is a virtual explosion of computerized marketing management support systems ranging from "information systems" to "marketing creativity-enhancement programs".[13]

5. The fifth era, starting in the 1990's, may be characterized by an increase in routinized model applications. Bucklin et al. (1998) predict that in the coming decades, the age of marketing decision support will usher in an era of *marketing decision automation*, partly due to the "wealth" of data that can inform decision making in marketing. We also expect that firms increasingly customize their marketing activities to individual stores, customers and transactions.[14] If models and decision support systems take care of routine marketing decisions, then the manager has more opportunity to focus on the non-routine decisions which may require creative thinking. Examples of marketing decisions appropriate for automation are:[15]

- assortment decisions and shelf space allocation decisions for individual stores;
- customized product offerings including individualized pricing and promotion;
- targeting of direct mail solicitations;
- coupon targeting;
- loyalty reward and frequent shopper club programs;
- the creation of promotion calendars, etc.

In Chapter 21 we consider likely future developments in more detail.

In this book we concentrate on the steps in the model-building process that is especially representative of the fourth era. Although we pay attention to models that advance marketing knowledge, our emphasis is on marketing decision models. In the next section we discuss the outline of this book.

1.2 Outline

This book consists of four parts:

- Part I: Introduction to marketing models – Chapters 1–4;
- Part II: Specification – Chapters 5–14;
- Part III: Parameterization and validation – Chapters 15–18;
- Part IV: Use/Implementation – Chapters 19–21.

---

11. See also Plat (1988).
12. Bucklin et al. (1998).
13. Wierenga, van Bruggen (1997) and Chapter 15.
14. See, for example, Hoekstra, Leeflang, Wittink (1999).
15. Bucklin et al. (1998).

Part I deals with the definition of a model, the degree of explicitness in modeling a decision problem, the benefits to be derived from model building, and a typology of marketing models. In Chapter 1, we define the model concept. In Chapter 2, we classify models according to the degree of explicitness, and we distinguish implicit, verbal, formalized, and numerically specified models. One question a potential model user will ask is how a model can help the user. We discuss model benefits in Chapter 3. In this chapter we also discuss models that advance marketing knowledge. Two important determinants of model specification are the intended use of the model and the desired level of behavioral detail. We provide a typology of marketing models based on these two dimensions in Chapter 4. Chapter 4 is the basis for Chapters 8–10 of Part II.

In Chapter 5 we review the main steps of the model-building process, the components of a mathematical model, and some elementary notions of model specification. The sequence of the "traditional" steps, Specification, Parameterization, Validation and Use/Implementation constitutes the structure of what follows.

Marketing is in essence dynamic. In Chapter 6 we discuss the modeling of marketing dynamics. In Chapter 7 we discuss implementation criteria with respect to model structure.

In Chapter 8 we give examples of models specified according to intended use, i.e. according to whether the primary intention is to have a descriptive, predictive, or normative model. One class of predictive models consists of the demand models. We study these models in some detail in Chapter 9. In Chapter 10 we distinguish models according to the amount of behavioral detail (little, some, much).

In Chapters 11–14 we discuss model specifications. In Chapter 11 we introduce models to diagnose competition and game-theoretic approaches, and focus our attention on models parameterized with aggregate (macro) data. In Chapter 12 we introduce models that describe individual choice behavior. We also discuss the modeling of competitive structures based on individual/household (micro) data.

Most firms offer multiple products in the marketplace. In Chapter 13 we discuss the different forms of interdependence between products and illustrate modeling approaches with explicit treatment of some forms of interdependence.

We end Part II with a discussion of specification issues such as aggregation, pooling, the definition of the relevant market, asymmetry in competition, and we introduce hierarchical models (Chapter 14).

Collecting data is the first step of parameterization. The organization of useful data is the central theme of Chapter 15. We also discuss decision-support systems and data sources in this chapter.

In Chapter 16 we consider methods and procedures for parameter estimation, including pooling methods, generalized least squares, simultaneous equation systems, nonparametric and semiparametric estimation, and maximum likelihood estimation. Both estimation from historical data and subjective estimation are discussed. Given that statistical inferences are inherent in the use of results, we also discuss statistical tests that can identify violations of assumptions about the disturbances.

In Chapter 17 we continue with model specification issues and associated estimation methods. We introduce a structural equation model with latent variables, mixture regression models for market segmentation, time series models, and varying parameter models.

Validation is an assessment of model quality. We discuss validation criteria, criteria for model selection, and relevant statistical tests in Chapter 18.

Aspects of implementation are given particular attention in Part IV. In Chapter 19, we discuss organizational aspects of model building, implementation strategy, the relation between model builder and user, and ease of use. Chapter 20 contains a number of cost-benefit considerations relevant to model use. We end with a discussion of the future of models for marketing decisions in Chapter 21. In this final chapter, we also consider the nature of modeling in the fifth era of marketing models.

In practice, model-building exercises often start with an inspection of available data, and a model specification that is based on whatever practical limitations exist. The intent of this book is to provide model builders and users with a broader perspective. We purposely include details about, for example, the process of model building so that both model builders and users can contemplate options that fit specific purposes. Nevertheless, we have decreased the relative emphasis in this book on implementation criteria, compared with BIMM. This change is a reflection of a shift in attention in model applications. Given the availability of large databases and the need for managers to incorporate model-based results in their decisions, it is appropriate to favor data collection, data handling, model specification, parameter estimation, model validation, and decision support issues.

Much of the modeling of marketing phenomena does not follow this sequence, however, and is ad hoc. From a theoretical perspective it is desirable to start with primitives and to derive a model with testable implications. In practice, the demand for unconditional and conditional forecasting tools often negates the development of structurally complete model specifications.

The material we present and discuss reflects of course our own expertise, experience and interests. Thus, many of the applications come from consumer goods manufacturers, which is also consistent with existing papers in the marketing journals. Increasingly, however, we also see useful applications in industrial marketing,[16] international marketing,[17] retail marketing,[18] and the marketing of services.[19] In addition,

16. See, for a survey, Brand and Leeflang (1994).
17. See, for example, Putsis, Balasubramanian, Kaplan and Sen (1997), Ter Hofstede, Steenkamp and Wedel (1999).
18. See, for example, Krishnan, Soni (1997), Popkowski Leszczyc, Timmermans (1997), Bell, Ho, Tang (1998), Iyer (1998), Lal, Villas-Boas (1998), Sirohi, McLaughlan and Wittink (1998).
19. See the special issues of *Management Science*, November, 1995, and September, 1999, Boulding, Kalra, Staelin, Zeithaml (1993), Boerkamp (1995), Bolton (1998), Bolton, Lemon (1999), Putsis, Sen (1999).

our experience is primarily with models based on aggregated data.

Increasingly, household purchase and preference data are used to learn about real-world market behavior. There are important benefits that result from a focus on disaggregate data. One is that at the disaggregate level model specifications tend to be more consistent with plausible conditions of utility maximizing consumers. Another is that heterogeneity in consumer behavior can be observed and fully exploited. A logical consequence of this orientation is that models of aggregate data will be respecified to be consistent with disaggregate models.[20] At the same time, there is an emerging interest among researchers and practitioners to determine the relative advantages and disadvantages of, for example, household- and store-level purchase data.[21]

1.3 The model concept

We now define what we mean by a model and propose the following definition:

A model is a representation of the most important elements of a perceived real-world system.

This definition indicates that models are condensed representations or simplified pictures of reality. We can think of models as structures that are necessary, or at least useful, for decision makers to understand the systematic parts of an underlying reality.

To provide a more detailed perspective, we next discuss the components of this definition.

1. *Real-world system.* We can take the perspective of a manager for whom the system captures the relevant parts of the environment in which the manager makes decisions. The system consists of all elements that have or can have a bearing on the problem under study. The real-world system relevant to this book is the part that deals with the marketing environment (including "non-marketing elements" that have a bearing on marketing decisions). In a narrow sense, we can distinguish marketing models from production models, finance models and corporate models. However, models as representations of the important elements of a system are not restricted to the management sciences but can be found in all sciences. Thus, we can also distinguish physical, psychological, sociological and economic models.[22]

2. *Perceived.* A model is said to be representative of a perceived real-world system. This descriptor is used to indicate that model building is a subjective process. Although researchers may agree on what is to be accomplished, the elements selected and the manner in which the elements are related to each other will vary between model builders. Of course, the outcome of the model-building process also depends

---

20. See Gupta, Chintagunta, Kaul and Wittink (1996), for an example.
21. See Bodapati and Gupta (1999), for an analysis of conditions under which store-level data can provide superior results inclusive of household heterogeneity.
22. Tinbergen (1966, p.6).

on the user, the interactions between model builder and user, and the intended use.[23] Importantly, by describing the subjective interpretation of the real-world system, the model builder explicates the perceptions. Thus, others can debate whether important elements are omitted, whether the relationships expressed are inadequate, etc.

3. *Most important elements.* The purpose of a model is often for the user to obtain a better understanding of the real world it represents. Perhaps especially in marketing, because it deals with human behavior, the relevant part of the real world is potentially very complex. For example, consumer purchase decisions are influenced by economic as well as psychological and sociological motivations. Marketing managers use a diversity of appeals directed at many different segments of consumers. Thus, the demand functions which represent the central part of model building in marketing can potentially contain an almost infinite number of factors.

Models are intended to capture the most important elements out of this complexity. One reason is that it is truly impossible to provide a complete representation of the part of the real world relevant to a marketing manager. Another reason is that managers can obtain a better understanding of the real world by focusing only on the most critical elements. This idea is also reflected in other definitions of models such as the descriptions of models as simplified pictures[24] or stylized representations.[25]

Complex marketing systems can be simplified by, for example:[26]

- neglecting those elements that individually should have small effects;
- compartmentalizing the system into subsystems, and treating the subsystems independently (which implies that dependencies between the subsystems are ignored);
- aggregating data.

For each of these simplifying schemes, it is critical that the model builder decides that the benefits expected from simplification exceed the costs. In addition, the importance of including specific elements in the model depends on the model's intended use. For example, models intended to provide unconditional forecasts should usually be much simpler than models intended to provide substantively useful forecasts conditional upon the marketing activities to be selected by the manager.

4. *Representation.* We can represent the system being studied not only by choosing the most important elements, but also through the form in which the system is expressed. Perhaps the simplest form of representation is the *verbal* one.[27] Another simple form is an *analog* one which is used to show physical measures such as speed

---

23. The idea that no unique representation of a system exists has been referred to by Lilien (1975, p.12) as "model relativism".
24. Leeflang (1974, p.8).
25. Lilien, Rangaswamy (1998, p.6).
26. We return to this issue in Section 7.2.1.
27. We can also use implicit models but these tend to suffer from a lack of transparency.

(speedometer) or temperature (thermometer). In some fields, such as manufacturing or architecture, one uses small-scale models of physical configurations, referred to as *iconic* models.

We focus on representations of marketing relations by way of *mathematical* or *symbolic* models. In these models mathematical symbols are used to represent the most important elements of a system. To obtain the greatest benefit from model use it is advisable for the model builder to make explicit the relationships between the elements in the system being modeled. Models that do not contain a numerical specification of these relationships are defined as *formalized* models. By contrast, the models of greatest interest to us are *numerically specified* models. In these models we show not only the direction of relationships between variables but also the magnitudes of effects.

We discuss ways to represent marketing systems more extensively in Chapter 2.

Classifying marketing models according to degree of explicitness

In Chapter 1 we defined a model as a representation of the most important elements of a perceived real-world system. In this chapter, we consider a number of ways of representing these elements, the differentiating dimension being the "degree of explicitness". We distinguish implicit models, verbal models, formalized models, and numerically specified models, and illustrate different methods of representing systems with an example.

2.1 Implicit models

In marketing practice, it is often said that managers approach problems in an intuitively appealing manner and use experience to solve problems in an ad hoc manner. One might be tempted to believe that these decision makers do not use models. This, however, is not the case. If intuition and experience are the basis for a solution, decision makers have implicitly made use of *a model*. But the model is not necessarily recorded in a communicable form; it is *an implicit model* which so far is present only in the brain of the decision maker.

The very fact that a manager is capable of making decisions implies that he has some *representation* in his mind, no matter how rudimentary, of the environment relevant to the problem he faces, where environment includes all aspects pertaining to his problem. In this sense, all decisions are in fact model based. Details of the implicit model can sometimes be inferred from the decisions made and the associated characteristics of the environment. Alternatively, the decision maker can describe how he proceeds.

2.2 Verbal models

The first step in making a model explicit is for a manager to state in *words* what he perceives as the important elements surrounding a problem. This is more easily said than done. There are many examples in the (marketing) literature which illustrate the difficulty of communicating one's thinking. A case in point is a descriptive model[1] of a pricing decision process constructed by Howard and Morgenroth (1968), based on interviews held with company executives over a period of two years.[2] The executives felt that it was virtually impossible for them to describe how they arrived at pricing decisions. Interestingly, the descriptive model ultimately obtained was relatively simple, and its predictions corresponded closely to actual decisions. This illustrates that the executives had a well-structured perception of the environment surrounding the pricing decisions, but had great difficulty in verbalizing or otherwise communicating their views.

We consider a simple example to illustrate the notion of a *verbal* model. Take a monopolist who produces and sells one product. For the last five years, price (in real dollars) has remained constant and sales per capita have also been quite stable. He wonders whether the current price is optimal in a profit maximizing sense. He believes that a price reduction will lead to increased unit sales, and a price increase to reduced unit sales. However, a price reduction will also result in a smaller unit contribution (unit price – unit cost), while a price increase will make the unit contribution higher. Thus the monopolist realizes that there is a trade-off between changes in the number of units sold and changes in the contribution per unit, and that there is a price that maximizes his total contribution to fixed costs and profit. What he is really saying is that there exists a demand curve, and by changing the (real) price he can learn how price influences demand. In this manner the monopolist can communicate elements that are the basis for a verbal model.

Our monopolist wants to determine the price leading to optimal profit by trial and error. He is aware of the fact that by using such a procedure, it is unlikely for him to obtain the exactly optimal price and corresponding profit. Specifically, he will continue to change his price until the improvement in profit, $\Delta\pi$, is smaller than a predetermined amount δ. He might also have other insights such as: "I will not increase my price by more than twenty percent, because then I would be inviting potential competitors to enter the market. In the long run, my profit figure would shrink". His view of the market environment is now somewhat broader. He now wants to maximize profit, subject to a price constraint p_c, reflecting his belief in limit pricing, although he has probably never heard of this term.[3] We could go on and see what other influences he perceives, such as the role of advertising and distribution, but the preceding illustrates what we mean by a verbal model.

---

1. A descriptive model, as the name indicates, describes a situation or a decision-making process. The notion of a descriptive model will be discussed in Sections 4.1 and 8.1.
2. The ultimate model is a logical flow model, but this was constructed on the basis of verbal descriptions of the elements of the model and their interactions. The notion of a logical flow model is defined in Section 2.3. A recent example can be found in Brand (1993). Brand describes the complex organizational buying process of heat exchangers with a so-called buying process-simulation model; see Section 8.1.
3. A *limit price* has the property that prices above its value will stimulate entry by competitors, whereas lower prices will discourage entry.

> *"I will change my price in steps with each change equal to plus or minus Δp, until the increase in profit is less than a predetermined amount δ, with the restriction that price stays below the value p_c."*

Figure 2.1 Verbal model for profit satisficing monopolist.

The verbal model can be represented as in Figure 2.1.[4]

2.3 Formalized models

In most marketing problems, there is a variety of variables which can play an important role. These variables may have complex effects on the demand. For a description of the relationships in words it may be difficult or even impossible to keep all relevant characteristics and conditions in mind. To illustrate the idea, we complicate the example given in Section 2.2 by adding advertising as a second marketing instrument. Increases in advertising expenditures may lead to increased sales, but total costs will increase as well. The complexity of sales effects is indicated by the idea that advertising expenditures in period t (say April, 1999) may not only lead to increases in sales in period t but also to increases in period $t + 1$ (say May, 1999), and possibly may contribute to increases in sales in the periods after $t + 1$. Increases in sales in April, 1999 will result in changes in the total contribution (= per unit contribution times number of units sold) in April, 1999 and this may lead to changes in advertising expenditures in future periods.[5] Thus relations may exist between:

- advertising expenditures in t and unit sales in t;
- advertising expenditures in t and sales in $t + 1$;
- advertising expenditures in t and sales in $t + 2$ (and perhaps later periods);
- sales in t and advertising expenditures in $t + 1$; etc.

In order to make relationships more precise it is necessary to formalize them. This means that we specify which variables influence which other variables and what the directions of causality between these variables are. The representation of a system through formalized relationships between the most important variables of a system is called a formalized model. Within the class of formalized models we make a further distinction between logical flow models and formalized mathematical models.

---

4. See for other examples: Montgomery and Urban (1969, pp. 9-12), Boyd and Massy (1972, pp. 17-21), Lilien, Kotler, Moorthy (1992, pp. 1-7).

5. This is based on the fact that many firms determine advertising expenditures on the basis of past revenue performance. While this runs contrary to the general belief that advertising is a determinant of sales and not the other way around, fixing the level of the advertising budget as a percentage of past sales nevertheless remains a common corporate practice. See Schmalensee (1972, Chapter 2), Cooil, Devinney (1992) and Batra, Myers, Aaker (1996, p. 551).

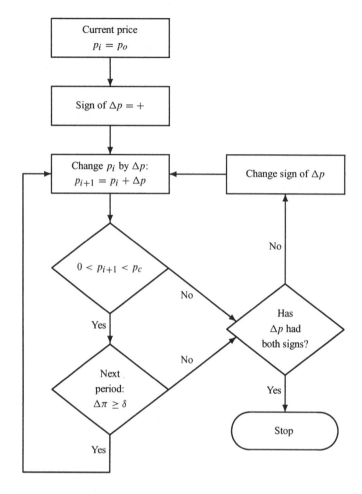

Figure 2.2 Logical flow model for profit satisficing monopolist.

A *logical flow model* represents an extension of the verbal model by the *use of a diagram*. This diagram shows the sequence of questions and of actions leading to a solution of the problem. This kind of model is also known as a *graphical* or a *conceptual model*. The flow diagram makes clear, or more explicit, what the manager has put in words. Such a diagram can serve as a basis for discussions. The diagram may show discrepancies between the formalized model and the decision maker's thinking. It can also be used to identify possible inconsistencies in the model.

A *formalized mathematical model* represents a part of the real-world system by specifying relations between some explanatory (predictor) variables and some effect (criterion) variable(s).

We now return to the example of the monopolist described in Section 2.2. Our decision maker wants to try a price increase first, and he wants to change price in increments equal to Δp. The *logical flow model* representing the monopolist's problem

$$\max_p \pi = (p - c)q - FC \quad (2.1)$$
subject to
$$0 < p < p_c \quad (2.2)$$
where
$$q = f(p). \quad (2.3)$$

Figure 2.3 *Formalized mathematical model for profit optimizing monopolist.*

is shown in Figure 2.2.

In this figure, the following notation is used:

p_o = original or current price,

$\Delta\pi$ = change in profit,

δ = a predetermined amount of $\Delta\pi$ used as a termination measure for the trial-and-error procedure, and

p_c = limit price above which competitive entry becomes likely.

We emphasize that this example is only an illustration. We do not suggest that firms will actually arrive at (almost) optimal prices on the basis of a trial-and-error procedure applied in the market place. There are several aspects that restrict managers' abilities to learn about the demand curve in such a trial-and-error procedure. For example, markets may not adjust instantaneously to price changes. Also, the environment cannot be assumed to remain constant. Thus, the demand for the product may change because of factors not yet considered explicitly. Even if the environment were to remain constant the relation between demand and price is not deterministic. If the observed demand after each price change is subject to an unknown amount of uncertainty, then the flow model shown in Figure 2.2 can produce incorrect results. We also note that the model's adequacy depends on the actual shape of the demand function.

If we assume that price is the only variable which determines sales of the product, the *formalized mathematical model* can be represented as in Figure 2.3.

The mathematical symbols are defined as follows:

π = total profit,

p = price per unit,

c = variable cost per unit (assumed constant),

q = number of units sold,

FC = fixed costs,

p_c = limit price above which competitive entry becomes likely, and

q = $f(p)$ indicates that q is a function of the price per unit.

Equation (2.1) states that profit is equal to sales revenue (pq), minus variable production costs (cq), minus fixed costs (FC). This type of model is not very useful from a managerial decision making point of view because nothing is said about *how* demand (q) depends on price. In the logical flow model this relation is *approached* by trial-and-error. If the manager wants to have a clear description of how decisions are currently made, a logical flow model may be sufficient. In the following section and in Chapter 5, we shall devote extensive attention to the specification of the demand relations.

2.4 Numerically specified models

In numerically specified models, the various components and their interrelations are quantified. The decision maker's objective is now to disentangle the kind of relationships described in Section 2.3. A set of mathematical relations written "on the back of an envelope" may do the job, which suggests that the model purpose has implications as to the desired "degree of explicitness". For this reason we classify models along that dimension.

Even if optimization is the ultimate reason for modeling a particular problem, having a numerically specified model is not always a prerequisite. For example, the logical flow model in Section 2.3 may, under certain conditions, allow the decision maker to find a near-optimal price, without having to specify the demand function numerically. Nevertheless, numerically specified models are, in many situations, the most appropriate representations of real-world systems. Below we examine why a numerically specified model might be more appropriate than a flow model.

First of all, a numerically specified model will allow the decision maker to quantify the effects of multiple, and potentially conflicting forces. Consider, for example, the monopolist decision maker who realizes that "there is a trade-off between changes in sales and changes in (unit) contribution". Specifying a model numerically will provide precision to the statements that a price increase results in a sales decrease and an advertising increase results in a sales increase.

Secondly, we may say that if a numerically specified model constitutes a reasonable representation of a real-world system, it can be used to examine the consequences of alternative courses of action and market events. We can imagine that a properly numerically specified model provides the decision maker with an opportunity to conduct experiments. Once various relationships are quantified, the decision maker can contemplate how the demand varies with price and other changes. It should be clear that such experiments are inexpensive, and less risky than the market experiments conducted by the monopolist (in Sections 2.2 and 2.3). If a decision maker changes a product's actual price frequently in order to determine the near-optimal price, many consumers may be turned away, with potentially long-term consequences.

Thus, a numerically specified model gives management the opportunity to explore the consequences of a *myriad of actions*, a capability which cannot normally be duplicated in the real world. These considerations lead to the use of simulation models, both in the sense of providing answers to "what if" types of questions and in the sense of dealing with stochastic (uncertain) elements. Of course, the representation of real-world systems by numerically specified models provides advantages, conditional

$$\max_p \pi = (p - c)q - 100 \quad (2.1a)$$
subject to
$$0 < p < p_c \quad (2.2a)$$

$$q = 10\,p^{-2}. \quad (2.3a)$$

Figure 2.4 Numerically specified model for a profit optimizing monopolist.

upon the model being a reasonable representation of reality. How to construct and evaluate such representations is an important objective of this book.

Having presented some advantages, we should also consider disadvantages. Building and using models costs money, and the more complicated and the more explicit models become, the more expensive they will be. Thus weighing the costs against the benefits will always be a necessary step in the modeling process.

We conclude this chapter by showing in Figure 2.4 a numerical specification for the example of the preceding sections. The symbols are the same as in Figure 2.3. In Figure 2.4 we assume that the fixed costs (*FC*) are equal to $100. The difference between Figure 2.3 and Figure 2.4 is the numerically specified relation[6] between q and p (relation 2.3a). This relation is of the form:

$$q = \alpha p^\beta \tag{2.4}$$

generally known as a multiplicative function or relation. The coefficients α and β are referred to as the model parameters, are unknown, but can be estimated (i.e., approximate values can be obtained) in a number of ways. In some cases, an analysis of historical data will be possible. Alternatively we can use subjective estimation methods.

In order to illustrate how the optimal value for the price variable can be obtained, we assume that the optimal price is smaller than p_c. Once the parameters have been determined (as in (2.3a)), the optimal price can be obtained by differentiating the profit function with respect to price, setting it equal to zero, and solving for price. This is shown below. We start by substituting (2.3a) in (2.1a):

$$\pi = (p - c)10\,p^{-2} - 100 \tag{2.5}$$
$$= 10\,p^{-1} - 10\,cp^{-2} - 100.$$

Differentiating this equation with respect to p (assuming c to be constant):

$$\frac{d\pi}{dp} = -10\,p^{-2} + 20\,cp^{-3}. \tag{2.6}$$

---

6. The terms "numerically specified marketing model" and "marketing model" will be used interchangeably from now on unless otherwise indicated.

Setting (2.6) equal to zero and solving for p we obtain:

$$p = 2c \tag{2.7}$$

which implies that the monopolist should use a markup of 100 percent. To make sure that $p = 2c$ corresponds to a maximum, second-order conditions should be examined. For reasonable specifications of demand and profit functions, these will generally be satisfied. The expression for the second-order condition in our example is:

$$\frac{d^2\pi}{dp^2} = +20p^{-3} - 60\,cp^{-4} \tag{2.8}$$

which for a maximum should be negative.

Substituting $p = 2c$ in (2.8) we get:

$$\frac{d^2\pi}{dp^2} = \frac{20}{8c^3} - \frac{60\,c}{16\,c^4} = \frac{-20}{16\,c^3} < 0 \tag{2.9}$$

which means that $p = 2c$ leads to a maximum value of π.

We want to emphasize that the procedure described above has limited real-world applicability. The demand function was assumed to be deterministic whereas in reality all coefficients are estimates, and we would want to know the quality of these estimates, and how sensitive optimal price and optimal profits are to changes in their values. Furthermore, in Section 2.4, the limit price was not considered. Adding this constraint makes the optimization procedure somewhat more difficult. We should also bear in mind that the example discussed in this chapter was kept unrealistically simple. Marketing problems generally involve more than one decision variable, multiple objectives (for example, market expansion in addition to a profit goal and some constraints), multiple products[7] and multiple territories. In addition, unit variable production cost may vary with quantity produced and thus with price. Finally, monopolies being the exception rather than the rule, models will have to account for competitive activity.[8] Nevertheless, the example illustrates that part of a real-world system can be represented in different ways, according to the degree of explicitness chosen.

---

7. See Chapter 13.
8. See Chapter 11.

CHAPTER 3

Benefits from using marketing models

Before delving into details of marketing model building, we discuss the potential benefits that can be derived from models.

In Section 3.1, we examine whether marketing problems are in fact quantifiable, and to what extent.

In Section 3.2, we examine direct and indirect benefits of models, the primary purpose of a model being to provide decision support for marketing management.

We recognize that models may be developed for different reasons. For example, models can be helpful for the discovery of lawlike generalizations, which may improve our knowledge and understanding of marketing phenomena. We elaborate on this type of model building in Section 3.3. We note that the approaches presented in Sections 3.2 and 3.3 are complementary. Models for decision making are often short-term oriented. In the process of building such models, we will learn about marketing relationships, and this learning may lead to the discovery of lawlike generalizations. At the same time, decision models should incorporate any generalizable knowledge that already exists. In this sense the approaches inform each other.

We conclude Chapter 3 with a short case study in Section 3.4. This case serves to clarify the basic model concepts defined in Chapter 1, and at the same time it illustrates some of the benefits listed in Section 3.2.

3.1 Are marketing problems quantifiable?

Intuition is the basis for much marketing problem solving. This is generally justified by the argument that, because of their complexity, marketing problems are of a non-quantifiable nature. This complexity is sometimes used as an excuse for a reluctance to build a model. We do not pretend that a mathematical model can be used to approach every marketing problem, nor that each problem is completely quantifiable. In general, marketing problems are neither strictly quantitative nor strictly qualitative, and we believe that both quantitative and qualitative approaches are necessary to solve marketing problems. Just as a vector has not only a direction but also a length, marketing phenomena may be considered as consisting of two components, a qualitative and a quantitative (or quantifiable) one. Thus, we do not support the argument that a mathematical model can constitute a complete solution for every marketing problem. But we also do not subscribe to the notion that sophisticated approaches are useless for the ill-structured problems that are common in marketing. To illustrate the tensions consider the following example.[1]

The marketing director of a company wants to determine the size of his sales force.[2] He knows that a strong sales force is important, but also that at some point increases in the size are subject to the law of diminishing returns. His intuition cannot tell him whether the size of the sales force should be, say, 5, 10 or 15 persons. Estimates of the expected returns from sales forces of various sizes may assist him in the choice of a number that strikes a balance between the demand for immediate return on investment in the sales force and a desire for investment in sales growth. To this end he needs a formalized model, data and a numerical specification obtained from data. However, the marketing director is faced with the problem that the fluctuations in his sales force have been modest over time: the size has varied from seven to ten representatives. He believes that past data cannot be used to infer what the relation will be between returns and size outside the range of values that have occurred in the past. This lack of variability in the data can be overcome by collecting subjective judgments (see below).

Once an optimal budget for the sales force is determined, the marketing manager still has to formulate the manner in which the sales people should divide their time between large and small customers and/or between acquiring new customers and keeping existing ones. An analytical treatment of an experiment can indicate how salespeople should allocate their time. A distribution of customer sizes plus a measure of the effectiveness of the sales force may indicate how many customers the sales force should concentrate on and how much time should be spent on holding current and on converting new customers. The marketing director and the sales people already know that it is harder to acquire a customer than to keep one. Their intuition fails to tell them *how much* harder this is. They also know that it is important to concentrate on large customers. However, their intuition can not tell them whether this should be, say, the 500 largest, the 1,000 largest or the 5,000 largest.

From this example it is clear that the *direction* of a solution for a marketing problem can often be found by a qualitative analysis. A more quantitative treatment of the problem can be instrumental in finding the "approximate length" of the solution. Models and data are necessary, although not always sufficient to determine this "length".

If market data are not available for model estimation, marketing scientists can rely on managerial judgments. These subjective judgments can be used to calibrate a model. This approach is used, for example, in the CALLPLAN model for Syntex (Lodish, 1971). This approach represents the best one can do with the limited information at hand but it can leave everyone somewhat uneasy.[3] On using subjective estimates, the Syntex senior vice-president of sales and marketing concluded:

---

1. See also Herniter and Howard (1964, p. 38).
2. This example is taken from Leeflang (1995) and based on ideas of a model developed by Rangaswamy, Sinha and Zoltners (1990). See also LaForge, Cravens (1985) and Blattberg, Hoch (1990).
3. See Chakravarti, Mitchell, Staelin (1981).

"Of course, we knew that the responses we estimated were unlikely to be the 'true responses' in some absolute knowledge sense, but we got the most knowledgeable people in the company together in what seemed to be a very thorough discussion, and the estimates represented the best we could do at the time. We respect the model results, but we will use them with cautious skepticism"

(Clarke, 1983, p.10).

The next example illustrates how a qualitative and a quantitative approach are complementary.[4] In the Netherlands, 1989 was a crucial year in the development of the television advertising market. In October 1989, private broadcasting was introduced (RTL4) and there was a substantial expansion of air-time available for TV commercials on the public broadcasting channels.

Based on pressure from various parties, the Dutch government had to face the problem whether or not to permit the introduction of private broadcasting in the Netherlands in 1988. This issue is closely related to other problems connected with the laws and rules surrounding the public broadcasting system. In this system, the total time available for commercials was restricted, and for years there had been an excess demand for broadcast commercials. In some periods the demand for television advertising was three times the supply. The government restricted the time available for commercials to minimize the transfer of advertising expenditures from daily newspapers and magazines to television. This transfer was a threat to the survival of many of the smaller newspapers and magazines, and their survival was considered essential to the preservation of a pluriform press.

International developments (such as adaptations in laws, as a consequence of the birth of the internal European market (after 1992), the entry of European satellite broadcasting stations), and the lobby and pressure of advertisers and advertising agencies led the government to reconsider the amount of air time available for advertising on public television. In order to obtain a basis for sound decision making, several marketing scientists were invited by the Dutch government to study:

a. the impact of an increase in the availability of commercial time in the *public* broadcasting system on the demand for advertising in newspapers and magazines;
b. the effects of the introduction of *private* broadcasting on the advertising volume in newspapers, magazines *and* public broadcasting.

Econometric models were used to estimate the effect of an expansion of public broadcasting advertising time on the allocation by firms of advertising expenditures to daily newspapers and magazines. The results of this analysis are described elsewhere.[5] However, these models could not predict the effects of new entrants. Hence, the challenge was to develop and use a research method to obtain quantitative predictions of the effects of the introduction of private broadcasting on advertising expenditures in other media. For this, the researchers employed an intention survey which was

---

4. This example is taken from Alsem, Leeflang (1994).
5. See Alsem, Leeflang, Reuyl (1990, 1991), Leeflang, Alsem, Reuyl (1991).

administered to advertisers and advertising agencies. This survey is discussed in more detail in Chapters 16 and 18.

We conclude by repeating that the "direction" of a solution can often be found by a non-quantitative analysis. A quantitative treatment of the problem, however, can be instrumental in finding the "approximate length" of the solution.

3.2 Benefits from marketing decision models

In this section, we consider benefits which may result from building and using marketing models. A more complete discussion of benefits and possible disadvantages ("costs") is postponed until Chapter 20.

We first consider *decision* models. These models focus, or at least they should focus, on the manager's perception of the environment in which he operates. A marketing scientist attempts to describe this world with models in such a way that he can give the decision maker assistance.[6] Typically one starts with a specific problem in one particular firm, with a manager looking for help in making decisions. The resulting models do not provide *final answers* to the *general problems* of new-product selection, marketing mix decisions, sales force allocation, media selection, etc. Instead, the models should be helpful in specific situations, which of course does not preclude that learning will take place, eventually resulting in knowledge of a more general nature. Models that focus exclusively on the generation of knowledge do not satisfy the criteria of decision models.

Since decision models are built originally for solving specific problems, some solution is required in the immediate future. As a result, decision models are based on what we know, or on what we think we know. The decision maker does not have the luxury to wait for additional or new knowledge to be developed elsewhere. Thus, decision models must be directly applicable. In that case the models are often referred to as being relevant. We call this a managerial or operational definition of relevance. Not all the work in marketing science fits this narrow definition. For example, academic research which is currently considered non-implementable in practice, might become operational a few years hence. Therefore it would be a mistake to require all model building to be directly applicable. Such a requirement would reflect a very short-term view, which affects long-run progress in the field negatively.

We now turn to the expected benefits. Here we make a distinction between direct and indirect benefits. Although the line between these two types of benefits is not always easy to draw, we define indirect benefits to be those that are not related directly to the reasons for which the model was built in the first place. In this sense, most indirect benefits will only be realized slowly over time.

---

6. This is reminiscent of Bowman's (1967) early work on consistency and optimality in management decision making.

Direct benefits[7]

Companies invest in model building presumably because it leads to better decisions. "Better" is understood here as contributing to the fulfillment of the company's goals. For example, if the firm's single objective is to maximize profit, the benefits of a model can be defined as the incremental discounted profit generated by having the model as opposed to not having it.[8] This requires knowledge of the amount of incremental profit over time, or of some proxy measure. Furthermore, the relevant time horizon has to be determined, and a discount rate defined.

We provide a few examples to suggest how direct benefits may materialize:

1. Suppose a model indicates that a firm is overspending on advertising, i.e. the marginal cost from advertising exceeds the marginal revenue. Adjusting the spending level will result in higher profitability.
2. A promotion budget can be allocated over different instruments such as displays, featuring (support of retailers' advertising by manufacturers), bonuses, refunds, samples, etc. A model can help in this allocation process by showing how the different instruments contribute to the profit resulting from any possible allocation.
3. Marketing managers are often faced with the question whether they should increase their advertising budget *or* whether they should decrease their prices. It has been found, however, that the optimal price also depends on the advertising budget.[9]
4. In sealed competitive bidding, candidates submit a price and the lowest bidder wins.[10] Systematizing information on past bidding behavior into a model may result in a pricing strategy that will lead to an increase in expected profit.

In some cases it is difficult to measure the benefits directly while in other cases it is straightforward. Examples of both are given in Section 20.3. The measurement is complicated by the fact that a cost-benefit evaluation should be carried out before (1) the model is built and (2) before it is implemented.

Indirect benefits

1. A marketing manager does not have to be explicit about his understanding of the environment in which he operates. He may decide on a multi-million dollar advertising budget without detailed knowledge about the effectiveness of advertising in influencing sales. A model would force him to explicate how the market works. This explication alone will often lead to an *improved understanding* of the role of advertising and how advertising effectiveness might depend on a variety of other

---

7. The discussion of benefits follows Naert (1977).
8. We note that the model itself will often be used to compute the incremental profit. This is not without danger, as is discussed in Section 20.3.
9. See Bemmaor, Mouchoux (1991), Kaul, Wittink (1995).
10. There are other schemes, such as awarding the contract to the bidder closest to the average bid price, where the average is computed on all bids, excluding the lowest and the highest. For a survey of alternative procedures, see Weverbergh (1977) and Lilien, Kotler, Moorthy (1992, pp. 209-212).

marketing and environmental conditions. Managers may force themselves to specify how marketing activities affect consumer demand. This confrontation shows what managers believe they know well and what they are uncertain about. If the confrontation occurs in a group, the discussion can provide valuable reasons why marketing activities should provide specified types of effects. Such an exercise is also very useful prior to model estimation. It puts management beliefs on record, and this allows for a comparison between model results with those beliefs. It has also been found that model-building exercises have encouraged managers to state their views and assumptions more clearly and explicitly than ever before.

2.   Models may work as *problem-finding* instruments. That is, problems may emerge after a model has been developed. Managers may identify problems by discovering differences between their perception of the environment and a model of that environment. To illustrate, Leeflang (1977a) observed a negative partial relation between the market share of a detergent brand and the penetration of the number of automatic washing machines. One interpretation of this relation is that the brand was perceived by households as being less appropriate to use in these machines (relative to other brands).

3.   Information is often available but not used. There are many examples of decisions which would have been *reversed* if available information had been used. Management may not know that data exist, or may lack methods for handling the information. Models can be instrumental *in improving the process by which decision makers deal with existing information.*

4.   Models can help managers decide *what information should be collected.* Thus models may lead to improved data collection, and their use may avoid the collection and storage of large amounts of data without apparent purpose. Clearly, model development should usually occur before data collection.[11]

5.   Models can also *guide research* by identifying areas in which information is lacking, and by pointing out the kinds of experiments that can provide useful information. By using models, managers have a better understanding of what they need to know and how experiments should be designed to obtain that information. To illustrate, suppose that *by parameterization* of a model we learn that the average effect of advertising on sales in some periods differs from the average effect in other time periods. To explain such differences we need additional information about changes in advertising messages, the use of media, etc.

6.   A model *often allows management to pinpoint changes in the environment faster* than is possible otherwise. This is illustrated in Figure 3.1. Consider the time periods starting with period 16, which show both forecasted and observed values (part B). We note that through period 20, forecasted and actual sales are very close. In period 21, a decrease is forecasted, but actual sales fall even more. The difference between fore-

---

11.   See, e.g. Forrester (1961) and Urban (1974).

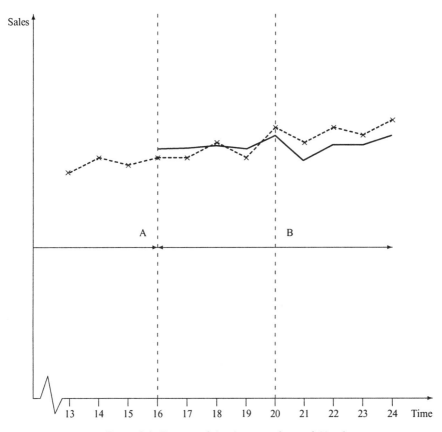

Figure 3.1 Forecasted (- - -) versus observed (-) sales.

casted and observed values persists in subsequent periods. This points to a very useful aspect of models namely, their *diagnostic capacity*. Since the deviation in period 21 is larger than in previous periods, the managers may conclude that something has changed in the environment. It remains to be determined exactly what has changed, but the model warns the manager faster than is usually possible without it.

The difference between actual and forecasted sales may be due to competitive activity, such as a new product being marketed with substantial marketing effort, or a price decrease by a competitor or another factor that influences sales but is omitted from the model. The model helps the manager to detect a possible problem more quickly, by giving him an early signal that something outside the model has happened.[12]

7.   Models provide a *framework for discussion*. If a relevant performance measure (such as market share) is decreasing, the model user may be able to defend himself to point to the effects of changes in the environment that are beyond his control, such as new product introductions by the competition. Of course, a top manager may also

---

12. This point is also emphasized by Little (1975b).

employ a model to identify poor decisions by lower-level managers.

To illustrate, consider the framework developed by Hulbert and Toy (1977). Their framework is used to evaluate marketing performance versus plan. They decompose a variance (difference) in profit contribution in the following way:

$$q_a cm_a - q_p cm_p = \text{var} \cdot (\text{price/cost}) + \text{var} \cdot (\text{market size}) \qquad (3.1)$$
$$+ \text{var} \cdot (\text{share})$$

where

$$\text{var} \cdot (\text{price/cost}) = q_a(cm_a - cm_p),$$
$$\text{var} \cdot (\text{market size}) = m_p cm_p(Q_a - Q_p),$$
$$\text{var} \cdot (\text{share}) = Q_a cm_p(m_a - m_p),$$
$$q_a, q_p = \text{actual respectively planned brand sales,}$$
$$cm_a, cm_p = \text{actual/planned contribution margin,}$$
$$Q_a, Q_p = \text{actual/planned product class sales,}$$
$$m_a, m_p = \text{actual/planned market share.}$$

Thus a variance in *profit* contribution could arise from differences between actual and planned: (1) contribution per unit, (2) product class sales, and (3) market share. In this decomposition price and quantity are assumed to be independent, while in most cases they are interrelated. An analyst of profit contribution variance should, of course, use appropriate market response functions. Albers (1998) developed a principle that decomposes the profit contribution variance into separate variances associated with the effects of single marketing instruments.

8. Finally, a model may result in a *beneficial reallocation of management time*, which means less time spent on programmable, structured, or routine and recurring activities, and more time on less structured ones. Examples of structured activities are media-allocation decisions, inventory decisions, decisions on the allocation of the sales force over areas, customers or products, decisions on how many mailings to send to each of many (potential) customers, etc.

3.3 Building models to advance our knowledge of marketing

In this section, we concentrate on the development of models when the primary purpose is the advancement of knowledge. New knowledge is acquired when generalizable phenomena are found, resulting in laws of marketing. In that sense, the approach is more long-term oriented and it transcends the specificity of a particular problem.

A well-known advocate of this approach to model building is Ehrenberg. His basic model-building philosophy is described in a book on repeat buying (1972), and various other sources.[13] He distinguishes two kinds of research traditions in market-

---

13. See Ehrenberg (1990, 1994, 1995). For some models see Chapter 12.

ing viz.: the Theoretical-in-Isolation or TiI and the Empirical-then-Theoretical or EtT approaches (Ehrenberg, 1994). The two research traditions can each be characterized in two steps:

Theoretical-in-Isolation or TiI or TE (first Theory then Empirical generalization):

1. Construct a theoretical model or analysis approach.
2. Test it on a set of data.

Empirical-then-Theoretical or EtT or ET (first Empirical generalization then Theory):

1. Establish a (generalizable) empirical pattern.
2. Develop a (low-level) theoretical model or explanation.

In marketing, TiI became popular in the 1960s and 1970s. This tradition is greatly facilitated by the availability of data, computers, and what Ehrenberg (1994, p.80) calls "seemingly objective statistical tests of significance". Ehrenberg (1970) criticizes the use of TiI as *Sonking:* Scientification of Non-Knowledge. He also maintains that few lasting results have emerged from TiI.

ET seeks to first establish some empirical patterns that exist across a variety of product categories, time periods, geographic areas, etc. If the patterns hold in many different situations, generalizable findings exist and one can establish under what empirical conditions the findings generalize to form a "law". A criticism of ET is that the results are "merely descriptive". But if generalizable findings emerge, it follows that ET (or so-called models-of-fact) will be long-term oriented, both because of the time required to discover generalizable knowledge and because the findings are not time dependent. A manager, however, faced with current problems cannot wait until "laws of marketing" become available. She wants answers within a short time span. Generalizations that have already been established should, of course, be taken into account in the development of decision models, and in that sense Ehrenberg's approach becomes complementary to the prevailing approach in building decision models. For example, the development of laws of marketing might lead to theoretical premises about certain model parameters, e.g. restrictions could be imposed a priori on the parameter values. The relevance of such theoretically-based restrictions can be investigated when models are validated.

Among the regularities Ehrenberg has found are the following (Uncles, Ehrenberg, Hammond, 1995). For most frequently purchased branded goods, the market shares differ strongly across brands. The brands also tend to have different numbers of households purchasing the brands, and these numbers are related to the brands' market shares. Thus smaller brands have fewer buyers. However, buyers of smaller brands also tend to make fewer purchases, in a given time period. These two negatives for brands with smaller market shares are often jointly referred to as "double jeopardy". Fader and Schmittlein (1993) found a third important advantage for high-share brands: unusually high behavioral loyalty. We note that even the research on empirical generalizations advocated by Ehrenberg is not devoid of theory. Some initial theoretical development prior to data analysis is required to know what to focus on. However, much of the theoretical analysis occurs after patterns in the data have been noted (induction).

Is "sonking" (TE) really bad? There are certainly many marketing scientists who do not think so, and want to "sonk" because they want to learn. A typical example is the observation by Forrester (1961), who argues that the first step in model building does not consist of an extensive data collection exercise. Instead, a model should come first, and it should be used to determine what data need to be collected. Forrester's view is in sharp contrast with Ehrenberg's models of fact approach, and Ehrenberg might put Forrester's way of building models in the category of sonking. The rationale underlying Forrester's work is that model building is one approach for finding out what we do not know, or for discovering what kinds of things would be of interest to know. Unlike Ehrenberg, we believe this kind of modeling can be very valuable, as long as we do not call the outcome "the theory". Instead, the TE approach is useful for the development of new hypotheses or conceptualizations. In addition, once empirical generalizations are formed they cannot be taken for granted and they are subject to falsification in a Popperian sense.

We believe that both ET and TE types of research can be productively employed in marketing. For Ehrenberg's approach to be successful, the data patterns must be relatively easily observable. Powerful, but simple, ideas are used to develop explanations for these patterns. In applied econometrics the ET approach may focus on main effects for marketing variables (e.g. what is the price elasticity) and on the use of data that do not require complex estimation techniques (e.g. experimental data).

More extensive theory development, prior to data analysis, may be required to propose more complex relationships. We imagine that many interaction effects will not be discovered from Ehrenberg's approach. Both theoretical and analytical work may be prerequisites for the specification of higher-level models. In addition, sophisticated estimation procedures may be needed to obtain empirical evidence in support of the theory. For example, data on the sales of products receiving promotional support (such as a temporary price cut) often show no evidence of a dip in sales after the promotion is terminated. Such a dip is expected if consumers engage in stockpiling. Thus, the ET approach is likely to ignore the possibility of a dip, whereas the TE approach would, after a failure to observe dips in simple models, consider more complex models that can capture the phenomenon.

In more mature scientific work any descriptive result would be followed by further empirical testing (E), more well-based theorizing (T) and speculation, more empirical testing (E), and so on. In this way science traditionally moves into "more characteristically looped ETET . . . models". Thus "in the long run" the difference between ET and TE would largely disappear if the initial theory in TE is tested not on a Single Set of Data (SSoD) but on Many Sets of Data (MSoD).[14] In this regard Ehrenberg (1995, p. G27) speaks about:

---

14. See for this discussion also Bass (1995).

"a design switch away from collecting a Single Set of Data (SSoD) toward explicitly collecting Many (differentiated) Sets of Data (MSoD)."

In the more recent TiI-based marketing science literature many *empirical generalizations* or "laws" using "*meta-analysis*" are described. Meta-analysis refers to the statistical analysis of results from several individual studies for the purpose of generalizing the individual findings (Wold, 1986). The primary benefit of meta-analysis in marketing is that it delivers generalized estimates of various *elasticities, quantitative characteristics* of *buyer behavior* and *diffusion models,* and the accuracy associated with estimated parameters and model fits. The assumption is that different brands and different markets are comparable at a general level but that at the same time model parameters to some extent vary systematically over different brand/model settings in an identifiable manner (Farley, Lehmann, Sawyer, 1995, p. G.37). The empirical generalization

... *"is a pattern or regularity that repeats over different circumstances and that can be described simply by mathematical, graphic or symbolic methods. A pattern that repeats but need not be universal over all circumstances"*

(Bass, 1995, p. G7).

In the marketing literature an increasing number of meta-analyses and empirical generalizations are found. In one of the early studies Leone and Schultz (1980) observed that:

- the elasticity of (selective) advertising on brand sales is positive but small;
- increasing store shelf space has a positive impact on sales of nonstaple grocery items.

In meta-analyses conducted by Assmus, Farley, Lehmann (1984) and Lodish et al. (1995a) somewhat higher advertising elasticities are reported. Lodish et al. (1995a) also found that the advertising elasticities of new products are much higher than the average advertising elasticities. Other meta-analyses refer to the long-term effects of advertising.[15]

In other meta-analyses mean[16] price elasticities are reported. Yet empirical generalizations do not always result in "numbers". Kaul and Wittink (1995) describe the relationship between advertising and price sensitivity, and generate a set of three empirical generalizations:

- an increase in *price advertising* leads to higher price sensitivity among consumers;
- the use of *price advertising* leads to lower prices;
- an increase in *nonprice advertising* leads to lower price sensitivity among consumers.

---

15. See, e.g. Leone (1995), Lodish et al. (1995b) and Section 18.3.
16. Many other examples of price elasticities are found in Lambin (1976), Verhulp (1982), Tellis (1988b), Hanssens, Parsons, Schultz (1990, Chapter 6) and Ainslie, Rossi (1998).

The increasing amount of research on the effects of promotions has also led to generalizations such as (Blattberg, Briesch, Fox, 1995):

- promotions significantly increase sales;
- higher market share brands are less "promotion" elastic;
- the greater the frequency of promotions, the lower the increase in sales, etc.

Other generalizations refer to the diffusion of new products, first-mover advantages (Van der Werf, Mahan, 1997), repeat buying, the stationarity of market shares, the relation between market share, distribution and sales effort, etc.[17]

3.4   On the use of a marketing model: a case study

We conclude this chapter by presenting a case study to clarify some of the concepts introduced in Chapters 1 to 3. In this hypothetical - yet quite realistic - example, the reader should recognize:

1. the use of the concepts, system (everything that relates to a manager's problem), model (representation of the most important elements of a perceived real-world system) and what is meant by these "most important elements";
2. the process that ultimately leads to a model;
3. the relation between intended use and degree of model explicitness;
4. the benefits and costs inherent in marketing modeling.

The Good Food Company case[18]
The Good Food Co. sells many food products. These are packaged in a large number of plants, and are shipped to retailers through a network of warehouses. At present, Good Food Co. makes 500 different products at 50 plants. The firm sells to over 2,000 retailers (mostly supermarkets) and currently has 60 warehouses. Mark Cent, the company's treasurer, has felt for a long time that the cost of distribution is excessive. On various occasions he argued with the President of the Board that something ought to be done about the high and increasing cost of distribution. Although there was agreement that the situation deserved attention, little or no action was taken. In February of 1996, Mark Cent prepared another presentation for the Board on the distribution issue. This time, however, he collected some figures to make his point. Distribution costs for the last ten years are given in Table 3.1.[19] The second column in this table shows that the percent increase over the previous year is going up dramatically with the most recent percentages being over 10 percent.
Corresponding revenues over the last five years also increased, but at a much lower rate, of approximately 4 percent per year. Mr. Cent's latest figures finally convince

---

17. See for a survey of generalizations in marketing the special issue of *Marketing Science*, vol. 14, nr. 3, part 2, 1995 and more specifically the survey in Bass, Wind (1995). See also Hanssens et al. (1990, Chapter 6).
18. The problem description has to a certain extent been inspired by the Heinz Co. case, available from Harvard Clearing House.
19. The values in Table 3.1 and in the rest of the discussion are given in real dollars, i.e. they have been deflated.

Table 3.1 Good Food Co. distribution costs.

Year	Distribution cost (in millions of dollars)	Percent increase over previous year
1986	7.5	
1987	7.6	1.3
1988	7.9	4.0
1989	8.1	2.6
1990	8.6	6.2
1991	9.0	4.7
1992	9.7	7.8
1993	10.5	8.2
1994	11.6	10.5
1995	12.9	11.2

the Board that action is called for. All members agree that the distribution costs are excessive, and that the distribution network should be examined to discover potential savings. They realize that the problem is complicated, and that outside help is required. In April 1996, Wareloc Consultants was invited to work on the project. The consultants formulated the problem as one of minimizing the total cost of distributing 500 products to 2,000 retailers.

In the Good Food Co. case, the problem, system and model can be defined as follows.

The problem

As formulated by management and as perceived by Wareloc Consultants, the *problem* was to determine the number of plants and warehouses, where to locate them, what to produce where, and to obtain a transportation schedule to minimize the total cost of distribution. After further consultation with Good Food Co. management, the solution space became somewhat constrained. No new plants were to be added and there could be no technology transfer from one plant to another, which meant that the current product mix at each plant could not be changed. Within prevailing capacity limits, the production of specific products could be increased as well as decreased or even eliminated.

The system

With this information, the elements of the system would include:

- the production capacity for each product at each plant;
- all possible locations for warehouses;
- the cost of building or renting warehouses at each possible location;

- the cost of transporting a particular product from a particular plant to a particular warehouse and to a particular retailer, as a function of the number of units;
- the expected demand for each product at each retail outlet.

The model

It is not difficult to see that the development of a model with all these elements is a demanding task. A first step is to determine which *elements* Wareloc Consultants should try to model.[20] They did this through a series of discussions with Good Food Co. management. Based on these discussions a consensus developed that the following *simplifications* (i.e. eliminating *less important elements*) would only marginally decrease the usefulness of the results:

- expected demand for each product at each retail outlet is last year's sales plus four percent;
- transportation costs are assumed to be constant per unit.

How to deal with all possible warehouse locations was more difficult. *A priori* this number is indeed very large. The following simplifications were considered acceptable. One is that warehouses should be located near concentrations of demand (i.e. close to cities). Two, the exact sites were of little importance now, and could be considered outside the model. This means that if it was decided to add a warehouse in a particular area, one would then search for an appropriate location as a separate problem.[21]

At this point, the problem had become more manageable, without yielding a model so different from the (perceived) real problem as to make it useless. This representation of the system was then modeled by Wareloc Consultants, and a heuristic was developed to search for a "good" distribution network.[22] As a result of their effort, Wareloc Consultants reported on September 20, 1996 that total distribution costs for 1996 could be reduced to $12.3 million, a saving of $0.6 million over 1995 and a saving of perhaps $2 million over the projected distribution costs for 1997. This result is quite encouraging, in particular since it is based on an overall increase in sales of four percent.[23] Mr. Cent was very pleased, and so was the Board. One of the outcomes of the study was that twenty of the existing warehouses could be phased out, and only five new locations would be needed.

A few days later, Mr. Sell, Vice-President of Marketing, was given a copy of the report. He read it with much scepticism. From the beginning, he had negative feelings about the project, partly because he had not been consulted. The Board felt that the

---

20. Peterson's (1965) fable of the wizard who oversimplified would be very useful reading at this point.
21. This relates to the issue of a hierarchy of models which is dealt with in Chapter 19.
22. A *heuristic* is a systematic procedure to find increasingly better solutions to a particular problem. This is also true for an *algorithm*, the difference being that algorithms can guarantee convergence, i.e. an optimum will be found, while heuristics cannot. A typical example of an algorithm is the Simplex Method of Linear Programming. Heuristics are used when no analytical solutions are available, or when the problems are too large in size to be amenable for solution by algorithmic methods. The distribution system in the case is a typical example of a large scale problem. A possible heuristic for solving problems analogous to the one being discussed here, was proposed by Kuehn and Hamburger (1963).
23. Of course the solution can no longer be implemented in 1996. But, if it had been, a saving would have resulted.

Table 3.2 Relation between distribution cost and service rate
for Good Food Co.

Alternative	Distribution cost (in millions of dollars)	Percent served within 24 hours	48 hours
1	12.3	60	70
2	12.7	67	80
3	13.1	70	85
4	13.1	75	82
5	13.1	68	88
6	13.5	72	87
7	13.5	70	89

project was intended to reduce distribution costs, and that the marketing people would not be of much help. After he had studied the report in depth, especially the location of the warehouses in the proposed plan, Mr. Sell concluded that sales would be badly affected if the plan were implemented. In the past, the company had been able to fill about 70 percent of the orders within 24 hours, and about 85 percent within 48 hours. In Mr. Sell's opinion, this rate of service would not be possible under the proposed plan. Good Food's high service rate had been one of the company's strongest competitive advantages. Mr. Sell felt that without this advantage sales would decline. He discussed the matter at the next Board meeting on October 31, 1996 and after much debate a decision was made to ask Wareloc Consultants to examine some alternative warehouse location plans and the corresponding service rates.

Wareloc Consultants spent another two months relating cost *of distribution to rate of service*. Some of the options are shown in Table 3.2. From Table 3.2 we can draw the following conclusions. With the plan originally proposed by Wareloc Consultants (alternative 1), a substantial decline in the service rate is expected. With the current rate of 70 percent served within 24 hours, and 85 percent within 48 hours, distribution cost is estimated to be $13.1 million dollars (alternative 3). This represents an increase in the distribution cost of almost 1.6 percent [{(13.1 − 12.9)/12.9} × 100%] over last year for an estimated 4 percent increase in sales. This indicates the existence of potential savings, based on the projected increase in distribution costs, even if the service rate is not affected. The table further indicates that, for a given distribution cost, a trade-off exists between 24 and 48 hour service rates. Management now can contemplate the value of (high) service rates versus (low) distribution costs.

This discussion provides insight into the following aspects:

1. The concepts problem, system and model were illustrated as was the selection of the most important elements. In the Good Food Co. example the problem itself was perhaps perceived incorrectly. It was seen as one of excessive distribution cost, when in fact one should look at the global performance of the company.[24] We can still examine the distribution network but we should do so by keeping in mind the

---

24. The study of global systems presents problems of its own as indicated in Chapter 19.

company's objective, such as long-term profit maximization. Instead of a search for a minimum-cost distribution network we would look for a balance between distribution cost, on the one hand, and service rate on the other, leading to a satisfactory profit performance.[25]

We should also point out that the problem definition is often quite difficult, because, as has been indicated in Section 3.2, problems will often emerge or become transparent after an initial model has been developed. In any case, it is critical for managers to spend sufficient time and effort in the problem definition stage. This requires discussions with all parties who might be able to help. The Good Food Co. case illustrates that early involvement of the marketing vice-president might have avoided some problem definition difficulties.

In other instances the system is ill-defined. In general, it is no trivial task to determine all the elements which relate to a problem. It is quite conceivable that some important elements have simply been omitted during the transition from problem to system. Often difficulties will arise because the model is poorly constructed. For example, some elements of the system may be interrelated, whereas, in the model, they are assumed to be independent.

2.   The process of problem finding, model building, redefined problem finding, and redefined model building has been elucidated.

3.   The intended use of the model could ultimately be defined as searching for a balance between distribution cost, on the one hand, and service rate on the other hand, leading to a satisfactory profit performance. This means that the initial model does not provide a correct answer to the question what distribution network will lead to maximum profit. Getting a correct answer requires the determination or estimation of a relationship between demand and service rate into the model. At this point, the company does not know how demand and service rate are related. Subjective estimates could be obtained. Alternatively the company might decide that this problem deserves a separate study. In other words, the original modeling effort has resulted in the identification of a new problem. Also, even if the dependence of demand on the service rate were known, it may or may not be useful to do extensive modeling. For example, the model may become too complex, and the search for a solution too difficult, relative to the expected benefits. This points to the need for management to consider cost-benefit aspects in model building.

4.   The direct benefit of a model is observable in the profit increases expected from model use. As indirect benefits we have:

• improved understanding of the problem resulting in a redefinition;
• insights that suggest the need for additional data collection;
• identification of areas in which data are needed.

---

25. Because of the complexity of the problem, the company will normally be satisfying rather than optimizing.

CHAPTER 4

A typology of marketing models

Marketing models can be classified on many dimensions. In this chapter, we present several classifications. In model building, the following dimensions are of particular relevance:

1. intended use;
2. level of demand;
3. amount of behavioral detail;

and it is also useful to distinguish:

4. time series versus causal econometric models; and
5. models for single products versus models for multiple products.

We discuss the meaning and significance of these dimensions in this chapter. This should facilitate the reading of Chapters 8, 9 and 10 which deal with intended use, level of demand, and amount of behavioral detail. The typologies are also relevant for the discussion of problems and issues in parameterization (Chapters 16 and 17) and validation (Chapter 18) of models.

4.1 Intended use: descriptive, predictive, normative models

Models can be classified according to purpose or intended use, i.e. why might a firm engage in a model-building project. Different purposes often lead to different models. To illustrate, we refer to the example in Section 2.2 about a firm that wanted to improve its pricing-decision process. For that purpose the firm examined the various steps, and their sequencing, it used to arrive at pricing decisions. In that case, the desired outcome of the model-building effort is a descriptive model and not a model of how the firm should (i.e. a normative model) determine its prices. This example shows how a model's intended use is an important determinant of its specification.

We distinguish between descriptive, predictive, and normative models. *Descriptive models* are intended to describe decision- or other processes. A descriptive model of a decision process may be an end in itself, in the sense that decision-making procedures are often quite complicated and not well understood. A decision maker may wonder *how particular decisions are arrived at* in her organization or by her customers. The decision maker may want to trace the various steps that lead to the decisions, and identify the forces that influence the outcome(s) of the decision processes.

The purpose of a descriptive model may also be to find out whether there is a structure that would *allow for automation* of part or of the entire decision process. The objectives may be restricted to a desire to describe the existing procedure, and the modeling process itself will not necessarily improve the firm's performance. It is possible, however, that a descriptive model of an existing decision process will show opportunities for improvement. Thus, a modeling effort may start in the descriptive phase and ultimately reach the normative phase.

The degree of explicitness will vary from one situation to another. In many cases, however, descriptive models will be of the logical flow type, with parts of the model expressed in mathematical terms. We show examples in Section 8.1.

Process models constitute a specific subset of descriptive models. Such models describe processes of decision makers. A process model consists of a sequential specification of relations. The model is specified in such a way that the effect of a change in one variable on other variables via intermediate relations can be examined. An example is the process model developed by Hoekstra (1987) to describe the behavior of heroin users. Model components include the process of obtaining money and heroin, getting imprisoned, abstaining from heroin, and enrolling in methadone programs. It is based on a logical flow diagram in which the steps in the process are made explicit. The behavior of heroin users is described based on information obtained from interviews. The model has been used to carry out scenario analyses to examine the effects of policy-based activities such as methadone treatment and law enforcement. While process models can describe complex purchase situations, it is not possible to aggregate the described behavior over heterogeneous members of the population(Lilien, Kotler, Moorthy 1992, p.56).[1]

Descriptive models are not restricted to decision problems. For example, one may describe a market by the structure of brand loyalty (the percentage of people buying product i in period $t + 1$, who bought the same brand on the previous purchase occasion), and brand switching (percentage of people changing from brand i to brand j). That is, the market could be described by a stochastic brand choice model. We discuss such descriptive models in Chapter 12.

By *predictive models* we mean models to forecast or predict future events. For example, a firm may want to predict sales for a brand under alternative prices, advertising spending levels, and package sizes. While the purpose of a predictive model is, as the word indicates, prediction, it is possible that, in order to arrive at a predictive model, we start with a descriptive model, perhaps in terms of current procedures, but also in terms of the elements relating to the problem. For illustrations, see the new-product evaluation model in Section 10.3 and stochastic brand choice models in Chapter 12.

Forecasting or prediction does not always mean answering "what if" types of

---

1. Other examples can be found in e.g. Zwart (1983), Brand (1993) and Pham, Johar (1996).

questions, such as, how does the demand change if price is increased by ten percent. In some brand choice models, the structure of brand loyalty and switching is summarized in a transition probability matrix. A general element of that matrix, $p_{ij,\,t+1}$, represents the probability that a person who buys brand i in period t will buy brand j in period $t + 1$.[2] Based on the transition probabilities and the current distribution of market shares, we can predict the evolution of market shares in future periods. In this case, the forecasts are not conditional on marketing activities.

Demand models make up a special class of predictive models. We refer to a demand model when we have a performance variable related to a level of demand. This performance variable may depend on a number of other variables, such as marketing decision variables employed by the firm and its competitors. We discuss this important class of predictive models further in Section 4.2 and in Chapter 9.

The final category consists of the *normative or prescriptive models*. A normative model has, as one of its outputs, a recommended course of action. This implies that an objective is defined against which alternative actions can be evaluated and compared. For example, the objective function in a media allocation model may be the maximization of profit, or at an intermediate level, the maximization of exposure value. We show an example related to the optimization of advertising spending in Section 8.3.

We conclude this section with a few observations. Researchers often believe that the ultimate output should be a normative model and that descriptive and predictive models are logical conditions. That is, one first describes the problem or one systematizes the various elements of a problem in a descriptive sense. Next one tries to answer "what if" types of questions. For example, what will sales be if the firm spends twenty percent more on advertising. Finally, the "what should" stage is reached. For example, how much should be spent on advertising in order to maximize profit.

In some cases the sequence is indeed from descriptive to predictive to normative models. In other situations, as noted earlier, a descriptive model may be sufficient. In still other cases, one may stop at the predictive stage, even if optimization is analytically or numerically possible. One reason for this is that the objective function is often hard to quantify. A firm usually has multiple objectives, and has to satisfy various constraints. For example, an objective of profit maximization may be constrained by requirements such as maintaining market share at least at its current level, and limiting the advertising budget to a certain percentage of last year's sales revenue. The latter constraint may seem artificial but could simply reflect the limited cash resources a firm has. Also, other entities in the company may compete for their share of those scarce resources. In that case, one might prefer to evaluate various alternatives one at a time, given that these constraints are satisfied, over the use of an algorithm to find the optimal solution.

---

2. At the aggregate level, "probability" becomes "percentage of people". The notion of transition probabilities is dealt with in more detail in Chapter 12.

Early model building in marketing was often of the normative kind with a concentration on the development of solution techniques. One reason for this is that operations research was still a young discipline with little or no contact with managers. Now that the discipline has matured, there are many more models of the predictive and descriptive, rather than of the normative, variety. Of course, proper discussions among marketing scientists and managers will allow the normative models to be useful.

4.2 Demand models: product class sales, brand sales, and market share models

In a demand model, the performance variable is a measure of demand. Many demand models belong to the subset of predictive models.

We distinguish individual demand and aggregate demand. Aggregate demand may refer to:

1. The total number of units of a product category purchased by the population of all spending units. The corresponding demand model is called an *industry sales*, or *product class sales* model.
2. The total number of units of a particular brand bought by the population of all spending units. The demand model is then a *brand sales model*.
3. The number of units of a particular brand purchased by the total population, relative to the total number of units purchased of the product class, in which case the demand model becomes a *market share* model.[3]

We can define the same measures at the segment level and at the level of the individual consumer leading to models with different levels of aggregation: market, store, segment, household and so on. Thus we define, for example:

1. category sales for a given household;
2. brand sales for the household;
3. the proportion of category sales accounted for by the brand, for the household.

From these definitions it follows that market share of brand j is equal to the ratio of brand sales of j and product class sales (i.e. brand sales summed over all brands). For example, consider total sales of cigarettes in period t, sales of, say, Lucky Strike in the same period, and the ratio of the latter over the former which is Lucky Strike's market share in period t. Note that all these variables can be defined in terms of units or dollars. It is common for demand variables to represent *unit* sales, in model specifications. One reason is that dollar sales is the product of two variables, unit sales and price per unit, and the use of such combinations inhibits the interpretation

---

3. The terminology adopted here is not unique. Product class sales, brand sales, and market share models are also referred to as primary demand, secondary demand, and selective (or relative) demand models. See, for example, Leeflang (1976, 1977a), Schultz, Wittink (1976).

of effects on demand. Nevertheless, especially if brands differ considerably in prices within a product category, managers should be interested in tracking performance in dollars as well as in units.

We can use two of the three measures as part of a more complex model. For example, to describe, explain and predict unit sales of a brand, we can develop a product class sales model and a market share model. By multiplying these two performance measures, product class sales and market share, we obtain brand sales. In Chapter 9, we discuss why it can be preferable to predict brand sales in this manner, rather than to relate brand sales to marketing instruments and environmental variables[4] directly. The core of the argument, however, centers around the fact that different levels of demand require different sets of variables for explanation. For example, it makes sense for the marketing variables used to predict market share, to use relative measures. Thus, if advertising is one of the variables that determine market share, advertising share of the brand may be used.

4.3 Behavioral detail

Another classification, is the amount of behavioral detail a model contains.[5] We distinguish the following three classes:

1. no behavioral detail;
2. some behavioral detail;
3. a substantial amount of behavioral detail.

Since the amount of behavioral detail is a continuous variable, and therefore is not easily discretized, only the first class can be unambiguously defined.

In models with *no behavioral detail*, marketing instruments and environmental variables are directly related to a performance measure, such as sales or market share. In this case intervening variables such as awareness and attitude are not considered, and the stimuli (instruments and environmental variables) are directly related to response (performance) measures or variables. The manner in which stimuli cause a response is treated as a black box. Thus, in these models inputs are directly related to output: see Figure 4.1.

The second category consists of models where *some behavioral detail* is explicitly shown. This can be done in different ways. One such type of model, in which the detail is provided at an aggregate level is the aggregate flow model. An example is the new-product evaluation model SPRINTER (Mod. I-Behavioral Option) developed

---

4. In Section 5.2 we define environmental variables as variables which are outside the marketing system or beyond the control of decision makers.
5. There are other possible distinctions with respect to model detail. For example, one could build company or corporate models, or models of functional areas; or models dealing with a product category, or a brand, or models related to specific marketing instruments. The focus would then be on the degree of model integration. We touch upon these ideas in Sections 5.1 and 19.2.3.

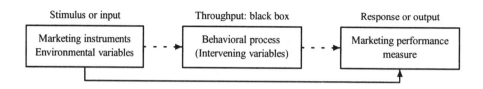

Figure 4.1 Model with no behavioral detail.

by Urban (1969a), in which some of the intervening variables appear in a "hierarchy-of-effects" fashion. For example, advertising may first cause some people to become exposed to the product. Some percentage of them will become aware of the product. Of those who have become aware, some will develop a favorable attitude and an intent to buy, etc.

In Urban's model, buyers move from one stage or state (e.g. the potential triers class) to another (e.g. the potential repeaters) after each purchase occasion. This means that the model tracks the flow of the buyers through a network of possible states, which explains why it is called *an aggregate flow model.*[6]

The benefits of more behavioral detail include the following. One is that we force ourselves to be explicit about at least some of the stages in the behavioral process. Just as we discussed with regard to the benefits of models in general, more detail provides opportunities for debate and reflection. Another advantage is that if a model does not perform well, we want to know how we can improve it. With more detail there is greater opportunity to identify the model's weaknesses.

Of course, with more behavioral detail we also face additional measurement and estimation problems. In the context of the SPRINTER model, we need to realize that intervening variables such as awareness and attitude have been given many different definitions.[7] And, no matter the definition, the measurement of attitudes in particular is difficult. Also, there is no agreement about exactly how the intervening variables affect behavior. The "hierarchy-of-effects" concept is controversial, and there are many alternative conceptualizations.

Brand choice models, in which transition probabilities are related to marketing instruments, can also be considered as belonging to the class of models with some behavioral detail. They can be defined at the individual- as well as at the aggregate level. Stimuli are not directly related to ultimate response or behavior but to a set of intermediate variables, the transition probabilities. MacLachlan (1972) refers to *models of intermediate market response.* Thus, if the transition probabilities are treated as behavioral quantities, these models contain some behavioral detail. The behavioral

---

6. Some aggregate flow models contain just a few behavioral elements. Others contain many more. Urban's Mod. I version (1969a) of the SPRINTER model is an example of the former, his Mod. III version (1970), an example of the latter. See Nijkamp (1993) for an extensive survey and evaluation of these models. The SPRINTER model is discussed in Section 10.2.

7. McGuire (1969, p. 142) writes in this respect: "Allport reviewed 16 earlier definitions of attitude before he ventured his own as a seventeenth. Nelson listed 30 such definitions, and Campbell and DeFleur and Westie, among others, many more."

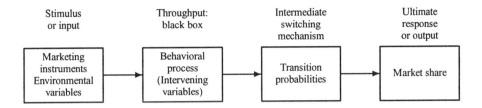

Stimulus or input	Throughput: black box	Intermediate switching mechanism	Ultimate response or output
Marketing instruments Environmental variables	Behavioral process (Intervening variables)	Transition probabilities	Market share

Figure 4.2 Model with some behavioral detail: a model of intermediate market response.

process explaining or causing the effect of stimuli on the transition probabilities, however, remains a black box, as illustrated in Figure 4.2.[8]

Finally, we have models containing a *substantial amount of behavioral detail*. These models focus on the description of behavioral processes. The detail can be explicitly modeled at the individual consumer level. An important subset of these models are the *micro-analytic simulation models*. In these, the demand is obtained by simulating the behavior of individual consumers, and then aggregating across consumers. Examples of such models are the consumer behavior model developed by Amstutz (1967) and the Howard and Sheth (1969) model, put in an empirically verifiable form by Farley and Ring (1970). More recently, the models of consumer behavior tend to be *partial models* which have a restricted number of relations between a limited number of variables. Examples are the relations between (1) involvement and persuasive communications, and (2) involvement and motivation. In the Elaboration Likelihood Model (ELM) developed by Petty and Cacioppo (1986), relations between these and other variables have been modeled through a logical flow model. The relations have been numerically specified by Nillesen (1992). Other models with a substantial amount of detail exist for the marketing of services.[9]

Since the early eighties there have been unparalleled developments in research methods which can be applied to models containing a substantial amount of behavioral detail. Much of this has occurred in the fields of psychometrics and statistics with additional contributions made by marketing researchers.[10] One such development is the Structural Equation Model (SEM). Most structural equation models are estimated with LISREL (Jöreskog, Sörbom, 1989).[11] The models contain latent or unobservable variables. These constructs are measured by a set of indicators, also called observed variables. The incorporation of latent variables in a model offers additional possibilities to construct models with a substantial amount of behavioral detail. The LISREL methodology is introduced in Section 17.1.

Models with much behavioral content generally consist of a large number of equations and parameters. Thus when we move from models with no behavioral detail

8. For a more elaborate discussion, see Leeflang (1974, Chapter 7), Naert, Bultez (1975), Leeflang, Boonstra (1982).

9. See, e.g. Boulding, Kalra, Staelin, Zeithaml (1993).

10. See, e.g. Bagozzi (1994a).

11. LISREL is a powerful multi-purpose computer program that facilitates the estimation of a variety of models. See, e.g. Sharma (1996, p. 426).

to models which contain a substantial amount of detail, there is, on the one hand, an increasing richness of representation of system phenomena and, on the other hand, greater complexity of measurement, estimation and validation. We return to these questions in Chapter 20.

4.4 Time series and causal models

Time series (models) capture response behavior over time from the systematic patterns in variables and disturbances. The main interest is to explain the variability in one or more variables over time without explicitly formulated causal variables. The response variable's fluctuations may be explained, for example, by lagged independent variables and/or time. Consider relation (4.1) in which the sales of a brand in period t is explained by two lagged sales variables.[12]

$$q_t = \alpha + \beta_1 q_{t-1} + \beta_2 q_{t-2}, \quad t = 3, 4, \ldots, T \tag{4.1}$$

where α is a constant term, β_1 and β_2 are response parameters, and T is the number of observations.

An alternative time-series model is relation (4.2):

$$q_t = \gamma + \delta_1 t + \delta_2 t^2, \quad t = 1, 2, 3, \ldots, T \tag{4.2}$$

where

$$\gamma, \delta_1, \delta_2 = \text{parameters}.$$

Relation (4.2) can be estimated, for example, by monthly data covering a two-year period ($T = 24$). If the estimated values of δ_1 and δ_2 are respectively positive and negative we obtain a bell-shaped curve which would represent part of the well-known curve of the product life-cycle.

Time-series models can be used to yield accurate forecasts for management but they usually do not produce useful knowledge about response behavior.[13] The approach does not reflect the idea that a performance measure such as sales can be controlled by the manipulation of decision variables such as price and advertising. By contrast causal models assume that variables under management control and environmental and other variables affect response in a direct and explicit way. The models focus on the relations between variables. Consider for example:

$$q_t = \alpha + \beta_1 p_t + \beta_2 a_t + \beta_3 temp_t + \beta_4 p_t^c + \beta_5 a_t^c, \quad t = 1, \ldots, T \tag{4.3}$$

where

$$p_t = \text{price per unit of a brand in period } t \text{ (in dollars)},$$
$$a_t = \text{advertising expenditures (in millions of dollars) of a brand}$$

12. In (4.1) - (4.3) a disturbance term is omitted for convenience.
13. In time series models the effects of independent variables can be estimated through so-called transfer function specifications: see Section 17.3.8.

in period t,

$temp_t$ = the average temperature in period t (degrees of Fahrenheit),

p_t^c = price per unit of a competing brand in period t,

a_t^c = the advertising expenditures (in dollars) of a competing brand in period t.

In relation (4.3) fluctuations in the sales of a brand are explained by the brand's own marketing instruments (price and advertising), an environmental variable (temperature), and marketing variables referring to the brand's competitor (p_t^c, a_t^c). The environmental variable, temperature, is an explanatory variable that is outside the control of the brand's management. This variable is a candidate for the explanation of fluctuations in the sales of products that depend on seasonal influences, such as beer, clothing and canned soup.

The term "causal" is also used in other contexts. In LISREL models "causal paths" between variables are identified (Section 17.1), and "causality" has also a specific meaning in validation (Section 18.4).

4.5 Models of "single" versus "multiple" products

Much of market modeling has dealt with descriptions, predictions and normative decisions concerning single products as brands. Yet, most firms manage multiple products. If a firm has several brands that belong to the same product line, it is important to consider the total performance across the various brands. For example, at the product line or category level we should monitor cannibalization, that is, the degree to which one brand gains market share at the expense of other brands of the same firm. More specifically, suppose that a given brand is offered in four different package sizes. Either because larger sizes have scale economies which reduce unit cost or because consumers who prefer larger sizes are more price sensitive, it is common for the unit price to be lower for larger package sizes. However, if smaller sizes are temporarily discounted, it is conceivable that many consumers temporarily switch to smaller sizes. In this case, a category-level approach is required to accommodate the switching between different sizes.

Cannibalization may also occur between different varieties or different sizes of a given brand, and between different brands offered by the same firm. For this reason, Procter & Gamble added a product category manager to minimize the competition between managers of alternative brands designed to serve similar consumer needs. Thus it is useful to model dependencies within a product line. The multiproduct firm is receiving an increasing amount of attention in the strategic management and marketing literatures.[14] Here "multiproduct" may refer to diversification in different product groups or product lines and to product variation (e.g. the items s', $s' = 1, \ldots, S'$ of

---

14. See, for example, Gijsbrechts, Naert (1984), Rao (1993).

brand j). The strategic management approaches have been primarily concerned with the problem of defining a portfolio of product groups.

In this book we concentrate on the modeling of single products. We discuss multi-product marketing models in Chapter 13 and in Sections 14.4-14.6. The multiproduct models we discuss in Chapter 13 deal with:

- product line interdependencies, especially product line pricing;
- resource allocation decisions, such as: shelf space allocation, and the allocation of an advertising budget over products and media.

In Chapter 14 we discuss models that account for the competition between items, i.e., brand-variety combinations. The models in Chapter 14 can account for the competition between items belonging to the same brand as well as the competition between items of different brands.

PART TWO

Specification

CHAPTER 5

Elements of model building

The classic approach to model building consists of three major parts:

1. specification;
2. parameterization;
3. validation.

However, the model-building process requires additional steps, some occurring before model specification, and other steps occurring after model validation. Accordingly, we place the three major parts of the classic approach in an implementation context in Section 5.1.

We introduce the basic terminology related to models, such as dependent variables, explanatory variables, parameters, disturbance terms, lagged effects, behavioral relations, etc. in Section 5.2.

Since behavioral relations form the core of a marketing model, several simple examples that show the specification of such relations are given in Section 5.3. These relations are mainly static. In Chapter 6 we discuss dynamic relations.

Implementation considerations lead to a number of criteria which the model structure or specification must satisfy. These criteria are reviewed in Chapter 7.

Specification is discussed extensively in Chapters 8 to 14, parameterization in Chapters 15, 16 and 17, and validation in Chapter 18.

5.1 The model-building process

Experience in model building among econometricians, statisticians, management scientists and operations researchers has led to the formulation of a sequence of steps for the development of mathematical models. Two alternative sequences are discussed in this section. We label the first a traditional view, and the second an implementation view.

A traditional view
Traditionally one often distinguishes the following steps:

a. *Specification (or Representation or Structure)* is the expression of the most important elements of a real-world system in mathematical terms. This involves two major steps:

1. Specifying the variables to be included in the model, and making a distinction between those to be explained (the dependent variables), and those providing the explanation (the explanatory or independent variables). For example, to explain market share of brand j (dependent variable) we could propose the following explanatory variables: price, advertising expenditures, promotions, distribution, quality, and measure these variables for brand j and for competing brands. Often, this also involves a choice of the statistical distribution of those variables, or a distribution of the error term of the dependent variable.

2. A second aspect is the specification of a functional relationship between the variables. For example, the effects of the explanatory variables can be linear or non-linear, immediate and/or lagged, additive or multiplicative, etc.[1] A choice among these options may be based on *a priori* reasoning. Our preference for one formulation over another could be based on certain arguments. An additive relationship, for example, implies that the explanatory variables do not interact, while a multiplicative specification assumes a specific type of interaction. Also, an S-shaped function indicates increasing returns to scale for low values of an explanatory variable and decreasing returns for high values. Empirical comparisons of alternative specifications can also assist us in choosing among options.

b. *Parameterization (or Estimation)* is the determination of parameter estimates for a model. For this, data are sometimes available or can be obtained without much effort. For example, a firm's advertising history may be available in the accounting department. One should, however, be careful with such data. From the point of view of the accounting department, advertising expenditures are incurred in the months in which advertising bills are paid to agencies and media. From the point of view of the model builder who wants to assess the effectiveness of advertising, expenditures are incurred at the time the advertising message is shown on television, heard on the radio or printed in newspapers and magazines. In other cases, specific measurement instruments have to be developed, or the data exist but are more difficult to obtain, such as, for example, advertising spending by competitors.

We mentioned in the preceding chapter *"unobservable"* or *"latent"* variables. Attitudes about products, intentions to purchase, feelings, but also demand are unobservable variables.[2] Sometimes such unobservable variables are omitted from the model, as in the stimulus-response models: the models with no behavioral detail. Alternatively one can develop instruments to measure the unobservable variables, either directly or as a function of *observable* or *indicator* variables. Which solution is chosen depends on the purpose of the research.

Apart from data collection issues, we need to identify techniques to be applied for extracting estimates of the model parameters from the data collected. The choice of a technique depends on:

- the kind of data available and/or needed;

---

1. For a definition of these terms, see Section 5.3.
2. See also, e.g. Hanssens, Parsons, Schultz (1990, p.33).

- the kind of variables (observable/unobservable) in the model;
- the assumptions (of a statistical nature) that are necessary and/or acceptable;
- the computational effort and expense considered to be reasonable.

We note that there is often a trade-off between statistical qualities of the estimators, and flexibility (and realism) in the specification. Based on data availability, we consider in Chapter 16:

1. data-based parameterization: parameter estimation from historical data;
2. subjective estimation: judgment-based parameter estimation.

c. *Validation (or Verification or Evaluation)* of a model and its parameters implies assessing the quality or the success of the model. Possible criteria are:

1. the degree to which the results are in accordance with theoretical expectations or well-known empirical facts;
2. the degree to which the results satisfy statistical criteria or tests;
3. the degree to which the result is relevant to the original purpose:
   - is the model useful for clarifying and describing market phenomena?
   - does the model provide an acceptable degree of predictive accuracy?
   - are the model results suitable for the determination of optimal marketing-policies?

d. *Application or Use of a model.* This step means experience with the model, given successful validation, opportunities for continued testing as well as model adjustments, model updating, etc.

An implementation view
In the traditional view, no explicit attention is given to implementation in the model-building process. We propose a process that is designed for model implementation. This process is described in Figure 5.1 and is explained below.

1. *Opportunity identification*
In this stage a model builder has to evaluate whether the development/use of a model can improve managerial decision making. The model builder will often be invited to consider the opportunity by a manager who is overwhelmed by demands on his/her time or who believes that the effectiveness or efficiency of decision making can be improved. Ideally the model builder and manager work together to define the problem, to agree on an approach and to determine that the expected benefits exceed the costs of model building. It is also important to establish that the model builder knows the right tools and does not unduly favor specific approaches.[3]

2. *Model purpose*
The intended use of the model should be defined as precisely as possible. For example, the manager may need a model to obtain accurate sales forecasts. The model

---

3. See also Urban (1974) who calls these approaches "priors".

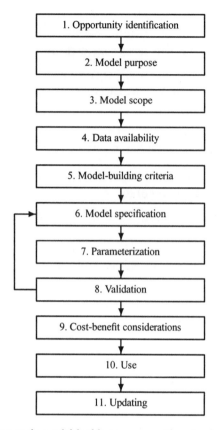

Figure 5.1 Stages in the model-building process with an implementation focus.

builder needs to know the level of detail for which forecasts are required. The model builder also needs to learn what the manager believes to be the relevant determinants of sales so that model-based conditional forecasts can be developed. In this step both the level of demand and the amount of behavioral detail should receive attention.

3. *Model scope*

Model building can take place for a specific type of decision or for a broader set of decisions. The manager may want the model-building effort to focus on a single decision variable. Thus, the desired outcome may be a model of advertising effects. Alternatively, the manager may desire to have a model that includes the effects of all relevant marketing activities. The latter is actually desirable for at least two reasons. One is that marketing activities may be correlated in historical data. In that case, in order to be able to learn the effect of only one variable, the other variables must be included in the model. Another reason is that even if the variables can be manipulated experimentally (such that the variables can be uncorrelated), their joint movement may produce greater or smaller effects than the sum of their individual effects.

Similar arguments may apply to other decision variables pertaining to non-marketing activities. For example, promotions such as temporary price cuts often have strong effects on sales which may require intensive adjustments in production and distribution. The financial consequences of those adjustments need to be taken into account by the manager to determine the total profit impact of the marketing activity.

4. *Data availability*

One reason a manager may ask for a model-building effort is the increasing availability of large amounts of data. For example, in packaged, non-durable consumer goods industries market feedback was provided to managers in the U.S. by means of bimonthly store audits, until the mid 1980's. The ACNielsen Company did not encourage model building based on these data largely because of the highly aggregated nature of the data. With the introduction of scanners into supermarkets, managers could obtain much more detailed market feedback much more frequently.[4]

To a certain extent the data available through historical records determine the types of model that can be developed. The model builder should, however, recognize that experimental methods can provide more powerful insights. Also if the risk or time required for experimentation is too high and historical data are insufficient, the possibility of using subjective estimation methods remains. In this step the power of historical data needs to be established relative to the desired model purpose. See also Section 15.1.

5. *Model-building criteria*

For a model to be implemented its structure should satisfy various criteria. Little (1970) proposed that a model should be:

a. simple;
b. complete on important issues;
c. adaptive;
d. robust.

It is easy to see that some of these criteria are in conflict. Thus, none of the criteria should be pushed to the limit. Instead, we can say that the more each individual criterion is satisfied, the higher the likelihood of model acceptance.

Briefly, models should be as simple as possible. Simplicity is a virtue in that simple models are easy to understand and communicate. Since no model is complete, the more a manager understands its structure, the better the model user can recognize the model's limitations. However, simplicity will not be acceptable if the cost is that the model becomes incomplete on important issues. All, relevant variables need to be incorporated even if the manager is interested in learning about the effect of a single variable.

If the effect(s) of interest can change over time or over units, the model should be adaptive. Finally, robustness means that the model is unlikely to generate implausible answers. We discuss these aspects in more detail in Chapter 7.

---

4. See McCann, Gallagher (1990).

6.-8.

The stages of *model specification, parameterization* and *validation* are discussed under the traditional view (a-c).

9. Cost-benefit considerations

We mentioned that in stage 1 *(opportunity identification)* one should establish that the expected benefits exceed the (expected) costs of model building. At this point both benefits and cost should be known with a fair amount of precision. Before the model is implemented and incorporated in a manager's decision-making process, it is appropriate to re-examine the cost-benefit tradeoff. The question now is not whether the model-building effort is worthwhile. Instead, it is useful to determine if the insights gained appear to be more beneficial than the costs. One way to make this practical is to compare, in the next stage, the decisions that will be made with the benefit of the model to the decisions that would otherwise occur. In this manner it is possible to determine whether the model should in fact be used. If the model fails on this criterion, we can return to earlier stages if there is sufficient promise for a modified approach to be successful.

10. Use

This stage should correspond to part d. under the traditional view. However, we place the comments made under d. under our last stage called *"updating"*. In a direct sense, use of the model requires that the manager fully understands both its strengths and its weaknesses. We do not need to say much about this stage if the model is truly simple (see stage 5). However, as model complexity increases, implementation will require appropriate support. One way to accomplish this is for the model builder to construct a market simulation capacity. With that the manager should be able to explore how the market will behave under a variety of conditions which can be influenced by the manager.

There are several advantages associated with the creation of a market simulation capacity. One is that the manager does not have to use a mathematical model. Instead, the implications of the model can be explored. In this case the model builder does need to place constraints on such explorations, for example, to rule out combinations of marketing activities for which the model would in fact give implausible forecasts.

11. Updating

Over time, the manager may develop a better understanding of the marketplace, and this could require modifications in the model. Even without this, the continued comparison of actual outcomes with those predicted by the model may suggest that the model needs to be expanded (e.g. an additional variable or greater complexity in effects) or that the parameters need to be updated. Thus, the updating in this stage refers to updating of both the model specification and the parameterization.

The continued comparison of actual outcomes with predictions requires that differences (errors) be analyzed so that one can distinguish between errors due to e.g. model specification, measurement error, aggregation, and changes in the environment. The model modifications desired depend on which of these types of causes is responsible for the errors. In this regard it is critical to distinguish between systematic and random error. Practically, error magnitudes that fall within what can be expected based on the uncertainty of parameter estimates are considered random. As the number of observable prediction errors increases it also becomes easier to detect systematic patterns.

The "implementable model-building process" is an iterative procedure. The procedure, in its entirety or with only a few stages, can be repeated until an acceptable model is specified and estimated. This is a labor-intensive activity. If the knowledge of the analyst can be captured in the computer, resulting in a knowledge-based system, we have what McCann and Gallagher (1990) call a "MarketMetrics Knowledge System (M^2KS)". This system is a "marriage" of theory and the application which may lead to a Generalized Modeling Procedure (GMP). A GMP includes testing the data, testing the specification, and testing the statistical properties of the developed model. The GMP starts with data retrieval and data checks. Based on an initial data check, the GMP formulates a model which contains variables that, for example, pass the data check for sufficient observations *and* sufficient variation. After the initial model estimation, various statistical tests and checks are applied and the model is corrected. An iterative procedure is used to arrive at a final model. The final model is stored in the system (McCann, Gallagher, 1990, pp. 106-107).

5.2 Some basic model-building terminology

In Section 1.2 a model is defined as a representation of the most important elements of a perceived real-world system. A mathematical model describes such a system by means of one or more mathematical relations between its elements or variables. In this section[5] we define the basic terminology of:

1. the components or elements of a model;
2. the relations which may exist between these elements.

Elements
The various elements or components of a relation between variables can be seen in the following equation:

$$q_{jt} = \alpha_j + \beta_j a_{jt} + u_{jt}, \quad t = 1, 2, \ldots, T \qquad (5.1)$$

where

q_{jt} = sales (in units) of brand j in period t,
α_j = an unknown constant (intercept),
β_j = an unknown slope (effect) parameter,[6]
a_{jt} = advertising expenditures (in dollars) of brand j in period t,
u_{jt} = a disturbance term, and
T = the number of observations.

---

5. This section can easily be omitted by readers who are familiar with the basic terminology of econometrics.

The objective of the specification of relation (5.1) is to explain variation in the unit sales of brand j. Thus, q_{jt} is the *variable to be explained, the dependent variable* or the *criterion variable*. For this purpose one specifies:

1. the variable(s) that can explain the variation in the dependent variable, referred to as *explanatory variable(s), independent variables* or *predictors* (a_{jt});
2. the *mathematical form* between the criterion variable and predictor(s);
3. a disturbance term which captures the part of the criterion variable that cannot be explained by the predictors.

The mathematical form of (5.1) is simple: it is a linear relation containing a constant term α_j and an effect parameter β_j that indicates the change in the number of units sold when a_{jt} increases by one unit (in this case, one dollar). Parameterization of (5.1) leads to numerical specification of α_j and β_j. The estimated values of α_j and β_j are indicated by $\hat{\alpha}_j$ and $\hat{\beta}_j$. This is illustrated in Figure 5.2, where the values of monthly sales of brand j observed in 1997 are plotted against the corresponding monthly advertising expenditures. The data clearly suggest that there is a relation between a_{jt} and q_{jt}. Low values of q_{jt} correspond to low values of a_{jt}, and similarly for high values. Since the observations do not all fall on the straight line, equation (5.1) does not explain all variation in sales by variation in advertising. But, one will try to determine $\hat{\alpha}_j$ and $\hat{\beta}_j$ in such a way that the estimated relation is the "best" one can obtain. "Best" implies that there exists a criterion against which different sets of estimates can be compared. In *classical* statistics and econometrics, estimates can be obtained through the minimization of the sum of the squared deviations between observed values q_{jt} and estimated ones $\hat{q}_{jt} = (\hat{\alpha}_j + \hat{\beta}_j a_{jt})$, i.e., $\hat{\alpha}_j$ and $\hat{\beta}_j$ are the values which minimize $\sum_{t=1}^{T} \hat{u}_{jt}^2$ where[7] $\hat{u}_{jt} = q_{jt} - \hat{q}_{jt}$. If this criterion is adopted, one refers to estimation by *the method of least squares*.[8] This method is also known as ordinary least squares (OLS). The method assumes a *quadratic loss function*, which means that the degree to which deviations from observed values should be penalized is proportional to the squared deviations. The least squares criterion also assumes that overestimation and underestimation are equally bad.

For the data presented in Figure 5.2 the following estimates are obtained: $\hat{\alpha}_j = 200$, and $\hat{\beta}_j = 0.5$. Also indicated are two values of the estimated disturbance terms (also called the *residuals*), $\hat{u}'_{jt}$, and $\hat{u}''_{jt}$, corresponding to values $a_{jt} = 600$, and 1100, respectively. We note that the least squares criterion is one of several possible criteria, on the basis of which best estimates can be found.[9]

---

6. In regression analysis, α_j and β_j are called the regression coefficients; β_j is also known as a response or slope parameter.

7. The sign $\sum_{t=1}^{T}$ is a summation sign, indicating that T terms (from $t = 1$ to $t = T$) will be added. In the example $\sum_{t=1}^{T} \hat{u}_{jt}^2$ is the compact notation for $\hat{u}_{j1}^2 + \hat{u}_{j2}^2 + \ldots + \hat{u}_{jT}^2$.

8. For a detailed description of this method we refer to econometrics textbooks, such as Amemiya (1994, Chapters 1 and 2), Judge, Griffiths, Hill, Lütkepohl and Lee (1985), Wittink (1988), Stewart (1991), Greene (1997), Goldberger (1998). See also Chapter 16.

9. If, for example, the cost of underpredicting is greater than the cost of overpredicting, one could choose an appropriately asymmetric loss function.

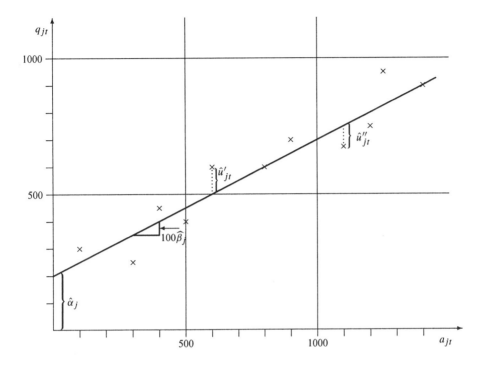

Figure 5.2 Sales in units and advertising expenditures (1).

Because advertising spending does not fully determine sales, the relation:

$$q_{jt} = \alpha_j + \beta_j a_{jt} \tag{5.2}$$

is inadequate. To make the equation complete, a *disturbance term* u_{jt} is added to the right-hand side. A disturbance term is ideally a *random or stochastic variable*. The main characteristic of such a variable is that it assumes different values (or falls into different value intervals), according to some probability distribution. If u_{jt} is stochastic, q_{jt} is stochastic as well. For statistical estimation and testing of the model, the probability distribution of the disturbance term is very important. In Chapter 16, we discuss this in greater detail.

In the above definition, the disturbance term represents the part of sales which one is unable to predict, given knowledge of advertising spending. It is the unexplained part of the relation. The disturbance usually is more than just random error:

1. The larger the *error of measurement* in the variables, the larger the error compo-
nent u_{jt} will be. One reason for such error is sampling. For example, sales of brand j in period t may be obtained from a sample of all retail outlets. Worse, there may also be systematic measurement errors involved. If some outlets are unavailable for inclusion (e.g. a retailer may refuse the market research company access) the error can be systematic.

The advertising expenditures may be obtained through an agency collecting information on advertising space in newspapers and magazines, and advertising spots on radio and television. But the agency may miss information on outdoor advertising and sponsorship of sport events. Errors in measurement may also result from poor measurement instruments or from the use of approximate (or proxy) variables. For example, sales may depend not so much on how much is spent on advertising as on the quality of the copy.

2. The disturbance term also represents *the error due to missing or omitted variables*. It is clear that, in general, sales also depend on variables other than advertising. Excluding those variables means that their effects become part of the disturbance term. Possible reasons for omitting variables are that no data are available, or that neither the manager nor the model builder imagines their relevance.

There will also be many variables which are difficult or impossible to identify, but which each have a negligible effect on sales. Collecting information on these variables, and incorporating them in the model structure will not be worth the cost. It is possible to assume that the disturbance term is truly random if this condition applies.

3. Not including relevant variables is one possible form of *misspecification or specification error*. Another relates to error in the functional relationship. For example, in (5.1) the relation between sales and advertising is assumed to be linear. If there are decreasing returns to scale in advertising, a linear model (which assumes constant returns) is inappropriate. Incorrect specification of the functional form also contributes to the disturbance term.

All elements of equation (5.1) have now been defined.

Other elements of mathematical models can be defined by considering the following set of *"structural relations"* (describing the structure of a market phenomenon):

$$m_{jt} = \beta_{0j} + \beta_{1j} \frac{a_{j,t-1}}{\sum_{r=1}^{n} a_{r,t-1}} + \beta_{2j} \frac{p_{jt}}{\frac{1}{n}\sum_{r=1}^{n} p_{rt}} + \beta_{3j} m_{j,t-1} + u_{jt} \quad (5.3)$$

$$Q_t = \gamma_0 + \gamma_1 \sum_{r=1}^{n} a_{r,t-1} + \gamma_2 Inc_t + v_t \quad (5.4)$$

$$q_{jt} = m_{jt} Q_t \quad (5.5)$$
$$R_{jt} = p_{jt} q_{jt} \quad (5.6)$$
$$TC_{jt} = c_j q_{jt} + FC_j + a_{jt} \quad (5.7)$$
$$\pi_{jt} = R_{jt} - TC_{jt} \quad (5.8)$$
$$\pi_{jt}^{a} = (1-\tau)\pi_{jt} \quad (5.9)$$

where

m_{jt} = market share of a brand j in period t,

$$a_{jt} = \text{advertising expenditures of brand } j \text{ in period } t,$$
$$p_{jt} = \text{price per unit of brand } j \text{ in period } t,$$
$$u_{jt}, v_t = \text{disturbance terms,}$$
$$Q_t = \text{product class sales in period } t,$$
$$Inc_t = \text{disposable income in period } t,$$
$$q_{jt} = \text{sales (in units) of brand } j \text{ in period } t,$$
$$R_{jt} = \text{revenue of brand } j \text{ in period } t,$$
$$TC_{jt} = \text{total cost of brand } j \text{ in period } t,$$
$$c_j = \text{variable cost per unit of brand } j,^{10}$$
$$FC_j = \text{fixed costs of brand } j,$$
$$\pi_{jt} = \text{profit (before tax) from marketing brand } j \text{ in period } t,$$
$$\pi_{jt}^a = \text{after tax profit,}$$
$$\tau = \text{tax rate,}$$
$$t = 1, \ldots, T, \text{ and}$$
$$T = \text{total number of observations.}$$

In relation (5.3) market share is a function of the price of j in period t, which is defined relative to the average price of the product class.[11] It is also a function of advertising share in period $t-1$, based on the belief that advertising does not influence purchases instantaneously. Also in (5.3) market share in t is a function of its value in period $t-1$. This is a reflection of market inertia or of the fact that advertising share in periods prior to $t-1$, and relative price in periods prior to t have longer-term effects.[12]

Relation (5.4) shows that variation in *product class* sales is explained by variation in total advertising expenditures of all brands, and by variation in disposable income.

From the definitions above, it follows that m_{jt} is a criterion variable in relation (5.3). However, m_{jt} also defines, together with Q_t, the unit sales variable in (5.5). In general, variables are placed in two distinct groups according to whether or not they are explained in the model. *Endogenous* variables are those which are to be determined by the phenomena expressed in the model. *Exogenous* variables, on the other hand, are determined outside the model. Thus, we can say that a model represents the determination of endogenous variables on the basis of exogenous variables. In the model described in relations (5.3)-(5.9), the following variables are endogenous: m_{jt}, Q_t, q_{jt}, R_{jt}, TC_{jt}, π_{jt}, π_{jt}^a. These variables are explained by equations (5.3)-(5.9). In this case, the number of endogenous variables is equal to the number of equations. The exogenous variables are: $a_{j,t-1}$, $\sum_{r=1}^{n} a_{r,t-1}$, p_{jt}, $\frac{1}{n}\sum_{r=1}^{n} p_{rt}$, Inc_t, c_j and FC_j.

The exogenous variables can further be classified as:

1. decision variables (also called instruments or controllable variables), and

---

10. Variable cost could also be time varying, in which case c_j becomes c_{jt}.
11. Here, the average price is obtained as a simple arithmetical average. A sales weighted price could be used instead.
12. We discuss this in Chapter 6.

2. environmental variables.

The decision variables include variables controlled by firm j and variables controlled by j's competitors. Examples of the former are $a_{j,t-1}$ and p_{jt}; examples of the latter are $a_{r,t-1}$ and $p_{rt}, r = 1, \ldots, n, r \neq j$.

The environmental variables capture important phenomena relevant to the modeled system that cannot be controlled by the decision makers. In the system of equations (5.3)-(5.9) Inc_t is an environmental variable.

In relation (5.3) market share of brand j in period t is an endogenous variable which depends, among others, on the market share of j in the preceding period $t-1$, a lagged endogenous variable. This requires that we reformulate our statement with respect to the relation between endogenous and exogenous variables. The function of a system such as (5.3)-(5.9), is to *describe the current* (i.e. non-lagged) *values of the endogenous variables in terms of current and lagged values of the exogenous variables and of lagged values of the endogenous variables.* The current endogenous variables are called *jointly dependent,* and the set of all current and lagged exogenous variables plus the lagged endogenous variables *predetermined.* To summarize, we distinguish the following kinds of variables:

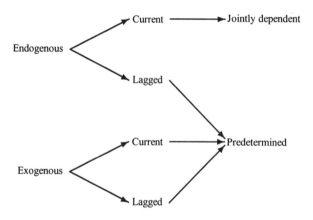

This classification of variables is especially relevant when parameters are estimated in systems of relations (Section 16.4 and Section 17.1). By expressing the jointly dependent variables in terms of predetermined variables only, we obtain *"reduced-form relations"* of a model.[13] Assuming that the unknown parameters have been estimated, and ignoring the disturbance terms, the following reduced-form can be

---

13. It is also possible to express the current endogenous variables in terms of current and lagged exogenous variables only. This expression is called a *final form,* and is obtained by a repeated elimination of all lagged endogenous variables from the reduced-form relation. See, for example, Judge et al. (1985, p. 661).

obtained:

$$\widehat{\pi_{jt}^a} = (1 - \tau)\left\{(p_{jt} - c_j)(\hat{\beta}_{0j} + \hat{\beta}_{1j}\frac{a_{j,t-1}}{\sum_{r=1}^{n} a_{r,t-1}} + \hat{\beta}_{2j}\frac{p_{jt}}{\frac{1}{n}\sum_{r=1}^{n} p_{rt}}\right. \quad (5.10)$$

$$\left. + \hat{\beta}_{3j}m_{j,t-1})(\hat{\gamma}_0 + \hat{\gamma}_1\sum_{r=1}^{n} a_{r,t-1} + \hat{\gamma}_2 Inc_t) - FC_j - a_{jt}\right\}.$$

Similarly, reduced forms for $\widehat{\pi}_{jt}$, $\widehat{TC}_{jt}$, $\widehat{R}_{jt}$, and $\hat{q}_{jt}$ can be obtained. The jointly dependent variables m_{jt} and Q_t are already expressed in terms of predetermined variables, in relations (5.3) and (5.4) respectively.

The variables in a marketing model can not always be measured on a metric scale.[14] For some variables only the presence or absence of an activity can be registered. We then refer to *qualitative variables*. A special class of these consists of so-called *dummy variables*. Typically, these variables are *assigned* a value of one in the presence, and zero in the absence, of a given characteristic. As is shown in subsequent chapters, dummy variables may be introduced in order to account for unusual or special events. For example, let Q_t in (5.4) represent product class sales of detergents. In the summer months (June, July, August) the sales of detergents may increase because people spend more time outside and clothes have to be washed more frequently. It is also possible, however, that there are less sales because people wear less clothes. Anyhow, we may observe a temporary shift in the demand curve. We can accommodate this by adding a dummy variable to equation (5.4):

$$Q_t = \gamma_0 + \gamma_1\sum_{r=1}^{n} a_{r,t-1} + \gamma_2 Inc_t + \gamma_3\delta_t + v_t \quad (5.4a)$$

where

$$\delta_t = 1 \text{ for } t = \text{June, July, August, 0 otherwise.}$$

Thus, if $\hat{\gamma}_3 > 0$, predicted sales shifts upward and if $\hat{\gamma}_3 < 0$ it shifts downward in June, July, August, holding other things constant, and will return to its normal level afterwards. We note that in (5.4a) we assume that the change in sales is the same for all three months. If this is not realistic, (5.4a) can be modified by introducing additional dummy variables. Specifically, use of the stockpiled product will correspond to a reduction in sales.

Another example of a model with dummy variables is the SCAN*PRO model. This model proposed by Wittink, Addona, Hawkes and Porter (1988) was developed for commercial purposes and has been used in over 2000 commercial applications in the United States, Canada, Europe, and elsewhere. This model captures the effects of temporary price cuts, displays, and feature advertising for multiple brands on one brand's unit sales in a metropolitan area. This brand sales model, where the brand

---

14. Variables measured on an interval or ratio scale are called metric. If measured on a nominal or ordinal scale they are non-metric. See, for example, Torgerson (1959).

sales are measured at the store level, contains many qualitative variables to account for:

- Seasonality of sales, using weekly indicator variables.
- Heterogeneity in store size, using store indicator variables.
- Promotional variables such as the use of displays, featuring and the combination of displays and featuring. The indicator variables for these promotions have a value of one if a brand is promoted by a store in a (weekly) period t and zero otherwise.

The weekly indicator variables in the SCAN*PRO model are also used to account for the possible effects of *omitted variables*. The "classical" SCAN*PRO model does not include, for example, coupon distributions or manufacturer advertising variables.

The indicator variables which measure the promotions are *proxy variables*. Displays of products by retailers can differ in location, size, etc. Similarly, a retailer can feature a brand in a weekly advertisement in different ways. Until more precise measures of these promotions are taken, one has to be concerned about measurement error in these proxy variables. The SCAN*PRO model is introduced in Section 9.3.

Few if any *metric* variables are measured or observed without *error*. Variables are often measured with some uncertainty or are recorded inadequately. For example, the endogenous variable "sales" can be measured at the consumer level, by means of a household panel, which is subject to error due to cooperation refusals, or at the retail level using a sample of stores. Data on sales can also be obtained using ex-factory sales. *External* data on inventories at the retail and wholesale level can be used to correct the *"internal"* ex-factory sales data for such fluctuations. Sales data are not only measured at different *levels* but also by different *methods*. For example, sales data are obtained at the retail level either with scanners or through traditional store audits. It has been demonstrated[15] that the different methods of registration and the levels at which sales are measured can lead to large differences in sales amounts. The same can hold for other relevant marketing variables such as price, distribution and advertising. Less is known about the sensitivity of parameter estimates to the kind of data used to parameterize relations. However, models which have the same (mathematical) structure and the same variables but which are based on data obtained by different methods or measured at different levels can lead to substantially different marketing decisions.[16]

Some variables of considerable interest are *unobservable*. The problem of unobservable variables takes on greater importance as researchers explore new areas of empirical research.[17] These models include theoretical or abstract variables, for which the measures are known to be imperfect or the scales of measurement do not exist

---

15. See Leeflang, Olivier (1980, 1982, 1985), Leeflang, Plat (1988), Foekens, Leeflang (1992).
16. See Leeflang, Olivier (1980, 1985), Shoemaker, Pringle (1980).
17. Compare Judge et al. (1985, p. 707).

at all. Examples of such variables are utility, attitude, advertising goodwill, brand equity, buying intention but also "demand". *Unobservable* or *latent* variables may be distinguished from observable variables or indicators. Indicators may be related to latent variables in, for example, the following way:

$$q_t^{cp} = \xi^{cp} + \gamma_1 \eta_t + \zeta_t \tag{5.11}$$

where

$$q_t^{cp} = \text{sales measured by a consumer panel } (cp) \text{ in } t,$$
$$\xi^{cp} = \text{an unknown, parameter,}$$
$$\eta_t = \text{the "true" sales in } t,$$
$$\gamma_1 = \text{a parameter linking the indicator to the latent variable,}$$
$$\zeta_t = \text{a disturbance term.}$$

In (5.11) η_t is the latent variable "true" sales and q_t^{cp} is an observable variable. The disturbance term represents the measurement error. The true sales may be indicated by different observable variables.

$$q_t^{cp} = \xi^{cp} + \gamma_{11} \eta_t + \zeta_{1t}$$
$$q_t^{ra} = \xi^{ra} + \gamma_{12} \eta_t + \zeta_{2t} \tag{5.12}$$
$$q_t^{ef} = \xi^{ef} + \gamma_{13} \eta_t + \zeta_{3t}$$

where

$$q_t^{ra} = \text{sales measured by a retail audit } (ra) \text{ in period } t,$$
$$q_t^{ef} = \text{sales measured by "ex-factory sales" } (ef) \text{ in period } t, \text{ and}$$
$$\zeta_{1t}, \zeta_{2t}, \zeta_{3t} = \text{disturbance terms.}$$

In these equations, for reasons of identification one of the γ parameters needs to be set to one, e.g., $\gamma_{11} = 1$. We return to this and other issues in Section 17.1.

Summary: Variables can be classified into observable and unobservable variables. Observable variables can be specified to depend on unobservable variables. The advantages of doing this is that we make the role of measurement error explicit. An other useful classification of variables consists of *metric* (quantitative) and *non-metric* (qualitative) variables. Qualitative variables can be incorporated into a model using dummy variables.

Relations
We can distinguish the following kinds of relations or equations:[18]

1. behavioral equations;
2. definition equations;

---

18. See, for example, Klein (1962, pp. 225-226), Theil (1971, pp. 1-4).

3. technical equations;
4. institutional equations.

Furthermore we can distinguish:

5. micro- and macro relations;
6. static and dynamic relations.

Each of these is briefly described below.

Behavioral equations
Behavioral relations refer to system behavior. For example, equation (5.3) relates the aggregate behavior of buyers of a brand, expressed in terms of market share, to price, advertising, and past buying behavior. Similarly, equation (5.4) relates the aggregate behavior of buyers of a product class, in terms of product class sales, to total advertising spending and to disposable income. We discuss other examples of behavioral equations in Section 5.3.

Definition equations
Definition relations feature known identities. We distinguish:

• *Stock-type definition equations relating to points in time*, i.e.:

$$Q_t = \sum_{r=1}^{n} q_{rt} \tag{5.13}$$

where

Q_t = product class sales in period t (say, April 1997),
q_{rt} = sales of brand r in period t, and
n = total number of brands.

• *Flow-type definition equations relating to changes over time*, i.e.:

$$Q_t - Q_{t-1} = \Delta Q_t = \sum_{r=1}^{n}(q_{rt} - q_{r,t-1}) = \sum_{r=1}^{n} \Delta q_{rt} \tag{5.14}$$

which indicates that the change in product class sales in period t, from period $t - 1$, is equal to the sum of changes in sales of all brands $r = 1, \ldots, n$, assuming that the total number of brands remains equal to n. Both (5.13) and (5.14) are identities, provided the definitions of the variables appearing in (5.13) and (5.14) are mutually consistent.

From (5.13) to (5.14) it is clear that the *stock type* (5.13) definition relations and the *flow type* (5.14) definition relations are interrelated.

In some cases, definition relations can be substituted into other relations of a model, which may reduce the number of variables and equations.

Technical equations
In these equations, variables are related on the basis of their technical connection. Examples are production functions that describe quantitative relationships between inputs and outputs. Technical coefficients describe how the former are transformed into the latter.

If c_j and FC_j are known, (5.7) is a definition equation. It is a technical equation, if the c_j and FC_j are unknown values. The relation to be estimated could then be written as:

$$TPC_{jt} = \alpha_0 + \alpha_1 q_{jt} + w_t \tag{5.15}$$

where

$$TPC_{jt} = TC_{jt} - a_{jt} = \text{total production cost, and}$$
$$w_t = \text{a disturbance term.}$$

Obtaining estimated values $\hat{\alpha}_0$, $\hat{\alpha}_1$ would give us estimates of FC_j and c_j respectively.[19]

Institutional equations
In institutional equations, parameters result from decisions made by institutions such as governments (at various levels). An example is equation (5.9) relating before- to after-tax profit, the parameter τ being determined by fiscal authorities. Another example is the relation between the interest rate on savings paid by banks, and the length of time savings must remain deposited.

Micro- and macro-relations
Relations can be specified at different levels of aggregation. For example, the demand for brand j, in period t can be specified at the household level (a micro-relation), at the store level, at the chain level, where a chain consists of different stores, at the regional, national or cross national level. Micro- and macro-relations refer to the degree of aggregation over entities. A relation is a macro-relation if measurement covers multiple entities. An analysis of the relationship between micro- and macro-relations deals with the theory of aggregation. We pursue this in Chapter 14.

Static and dynamic relations
When variables differ in time subscripts but occur in the same equation, as is the case in (5.3) and (5.4), we speak about a *dynamic* relation. Otherwise the relation is said to be *static*, as is true of (5.7). In Chapter 6 we discuss the modeling of dynamic relations.

---

19. The cost function in (5.15) assumes constant variable cost per unit. More complex cost functions are, of course, possible.

5.3 Specification of behavioral equations: some simple examples

We now describe examples of behavioral equations and distinguish three types of mathematical forms:

1. linear in both parameters and variables;
2. non-linear in the variables, but linear in the parameters;
3. non-linear in the parameters and not linearizable.

The distinction is important from the point of view of estimation. Forms 1, and 2 are estimable by classic econometric methods, whereas 3 is not.

5.3.1 MODELS LINEAR IN PARAMETERS AND VARIABLES

Models linear in parameters and variables have the following structure.[20]

$$y_t = \alpha_0 + \sum_{\ell=1}^{L} \alpha_\ell x_{\ell t} \tag{5.16}$$

where

$$y_t = \text{value of the dependent variable in period } t,$$
$$x_{\ell t} = \text{value of independent variable } \ell \text{ in period } t, \text{ and}$$
$$\alpha_0, \alpha_1, \ldots, \alpha_L = \text{the model parameters.}$$

Equation (5.16) is an example of a linear, additive model. It is additive in the sense that each predictor contributes only a single effect to the determination of the criterion variable. While this is the simplest possible representation, it also has serious drawbacks. The linearity assumption implies constant returns to scale with respect to each of the independent variables. This can be seen by taking the first-order partial derivative of y_t with respect to any of the independent variables $x_{\ell t}$:

$$\frac{\partial y_t}{\partial x_{\ell t}} = \alpha_\ell, \quad \ell = 1, \ldots, L \tag{5.17}$$

which means that increasing $x_{\ell t}$ by one unit results in an increase of y_t by α_ℓ units holding the other variables constant. This assumption of constant returns to scale is unreasonable most of the time. For example, if x_ℓ is advertising and y sales, we might expect an increment in x_ℓ to have more effect when x_ℓ itself is lower than when it is higher. This means that we expect advertising to have decreasing returns to scale.[21]

Another drawback of the linear additive model is that it assumes no interactions between the variables. This can again be seen by looking at the first-order derivative in (5.17). Since it is constant, it follows that the effect of x_ℓ on y does not depend on

---

20. In most of this section the disturbance term is omitted for convenience.
21. This is confirmed in studies by Little (1979). More generally, one expects advertising to show increasing returns first, then decreasing returns. We show examples of how to model this in Section 5.3.2.

the values of other independent variables. Once again, this assumption is often unreasonable. For example, advertising will have a greater effect on sales if the brand is available in more rather than in fewer retail stores. At decreasing levels of availability, advertising should have increasingly smaller effects (and zero effect if the product is not available at all).

5.3.2 MODELS LINEAR IN THE PARAMETERS BUT NOT IN THE VARIABLES

A second class of models are those which are non-linear in the variables, but linear in the parameters. They are also called *non-linear additive models*. Equation (5.18) is an example of such a model:

$$y_t = \alpha_0 + \alpha_1 e^{x_{1t}} + \alpha_2\sqrt{x_{2t}} + \alpha_3 x_{3t} + \alpha_4 \ln x_{4t} \tag{5.18}$$

in which three variables (x_{1t}, x_{2t}, and x_{4t}) are assumed to have non-linear effects. This model can be transformed into the following linear additive relation:

$$y_t = \alpha_0 + \sum_{\ell=1}^{4} \alpha_\ell x_{\ell t}^*. \tag{5.19}$$

This is accomplished by simply defining:

$$x_{1t}^* = e^{x_{1t}}$$
$$x_{2t}^* = \sqrt{x_{2t}}$$
$$x_{3t}^* = x_{3t}$$
$$x_{4t}^* = \ln x_{4t}$$

and the $x_{\ell t}^*$ are themselves, except for x_{3t}^*, non-linear functions of the underlying variables. Thus, from the point of view of estimation, equations (5.16) and (5.18) are similar.

The proposed relation between each independent variable and the dependent variable should be based on *theory* or *experience*. If we know that advertising shows decreasing returns to scale we can focus our attention on possible mathematical formulations. In addition, as we show in Chapter 7, model-building criteria can provide direction with regard to the specification of a model.

We next discuss a few formulations, with their characteristics, advantages, and disadvantages. Consider the following relation:

$$q_{jt} = \alpha_0 + \alpha_1 a_{jt} + \alpha_2 a_{jt}^2 + u_{jt} \tag{5.20}$$

where

q_{jt} = sales in units of brand j in period t,
a_{jt} = advertising expenditures of brand j in period t, and
u_{jt} = disturbance term.

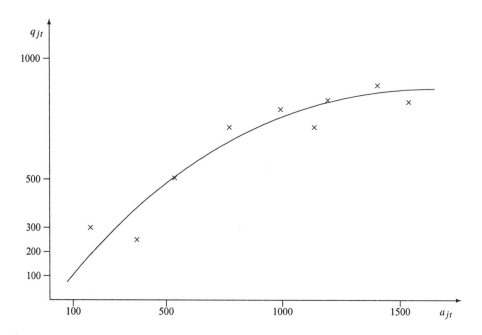

Figure 5.3 Sales in units and advertising expenditures (2) (equation (5.20)).

Figure 5.3 suggests that (5.20) provides a better fit than the straight line shown in Figure 5.2. would have. In Figure 5.3 the fitted sales will increase with advertising, but at a decreasing rate, i.e. the increases in sales become smaller as a_{jt} gets larger. To understand the nature of effects, we can use the first derivative of q_{jt} with respect to a_{jt}:

$$\frac{dq_{jt}}{da_{jt}} = \alpha_1 + 2\alpha_2 a_{jt}. \tag{5.21}$$

If $\alpha_1 > 0$ and $\alpha_2 < 0$, we have decreasing returns to scale. But if

$$a_{jt} > \frac{\alpha_1}{-2\alpha_2}$$

sales would decline with further increases in advertising. This phenomenon is known as *supersaturation* (Hanssens et al., 1990, p.42). Supersaturation results if excessive marketing effort causes a negative response.[22] If this phenomenon runs counter to our prior beliefs, we could reject the model specified in equation (5.20). Nevertheless, the model may perform well within a certain range of values of a_{jt}. For example, in Figure 5.3, a_{jt} ranges between \$175 and \$1,600. Perhaps we should restrict the use of the parameter estimates $\hat{\alpha}_0$, $\hat{\alpha}_1$, and $\hat{\alpha}_2$ to this range of variation. Indeed, if we

---

22. Supersaturation, is perhaps more realistic if the advertising variable a_{jt} in (5.20) is replaced by personal selling efforts. An excessive number of visits by sales persons may have a negative effect on sales.

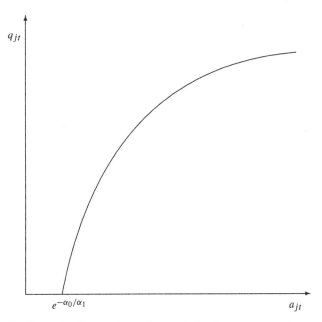

Figure 5.4 Example of a semi-logarithmic relation ($q_{jt} = \alpha_0 + \alpha_1 \ln a_{jt}, \alpha_1 > 0$).

have no confidence in the estimated model outside a specific range[23] of variation, we should make this explicit. We discuss this point in more detail in Chapter 7.

There are other ways to represent decreasing returns to scale. Two alternatives to (5.20) are shown in (5.22) and (5.24). A first possibility is to express the dependent variable, say sales, as a function of the *square root* of the independent variable, say advertising,

$$q_{jt} = \alpha_0 + \alpha_1 \sqrt{a_{jt}}. \tag{5.22}$$

The first-order derivative of q_{jt} with respect to a_{jt} is:

$$\frac{dq_{jt}}{da_{jt}} = \frac{\alpha_1}{2\sqrt{a_{jt}}} \tag{5.23}$$

which shows decreasing returns to scale, and tends to zero when a_{jt} is very large.

Another frequently used mathematical form is the *semi-logarithmic* one, i.e.,

$$q_{jt} = \alpha_0 + \alpha_1 \ln a_{jt} \tag{5.24}$$

where $\ln a_{jt}$ is the natural logarithm of a_{jt}. An example is shown in Figure 5.4. Now for some values of a_{jt}, predicted sales is negative:

---

23. The main reason for this is the fact that one never knows the "true" model. Experience and experimentation, however, may help to reduce uncertainty.

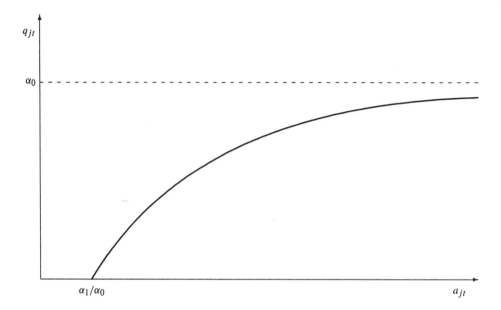

Figure 5.5 Reciprocal sales-advertising relation (5.26a).

$$\alpha_0 + \alpha_1 \ln a_{jt} \ < \ 0, \ \text{if}$$
$$\ln a_{jt} \ < \ \frac{-\alpha_0}{\alpha_1},$$

or

$$a_{jt} \ < \ e^{-\alpha_0/\alpha_1}.$$

Thus, this model is not acceptable when this condition applies. However, equation (5.24) shows decreasing returns to scale over the whole range of a_{jt}, since:

$$\frac{dq_{jt}}{da_{jt}} = \frac{\alpha_1}{a_{jt}} \tag{5.25}$$

which decreases with a_{jt}. Again, returns to advertising tend to zero as a_{jt} becomes very large.

The sales-advertising relations (5.20), (5.22), and (5.24) all represent decreasing returns to scale. All three, however, are deficient for high values of advertising: the first one (5.20) because for high values of a_{jt}, q_{jt} starts to decline; the second and third ones, because q_{jt} tends to infinity, when a_{jt} tends to infinity. Since we know that maximum sales potential is a finite quantity, we prefer sales-advertising models

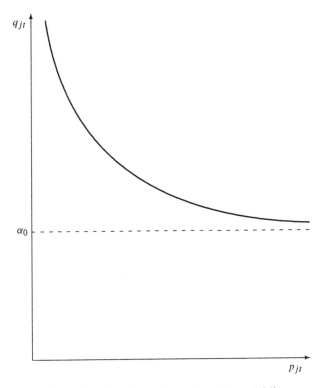

Figure 5.6 Reciprocal sales-price relation (5.26b).

in which sales approaches a saturation level as advertising grows large.[24] A simple
example is the *reciprocal relation*:

$$q_{jt} = \alpha_0 + \frac{\alpha_1}{a_{jt}}, \text{ with } \alpha_0 > 0, \alpha_1 < 0. \tag{5.26a}$$

As a_{jt} increases, q_{jt} approaches α_0 asymptotically (see Figure 5.5). Note that if $a_{jt} <$
α_1/α_0, q_{jt} is negative. Thus, while a reciprocal relation leads to a finite asymptote for
q_{jt} for increasing a_{jt}, it can still be problematic for very low values of a_{jt}.

Another example of a reciprocal relation is:

$$q_{jt} = \alpha_0 + \frac{\alpha_1}{p_{jt}}, \text{ with } \alpha_0, \alpha_1 > 0 \tag{5.26b}$$

where

$$p_{jt} = \text{ price of brand } j \text{ in period } t.$$

An illustration of equation (5.26b) is shown in Figure 5.6. It is clear that (5.26b) may
not be meaningful for extremely low values of p_{jt}: as p_{jt} goes to zero, q_{jt} goes

---

24. We analyze this problem further in Chapter 7. One of the implementation criteria concerns model behavior
for extreme values of the explanatory variables.

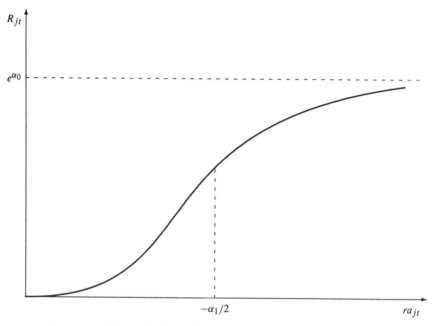

Figure 5.7 Logarithmic reciprocal relation (5.27).

to infinity. Equation (5.26b) may, therefore, only be a reasonable approximation of reality within a restricted range of values for p_{jt}.

If one wants a response function to show increasing returns to scale first, then decreasing returns, the *logarithmic reciprocal* relation given in (5.27) may be used:

$$\ln R_{jt} = \alpha_0 + \frac{\alpha_1}{ra_{jt}} \tag{5.27}$$

where

$\quad R_{jt} \;=\;$ revenues, obtained by a retailer, for product group j
$\qquad\qquad$ in period t, and

$\quad ra_{jt} \;=\;$ number of products (e.g. sizes and brands) in product
$\qquad\qquad$ group j in t (range).

In Figure 5.7, we see that this curve, for $\alpha_0 > 0$ and $\alpha_1 < 0$, shows increasing returns to scale for $ra_{jt} < -\alpha_1/2$, and decreasing returns for $ra_{jt} > -\alpha_1/2$. This is demonstrated below. Relation (5.27) can also be written as:

$$R_{jt} = e^{(\alpha_0 + \alpha_1/ra_{jt})}. \tag{5.28}$$

Differentiating (5.28) with respect to ra_{jt} we get:

$$\frac{dR_{jt}}{d\,ra_{jt}} = \frac{-\alpha_1}{ra_{jt}^2} e^{(\alpha_0 + \alpha_1/ra_{jt})}. \tag{5.29}$$

The second-order derivative is:

$$\frac{d^2 R_{jt}}{d\, ra_{jt}^2} = \frac{\alpha_1^2}{ra_{jt}^4} e^{(\alpha_0 + \alpha_1 / ra_{jt})} + \frac{2\alpha_1}{ra_{jt}^3} e^{(\alpha_0 + \alpha_1 / ra_{jt})} \tag{5.30}$$

$$= \left[\frac{\alpha_1^2 + 2\alpha_1 ra_{jt}}{ra_{jt}^4} \right] e^{(\alpha_0 + \alpha_1 / ra_{jt})}.$$

It follows that the inflection point is $ra_{jt} = -\alpha_1/2$. Equation (5.28) has an asymptote e^{α_0} as ra_{jt} increases.[25]

So far, we have focused on the issue of varying returns to scale. In Section 5.3.1. we indicated that a second deficiency of the model linear in parameters and variables is that it does not allow for interactions. One way to overcome this deficiency is to add interaction variables. For example, with two predictors x_1 and x_2 we can add the product $x_1 \cdot x_2$:

$$y_t = \alpha_0 + \alpha_1 x_{1t} + \alpha_2 x_{2t} + \alpha_3 x_{1t} x_{2t}. \tag{5.31}$$

The effect of a marginal change in x_{1t} on y_t is now:

$$\frac{\partial y_t}{\partial x_{1t}} = \alpha_1 + \alpha_3 x_{2t}. \tag{5.32}$$

With α_3 positive, (5.32) indicates that the marginal effect of x_{1t} increases with x_{2t}. For example, if x_{1t} is advertising, and x_{2t} distribution, measured by the number of retail stores carrying the brand, (5.32) allows for advertising to have a larger effect if more stores sell the brand.

A disadvantage of the interaction term formulation becomes apparent when the number of predictor variables exceeds two. For example, with three predictors, a full interaction model becomes:

$$y_t = \alpha_0 + \alpha_1 x_{1t} + \alpha_2 x_{2t} + \alpha_3 x_{3t} + \alpha_4 x_{1t} x_{2t} + \alpha_5 x_{1t} x_{3t} + \alpha_6 x_{2t} x_{3t} +$$
$$\alpha_7 x_{1t} x_{2t} x_{3t} \tag{5.33}$$

and

$$\frac{\partial y_t}{\partial x_{1t}} = \alpha_1 + \alpha_4 x_{2t} + \alpha_5 x_{3t} + \alpha_7 x_{2t} x_{3t}. \tag{5.34}$$

In general, with L predictor variables, a full interaction model contains 2^L terms. It can easily be seen that both estimation and interpretation will become problematic, even for fairly small values of L. Thus, it is often necessary for a model builder to specify in advance which of many possible interaction variables to include.

---

25. This model has been used for non-frequently purchased consumer goods by Brown and Tucker (1961). Bemmaor (1984) used this model in his study of an advertising threshold effect. See for another application Leeflang (1975).

One of the most frequently encountered marketing response functions is the so-called *multiplicative model:*[26]

$$y_t = \alpha_0 x_{1t}^{\alpha_1} x_{2t}^{\alpha_2} \dots x_{Lt}^{\alpha_k} \tag{5.35}$$

or more compactly:[27]

$$y_t = \alpha_0 \prod_{\ell=1}^{L} x_{\ell t}^{\alpha_\ell}. \tag{5.36}$$

Response function (5.35) has the following desirable characteristics. First, it accounts for a specific form of interaction between the various instruments. This can easily be seen by looking at the first-order derivative with respect to, say, instrument x_ℓ:

$$\frac{\partial y_t}{\partial x_{\ell t}} = \alpha_0 \alpha_\ell x_{1t}^{\alpha_1} x_{2t}^{\alpha_2} \dots x_{\ell t}^{\alpha_\ell - 1} \dots x_{Lt}^{\alpha_L} \tag{5.37}$$

which can be written as:

$$\frac{\partial y_t}{\partial x_{\ell t}} = \frac{\alpha_\ell y_t}{x_{\ell t}}. \tag{5.38}$$

The impact of a change in $x_{\ell t}$ on y_t is therefore a function of y_t itself, which means that it depends not only on the value of $x_{\ell t}$ but on all the other variables as well.

Secondly, model (5.35) has a simple economic interpretation. Letting η_ℓ be the elasticity of y with respect to variable x_ℓ, i.e.:

$$\eta_\ell = \frac{\partial y_t}{\partial x_{\ell t}} \frac{x_{\ell t}}{y_t}$$

and using (5.38) we find; $\eta_\ell = \alpha_\ell$, which means that the exponents in a multiplicative response model are constant elasticities (This is a disadvantage if one wants η_ℓ to depend on x_ℓ or on $x'_\ell, \ell' \neq \ell$). A third advantage of the model is that, although it is non-linear in the parameters (they appear as exponents), a simple transformation can make it linear. Taking the logarithm of (5.35) we obtain:

$$\ln y_t = \ln \alpha_0 + \alpha_1 \ln x_{1t} + \alpha_2 \ln x_{2t} + \dots + \alpha_L \ln x_{Lt}. \tag{5.39}$$

Equation (5.39) is linear in the parameters $\alpha_0^*, \alpha_1, \alpha_2, \dots, \alpha_L$, where $\alpha_0^* (= \ln \alpha_0)$.[28] Equation (5.39) is sometimes referred to as a *double-logarithmic* relation in contrast to a *semi-logarithmic* one, such as (5.24), where logarithms only appear in the right-hand side of the equation.

---

26. Also referred to as Cobb-Douglas response functions because the structure is identical to that of Cobb-Douglas production functions, $Q = \alpha L^\beta C^\gamma$ (Q = quantity, L = labor, C = capital).

27. $\Pi_{\ell=1}^{L}$ is a product sign indicating that L terms from $\ell = 1$ to $\ell = L$ will be multiplied. For example, $\Pi_{\ell=1}^{L} x_\ell$ is the compact notation for $x_1 \cdot x_2, \dots, \cdot x_L$.

28. In fact we saw a similar example before. Model (5.28), is non-linear in the parameters α_0 and α_1. Taking logarithms, however, makes it linear (see equation (5.27)).

With regard to interaction effect, shown in (5.37) we note that there are many examples of interaction effects in the marketing literature (Gatignon, 1993, Logman, 1995). Consider, for example the interaction between communication expenditures and price. There are alternative theories, i.e. "the advertising as market power" and "the advertising as information" schools of thought. According to the first school, high communication expenditures (in particular advertising) allow firms to obtain market power, in part because consumers become less price sensitive (Conamor, Wilson, 1974, Krishnamurthi, Raj, 1985). However, supporters of the "advertising as information" school argue that increased communication encourages brand comparisons which will increase price sensitivity (Prasad, Ring, 1976, Wittink, 1977 and Kanetkar, Weinberg and Weiss, 1992)[29].

Many other interaction effects are discussed in Logman (1995). One of the relations which is quite often used to study interactions is a so-called "extended multiplicative relation" (Logman, 1995):

$$\ln y_t = \ln \alpha_0 + \alpha_1 \ln x_{1t} + \alpha_2 \ln x_{2t} + \alpha_3 \ln x_{1t} x_{2t} \tag{5.40}$$

which is a combination of (5.39) and (5.31). Equation (5.40) allows the elasticity, of, say, x_1, to depend on x_2.

To see the functional form of relations in the multiplicative model, consider the case with only one explanatory variable:

$$y_t = \alpha_0 x_{1t}^{\alpha_1}. \tag{5.41}$$

Figure 5.8 shows (5.41) for various values of α_1. Curve I represents the case $\alpha_1 > 1$, i.e. increasing returns to scale. Curve II is typical for $0 < \alpha_1 < 1$, i.e. decreasing returns to scale. This is what we might expect if x_1 were advertising. Curve III illustrates the case $-1 < \alpha_1 < 0$, and finally curve IV, $\alpha_1 < -1$. The latter two might apply when x_1 is a price variable, curve III representing inelastic demand and curve IV elastic.

Multiplicative demand functions have been used in empirical studies for a very long time.[30] In empirical research in marketing of the econometric variety, it is one of the most popular specifications.

There are many other linearizable forms besides the multiplicative model. One is the *exponential model*:

$$y_t = \alpha_0 e^{\alpha_1 x_{1t}} \tag{5.42}$$

which, after taking logarithms, becomes linear in the parameters $\gamma_0 \, (= \ln \alpha_0)$ and α_1, i.e.:

$$\ln y_t = \gamma_0 + \alpha_1 x_{1t}. \tag{5.43}$$

---

29. For more thorough discussions of this "controversy" in interactions, see Popkowski-Leszczyc, Rao (1989) and Kaul, Wittink (1995).
30. See, for example, Moore (1914) and Schultz (1938).

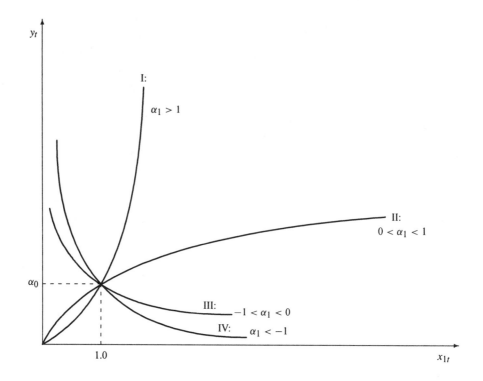

Figure 5.8 Examples of multiplicative relations.

The exponential model is represented in Figure 5.9. This model may, also, with α_1 negative, be appropriate for a sales-price relation. For price (x_{1t}) equal to zero, sales equal α_0, whereas for price going to infinity, sales tend to zero.[31] However, for $\alpha_1 >$ 0, (5.42) has no saturation level. Yet for almost all products in virtually any market it holds that no matter how much marketing effort is expended, there is a finite upper limit to sales. We show later how the saturation level is a finite quantity in the modified exponential model (5.50), which is an intrinsically non-linear model.

Another popular specification in empirical research in marketing is the logit model, which is discussed in detail in Chapters 9 and 12. A specific version of a logit model is the *logistic* specification (5.44):[32]

$$y_t = \frac{1}{1 + \exp{-(\alpha_0 + \sum_{\ell=1}^{L} \alpha_\ell x_{\ell t})}}. \tag{5.44}$$

This relation can be linearized and rewritten as:

$$\ln\left(\frac{y_t}{1 - y_t}\right) = \alpha_0 + \sum_{\ell=1}^{L} \alpha_\ell x_{\ell t}. \tag{5.45}$$

---

31. Cowling and Cubbin (1971) used this functional form to explain the United Kingdom market for cars in terms of quality-adjusted price.
32. See Nooteboom (1989) for an application.

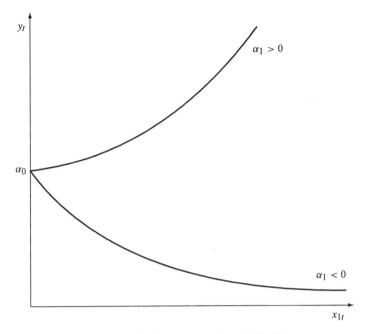

Figure 5.9 The exponential model (5.42).

We can also use the *Gompertz model*, which has a S-shaped form:

$$y_t = \alpha_0 \cdot \alpha_1^{\alpha_2^{x_{1t}}} \tag{5.46}$$

with $\alpha_0 > 0$, and $0 < \alpha_1, \alpha_2 < 1$. Equation (5.46) is shown in Figure 5.10. For x_{1t} going to zero, y_t approaches $\alpha_0 \cdot \alpha_1$ asymptotically. When x_{1t} tends to infinity, y_t goes to α_0. By taking logarithms, (5.46) becomes:

$$\ln y_t = \ln \alpha_0 + \alpha_2^{x_{1t}} \ln \alpha_1 \tag{5.47}$$

which remains non-linear in the parameters. A special case frequently encountered in the literature is:[33]

$$y_t = \alpha_1^{\alpha_2^{x_{1t}}} \tag{5.48}$$

which corresponds to α_0 being equal to one in (5.46). This could be appropriate for a market share model, where one must be the upper limit. With $\alpha_0 = 1$, (5.47) becomes:

$$\ln y_t = \alpha_2^{x_{1t}} \ln \alpha_1.$$

Taking logarithms of this expression, a linear model is obtained:

$$\ln \ln y_t = \beta_1 + \beta_2 x_{1t}$$

---

33. See, for example, Montgomery and Urban (1969, p. 340), where $x_{1t} = t$.

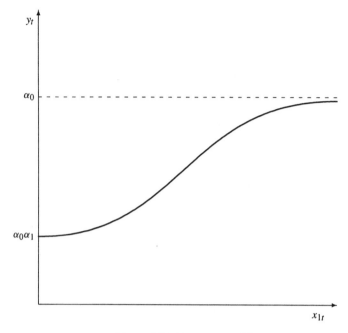

Figure 5.10 Gompertz model.

where

$$\beta_1 = \ln \ln \alpha_1, \text{ and}$$
$$\beta_2 = \ln \alpha_2.$$

In the SCAN*PRO model, developed by Wittink et al. (1988) which is discussed in Section 9.3, we introduce so-called multipliers. These are parameters with dummy variables as exponents. The partial relation between the dependent variable (here sales) and the dummy variables can be written as:

$$y_t = \alpha_0 \gamma_1^{\delta_{\ell t}} \tag{5.49}$$

where

$$\gamma_1 = \text{multiplier},$$
$$\delta_{\ell t} = \text{an indicator variable for promotion } \ell : 1 \text{ if the brand is}$$
$$\text{promoted in } t, \text{ and } 0 \text{ otherwise.}$$

A multiplier value of 2 for, for example, $\ell = 1 = $ own display activity, means a doubling of brand sales when the brand is on display. Relation (5.49) is a special case of (5.46).

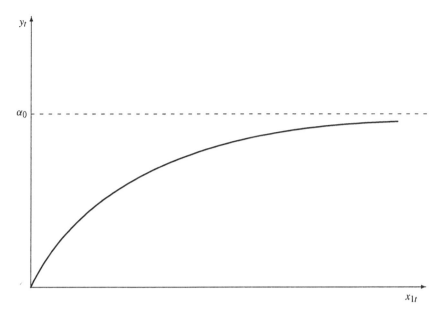

Figure 5.11 Modified exponential model (5.50).

5.3.3 MODELS NON-LINEAR IN THE PARAMETERS AND NOT LINEARIZABLE

It should be clear by now that marketing relations are generally non-linear in either variables or parameters or both. These relations sometimes are linearizable while at other times they are not. In the latter case the model is called *intrinsically non-linear* or *intractable*.[34] In the past, model builders often went to great efforts to make their models linearizable. This was primarily due to the fact that estimation methods in econometrics generally assumed models to be linear in the parameters. In recent years, however, powerful non-linear estimation techniques have been developed, and their availability as computer routines is increasing. Such techniques are discussed in Goldfeld and Quandt (1972, 1976), Amemiya (1983, 1985) and Judge et al. (1985). Other researchers have adapted non-linear programming algorithms for non-linear estimation.[35] Thus, from an estimation point of view, intrinsic non-linearity is no longer problematic in a purely technical sense. It remains true, however, that the statistical properties of non-linear estimation techniques are not as well known as those of linear models. We return to this point in Chapter 16.

As a first example of an *intrinsically non-linear* model, consider the *modified exponential model*:

$$y_t = \alpha_0(1 - e^{-\alpha_1 x_{1t}}), \quad \text{with } \alpha_0 > 0, \text{ and } \alpha_1 > 0. \tag{5.50}$$

---

34. Intractable is the designation used by, for example, Wonnacott and Wonnacott (1970, p. 98).

35. For example, Naert and Bultez (1975) adopted the Sequential Unconstrained Minimization Technique (SUMT) developed by Fiacco and McCormick (1968) for non-linear estimation. Little (1975b) made use of their suggestion in examining the historical data for his marketing mix model BRANDAID. Other examples are found in Horsky (1977a), Metwally (1980), Rangan (1987), Srinivasan, Weir (1988).

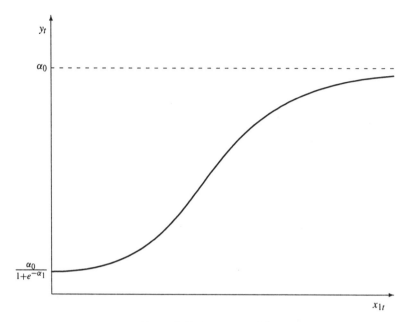

Figure 5.12 Logistic model (5.53).

Equation (5.50) is shown in Figure 5.11. If x_{1t} equals zero, y_t also equals zero. As x_{1t} goes to infinity, y_t approaches α_0 asymptotically. An interesting characteristic of the model is that the marginal sales response is proportional to the level of untapped potential $(\alpha_0 - y_t)$. This is easily demonstrated as follows. The first-order derivative of y_t with respect to x_{1t} is:

$$\frac{dy_t}{dx_{1t}} = \alpha_0 \alpha_1 e^{-\alpha_1 x_{1t}}. \tag{5.51}$$

Untapped potential is:

$$\alpha_0 - y_t = \alpha_0 e^{-\alpha_1 x_{1t}}$$

and it follows from (5.51) that the marginal sales response is proportional to $(\alpha_0 - y_t)$, with α_1 serving as the proportionality factor.

Applications of (5.50) are Buzzell (1964, pp. 136–156), and Lodish, Montgomery and Webster (1968). In their models x_{1t} represents selling effort. In Little and Lodish (1969), it is advertising effort. Rangan (1987) developed a more general (multivariate) modified exponential model:

$$y_t = \alpha_0 \left(1 - e^{-\alpha_1 - \sum_{\ell=2}^{L} \alpha_\ell x_{\ell t}} \right). \tag{5.52}$$

The dependent variable (y_t) in Rangan's model is market share at time t. The parameter α_0 is the maximum achievable market share with channel effects alone. The $x_{\ell t}$ are channel function components such as sales force calling effort, inventory level, delivery time, etc.

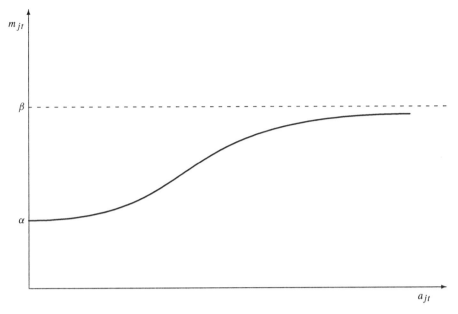

Figure 5.13 $m_{jt} = \alpha + (\beta - \alpha)a_{jt}^{\delta}/(\gamma + a_{jt}^{\delta})$, *and* $\delta > 1$ *(5.54)*.

A second example is the logistic model:

$$y_t = \frac{\alpha_0}{1 + e^{-(\alpha_1 + \alpha_2 x_{1t})}}, \quad \alpha_0, \alpha_1, \alpha_2 > 0 \tag{5.53}$$

shown in Figure 5.12. This is a more general specification than (5.44) in which the saturation level $\alpha_0 = 1$. With $x_{1t} = 0$, $y_t = \alpha_0/(1 + e^{-\alpha_1})$, and with x_{1t} going to infinity, y_t tends to α_0.

In the literature, a number of other S-shaped models have been proposed. We restrict ourselves to just a few. The first is one proposed by Little (1970) in his advertising budgeting model ADBUDG. The dependent variable is market share of brand j, m_{jt}, and the explanatory variable is advertising expenditures of brand j, a_{jt}. The following market share response function is postulated:

$$m_{jt} = \alpha + (\beta - \alpha)\frac{a_{jt}^{\delta}}{\gamma + a_{jt}^{\delta}}. \tag{5.54}$$

Assuming that all parameters are positive and $\beta > \alpha$, we obtain the graphical representations shown in Figures 5.13 and 5.14 for $\delta > 1$ and $\delta < 1$ respectively.[36,37]

---

36. The difference is easily understood by looking at the first- and second-order derivatives:

$$\partial m_{jt}/\partial a_{jt} = (\beta - \alpha)\gamma\delta a_{jt}^{\delta-1}/(\gamma + a_{jt}^{\delta})^2, \text{ and}$$

$$\partial^2 m_{jt}/\partial a_{jt}^2 = (\beta - \alpha)\gamma\delta a_{jt}^{\delta-2}(\gamma(\delta - 1) - (\delta + 1)a_{jt}^{\delta})/(\gamma + a_{jt}^{\delta})^3.$$

37. We return to this particular market share response function in Sections 7.5 and 16.9.

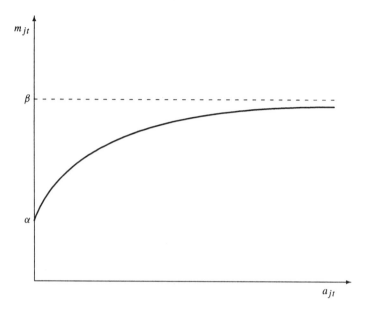

Figure 5.14 $m_{jt} = \alpha + (\beta - \alpha)a_{jt}^\delta/(\gamma + a_{jt}^\delta)$, *and* $\delta < 1$ *(5.54)*.

Johansson (1973, 1979) proposed the following model:

$$\frac{m_{jt} - \alpha}{\beta - m_{jt}} = \eta(a_{jt}^*)^\delta \tag{5.55}$$

where, $a_{jt}^* = a_{jt}/(a_{jt} + a_{ct})$, and with a_{ct} the advertising spending level of competition. In (5.55) α represents the lower and β the upper limit of market share. Specifications (5.54) and (5.55) are closely related as is demonstrated below. From (5.54) we have:

$$m_{jt} - \alpha = (\beta - \alpha)a_{jt}^\delta/(\gamma + a_{jt}^\delta) \tag{5.56}$$

and

$$\beta - m_{jt} = (\beta - \alpha) - (\beta - \alpha)a_{jt}^\delta/(\gamma + a_{jt}^\delta). \tag{5.57}$$

Dividing (5.56) by (5.57) we obtain:

$$\frac{m_{jt} - \alpha}{\beta - m_{jt}} = \frac{a_{jt}^\delta}{\gamma}.$$

Replacing $1/\gamma$ by η and a_{jt} by a_{jt}^* we obtain (5.55). The extension to other variables is straightforward, and in its most general form (5.55) can be written as:

$$\frac{y_{jt} - \alpha}{\beta - y_{jt}} = \eta x_{1t}^{*\delta_1} \cdot x_{2t}^{*\delta_2} \cdots x_{Lt}^{*\delta_L} \tag{5.58}$$

where, $x_{\ell t}^*$, $\ell = 1, \ldots, L$, could either be $x_{j\ell t}$, or $x_{j\ell t}/(x_{j\ell t} + x_{c\ell t})$, or $x_{j\ell t}/x_{c\ell t}$, and $x_{j\ell t} = $ value of the independent variable ℓ of brand j in t, $x_{c\ell t} = $ value of the independent variable ℓ of a competing brand.

An interesting special case is obtained with $\alpha = 0$, and $\beta = 1$, in which case the model becomes linearizable. With y_{jt} being market share, these lower and upper bounds are the theoretical limits within which market share can vary. Equation (5.58) becomes:

$$\frac{m_{jt}}{m_{ct}} = \eta x_{1t}^{*\delta_1} \cdot x_{2t}^{*\delta_2} \cdots x_{Lt}^{*\delta_L} \tag{5.59}$$

where $m_{ct} = 1 - m_{jt} = $ market share of competition. Equation (5.59) is a multiplicative model such as (5.36), and therefore is linear after taking logarithms:

$$\ln \frac{m_{jt}}{1 - m_{jt}} = \ln \eta + \delta_1 \ln x_{1t}^* + \ldots + \delta_L \ln x_{Lt}^* \tag{5.60}$$

which is again the linear logit model (5.44).

CHAPTER 6

Marketing dynamics

Marketing is in essence dynamic. This means that new products are developed, tested, and launched, that more and better packaging is introduced, that competitors come and go, and so on. But it also means that the effect of, for example, an advertising campaign does not end when the campaign is over. The effect, or part of it, will remain perceptible for some future periods. Or, looked at somewhat differently, sales in period t will be determined by advertising in t, but by spending in $t-1, t-2, \ldots$ as well. Thus, one can refer to the *lagged effects* of advertising. For trade and consumer promotions the same *effects may* occur.[1] The dynamic aspects of marketing are not only exhibited in lagged effects but also in *lead effects*, i.e. consumers or competitors anticipate a marketing stimulus and adjust their behavior before the stimulus actually occurs.[2] So, for example, consumers may anticipate future price cuts or promotions.

In this chapter we first discuss the modeling of marketing dynamics in the case of one explanatory variable. Issues related to having more than one independent variable are dealt with in 6.2. In Section 6.3 we discuss the selection of dynamic models. Finally in Section 6.4 we give attention to lead effects.

6.1 Modeling lagged effects: one explanatory variable

Marketing dynamics in the one variable case often deals with the time effect of advertising. Most of the discussion in this section will, therefore, be concerned with advertising. As we indicate in Section 2.3, the effect of a campaign in period t will generally not be exhausted by the end of the period, but will linger on into the future. That means that the effect is cumulated over time, and thus one refers to the *cumulative effects of advertising*. Cumulative effects of advertising can be represented, for example, by the demand function (6.1):

$$q_t = \alpha + \beta_1 a_t + \beta_2 a_{t-1} + \ldots + \beta_{s+1} a_{t-s} + u_t \qquad (6.1)$$

where

---

1. See, e.g. Blattberg, Neslin (1989, 1990, 1993), Blattberg, Briesch, Fox (1995), van Heerde, Leeflang, Wittink (1999c).
2. This description is based on Hanssens, Parsons and Schultz (1990, p. 213).

$$q_t = \text{sales in period } t,$$

$$a_t, a_{t-1}, \ldots = \text{advertising expenditures in period } t, \quad t-1, \ldots$$
$$\text{respectively, and}$$

$$u_t = \text{a disturbance term.}$$

Equation (6.1) indicates that advertising has an effect up to s periods into the future. The lagged effect of marketing activities on sales has long been recognized as one of the complicating features of market measurement. Its existence means that promotional programs should be evaluated over a period longer than that of each campaign. Failure to measure it adequately leads to under-estimation of the impact of the promotions in media concerned (Jones, 1986), and is one probable reason for the typical switch of marketing expenditures from the long-term brand building offered by advertising, to short-term oriented, but easily measured, sales promotions (Magrath, 1988).

We make a distinction between delayed-response effects and customer-holdover effects. Delayed-response effects arise from the delay between marketing money being spent and sales occurring.[3] It can happen because of:

- execution delay: e.g. the time between management spending money or preparing an ad and the ad appearing;
- noting delay: e.g. the time between a magazine being published and read;
- purchase delay: the time between a consumer recieving the stimulus to purchase and a purchase being made.

The *delayed-response* effect can be simply represented by a relation such as (6.2):

$$q_t = \alpha + \beta_1 a_{t-s} + u_t \tag{6.2}$$

where s is the number of time periods between, say, the time the advertising money is spent and the sales that result from this expenditure.

Customer-holdover effects occur because customers sometimes make repeated purchases for some time, $t, t+1, t+2, \ldots, t+s$ after the initial stimulus in t, either as:

- new buyer holdover effects, where marketing activity creates new customers who make repeat purchases, or
- increased purchase holdover effects, where the marketing stimulus increases the average quantity purchased per period for some time.

The estimation of lagged effects in the demand function (6.1) is difficult for at least three reasons. First, one has to decide how many lagged terms to include in the specification, i.e. one has to decide how long the advertising effect lasts. In what follows, we refer to this as the *duration interval*, and determining the correct value of s is called the *truncation problem*. Secondly, with s lagged terms in the model,

---

3. See, Lilien, Kotler (1983, p. 80), and Leeflang, Mijatovic, Saunders (1992).

the number of parameters becomes $s + 2$. Since data are often a scarce commodity, statistical problems are likely to arise because of loss of *degrees of freedom*.[4] This results both from an increase in the number of parameters and from a decrease in the number of usable observations. Suppose we have thirty-six monthly observations ($T = 36$) on sales and advertising spending from January 1995 to December 1997. For 1/95, January 1995, and assuming $s = 10$, (6.1) becomes:

$$q_{1/95} = \alpha + \beta_1 a_{1/95} + \beta_2 a_{12/94} + \ldots + \beta_{11} a_{3/94} + u_{1/95}.$$

This is not a usable observation, since $a_{12/94}, \ldots, a_{3/94}$ are unknown. The first usable observation is then 11/95, November 1995, for which (6.1) becomes:

$$q_{11/95} = \alpha + \beta_1 a_{11/95} + \beta_2 a_{10/95} + \ldots + \beta_{11} a_{1/95} + u_{11/95}.$$

In general, with s the number of lags, the number of usable observations is $T - s$, and the number of degrees of freedom of the error term is $T - 2 - 2s$. A third difficulty with direct specification of lags is that the larger s, the higher the chance that the explanatory variables become collinear.[5]

The three reasons above have led researchers to consider relations between the various β_i in (6.1) in order to arrive at a simpler model. A simpler model will have fewer parameters and will be less troublesome to estimate. One should, of course, be careful not to loose the true structure for simplification.

Many alternative specifications of a relation between the β_i's have been proposed in literature. We consider the most common ones.[6] The most popular lag structure in marketing studies is no doubt the following. First (6.1) is rewritten with an infinite number of terms, which means that the entire advertising history is taken into account:

$$q_t = \alpha + \sum_{\ell=0}^{\infty} \beta_{\ell+1} a_{t-\ell} + u_t. \tag{6.3}$$

It is now assumed that:

$$\begin{aligned}
\beta_2/\beta_1 &= \lambda, \\
\beta_3/\beta_2 &= \lambda, \text{ or} \\
\beta_3/\beta_1 &= \lambda^2, \tag{6.4}
\end{aligned}$$

---

4. In Section 5.2 we saw that the typical objective function in estimating parameters is to minimize $\sum_{t=1}^{T} \hat{u}_t^2$. If the number of observations is exactly equal to the number of parameters, an exact fit can be obtained and, therefore, $\sum_{t=1}^{T} \hat{u}_t^2 = 0$. Thus to obtain information on the nature of the error term of (6.1), we need more than $T - s - 2$ observations. One refers to $T - s - 2$ as the number of degrees of freedom for the error term. The larger s, the smaller this number of degrees of freedom becomes. See also Chapter 16 on parameterization.

5. Collinearity or multicollinearity relates to the correlation between explanatory variables. A more exact definition will be given in Chapter 16. We limit ourselves here to stating that collinearity has the disadvantage of making the coefficients less reliable.

6. For extensive surveys, we refer to Griliches (1967) and Dhrymes (1981), Judge, Griffiths, Hill, Lütkepohl and Lee (1985, Chapters 9 and 10) at the more theoretical level, and Yon (1976, Chapter 4), Hanssens et al. (1990, Chapter 7), Leeflang et al. (1992) in a marketing context.

$$\vdots$$

$$\beta_{\ell+1}/\beta_1 = \lambda^\ell,$$

$$\vdots$$

where, $0 \le \lambda < 1$. The lag structure specified in (6.4) assumes that the advertising effect is geometrically (or exponentially in the continuous case) decreasing over time. This model is known as the geometric lag model or Koyck model.

In the literature on lag structures, one often encounters the term *distributed lags* or *lag distribution*. The meaning of this terminology relates to the similarity in the properties of lag coefficients and those of a probability mass function, as is shown below. In general, we can rewrite (6.3) as:

$$q_t = \alpha + \beta_1 \sum_{\ell=0}^{\infty} \omega_\ell a_{t-\ell} + u_t \tag{6.5}$$

where the ω_ℓ terms represent the lag structure. Distributed lags are then assumed to have the following properties:

$$\omega_\ell \ge 0, \text{ for all } \ell \text{ and} \tag{6.6}$$

$$\sum_{\ell=0}^{\infty} \omega_\ell = 1 \tag{6.7}$$

i.e. the lag coefficients are assumed to be non-negative and to sum to one.[7]

Since the lag structure defined in (6.4) implies $\omega_\ell = \lambda^\ell$, it satisfies (6.6) but not (6.7). In order for the geometric lags to sum to one they should be defined as:

$$\omega_\ell = (1 - \lambda)\lambda^\ell. \tag{6.8}$$

The lag structures as defined in (6.4) and (6.8) are, of course, not fundamentally different. We will therefore adhere to the former, because in the literature it is most frequently applied under that form. Substituting (6.4) in (6.3) we obtain:

$$q_t = \alpha + \beta_1 a_t + \beta_1 \lambda a_{t-1} + \beta_1 \lambda^2 a_{t-2} + \ldots + \beta_1 \lambda^L a_{t-L} + \ldots + u_t. \tag{6.9}$$

Now we lag equation (6.9) one period and multiply by λ:

$$\lambda q_{t-1} = \lambda \alpha + \beta_1 \lambda a_{t-1} + \beta_1 \lambda^2 a_{t-2} + \ldots + \beta_1 \lambda^{L+1} a_{t-L-1} \tag{6.10}$$
$$+ \ldots + \lambda u_{t-1}.$$

Subtracting (6.10) from (6.9) gives:

$$q_t - \lambda q_{t-1} = \alpha(1 - \lambda) + \beta_1 a_t + u_t - \lambda u_{t-1}.$$

---

7. The requirement of non-negativity is not always realistic. Sales in a period after a promotion may be below the normal level, which implies that the corresponding parameter of the lagged variable is negative.

*Table 6.1 Implied duration interval as a function of
             the data interval.*

Data interval	$\hat{\lambda}$	90% duration interval in months	Number of studies
Weekly	.537	0.9	2
Monthly	.440	3.0	10
Bimonthly	.493	9.0	10
Quarterly	.599	25.1	10
Annual	.560	56.5	27

Source: Clarke (1976, p. 351).

With $\alpha^* = \alpha(1 - \lambda)$, and $u_t^* = u_t - \lambda u_{t-1}$, we obtain:

$$q_t = \alpha^* + \lambda q_{t-1} + \beta_1 a_t + u_t^*. \tag{6.11}$$

The procedure is due to Koyck (1954), and is generally referred to as the Koyck transformation. The estimation problems are now greatly reduced since only three parameters remain. Also β_1 will measure the direct (short term) effect of advertising, while λ measures how much of the advertising effect in one period is retained in the next. One often refers to λ as the *retention rate*. The long-term advertising effect is obtained as follows. If the advertising investment is kept constant ($a_t = a$ for all t), in equilibrium we have $q_t = q_{t-\ell} = q$. Or from (6.11), and omitting the error term $q = \alpha^* + \lambda q + \beta_1 a$, or:

$$q = \alpha + \frac{\beta_1}{1 - \lambda}a. \tag{6.12}$$

Thus $\beta_1/(1-\lambda)$ measures the (total) effect of advertising. Given (6.4), the parameters β_1 and λ suffice to measure the short-term and long-term effect of advertising.[8]

The Koyck model, however, is not without problems. First if u_t satisfies the assumptions of the classical linear regression model, then u_t^* does not.[9] We do not discuss this issue here, but refer to any standard econometrics text.

The duration interval of advertising implied by the Koyck model has been studied by Clarke (1976) on the basis of a survey of 59 cases. Since (6.11) is an additive model, the same relation holds for, say, $q_t^* = q_t + q_{t-1}$ and $a_t^* = a_t + a_{t-1}$. Hence the implied duration interval should not vary with the periodicity of the data, expressed by the data interval. However, from the figures in Table 6.1 it is clear that the implied duration interval is a function of the periodicity of the data.

---

8. In an applied setting, estimated values $\hat{\alpha}$, $\hat{\beta}_1$, and $\hat{\lambda}$ will be used. These estimates are obtained from the numerical specification of (6.11). Since $\hat{\beta}_1$ and $\hat{\lambda}$ are estimated, $\hat{\beta}_1/(1 - \hat{\lambda})$ will be estimated as well. One difficulty is that the distributional properties of that ratio are not well known.
9. In particular, if the residuals u_t of the original model are uncorrelated, then the u_t^* must be autocorrelated.

Table 6.2 Parameter estimates and implied duration intervals for cigarettes as a function of the data interval.

	Annual data	Bimonthly data	Monthly data
Advertising $(\hat{\beta}_1)^a$	0.15	0.06	0.04
Lagged sales $(\hat{\lambda})$	0.57	0.65	0.75
Total effect of advertising $(\hat{\beta}/1 - \hat{\lambda})$	0.35	0.16	0.14
Average lag in months	16	4	3
90% implied duration interval (months)	49	11	8

[a] In this study q_t and a_t refer to values aggregated over firms/brands.

Source: Leeflang and Reuyl (1985a, p. 97).

The table shows the average value of $\hat{\lambda}$, and the average 90% duration interval, which means the time it takes for advertising to reach 90 percent of its total effect, for each of the five data intervals. The results indicate a large increase in the implied duration time as the data interval increases, pointing to a data interval bias. The problem is even more striking when very different implied duration intervals are obtained from one and the *same* data set. A case in point is the relation between industry sales and industry advertising expenditures for the West-German cigarette market. The relation has been estimated by Leeflang and Reuyl (1985a) using annual, bimonthly and monthly data covering the same time period (1960-1975). Table 6.2 shows the estimated values of the advertising parameter and the parameter for lagged primary demand of the calibrated Koyck-model. Furthermore the long-term elasticity of advertising and the 90% duration interval in months are specified.

Leone (1995) provides a theoretical explanation for the inconsistent findings from previous econometric analyses of aggregated data concerning the duration of advertising carry-over effects. He also adjusted the lagged sales parameter in models with a data interval/aggregation bias. He found that the average carry-over effect is between six and nine months. A similar conclusion is based on a meta-analysis performed by Assmus, Farley, Lehmann (1984) and it is also consistent with the findings of Lodish et al. (1995b). They summarized advertising carryover effects based on a summary of 55 in-market estimates of the long-term effects of TV advertising using experimental (Behavior Scan) tests. We return to this issue in Section 14.1.3.

We now turn our attention to the *shape of the lagged effects*. A geometrically decaying lag structure implies that a campaign in period t has its greatest effect in the same period. This may or may not be realistic, depending, among other things, on the periodicity of the data. For example, decreasing lagged effects might be quite reasonable for annual or even for quarterly data. With monthly data, it is possible that advertising will reach its peak effect after a few periods. For example, in their study of the dynamic effects of a communications mix for an ethical drug, Montgomery and Silk (1972) found that direct mail had its peak effect in the month after the mailing. Samples and literature similarly peaked after a one-month lag. Journal advertising showed a peak, although a modest one, three months after the advertising appeared in the medical journals.

There are various ways of dealing with such more complex lag structures. The most obvious way is to include a number of direct lags, the geometric decay taking effect after a few periods. In that case, the sales-advertising equation becomes, for example:

$$q_t = \alpha + \beta_1 a_t + \beta_2 a_{t-1} + \beta_3 a_{t-2} + \beta_4 a_{t-3} + \beta_4 \lambda a_{t-4} \tag{6.13}$$
$$+ \beta_4 \lambda^2 a_{t-5} + \ldots + u_t.$$

Applying the Koyck transformation to (6.14), we obtain after rearranging terms:

$$q_t = \alpha(1 - \lambda) + \lambda q_{t-1} + \beta_1 a_t + (\beta_2 - \beta_1 \lambda)a_{t-1} \tag{6.14}$$
$$+ (\beta_3 - \beta_2 \lambda)a_{t-2} + (\beta_4 - \beta_3 \lambda)a_{t-3} + u_t - \lambda u_{t-1}$$

and the relation to be estimated is:

$$q_t = \alpha^* + \lambda q_{t-1} + \beta_1 a_t + \beta_2^* a_{t-1} + \beta_3^* a_{t-2} + \beta_4^* a_{t-3} + u_t^* \tag{6.15}$$

where

$$\alpha^* = \alpha(1 - \lambda),$$
$$\beta_i^* = \beta_i - \beta_{i-1} \cdot \lambda, \quad i = 2, 3, 4,$$
$$u_t^* = u_t - \lambda u_{t-1}.$$

Equation (6.15) contains six parameters. Their estimates suffice to obtain estimates of the parameters in the original model (6.14). Although this formulation allows for more flexibility in the nature of lagged effects, it reintroduces some of the difficulties (loss of degrees of freedom and multicollinearity) which we want to avoid.

The combination of direct lags with geometrically declining lags has been applied by a number of authors. Lambin (1972a) uses it in relating sales to advertising of gasoline based on quarterly data. Similar approaches are used by Montgomery and Silk (1972), Doyle and Saunders (1985), Leeflang et al. (1992).

Bass and Clarke (1972) examine a number of alternative specifications in their study of the advertising effectiveness for a dietary product. Their point of departure is equation (6.5), for which six alternative specifications of the ω_ℓ are considered. In Model I, $\omega_\ell = (1 - \lambda)\lambda^\ell$, resulting after transformation in:

$$q_t = \alpha(1 - \lambda) + \lambda q_{t-1} + \beta_1(1 - \lambda)a_t + u_t - \lambda u_{t-1}. \tag{6.16}$$

In Model II one specific lag is introduced before the geometric decay function becomes applicable, in which case we obtain:[10]

$$q_t = \alpha(1 - \lambda) + \lambda q_{t-1} + \beta_1 \alpha_0 a_t + \beta_1 \alpha_1 a_{t-1} + u_t - \lambda u_{t-1}. \tag{6.17}$$

---

10. For a more detailed exposition on, among other things, the constraints on the parameters to ensure non-negativity of the lag coefficients, we refer to the Bass and Clarke article. A full understanding requires knowledge of lag-generating functions and the algebra of lag operators, for which we refer to Dhrymes (1981).

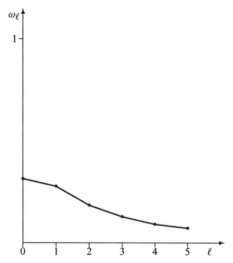

Figure 6.1 Pascal distributed lag structure ($r = 2$, $\lambda = 0.4$).

Model III is an expansion of the Koyck model to a second-order lag function:

$$q_t = \alpha(1 - \lambda_1 - \lambda_2) + \lambda_1 q_{t-1} + \lambda_2 q_{t-2} + \beta_1 \alpha_0 a_t + u_t \qquad (6.18)$$
$$-\lambda_1 u_{t-1} - \lambda_2 u_{t-2}.$$

A natural extension is to have one direct lag in the explanatory variable a_{t-1} in addition to the two lagged dependent variables. The result is Model IV:

$$q_t = \alpha(1 - \lambda_1 - \lambda_2) + \lambda_1 q_{t-1} + \lambda_2 q_{t-2} + \beta_1 \alpha_0 a_t + \beta_1 \alpha_1 a_{t-1} \qquad (6.19)$$
$$+ u_t - \lambda_1 u_{t-1} - \lambda_2 u_{t-2}.$$

Model V has three lagged dependent variables:

$$q_t = \alpha(1 - \lambda_1 - \lambda_2 - \lambda_3) + \lambda_1 q_{t-1} + \lambda_2 q_{t-2} + \lambda_3 q_{t-3} \qquad (6.20)$$
$$+ \beta_1 \alpha_0 a_t + u_t - \lambda_1 u_{t-1} - \lambda_2 u_{t-2} - \lambda_3 u_{t-3}$$

while Model VI has, in addition, one lagged explanatory variable:

$$q_t = \alpha(1 - \lambda_1 - \lambda_2 - \lambda_3) + \lambda_1 q_{t-1} + \lambda_2 q_{t-2} + \lambda_3 q_{t-3} \qquad (6.21)$$
$$+ \beta_1 \alpha_0 a_t + \beta_1 \alpha_1 a_{t-1} + u_t - \lambda_1 u_{t-1} - \lambda_2 u_{t-2} - \lambda_3 u_{t-3}.$$

Models I, III, and V have monotonically decreasing lag structures, whereas Models II, IV, and VI do not. See Section 6.3 for a discussion of some results.

Models I through VI are all variants of the Koyck model. There are, of course, many *alternative* ways of allowing for non-monotonicity in the lag structure. Usually a distinction is made between *infinite* and *finite* distributed lags.[11] Equation (6.3) is an example of an infinite and (6.1) of a finite distributed lag model.

---

11. See Judge et al. (1985).

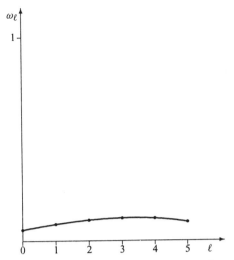

Figure 6.2 *Pascal distributed lag structure (r = 2, λ = 0.8).*

The *Pascal lag* structure offers opportunities to estimate a model that contains an infinite number of parameters. The Pascal lag was proposed and applied by Solow (1960). The Pascal distribution, also called the *negative binomial distribution*, has the following structure:

$$\omega_\ell = \frac{(r + \ell - 1)!}{(r - 1)!\ell!}(1 - \lambda)^r \lambda^\ell, \quad \ell = 0, 1, 2, \ldots \quad (6.22)$$

Taking $r = 2$ as a special case, we obtain:

$$\omega_0 = (1 - \lambda)^2$$
$$\omega_1 = 2(1 - \lambda)^2 \lambda$$
$$\omega_2 = 3(1 - \lambda)^2 \lambda^2$$
$$\omega_3 = 4(1 - \lambda)^2 \lambda^3$$

$$\cdots$$

$$\omega_\ell = (\ell + 1)(1 - \lambda)^2 \lambda^\ell, \ldots$$

For some values of λ, the series will decrease monotonically (for example, $\lambda = 0.4$), while for others it will first increase to a maximum, then decline (for example, $\lambda = 0.8$). These two cases are illustrated in Figures 6.1 and 6.2. We further observe that for $r = 1$, (6.22) reduces to (6.8), the geometric lags.

Mann (1975) used the 647 monthly observations in the Lydia Pinkham data base to fit the Pascal model.[12] He tried values for r ranging from 1 to 10, and obtained a best fit for $r = 4$. Bultez and Naert (1979) used the subset of the data published in Palda (1964). They obtained a best fit for $r = 6$, for r ranging from 1 to 12. Their

---

12. The Lydia Pinkham's vegetable compound data were first examined by Palda (1964) and have been used in many econometrics studies since.

objective was not to obtain a best estimate of the lag structure, but to examine whether or not lag structure matters in optimizing advertising spending. For that purpose, optimal values were derived corresponding to a number of alternative lag structures (no dynamic effect at all, $r = 1$, $r = 2, \ldots, r = 6$). The sensitivity of profit was examined with respect to using one model to estimate the parameters (for example, the static model), when in fact another model (for example, $r = 6$) is the correctly specified one. They concluded that, at least for this data base, lag structure does not matter much in optimization, the implication being that the emphasis in the literature on finding the best lag structure may be somewhat misplaced.[13]

Almon (1965) proposed a method to estimate a model with finite distributed lags. The relation between the β_t's in (6.1) and the lag length is approximated by a continuous function of the form:

$$\beta_t^* = \phi_0 + \phi_1 t^* + \phi_2 t^{*^2} + \ldots \phi_r (t^*)^r, \quad r \le s. \tag{6.23}$$

This equation is a polynomial in t^*, and if r is strictly less than s, the use of this approximation imposes restrictions on β_t^*, $t^* = 1, \ldots, s$ (Stewart, 1991, p.181). The parameters ϕ_i may be estimated by substituting (6.23) into (6.1) and applying least squares. This model has been widely used in applied econometric work because of the flexibility of the polynomial lag shape, the decrease in the number of parameters that must be estimated, the ease of estimation, and the reduction in multicollinearity. In marketing this model has been applied by van Heerde et al. (1999c) to model dynamic effects of promotions.[14]

In the marketing literature several other distributed lag models have been developed and applied. We discuss two of them. The first model is based on the current-effects model:

$$q_t = \alpha + \beta_1 a_t + u_t. \tag{6.24}$$

In the current-effects model it is assumed that the disturbances u_t are *not* correlated with the disturbances in preceding periods. That is: there is *no* autocorrelation. If, however, the u_t are correlated with, for example, u_{t-1} we have:

$$u_t = \rho u_{t-1} + \varepsilon_t \tag{6.25}$$

where

ρ = the autocorrelation coefficient, $\rho \ne 0$, and

ε_t = an error term.

Subsituting (6.25) into (6.24), specifying (6.24) for $t - 1$ and substituting the resulting expression for u_{t-1} in the modified (6.24), we get:

$$q_t = \alpha(1 - \rho) + \beta_1 a_t + \rho q_{t-1} - \rho \beta_1 a_{t-1} + \varepsilon_t. \tag{6.26}$$

---

13. See also Bultez, Naert (1988a) and the discussion in Magat, McCann and Morey (1986).

14. Almon's distributed lag model, however, is beset with difficulties because the estimators have sampling distributions and properties that are unknown due to complicated pretesting schemes. See Judge et al. (1985, p. 357).

Relation (6.26) can also be written as:

$$q_t - \rho q_{t-1} = \alpha(1 - \rho) + \beta_1(a_t - \rho a_{t-1}) + \varepsilon_t \qquad (6.27)$$

which is a linear relationship between a change in the level of demand and a change in the level of advertising expenditure. If there is *no* autocorrelation and $\rho \approx 0$, (6.27) reduces to (6.24). However if $\rho \neq 0$ we have a *dynamic specification*. This *autoregressive current-effects model* (6.27) is often used by researchers (Kanetkar, Weinberg, Weiss, 1986).

Another well-known dynamic model is the *partial adjustment model*. This model is based on the notion that there are levels of marketing instruments which are associated with desired sales q'_t:

$$q'_t = \alpha' + \beta'_1 a_t + u'_t \qquad (6.28)$$

while the actual sales achieved only adjusts partially toward the desired sales amount (Nerlove, 1956):

$$q_t - q_{t-1} = (1 - \lambda)(q'_t - q_{t-1}) \qquad (6.29)$$

where

$$\lambda = \text{the adjustment rate}, \quad 0 < \lambda < 1.$$

This phenomenon may occur if, say, repetitions of a television ad are needed before all members of the target market comprehend it or repetitions are needed to convince some consumers to buy.

By substituting (6.28) into (6.29), the partial adjustment model is obtained:

$$q_t = \alpha + \beta_1 a_t + \lambda q_{t-1} + u_t \qquad (6.30)$$

where

$$\alpha = \alpha'(1 - \lambda),$$
$$\beta_1 = \beta'_1(1 - \lambda),$$
$$u_t = (1 - \lambda)u'_t.$$

The partial-adjustment model (6.30) and the autoregressive current-effects model (6.26) have similar structure, albeit that the parameter ρ represents the autocorrelation of the disturbances, whereas the parameter λ in (6.30) represents the adjustment rate! If one adds a lagged advertising variable to (6.28) equations (6.26) and (6.30) have exactly the same variables, but (6.26) has a restriction among the parameters.

The differences in the disturbance terms account for the difference between the partial adjustment model (6.30) and the geometric lag model (6.11). In (6.11) $u_t^* = u_t - \lambda u_{t-1}$, where λ is the retention rate which equals the autocorrelation parameter. In (6.30) $u_t = (1 - \lambda)u'_t$, where u'_t is a disturbance term with no autocorrelation. These comparisons indicate that it may be very difficult to discriminate the different distributed lag models. Testing procedures have been proposed by e.g. Griliches

(1967), Bass, Clarke (1972) and Weiss, Windal (1980). We return to these tests in Section 6.3 and Section 18.4.2.

To conclude this section, we return to (6.6), i.e. $\omega_\ell \geq 0$ for all ℓ, introduced when we discussed the meaning of distributed lags. We said in passing that non-negativity is not always a realistic requirement. An example is the dynamic effect of a cents-off (price cut) promotion. During a promotion for a frequently purchased food product, sales tend to increase above the normal sales level. It is possible that sales in the week after a promotion will be below the normal level.[15] An explanation is the result that a promotion may not only attract new buyers, but it may also result in loyal buyers stocking up on the product, which in turn leads to a decrease in sales in the period immediately following a promotion. The dynamics of a promotion, pr_t (excluding all other variables for simplicity), could therefore be modeled as follows:

$$q_t = \alpha + \beta_1 pr_t + \beta_2 pr_{t-1} + u_t \tag{6.31}$$

where

$$\beta_1 > 0, \beta_2 < 0, \text{ and } \beta_1 \text{ larger than } \beta_2 \text{ in absolute value.}$$

This phenomenon is known as a negative lag effect (Doyle, Saunders, 1985). The distributed lags for which $\omega_\ell \geq 0$, are known as positive lag effects.

6.2 Modeling lagged effects: several explanatory variables

So far, we have just considered the dynamics of advertising. In marketing applications we often see that after equation (6.11) is derived, one just adds other variables to it. For example, with price (p_t) and distribution (d_t) as additional variables, one then writes:

$$q_t = \alpha^* + \lambda q_{t-1} + \beta_1 a_t + \beta_2 p_t + \beta_3 d_t + u_t^*. \tag{6.32}$$

This may seem quite plausible. It implies, however, that price and distribution have the same lagged effect as advertising. This means that (6.32) is obtained by applying the Koyck transformation to:

$$q_t = \alpha + \beta_1 a_t + \beta_1 \lambda a_{t-1} + \beta_1 \lambda^2 a_{t-2} + \ldots + \beta_2 p_t + \beta_2 \lambda p_{t-1} \tag{6.33}$$
$$+ \beta_2 \lambda^2 p_{t-2} + \ldots + \beta_3 d_t + \beta_3 \lambda d_{t-1} + \beta_3 \lambda^2 d_{t-2} + \ldots + u_t$$

as can be easily verified.

To state that price and advertising have the same lag structure is a heroic assumption. It is generally accepted that price responses occur much faster. Suppose that price and advertising are the only explanatory variables, and that both follow a

---

15. This "postpromotion" dip in (aggregate) sales data was typically not found empirically. See Neslin, Schneider Stone (1996) for arguments, and van Heerde et al. (1999c) for specifications that produce empirical evidence.

geometrically declining lag structure, but with different parameters λ_1 and λ_2. The basic model becomes:

$$q_t = \alpha + \beta_1 a_t + \beta_1 \lambda_1 a_{t-1} + \beta_1 \lambda_1^2 a_{t-2} + \ldots \tag{6.34}$$
$$+ \beta_2 p_t + \beta_2 \lambda_2 p_{t-1} + \beta_2 \lambda_2^2 p_{t-2} + \ldots + u_t.$$

The model transformation now requires *two* steps. First, equation (6.34) is lagged one period, multiplied by λ_1 and subtracted from (6.34), yielding:

$$q_t - \lambda_1 q_{t-1} = (1 - \lambda_1)\alpha + \beta_1 a_t + \beta_2 p_t \tag{6.35}$$
$$+ (\lambda_2 - \lambda_1)(\beta_2 p_{t-1} + \lambda_2 \beta_2 p_{t-2} + \ldots) + u_t - \lambda_1 u_{t-1}.$$

Now (6.35) is lagged one period, multiplied by λ_2, and subtracted from (6.35). After rearranging terms, one obtains:

$$q_t = (1 - \lambda_1)(1 - \lambda_2)\alpha + \beta_1(a_t - \lambda_2 a_{t-1}) + (\lambda_2 - \lambda_1)\beta_2 p_{t-1} \tag{6.36}$$
$$+ \beta_2(p_t - \lambda_1 p_{t-1}) + (\lambda_1 + \lambda_2)q_{t-1}$$
$$- \lambda_1 \lambda_2 q_{t-2} + u_t^*$$

where

$$u_t^* = u_t - (\lambda_1 + \lambda_2)u_{t-1} + \lambda_1 \lambda_2 u_{t-2}.$$

We observe that (6.36) is not only much more complex than (6.32), but is also nonlinear in the parameters. The unknown parameters λ_1 and λ_2 appear both in the relation and in the expression for the disturbance terms (u_t^*). There are different solutions for this problem:

1. Non-linear estimation with Almon polynomials (finite distributed lags), Pascal distributed lag structures (infinite distributed lags) or other non-linear approaches; see Section 6.1.
2. Simplified search procedures by, say, a transformation of the data matrix. This has been demonstrated by Leeflang, Mijatovic (1988) who used a transformation developed by Zellner and Geisel (1970).
3. Non-linear estimation methods in a number of sequential steps. This procedure has been applied by Houston and Weiss (1974).

6.3   Selection of (dynamic) models

From the discussion at the end of Section 6.1 it appears that there are subtle differences between alternative dynamic specifications. The best among the alternative specifications can be chosen in different ways. We limit ourselves to highlighting a few points.[16]

---

16. A more detailed discussion on choosing the best model is given in Chapter 18.

First, the models can be evaluated on theoretical criteria. For example, if the theory states that all lagged effects should be non-negative, their estimates will have to satisfy a number of constraints. In relation (6.18), i.e. Model III of Bass and Clarke (1972), for example, imposing non-negativity constraints implies that the estimated parameters should satisfy the set of constraints (6.37):[17]

$$0 < \hat{\lambda}_1 < 2$$
$$-1 < \hat{\lambda}_2 < 1$$
$$1 - \hat{\lambda} - \hat{\lambda} > 0 \quad\quad\quad\quad (6.37)$$
$$\quad\quad\quad\quad (6.38)$$

$$hat\lambda_1^2 \geq -4\hat{\lambda}_2$$

$$\hat{\beta_1\alpha_0} \geq 0.$$

Bass and Clarke (1972) obtained the following estimates:

$$\hat{\lambda}_1 = 0.83, \quad \hat{\lambda}_2 = -0.27, \quad \widehat{\beta_1\alpha_0} = 0.12, \quad\quad\quad\quad (6.39)$$

and it is easy to see that the constraints are not satisfied, since $\hat{\lambda}_1^2$ is smaller than $-4\hat{\lambda}_2$. This suggests that the model should be rejected, in particular if, in addition, it can be demonstrated that the violation of the constraint is not due to chance.

The selection of models is also possible based on statistical tests. Such tests are easily applied if the models are "nested". Nesting is a means of selecting amongst alternative specifications where the parameters of lower-order equations are contained within the parameters of higher-order ones. For example, Model V of the Bass, Clarke model, i.e. (6.20), is nested in Model VI (6.21); Model IV is a specific version of Model VI where $\lambda_3 = 0$; Model II is nested in Model IV; etc. Not all "competing" models are nested. Although it can be demonstrated[18] that the Koyck model (6.11), the current-effects model (6.24), the autoregressive current-effects model (6.27) and the partial-adjustment model (6.30) are all nested into one master model (the autoregressive multiple geometric lag model) they are not mutually nested. The selection between non-nested models is possible using information criteria and specific tests developed for non-nested models: see Section 18.4.3.

6.4 Lead effects

It is possible to extend marketing dynamics to include anticipations as well as carry-over effects. Leads occur when customers and/or competitors anticipate a marketing action and adjust their behavior before the action takes place.[19] Consumers may expect prices to fall or a new product to be introduced. In these cases they may hold back purchases until the anticipated event occurs.

---

17. Taken from the Bass and Clarke (1972) article.
18. See Leeflang et al. (1992) and Section 18.4.2.
19. Hanssens et al. (1990, p.49).

Consumers may also decelerate their purchases in anticipation of a promotion. This produces a prepromotion dip. This theory has some support in the literature (Krishna, 1992) and has been recently confirmed empirically in a study by van Heerde et al. (1999c).

Leads may also occur because sales persons delay sales if they anticipate or know that selling commissions are to rise. Doyle and Saunders (1985) examined the sales of natural gas and gas appliances as a function of a number of variables. One of these variables is the commission structure for sales personnel. The hypothesis of interest was that a temporary increase in commission rate accompanying a promotion would be preceded by a dip in sales, if sales people attempted to get customers to purchase during the time their commission rates were higher. Doyle and Saunders (1985) calculated that about 7 percent of total sales during an 8-week promotion period consisted of sales that would have taken place prior to the promotion period had commission sales not been increased during that period.

Lead effects can be modeled in a similar manner as lagged effects, at least in principle. As an example we specify

$$q_t = \alpha + \beta_1 p_t + \beta_2 p_{t+1} + \beta_3 p_{t+2} + u_t \qquad (6.40)$$

where

$$p_t = \text{price per unit in period } t, \text{ and}$$

$$p_{t+1}, p_{t+2} = \text{the announced prices or expected prices one- and two}$$
$$\text{periods ahead, respectively.}$$

If consumers expect price increases in $t+1$ and $t+2$, $\beta_2, \beta_3 > 0$, i.e.: *positive* leads. Anticipation of price reductions result in *negative* leads, i.e.: $\beta_2, \beta_3 < 0$. Negative leads were found by Doyle, Saunders (1985) and van Heerde et al. (1999c).

CHAPTER 7

Implementation criteria with respect to model structure

In Chapter 5 we introduced some basic notions regarding the specification of marketing models. In this chapter we study criteria that a model structure should ideally satisfy in order to stand a good chance of being implemented. The likelihood of model acceptance depends also, as indicated in Chapter 4, on other criteria which have little or nothing to do with model structure. We consider those other criteria in Chapter 19.

In Section 7.1, we clarify what we mean by implementation criteria related to structure. We present five criteria in Section 7.2. The criterion of robustness deserves special recognition, and we observe in Section 7.3 that many of the models in the literature fail on that criterion. In Sections 7.4 and 7.5, we relate robustness to intended model use and the nature of the problem faced by management.

7.1 Introduction

Several authors have proposed specification criteria, i.e. criteria pertaining to model structure. Most authors have looked at these from the *model builder's* point of view. Some criteria are based on theoretical requirements such as the logic of the mathematical structure. Other criteria may be practical, and emphasize aspects relevant to parameter estimation. A few authors have considered criteria from the *user's* point of view.

In proposing criteria for a decision calculus, Little (1970) takes the user's point of view. As indicated in Chapter 1, the criteria belong to two aspects: model structure and ease of use. With regard to model structure, models should be:

1. simple;
2. complete;
3. adaptive;
4. robust.

To link the criteria "simple" and "complete", Urban and Karash (1971) introduced the notion of evolutionary model-building. This criterion is also added by Little (1975a) in his later work. The evolutionary character of model-building is not in fact a criterion related to structure, but to the implementation process. We return to this topic in Section 19.2.2. Evolutionary model-building is one way to reconcile simplicity with completeness. Therefore, we use five criteria (simple, evolutionary, complete, adaptive, and robust) for our frame of reference in Section 7.2.

We do not claim that any model that fails on one of the criteria is unacceptable. Rather, the criteria, described in detail below, are intended to illustrate desirable model characteristics. Thus, the more a given model satisfies each criterion, the greater its likelihood of acceptance.

7.2 Implementation criteria

7.2.1 MODELS SHOULD BE SIMPLE

All models are simplified representations of real-world phenomena. One way in which model simplicity can be achieved is by keeping the number of variables small, and only to include the important phenomena in the model. This can be achieved in one or more of the following ways:

a. *Clustering of variables.*
Clustering of variables, which is often done in econometric studies. For example, a large number of brands assumed to influence the performance of the brand under study, may be aggregated into "competition". Or marketing instruments are aggregated into a small number of classes, such as product, distribution, advertising, promotions, and price.[1] For example, advertising expenditures separated by media such as television, radio, newspapers, magazines and billboards would be aggregated into total advertising expenditures. We note that this aggregation implicitly assumes that the marginal effect of an extra investment in advertising does not differ across the media. If the data are sufficient, this assumption should be tested. Statistical procedures such as principal components analysis or other dimension reduction methods are sometimes used to group variables on the basis of their covariance structure.

b. *Introducing relative variables.*
Imagine an equation that specifies total product category expenditures (over time) in current dollars as a function of total disposable income, also in current dollars, an inflation index and total number of individuals in the population. This equation can be simplified as follows. Both product category expenditures and total disposable income can be expressed *per capita*, and in *constant dollars*. This reduces the number of predictor variables from three to one. Importantly, the three variables are likely to be highly correlated. Of course, the new equation does not predict total category expenditures in current dollars. Instead, it predicts per capita expenditures in constant dollars. For the purpose of understanding the relation between category expenditures and income this is likely to be an advantage. If one needs to forecast next year's product category expenditures in current dollars, appropriate multiplication figures are needed.

---

1. See, for example, Leeflang, Koerts (1973).

c. *Dividing variables into subproblem-classes.*
A problem is partitioned into subproblems, each of which is analyzed separately, which means one considers only those variables that relate to each particular sub-problem. When the subproblems have been modeled, they are combined to cover the problem completely. Examples are models of individual products belonging to a wider assortment. We say more about this when we discuss these models in Chapters 13 and 14.

d. *Phasing variables over different levels.*
In demand models, variables can be divided into classes according to the various levels of demand that can be distinguished. Fluctuations in *product class sales per capita* can be explained by fluctuations in environmental variables, such as disposable income *per capita*, a weather index and fluctuations in marketing instruments such as average price, product class advertising expenditures per capita, etc. And variations in *market share* can be explained by variations in relative or share values of the various classes of marketing instruments. The phasing of variables over different levels can be accomplished by decomposition of a dependent variable. For example, revenue for a given time period and a given territory can be decomposed as:[2]

Revenue = Price × Quantity

and, for the same period and territory:

$$\text{Quantity} = \text{Number of Buyers} \times \text{Average Size/Purchase} \qquad (7.1)$$
$$\times \text{ Frequency of Purchase.}$$

Other examples are models in which the impact of marketing variables on (1) category purchase (product class sales) (2) brand choice and (3) purchase quantity decisions of households for frequently purchased goods are determined.[3]

e. *Constraining parameter values.*
An example is given in Chapter 6, where the Koyck model (relation (6.9)) constrains the distributed lag coefficients λ_t, $t = 1, \ldots, \infty$ to be of the form λ^t which is a constrained, parsimonious specification.

Points a-e above represent different ways of obtaining simple structure, often through a reduction in the number of variables/parameters. This relates to the concern of many model builders, especially those with a background in statistics and econometrics, that models must be manageable and estimable. This calls for *parsimony of the models*, i.e. there should be a modest number of parameters, and *for simple structure,* which might mean that linear or linearizable models are preferred to non-linearizable ones.

---

2. Farris, Parry, Ailawadi (1992).
3. See, e.g., Chintagunta (1993a, 1999), van Heerde, Leeflang, Wittink (1999b). A model with a similar structure to explain the purchase timing of products offered by direct marketing has been developed by van der Scheer and Leeflang (1997). Other examples are found in Gupta (1988), Krishnamurthi, Raj (1988), Bucklin, Lattin (1991), Chiang (1991) and in Section 12.4.

The notions of simplicity favored by the model builder will not always be agreeable to the *user*. Consider a producer of a frequently purchased food product. One of her marketing mix elements is a temporary price cut or price promotion offered multiple times per year. The brand is supported by a limited amount of advertising throughout the year. During the times of promotion, however, advertising support is increased, primarily to make consumers aware of the price cut. If the model builder wants to estimate separate effects of promotion and advertising, he is likely to experience difficulties because these effects are confounded, since heavy advertising spending coincides with price cut campaigns. Thus he may have to combine the two variables and measure their joint effect. This, however, may not be acceptable to the model user. For her, promotion and advertising are separate instruments, even though in some periods, one might be used to support or complement the other. Combining them for estimation purposes may result in a loss of quality and prestige of both model and model builder in the eyes of the user.[4]

In such a situation, the model builder may have to educate the model user about some statistical difficulties and how those difficulties can be reduced. If a manager has perfect knowledge of consumer response to marketing activities, she has no need for the results obtainable with a model. All managers in fact have uncertainty about market response. The question is whether they are willing to admit the extent of their uncertainty. Some of this uncertainty can be reduced by analyzing historical data. However, the actions taken by managers reflect their beliefs about market response. Thus, if advertising support is always increased in the presence of a temporary price cut, the manager apparently believes that the effect of the price cut is sufficiently greater with this support. The only way to determine how beneficial this support truly is, is to vary it systematically. For example, the manager could have some price cuts not coincide with extra advertising, and implement a given price cut with a different amount of advertising support (at different times and/or in different markets). By experimenting with the marketing variables it is possible to enhance the learning about market response (see Little, 1970). Another possibility is to combine subjective with data-based estimation.

We now define more clearly what "simple" means for the user. We cannot expect managers to be experts in mathematics, statistics, econometrics, operations research and computer science. They are not, they do not pretend to be, nor do they want to be. The manager is often not interested in the detailed intricacies of the model. What she wants is a basic understanding of the logic of the model and of what it can do for her. For the user, a model will be simple if this basic understanding is provided. Communication and involvement are two means of achieving this.

Historically, communication between model builder and model user was almost non-existent. This was described in 1969 by Montgomery and Urban (p. 5). Decision makers did not understand the jargon of the operations researcher and management scientist, and model building took place to a large extent in isolation. The situation has much improved in recent years. Market research firms, such as AC Nielsen and

---

4. This is elaborated upon in Chapter 16.

IRI, and consulting firms, such as McKinsey, have become heavily involved in the development and estimation of market response models. Much of the development is based on client needs, and this requires that implementation of model results plays a large role. Thus, the model builders have to take into account how new models fit into the decision-making environment. Models have also become easier to communicate with as a result of the widespread availability of on-line computer systems and the development of knowledge-based systems (McCann, Gallager, 1990). We treat this in more detail in the section dealing with ease-of-use criteria in Chapter 19.

Involvement means that the important factors bearing on the problem are described by the decision makers and not by the model builder. Also the model structure should represent the decision makers' view of how the market works.

We should, of course, realize that the real world is not simple, and that when a model represents the most important elements of a system, it will often look uncomfortably complicated. It is for this reason that Urban and Karash (1971) suggested building models in an evolutionary way, i.e. starting simply and expanding in detail as time goes on.[5]

7.2.2 MODELS SHOULD BE BUILT IN AN EVOLUTIONARY WAY

The basic idea is that one does not build a model with all ramifications from the start. Manager and model builder begin by defining the important elements of the problem, and how these elements are related. Based on an initial meeting or set of meetings, the primary elements are specified. The manager should be fully involved, so that she is likely to understand what the model does, and is interested in this tool, because it should represent her view of the world. As the manager uses the model, and builds up experience with this decision aid, she will realize its shortcomings. The model will then be expanded to incorporate additional elements. The model is now becoming more complex, but the manager still understands it, because it is her realization that something was missing which led to the increase in complexity. In a sense the model becomes difficult, yet by using an evolutionary approach, it also remains simple because the manager has a clear understanding of what the model is supposed to do.

This approach can be accompanied by a two-step presentation. First, a formalized or *conceptual* model is presented to management. This model ultimately reflects management's own views about the nature of market response. Second, an empirical model or *statistical model* is used to convey to management, how much of the overall response is captured in the model (Hanssens, Parsons, Schultz, 1990, p. 336).

7.2.3 MODELS SHOULD BE COMPLETE ON IMPORTANT ISSUES

For a model to be a useful decision-support tool, it has to represent all relevant elements of the problem being studied. This means that a model should account for all important variables. If competitors matter, then the effects of their actions on a

---

5. Amstutz (1970) proposes something which is conceptually similar.

brand under study should be incorporated. The marketing dynamics should be built in, and so on.[6] Other relevant elements are parameters which account for heterogeneity of the supplier (e.g. competitive advertising effects vary across competitors) and/or the heterogeneity of demand (e.g. own-brand advertising effects, brand loyalty, price sensitivity, etc. vary by market segment).

It should be clear that completeness on all important issues is a criterion which may conflict with simplicity. As long as simple is roughly synonymous with understandable, then the model builder can resolve the conflict at least partially by adopting an evolutionary approach.

There may be other conflicts between the interests of the model user and the needs of the model builder. Suppose, for example, that the regular price is not an active marketing instrument, a typical situation in many oligopolistic markets. It will then be difficult, or impossible, to assess its impact on sales because it does not show sufficient variation. As a result, the regular price does not appear in the specification of an econometric model. In that case, the implication is not that price does not affect sales, but that its effect cannot be measured by analyzing historical data. To have a "complete" model of demand, the effect of price has to be assessed through other means.[7]

Completeness is, of course, a relative concept. It is relative to the problem, to the organization, and to the user. We briefly outline these three aspects here and discuss the first more extensively in Section 7.5 while we expand on the other two in Chapter 19.

Completeness relative to the *problem* can be illustrated as follows. In modeling the effects of advertising, we may wonder whether we should focus on total advertising, i.e. estimate its overall effectiveness, or whether we should differentiate between the various media vehicles available for the communication of advertising messages. An initial answer to this question is that it depends on the problem definition. If the model is intended to aid marketing mix planning at the brand management level, then the total effect of advertising is what is needed. In that case it may be appropriate to use the aggregate of all advertising expenditures. However, if the advertising manager wants to know how to allocate expenditures to the different media vehicles, data on each of these media are required. The advertising manager needs detailed understanding of the effects of alternative media vehicles as well as of different advertising copies and specific advertising campaigns (e.g. Montgomery, Silk, 1972).

This delineation of data needs corresponding to the needs of different managers may, however, not be sufficient. Even if the marketing manager is only concerned with the determination of total advertising expenditures, and not its breakdown, it is possible that the estimation of the effect of total advertising is estimated with

---

6. See also Leeflang (1974, Chapter 6), and Leeflang, Koerts (1975).

7. A simple way to combine a laboratory experiment to determine price elasticity with historical data analysis of other marketing instruments is proposed by Naert (1972). Other (field) experiments for this purpose are Gabor-Granger procedures and Brand-Price Trade-Off analyses. See, e.g. Leeflang, Wedel (1993), Kalyanam, Shively (1998), Wedel, Leeflang (1998). Survey experiments, such as provided by conjoint analysis, offer additional opportunities. See, for example, Currim, Weinberg, Wittink (1981), Mahajan, Green, Goldberg (1982).

greater validity and precision from a model in which the advertising components are separated.

The *organizational* structure of the firm will also be a determinant of completeness. A firm with a highly decentralized structure may generate a large number of relatively simple subproblems. The corresponding models will also be relatively simple and incomplete from the perspective of the firm.[8] Centralized firms will have a smaller number of separate problem statements each of which will require more complex models.

At the same time, the size of the organization may influence the desired degree of completeness. A marketing mix problem for a small firm operating at the regional level will not be the same as that of a firm selling a national brand. We consider this aspect in the discussion of costs and benefits in Chapter 20.

The desired level of completeness will also depend on the *user*. Larréché (1974, 1975) has observed that one manager's integrative complexity, i.e. her ability to integrate pieces of information into an organized pattern, is not the same as that of another manager. The desired level of complexity and completeness will, therefore, vary according to the user. This amplifies the need for intense involvement of the user in the model-building process.

7.2.4 MODELS SHOULD BE ADAPTIVE

Market change and market behavior are dynamic. Thus, it is not possible to think of model building as a one-time affair. Instead, models need to be adapted more or less continuously. This implies that either the structure and/or the parameters have to be adapted. For example, the entry or exit of a competitor may imply that certain model parameters change. In addition, the specification of the model may have to change.

The changes that require model adaptation can take many forms. The true values of model parameters can change if the set of consumers that makes product category purchases changes. We discuss this issue in detail in Section 17.4. Brand parameters may also change if the amount of advertising for all brands or the average price in the category changes. And modifications in product characteristics, which are rarely included in demand models, can change brand-level parameters as well. These examples suggest why model parameters may vary, even if the structure of the model can remain as is. All observable market changes that can be related to model characteristics give reason for the model builder to respecify the structure and/or reestimate the parameters. For example, if a firm has traditionally sold its products through independent distributors but has designed a wholly-owned distribution network, then the change in the structure of the selling process will require that a new model be created.

---

8. Of course, there remains the problem of coordinating the various subproblems in order to make sure that subunits do not pursue objectives that are in conflict with overall company objectives. Internal or transfer pricing can be successfully applied to overcome such potential conflicts. See, for example, Baumol and Fabian (1964) and Hess (1968).

Knowledge of the marketplace, and the changes that require a new model structure, is the primary determinant of adaptation. A secondary determinant is the difference between actual and predicted values (see Section 3.2 and the illustration in Figure 3.1). The greater this difference, to the extent that it cannot be attributed to statistical uncertainty, the more reason there is to adapt. Thus, the greater the prediction error the greater the need to respecify the model. Is there a missing variable? Should the functional form be modified? Do consumers respond differently?

It should be clear that both the use of logical arguments ("the model needs to change because the market environment is different") and a careful analysis of prediction errors are critical for continued model use. Alternatively, one can update parameter estimates routinely, by reestimation each time new data become available. Routine reestimation is advisable if there are, for example, gradual changes in the consumer population. It is conceivable that by tracking how the parameter estimates change over time, short-term projections can be made of how the parameters will change in the future. Little (1975b, p. 662) stresses the importance of adaptive control by continually measuring programs and monitoring systems to detect change. Formal systems for (adaptive) control of advertising spending have been proposed by Little (1966) and Horsky and Simon (1983).

An important determinant of the likelihood of model acceptance is that it is easily adaptable. It is always easy to replace previous parameter estimates. Adaptation to structural changes tends to be more difficult. A facilitating factor is the *modularity* of the model. For example, a marketing mix model may consist of a set of submodels, such as a price-, an advertising-, and a promotion module. The modular structure will prove particularly useful when a change does not involve all of the modules. An excellent example of modular model building is BRANDAID, a marketing mix model developed by Little (1975a, 1975b).

7.2.5 MODELS SHOULD BE ROBUST

Little (1970, p. B470) defines model *robustness*[9] as a quality characteristic which makes it difficult for a user to obtain bad answers. He suggest that robustness is achievable through the specification of a structure that constrains answers to a meaningful range of values. Application of the robustness criterion requires that the model builder has an understanding of marketplace behavior. This understanding is necessary for the model builder to identify relevant constructs, to define valid measures of the constructs, to specify meaningful functional forms (e.g. nonlinear effects), and to accommodate appropriate interaction effects.

Empirically, model robustness exists if the model results reflect:

a. Correct marginal effects and changes therein.[10] Broadly speaking, each marginal effect should be plausible over a wide range of possible values for the corresponding predictor variable (appropriate functional form).

---

9. Robustness has a different meaning in statistics and econometrics. According to Theil (1971, p. 615), a statistical test is called robust if it is insensitive to departures from the assumptions under which it is derived.
10. Mathematically, first- and second-order derivatives should have the right signs.

b. Meaningful interaction effects. The marginal effect of a given predictor variable may depend on the value of another predictor variable: for example, there is a large body of evidence to support the view that the price elasticity of a brand depends on the amount of advertising support (Kaul and Wittink, 1995).

c. The endogeneity of variables for which the models are intended to produce marginal effects. If a predictor variable is manipulated by management based on realized values of the criterion variable then this "reverse causality" must be taken into account in the model-building process (Kadyali, Chintagunta, Vilcassim, 1999).

In practical applications, the argument is often made that it is sufficient to obtain an estimated equation that produces plausible predicted values over the range of observed values that occur in the sample for the predictor variables. This is a myopic perspective. The objective of model building is to enrich our understanding of relationships beyond historical practices, as much as possible. New insights are especially likely to occur if we conduct experiments. That is, we vary marketing activities, in part, to learn about effects that are difficult or impossible to discern from existing data. But in the absence of such experiments, we should attempt to learn as much as possible from models of historical data. The best opportunity to do this is to use a model specification that can provide plausible predictions outside the range of sample values as well as within. In this regard it is useful to note that empirical researchers seldom indicate that an estimated equation can only be used for restricted ranges of values for the predictor variables. For some criterion variables, it is possible to specify constraints. For example, if the criterion variable represents a brand's market share, robustness is violated if predicted values are less than zero or more than one. Since market share is bounded by zero and one, it is appropriate to require that predicted market shares satisfy the same constraints. And, if all brands belonging to a product category are modeled together, we may insist on an additional constraint: the predicted market shares should sum to one. Thus, when actual values are subject to certain constraints, their model counterparts should satisfy the same constraints. Such models are called *logically consistent* (see, for example, Naert and Bultez, 1973) or *consistent sum-constrained*. Consistent sum-constrained models are models, specified in such a way that the sum-constraint is automatically satisfied, which means that the *estimated* values of the dependent variables (e.g. market shares) or a subset of the dependent variables sum to a known number. Let q_{jt} be the demand for brand j in period t, and $restr_{.t} = \sum_{j=1}^{n} q_{jt}$ = product class sales in period t. For sum-constrained models we require:

$$\sum_{j=1}^{n} \hat{q}_{jt} = \sum_{j=1}^{n} q_{jt} = restr_{.t}. \tag{7.2}$$

Consistent sum-constrained models have to satisfy a number of conditions which have implications for their structure.[11]

---

11. See, e.g. McGuire, Farley, Lucas, Ring (1968), McGuire, Weiss (1976), Weverbergh, Naert, Bultez (1977), Leeflang, Reuyl (1979), Reuyl (1982).

While robustness is a desirable characteristic, it is, just as completeness, a relative concept. We demonstrate why and in what sense in Sections 7.3 to 7.5.

7.3 Can non-robust models be good models?[12]

Suppose we take a pragmatic view of the meaning of the label "good model", namely, a model is good if it works well. For example, if a model has been developed to forecast sales, and if the model's predictions stay within, say, one half percent of actual sales, management might decide that the model is excellent. With this level of forecast accuracy, management may not care much about how the model works, or whether or not its structure is robust.[13]

It turns out that there are many examples of models that are non-robust but nevertheless, within reasonable limits, work well.

We begin with a simple example. Consider the following multiplicative sales response function:[14]

$$q_t = \alpha p_t^{\beta_p} a_t^{\beta_a} \tag{7.3}$$

where

$$q_t = \text{unit sales in period } t,$$
$$p_t = \text{price in period } t,$$
$$a_t = \text{advertising expenditures in period } t, \text{ and}$$
$$\alpha, \beta_p, \beta_a = \text{model parameters.}$$

The parameters β_p and β_a are respectively the price and advertising elasticities. Normally β_p will be negative and larger than one in absolute value (see Tellis, 1988b), and β_a will be between zero and one (see Assmus, Farley, Lehmann, 1984). The question now is: what happens to sales as price and advertising vary? For $a_t = a_0$ $(a_0 > 0)$, and with price becoming very high, sales tend to zero as expected. On the other hand, as price goes to zero, unit sales go to infinity. However, since sales cannot exceed the total market potential, a finite quantity, this implication is not realistic. Therefore, following the definition given in Section 7.2.5, the model is not robust. And what about advertising? Given $p_t = p_0$ $(p_0 > 0)$, and letting advertising go to infinity, we observe from equation (7.3) that sales also go to infinity. In addition, with advertising equal to zero, sales are also zero. One might argue that it is realistic to expect zero unit sales in the absence of advertising. For a new brand about which consumers have no awareness nor knowledge, this implication may be realistic: brand awareness is often a necessary condition prior to purchase. However, for established brands, zero advertising will not result in zero unit sales, at least not immediately. Thus, we need to know more about the type of brand and the characteristics of the marketplace before

---

12. See also Naert (1974).
13. In a sense this argument is within the realm of positive economics. See, for example, Friedman (1953).
14. For simplicity of exposition we omit error terms.

we can make a proper judgment about the extent to which equation (7.3) is or is not robust.

Some additional problems arise with market share functions. Suppose we use:

$$m_{jt} = \alpha_j \left[\frac{p_{jt}}{p_{ct}} \right]^{\beta_{pj}} \left[\frac{a_{jt}}{a_{ct}} \right]^{\beta_{aj}} \tag{7.4}$$

where

$$
\begin{aligned}
m_{jt} &= \text{market share of brand } j \text{ in period } t, \\
p_{jt}, a_{jt} &= \text{price, and advertising, for brand } j \text{ in period } t, \\
p_{ct}, a_{ct} &= \text{a competitive price index, and a competitive} \\
&\quad \text{advertising index, and} \\
\alpha_j, \beta_{pj}, \beta_{aj} &= \text{parameters for brand } j.
\end{aligned}
$$

For realistic values of variables and parameters, market share in equation (7.4) will be non-negative. But, in addition to having the same non-robust characteristics as (7.3), equation (7.4) would predict an infinite market share if company j has a positive advertising budget, if competitors do not advertise.[15] Yet, by definition, market share should lie between zero and one.

Market share functions should ideally also satisfy the constraint that *predicted* market shares across brands sum to one. This may seem trivial, yet it is not. To show why, first consider a linear model with two firms j and c:

$$
\begin{aligned}
m_{jt} &= \lambda_j m_{j,t-1} + \gamma_j a_{jt}^* \\
m_{ct} &= \lambda_c m_{c,t-1} + \gamma_c a_{ct}^*
\end{aligned}
\tag{7.5}
$$

where

$$
\begin{aligned}
m_{jt}, m_{ct} &= \text{market share of brand } j \text{ and brand } c \text{ in period } t, \\
m_{j,t-1}, m_{c,t-1} &= \text{lagged market share,} \\
a_{jt}^*, a_{ct}^* &= \text{advertising share,}[16] \text{ and} \\
\lambda_j, \lambda_c, \gamma_j, \gamma_c &= \text{model parameters.}
\end{aligned}
$$

The observed market share values will, by definition, sum to one. As suggested above, it is desirable (and it is a necessary condition for robustness) to have *esti-mated* values satisfy the same condition. Naert and Bultez (1973) have shown that for estimated market shares to sum to one, the following constraints should be imposed

---

15. This problem can be avoided by placing $p_{jt} + p_{ct}$ and $a_{jt} + a_{ct}$ in the denominators. However, the drawback then is that market share does not depend on own-brand advertising, if competitors do not advertise.

16. $a_{jt}^* = a_{jt}/(a_{jt} + a_{ct})$, $a_{ct}^* = a_{ct}/(a_{jt} + a_{ct})$.

on the parameters of (7.5):[17]

$$\lambda_j = \lambda_c = \lambda$$
$$\gamma_j = \gamma_c = \gamma$$
$$\lambda + \gamma = 1.$$

But imposing these constraints to achieve robustness creates new problems, since they imply that different brands have the same marginal effect for advertising. It follows that *linearity* and *robustness* do not go well together, if we want to allow for heterogeneity in the response parameters across brands.

We now consider whether a multiplicative structure might be robust. The multiplicative equivalent of the set of equations (7.5) is:

$$m_{jt} = m_{j,t-1}^{\lambda_j} a_{jt}^{*\gamma_j} \tag{7.6}$$
$$m_{ct} = m_{c,t-1}^{\lambda_c} a_{ct}^{*\gamma_c}.$$

Unfortunately, with this type of multiplicative market share functions, no constraints on the parameters exist that will ensure the predicted market shares sum to one.[18]

We conclude that the linear and multiplicative market share functions shown in (7.5) and (7.6) are non-robust. Yet, as we discussed in Chapter 5, these market share functions are used frequently in empirical marketing studies, and in many cases the estimated functions do have descriptive validity as illustrated below.

For three alternative market share models, the fluctuations in bimonthly market shares of four brands of the German cigarette market are explained by advertising shares and lagged market shares.[19] The linear additive model is specified as:

$$m_{jt} = \alpha_j + \beta_{1j} a_{jt}^* + \beta_{2j} m_{j,t-1}. \tag{7.7}$$

The multiplicative version is:

$$m_{jt} = \alpha_j \cdot a_{jt}^{*\beta_{1j}} m_{j,t-1}^{\beta_{2j}}. \tag{7.8}$$

As we discussed, models (7.7) and (7.8) are non-robust models: there is no guarantee that the predicted market shares sum to one ((7.7) and (7.8)) or are between zero and one ((7.7)).

A class of *robust* market share models are the so-called attraction models. An example of an attraction model is (for $j = 1, .., 4$):

$$m_{jt} = \frac{\alpha_j \cdot a_{jt}^{*\beta_{1j}} m_{j,t-1}^{\beta_2}}{\sum_{r=1}^{n} \alpha_r \cdot a_{rt}^{*\beta_{1r}} m_{r,t-1}^{\beta_2}} \tag{7.9}$$

where

---

17. Constraints for the general linear model (with constant term) were derived by Schmalensee (1972) and Naert and Bultez (1973). See also McGuire and Weiss (1976) and Weverbergh (1976). For a further discussion, see Chapter 9.
18. Except for such trivial and meaningless constraints as $\lambda_j = \lambda_c = 0$, $\gamma_j = \gamma_c = 1$, or $\gamma_j = \gamma_c = 0$, $\lambda_j = \lambda_c = 1$.
19. The example is taken from Leeflang, Reuyl (1984a).

Table 7.1 Parameter estimates of market share models.

Specification		Advertising share				Lagged market share			
		β_{11}	β_{12}	β_{13}	β_{14}	β_{21}	β_{22}	β_{23}	β_{24}
Linear additive	(7.7)	0.04^b	-0.01	0.04^b	-0.02	0.50^a	0.81^a	0.67^a	0.70^a
Multiplicative	(7.8)	0.13^b	0.01	0.07^a	-0.02	0.46^b	0.84^a	0.81^a	0.70^a
Attraction	(7.9)	0.60^a	-0.02	0.06^b	-0.34		$\leftarrow 0.86^a \rightarrow$		

[a,b]Estimates significant at the 1% and 5%-level respectively.

Source: Leeflang, Reuyl (1984a, p. 214).

n = the number of brands (n = 4).

The estimates of the response parameters of (7.7)-(7.9) are shown in Table 7.1. From Table 7.1 we conclude that there are *marked differences* between the advertising (share) parameters across the brands (within each of the three equations). For brands 1 and 3 the advertising parameter estimates have the expected sign and are statistically significant.[20] For other brands, however, the results are less satisfactory. Two brands have negative coefficients for advertising share in the linear additive and attraction specifications. The multiplicative specification shows only one negative advertising effect. Fortunately, none of the negative coefficients are significant. On the other hand, the lagged market share effect is almost always highly significant. The results are plausible for two of the four brands, suggesting a modest amount of descriptive validity.

For another example of a multiplicative market share function, we use Lambin, Naert and Bultez (1975), who estimated market share of an inexpensive consumer durable as a function of lagged market share, relative price $p^r_{jt}(= p_{jt}/p_{ct})$, relative advertising $a^r_{jt}(= a_{jt}/a_{ct})$, and relative quality $\tilde{x}^r_{jt}(= \tilde{x}_{jt}/\tilde{x}_{ct})$:

$$m_{jt} = \alpha_j (m_{j,t-1})^{\lambda_j} (p^r_{jt})^{\beta_{pj}} (a^r_{jt})^{\beta_{aj}} (\tilde{x}^r_{jt})^{\beta_{xj}}. \tag{7.10}$$

We show the parameter estimates in Table 7.2. The results indicate that (7.10) offers a plausible description of how market share depends on lagged market share, and the company's decision variables (relative to competitors). All marginal effects have the expected signs and are statistically significant. However, the earlier criticism of the multiplicative market share function still applies.

---

20. For completeness, we provide a brief explanation of statistical significance for parameter estimates. The null hypothesis H_0 is that the parameters β_{1j} and β_{2j}, $j = 1, .., 4$, are equal to zero. A statistical test (t-test) is applied to test each of these hypotheses. For all three models the null hypothesis is not rejected for β_{12} and β_{14}. The null hypothesis is rejected for all other parameters of (7.7). However, there is a one percent (a), respectively five percent (b), chance that H_0 is erroneously rejected. The tests are two-tailed which means that expectations about signs of coefficients are not taken into account. Two-tailed tests are more conservative than one-tailed tests if the chance of incorrectly rejecting H_0 is held constant.

Table 7.2 Parameter estimates of a multiplicative market share response function.

Variable	$m_{j,t-1}$	p^r_{jt}	a^r_{jt}	$\tilde{x}^r_{jt}$	Intercept (α_j)
Parameter estimate	0.34^c	-3.73^b	0.15^a	0.58^b	0.60^a

a,b,c One-tailed t-test significant at the 1%, 2.5% and 10%-level respectively.

Source: Lambin, Naert, Bultez (1975, p. 121).

In a number of well-known and commercially successful models such as the SCAN*PRO model (Wittink, Addona, Hawkes, Porter, 1988), PROMOTIONSCAN (Abraham, Lodish, 1992), DEALMAKER (McCann, Gallagher, 1990), "brand sales" is the criterion variable. Although the empirical results tend to be plausible, one can provide the following criticism of non-robustness. For example, the criterion variables in the SCAN*PRO model are brand unit sales (j) at the store level (k) in week t. The model estimates the effect of promotional variables implemented by retailers. Now, brand sales q_{kjt} can be aggregated over stores ($q_{.jt}$) over brands ($q_{k.t}$), over brands and stores ($q_{..t}$), over time, etc. However, there is no guarantee that:

$$\sum_{r=1}^{n} \hat{q}_{krt} = q_{k.t} \text{ or} \tag{7.11}$$

$$\sum_{k=1}^{K} \hat{q}_{kjt} = q_{.jt}$$

where

n = the number of brands and K the number of stores.

In this sense the SCAN*PRO model is non-robust.

Similar problems of non-robustness occur in disaggregate models of demand. Take for example the linear probability model (7.12) which models individual choice behavior:

$$\pi_j = \alpha_{0j} + \sum_{\ell=1}^{L} \alpha_{\ell j} x_{\ell j} \tag{7.12}$$

where

π_j = the probability that a consumer purchases brand j,

α_{0j} = an intercept term,

$\alpha_{\ell j}$ = parameters capturing the effects of marketing variables,

$x_{\ell j}$ = marketing variables.

The linear probability model may yield predictions of the purchase probability outside the (0, 1) interval, dependent on the values of marketing variables and parameters, and is thus logically inconsistent. A so-called (multinomial) logit model describing purchase probability uses a formulation that is similar to that of an attraction model for market shares and resolves the problem of logical inconsistency:

$$
\pi_j = \frac{\exp\left(\alpha_{0j} + \sum_{\ell=1}^{L} \alpha_{\ell j} x_{\ell j}\right)}{\sum_{r=1}^{n} \exp\left(\alpha_{0r} + \sum_{\ell=1}^{L} \alpha_{\ell r} x_{\ell r}\right)}.
\tag{7.13}
$$

In this formulation the predicted probabilities are between 0 and 1. An alternative disaggregate choice model that is logically consistent is the multinomial probit model, (Chapter 12). Similar problems of logical inconsistency occur in other disaggregate models, for example in purchase frequency models, in which the predicted frequencies need to be restricted to the positive domain.

In this section we examined some non-robust marketing models. The market share and choice models give bad answers for extreme values of the predictor variables, and over the whole range of possible values some of the models do not have the property that the predicted market shares sum to one across brands. Nevertheless, these same models have been used in empirical studies, and they often fit the data well and seem to have descriptive value. This leads us to believe that the requirement of robustness should be linked to the use one intends to make of the model. We explore this further in the next section.

7.4 Robustness related to intended use

In this section we show that data generated from one model can sometimes be fitted quite well with other models. The primary reason is that predictor variables often do not show much variation in the sample. We use an example to show that robustness is not sufficient for model quality.

Suppose the true relation between unit sales and advertising of brand j is:

$$
q_{jt} = \alpha + (\beta - \alpha) \frac{a_{jt}^{\delta}}{\gamma + a_{jt}^{\delta}}.
\tag{7.14}
$$

This equation has a robust functional form, the properties of which we examined in Section 5.3.3, which follows a S-curve.[21] Assume that the parameters are $\alpha = 100,000$, $\beta = 400,000$, $\gamma = 200$, $\delta = 0.5$. We show the corresponding function in Figure 7.1, which we refer to as "real S" (the true S-curve):

$$
q_{jt} = 100,000 + 300,000 \frac{a_{jt}^{0.5}}{200 + a_{jt}^{0.5}} + \varepsilon_t
\tag{7.15}
$$

---

21. In Section 7.5 we show that (7.14) is in fact robust only in a limited sense.

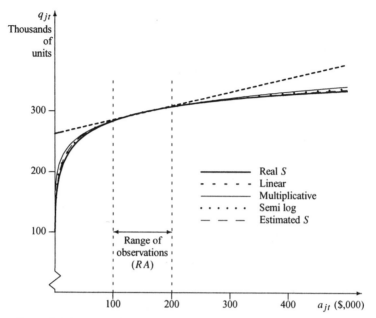

Figure 7.1 Sales as a function of advertising for alternative model specifications.

where ε_t is a normally distributed error term with mean zero and a standard deviation of 1,000. To simulate unit sales we took as values for a_{jt}: $100,000, $105,000,\ldots$, $200,000. Thus in the simulated period of observation, advertising varies between $100,000 and $200.000. In Figure 7.1 this is the interval RA. We assume that the company has never operated outside that range.

Suppose now that we postulate a linear relation between q_{jt} and a_{jt}:

$$q_{jt} = \alpha' + \beta' a_{jt} + \varepsilon'_t. \tag{7.16}$$

Estimating α' and β' from the simulated data gives:

$$\hat{q}_{jt} = \underset{(237.0)}{263,000} + \underset{(35.7)}{0.23} \, a_{jt}, \quad R^2 = 0.986 \tag{7.17}$$

where the figures in parentheses are the t-statistics.[22]

---

22. The coefficient of determination R^2 measures how much of the variation in the criterion variable is explained by the model, i.e. by the predictor variables. Applied to equation (7.17),
$R^2 = \sum_{t=1}^{T} (\hat{q}_{jt} - \bar{q}_{jt})^2 / \sum_{t=1}^{T} (q_{jt} - \bar{q}_{jt})^2$, where T is the number of observations, and $\hat{q}_{jt}$ and $\bar{q}_{jt}$ are estimated and average brand sales respectively.

It can be shown that in a model which is linear in the parameters, an OLS estimator $\hat{\beta}$ of a parameter β follows a normal distribution, or $(\hat{\beta} - \beta)/\sigma_{\hat{\beta}}$, where $\sigma_{\hat{\beta}}$ is the standard deviation of $\hat{\beta}$, follows a standard normal distribution if the error term satisfies certain desirable properties. The standard deviation $\sigma_{\hat{\beta}}$ is a function of σ_{ε}, the standard deviation of the error term. Since the latter is unknown, so will be $\sigma_{\hat{\beta}}$, and thus we rely on an estimated value $\hat{\sigma}_{\hat{\beta}}$. It can then be demonstrated that $(\hat{\beta} - \beta)/\hat{\sigma}_{\hat{\beta}}$ follows a student or t-distribution with $T - s$ degrees of freedom, where s is the number of parameters. The reported t-values in (7.17) are $\hat{\beta}/\hat{\sigma}_{\hat{\beta}}$, i.e. they correspond to testing the null hypotheses $H_0 : \alpha' = 0$ and $\beta' = 0$ respectively. See also Chapter 16.

Similarly, we consider a multiplicative form:

$$q_{jt} = \alpha'' a_{jt}^{\beta''} e^{\varepsilon_t''} \tag{7.18}$$

which, as indicated in Section 5.3.2, can be estimated by linear regression after taking logarithms. The regression results are:

$$\widehat{\ln q_{jt}} = \underset{(92.0)}{11.26} + \underset{(11.0)}{0.11} \ln a_{jt}, \quad R^2 = 0.870. \tag{7.19}$$

Finally, a semi-logarithmic model is postulated:

$$q_{jt} = \alpha''' + \beta''' \ln a_{jt} + \varepsilon_t''' \tag{7.20}$$

which is estimated as:

$$\hat{q}_{jt} = \underset{(-10.5)}{-93,221} + \underset{(44.0)}{32,809} \ln a_{jt}, \quad R^2 = 0.991. \tag{7.21}$$

The true model (7.14) is nonlinear in the parameters, but can be linearized as follows:[23]

$$\frac{q_{jt} - \alpha}{\beta - q_{jt}} = \frac{a_{jt}^\delta}{\gamma}. \tag{7.22}$$

Taking logarithms we obtain:

$$\ln \frac{q_{jt} - \alpha}{\beta - q_{jt}} = \gamma^* + \delta \ln a_{jt} \tag{7.23}$$

where $\gamma^* = \ln \gamma$. In order to estimate (7.23), α and β have to be known. In the simulation, an iterative "grid" search procedure was applied using maximization of the coefficient of determination R^2 as the choice criterion.[24] The following equation was ultimately obtained:

$$\left[\widehat{\ln \frac{q_{jt} - \alpha}{\hat{\beta} - q_{jt}}} \right] = \underset{(-35.9)}{-2.94} + \underset{(40.9)}{0.28} \ln a_{jt}, \quad R^2 = 0.989 \tag{7.24}$$

with $\hat{\alpha} = 5,000$, and $\hat{\beta} = 490,000$.

From the results described in (7.15), (7.17), and (7.21), it is clear that a linear, a multiplicative, and a semi-logarithmic model, each with only two parameters, fit the data, simulated from a four-parameter model, quite well. The statistical results (shown here) alone may be inadequate for a decision as to which model is the best one.

---

23. See Section 5.3.3.
24. For a more detailed description, see Naert (1974). Both α and β were varied in steps of 5,000. Variation in smaller amounts were not useful, because of the low sensitivity of R^2 to α and β in the neighborhood of the optimum.

Next we evaluate the predictive abilities of the various models. Figure 7.1 shows the real S-curve as well as the four estimated curves. From this figure, it is clear that the four curves do just about equally well as long as the advertising budget falls within the interval RA. However, outside this interval, we know that (7.15), (7.17), and (7.21) do not approach a finite limit, but predicted sales continues to increase with advertising. In that sense (7.24) would seem to be more appropriate. When advertising goes to zero, we know that (7.21) (the semi-logarithmic function) breaks down, since it predicts sales of minus infinity when there is no advertising spending. For the S-curve, the linear function and the multiplicative function, the predictions for low advertising spending are robust and we cannot reject any of these (although we may object to positive sales for zero advertising in the linear model).

We note that for all of the above models, the forecast accuracy decreases as we move further away from the interval RA. That is, the standard error of the forecast is at a minimum at the mean value of the predictor variables in the sample data.[25] Also, outside RA we can only guess how unit sales responds to advertising since we have no data to support the argument. However, we expect that outside RA the linear model will not perform well, because generally advertising shows decreasing returns to scale beyond a certain level of expenditures.

Even if the model specification is considered theoretically desirable, as we may conclude about the equation that produces the S-curve, the empirical results may show limitations. For example, a comparison of the true parameter values in (7.15) with the estimated parameter values in (7.24) shows remarkably large differences. When advertising is zero, the true amount of unit sales is $100,000$ whereas the predicted amount is only $5,000$. Thus, an apparently attractive model specification which is known to be correct in a simulation study can still produce predicted values with a high amount of error. The very limited range of variation in advertising that occurs in the simulation makes it difficult to obtain accurate predictions for extreme conditions such as zero advertising.

We now consider a normative model. Suppose we evaluate the profitability of advertising, and we determine the advertising budget that maximizes profit. We show below that the linear model cannot be used. Profit, π_{jt}, is:

$$\pi_{jt} = (p - c)q_{jt} - a_{jt} \tag{7.25}$$

where

  p = price per unit, and

  c = average unit cost.

If $q_{jt} = \alpha + \beta a_{jt}$, (7.25) becomes:

$$\pi_{jt} = (p - c)(\alpha + \beta a_{jt}) - a_{jt}. \tag{7.26}$$

In (7.26) we have, on the one hand, the contribution margin, $(p - c)$, multiplied by the demand, $(\alpha + \beta a_{jt})$, and, on the other hand, the cost of advertising, a_{jt}.

---

25. See, for example, Wittink (1988, p.46). See also Section 18.5.

Table 7.3 Optimal advertising budget derived from alternative specifications.

Model	Optimal advertising (in thousands of $)	Optimal predicted profit ($)	Real profit ($)
S (real)	166	1,340,117	1,340,117
S (estimated)	163	1,339,987	1,340,091
Multiplicative	171	1,339,476	1,340,019
Semi-logarithmic	164	1,339,610	1,340,107

If $(p - c)\beta > 1$, profit increases with advertising, and the model would suggest that management spend as much on advertising as possible. If $(p - c)\beta \leq 1$, profit would be maximized at zero advertising. Managers will reject such implications as being nonsensical. Yet the linear model is robust for predictions within the range RA.

The other three models give meaningful normative implications for the advertising budget, although the semi-logarithmic model is not robust for small levels of advertising spending, and neither the multiplicative nor the semi-logarithmic model is robust for very high levels of advertising spending.

Table 7.3 shows the optimal advertising budgets for each of the models (excluding the linear one), the corresponding optimal predicted profit amounts and the real profit amounts, by assuming a contribution margin of $5. We see that the spending levels are quite similar across the models, and that the corresponding real profit levels differ even less. The latter is due to the insensitivity of profit to changes in advertising spending in a wide range around the optimum.[26]

The predictive power of (non-robust) linear and multiplicative market share models and (robust) attraction models has been compared in a number of studies.[27] The results show that the attraction models do not always have significantly greater predictive power than their non-robust counterparts. Thus, even though the attraction models have advantages on theoretical grounds this does not imply that better predictions are obtained. One problem with these empirical comparisons is that insufficient attention is paid to the characteristics of the data used for predictions. Robust models will outperform other models only if the data allow the advantage of robustness to exhibit itself.

It should be clear from this discussion that the desired robustness for a model depends on model use. Given their theoretical advantages and that, nowadays, these models are not difficult to estimate, robust specification should generally be preferred.

---

26. For evidence that low sensitivity is also frequently observed in the real world, see Naert (1973), and Bultez and Naert (1979).
27. See Naert, Weverbergh (1981a, 1985), Brodie, de Kluyver (1984), Ghosh, Neslin, and Shoemaker (1984), Leeflang, Reuyl (1984a).

7.5 Robustness related to the problem situation

In his illustration of a decision calculus, Little (1970) uses a functional relation such as (7.14), but with sales replaced by market share:[28]

$$m_{jt} = \alpha_j + (\beta_j - \alpha_j) \frac{a_{jt}^{\delta_j}}{\gamma_j + a_{jt}^{\delta_j}}. \tag{7.27}$$

Assuming $0 \le \alpha_j \le \beta_j \le 1$, it turns out that this model constrains predictions to a meaningful range of values. Thus this model seems to satisfy the criterion of robustness. Yet, in a strict sense, this market share function also proves to be problematic. For example, suppose we consider how j's market share changes if competitors double their advertising, while j's advertising remains unchanged. From equation (7.27) we see that market share remains the same. This suggests that the model is not robust. However, our conclusion may be different if we take the problem situation being modeled into account.

Suppose that the market consists of ten firms, with company j having about 50 percent market share, and the second largest firm about 10 percent. For such a market, equation (7.27) is much more acceptable. Company j is clearly the leading firm and it is unlikely that a leading firm will keep its advertising constant if competitors double theirs. More likely is a scenario in which competitors react to changes in the leading firm j's advertising spending. All these reactions will be reflected, in an average way, in the coefficients. Although the model does not explicitly consider the effect of competitors' advertising on brand j's sales nor the competitive reactions, it does so implicitly through the coefficients. Thus the decision maker may still be able to use the model to evaluate the effect of changes in the advertising budget for brand j on market share and profit, especially if brand j's advertising share is much larger than 50 percent. However, we expect that marketing actions are improved if those other aspects are explicitly modeled.

By adding other features to the model in (7.27), such as replacing a_{jt} by a_{jt}/a_{ct} with a_{ct} equal to competitive advertising, the predictive ability of the model may also improve. But such additions need to be justified in a cost-benefit sense. The question is whether the incremental gain to management from increased accuracy in predictions exceeds the incremental cost of collecting data on the advertising spending of competitors.

Finally, consider a different problem situation. Suppose that the market consists of two firms, each of which has approximately 50 percent market share. It is obvious that competitive activity should now be considered explicitly in the model, in particular if an increase in advertising by one firm is followed by a similar increase by the other firm, and industry sales tend to remain constant. In this problem situation, equation (7.27) cannot be a robust representation of reality.

---

28. Index j has been added for clarity (relative to equation (7.28) below).

We note that if the same type of market share function is defined for a competing firm:

$$m_{ct} = \alpha_c + (\beta_c - \alpha_c) \frac{a_{ct}^{\delta_c}}{\gamma_c + a_{ct}^{\delta_c}} \tag{7.28}$$

no meaningful restrictions can be imposed on the parameters to satisfy range and sum constraints on market shares. This aspect of non-robustness remains even when a_{jt} is replaced by a_{jt}/a_{ct} and a_{ct} by a_{ct}/a_{jt}.

We conclude that a model should not produce absurd predictions when predictor variables take extreme values. The importance of robustness in this sense depends, however, on the problem situation being modeled, and on the intended model use. For example, if extreme values never occur in practice, model behavior at such values is not critical. However, if the predictions are absurd at extreme values, model implications may not be very good at less extreme values. In addition, the model builder may not know the intention of the model user.

Everything else being equal, robustness is a desirable criterion. But robustness perse is not a panacea. The example in Section 7.4 shows that a model with desirable structure can have unreliable parameter estimates.[29] Thus, multiple, and possible conflicting, aspects need to be considered jointly.

---

29. See also Leeflang (1977b).

CHAPTER 8

Specifying models according to intended use

In this chapter, models are classified according to the primary purpose or intended use. We distinguish:

1. descriptive models intended to describe decision processes of managers or customers;
2. predictive models to forecast or predict future events or outcomes;
3. normative models on the basis of which recommended or optimal courses of action can be determined.

We note that a given model can be intended to be descriptive, predictive *and* normative. Indeed, one can argue that for a model to have valid normative implications, it must have predictive value and at least some descriptive power. However, a descriptive model does not necessarily have normative implications. And a predictive model may also not be useful for normative considerations. Therefore, we distinguish models as to their *primary* purpose.

We present two examples of a descriptive model in Section 8.1. The first shows a representation or description of important elements of a pricing decision by means of a logical flow model. The other example shows a description of a complex organizational buying process.

We discuss a predictive model in Section 8.2 that shows how the effects of alternative marketing programs on performance measures of a firm can be predicted.

Finally, in Section 8.3, normative models are developed. An example illustrates the sequence from descriptive to predictive to normative models. The chapter concludes with a small survey of applications of allocation models.

8.1 Descriptive models

There are multiple reasons for the development of models of decision processes. In Section 4.1, we argued that such models may result from a desire to make existing decision procedures explicit, or to examine whether those processes allow for automation or improvement. A descriptive model may also be a first step in a larger modeling effort with prediction or even optimization as the ultimate aim. The distinction between these three model types is important since model requirements when the purpose is only descriptive are generally less exacting than the requirements for models predicting the impacts of decision- and environmental variables. This is demonstrated by the simulated example in Section 7.4.

In this section, we first discuss the study of Howard and Morgenroth (1968), referred to in Section 2.2. The objective of their study was to describe the pricing procedure by a large company operating in an oligopolistic market. In this company executives had great difficulty verbalizing the process through which price decisions were made. Indeed the procedure was felt to be so complex that describing it was considered virtually impossible. Yet, the flow diagram resulting from lengthy discussions between executives of the company and the authors is fairly simple, as can be seen in Figure 8.1.

The descriptive model in Figure 8.1 is of the logical flow type.[1] The figure shows that the procedure begins by watching p_{wilt}, the wholesale (w) price of the initiator (i) in a local market (l) at time t (see box 1). Three alternative outcomes are possible:

1. If p_{wilt} does not change and differs from p_{wxlt}, where p_{wxlt} is the wholesale (w) price of our company (x) in l at t, no action is taken (box 2).
2. If p_{wilt} increases (box 3), there are various possible reaction patterns depending on the attitude of the district sales office (DSO):

    • if the DSO agrees, the price increase is followed (boxes 4 and 5);
    • if the DSO does not agree to a price increase, it can be overruled by the decision maker (DM), if she thinks other competitors will also increase their price (p_{wo}) (box 6);
    • if the DSO does not agree to a price increase, and the DM feels that other competitors will not increase their price, a holding period is enforced (box 7), and price is increased only if other competitors raise their price. If p_{wo} does not go up, no action is taken.

3. If p_{wilt} decreases, and differs from p_{wxlt}, DSO is again contacted, competitors' sales volumes in the local market are taken into account, waiting periods are observed, and steps are taken to prevent the price cut from spreading to adjacent market areas.[2]

From Figure 8.1 and its description we conclude that company x does not initiate price changes. The company is a "follower", the initiating company the price "leader". Another point is that the reaction to an initiator's price increase differs substantially from that of a price decrease.

The procedure seems simple enough. But does this flow diagram really model the decision process? To answer the question, we have to put the model to a test, which requires advancing one step, from the descriptive phase to the predictive phase. Howard

---

1. Some symbols have been adapted to be consistent with our notation.
2. The complete procedure in case of a price decrease can be deduced from Figure 8.1, similar to the description given for a price increase.

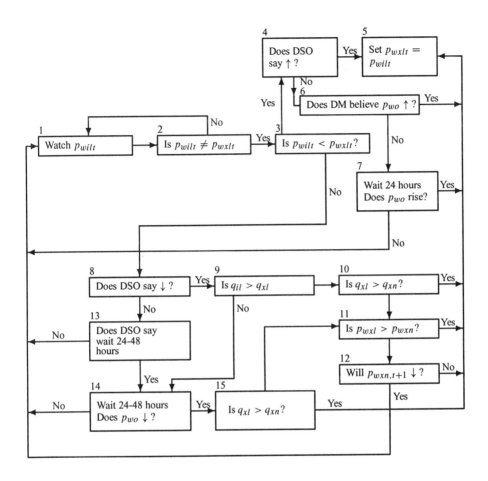

Symbols: p = price, w = wholesale, x = our company, o = other major competitors in local markets, i = initiator, t = time, at present, q = quantity, i.e. sales volume in physical terms, l = local market in which price change is being considered, n = nearby market with funnel influences, DSO = District Sales Office (District Sales Manager), ↑ = raise price, ↓ = drop price, DM = decision maker.

Source: Howard and Morgenroth (1968, p.419).

Figure 8.1 Descriptive model of a pricing decision process.

and Morgenroth tested their model on 31 actual decisions. Managers made decisions without the model, using existing company procedures. The model was applied independently to the same 31 situations. The model predictions were then compared to the actual decisions, and the degree of agreement was found to be acceptable.[3]

---

3. This is a test of the accuracy of the model's output. Howard and Morgenroth also present a test of the process, which asks whether the model describes the decision-making process used by the manager.

The Howard-Morgenroth study is an example of a descriptive model of the logical flow type. Descriptive models which are a combination of a logical flow model and a numerically specified model have been developed to model, for example, organizational buying behavior.[4,5] Many industrial markets are characterized by heterogeneous supply and demand. Products may be uniquely developed for small segments that sometimes consist of just one organization. Industrial marketing data are often difficult to obtain. There are not many individual firms that keep systematic records, while systematic data gathering by commercial market research agencies tends to be limited to a few large product categories (such as electronic components). Sometimes, it is virtually impossible to collect data. Products, prices and services are often customer specific and not public. As a result, the actions of competitors are often unobservable.

The organizational buying processes are complex. There are multiple buying influences, many process stages and formal procedures. Formalizing these processes may require the development of complex models, which are usually difficult for users to understand and implement. Different models have been developed to address these and other problems, viz.:

- small sample descriptive models (because of unique complexities, descriptive models tend to be based on small samples);
- judgment-based models (managerial judgment about the effect of marketing actions is quantified, either by collecting subjective parameter estimates or by inferring estimates from judgments about outcomes; see also Section 16.9);
- models based on cross-sectional comparisons (this is often done when time series data are inadequate; for an application to industrial advertising, see the ADVISOR project, Lilien, 1979).

We distinguish three methods, each being suitable for the development of *small sample descriptive models*: protocol analysis, script analysis and processs simulation.[6]

Protocol analysis is based on the information-processing theory of Newell and Simon (1972), which states that individuals go through complex cognitive processes in distinct stages. Crow, Olshavsky, and Summers (1980) applied this theory in a study in which they asked fourteen purchasers to phrase their thoughts during hypothetical, modified repurchase decisions. The subjects were all members of medium-sized or large organizations. Vyas and Woodside (1984) used protocol analysis of real purchase situations. They gathered additional information by observing meetings between buyers and sellers and studying documents, such as records and quotations. This combination of data gathering is based on decision systems analysis (Capon and Hulbert, 1975). Vyas and Woodside studied 62 individuals who constituted 18 buying centers. The buying decisions concerned long-term purchasing agreements. The studies show what specific decision criteria and decision rules are used in different

---

4. Other examples can be found, for example, in Cyert and March (1963).
5. See also Lilien, Kotler, Moorthy (1992, Chapter 3) and Brand, Leeflang (1994). The discussion about industrial markets is based on Brand, Leeflang.
6. The following text is based on Brand (1993).

stages of the buying process and in various buying situations.

Script analysis is based upon the concept of "cognitive scripts" derived from cognitive psychology (Abelson, 1976). A cognitive script is a prescribed range of behavioral actions that are stored in the brain of a human being who repeatedly experiences the same situation. The script influences an individual's expectations about others and the individual's interpretation of received information. Leigh and Rethans (1984) collected the cognitive scripts of 36 purchasers for four different situations. They found repurchases and new tasks differ greatly with respect to the information search process. For repurchases, the present supplier is usually the sole informant on possible solutions to a problem, whereas for new tasks the buyer engages in a more elaborate information search. The usefulness of the script analysis is high at the individual level. A study of scripts across respondents may not show a consistent description of the process.

The process simulation approach comprises two steps:

- the detailed description of a specific process which results in a formalized model;
- the simulation of the process which involves calculating the model's outcome(s) given a set of input values.

We illustrate the development of a "small sample descriptive model" with a study by Brand (1993). She studied the buying process of heat-exchangers of two large (Dutch) dairy organizations. In Figure 8.2 we show a flow diagram consisting of eight steps in this purchase process, viz.:

1. need recognition;
2. budget approval;
3. formulation of specifications;
4. the identification of potentially acceptable suppliers;
5. the assignment of Request For Quotations (RFQ);
6. the awarding of the contract;
7. the negotiation about delivery and details;
8. evaluation of purchase.

The sequence in which the steps occur is not fixed. Steps can occur simultaneously, steps can be skipped in certain situations, and there exists feedback between various steps. If, for example, a new heat-exchanger is urgently required, the early stages receive minimal attention. Brand (1993) focused her modeling of the buying process on those steps in which a supplier can use marketing instruments to influence the buyer's deliberations. Each of these steps, the selection of potential suppliers (4), the selection of potential suppliers who are asked to submit a quotation (5) and the selection of the preferred suppliers (6), has an identifiable outcome which becomes a criterion variable of the model. In step 4, the criterion variable is membership on the bidlist; in step 5 it is whether or not a request for quotation (RFQ) is issued to a supplier, while in step 6 it is whether or not the contract is obtained.

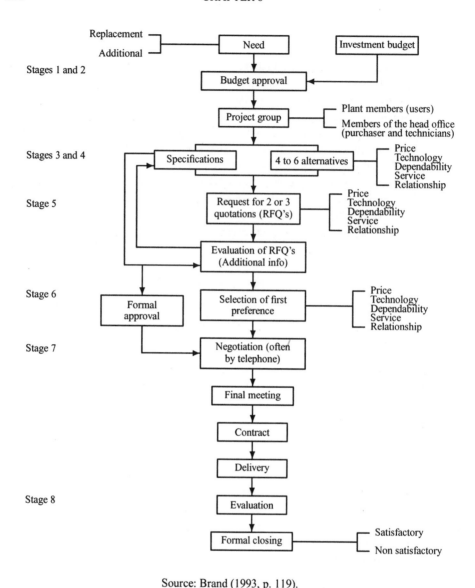

Source: Brand (1993, p. 119).

Figure 8.2 Flow diagram of the purchase of heat-exchangers.

Brand obtained a description of the buying process through semi-structured interviews with decision makers, influencers, users and other relevant parties. In a second round of face-to-face interviews with the primary decision makers and users, she obtained information about the relevance or influence of possible marketing instruments and other factors on outcomes of the decision-making process. The decision makers described five dimensions which determine the outcomes in one or more of the three steps; viz. price, technology, dependability, service and relationship. Subsequently these decision makers were asked to identify indicators for each of these five dimensions. In this manner Brand defined 51 indicators. The weights for these indicators depend on the step in the buying process. For example, image and reputation play an important role during the early stages of the buying process, whereas specific elements of the suppliers' communication mix and the quotation are more important in later steps. The decision makers involved in the relevant steps of the buying process also evaluated each of the suppliers on scales for the indicators, ranging from 1 (low) to 5 (high). With the scores on all relevant indicators for each supplier and buyer-specific weights for the indicators relevant to a stage in the decision-making process, the attractiveness of each supplier can be determined in each stage for a given buyer. In case of multiple decision makers, weighted averages scores (and indicator weights) were defined. The description of the buying process (1), the weights (2), and scores (3) can be used to develop models that describe decision rules. In the research by Brand, these rules turned out to be largely determined by two factors, viz.:

- the presence of an approved vendor list (AVL) in the buying organization (stages 4 and 5),
- the time pressure of the purchase (stages 5 and 6).

If the buying organization uses an approved vendor list, stage 4 of the buying process is redundant. In stage 5 RFQ's are then sent to a limited number of suppliers on the AVL. A current supplier of heat-exchangers has an additional advantage.

If the buyer faces time pressure, stage 4 proceeds at a faster rate. In stages 5 and 6 delivery time tends to have much weight, while price is accorded less weight than in earlier stages. The search for a supplier is also more concentrated; only two or three suppliers are asked to prepare a quotation.

Combining these two factors and three stages, different decisions rules can be formulated. To illustrate, we show in Figure 8.3 the decision rule in stage 4 for a buying organization that uses an AVL. For this buyer AVL-suppliers are automatically admitted to stage 5. Non-AVL suppliers need to obtain a maximum score on either price ($P = 5$) or technology ($T = 5$), and at least average on three other dimensions (excluding R=relationship) or have both P and T equal to 4 (and at least average on two other dimensions excluding R), in order to be admitted to stage 5. From Figure 8.3 it is clear that this buyer cares primarily about price and technology, and secondarily about dependability and service, in stage 4.

Brand used descriptive models to determine the effectiveness of a supplier's instrument. Overall, technical quality (T) and the buyer/seller relationship (R) appeared to be dominant criteria. Price and other variables are especially important in step 6.

Major advantages of process simulation, of protocol- and script analyses are that the model can include more complexities, such as a multi-person buying center, and that a range of "what if" questions can be considered.

Although the primary objective of descriptive models is to describe existing decision processes, it is often useful to evaluate the validity of these models by com-

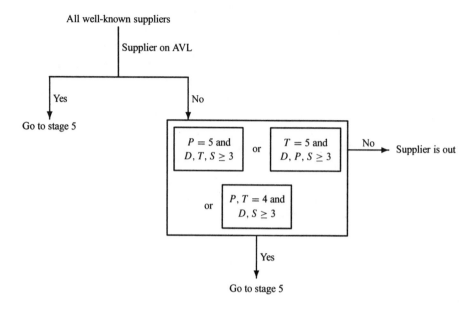

Source: Brand (1993, p. 132).

Figure 8.3 Decision rule of an AVL-buyer in step 4.

paring predictions with actual decisions. In the next section we describe models developed specifically for predictive purposes.

8.2 Predictive models

The purpose of predictive models is to forecast or predict future events or outcomes. We distinguish:

- unconditional forecasting;
- conditional forecasting.[7]

An unconditional forecast in marketing is not dependent on the marketing activities for a firm or a product, except as these pertain to fixed matters such as product characteristics. Thus the prediction process that leads to an unconditional forecast does not take the firm's marketing inputs explicitly into account. Although many new-product models include awareness (as a function of advertising) and availability (as a function of distribution), other models generate unconditional sales forecasts of a new product prior to test market and/or market introduction.[8] Diffusion models that present the level of spread of an innovation among prospective adopters over time also often provide unconditional forecasts. The purpose of a diffusion model is to depict successive

7. See, for example, Boyd, Massy (1972, p. 145).
8. See for examples, Urban (1993).

increases in the number of adopters and to predict the continued development of a diffusion process already in progress.[9] Models that represent life-cycles[10] and many product class sales models also tend to provide unconditional forecasts. We discuss some new-product models, both unconditional and conditional ones, in Section 10.2. Examples of predictive models that lead to unconditional forecasts can also be found in Section 4.4 (relations (4.1) and (4.2)) and in Section 17.3 (time series).

A specific class of unconditional forecasting models is the naive sales/market share model. Naive model-based predictions are often compared with the (conditional) forecasts of econometric or causal models.[11] An example of a naive market share model is given in (8.1):

$$m_{jt} = \alpha_{0j} + \alpha_{1j} m_{j,t-1} + u_{jt} \tag{8.1}$$

where

m_{jt} = market share of brand j in t,

u_{jt} = disturbance term.

A special case of this naive model sets $\hat{\alpha}_{0j} = 0$ and $\hat{\alpha}_{1j} = 1$. In that case the *prediction* for this period is the *actual* outcome in the previous period.

The purpose of conditional forecasting models is to predict the outcome of a proposed marketing program or to predict the consequences on own-brand sales or market share of competitors' possible programs. Such "if-then" types of forecasts can only be derived from causal models. The intended model use and the availability of (causal) data determine whether unconditional or conditional forecasting methods are used. Thus, if no "causal data" on marketing instruments are available one can only generate unconditional forecasts, unless subjective data are generated (see Section 16.9).

We illustrate conditional forecasting with a simplified model developed to examine the likely impact of changes in marketing decision variables on performance measures.[12] The model is based on a numerically specified market share model that has been calibrated on data of the detergent market in the Netherlands. For additional discussion and critical evaluation of this model, see Section 15.4.[13]

The estimated equation is:

$$\hat{m}_{jt} = 6.9 + 7.9 \frac{a_{j,t-1}}{A_{t-1}} - 7.2 \frac{p_{jt}}{P_t} + 9.2 d_{jt} \tag{8.2}$$

where

---

9. See, for a survey, e.g. Mahajan, Muller, Bass (1990, 1993).

10. See Cox (1967), Brockhoff (1967), Tellis, Crawford (1981), Easingwood (1987), Balasubramanian, Ghosh (1992), Paich, Sterman (1993).

11. See, for example, Armstrong, Brodie, McIntyre (1987), Brodie, de Kluyver (1987), Alsem, Leeflang Reuyl (1989), Danaher (1994), Kumar (1994), Brodie, Danaher, Kumar, Leeflang (2000).

12. See Leeflang (1976, 1977a). The system of relations has about the same structure as the relations (5.3)-(5.9).

13. More sophisticated models that satisfy the criteria discussed in Chapter 7 also have been developed for this market. See, e.g. Foekens, Leeflang, Wittink (1997). We keep (8.2) for simplicity of the argument, not because of its realism.

$\hat{m}_{jt}$ = predicted unit market share of brand j in period t, measured in percentage points,

$a_{j,t-1}$ = advertising expenditures of brand j, in thousands of Dutch guilders in $t-1$,

A_{t-1} = $\sum_{r=1}^{n} a_{r,t-1}$ = total advertising expenditures for n brands in $t-1$, in thousands of Dutch guilders, where $n = 7$ is the number of relevant detergent brands,

p_{jt} = price per kilogram of brand j in Dutch guilders in t,

P_t = $\dfrac{\sum_{r=1}^{n} p_{rt}}{n}$ = (unweighted) average price per kilogram in Dutch guilders in t,

d_{jt} = market coverage of brand j in t, measured as a fraction of the total number of outlets where the product class is sold.

In this example t is a bi-monthly period. Given the mathematical form of (8.2) and the discussion on model robustness in the previous chapter, it is clear that (8.2) has only limited usefulness as a predictive model. Because of this we could warn model users not to go outside the range of values for the decision variables present in the historical data. Thus we could take precautions by explicitly adjoining range constraints to the model. For example:

$$a_j^L \leq a_{jt} \leq a_j^U, \text{ for all } t$$

where a_j^L and a_j^U are the lower and upper bounds on advertising expenditures observed in the historical data.

In order to be able to predict unit sales we also should relate product class sales Q_t to a number of explanatory variables. However, for simplicity, we use an unconditional estimated value of Q_t, expressed in thousands of kilos:[14]

$$\widehat{Q}_t = 8,500. \tag{8.3}$$

From the definitions of m_{jt} and Q_t it follows that the predicted value of brand sales, q_{jt}, equals:

$$\hat{q}_{jt} = \hat{m}_{jt} \widehat{Q}_t / 100 \tag{8.4}$$

or

$$\hat{q}_{jt} = 85 \, \hat{m}_{jt}. \tag{8.5}$$

---

14. It should be clear, however, that to fully exploit the example, one should be able to assess the impact on product class sales of price and advertising of all of the brands on Q_t. This, of course, requires the use of the product class equation, and not one expected value: see equation (15.2) for a discussion.

To assess the impact of alternative marketing programs on profit, we have to relate sales and market share to revenue, costs and, ultimately, to before- and after-tax profit. The producer's revenue (in thousands of Dutch guilders), after sales tax, is:[15]

$$\widehat{R}_{jt} = 0.851(p_{jt} - rm_{jt})\hat{q}_{jt} \tag{8.6}$$

where, p_{jt} is retail price, and rm_{jt} retailer's margin, which for this product amounts to 30 percent of the retail price:

$$rm_{jt} = 0.3 \cdot p_{jt}. \tag{8.7}$$

Substituting (8.7) in (8.6), we obtain:

$$\widehat{R}_{jt} = 0.5957 \cdot p_{jt} \cdot \hat{q}_{jt}. \tag{8.8}$$

Estimated total cost $(\widehat{TC}_{jt})$ is obtained as follows:

$$\widehat{TC}_{jt} = c_{1j}\hat{q}_{jt} + c_{2j}\exp(c_{3j}d_{jt}) + FC_j + a_{jt} \tag{8.9}$$

where

$$
\begin{aligned}
c_{1j} &= \text{variable cost per unit } (1.00 \text{ guilder)},^{16} \\
c_{2j}, c_{3j} &= \text{parameters of the (exponential) distribution function,} \\
&\quad \text{we assume } c_{2j} = 0.9 \text{ and } c_{3j} = 5.7, \\
FC_j &= \text{fixed costs} = 100,000 \text{ guilders in each period } t.
\end{aligned}
$$

Profit before-, π_{jt}, and after-, π_{jt}^a, taxes is:

$$\hat{\pi}_{jt} = \widehat{R}_{jt} - \widehat{TC}_{jt} \tag{8.10}$$
$$\hat{\pi}_{jt}^a = (1-\tau)\hat{\pi}_{jt} = 0.65\,\hat{\pi}_{jt}. \tag{8.11}$$

By combining the above equations, we obtain the following reduced-form relation:

$$\hat{\pi}_{jt}^a = 0.65\left[(0.5957\,p_{jt} - 1)0.85\left(6.9 + 7.9\frac{a_{j,t-1}}{A_{t-1}} - 7.2\frac{p_{jt}}{P_t}\right.\right. \tag{8.12}$$
$$\left.\left. +9.2\,d_{jt}\right) - 100,000 - a_{jt} - 0.9\exp(5.7d_{jt})\right].$$

The reduced-form equation can now be used to explore the impact of alternative marketing programs on net profit after tax. In Table 8.1 we show a detailed calculation for specific values of the decision variables, viz.:

$$a_{j,t-1} = 207, \quad A_t = 4,000, \quad p_{jt} = 3.40, \quad P_t = 2.86, \quad \text{and} \quad d_{jt} = 0.85.$$

Tables 8.2-8.8 show the predicted effects of other alternative marketing programs along with a few random variations in competitors' patterns. The last column in

---

15. Where $0.851 = 1/(1 + 0.175)$, representing a sales tax of 17.5 percent.
16. Variable cost per unit is assumed to be constant. For the range limits we imposed, this assumption is reasonable.

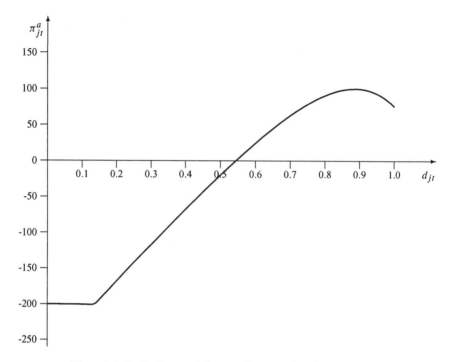

Figure 8.4 Profit after tax (π_{jt}^{a}) as a function of market coverage (d_{jt}).

Tables 8.1-8.3 shows a return to the original values to accommodate the lagged ad-vertising effect. These examples suggest the benefits of "what if" types of predictive models. The models provide the marketing manager with opportunities to explore alternative marketing programs based on an estimated market share model. Such explorations may suggest actions to avoid as well as desirable activities to initiate. Importantly, these actions can be considered in a simulation which avoids a lot of potentially undesirable experimentation in the market place.

The model structure and the predicted effects of alternate marketing programs shown in Tables 8.1-8.8 in fact demonstrate that the advertising budget that maxi-mizes profit is zero. Thus this model is "nonsensical" in light of the discussion in Section 7.4. The value of market coverage that maximizes profit can be derived from Figure 8.4. The profit sensitivity to market coverage seems realistic with a maximum close to 90 percent coverage.

We note that the foregoing sensitivity calculations assume the lack of uncertainty in predicted values. There are two considerations relevant to this. One is that it is possible to construct confidence intervals around the predicted values so as to quan-tify the statistical uncertainty. The other is that optimal decisions may incorporate asymmetries in uncertainties or risk.

Experience in model building has resulted in some guidelines to improve the pre-dictive accuracy of causal models, relative to naive models. In general the predictive accuracy of causal models is improved if,

- disaggregate data are used for model building;[17]
- there is high variability in the causal variables;[18]
- the number of observations is large;[19]
- the parameters are stable over time.[20]

We discuss other issues regarding predictive accuracy and predictive validity in Chapters 14 and 18 respectively.

17. See, for example, Wittink (1987), Chen, Kanetkar, Weiss (1994), Foekens, Leeflang, Wittink (1994), Christen, Gupta, Porter, Staelin, Wittink (1997).
18. Wittink (1987), Kumar (1994).
19. Danaher, Brodie (1992).
20. Foekens, Leeflang, Wittink, (1994).

Table 8.1 Starting values.

	t
INPUT VARIABLES	
Price brand j	3.40
Average price	2.86
Advertising brand j	207
Total advertising	4,000
Market coverage	0.85
PRODUCT CLASS SALES	
Units (000)	8,500
Guilders (000)	24,310
BRAND SALES/MARKET SHARE	
Market share	6.57
Sales brand j in units (000)	558
Sales brand j in guilders (000)	1,899
FINANCIAL STATEMENT[a] (000)	
Sales brand j	1,899
Retailer margin	570
Sales tax	198
Revenue after tax sales	1,131
Variable cost	558
Gross profit	573
Fixed cost	100
Advertising cost	207
Distribution cost	114
Net profit before tax	151
Tax	53
Net profit after tax	98

[a]Figures are rounded to the next integer.

Table 8.2 Advertising expenditures of brand j up by 50 percent (no competitive reaction in t).

	t	$t+1$
INPUT VARIABLES		
Price brand j	3.40	3.40
Average price	2.86	2.86
Advertising brand j	311	207
Total advertising	4,104	4,000
Market coverage	0.85	0.85
PRODUCT CLASS SALES		
Units (000)	8,500	8,500
Guilders (000)	24,310	24,310
BRAND SALES/MARKET SHARE		
Market share	6.57	6.76
Sales brand j in units (000)	558	575
Sales brand j in guilders (000)	1,899	1,953
FINANCIAL STATEMENT[a] (000)		
Sales brand j	1,899	1,953
Retailer margin	570	586
Sales tax	198	204
Revenue after tax sales	1,131	1,164
Variable cost	558	575
Gross profit	573	589
Fixed cost	100	100
Advertising cost	311	207
Distribution cost	114	114
Net profit before tax	41	168
Tax	17	59
Net profit after tax	31	109

[a] Figures are rounded to the next integer.

Table 8.3 Advertising expenditures of brand j up by 50 percent in t; total advertising expenditures up by 50 percent in t + 1.

	t	t + 1	t + 2
INPUT VARIABLES			
Price brand *j*	3.40	3.40	3.40
Average price	2.86	2.86	2.86
Advertising brand *j*	311	207	207
Total advertising	4,104	6,000	4,000
Market coverage	0.85	0.85	0.85
PRODUCT CLASS SALES			
Units (000)	8,500	8,500	8,500
Guilders (000)	24,310	24,310	24,310
BRAND SALES/MARKET SHARE			
Market share	6.57	6.76	6.43
Sales brand *j* in units (000)	558	575	547
Sales brand *j* in guilders (000)	1,899	1,953	1,859
FINANCIAL STATEMENT[a] (000)			
Sales brand *j*	1,899	1,953	1,859
Retailer margin	570	586	558
Sales tax	198	204	194
Revenue after tax sales	1,131	1,164	1,108
Variable cost	558	575	547
Gross profit	573	589	561
Fixed cost	100	100	100
Advertising cost	311	207	207
Distribution cost	114	114	114
Net profit before tax	41	168	139
Tax	17	59	49
Net profit after tax	31	109	91

[a]Figures are rounded to the next integer.

Table 8.4 Price decrease of brand j by 5 percent (no reaction).

	t
INPUT VARIABLES	
Price brand j	3.23
Average price	2.84
Advertising brand j	207
Total advertising	4,000
Market coverage	0.85
PRODUCT CLASS SALES	
Units (000)	8,500
Guilders (000)	24,140
BRAND SALES/MARKET SHARE	
Market share	6.94
Sales brand j in units (000)	590
Sales brand j in guilders (000)	1,905
FINANCIAL STATEMENT[a] (000)	
Sales brand j	1,905
Retailer margin	572
Sales tax	199
Revenue after tax sales	1,135
Variable cost	590
Gross profit	545
Fixed cost	100
Advertising cost	207
Distribution cost	114
Net profit before tax	124
Tax	43
Net profit after tax	80

[a] Figures are rounded to the next integer.

*Table 8.5 Price decrease of brand j by 5 percent in t; market follows in t + 1
with equal price decrease.*

	t	$t + 1$
INPUT VARIABLES		
Price brand j	3.23	3.23
Average price	2.84	2.72
Advertising brand j	207	207
Total advertising	4,000	4,000
Market coverage	0.85	0.85
PRODUCT CLASS SALES		
Units (000)	8,500	8,500
Guilders (000)	24,140	23,120
BRAND SALES/MARKET SHARE		
Market share	6.94	6.58
Sales brand j in units (000)	590	559
Sales brand j in guilders (000)	1,905	1,806
FINANCIAL STATEMENT[a] (000)		
Sales brand j	1,905	1,806
Retailer margin	572	542
Sales tax	199	188
Revenue after tax sales	1,135	1,076
Variable cost	590	559
Gross profit	545	517
Fixed cost	100	100
Advertising cost	311	207
Distribution cost	114	114
Net profit before tax	124	95
Tax	43	33
Net profit after tax	80	62

[a] Figures are rounded to the next integer.

Table 8.6 Increase of market coverage from 85 to 95 percent.

	t
INPUT VARIABLES	
Price brand j	3.40
Average price	2.86
Advertising brand j	207
Total advertising	4,000
Market coverage	0.95
PRODUCT CLASS SALES	
Units (000)	8,500
Guilders (000)	24,310
BRAND SALES/MARKET SHARE	
Market share	7.49
Sales brand j in units (000)	637
Sales brand j in guilders (000)	2,164
FINANCIAL STATEMENT[a] (000)	
Sales brand j	2,164
Retailer margin	649
Sales tax	226
Revenue after tax sales	1,289
Variable cost	637
Gross profit	653
Fixed cost	100
Advertising cost	207
Distribution cost	202
Net profit before tax	144
Tax	50
Net profit after tax	93

[a] Figures are rounded to the next integer.

Table 8.7 Increase of market coverage from 85 to 90 percent.

	t
INPUT VARIABLES	
Price brand j	3.40
Average price	2.86
Advertising brand j	207
Total advertising	4,000
Market coverage	0.90
PRODUCT CLASS SALES	
Units (000)	8,500
Guilders (000)	24,310
BRAND SALES/MARKET SHARE	
Market share	7.03
Sales brand j in units (000)	597
Sales brand j in guilders (000)	2,031
FINANCIAL STATEMENT[a] **(000)**	
Sales brand j	2,031
Retailer margin	609
Sales tax	212
Revenue after tax sales	1,210
Variable cost	597
Gross profit	613
Fixed cost	100
Advertising cost	207
Distribution cost	152
Net profit before tax	154
Tax	54
Net profit after tax	100

[a] Figures are rounded to the next integer.

Table 8.8 Decrease of market coverage from 85 to 75 percent.

	t
INPUT VARIABLES	
Price brand j	3.40
Average price	2.86
Advertising brand j	207
Total advertising	4,000
Market coverage	0.75
PRODUCT CLASS SALES	
Units (000)	8,500
Guilders (000)	24,310
BRAND SALES/MARKET SHARE	
Market share	5.65
Sales brand j in units (000)	480
Sales brand j in guilders (000)	1,633
FINANCIAL STATEMENT[a] (000)	
Sales brand j	1,633
Retailer margin	490
Sales tax	170
Revenue after tax sales	973
Variable cost	480
Gross profit	492
Fixed cost	100
Advertising cost	207
Distribution cost	65
Net profit before tax	121
Tax	42
Net profit after tax	78

[a] Figures are rounded to the next integer.

8.3 Normative models

The third class of models consists of normative or prescriptive models. Their purpose is to determine a recommended course of action that should improve performance. In other words, one wants to determine which decision is best for an objective such as profit maximization. In Section 8.3.1, we discuss a marketing mix problem to illustrate a normative model for profit maximization.

Many of the normative models in marketing are allocation models, in which a certain amount of a particular quantity (money, time, space) is available, and the objective is to allocate it between alternative uses in an optimal way. We enumerate some existing allocation models in Section 8.3.2.

8.3.1 A PROFIT MAXIMIZATION MODEL

We apply profit maximization to a marketing mix problem, and concern ourselves with one element, advertising. The objective is to evaluate the profitability of advertising, holding other variables constant.

The product concerns a well-established, frequently purchased consumer good sold in Belgium. The idea is to estimate a demand function which can be used to predict sales, and to choose the optimal level of advertising spending. We consider a demand function estimated by Lambin (1969), and discussed by Naert (1973).

The numerically specified demand function has the following form:

$$\hat{q}_t = -32,733 + 12,423 \log Inc_t + 0.507 \, q_{t-1} + 1,777 \log_{10} a_t \qquad (8.13)$$
$$-2.2 \, wi_t + 843 \log f_t$$

where

$$q_t = \text{sales per 1,000 potential consumers (in the age group}$$
$$\text{to 25 years)},$$
$$Inc_t = \text{real private disposable income},$$
$$q_{t-1} = \text{lagged sales,}[21]$$
$$a_t = \text{real advertising expenditures per 1,000 potential}$$
$$\text{consumers},$$
$$wi_t = \text{weather index (rainfall), and}$$
$$f_t = \text{visit frequency to sales outlets by sales person},$$
$$t = \text{year.}$$

There is no price variable among the explanatory variables in the demand equation. In the original specification, price was included but it was dropped because the estimated

---

21. As shown in Section 6.2 this may result from the assumption of a geometric decaying lag structure. However, the implication may be that there is an identical lag parameter for the visit frequency to sales outlets, a hardly tenable proposition. The database consisted of yearly data. Based on the discussion in Section 6.1, a data interval bias is likely to be present, if the interpretation of the lagged sales coefficient is with regard to cumulative advertising effects.

effect was statistically insignificant. This is one of the dilemmas often faced in applied econometrics. We know that price affects demand in general. However, if price (or any other variable for that matter) is relatively stable over the period of observation, then it cannot have much explanatory power in the sample. If price is excluded, its effect will be taken up by the constant term, the implication being that, on the basis of historical data, nothing can be said about the impact of price on sales. Thus, if the objective is to determine the optimal marketing mix, the information contained in the historical data would be insufficient. Other means, such as experimentation or subjective judgment may provide useful insights. The lack of sufficient price variation is of no consequence if the model is to be used for a determination of optimal advertising spending, under the assumption that the actual level of advertising does not depend on price. The output is a recommended budget. In this sense, the model is normative. However, from a practical point of view, the word "normative" is perhaps too strong. What one is really interested in is to determine whether current advertising expenditures are too high, too low, or about right. The model can produce a specific figure but it is useful to take it as a guideline rather than as something absolute. We provide the following reasons why we might not use the word "normative" in an absolute sense:

1. the demand equation is estimated, which implies that there is uncertainty about the true values of the response coefficients;[22]
2. advertising is only one instrument in the firm's marketing mix;
3. the firm faces multiple objectives, while most models assume the existence of a single objective such as profit maximization;[23]
4. the effectiveness of advertising depends on the quality of the copy, the selection of media, and so on. The regression coefficient gives at best an idea of an average effect.[24]

We now derive an optimal advertising budget for the profit-maximizing firm whose demand function is given by (8.13). We first show how to optimize advertising expenditures when lagged effects of advertising are *not* taken into account. After that an optimal solution is derived which assumes that the lagged sales variable represents advertising dynamics.

Determination of the short-term advertising budget
Since advertising spending is the object of the study, we assume that other variables (price, visit frequency) have been decided upon, and uncontrollable variables have been predicted. For example, national statistics can be used to predict future levels of

---

22. Given footnote 21 related to the assumed lag structure, there will not only be substantial variance in the estimated parameters, but the estimates themselves could be biased, i.e. their expected values might differ from the true parameter values.
23. We note that other objectives, such as short-term sales maximization and growth maximization can be consistent with an overall objective of long-term profit maximization.
24. Given a specific campaign, with a specific copy and media plan, one could make an appropriate adjustment in the advertising parameter. The idea of combining databased parameterization with subjective parameterization was first suggested by Lambin (1972b). We elaborate on this in Chapter 16.

disposable income. Substituting the values of these variables, equation (8.13) reduces to:[25]

$$\hat{q}_t = -2,231 + 1,777 \log_{10} a_t. \tag{8.14}$$

The objective of the firm is to maximize profit per 1,000 potential consumers, π_t:

$$\hat{\pi}_t = (p_t - c_t)\hat{q}_t - a_t \tag{8.15}$$

where c_t is unit variable cost. In the remainder of this discussion, we assume that c_t is constant, i.e. $c_t = c$ for all t. In other words, variable cost (c) and marginal cost (MC) are equal. Fixed costs were not given in Lambin (1969) but can be ignored since these do not affect the optimal level of advertising spending. Given that price is predetermined, we let p_t equal p, so that (8.15) reduces to:

$$\hat{\pi}_t = (p - c)\hat{q}_t - a_t. \tag{8.16}$$

To maximize profit, the following relationship has to be satisfied:[26]

$$\mu = 1/w \tag{8.17}$$

where

$$\mu = p\frac{\partial q}{\partial a} = \text{marginal revenue product of advertising,}[27] \text{and}$$

$$w = \frac{p - MC}{p} = \frac{p - c}{p} = \text{percent gross margin.}$$

Currently average advertising expenditure for 1,000 potential consumers is $\bar{a} = 3,440$ BF (Belgian Francs), with corresponding sales, $\bar{q} = 4,060$.

The price is 6 BF (average price paid by the retailer to the manufacturer) and marginal cost (assumed constant over the relevant range) is 2.7 BF. The percent of gross margin for the manufacturer is then:

$$w = (6 - 2.7)/6 = 0.55. \tag{8.18}$$

From (8.17) we find that at the optimum the marginal revenue product of advertising should satisfy:

$$\mu = 1/0.55 = 1.818. \tag{8.19}$$

Since $\mu = p\frac{\partial q}{\partial a}$, at optimality we should have:

$$\partial q/\partial a = (1.818)/6 = 0.303. \tag{8.20}$$

---

25. This is not shown in Lambin's (1969) paper but it can be derived from Naert (1973). Although the constant term being negative suggests the model may be misspecified, it need not trouble us here, as will appear from the subsequent discussion. We note that robustness should be considered from the point of view of intended model use.

26. Following the Dorfman-Steiner (1954) theorem derived in the Appendix to this chapter.

27. Since in (8.14) sales is only a function of advertising, we could write dq/da. We continue to write $\partial q/\partial a$ to remind us that (8.14) was derived from a demand function with other explanatory variables, especially the sales call frequency.

In general, $\partial q / \partial a$ can be written as follows:[28]

$$\frac{\partial q}{\partial a} = \left[\frac{\partial q}{\partial \log_{10} a} \right] \left[\frac{d \log_{10} a}{d \ln a} \right] \left[\frac{d \ln a}{da} \right]$$

which is

$$\frac{\partial q}{\partial a} = \left[\frac{\partial q}{\partial \log_{10} a} \right] \left[\frac{0.4343}{a} \right]. \tag{8.21}$$

It follows from (8.21) that the optimal advertising spending level a^* should satisfy:

$$a^* = \frac{(\partial q / \partial \log_{10} a)(0.4343)}{\partial q / \partial a}. \tag{8.22}$$

From (8.13) we know that $\partial q / \partial \log_{10} a = 1,777$, and from (8.20) $\partial q / \partial a = 0.303$. Thus a^* equals:

$$a^* = (1,777)(0.4343)/0.303 = 2,545 \text{ BF}.$$

Compared to actual expenditures of 3,440 BF, it appears that the firm is overspending on (short-term) advertising. It is, however, instructive to determine how sensitive profit is to changes in advertising spending. We first examine the profit when the firm continues the current advertising spending. Profit is predicted to be:

$$\hat{\pi} = (p - MC)\hat{q} - a = 3.3\hat{q} - a.$$

With $\bar{a} = 3,440$ BF, we found $\bar{q} = \hat{q} = 4,060$, so that current profit is predicted to be:

$$\hat{\pi} = 3.3 \times 4,060 - 3,440 = 9,958 \text{ BF}.$$

At optimality, $a^* = 2,545$ BF, with corresponding sales:

$$\begin{aligned} \hat{q} &= -2,213 + 1,777 \log_{10} 2,545 \\ &= -2,213 + 1,777 \times 3.4057 = 3,839. \end{aligned}$$

Maximum profit is then:

$$\hat{\pi} = 3.3 \times 3,839 - 2,545 = 10,124 \text{ BF}.$$

We see that, if only short-term effects are considered, actual advertising expenditures exceed the optimal level by about 35 percent. However, current profit is only about 1.5 percent below its maximum value. This suggests that profit is quite insensitive to changes in advertising expenditures.

Determination of the long-term advertising budget
The effect of advertising in period t also occurs in later periods. Let λ be the retention

---

28. This rather complex expression results from the fact that in equation (8.13) logarithms to the base ten were used.

rate of advertising. An advertising investment of a_t in period t, yields q_t sales in t, λq_t in $t + 1$, $\lambda^2 q_t$ in $t + 2, \ldots$ However, given that a dollar of profit in the future is less valuable than the same profit today, we adjust for the time value of money when we evaluate an advertising investment. Let the discount rate be i. The present value of the long term (LT) profit stream $\pi(LT)$ generated by an advertising expenditure of a dollars is:[29]

$$\pi(LT) = q(p - c) \left[1 + \frac{\lambda}{1 + i} + \frac{\lambda^2}{(1 + i)^2} + \frac{\lambda^3}{(1 + i)^3} + \cdots \right] - a. \tag{8.23}$$

Since $0 \leq \lambda < 1$, we also have $0 \leq \dfrac{\lambda}{1 + i} < 1$, and (8.23) reduces to:

$$\pi(LT) = \frac{q(p - c)}{1 - \lambda/(1 + i)} - a. \tag{8.24}$$

At optimality we should have:[30]

$$\frac{\mu}{1 - \lambda/(1 + i)} = \frac{1}{w}. \tag{8.25}$$

Recall from equation (6.11) that the coefficient of lagged sales q_{t-1}, in equation (8.13) is an estimate of λ. Thus $\lambda = 0.507$, and if we further assume a discount rate of $i = 8$ percent, the long-term optimal value of μ is:[31]

$$\mu = 1.818 \left(1 - \frac{0.507}{1 + 0.08} \right) = 0.965, \text{ and therefore}$$

$$\partial q / \partial a = 0.965/6 = 0.161.$$

If the firm takes a long-term view, the optimal advertising budget is:

$$a_{LT} = (1, 777)(0.4343)/0.161 = 4, 801 \text{ BF}.$$

Corresponding expected sales are:

$$\hat{q}_{LT} = -2, 213 + 1, 777 \log 4, 801 = 4, 329$$

and expected long-term profit is:

$$\hat{\pi}_{LT} = \frac{(4, 329)(3.30)}{0.5306} - 4, 801 = 22, 125 \text{ BF}.$$

29. The optimal long-term value of advertising spending obtained here is an equilibrium value as is easily demonstrated. We therefore eliminate the time index. For a discussion of the dynamic process, see Lambin, Naert and Bultez (1975) which includes an example of optimal advertising spending over time.

30. $\dfrac{\partial \pi(LT)}{\partial a} = \dfrac{(p - c)(\partial q/\partial a)}{1 - \lambda/(1 + i)} - 1 = 0$, or $\dfrac{p\partial q/\partial a}{1 - \lambda/(1 + i)} = \dfrac{p}{p - c} = \dfrac{p}{p - MC} = \dfrac{1}{w}$.

31. The parameter λ has been estimated from annual data. From Section 6.1 we know that $\hat{\lambda}$ may be biased upward.

If advertising expenditures remain at the *current* level, expected long-term profit is:

$$\hat{\pi}_{LT} = \frac{(4,060)(3.30)}{0.5306} - 3,440 = 21,811 \text{ BF.}$$

Thus, by taking into account the lagged effects of advertising, we find that actual spending is an estimated 28 percent *below* the optimal amount. Importantly, with positive lagged effects, the optimal advertising expenditure increases relative to the case when we ignore these effects. As before, if we increase the advertising budget to the optimal level, the expected profit increases by only 1.43% percent.

We note that sensitivity analyses frequently demonstrate that large percentual changes in advertising expenditures result in only small percentual changes in profits over a wide range of expenditure levels. This phenomenon is known as the flat maximum principle (Hanssens, Parsons, Schultz, 1990, p. 26). In this respect we refer to Chintagunta (1993b) and to the discussion whether lag structure matters in the optimization of advertising expenditures in Section 6.1. We note that profit is more sensitive to departures of price from its optimal level than it is to departures from optimal advertising expenditures.

We have to be careful in the application of optimization rules. In the discussion above we implicitly assumed that there are no profitable alternatives to advertising spending. Indeed, the condition $\mu = 1/w$ implies that at the optimum:

$$(p - MC)\frac{\partial q}{\partial a} = 1.$$

Stated in words, this means that the last dollar invested just pays for itself but nothing more. In fact the firm can do better, by investing that last dollar in some other venture where it can earn a return of re percent. The return on the best possible alternative investment should be considered as an opportunity cost. With an opportunity cost of re percent, the optimality condition becomes:

$$\mu = \frac{1 + re}{w}.$$

With $re = 0.20$, and $\mu = (1 + 0.20)/0.55 = 2.18$, at optimality $\partial q/\partial a$ should equal $\mu/p = 2.18/6 = 0.36364$. Applying (8.22) for example, we find an optimal short-term advertising budget of 2,122 BF, instead of 2,545 BF which we obtained when the opportunity cost was (implicitly) assumed to zero.

One final note about the specific normative model discussed in this section: it concerned a monopolist.[32] Since monopolies are the exception in the marketplace, rather than the rule, it is important to study marketing mix decisions and the profitability of advertising in, say, oligopolies. Some studies applicable to competitive environments are reviewed in Bultez (1975), Lambin (1976), Hanssens et al. (1990, Chapter 8), and Erickson (1991). This topic receives much attention in the more recently developed

---

32. That is the demand equation did not take into account any element of competitive rivalry, i.e. a monopoly was assumed. Also the Dorfman-Steiner theorem was derived for a monopoly. An extension to oligopolistic markets was provided by Lambin, Naert and Bultez (1975), and will be touched upon in Chapter 9.

game theoretic models in marketing. We discuss some of these models in Section 11.4.

Several normative models have been successfully developed to determine the optimal *sales force*. Examples are Lodish's CALLPLAN (1971), Lodish, Curtiss, Ness and Simpson (1988), Rangaswamy, Sinha and Zoltners (1990) and Gopalakrishna and Chatterjee (1992).[33] CALLPLAN is an interactive system that supports the sales force for the planning of visits. It requires managerial judgments about response functions and information about traveling expenses and available time. The built-in search procedure identifies the sales plan that optimizes expected revenue minus traveling expenses. The model was later refined by adding managerial judgments about the (relative) effectiveness of each sales representative for each account.

Lodish et al. (1988) developed a model based on estimates of response functions, made by a team of managers in a Delphi-like setting. We discuss the Delphi method in Section 16.9. The response functions describe two situations:

1. changes in the emphasis on particular products during sales presentations;
2. changes in the number of sales calls in various market segments.

In an application, additional archival data were collected, including cost per sales representative, other expenses, management time, production and distribution costs, and the current allocation of sales force effort. The model results include the optimal size and allocation of a company's sales force.

Rangaswamy et al. (1990) proposed a normative sales force model. In an application for a pharmaceutical firm, they used a combination of judgmental data (obtained with the Delphi process) and historical data to calibrate several thousands of parameters. Their model generates the optimal number of sales force teams, their sizes, and the deployment of the total sales force by product and market segment. In 1990, this model-based approach for sales-force structuring had been implemented in over 100 settings in more than 20 countries.

Gopalakrishna and Chatterjee (1992) developed a model that explains the realized share of sales potential by advertising expenditures, personal selling expenditures, and competitive variables. The model can be used to assess the joint impact of advertising and personal selling effort on performance. An application at a US industrial firm suggests that this approach can raise profits substantially.

Other normative models have been constructed to specify *salesforce compensation plans*. These plans determine fixed payments (salary) and variable payments (commissions, bonuses). Optimal compensation plans can be constructed by maximizing the expected profit. If sales are assumed to be stochastic, it can be demonstrated that the optimal compensation plan is a function of the risk tolerance of the salesperson, the environmental uncertainty, the efficiency of the production process, and alternative job opportunities (Basu, Lal, Srinivasan, Staelin, 1985). Lal and Staelin (1986) modified the model in such a way that it can be applied in situations in

---

33. See also Brand, Leeflang (1994).

which the sales force has more knowledge of prospects and clients than management does (asymmetric information) and the sales force is considered to be heterogeneous with respect to risk tolerance and ability. Lal and Staelin demonstrate that the presence of asymmetric information and heterogeneous salespeople leads to an optimal strategy of offering multiple contracts. In this situation, different salespeople choose different schemes leading to improved individual performance and organizational profit.

Neslin and Shoemaker (1983) devised a normative decision calculus model for planning *coupon promotions*. Dhar, Morrison and Raju (1996) apply a normative model to study the relative impact of package coupons on profits. For examples of normative models to determine optimal *prices* see Hanssens et al. (1990, pp. 240-246), Zoltners (1981), Narasimhan (1988) and Rao (1993).

Zoltners (1981) distinguished normative models as: theoretical models and decision models.[34] Theoretical models are designed to develop normative theory, whereas decision models are designed to provide solutions to specific decision problems. The decision models have a real-world focus and have an empirical basis. The models we discussed so far belong to the set of decision models. Normative theoretical models typically employ mathematical representations of market behavior. They are generally solved analytically or embedded in a simulation analysis.

An important subset of "theoretical, non-empirical, normative models" consists of dynamic optimal control models. Most of these models have been developed to determine optimal *advertising* expenditures over time, subject to dynamics that define how advertising expenditures translate into sales and in turn, into profits for a firm or even for a group of firms.[35] Optimal control theory has also been applied to find optimal *pricing policies over time*.[36] Rao and Thomas (1973) used dynamic programming to schedule promotions optimally over a time horizon.

Theoretical normative models have also been developed that model "normative" *purchase behavior*. Examples are the models of Krishna (1992, 1994) and Assunçao, Meyer (1993). In these models the impact of consumer price expectations, dealing patterns and price promotions on consumption have been examined.

8.3.2 ALLOCATION MODELS

The marketing literature contains several allocation models. These have the following characteristics. Resources are available in limited quantities; for example, an advertising manager has a budget, a sales person can work eight hours a day, potentially supplemented by a few of hours overtime. The purpose of such models is to allocate this quantity to subvariables (media, market segments, sales accounts ...) so as to

---

34. We closely follow Zoltners (1981, pp. 58-59).
35. For comprehensive surveys of these models see Sethi (1977), Hanssens et al. (1990, Chapter 9) and Feichtinger, Hartl and Sethi (1994).
36. See Hanssens et al. (1990, Chapter 8) and Rao (1993) for surveys.

optimize an objective function (profit, sales, . . .). We consider a few examples in the areas of advertising, selling, and distribution.

Blattberg and Neslin (1990, p. 391) suggest that the promotion planning process consists of three levels of budgeting decisions: the total marketing budget, the allocation of that budget to promotions (versus advertising and other marketing mix elements), and the preparation of individual promotion budgets or "individual events". The allocation of the *total marketing budget* over promotions, advertising and other marketing mix elements can be accomplished by the normative models discussed in Section 8.3.1.[37] A model which allocates the promotion budget over advertising and trade promotion expenditures was developed by Neslin, Powell and Schneider Stone (1995). This model represents the manufacturer's attempt to maximize profits by advertising directly to consumers and offering periodic discounts to the retailer in the hope that the retailer will in turn "pass through" a promotion to the consumer. The model considers the allocation in a manner that appears to fit the last two levels of budgeting decisions defined by Blattberg and Neslin.

The best-known allocation models are the *media allocation* models. Some of these only consider the allocation of a given advertising budget to a number of alternative media vehicles. Examples are Lee and Burkart (1960), Lee (1962), and Ellis (1966). Others have modeled the timing of the insertion in the various media. Examples are, Lee (1963), Taylor (1963), Little and Lodish (1969), Srinivasan (1976), Mahajan, Muller (1986), Hahn, Hyun (1991), Feinberg (1992), Mesak (1992), Bronnenberg (1998), Naik, Mantrala, Sawyer (1998). Reddy, Aronson and Stam (1998) developed the SPOT (Scheduling Programs Optimally to Television)-model. This model is used for optimal prime-time TV program scheduling. Because the advertising revenues of TV-networks are linked directly to the size of the audience delivered to the advertiser, this type of scheduling model is also relevant for decision makers in marketing. The issue of advertising schedules, specifically whether advertising should be steady (constant) or turned on and off (pulsed), has received attention from authors of the more recent studies. Objective functions in media allocation models vary from the maximization of reach to maximization of a discounted profit stream over a finite time horizon. Pedrick and Zufryden (1991) developed a model to analyze the impact of advertising media plans and point-of-purchase marketing variables on several brand market performance measures (market share, penetration, and depth of repeat purchase patterns).

An advertising budget can be allocated to subvariables other than media vehicles as well. The subvariables could be market segments such as, for example, different geographic regions. Applications include Zentler and Ryde (1956), Friedman (1958), and Urban (1971). Alternatively an advertising budget can be allocated to different products. This is considered by Doyle and Saunders (1990) and discussed in Chapter 13.

The allocation of *sales effort* has also been the subject of numerous studies.

---

37. It is also conceivable, of course, to have both budget determination and allocation in one single model. An example is the "integrated model for sales force structuring" developed by Rangaswamy et al. (1990).

Nordin (1943), Zoltners (1976), Zoltners, Sinha (1983), Skiera and Albers (1998) examined the spatial allocation of a sales force. Brown, Hulswit, and Ketelle (1956) studied the optimal frequency of visiting actual and potential buyers. André (1971) and Lodish (1971) developed procedures to optimize a salesmen's allocation of time spent on different accounts. Montgomery, Silk and Zaragoza (1971) present a procedure to help a salesperson in determining how much time to spend on various products to be sold.

The allocation of the *promotion budget* to individual events deserves more attention. Relevant to this question is the empirical result that the frequency and magnitude of price discounts have significant effects on the (own)price elasticities.[38] Higher and more frequent discounts lead to less negative price elasticities. Thus the timing and the determination of the size of the discount are important determinants of the managers' profit optimization problem.[39] However, the allocation of the total amount to discounts in specific time periods and the magnitude of each discount remain important optimization questions.

We note that the allocation of *shelf space* requires the development of idiosyncratic models. We discuss such models in Chapter 13.

---

38. See, for example, Raju (1992), Foekens, Leeflang, Wittink (1999).
39. See also Tellis and Zufryden (1995)

Appendix: The Dorfman-Steiner theorem

Let $q = q(p, a, \tilde{x})$, be demand (q) as a function of price (p),
advertising (a), and quality ($\tilde{x}$).

$c = (q, \tilde{x})$, be variable cost per unit, and

$FC =$ fixed cost.

Profit π is:

$$\pi = p\,q(p, a, \tilde{x}) - c(q, \tilde{x})q(p, a, \tilde{x}) - a - FC. \tag{8.A.1}$$

If the objective is to maximize profit, at optimality we should have:[40]

$$\frac{\partial \pi}{\partial p} = q + p\frac{\partial q}{\partial p} - c\frac{\partial q}{\partial p} - q\frac{\partial c}{\partial q}\frac{\partial q}{\partial p} = 0 \tag{8.A.2}$$

$$\frac{\partial \pi}{\partial a} = p\frac{\partial q}{\partial a} - c\frac{\partial q}{\partial a} - q\frac{\partial c}{\partial q}\frac{\partial q}{\partial a} - 1 = 0 \tag{8.A.3}$$

$$\frac{\partial \pi}{\partial \tilde{x}} = p\frac{\partial q}{\partial \tilde{x}} - c\frac{\partial q}{\partial \tilde{x}} - q\frac{\partial c}{\partial q}\frac{\partial q}{\partial \tilde{x}} - q\frac{\partial c}{\partial \tilde{x}} = 0. \tag{8.A.4}$$

Dividing (8.A.2) by ($\partial q/\partial p$) we obtain:

$$\frac{q}{\partial q/\partial p} + p - c - q\frac{\partial c}{\partial q} = 0. \tag{8.A.5}$$

Total variable production cost equals $c \cdot q$. Marginal cost (MC) is then:

$$MC = \frac{\partial(cq)}{\partial q} = c + q\frac{\partial c}{\partial q}. \tag{8.A.6}$$

Using (8.A.6), we can write (8.A.5) as:

$$\frac{-q}{\partial q/\partial p} = p - MC.$$

Dividing both sides by p, and letting:

$$w = \frac{p - MC}{p} = \text{percentage of gross margin}$$

we obtain:

$$-\eta_p = 1/w \tag{8.A.7}$$

where

---

40. We assume that second-order conditions are satisfied.

$$\eta_p = \frac{\partial q}{\partial p}\frac{p}{q} = \text{price elasticity.}$$

Dividing (8.A.3) by $(\partial q/\partial a)$,

$$p - c - q\frac{\partial c}{\partial q} - \frac{1}{\partial q/\partial a} = 0$$

or

$$p - MC = \frac{1}{\partial q/\partial a}.$$

After dividing both sides by p, we find:

$$\mu = 1/w \qquad\qquad\qquad\qquad (8.A.8)$$

where

$$\mu = p\frac{\partial q}{\partial a} = \text{marginal revenue of product advertising.}$$

Finally, we divide (8.A.4) by $\partial q/\partial \tilde{x}$:

$$p - c - q\frac{\partial c}{\partial q} - q\frac{\partial c/\partial \tilde{x}}{\partial q/\partial \tilde{x}} = 0$$

or

$$\frac{p - MC}{p} = \frac{q\,\partial c/\partial \tilde{x}}{p\,\partial q/\partial \tilde{x}}$$

or

$$\eta_{\tilde{x}}\frac{p}{c} = 1/w \qquad\qquad\qquad\qquad (8.A.9)$$

where

$$\eta_{\tilde{x}} = \frac{(\partial q/\partial \tilde{x})/q}{(\partial c/\partial \tilde{x})/c}.$$

At optimality (8.A.7), (8.A.8), and (8.A.9) should hold simultaneously, or:

$$-\eta_p = \mu = \eta_{\tilde{x}}\frac{p}{c} = \frac{1}{w}. \qquad\qquad (8.A.10)$$

This result is generally known as the Dorfman-Steiner (1954) theorem. This theorem has been modified and extended in many directions. Examples are the models of Lambin (1970), Lambin, Naert, Bultez (1975) (see Chapter 11), Leeflang, Reuyl (1985b), Plat, Leeflang (1988).

CHAPTER 9

Specifying models according to level of demand

In Section 4.2, we proposed three classes of demand functions: product category/ product class sales, brand sales, and brand market share models.[1] Such a classification is useful because model specification - both in terms of variables and mathematical form - can have features that are distinct for each of these three categories. In addition, we can distinguish models of individual- and aggregate demand, which we discuss in Section 9.1. Individual demand refers to the individual- or household level. Aggregate demand can be measured at levels such as store-, chain- and market demand. Further distinctions can be made between segments, regions, etc. In this chapter we concentrate on aggregate demand models for the three classes of demand functions, mentioned above. In Section 9.2, we discuss product class sales models.

The second class, brand sales, can either be modeled separately as a function of decision- and environmental variables, or it can be obtained from the product of product class sales and market share. We illustrate both approaches in Section 9.3.

A detailed analysis of market share models is given in Section 9.4, with particular attention to robust market share specifications.

9.1 An introduction to individual and aggregate demand

Aggregate demand models can either describe market behavior directly, or indirectly through individual behavior models from which outcomes are aggregated to determine market response.[2] An aggregate response model, if postulated *directly*, is applied to aggregate data and has its own component of response uncertainty (represented by the properties of the error term). The probabilistic properties of the *indirectly* specified aggregate models are derived from the perspectives of the individual component models.

---

1. The literature contains a number of synonyms for product class sales, such as primary demand (see, for example, Leeflang, 1977a), industry sales or demand (see, for example, Lambin, Naert, Bultez, 1975), and generic demand (Hughes, 1973, p. 2). In analogy to product class sales being called primary demand, brand sales is also referred to as secondary demand.
2. See Lilien, Kotler, Moorthy (1992, p. 672).

The increasing availability of scanner-type data at the household level has led to strong interest in models of individual buyer behavior[3] and methods for aggregation. The unique opportunities for understanding consumer behavior and deriving implications for marketing actions include:[4]

- analyzing household brand switching and brand loyalty over time;
- monitoring new brand performance through measures such as trial and penetration rates;
- modeling household heterogeneity in purchase behavior and exploiting household differences for segmentation and targeting marketing actions, such as direct mail campaigns;[5]
- understanding the impact of marketing variables on the timing of households' purchases and stockpiling behavior for the planning of promotions by retailers;[6]
- testing theories of consumer behavior.

The modeling of aggregate response from the addition of behavior across individuals ideally reflects heterogeneity across households in their intrinsic brand preferences and in their sensitivities to marketing variables (Chintagunta, Jain, Vilcassim, 1991). Different approaches are available to account for household heterogeneity at the disaggregate level.[7] These approaches exploit the information contained in the set of purchases available from each individual or household. The question is how to accommodate differences across households in their brand preferences and sensitivities to marketing variables in models of aggregate data. Related aggregation questions apply to the aggregation of store data to the market level.[8] We consider the aggregation problem in Chapter 14.

Some models have been developed which have about the same structure at the individual (micro) level and at the aggregate (macro) level. For example, Markov models are often used to accommodate the idea that the last brand chosen (in period t) affects the current purchase (in period $t + 1$). A first-order Markov model applies when *only* the last purchase has an influence on the next one, i.e.

$$P(X_{t+1} = j \mid X_t = r, \ X_{t-1} = k, \ldots) = P(X_{t+1} = j \mid X_t = r) = p_{rjt} \qquad (9.1)$$

where $P(X_{t+1} = j \mid X_t = r, \ X_{t-1} = k, \ldots)$ is the probability that the brand purchased at time $t + 1$ is j, given that the brand purchased at t was r, at $t - 1$ was $k, \ldots$. These probabilities are called *transition probabilities*. The Markov model is *zero-order* if the probability of purchasing a particular brand at $t + 1$ does not depend on purchasing behavior at $t, t - 1, t - 2, \ldots$. In other words a zero-order model applies

---

3. For some surveys, see Lilien et al. (1992, Chapter 2).
4. Based on Gupta, Chintagunta, Kaul, Wittink (1996, p. 383).
5. See, for example, Bult, Wittink (1996).
6. See Tellis, Zufryden (1995), Neslin, Schneider Stone (1996).
7. Guadagni, Little (1983), Jones, Landwehr (1988), Kamakura, Russell (1989), Chintagunta (1992b, 1993a), Fader, Lattin (1993), Gönül, Srinivasan, (1993a) Gupta, Chintagunta (1994), Rossi, Allenby (1994), Wedel, Kamakura (1998).
8. See Christen, Gupta, Porter, Staelin, Wittink (1997).

when the current (and future) purchasing behavior does not in any way depend on past purchases. A *first-order* Markov model applies when only the most recent purchase has an influence on the current one. In a *stationary* first-order Markov model the transition probabilities are constant over time: $p_{ijt} = p_{ij}$. The transition probabilities are related to the (individual) brand choice probabilities ($\pi_{j,t+1}$) as:

$$\pi_{j,t+1} = \sum_{r=1}^{n} p_{rj}\pi_{rt}, \text{ for every } j = 1, \ldots, n, \quad t = 1, \ldots, T \quad (9.2)$$

where

$\pi_{j,t+1}$ = probability brand j is chosen at $t + 1$ by an individual consumer/household,

n = total number of brands.

The unconditional (π_{rt}) and conditional (p_{rj}) probabilities are distributed over the population of consumers. One may account for heterogeneity by making assumptions about these distributions.[9] Under the assumption of consumer homogeneity, i.e. consumers have the same p_{rj} and π_{rt} values, it can be demonstrated that relation (9.3) holds at the aggregate level:

$$m_{j,t+1} = \sum_{r=1}^{n} \tilde{p}_{rj}m_{rt}, \text{ for every } j = 1, \ldots, n, \quad t = 1, \ldots, T \quad (9.3)$$

where

$m_{j,t+1}$ = market share of brand j in period $t + 1$,

$\tilde{p}_{rj}$ = fraction of consumers who buy brand r in t and brand j in $t + 1$.

The fractions $m_{j,t+1}, m_{jt}, \tilde{p}_{rj}$ follow the multinomial distribution with means $\pi_{j,t+1}$, π_{jt} and p_{rj}. Although (9.2) and (9.3) have the same structure, the definitions of the variables are clearly different between the individual- and the aggregate levels.

A second example of similarity in structure between individual- and aggregate models is the specification of the logit model (see relations (5.44), (5.53) and (5.60) for the aggregate-level specification). The multinomial logit model is a popular model in the marketing science literature since the pioneering research by Guadagni and Little (1983). We introduce the model specification at the individual/household level.[10] Consider an individual i confronted with a choice from a set of alternatives, CS_i, such as different brands in a product category. The utility that consumer i expects from alternative (brand) j is U_{ji}. This utility can be divided into two components, a systematic part (V_{ji}) and a random component (ε_{ji}). Thus:

$$U_{ji} = V_{ji} + \varepsilon_{ji}. \quad (9.4)$$

9. See, for example, Morrison (1966), Jones (1973), Leeflang (1974, Chapter 7).
10. We closely follow Guadagni, Little (1983). See also Lilien et al., (1992, Chapter 2), Roberts, Lilien (1993).

Given a specific set of alternatives, individual i chooses the option with the highest utility. The probability of choosing j is:

$$\pi_{ji} = P[U_{ji} > U_{ri} , \ r, j \in CS_i]. \underset{r \neq j}{} \tag{9.5}$$

If the ε_{ji} in (9.4) are independently distributed random variables with a double exponential distribution, then it can be shown[11] that individual i's choice probabilities have the (simple) form:

$$\pi_{ji} = e^{V_{ji}} / \sum_{r \in CS_i} e^{V_{ri}}. \tag{9.6}$$

The systematic, deterministic component of a consumer's utility for alternative j can be expressed as a linear function of observed variables relevant to j ($x_{\ell ji}$, $\ell = 1, \ldots, L$):

$$V_{ji} = \alpha_{0j} + \sum_{\ell=1}^{L} \alpha_{\ell j} x_{\ell ji}. \tag{9.7}$$

Substituting (9.7) in (9.6) we obtain the expression for the multinomial logit model at the individual level:

$$\pi_{ji} = \exp\left(\alpha_{0j} + \sum_{\ell=1}^{L} \alpha_{\ell j} x_{\ell ji}\right) / \sum_{r \in CS_i} \exp\left(\alpha_{0r} + \sum_{\ell=1}^{L_r} \alpha_{\ell r} x_{\ell ri}\right) \tag{9.8}$$

where

$L_r =$ the number of predictor variables for alternative r.

A similar expression is available at the aggregate level, as discussed in Section 9.4.[12]

From the disaggregate logit model in equation (9.8), forecasts of aggregate demand and market shares can be obtained. The essence is that a prediction of the share of choices of a brand, needs to be computed from the individual-level choice probabilities. If the model would have been calibrated on the whole population of I consumers, this approach would be conceptually simple: the expected market share of brand j would equal the average of the choice probabilities of the I individuals in the population:

$$m_j = \sum_{i=1}^{I} \pi_{ji} / I. \tag{9.9}$$

However, in most cases the individual-level choice probabilities are not known for all individuals in the population, since the levels of the predictors are unknown outside

---

11. Theil (1969), McFadden (1974).

12. Allenby and Rossi (1991a) have demonstrated, that under a number of conditions, the micro specification (9.8) is related to a macro specification, such as (9.27) substituted in (9.25). See also Gupta et al. (1996).

the sample. However, some appropriate distribution of the predictors may be assumed, for example the normal distribution. For simplicity we take the case of a single predictor, i.e. $L = 1$ in (9.8), two brands, i.e. $n = 2$, and coefficients that are constant across brands. Denoting the normal distribution of the predictor by $\phi(x_j, \mu_j, \sigma_j^2)$, an estimate of market share can be obtained by integrating over the distribution of the predictor:

$$m_j = \int \pi_{ji}(x)\phi(x_j, \mu_j, \sigma_j^2)dx_j. \tag{9.10}$$

This problem has been solved by McFadden and Reid (1975). The idea is that the difference between the value of the predictor for a particular subject, and its mean in the population $x_{ji} - \bar{x}_j$, follows a normal distribution with zero mean and variance σ^2. Formulating (9.4) in this case as:

$$U_{ji} = \alpha_0 + \alpha_1 \bar{x}_j + \alpha_1(x_{ji} - \bar{x}_j) + \varepsilon_{ji} = \alpha_0 + \alpha_1 \bar{x}_j + \varepsilon_{ji}^* \tag{9.11}$$

assuming ε_{ji}^* are $N(0, 1)$ distributed, and applying equation (9.5) yields:

$$\pi_{1i} = P[\alpha_1(\bar{x}_1 - \bar{x}_2) > (\varepsilon_{2i}^* - \varepsilon_{1i}^*)]. \tag{9.12}$$

This equation can be shown to result in the aggregate binary probit model:

$$m_j = \Phi\left(\frac{\alpha_1(\bar{x}_1 - \bar{x}_2)}{\sqrt{1 + \sigma^2}}\right) \tag{9.13}$$

with $\Phi(\cdot)$ the cumulative normal distribution. Thus, the aggregate share is the same as the individual choice probability evaluated at the population mean of the predictor, but the variance of the disturbance is increased to $1 + \sigma^2$, so that the scale of the aggregate model is smaller than that of the individual-level model (see Ben-Akiva and Lerman, 1985, pp. 143-144, who also give extensions to more predictors and choice alternatives).

The explicit integration procedure is elegant, but not without problems. One problem is that the assumption of the normal distribution may not be tenable. This holds for example if some of the predictors take on only a limited set of discrete values (summations would replace the integral). The second problem is that for larger numbers of predictors the computation of the shares lead to numerical difficulties, and one needs to resort to simulation methods. Therefore, a number of approximate methods have been proposed. Ben-Akiva and Lerman (1985) provide an excellent overview, here we give two particular examples:

1. the average individual method, and
2. sample enumeration.

The average individual method computes a "representative" individual (RI), identified by the mean of L predictors $\bar{x}_{lj}$. Subsequently, the choice probability is evaluated at the average values of those predictors:

$$m_j^{RI} = \pi_{ji}(\bar{x}_{1j}, \ldots, \bar{x}_{Lj}). \tag{9.14}$$

From equation (9.10) this procedure can be seen to neglect the heterogeneity in the distribution of the predictors in the population: it involves an approximation of the distribution of those predictors by their means. The difference between (9.14) and (9.10) increases as the variances of the predictors increase.

Sample enumeration (SE) uses the random sample of N individuals from the population as representative of that population and uses the predicted share in the sample as an estimator of the population market share:

$$m_j^{SE} = \sum_{i=1}^{I} \pi_{ji}/N. \tag{9.15}$$

where

I = total number of consumers in the population.

The sample enumeration estimator has the attractive property that it is a consistent estimator of the population share if the parameter estimates in the choice model are consistently estimated. In addition, sample enumeration is an attractive procedure to obtain forecasts of market shares in a-priori delineated market segments, defined by e.g. geographical regions or socio-economic classes, and it is easy to use "what if" market forecasting scenarios. Sample enumeration appears to be an attractive alternative of obtaining aggregate forecasts, given the potential bias of the representative individual and the computational cost of the explicit integration methods (Ben-Akiva and Lerman, 1985).

The most important ways of representing heterogeneity in disaggregate models currently in use are through either a continuous or a discrete mixture distribution of the parameters. To illustrate, assume a model with individual-level parameters α_i for $i = 1, \ldots, N$ consumers. Consider, for example, the application of a multinomial logit model to household scanner data, given by equation (9.8) (McFadden, 1977). We are interested in the distribution of the individual-level parameters, which we call the mixing distribution $f(\alpha_{(i)} \mid \Theta)$, where $\alpha_{(i)}$ is a $L + 1$ vector of individual's i parameters $\alpha_{0i}, \ldots, \alpha_{Li}$, where we assume that Θ is a set of parameters indexing the mixing distribution. For simplicity, we suppress dependence on other parameters of interest. The discussion, based on Wedel et al. (1999), focuses on the form of the mixing distribution.

Homogeneous models of choice (Guadagni and Little, 1983) are the simplest models which assume a homogeneous population. In homogeneous models, the $(L+1)$ vector of choice parameters $\alpha_{(i)}$ does not vary across the population and there is no mixing distribution; variation enters the model only through the predictors. Early approaches to heterogeneity in the marketing and econometrics literature treated heterogeneity as a nuisance, and included individual-level intercept terms in the choice model to eliminate heterogeneity. Fixed-effects approaches were used, in which for each individual a mean parameter was estimated. Subsequently, a distribution was assumed for the intercept term, which was approximated by a discrete number of support points and probability masses (Chintagunta, Jain and Vilcassim, 1991), which involves $f(\alpha_{(i)} \mid \Theta) = \pi_s$, for $s = 1, \ldots, S$, where $f(\cdot)$ is a discrete distribution and S is the total number of support points. These can be interpreted as segments (Section 17.2).

Later, heterogeneity became of fundamental interest in marketing. The support point was extended to capture heterogeneity across all the parameters in a choice model. Thus, finite mixture regression models arose that connected well to marketing theories of market segmentation (Wedel and Kamakura, 1998). Such finite mixture models have enjoyed considerable success and are discussed more extensively in Chapter 17. Managers are comfortable with the idea of market segments, and the models appear to do a good job of identifying useful groups. However, market segments cannot account fully for heterogeneity if the true underlying distribution of the parameters is continuous. In addition, some practitioners, such as direct and database marketers, prefer to work at the level of the individual respondent.

While a discrete mixing distribution leads to finite mixture models, continuous mixing distributions lead to random coefficients (e.g. probit or logit) models. Random coefficient logit models have received considerable attention in marketing and related fields (Allenby, Ginter, 1995, Rossi, McCulloch, Allenby, 1996, Elrod, Keane, 1995, Haaijer, Wedel, Vriens and Wansbeek, 1998). Typically a multivariate normal distribution is assumed for all regression parameters in the model, i.e. $f(\alpha_{(i)} \mid \Theta) = MVN(\mu, \Sigma)$. The use of a continuous heterogeneity distribution has several advantages: it characterizes the tails of the heterogeneity distribution better and it predicts individual behavior more accurately than finite mixture models.

Some researchers have argued that the assumption in finite mixture models of a limited number of segments of individuals who are perfectly homogeneous within segments is too restrictive (Allenby and Rossi, 1999), and that the finite mixture model leads to an artificial partition of the continuous distribution into homogeneous segments. In many fields within marketing, emphasis is now on individual customer contact and direct marketing approaches. Individual-level response parameters may be required for optimal implementation of direct- and micro marketing strategies. On the other hand, proponents of the finite mixture approach argue that the estimates of models with continuous heterogeneity distributions may be sensitive to the specific distribution assumed for the parameters (i.e. the normal), which is determined subjectively by the researcher. Further, most models that approximate heterogeneity through a number of unobserved segments have great managerial appeal: models formulated at the segment-level have an edge if there are scale advantages in production, distribution, or advertising. Still, combinations of the discrete- and continuous heterogeneity approaches, that account for both discrete segments and within-segment heterogeneity, have been developed, (Allenby, Arora and Ginter, 1998, Allenby and Rossi, 1999).

9.2 Product class sales models

Observations used for the estimation of product class sales can be of two varieties:

1. *Cross-sectional data:* product class sales and other data are available across, say, geographical areas or individuals at a certain point in time.
2. *Time-series data:* the values of product class sales for a given region or individual, and the corresponding explanatory variables, are observed over a number of time periods.

The observations may also consist of a combination, or - as it is generally referred to in the literature - a *pooling* of cross-section and time-series data. Pooling calls for special estimation procedures which are introduced in Chapters 14 and 16.

If product class sales is to be explained from cross-sectional data, the explanatory variables are often socio-economic and demographic variables, such as age, sex, education, occupation, income, location, family size, as well as marketing variables. However, the effects of marketing instruments cannot be obtained unless the marketing instruments vary across individuals, or groups of individuals, or cross sections. Many examples of these models can be found in the economic and econometric literature. See, e.g. Duesenberry (1949), Klein, Lansing (1955), Kapteyn, Wansbeek, Buyze (1980), Kapteyn, van de Geer, van de Stadt, Wansbeek (1997).

An example of a marketing model estimated with cross-sectional data is a model that captures differences in trade show effectiveness across industries, companies and countries. The authors of this model (Dekimpe, François, Gopalakrishna, Lilien, Vanden Bulte, 1997) provide results about the effects of various show types and tactical variables (booth size, personnel) on observed performance.

In time-series data, the predictors often consist of both environmental and marketing variables. Examples of environmental variables are: population size, a weather index, and information on economic activity. For cross-sectional data it is common for researchers to use aggregate values of marketing instruments, meaning that aggregation is performed over all brands that constitute the product class. Examples are total advertising expenditures, total number of retail outlets and average price.

In Section 8.3.1 we presented a product class sales model estimated from times-series data. In that example, however, product class sales and brand sales were identical, given that the market under consideration was monopolistic. Below we give some examples of product class sales models for oligopolistic markets. The purpose of these examples is to illustrate the types of variables that are used to explain product class sales.

Demand for gasoline is a derived demand in the sense that it depends on the number of automobiles. Thus, car ownership may be an explanatory variable. An example is Lambin's (1972a) estimation of per capita demand for gasoline in Italy, as a function of per capita car ownership.

$$\frac{\widehat{Q_t}}{N_t} = 94 \left[\frac{PA_t}{N_t}\right]^{0.77} \left[\frac{\frac{1}{n}\sum_{r=1}^{n} Prt}{PI_t}\right]^{-0.39} [sd_1]^{-0.06}[sd_2]^{0.04}[sd_3]^{0.09} \qquad (9.16)$$

where

$$
\begin{aligned}
Q_t &= \text{product class sales,} \\
N_t &= \text{population size,} \\
PA_t &= \text{car ownership,} \\
p_{rt} &= \text{price of gasoline brand } r, \\
n &= \text{number of brands in the product class,} \\
PI_t &= \text{general price index, and} \\
sd_1, sd_2, sd_3 &= \text{dummy variables to account for seasonal} \\
&\quad \text{variation (\textit{seasonal dummies}).}
\end{aligned}
$$

A similar case is Leeflang's (1976, 1977a) study of the Dutch detergent market, where sales depend on the ownership of automatic washing machines,[13]

$$
\widehat{Q}_t = e^{7.57} \left[\frac{Inc_t^*}{PI_t} \right]^{0.40} \left[\frac{\frac{1}{n} \sum_{r=1}^{n} p_{rt}}{PI_t} \right]^{-0.23} [AW_{t-1}]^{0.11} \tag{9.17}
$$

$$
\cdot \left[\sum_{r=1}^{n} a_{rt}^e \right]^{-0.02} \cdot \left[\sum_{r=1}^{n} a_{rt}^p \right]^{0.02}
$$

where

$$
\begin{aligned}
Inc_t^* &= \text{disposable income (in nominal terms),} \\
AW_{t-1} &= \text{ownership of automatic washing machines,} \\
a_{rt}^e &= \text{radio and television advertising expenditures of brand } r, \text{ and} \\
a_{rt}^p &= \text{press advertising expenditures of brand } r.
\end{aligned}
$$

For the other variables we refer to the legend following equation (9.16).

In Section 6.1 we briefly discussed the relation between industry sales and variables such as industry advertising expenditures in the West-German cigarette market. One of the *non-dynamic* relations is relation (9.18):

$$
\frac{Q_t}{N_t^*} = e^{\alpha_0 + u_t} \frac{\left(\sum_{r=1}^{n} a_{rt} \right)^{\alpha_1}}{N_t^*} \frac{(C_t)^{\alpha_2}}{N_t^*} \frac{(QR_t)^{\alpha_3}}{N_t^*} \frac{(QP_t)^{\alpha_4}}{N_t^*} \frac{(QC_t)^{\alpha_5}}{N_t^*} \tag{9.18}
$$

where

$$
\begin{aligned}
Q_t &= \text{total number of cigarettes in } t, \\
N_t^* &= \text{number of persons over 15 years of age in } t, \\
u_t &= \text{a disturbance term,}
\end{aligned}
$$

---

13. A market share demand function for the same market was given in Section 7.2. See for an alternative specification of (9.17), equation (15.2).

Table 9.1 Parameter estimates and statistics of relation (9.18).

Variable	Parameter estimate
Advertising $\left(\sum_{r=1}^{n} a_{rt}\right)/N_t^*$	0.04^c $(0.02)^a$
Household consumption $(C_t)/N_t^*$	0.60^b (0.09)
Roll your own tobacco $(QR_t)/N_t^*$	-0.07^c (0.03)
Pipe tobacco $(QP_t)/N_t^*$	-0.07 (0.04)
Cigars $(QC_t)/N_t^*$	-0.08 (0.05)
R^2	0.85

[a] The number in parentheses are standard errors
[b,c] Estimates significant at the 1% and 5%-level respectively

Source: Leeflang and Reuyl (1985a, p. 96).

a_{rt} = advertising expenditures measured in German marks of brand r,
C_t = household consumption measured in German marks in t,
QR_t = industry sales of "roll your own" tobacco, measured in grams in t,
QP_t = industry sales of pipe tobacco, measured in grams in t, and
QC_t = industry sales of cigars, measured in number of units in t.

All variables are defined per capita (per person over 15 years of age). After all variables were regressed against time (to remove trends), the estimated parameters for the (adjusted) per capita variables in (9.18), obtained from monthly observations, are those in Table 9.1. Advertising has a significant effect on industry sales. In an other part of their analysis (not shown here) Leeflang and Reuyl demonstrate that this effect diminishes over time. The estimated coefficient for household consumption (per capita) indicates that the consumption of cigarettes is quite responsive to household consumption, albeit that a percentage increase in household consumption leads to a smaller percentage increase in cigarette consumption. The cross elasticities are all negative. The cross elasticy for roll your own tabacco is the only significant cross elasticy.

Many other examples of industry sales demand models can be found in the literature. See e.g. Lambin (1976), Leone, Schultz (1980), Lancaster (1984).[14]

---

14. Calls for advertising bans in different areas such as alcohol and cigarettes continue to echo around the world on a continuing basis. This explains why so many models have been developed in these areas. See, e.g. Duffy (1996), Franses (1991), Leeflang, Reuyl (1995) and Luik, Waterson (1996).

Consumer demand theory, as treated in economics, has yielded a large number of product class sales models. Given a utility function, consumer demand theory looks for the optimal allocation of consumer budgets over a number of product classes, and, in this manner demand for various product classes is explained. Unfortunately, product classes in these models are often very broadly defined, which makes them less useful for decision making purposes in marketing. These models are, therefore, not further discussed here. The interested reader is referred to, for example, Barten (1977), Brown and Deaton (1972) and Theil (1975, 1976). These models, however, have inspired marketing scientists to develop models for market structure analysis.[15]

9.3 Brand sales models

Recall that brand sales can either be modeled directly or indirectly. Directly means that sales of brand j are explained as a function of marketing variables of brand j, marketing variables of competing brands, and environmental variables. Indirectly means that brand sales (q_{jt}) obtains from the product of category sales (Q_t) and market share of the brand of interest (m_{jt}). Specification of product class sales was discussed in the previous section. We discuss market share models in Section 9.4.

Arguments in favor of modeling brand sales *indirectly* are:

1. It is possible to distinguish between changes in q_{jt} that are caused by changes in market size, Q_t, and those that come from changes in the relative position of brand j in that market, expressed by market share, m_{jt}.
2. Using market share rather than sales as the dependent variable has the following advantages: environmental variables, and seasonal or cyclical factors causing expansion or contraction of the entire market need not be included.[16] The share model concentrates attention on the competitive interactions between brands in the product class.[17]
3. By phasing variables over different levels we reduce the potential number of explanatory variables per equation, which reduces the multicollinearity (see Section 16.1).

Arguments in favor of modeling brand sales *directly* are:

1. To the extent that marketing activities for individual brands influence product category sales, it is implausible that those marketing effects are the same for equivalent increases across the brands that belong to a product category.
2. Product category sales result from the aggregation of sales across brands belonging to the category. Since brands are heterogeneous in marketing activities

---

15. See Clements, Selvanathan (1988), Vilcassim (1989).
16. The assumption being that such variables affect demand for each brand equally. This assumption will often be quite reasonable. If not, however, environmental variables affecting brands differently should be included in the market share function (as well as in the direct estimation of brand sales).
17. This is emphasized by, for example, MacLachlan (1972, p. 378) and Beckwith (1972, p. 171).

and tend to have unique parameters relating marketing variables to sales, the interpretation of product category demand model parameters is unclear.

3. If product category sales fluctuates, then a given brand's market share values are not really comparable. Alternatively, the more product category sales fluctuates, the more questionable the assumption of constant parameter values is.

We illustrate the direct approach with the well-known SCAN*PRO model (Wittink, Addona, Hawkes, Porter, 1988). This model uses brand sales as the criterion variable. The SCAN*PRO model is a store-level model developed to quantify the effects of promotional activities implemented by retailers on a brand's unit sales. The model accommodates temporary price cuts, displays, and feature advertising. In addition, it includes weekly indicator variables to account for the effects of seasonality and missing variables (such as manufacturer television advertising and coupon distributions) common to the stores in a metropolitan area, and store indicator variables. This model has been used in over 2000 different commercial applications in the United States, in Canada, in Europe, and elsewhere.

A slight modification of the original model is specified as follows, for brand j, $j = 1, \ldots, n$:

$$
q_{kjt} = \left[\prod_{r=1}^{n} \left(\frac{p_{krt}}{\bar{p}_{kr}} \right)^{\beta_{rj}} \prod_{\ell=1}^{3} \gamma_{\ell rj}^{D_{\ell krt}} \right] \left[\prod_{t=1}^{T} \delta_{jt}^{X_t} \right] \left[\prod_{k=1}^{K} \lambda_{kj}^{Z_k} \right] e^{u_{kjt}}, \tag{9.19}
$$

$$
k = 1, \ldots, K, t = 1, \ldots, T
$$

where

q_{kjt} = unit sales (e.g. number of pounds) for brand j in store k, week t,

p_{krt} = unit price for brand r in store k, week t,

$\bar{p}_{kr}$ = the median regular unit price (based on the non-promoted weeks) for brand r in store k,

D_{1krt} = an indicator variable for feature advertising: 1 if brand r is featured (but *not* displayed) by store k, in week t; 0 otherwise,

D_{2krt} = 0 an indicator variable for display: 1 if brand r is displayed (but *not* featured) by store k, week t; 0 otherwise,

D_{3krt} = an indicator variable for the simultaneous use of feature and display: 1 if brand r is featured *and* displayed; 0 otherwise,

X_t = an indicator variable (proxy for missing variables and seasonal effects): 1 if the observation is in week t; 0 otherwise,

Table 9.2 Average values of parameter estimates of the SCAN*PRO model.

Own-brand effects				Cross-brand effects			
Feature	Display	Feature and display	Price	Feature	Display	Feature and display	Price
1.63	2.25	3.07	-3.50	1.25	0.87	0.90	0.63

Source: Foekens, Leeflang and Wittink (1994, p. 260).

Z_k = an indicator variable for store k : 1 if the observation is from store k; 0 otherwise,

β_{rj} = the own price (deal) elasticity if $j = r$, or cross-price elasticity if $j \neq r$,

γ_{1rj} = the own feature and multiplier if $j = r$, or cross-feature ad multiplier if $j \neq r$,

γ_{2rj} = the own display multiplier if $j = r$, or a cross-display multiplier if $j \neq r$,

γ_{3rj} = the own display *and* feature multiplier if $j = r$, or a cross-display feature multiplier if $j \neq r$,

δ_{jt} = the (seasonal) multiplier for week t when the criterion variable represents brand j,

λ_{kj} = store k's regular (base) unit sales for brand j when there are no temporary price cuts and no promotion activities for any of the brands $r, r = 1, \ldots, n, r \neq j$

u_{kjt} = a disturbance term for brand j in store k, week t,

n = the number of brands used in the competitive set,

K = the number of stores in the sample for a major market, and

T = the number of weeks.

This model has been numerically specified in a study of the model's forecasting accuracy at different levels of aggregation (store, chain, market-level). We consider here the parameter estimates obtained from store-level data only. These estimates are obtained from UPC scanner data provided by ACNielsen, for one large metropolitan area in the United States. Weekly data were available for three national brands competing in a frequently purchased food category. The average values of the significant parameter estimates are shown in Table 9.2. The averages are averages over three brands and the 40 stores in the sample.[18]

---

18. See Foekens, Leeflang, Wittink (1994).

As expected, the own-brand price elasticity is negative, and the cross-brand elasticity is positive. The (promotion) multipliers with a value larger than 1 have a positive effect on unit sales, while values smaller than 1 have a negative effect. All cross effects, except feature, have the expected negative impact on q_{kjt}.

The SCAN*PRO model has been used in several studies in which aggregation effects are considered.[19] The model also constitutes the basis for the development of varying parameter models[20] (see Section 17.5), semiparametric models[21] (see Section 16.7) and models for the effects of dynamic lead- and lag effects.[22]

To *model brand sales indirectly,* we closely follow the derivation in Lambin, Naert and Bultez (1975). They observed that for profit maximization the Dorfman-Steiner theorem (derived in the Appendix to Chapter 8) remains valid independent of whether the market is a monopoly or an oligopoly, making a separate derivation for each case unnecessary.[23] For an oligopoly, however, brand sales elasticities can be decomposed.[24] We illustrate this below for the brand sales advertising elasticity.[25] We formulate the relation between brand sales-, product class sales-, and market share elasticities as follows. By definition, brand sales, q, equals product class sales, Q, times market share, m,[26]

$$q = Qm. \tag{9.20}$$

Differentiating brand sales with respect to advertising (a) gives,

$$\frac{\partial q}{\partial a} = m\frac{\partial Q}{\partial a} + Q\frac{\partial m}{\partial a}. \tag{9.21}$$

Multiplying both sides by a/q, we obtain,

$$\frac{a}{q}\frac{\partial q}{\partial a} = m\frac{a}{q}\frac{\partial Q}{\partial a} + Q\frac{a}{q}\frac{\partial m}{\partial a} \tag{9.22}$$

which can also be written as,

$$\frac{a}{q}\frac{\partial q}{\partial a} = \frac{a}{Q}\frac{\partial Q}{\partial a} + \frac{a}{m}\frac{\partial m}{\partial a} \tag{9.23}$$

---

19. Foekens, Leeflang, Wittink (1994), Gupta et al. (1996), Christen et al. (1997).
20. Foekens, Leeflang, Wittink (1999).
21. van Heerde, Leeflang, Wittink (1999a).
22. van Heerde, Leeflang, Wittink (1999c).
23. In normative marketing mix studies one generally seeks the optimal policy for one brand assuming particular competitive reaction patterns. This means that one does not derive a simultaneous optimum for all brands in the product class. The latter would call for a game theoretic approach. We discuss game theoretic approaches in Section 11.4.
24. The relation established is independent of normative considerations: it does not depend on an assumption of profit maximization or on any other objective function.
25. For a more formal treatment, extending to other variables as well, see Lambin, Naert, Bultez (1975, pp. 106-115). In that paper the special character of quality as a decision variable is also discussed. A generalization to multiproduct markets is given by Bultez (1975).
26. The time and brand index are omitted for notational convenience.

or

$$\eta_{q,a} = \eta_{Q,a} + \eta_{m,a}. \tag{9.24}$$

i.e., the brand sales elasticity with respect to advertising, $\eta_{q,a}$, is equal to the total product class sales elasticity, $\eta_{Q,a}$, plus the market share elasticity, $\eta_{m,a}$, with respect to the same variable. Thus the brand sales elasticity can be obtained *indirectly* from the sum of the product category sales- and the brand market share elasticities.

Relation (9.24) can be extended to account for competitive reactions. These reactions with the same (advertising) or other marketing instruments (for example, price) are called *indirect* effects. They may influence $\eta_{Q,a}$ and/or $\eta_{m,a}$ as will be discussed in Chapter 11.

9.4 Market share models

Market share models can be specified to be logically consistent, in the sense that predicted values satisfy range (being between zero and one) and sum (summing to one across brands) constraints. One class of models that satisfy these constraints are the *attraction models*. The attraction of a brand depends on its marketing mix. Let A_{jt} be the attraction of brand j in period t (note that this symbol is also used for total advertising expenditures). Market share attraction models are defined as:

$$m_{jt} = \frac{A_{jt}}{\sum_{r=1}^{n} A_{rt}} \tag{9.25}$$

where n is the number of brands on the market. If A_{jt} is specified to be nonnegative, the attraction model has the desirable characteristics of both satisfying the range constraint ($0 \leq m_{jt} \leq 1$ for all j), and the sum constraint ($\sum_{r=1}^{n} m_{rt} = 1$). In this section, we focus on this type of model. Other market share specifications have been discussed in Chapters 5 and 7.

Bell, Keeney and Little (1975) demonstrate that the following axioms necessarily lead to a market share attraction model

1. The attraction for each brand is non-negative, i.e. $A_{jt} \geq 0$ for $j = 1, \ldots, n$ and $t = 1, \ldots, T$, and total attraction exerted on the market is positive,

$$\sum_{r=1}^{n} A_{rt} > 0, \quad t = 1, \ldots, T.$$

2. Zero attraction implies zero market share.
3. Brands with equal attraction have identical market shares.
4. If the attraction of a brand changes by a given amount, market share of any of the other brands is affected equally, no matter which brand's attraction has changed.

The attraction model has a structure that logically follows from a number of plausible axioms.[27] Only axiom (4) needs to be justified. Essentially, axiom (4) implies that if one brand becomes more attractive, while other brands remain at the same level of attractiveness, its gain in market share will come from all other brands proportional to their current shares (and to their attractiveness levels). This axiom is analogous to the IIA assumption discussed later.

Axiom (4) does not imply that the effect of a change in a marketing variable on one brand's market share has equivalent effects on other brands' market shares. The reason is that the brands' attractions depend on the marketing variables, and these attraction functions can be specified in a variety of ways.[28] Thus, axiom (4) deals with how the market shares of (other) brands vary when the attractiveness of one brand changes. It does not say anything about how the brands' attraction values depend on marketing activities, i.e. the components of the attraction functions are not discussed in the axioms.

Equation (9.25) represents the overall structure. The attraction function itself remains to be specified. We present six different specifications. In Section 14.3 we discuss other specifications. Two well-known market share specifications are the MCI model and the MNL model. The attraction for brand j in the "Multiplicative Competitive Interaction" (MCI) model is specified as:[29]

$$A_{jt} = \exp(\alpha_j) \prod_{\ell=1}^{L} x_{\ell jt}^{\beta_\ell} \cdot \varepsilon_{jt} \qquad (9.26)$$

where

$x_{\ell jt}$ = the value of the ℓ-th explanatory variable for brand j,
in period t,

ε_{jt} = a disturbance term,

L = the number of marketing instruments.

Throughout it is assumed that L is independent of j.

The attraction for the MultiNomial Logit (MNL) market share model is specified as:

$$A_{jt} = \exp\left(\alpha_j + \sum_{\ell=1}^{L} \beta_\ell x_{\ell jt} + \varepsilon_{jt}\right). \qquad (9.27)$$

The structure of this component is similar to the specification of the numerator of the MNL model at the individual level (9.8).[30]

---

27. Cooper and Nakanishi (1988, pp. 24-26) discuss these and other axioms in more detail. See also Barnett (1976).
28. This is discussed in more detail in Chapter 14.
29. The MCI models have been developed by Nakanishi (1972) and Cooper: see Nakanishi, Cooper (1974, 1982). These and other market share models are discussed extensively in Cooper, Nakanishi (1988).
30. Basuroy and Nguyen (1998) identified the conditions under which the MNL market share models can be the basis for equilibrium analysis.

While the attraction specification (9.26) has attractive characteristics, there are also two disadvantages. First, the attraction is zero if one of the explanatory variables (for example, advertising) is zero in period t. This problem does not apply to the MNL model (9.27). Second, the response parameter for instrument ℓ is β_ℓ, which is assumed to be equal for each brand. As we mentioned about the lack of robustness for the linear model in Section 7.3, marketing executives, in general, find the assumption of equal response parameters across brands unacceptable.

An extension that allows a variable's response to vary across brands is the *extended attraction model* (versus the *simple attraction model* (9.26) and (9.27)). This model is also known as the *differential effects model*:[31]

MCI-Differential Effects model: (MCI-DE):

$$A_{jt} = \exp(\alpha_j) \prod_{\ell=1}^{L} x_{\ell jt}^{\beta_{\ell j}} \varepsilon_{jt}. \tag{9.28}$$

MNL-Differential Effects model: (MNL-DE):

$$A_{jt} = \exp\left(\alpha_j + \sum_{\ell=1}^{L} \beta_{\ell j} x_{\ell jt} + \varepsilon_{jt}\right). \tag{9.29}$$

Before we introduce the last two of the six attraction specifications, we present expressions for elasticities.

OWN-BRAND ELASTICITIES

Market share elasticities need to be determined separately for each attraction model. That is, the formula depends on the attraction specification. The *direct* or *own* market share elasticities (e_j^ℓ) for models (9.26)-(9.29) are (ignoring time subscript t):

$$
\begin{aligned}
\text{MCI} \quad &: \ e_j^\ell \ = \ \frac{\delta m_j}{\delta x_{\ell j}} \cdot \frac{x_{\ell j}}{m_j} = \beta_\ell(1 - m_j) \\
\text{MNL} \quad &: \ e_j^\ell \ = \ \beta_\ell(1 - m_j)x_{\ell j} \\
\text{MCI-DE} \quad &: \ e_j^\ell \ = \ \beta_{\ell j}(1 - m_j) \\
\text{MNL-DE} \quad &: \ e_j^\ell \ = \ \beta_{\ell j}(1 - m_j)x_{\ell j}.
\end{aligned}
\tag{9.30}
$$

Note that the four elasticities differ with regard to the homogeneity/heterogeneity of the marketing variable parameters and in the presence/absence of the marketing variable itself. Specifically, the DE versions have $\beta_{\ell j}$ (versus β_ℓ), indicating that the parameter is brand-specific (heterogeneous). And the MNL model expressions include $x_{\ell j}$. Apart from these distinctions, each elasticity expression includes a marketing effort responsiveness parameter and the share of the market not captured by

---

31. Cooper, Nakanishi (1988, Chapters 3 and 5).

the brand $(1 - m_j)$. Thus, even if the responsiveness parameters are homogeneous, the elasticities differ across brands according to the remaining share. The inclusion of this $(1 - m_j)$ term has the desirable property that the elasticity goes toward zero as the brand's market share goes to one.

The MNL-based elasticities differ from the corresponding MCI-based ones in the inclusion of $x_{\ell j}$, which measures the marketing effort for variable ℓ used by brand j.

Holding market share constant, the elasticity expression shows that an increase in marketing effort, for $\beta > 0$, increases the elasticity. However, we know that market share is affected by marketing activities. Also, it is generally accepted that it becomes harder to gain share as the marketing effort increases.[32] The MNL-based elasticity expression implies that if own-brand market share increases proportionally faster than the marketing effort, the own-brand market share elasticity will decrease with increasing $x_{\ell j}$. Cooper and Nakanishi (1988, p. 35) find that MNL-based elasticities increase to a point and then decrease.

CROSS-BRAND ELASTICITIES

We now turn to a discussion about *cross elasticities*, which are defined as:

$$e^{\ell}_{j,r} = \frac{\delta m_j}{\delta x_{\ell r}} \frac{x_{\ell r}}{m_j} \qquad (9.31)$$

where

$$x_{\ell r} = \text{value of marketing instrument } \ell \text{ of competitor } r, r \neq j.$$

The expressions for the cross elasticities of the four attraction models are:[33]

$$
\begin{array}{lll}
\text{MCI} & : e^{\ell}_{j,r} = -\beta_{\ell} m_r \\
\text{MNL} & : e^{\ell}_{j,r} = -\beta_{\ell} x_{\ell r} m_r \\
\text{MCI-DE} & : e^{\ell}_{j,r} = -\beta_{\ell r} m_r \\
\text{MNL-DE} & : e^{\ell}_{j,r} = -\beta_{\ell r} x_{\ell r} m_r.
\end{array}
\qquad (9.32)
$$

The four cross-elasticity expressions have properties that are similar to the own-brand elasticities. The effect of r's activity on brand j's attraction is either homogeneous $(-\beta_{\ell})$ or heterogeneous $(-\beta_{\ell r})$, and MCI and MNL differ with regard to the exclusion (MCI) or inclusion (MNL) of the effort for instrument ℓ by brand r. Also, all expressions include m_r, implying that the cross elasticity is more negative (stronger) as r's market share is larger. The cross elasticity does not depend on the share of the brand for which the marketing effort takes place. However, the actual change in a brand's share varies, reflecting its current level. The new share of any brand other

---

32. We assume $\beta_{\ell}, \beta_{\ell j} \geq 0$ for all ℓ, j which applies to variables such as distribution, selling effort, advertising, and sales promotions. For variables such as price for which $\beta_{\ell}, \beta_{\ell j} \leq 0$ an analogous reasoning can be formulated.
33. We closely follow Cooper, Nakanishi (1988) and Cooper (1993).

than r may be simply calculated by: new share of brand $j = (1-$ new share of brand $r) *$ old share of brand j, $j \neq r$.

Because the expressions (9.32) are independent of m_j, the effects of marketing variable $x_{\ell r}$ are distributed among its competitive brands *in proportion* to their market shares. This means that the competitive brands are equally substitutable. The models (9.26)-(9.29) constrain the competition to being *symmetric*. This symmetry is the result of the *Independence of Irrelevant Alternatives* (IIA) assumption.[34] This assumption implies that the ratio of two (market) shares does not depend on the presence or absence of other choice alternatives. That this assumption holds for the models (9.26)-(9.29) can be demonstrated easily by taking the ratio of the market share attractions of two brands j and r. These ratios are independent of the other brands r', $r' \neq j, r$. The IIA-properties also hold for the individual choice models such as, for example, (9.8).

An equality of cross elasticities, symmetry between brands, does not fit what we tend to observe in the market place. Brands belonging to a given product category are usually not equally substitutable. For example, Blattberg and Wisniewski (1989) found that consumers who normally purchase brands with *low* regular prices (e.g. store brands) are sensitive to temporary price cuts for (national) brands with *high* regular prices. On the other hand, consumers normally purchasing these national brands tend to be insensitive to temporary price cuts for store brands. Steenkamp and Dekimpe (1997), however, show that the power of store brands depends on the product category.

We discuss alternative ways to account for asymmetric competition in Sections 14.4 and 14.5.[35] Briefly, one possibility is to expand the differential effects models one step further. Relations (9.33) and (9.34) are (the numerators of) attraction models with differential cross-competitive effects, called *Fully Extended Attraction (FEA) models*. We consider two versions of FEA models.

Fully Extended MCI model (FEMCI):

$$A_{jt} = \exp(\alpha_j) \prod_{\ell=1}^{L} \prod_{r=1}^{n} x_{\ell rt}^{\beta_{\ell jr}} \varepsilon_{jt}. \tag{9.33}$$

Fully Extended MNL model (FEMNL):

$$A_{jt} = \exp\left(\alpha_j + \sum_{\ell=1}^{L} \sum_{r=1}^{n} \beta_{\ell jr} x_{\ell rt} + \varepsilon_{jt} \right). \tag{9.34}$$

---

34. See Luce (1959), Debreu (1960), Ben-Akiva, Lerman (1985), Allenby, Rossi (1991b), Sethuraman, Srinivasan and Kim (1999) and the discussion in Section 12.3.3.
35. See also Foekens (1995), Bronnenberg, Wathieu (1996), Cooper, Klapper, Inoue (1996), Foekens, Leeflang, Wittink (1997).

For the own- and cross elasticities the following expressions can be derived:

$$\text{FEMCI} \; : \; e_{j,r}^{\ell} \; = \; \beta_{\ell jr} - \sum_{r'=1}^{n} \beta_{\ell jr'} \cdot m_{r'}$$

$$\text{FEMNL} \; : \; e_{j,r}^{\ell} \; = \; \left(\beta_{\ell jr} - \sum_{r'=1}^{n} \beta_{\ell jr'} \cdot m_{r'} \right) x_{\ell r}.$$

(9.35)

These formulas apply to both own- and cross elasticities. The own elasticities are obtained from (9.35) by letting $j = r$. The above expressions indicate that the effects of changes in marketing variables differ between the brands. Thus the FEMCI- and FEMNL-models account for asymmetric competition.[36]

In their monograph on market share models and market share analysis, Cooper and Nakanishi (1988, p. 18) raise the question:

"Why, . . ., are the MCI and MNL models not used more extensively?"

given that these models are flexible in the parameters, are logically consistent, and can account for asymmetric competition.

"The answer is that for a time both of these models were considered to be intrinsically nonlinear models, requiring estimation schemes which were expensive in analysts' time and computer resources. This, however, turned out to be a hasty judgment because these models may be changed into a linear model (in the model parameters) by a simple transformation"

(Cooper, Nakanishi, 1988, p. 28).

These transformations, known as log-centering, are briefly introduced below[37] for the MNL model (equations (9.25) and (9.27)). First (9.27) is substituted in (9.25). Then taking logarithms on both sides yields:

$$\log m_{jt} \; = \; \alpha_j + \sum_{\ell=1}^{L} \beta_\ell x_{\ell jt} + \varepsilon_{jt}$$

(9.36)

$$- \log \left(\sum_{r=1}^{n} \exp \left(\alpha_r + \sum_{\ell=1}^{L} \beta_\ell x_{\ell rt} + \varepsilon_{rt} \right) \right).$$

Summing (9.36) over j ($j = 1, \ldots, n$) and dividing by n gives:

$$\log \tilde{m}_t \; = \; \bar{\alpha} + \bar{\varepsilon}_t + \frac{1}{n} \sum_{r=1}^{n} \sum_{\ell=1}^{L} \beta_\ell x_{\ell rt}$$

(9.37)

$$- \log \left(\sum_{r=1}^{n} \exp \left(\alpha_r + \sum_{\ell=1}^{L} \beta_\ell x_{\ell rt} + \varepsilon_{rt} \right) \right)$$

where

---

36. For a more thorough discussion see Cooper, Nakanishi (1988, pp. 62-65).
37. We closely follow Foekens (1995, pp. 168-169).

$$\tilde{m}_t = \text{geometric mean of } m_{jt}, \tilde{m}_t = \left[\prod_{r=1}^{n} m_{rt} \right]^{1/n},$$

$$\bar{\alpha} = \frac{1}{n} \sum_{r=1}^{n} \alpha_r,$$

$$\bar{\varepsilon}_t = \frac{1}{n} \sum_{r=1}^{n} \varepsilon_{rt}.$$

If we subtract (9.37) from (9.36) we obtain the following form, which is linear in the parameters:

$$\log m_{jt}/\tilde{m}_t = \alpha_j - \bar{\alpha} + \sum_{\ell=1}^{L} \beta_\ell x_{\ell jt} - \frac{1}{n} \sum_{r=1}^{n} \sum_{\ell=1}^{L} \beta_\ell x_{\ell rt} + \varepsilon_{jt} - \bar{\varepsilon}_t, \qquad (9.38)$$

$$= \alpha_j^* + \sum_{\ell=1}^{L} \beta_\ell \left(x_{\ell jt} - \frac{1}{n} \sum_{r=1}^{n} x_{\ell rt} \right) + \varepsilon_{jt}^*.$$

The intercepts α_j can be estimated up to an arbitrary constant. If $\alpha_1 = 0$ the above equation can be written as:

$$\log(m_{jt}/\tilde{m}_t) = \sum_{r=2}^{n} (d_r - \frac{1}{n})\alpha_r + \sum_{r=1}^{n} \sum_{\ell=1}^{L} (d_r - \frac{1}{n}) x_{\ell rt} \beta_\ell + \varepsilon_{jt}^* \qquad (9.39)$$

where

$$d_r = 1 \text{ if } r = j, \text{ and } 0 \text{ otherwise.}$$

Model (9.39) requires transformations of all the variables. There is an equivalent model of (9.39) which yields identical estimates for both intercepts and response parameters but does not require any variable transformation apart from taking logarithms of m_{jt}. This model has the form:[38]

$$\log m_{rt} = \alpha_0 + \sum_{r=2}^{n} d_r \alpha_r + \sum_{t'=2}^{T} D_{t'} \Theta_{t'} + \sum_{\ell=1}^{L} \beta_\ell x_{\ell rt} + \varepsilon_{rt} \qquad (9.40)$$

where

$$\alpha_0 = \text{overall intercept,}$$
$$D_{t'} = 1 \text{ if } t' = t \text{ and } 0 \text{ otherwise.}$$

---

38. See Nakanishi, Cooper (1982).

Equation (9.40) has the same structure as (9.38) where $\Theta_{t'} + \alpha_0$ is interpreted as an estimate for the logarithm of the denominator of (9.25) for period t'. Equation (9.40) involves T additional parameters α_0 and $\Theta_{t'}$, $t' = 2, \ldots, T$.[39,40]

---

39. This has consequences for the degrees of freedom and the estimated standard errors. See Foekens (1995, p. 169).

40. We do not discuss the assumptions of the disturbances nor the estimation techniques required to estimate these relations. For details, see Bultez, Naert (1975).

CHAPTER 10

Specifying models according to amount of behavioral detail

As we indicated in Section 4.3, model detail can be considered from different angles. In this chapter we concern ourselves with the amount of *behavioral* detail a model contains. The "amount of behavioral detail" is not easily measured. Therefore, we use qualitative descriptions for a comparison of models in terms of behavioral detail. A higher level of behavioral detail usually implies that the model contains a larger number of variables, especially intervening variables (see Figure 10.1). It also tends to mean more equations and more parameters to estimate.

We distinguish three categories:

1. models with no behavioral detail;
2. models with some behavioral detail;
3. models with a substantial amount of behavioral detail.

The demarcation between "some" and "a substantial amount" is subjective. We provide illustrations to suggest typical examples of the three categories. Distinguishing models by the "amount of behavioral detail" is important because the categorization is a major determinant of ease (or difficulty) of estimation and validation (Chapters 16, 17 and 18).

In Section 10.1, we define what is meant by models without behavioral detail. Many of the examples discussed in previous chapters fit into this category. We offer some new-product evaluation models as examples of models with some behavioral detail in Section 10.2.

In Section 10.3, we illustrate the case of a substantial amount of behavioral detail with a Structural Equation Model (SEM). We conclude this chapter by indicating differences in (ease of) estimation and validation based on the level of behavioral detail. We also argue that cost-benefit considerations should play a role in the model-building process with respect to the appropriate level of detail.

179

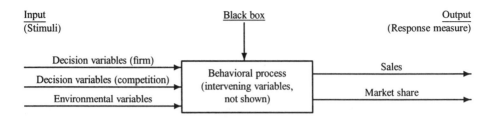

Figure 10.1 Model with no behavioral detail.

10.1 Models with no behavioral detail

By "behavioral detail" in a marketing model we mean that the model shows how marketing variables (e.g. advertising) influence variables such as brand awareness, brand knowledge, brand image, attitude toward a brand, motivation to purchase and similar psychological variables. These intervening variables in turn influence purchase behavior. In models with "no behavioral detail", the behavioral process, i.e. the process by which stimuli relate to intervening variables, and the process by which intervening and often unobservable variables relate to behavior, is not made explicit but is treated as a black box. Thus, models with no behavioral detail show only how response measures of ultimate behavior, such as sales and market share, relate to marketing decision variables (for a firm and its competitors) and environmental variables. We show this idea in Figure 10.1.[1]

We note that the illustrations in Chapter 9 fit the definition of a model with no behavioral detail. This is also true for many of the examples given in earlier chapters, such as the optimal advertising budget model in Section 8.3.1. We therefore do not provide other examples of this class of models.

10.2 Models with some behavioral detail

We distinguish between the inclusion of some behavioral elements at the individual level and at the aggregate level. Examples of the first category include some of the stochastic brand choice models in Chapter 12.

Models containing some behavioral detail at the aggregate level are called *aggregate flow* or *macro flow* models. Flow refers to the movements of consumers from one state to another until they reach the final state in which a decision to buy (or not to buy) is made. The aggregate level means that the model does not focus on states of individual consumers but instead focuses on aggregates of consumers.

In this book we discuss three kinds of macro flow models:

1. Models of intermediate market response. In these models stimuli are related to a set of intermediate variables, the transition frequencies. The transition frequencies

---

1. See also Figure 4.1.

represent the percentages of people moving from one state (brand choice in t) to another (brand choice in $t + 1$). These transition frequencies are linked to the ultimate response measure (market share). We discuss these models briefly in Chapter 12.

2. Diffusion models (see below).
3. Adoption models (see below).

Many new products introduced in the market place will not achieve the required results and will therefore be withdrawn from the market within a few years of introduction. Since a large part of the costs for new product development and introduction occurs after the research and development process is completed, managers need models to minimize costs. The models should provide accurate forecasts of new-product sales, and show how sales depend on product characteristics and marketing variables. Such diagnostic information allows managers to make adjustments in controllable variables, so that new-product success rates can be improved.

Diffusion models describe the spread of an innovation among a set of prospective adopters over time. A diffusion model depicts successive increases in the number of adopters and predicts the continued development of a diffusion process already in progress (Mahajan, Muller, Bass, 1993). The focus is generally on the generation of the product life cycle to forecast the first-purchase sales volume.

Diffusion models are based on the assumption that the diffusion of a new product is a social process of imitation. For example, early adopters influence late adopters to purchase the new product. Positive interaction between current adopters and later adopters is assumed to bring about the (rapid) growth of the diffusion process.

Category sales for a new durable product such as televisions for high definition (HDTV) broadcasts can be pictured as in Figure 10.2. Sales start out slowly but move at an increasing rate, then continue prior to t^* at a decreasing rate until a maximum is reached at t^*, after which sales decline. Sales do not tend to zero because new households (e.g. young couples) become potential buyers. Also, existing households will replace initial purchases and purchase additional units (see e.g. Bayus, Hong, Labe, 1989). Thus, once households purchase a second unit, or replace the first one, the interest in modeling goes beyond first-purchase sales volumes. The general shape of this curve has useful implications for the marketing and production of such products over their life cycle. The effectiveness of decisions depends on the availability of valid and reliable forecasts of the time (t^*) and the magnitude (Q_t^*) of peak sales.

Most ("classical") diffusion models assume the following:[2]

1. there are only two "consumer states", consumers who have adopted (i.e. made a first purchase) and consumers who have not (yet) adopted;
2. the total number of potential adopters is fixed;
3. the purchase volume per buyer is one unit, i.e. there are no replacements or repeat purchases and no multiple adoptions.

---

2. See also Lilien, Rangaswamy (1998, pp. 202-203).

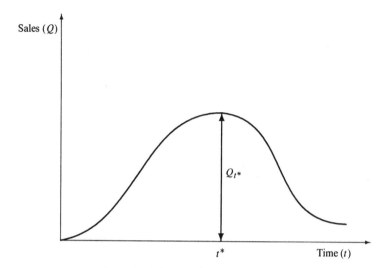

Figure 10.2 Sales of a new consumer durable over time.

Adoption models describe the stages of adoption processes.[3] Adoption processes represent the sequence of stages through which consumers progress from unawareness of an innovation to ultimate adoption. The adoption framework can be used by managers to determine the potential viability of a new product at *pre-test market* and *test market stages* of the new-product development process. By contrast, diffusion models are used to describe the early sales history of a new product and to forecast the time and the magnitude of peak sales. The differences between adoption and diffusion models have been characterized by Mahajan and Wind (1986, p. 15) as follows:

> *"Whereas the adoption models capture richness and reality, the diffusion models embrace simplicity and parsimony."*

Thus, adoption models generally contain more behavioral detail than diffusion models do.

DIFFUSION MODELS

The general structure of a *diffusion model* can be represented as:

$$\frac{dN(t)}{dt} = g(t)[\bar{N} - N(t)] = g[N(t)][\bar{N} - N(t)] \tag{10.1}$$

where

$N(t)$ = cumulative number of adopters at time t,

$g(t)$ = the coefficient of diffusion, which is usually
formulated as a function of $N(t)$,

3. The following text is partly based on Nijkamp (1993, pp. 53-54).

$\bar{N}$ = the total number of potential adopters, e.g.
consumers who ultimately adopt.

In the differential equation (10.1), the rate of diffusion of an innovation is assumed to be proportional to the difference between the total number of potential adopters $(\bar{N})$ and the number of adopters at that time. The term $[\bar{N} - N(t)]$ is often called the "untapped" potential, i.e., the remaining number of potential adopters. The proportionality coefficient is usually formulated as a function of the cumulative number of adopters:

$$g(t) = \alpha_0 + \alpha_1 N(t) + \alpha_2 (N(t))^2 + \dots. \tag{10.2}$$

In many diffusion models (10.2) is linear ($\alpha_2, \alpha_3, \dots = 0$):

$$g(t) = \alpha_0 + \alpha_1 N(t). \tag{10.3}$$

Substituting (10.3) in (10.1) gives:

$$\frac{dN(t)}{dt} = [\alpha_0 + \alpha_1 N(t)][\bar{N} - N(t)]. \tag{10.4}$$

For $\alpha_0, \alpha_1 > 0$, (10.4) is known as the *mixed-influence model*. An increase in $N(t)$ is modeled as the sum of two terms, each having its own interpretation. For $\alpha_1 = 0$, we obtain the *(single) external influence* model (10.5):

$$\frac{dN(t)}{dt} = \alpha_0 [\bar{N} - N(t)] \tag{10.5}$$

where

α_0 = the external conversion parameter.

The parameter α_0 represents the influence of a "change agent" in the diffusion process, which may capture any influence other than that from previous adopters. In (10.5) it is assumed that there is no interpersonal communication between consumers in the social system. Thus, the change in $N(t)$, $\frac{dN(t)}{dt}$ is assumed to be due to the effects of mass communications (advertising) (Mahajan, Peterson, 1985, Mahajan, Muller, Bass, 1993).

The *(single) internal influence* diffusion model (10.6) is based on a contagion paradigm that implies that diffusion occurs through interpersonal contacts:

$$\frac{dN(t)}{dt} = \alpha_1 N(t)[\bar{N} - N(t)]. \tag{10.6}$$

In (10.6) the rate of diffusion is a function of the interaction between prior adopters $N(t)$ and the (remaining) potential adopters $[\bar{N} - N(t)]$. The parameter α_1 can be interpreted as the word-of-mouth effect of previous buyers upon potential buyers.

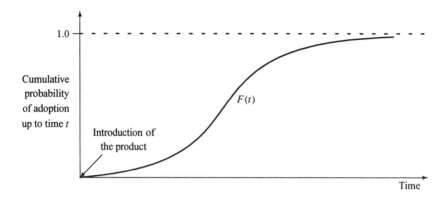

Source: Lilien, Rangaswamy (1998, p. 199).

Figure 10.3 Cumulative probability that a customer in the target segment will adopt the product before t.

The linear differential equation (10.4) can be solved to obtain:

$$N(t) = \frac{\bar{N} - [\alpha_0(\bar{N} - N_0)/(\alpha_0 + \alpha_1 N_0)] \exp\{-(\alpha_0 + \alpha_1 \bar{N})t\}}{1 + [\alpha_1(\bar{N} - N_0)/(\alpha_0 + \alpha_1 N_0)] \exp\{-(\alpha_0 + \alpha_1 \bar{N})t\}} \tag{10.7}$$

where

$$N_0 = \text{the cumulative number of adopters at } t' = 0.$$

In the *external* influence model (10.5) $\alpha_1 = 0$. Substituting this value in (10.7) and setting $N_0 = 0$ gives:

$$N(t) = \bar{N}[1 - \exp\{-\alpha_0 t\}] \tag{10.8}$$

which is the continuous formulation of the penetration model developed by Fourt and Woodlock (1960).

In the *internal* influence model (10.6), $\alpha_0 = 0$. Substituting this value into (10.7) gives:

$$N(t) = \bar{N} / \left[1 + \frac{\bar{N} - N_0}{N_0} \exp\{-\alpha_1 \bar{N}t\} \right] \tag{10.9}$$

which is a logistic curve (compare (5.53)).

A specific mixed-influence model is the Bass model (Bass, 1969b). The model can be formulated in absolute terms (number of adopters, sales) or in relative terms (the fraction of potential adopters who adopted the product at time t: $F(t)$). In *absolute terms* the Bass model can be specified as:

$$\frac{dN(t)}{dt} = [p + \frac{q}{\bar{N}} N(t)][\bar{N} - N(t)] \tag{10.10}$$

where

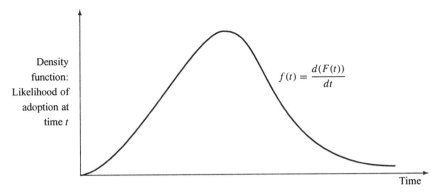

Source: Lilien, Rangaswamy (1998, p. 199).

Figure 10.4 Density function: likelihood that a consumer adopts the product at t.

p = the coefficient of innovation,
q = the coefficient of imitation.

Relation (10.10) can also be written as:

$$n(t) = \frac{dN(t)}{dt} = p[\bar{N} - N(t)] + \frac{q}{\bar{N}}N(t)[\bar{N} - N(t)] \qquad (10.11)$$

where

$n(t)$ = number of initial purchases at t.

The first term in (10.11) represents adoptions due to buyers who are not influenced in the timing of their adoption by the number of people who have already bought the product ("innovators"). The second term represents adoptions due to buyers who are influenced by the number of previous buyers ("imitators").

The Bass model is usually specified in *relative terms*: $F(t)$ is the (cumulative) probability that someone in the market or in the target segment will adopt the innovation by time t, where $F(t)$ approaches 1 as t gets larger. Such a function is depicted in Figure 10.3. The derivative of $F(t)$ is the probability density function (Figure 10.4) which indicates the rate at which the probability of adoption is changing over time.

Relation (10.11) can also be written as:

$$n(t) = p\bar{N} + (q - p)N(t) - \frac{q}{\bar{N}}(N(t))^2. \qquad (10.12)$$

The first-order differential equation (10.12) can be integrated to yield the S-shaped cumulative adopters distribution, $N(t)$. Once $N(t)$ is known, differentiation yields an expression for the non-cumulative number of adopters, $n(t)$, the time (t^*) and the magnitude of ($n(t^*)$ and $N(t^*)$) the peak of the adoption curve. We provide relevant expressions in Table 10.1.

Table 10.1 Analytical expressions for the Bass model.

Item	Expression
Cumulative number of adopters	$N(t) = \bar{N}\left[\dfrac{1 - e^{-(p+q)t}}{1 + \frac{q}{p}e^{-(p+q)t}}\right]$
Noncumulative number of adopters	$n(t) = \bar{N}\left[\dfrac{p(p+q)^2 e^{-(p+q)t}}{(p + qe^{-(p+q)t})^2}\right]$
Time of peak adoptions	$t^* = -\dfrac{1}{p+q}\ln\left(\dfrac{p}{q}\right)$
Number of adopters at the peak time	$n(t^*) = \dfrac{1}{4q}(p+q)^2$
Cumulative number of adopters at the peaktime	$N(t^*) = \bar{N}\left[\dfrac{1}{2} - \dfrac{p}{2q}\right]$
Cumulative number of adoptions due to innovators	$N_1(t) = \bar{N}\dfrac{p}{q}\ln\left[\dfrac{1 + \frac{q}{p}}{1 + \frac{q}{p}e^{-(p+q)t}}\right]$
Cumulative number of adoptions due to imitators	$N_2(t) = N(t) - N_1(t)$

Source: Mahajan, Muller, Bass (1993, p. 354).

Relation (10.12) can also be written in a simpler format:

$$n(t) = \beta_0 + \beta_1 N(t) + \beta_2 (N(t))^2. \tag{10.13}$$

Relation (10.13) is discretized by replacing continuous time t by discrete time periods, where t is the current period, $t + 1$ is the next period, and so on. With this modification the parameters of the following linear function can be estimated with ordinary least squares:[4]

$$n_t = \gamma_0 + \gamma_1 N_{t-1} + \gamma_2 N_{t-1}^2 + u_t \tag{10.14}$$

where

$$u_t = \text{a disturbance term.}$$

Bass applied this model to sales over time of eleven major appliance innovations, including air conditioners, electric refrigerators, home freezers, black-and-white television and power lawnmowers. We show the estimates for power lawnmowers in Table 10.2. The estimates of γ_0, γ_1 and γ_2 can be used to compute $\bar{N}$, p, q, t^*, and $N(t^*)$. In the case of power lawnmowers, the values are: $\bar{N} = 44{,}751{,}000$, $p = .009$, $q = .338$, $t^* = 10.3$, and "peak sales" ($N(t^*)$) is about 4,000,000. The peak actually occurred in period 10, and actual peak sales were about 4,200,000. Actual and predicted sales are shown in Figure 10.5.

---

4. The model can also be estimated with non-linear regression (Lilien, Rangaswamy, 1998). It has been shown that the non-linear least squares estimator is biased. Parameter estimates change systematically as one extends the number of observations used for estimation (Vanden Bulte, Lilien, 1997).

Table 10.2 Parameter estimates for power lawnmowers.

Symbol	Parameter Estimate	t Statistic
$\gamma_0(10^3)$	411	1.94
γ_1	0.33	7.41
$\gamma_2(10^{-7})$	−0.08	−4.74

The Bass model and its revised and extended forms have been used for forecasting innovation diffusion in retail service, industrial technology, agricultural, educational, pharmaceutical, and consumer durable good markets. Companies that have used the model include Eastman Kodak, RCA, IBM, Sears, and AT&T (Bass, 1986). Since the original publication of the Bass model, research on the modeling of the diffusion of innovations in marketing has resulted in an extensive literature.[5]

In the preceding description it is assumed that individual consumer response and aggregate response have identical functions. Since the decision to adopt an innovation is individual-specific, all potential adopters cannot have the same probability of adopting the product in a given time period. Thus, attempts have been made to develop diffusion models by specifying adoption decisions at the individual level.[6]

Some of the extended models incorporate price, advertising or firm size (Nooteboom, 1989).[7] Bass, Krishnan and Jain (1994) developed the Generalized Bass Model (GBM) that includes marketing decision variables. The GBM reduces to the Bass Model (BM) as a special case, i.e., if the decision variables are irrelevant. If percentage changes in period-to-period values of the decision variables are approximately, but not exactly, constant, the GBM provides approximately the same fit as the BM. On the other hand, if the coefficients of the decision variables are statistically significantly different from zero, the GBM provides explanations for deviations of the (actual) data from the smooth (fitted) curve of BM and an improved fit.

The GBM can be represented as follows:

$$P_t = [p + q F(t)]x(t) \tag{10.15}$$

where

P_t = probability of adoption at time t, given no adoption prior to t, and

$x(t)$ = current marketing effort.

The current marketing effort reflects the current effect of (dynamic) marketing variables on the conditional probability of adoption at time t. The dynamic part implies

---

5. For reviews of this literature see Mahajan, Muller, Bass (1990, 1993) and Nijkamp (1993). Putsis, Balasubramanian, Kaplan and Sen (1997) model the diffusion of sales in four product categories across ten European countries.
6. See, for example, Chatterjee, Eliashberg (1990).
7. See, for example, Kamakura, Balasubramanian (1988) and for a survey Bass, Krishnan, Jain (1994). See also Mahajan, Muller (1998), Kim, Bridges, Srivastava (1999).

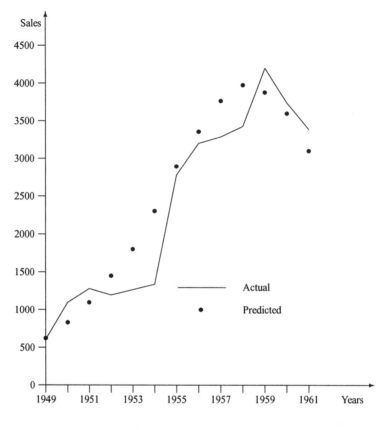

Source: Bass (1969b, p. 223).

Figure 10.5 Actual and predicted sales for power lawnmowers.

that $x(t)$ can incorporate lags in the decision variables.

ADOPTION MODELS

Aggregate adoption models differ from diffusion models in a number of ways. For example, adoption models usually deal with frequently purchased items although there are also examples of these models which forecast the adoption of durables.[8] The aggregate models are based on adoption processes conceptualized at the individual level. In these processes one may distinguish the following steps:[9]

1. *awareness,* in which the individual becomes cognizant of a new product in terms of its existence, but not necessarily with regard to the benefits offered by the product;

8. See Urban, Hauser, Roberts (1990), Urban (1993).
9. These steps were identified by Rogers (1962).

2. *interest,* the stage in which the individual is stimulated to seek more detailed information about the new product;
3. *evaluation,* in which the individual considers whether the new product provides sufficient value relative to its cost;
4. *trial,* the stage in which the individual tries the new product;
5. *adoption,* the stage in which the individual decides to make full and regular use of the new product.

The explicit specification of the fifth stage means that adoption models are particularly suited as *repeat purchase models.* We note that the *interactions* between adopters are not explicitly considered in adoption models.

The marketing literature includes a large number of adoption models,[10] which may be due to the high costs and high risks inherent in the introduction of a new product. Particularly important contributions were made by Urban. First for new industrial products[11] and later for frequently purchased consumer goods,[12] Urban created a new-product evaluation model with modular structure called SPRINTER, which stands for Specification of PRofit with INTERaction.[13] The interdependencies refer to the new brand and its relation to established brands in a product line of the firm that introduces the new brand. Although the SPRINTER model has been succeeded by other "more implementable" models, its structure is an excellent illustration of a macro flow adoption model.

In its simplest form[14] this new-product model contains the elements in Figure 10.6. Three consumer states or experience classes are distinguished. The *pretrial* class consists of potential triers who have no experience with the new brand. In a specific time interval some people of the pretrial class buy the new brand and move to the prerepeat class, which consists of potential repeaters. These "purchases" are shown in black in Figure 10.6. When these consumers buy the new brand again, they move to the preloyal class, the class of potentially loyal consumers of the new brand. They stay in this class when they repurchase the brand a second time, etc.

When consumers in an experience class purchase a competitive brand instead of a new brand, they move to the "preceding" experience class. This is denoted by the white arrows in Figure 10.6.

The SPRINTER model was programmed in a conversational mode. In other words, the model user interacts with the computer model via a terminal which feeds questions from the terminal to which the user responds. An example session is given in Table 10.3.[15] This table represents the main parts of the input for a SPRINTER Mod.I

---

10. See for some surveys Narasimhan, Sen (1983), Mahajan, Muller, Sharma (1984), Shocker, Hall (1986), Mahajan, Wind (1988) and Urban (1993).

11. Urban (1968).

12. See Urban (1969a, 1970) and Urban, Karash (1971).

13. Urban (1968). In another publication (Urban, 1970) the acronym SPRINTER stands for Specification of PRofits with INTERdependencies. See also Nijkamp (1993, p. 135).

14. Urban (1969a) labelled this SPRINTER version "Mod.I".

15. This is the simplest output option of Mod.I. The user's inputs are underlined.

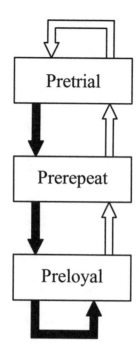

Source: Nijkamp (1993, p. 120).

Figure 10.6 Diagram of SPRINTER Mod. I.

version. We explain some points. In line 5, the user specifies the size of the target group. This number can either be constant over time or one can allow the size to vary, for example, due to seasonality. To accomplish this, one types ADD PERIOD, after which one can add a time index to let the target group size vary (in the example over 36 months).

The time period is usually taken as the smallest interpurchase time interval, for example one month. The illustration shows in line 8 that in time, five percent of the users buy every month, eight percent every two months, etc. For mature product categories, such a distribution can be obtained from survey or household purchase data.

The data provided by the model user (new product manager, marketing manager, etc.) in the terminal session (Table 10.3) are inputs in the new-product model shown in Figure 10.6.

The model predicts for each period the *number of people in each class* and the *number of buyers per class*. The output also contains market share information, profit per period, cumulative discounted profit (not shown in Table 10.3).[16]

---

16. For a number of other versions of SPRINTER see Nijkamp (1993).

Table 10.3 Example of a session of SPRINTER Mod.I.

1.	brand name	:	soapy
2.	period length	:	month
3.	name of first period	:	april
4.	number of periods	:	36
5.	size of the target group (in thousands)	:	add period

period 1: 14700
period 2: 14700
period 3: 13000
period 4: 13000
period 5: 13000

⋮ ⋮

period 36: 14600

6. trial rates (%)

period 1: 3.08
period 2: 2.86
period 3: 2.64
period 4: 2.42
period 5: 2.09

⋮ ⋮

period 36: 1.98

7.	maximum purchase interval	:	8
8.	% with interpurchase interval[a]		

1 month: 5
2 month: 8
3 month: 10
4 month: 12

⋮ ⋮

8 month: 3

9.	repeat after one trail (%)	:	70.0
10.	repeat after two trails (%)	:	90.0
11.	advertising budget (thousands of $)	:	add period

period 1: 352.0
period 2: 274.0

⋮

period 36: 122.0

12.	fixed costs (thousands of $)	:	300.0
13.	target rate of return (%)	:	33.0
14.	price	:	1.06
15.	gross profit margin (% of price)	:	43.50

[a]Distribution of interpurchase times.

The SPRINTER model requires a substantial amount of information in terms of inputs. Data collection is needed for the following:

1. the size of the target group;
2. the trial rates, i.e. the fraction of people in the target group who will try the product, in each period;
3. the distribution of interpurchase times;
4. the fraction of triers making a first repeat purchase;
5. the fraction of repeaters making an additional repeat purchase.

Clearly models with (more) behavioral detail require more data inputs than models with no behavioral detail.

Many *implementable* adoption models have been developed since the early eighties. Examples are BBDO's NEWS model,[17] the LITMUS[18] and ASSESSOR.[19]

ASSESSOR was initially marketed in the U.S. by Management Decision Systems, Inc. (MDS), then by Information Resources Inc. (IRI) and subsequently by M/A/R/C Inc.[20] In Europe ASSESSOR was introduced by NOVACTION.

As of 1997 both in Europe and in the USA, BASES accounts for the majority of pre-test-market new-product/concept evaluations. The services offered by BASES center around a system for consumer reactions to concepts or new products prior to test market or market introduction. The consumer reactions, along with planned media schedules, promotional activities and distribution, are used to predict sales volumes for the first two years. These predicted volumes are based on the information obtained from a sample of consumers who belong to the target market and who agree to participate after recruitment in a shopping mall. The consumers provide responses that allow BASES to estimate trial rates, repeat sales, transaction sizes and purchase frequencies. Importantly, due to the large number of commercial studies conducted, BASES uses its database to make various adjustments. For example, the first repeat rate, which is estimated from an after-use purchase intent, is adjusted for product-category specific and culture specific overstatements, price/value perceptions, intensity of liking perceptions, purchase cycle claims, etc. Thus, the usefulness of a service such as BASES is not indicated just by the quality of the modeling and the consumer responses. By linking actual new-product results to the consumer responses, based on factors such as product category and target market characteristics, one can improve the validity of market projections.

The ASSESSOR model is one of the few commercial models published in academic journals.[21] According to published results the success rate of new products that go through an ASSESSOR evaluation is 66 percent, compared with a success rate of

17. Pringle, Wilson, Brody (1982).
18. Blackburn, Clancy (1980).
19. See Silk, Urban (1978).
20. See Urban (1993).
21. See Urban, Katz (1983).

35 percent to products that do not undergo a formal pretest analysis.[22] By contrast, only 4 percent of new products that "failed" in ASSESSOR, but were introduced in the market anyway, succeeded. Also, the correlation between predicted and actual market shares is reported to be very high (0.95).

ASSESSOR and other pre-test-market models can be useful for marketing decisions in several ways. One is that test markets are expensive, take a long time, and can provide insights to competitors such that ultimate results are reduced. Thus, pretest market models can sometimes be used instead of test markets. If the pretest market model is an additional step in the new-product development process, one benefit is the reduction in risk. We discuss the expected financial impact of a pretest market module on the cost per successful new product in Chapter 20.

The ASSESSOR-model is based on two submodels:

- a trial and repeat model;
- a preference model.

The reason for having two models is that if these two models provide similar forecasts one can have more confidence in the forecasts. In case of differences in the forecasts, there is an opportunity to identify what unusual characteristics are present in the new product that require special attention. The trial-repeat model is estimated with consumer trials of products in a specially created store environment, and follow-up contacts to capture repeat in at-home use. The preference model is estimated from survey responses about the new product and established brands familiar to the respondents. Both models also use management judgment about variables such as brand awareness and -availability.

Consumers are typically screened in shopping malls. Given agreement to participate, they enter a testing facility. Participants complete a survey about awareness of existing brands and the consideration set of brands for purchases in the product category to which the new product might belong.[23] In addition, participants are asked about the brands in the product category they have purchased in the immediate past and their preferences for the brands in their consideration sets. The preference model transforms the measured preferences of the participants into choice probabilities.[24]

Participants who do not choose the new brand in the store laboratory receive a small size sample of the new brand. In this manner, all participants have an opportunity to try the new product. After a short period, sufficiently long for most consumers to experience product usage, the participants are contacted at their homes. Many of the questions are the same as those asked in the store laboratory. In addition, consumers are asked about product usage and are given an opportunity to (re)purchase the new product. Having collected trial and repeat data, it is then possible to predict the new product's market share. Similarly, the preference data after product usage are used to obtain a second prediction of market share. Both of these predictions are

---

22. Lilien, Rangaswamy (1998, p. 211).
23. For detailed descriptions, see Silk, Urban (1978), Urban (1993) or Lilien, Rangaswamy (1998, pp. 204-211).
24. See, for example, equation (9.8).

adjusted based on available information on such aspects as consideration set, brand awareness and -availability.

The (long-run) market share of the new product is predicted by the trial-repeat model as follows:

$$\hat{m}_j = \frac{\widehat{N(t)}}{N^*} \cdot \hat{\pi} \cdot w \tag{10.16}$$

where

$\hat{m}_j$ = the predicted value of the long-run market share of the new brand j,

$N(t)$ = the cumulative number of adopters,

N^* = the size of the target segment,

π = the proportion of those trying the new product who will become long-run repeat purchasers of the new product,

w = relative usage rate, with $w = 1$ the average usage rate in the market.

This model was originally formulated by Parfitt and Collins (1968). In ASSESSOR the components $N(t)/N^*$ and π are disaggregated in a number of macro flows:

$$\frac{\widehat{N(t)}}{N^*} = F \cdot K \cdot D + C \cdot U - (F \cdot K \cdot D)(C \cdot U) \tag{10.17}$$

where

F = long-run probability of trial assuming 100 percent awareness and distribution,

K = long-run probability of awareness,

D = long-run probability of availability in retail outlets (weighted distribution fraction),

C = probability that a consumer receives a sample,

U = probability that a consumer who receives a sample uses the sample.

The first right-hand term in (10.17), $F \cdot K \cdot D$, is quantified by the proportion of consumers who will be aware of the new brand (management judgment), have access to it in a store (management judgment) and try it (laboratory store results). The second term $C \cdot U$, represents the fraction of target market consumers who receive a sample of the new brand (management judgment) and use it (home contact). The third term adjusts for double counting those who both purchase the new product in a store for trial and receive a sample (since in the marketplace these two events are not mutually exclusive).

The repeat rate π is calculated as the equilibrium share of a two-state Markov process. It can be shown that:

$$\hat{\pi} = \frac{\hat{p}_{on}}{1 - \hat{p}_{nn} + \hat{p}_{on}} \qquad (10.18)$$

where

$\hat{p}_{on}$ = the estimated probability that a consumer who
purchases an other brand in period t, purchases the
new brand in $t + 1$,

$\hat{p}_{nn}$ = the estimated probability that a consumer purchases
the new brand in t and in $t + 1$.

We show in Section 12.3.1 how (10.18) is obtained. $\hat{p}_{on}$ is estimated from the proportion of consumers who did *not* "purchase" the new product in the test facility but say in the post-usage survey that they will buy the new product at the next purchase occasion. $\hat{p}_{nn}$ is the proportion of consumers who purchased the new product in the test facility and say in the post-usage survey that they will buy the product again.

10.3 Models with a substantial amount of behavioral detail

The models in this class are either:

1. *Micro-analytic simulation models,* which are models with behavioral details modeled at the individual consumer level, and for which the market response implications are explored via the technique of simulation; or
2. *Micro-analytic models,* where the behavioral details are also modelled at the individual consumer demand level, but where the market response implications are determined via analytic methods. Structural Equation Models (SEM) constitute a subset of these models. Other micro-analytic models with a substantial amount of behavioral detail are the purchase incidence models and the purchase timing models discussed in Chapter 12.

Simulation models provide a means for evaluating alternative marketing strategies in cases where analytical models are inadequate or inappropriate.[25] These models also permit interplay between empirical and subjective inputs.[26] Many micro-analytic simulation models have been developed in the sixties and seventies. Examples are Balderston, Hogatt (1962), Amstutz (1967, 1969) and Parasuraman, Day (1977).

Micro-analytic simulation models have also been developed to model the effects of promotions on consumer decision-making. Neslin and Shoemaker (1983) present a user-oriented model that simulates the effects of coupon promotions on sales and

---

25. Hanssens, Parsons, Schultz (1990, p. 274).
26. See for an example Lambin (1972b).

estimates net profitability. The model includes the actions of the manufacturer, retailers, and consumers. Krisha (1992, 1994) simulated the effects of consumer price expectations and retailer dealing patterns on consumer purchase behavior.

We use a structural equation model to illustrate a model with a substantial amount of behavioral detail. The model is described by Bagozzi (1994b) and is based on a study by Bagozzi, Baumgartner and Yi (1992). In this chapter we discuss the model's structure, but leave parameterization for Section 17.1.

The model is based on the theory of reasoned action (Fishbein, Ajzen, 1976, Ajzen, Fishbein, 1980). This theory posits that behavior is a function of a person's intention, which in turn is presumed to depend on that person's attitude toward the behavior and his/her subjective norms. An implication of the theory is that attitudes and subjective norms mediate the effects of other variables on intentions and that intentions mediate the impact of attitudes and subjective norms on behavior. A modification of the theory of reasoned action is that attitudes sometimes have direct effects on behavior. We show hypothesized relations in Figure 10.7.

In the model developed by Bagozzi et al. (1992), two segments of consumers are distinguished viz. action oriented- and state oriented consumers. Action orientation refers to a person's general tendency to approach (or avoid) things in a dynamic, active fashion: a high degree indicates readiness to act. Thus, for individuals who are action oriented the proportion of intentions that is transformed into behavior is high. People with a low self-regulatory capacity are state oriented. State orientation reflects inertia.

Bagozzi et al. developed a decision-related state- versus action-orientation scale with 20 forced-choice items. For each item one response alternative reflects state orientation and the other action orientation. It is hypothesized that attitudes influence intentions especially for action-oriented subjects, while subjective norms are expected to influence intentions especially for state-oriented subjects.

The model of Bagozzi et al. has been used to specify the antecedents of coupon usage for grocery shopping. For both groups of consumers the prior history of using coupons for grocery shopping is expected to play an important role in influencing intentions and current behavior.

Bagozzi's model of reasoned action is shown in the so-called path diagram of Figure 10.7. The structural or path model depicted in Figure 10.7 shows two types of constructs: observable and unobservable (latent). Unobservable constructs (ellipses in Figure 10.7) cannot be measured directly but can be related to indicators or observable variables. These indicators can, in principle, be measured and are indicated by squares in Figure 10.7. The relation between the latent variables in the structural model can be represented as:

$$\eta_2 = \beta_{21}\eta_1 + \gamma_{21}\xi_1 + \gamma_{23}\xi_3 + \zeta_2 \tag{10.19}$$

and

$$\eta_1 = \gamma_{11}\xi_1 + \gamma_{12}\xi_2 + \gamma_{13}\xi_3 + \zeta_1 \tag{10.20}$$

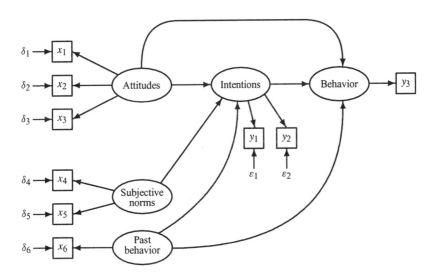

Source: based on Bagozzi (1994b, p. 366) .

*Figure 10.7 Relations between (coupon usage) behavior, intentions, attitudes, subjective norms
and past behavior.*

where

η_1 = intentions,

η_2 = behavior,

ξ_1 = attitudes,

ξ_2 = subjective norms,

ξ_3 = past behavior,

ζ_1, ζ_2 = disturbance terms.

The β_{21}-parameter represents the partial relation between the latent endogenous variables η_1 and η_2, while all γ-parameters represent partial relations between latent exogenous and endogenous variables. In this model it is assumed that coupon intentions are determined by the attitudes toward using coupons in the supermarket, subjective norms and past coupon usage. Coupon usage (behavior) is measured with a questionnaire which assesses people's self-reported coupon usage during a given week (y_3). Intentions are assessed by asking subjects to express their plans to use coupons in the same week. Two items (y_1 and y_2) are used to measure intentions viz. a seven-point likely/unlikely scale and a 11-point high/low probabilistic scale. Attitudes toward using coupons are assessed with three seven-point semantic differential scales: (x_1) pleasant/unpleasant, (x_2) good/bad and (x_3) favorable/unfavorable. Subjective norms are measured with two items, rated on seven-point scales, viz.

1. "most people who are important to me think I definitely should/definitely should not use coupons for shopping in the supermarket during the week" (x_4);
2. "most people who are important to me probably consider my use of coupons to be wise/foolish" (x_5).

Past coupon usage is measured with a single-item seven-point scale having endpoints of "I never use coupons" and "I use coupons every time I do my major shopping and generally redeem more than ten coupons" (x_6).

The latent variables are related to observable variables in the, so-called, measurement model. So, for example, the value of the variable "subjective norms" is determined by two observable variables x_4 and x_5:

$$x_4 = \lambda_{42}^* \xi_2 + \delta_4$$
$$x_5 = \lambda_{52}^* \xi_2 + \delta_5$$

(10.21)

where

$$x_4 = \text{the score on item 1,}$$
$$x_5 = \text{the score on item 2,}$$
$$\delta_4, \delta_5 = \text{measurement errors.}$$

For the other latent variables similar relations can be specified as is demonstrated in detail in Section 17.1. Cross-sectional data, measured at the individual level, are used to find "average" relations in this model with a substantial amount of behavioral detail.[27]

If we use the model-building criteria in Chapter 7, we find that models with a substantial amount of behavioral detail

• are not simple, and
• are not robust.

Although these types of models can provide useful insights, they are given limited attention in this book. This is because models with a substantial amount of behavioral detail are more difficult to implement, based on considerations of benefits and costs. Relative to models with no behavioral detail, an important benefit lies in the richness of representations of real-world phenomena. On the cost side we note that the inclusion of more behavioral detail implies:

a. models of greater complexity are more expensive to construct and use;
b. these models require more extensive forms of data collection;
c. parameter estimation is more difficult because there are alternative ways to define intervening variables, and measurement issues need to be addressed;
d. model validation is a more involved process.

---

27. Examples of other SEM's with a substantial amount of behavioral detail are Bagozzi, Silk (1983), Bearden, Teel (1983), Yi (1989), Oliver, De Sarbo (1988). See also Roberts, Lilien (1993), Bagozzi (1994b), Sharma (1996, Chapter 14).

We also note that richness of representation does not necessarily correlate positively with the benefits one derives from a model. This depends in part on the purpose of the model and on the problem one is trying to address. For example, marketing mix determination for an established brand in a mature market may be adequately accomplished with an (aggregate) market response model (assuming an absence of aggregation bias). Given a narrowly defined purpose it is unlikely that the addition of behavioral detail will improve a model's usefulness. On the other hand, if the problem is to make a GO-ON-NO decision for a new product, an aggregate flow model or a model of individual household adoption behavior should be more appropriate. Thus, a particular level of detail might be optimal in a cost-benefit sense for one type of problem, and not for another. The question of which level of detail is desirable will be easier to answer after we have studied the problem of parameterization in more depth. We, therefore, postpone further discussion until Chapter 20.

We have to keep in mind that the preceding evaluation is made from the point of view of the possible contributions of models to decision making in marketing. However, as we emphasized in Section 3.3, marketing models are also developed to discover generalizations that advance marketing knowledge. The value of many models with a substantial amount of behavioral detail may, to a large extent, be found in the area of theory construction. Thus, we restrict ourselves here to a discussion of the value of certain types of models from a usefulness perspective (in terms of cost-benefit considerations) for example, as decision aids, and not of their contribution to the development of the marketing discipline.

CHAPTER 11

Modeling competition

In modern marketing much attention is devoted to competition.[1] The intensity of competition may have increased over time because the economic climate of the (early) 1980s and (early) 1990s was characterized by minimal growth in many markets. Further, a higher rate of new-product introductions and reactions to new entries[2] may result from as well as contribute to a higher intensity of competition.

Many methods and models have been developed to diagnose competition. Day and Wensley (1988) dichotomize them into competitor-centered methods and customer-focused approaches. *Competitor-centered assessments* are based on direct management comparisons between the firm and a few target *competitors*. Such comparisons may include a determination of the relative strengths and weaknesses and a determination of the extent to which the marketing activities initiated by one firm are matched quickly by competitors. In Section 11.1 we discuss competitor-centered approaches in which competitive reactions are specified and calibrated.

Customer-focused assessments start with detailed analyses of customer benefits within end-use segments and work backward from the *customer* to the company to identify what actions are needed to improve performance. In Section 11.2 we describe one approach to customer-focused assessments by estimating market share response functions.

Given competitive reaction functions and market response functions the congruence between these two approaches can be identified as we show in Section 11.3.

In Section 11.3 we consider the "optimal" policies for *one* brand assuming particular reaction patterns of competition. The *simultaneous* optimum for all brands in the product class is studied in game-theoretic approaches which we introduce in Section 11.4. In this chapter we focus on models calibrated with aggregate (macro) data. In Chapter 12 we introduce models that describe competitive and market structures using individual/household (micro) data.

---

1. Sections (11.1)-(11.3) are based on Leeflang, Wittink (1992, 1994, 1996).
2. See, e.g. Robinson (1988), Gatignon, Anderson, Helsen (1989), Gatignon, Robertson, Fein (1997), Shankar (1997), Kalra, Rajiv, Srinivasan (1998).

11.1 Competitor-centered approaches to diagnose competition

Consider the following functions for Q, product class sales, and m, a brand's market share:

$$Q = Q_T(p, a, \tilde{x}, p_c, a_c, \tilde{x}_c, ev), \text{ and} \qquad (11.1)$$
$$m = m_j(p, a, \tilde{x}, p_c, a_c, \tilde{x}_c)$$

where

p, p_c = price of a brand (say brand j) and an index of
competitors' prices respectively,

$\tilde{x}, \tilde{x}_c$ = a quality measure for brand (j) and an index of
competitors' quality measures,

a, a_c = advertising expenditure of brand (j) and an index of
competitors' advertising expenditures, and

ev = a vector of environmental variables.

We do not use the index j for p, a and x to restrict the number of indices. We use (9.24) to define total brand j's sales elasticity with respect to its advertising ($\eta_{q,a}$) as the total product class elasticity ($\eta_{Q,a}$) plus the total market share elasticity with respect to brand j's advertising ($\eta_{m,a}$):

$$\eta_{q,a} = \eta_{Q,a} + \eta_{m,a}. \qquad (11.2)$$

These elasticity measures capture the effect of advertising for one brand on consumer demand. However, to capture the actual impact, we need to take into account how competitors react to changes in advertising for the brand and how this reaction modifies consumer demand. The competitive reactions belong to the set of competitor-centered approaches. Specifically, we distinguish *direct* and *indirect partial effects* of brand j's advertising on product class sales and brand j's market share. An indirect partial effect captures the following. If brand j changes its advertising expenditure level (Δa), competitors may react by adapting their spending level (Δa_c), and a_c in turn influences Q and/or m. In this explanation, as is usually assumed in oligopoly theory, competitors react with the same marketing instrument as the one which causes their reactions. Thus, competitors react to a change in price for j by a change in their prices, to a change in advertising by a response in advertising, etc. This type of reaction is defined as the *simple competitive reactions* case. It is more realistic, however, and consistent with the spirit of the *concept of the marketing mix* to accommodate *multiple competitive reactions*. In the latter case, a competitor may react to a change in price not just by changing his price, but also by changing his advertising as well as other marketing instruments.

We formalize the idea of having simple and multiple indirect reactions through reaction elasticities. With the general case of multiple competitive reactions we can write $\partial Q/\partial a$ and $\partial m/\partial a$ as follows:[3]

$$\frac{\partial Q}{\partial a} = \frac{\partial Q_T}{\partial a} + \frac{\partial Q_T}{\partial p_c}\frac{\partial p_c}{\partial a} + \frac{\partial Q_T}{\partial a_c}\frac{\partial a_c}{\partial a} + \frac{\partial Q_T}{\partial \tilde{x}_c}\frac{\partial \tilde{x}_c}{\partial a} \tag{11.3}$$

and

$$\frac{\partial m}{\partial a} = \frac{\partial m_j}{\partial a} + \frac{\partial m_j}{\partial p_c}\frac{\partial p_c}{\partial a} + \frac{\partial m_j}{\partial a_c}\frac{\partial a_c}{\partial a} + \frac{\partial m_j}{\partial \tilde{x}_c}\frac{\partial \tilde{x}_c}{\partial a}. \tag{11.4}$$

Multiplying both sides of (11.3) by a/Q, we obtain the product class elasticy, $\eta_{Q,a}$[4]:

$$\eta_{Q,a} = \eta_{Q_T,a} + (\rho_{p_c,a})(\eta_{Q_T,p_c}) + (\rho_{a_c,a})(\eta_{Q_T,a_c}) + (\rho_{\tilde{x}_c,a})(\eta_{Q_T,\tilde{x}_c}) \tag{11.5}$$

where

$\eta_{Q_T,a}$ = direct product class sales elasticity with respect to brand j's advertising,

η_{Q_T,u_c} = product class sales elasticity with respect to competitors' marketing instrument $u_c (= p_c, a_c,$ or $\tilde{x}_c)$, and

$\rho_{u_c,a}$ = reaction elasticity of competitors' instrument $u_c (= p_c, a_c,$ or $\tilde{x}_c)$ with respect to brand j's advertising expenditures.[5]

Similarly, $\eta_{m,a}$ can be decomposed as follows:

$$\eta_{m,a} = \eta_{m_j,a} + (\rho_{p_c,a})(\eta_{m_j,p_c}) + (\rho_{a_c,a})(\eta_{m_j,a_c}) + (\rho_{\tilde{x}_c,a})(\eta_{m_j,\tilde{x}_c}). \tag{11.6}$$

With (11.2) total brand sales elasticity $\eta_{q,a}$ is the sum of the components on the right-hand sides of (11.5) and (11.6):

$$\begin{aligned} \eta_{q,a} = {}& \eta_{Q_T,a} + (\rho_{p_c,a})(\eta_{Q_T,p_c}) + (\rho_{a_c,a})(\eta_{Q_T,a_c}) + (\rho_{\tilde{x}_c,a})(\eta_{Q_T,\tilde{x}_c}) \\ & + \eta_{m_j,a} + (\rho_{p_c,a})(\eta_{m_j,p_c}) + (\rho_{a_c,a})(\eta_{m_j,a_c}) + (\rho_{\tilde{x}_c,a})(\eta_{m_j,\tilde{x}_c}). \end{aligned} \tag{11.7}$$

Relations between specific elasticities, discussed in the literature, can be shown to be special cases of (11.7). We consider a few examples.[6] Bass (1969a) in a study of advertising and cigarettes, and Schultz (1971) in a study of competition between two airlines use:

$$\eta_{q,a} = \eta_{Q_T,a} + \eta_{m_j,a}. \tag{11.8}$$

This formulation allows product class demand to expand since $\eta_{Q_T,a}$ is not forced to be zero. However, no indirect effects are present. This may be an appropriate

---

3. In (11.3) and (11.4) $\partial Q_T/\partial a$, $\partial m_j/\partial a$ are the *direct* effects and $\partial Q/\partial a$, $\partial m/\partial a$ are the *total* effects.

4. To obtain $(\rho_{p_c,a})(\eta_{Q_T,p_c})$ multiply $\frac{\partial Q_T}{\partial p_c}\frac{\partial p_c}{\partial a}\frac{a}{Q}$ by $\frac{p_c}{p_c}$.

5. As other elasticities, $\rho_{u_c,a}$ is defined as $(\partial u_c/\partial a)(a/u_c)$.

6. The assumptions about competitive behavior are in many cases implicit.

representation for a *follower*, i.e. a competitor who assumes that other firms do not react to his decisions.

Lambin, Naert and Bultez (LNB) (1975) applied the concept of multiple competitive reactions to the market of a low-priced consumer durable good in West Germany. They used a multiplicative market share function, [7]

$$m_j = \alpha m^{\lambda}_{j,-1} (p^r)^{\beta_p} (a^r)^{\beta_a} (\tilde{x}^r)^{\beta_x} \tag{11.9}$$

where $u^r = u/u_c$, $u = p, a, \tilde{x}$ and $m_{j,-1} = m_{j,t-1}$. We showed in Section 5.3.2 that exponents in multiplicative relations are elasticities. Since $u^r = u/u_c$ it follows that:

$$\eta_{m_j,u^r} = \eta_{m_j,u} = -\eta_{m_j,u_c}. \tag{11.10}$$

If industry sales are insensitive to changes in marketing activities $\eta_{Q_T,u} = 0$. By using (11.10), we simplify (11.7) as follows:

$$\eta_{q,a} = (1 - \rho_{a_c,a})(\eta_{m_j,a^r}) - (\rho_{p_c,a})(\eta_{m_j,p^r}) - (\rho_{x_c,a})(\eta_{m_j,\tilde{x}^r}). \tag{11.11}$$

Estimation of (11.9) by Lambin et al. yielded the estimates:

$$\hat{\eta}_{m_j,a^r} = 0.147, \quad \hat{\eta}_{m_j,p^r} = -3.726 \text{ and } \hat{\eta}_{m_j,\tilde{x}^r} = 0.583.$$

The reaction elasticities were estimated from three multiplicative reaction functions,

$$u_c = \alpha_u p^{\rho_{u,p}} a^{\rho_{u,a}} \tilde{x}^{\rho_{u,\tilde{x}}} \tag{11.12}$$

where $u_c = p_c, a_c$, and $\tilde{x}_c$ for the three equations respectively. The estimates of the reaction elasticities to advertising for brand j were $\hat{\rho}_{a_c,a} = 0.273$, $\hat{\rho}_{p_c,a} = 0.008$, $\hat{\rho}_{x_c,a} = 0.023$.

Brand j's sales elasticity (here, the total market share elasticity, since $\eta_{Q_T,u} = 0$) can now be assessed by substituting the estimated market share and reaction elasticities in (11.11):

$$\hat{\eta}_{q,a} = (1 - 0.273)(0.147) - (0.008)(-3.726) - (0.023)(0.583),$$

i.e., the total brand sales elasticity $\hat{\eta}_{q,a}$ is 0.124 which compares with a direct (market share) elasticity of 0.147. Thus the net or total effect of advertising for brand j is smaller than the direct effect.

In the LNB-model it is assumed that the market consists of a leader who uses marketing instruments p, a and $\tilde{x}$ and a follower defined as the aggregate of the other firms. For example, $p_c = \sum_{r=2}^{n} p_r/(n - 1)$, $p = p_1$, $a_c = \sum_{r=2}^{n} a_r$, $a = a_1$, etc., where n = total number of brands and "1" indicates the leading brand.

In extended-LNB models, researchers made no distinction between leaders and followers. Instead they consider all brands separately in what amounts to a decomposition of competitive interactions. Leeflang and Reuyl (1985b) determined the interactions *for each set* of *two* brands. For L marketing instruments $x_\ell, \ell = 1 \ldots, L$

---

7. The time is omitted for convenience. Some of the variables in the reaction functions were specified with a one-period lag.

for each of n brands $j = 1, \ldots, n$, the following competitive reaction equations were estimated:

$$x_{\ell jt} = f[x_{\ell' rt}]_{\ell'=1,\ldots,L} \quad \ell, \ell' = 1, \ldots, L, \quad j, r = 1, \ldots, n, \quad j \neq r, \quad (11.13)$$
$$t = 1, \ldots, T$$

where $x_{\ell jt}$ is the value of the ℓ-th marketing instrument of brand j in period t. (Note that $\tilde{x}$, with a tilde, is a specific marketing instrument, viz. quality). In this extended model, the number of equations equals $Ln(n-1)$, compared with L equations for the LNB model. One difficulty with this model is that although all brands are allowed to compete with each other, each of the equations estimated uses predictors for only one other brand. Thus, the parameter estimates in (11.13) may be biased because relevant predictor variables are omitted.

Another example of an extended-LNB model is Hanssens' (1980b) model:[8]

$$x_{\ell jt} = f'([x_{\ell' rt}]_{\ell'=1,\ldots,L}, -[x_{\ell jt}]), \quad t = 1, \ldots, T. \quad (11.14)$$
$$r=1,\ldots,n$$

Equation (11.14) is more general than (11.13), in that it allows for joint decision making when $j = r$, that is, the possibility that changes in one variable are accompanied by changes in one or more *other* variables for a given brand. These relations between different variables for the same brand are known as *intrafirm* activities.

For (11.14) the number of equations to be estimated is Ln. While there are fewer equations than in (11.13), the large number of predictor variables may make the estimation of (11.14) difficult. For example, each equation may have $(Ln - 1)$ predictors, even if we do not consider time lags.

Gatignon (1984) and Plat and Leeflang (1988) extended Hanssens' (1980b) model in several directions. Gatignon's model simultaneously measures the effects of marketing mix variables on the reactions that may occur in different submarkets. The models Plat and Leeflang (1988) developed account for differences in the reactions of competitors operating in different market segments.

The data used to calibrate the reaction functions in the studies mentioned here concern manufacturers' actions and reactions. In the past, researchers used monthly, bimonthly, or quarterly data. With scanner data, researchers have new opportunities to study competitive reactions. Yet calibrating competitive reaction functions with weekly scanner data collected at the *retail level* also faces new problems. For example, changes in marketing activities may reflect actions and reactions of retailers as well as manufacturers. Price decisions for a brand, for example, are made ultimately by the retailers (Kim, Staelin, 1999). Temporary price cuts, displays, refunds, bonuses, etc. introduced at the retail level depend on the degree of acceptance (pass-through) of promotional programs by retailers. Thus, especially with scanner data, researchers who estimate competitive reaction functions should let the models reflect the roles of both manufacturers and retailers.

---

8. In (11.14), the "substraction" of $x_{\ell jt}$ means that instrument ℓ for brand j is *not* a predictor variable.

Leeflang and Wittink (1992) distinguish three categories of reactions: parallel movements, retailer-dominated reactions and manufacturer-dominated reactions. Competition between the seven brands in the market they consider is dominated by price and promotional programs.

Parallel movements are price or promotion fluctuations of brand j, $j = 1, \ldots, n$, that parallel the price fluctuations or promotional expenditures of other brands $r = 1, \ldots, n$, $j \neq r$ and occur in the same time period t or with a delay of one time period (one week). Such parallel movements may occur because of planned programs. For example, some retail chains may offer a price promotion for brand j when other chains do so for brand r. Parallel movements consist of a positive relation between competing brands' price variables (and between competing brands' promotions) and a negative relation between one brand's price movements and another brand's promotional expenditure changes.

Retailer-dominated reactions. If promotional activities in a product category are frequent, a retailer may run a promotional activity for one brand in one week followed by an activity for another brand in the next week. As a result, the price for brand j decreases as the price for brand r, $r \neq j$, increases, etc. In that case, we expect a negative relation between price movements for competing brands (and between promotions for competing brands) measured concurrently. Similarly a price decrease for one brand in week t may be followed by a promotional activity for another brand in week $(t + 1)$, resulting in a positive relation between those variables measured with a lag of one period in the reaction function. Retailer-dominated reactions are assumed to occur in the short run, either simultaneously or with a maximum lag of one period (one week).

In the longer run, within two to four weeks, retailers may react with price or promotion changes for brand j to changes in similar variables for competing brands. If these retailer activities are motivated by manufacturers' trade promotions, the nature and frequency of such activities for competing brands may reflect competitive reactions by manufacturers. In this case, partial relations with the same signs as those for parallel movements are expected.

Manufacturer-dominated reactions. For the measurement of manufacturers' reactions involving temporary price changes and other promotional variables, scanner data (showing retail sales and retailers' promotional activities) can reveal these reactions only if retailers cooperate with manufacturers. This cooperation often results from adaptive annual planning procedures which is assumed to take five to ten weeks. We expect these partial relations to have the same signs as those for parallel movements.

Leeflang and Wittink (1992) study the following marketing instruments: price *(p)*, sampling *(sa)*, refunds *(rf)*, bonus offers *(bo)* and featuring *(ft)* (retailer advertising). Competitive reaction functions are estimated for each of these marketing instruments for each brand. The criterion variables in the competitive reaction functions are expressed as changes. For price the logarithm of the ratio of prices in two successive periods is used. This is based on the idea that price changes for brands with different regular price levels are more comparable on a percentage than on an absolute basis.

Other promotional activities are specified in terms of simple differences, because zero values occur. To illustrate for the price of brand j (p_{jt}) the following competitive reaction function is specified:

$$\ln(p_{jt}/p_{j,t-1}) = \alpha_j + \sum_{\substack{r=1 \\ r \neq j}}^{n} \sum_{t^*=1}^{T^*+1} \beta_{jrt^*} \ln(p_{r,t-t^*+1}/p_{r,t-t^*}) \tag{11.15}$$

$$+ \sum_{t^*=2}^{T^*+1} \beta_{jjt^*} \ln(p_{j,t-t^*+1}/p_{j,t-t^*})$$

$$+ \sum_{r=1}^{n} \sum_{t^*=1}^{T^*+1} \sum_{x=1}^{4} \tau_{xjrt^*}(x_{r,t-t^*+1} - x_{r,t-t^*}) + \varepsilon_{jt},$$

$$\text{for } j = 1, \ldots, n \text{ and } t = (T^* + 2, \ldots, T)$$

where

$$x = 1 = sa, x = 2 = rf, x = 3 = bo, x = 4 = ft,$$
$$T^* = \text{the maximum number of time lags } (T^* = 10),$$
$$T = \text{the number of observations available,}$$
$$n = \text{the number of brands,}$$
$$\varepsilon_{jt} = \text{a disturbance term.}$$

Equation (11.15) includes lagged endogenous variables. This is done to account for the phenomenon that periods with heavy promotions are frequently followed by periods with relatively low promotional efforts.

An inspection of (11.15) makes it clear that the number of predictor variables is so large that it easily exceeds the number of observations.[9] Leeflang and Wittink (1992) used bivariate causality tests to select potentially relevant predictor variables.[10]

For all variable combinations, we show in Table 11.1 the number of times pairs of brands are "causally" related, based on bivariate tests. The maximum number for each of the cells in this table is 42 (excluding causal relations between different variables for the same brand). The largest number, 24, pertains to price-price relations. The smallest number, 2, refers to sampling-refund relations.

There are 256 significant relations (221+35) in Table 11.1, out of which 35 pertain to relations between variables for the same brand. These intrafirm activities are indicated in parentheses. Of the remaining 221 competitive reactions, 65 (29 percent) are simple (shown on the diagonal). This observed percentage is (significantly) different from an expected percentage of 20 percent if simple and other competitive relations are equally likely. Yet 156 (71 percent) of the estimated competitive reaction effects involve a different instrument. Thus, the results in Table 11.1 show that there is ample evidence of multiple competitive reactions.

---

9. For example, suppose that $n = 7$ (brands) each with five instruments, $T^* = 10$ (lagged periods), and $T = 76$.
10. For more detail on these tests, see Chapter 18.

Table 11.1 *Number of significant causal competitive reactions*
aggregated across all pairs of brands (with simple
competitive reactions shown cursively).

Predictor	Criterion Variable					
Variable	Price	Sampling	Refund	Bonus	Feature	Total
Price	*24*	4(1)	14(2)	11	9(5)	62(9)
Sampling	5(1)	*14*	2	4	18(13)	43(4)
Refund	5(3)	4(1)	*4*	6(2)	7(2)	26(8)
Bonus	12	8(1)	3(1)	*5*	9(2)	37(4)
Feature	13(4)	14(2)	4(2)	4(2)	*18*	53(10)
Total	59(8)	44(5)	27(6)	30(4)	61(12)	221(35)

Source: Leeflang, Wittink (1992, p.52).

The causality test results were used to specify the competitive reaction functions. Leeflang and Wittink obtained 171 significant reaction effects, of which some cases represent two different categories of reactions, such as, e.g. retailer- *and* manufacturer-dominated.

Table 11.2 summarizes the statistically significant effects with respect to the categorizations, stated in terms of parallel movements, short-run retailer-dominated reactions, long-run retailer-dominated reactions, and manufacturer-dominated reactions. For each criterion variable we show the frequencies with which each of the four types of reaction occur. The column totals show that the largest frequency of reaction effects occurs in the manufacturer-dominated reaction category, followed by the long-run retailer-dominated category. Similarly the row totals indicate that price is the most frequently used reaction instrument, followed by feature advertising.

These results illustrate the potential of competitive reaction function estimation. For a discussion of other models in which competitive reaction functions are calibrated, see Hanssens, Parsons and Schultz (1990, pp. 201-210) and more recently, Kadiyali, Vilcassim, Chintagunta (1999) and Vilcassim, Kadiyali, Chintagunta (1999). In all cases, the reaction functions attempt to capture how marketing instruments are used to react to changes in other instruments without regard to consumer response.

11.2 Customer-focused assessments to diagnose competition

A customer-focused approach to the use of marketing instruments is based on information about consumer sensitivity to changes in these instruments. Thus, a customer-focused assessment relies on estimated market response functions. These functions can be specified at different levels of demand. In this section we discuss an example in which the demand is specified at the market share level. In models of competitive interactions it is not realistic to assume that competitive behavior is symmetric. Sym-

Table 11.2 Frequency of statistically significant effects for four types of competitive reactions (excluding wrong signs and intrafirm effects).

Criterion variable	Parallel movement	Short-run Retailer-dominated reaction	Long-run Retailer-dominated reaction	Manufacturer-dominated reaction	Total
		Type of Reaction			
Price	11	5	9	25	50
Sampling	3	1	13	29	37
Refund	4	0	7	6	17
Bonus	2	3	7	12	24
Feature	12	3	11	17	43
Total	32	12	47	80	171

Source: Leeflang, Wittink (1992, p.55).

metric competitive behavior means that if the attraction of one brand changes by a given amount, the market share of any other brand is affected proportionally, no matter which brand's attraction has changed. However, competitive effects observed in the marketplace reveal that leading brands often take market share disproportionately from other brands (Cooper and Nakanishi, 1988, p. 56, Carpenter, Cooper, Hanssens and Midgley 1988, Foekens, Leeflang, Wittink, 1997, Cotterill, Putsis, Dhar, 1998 and the discussion in Section 9.4). Also price or quality leaders often have strong brand loyalties that prevent demand effects from being homogeneous across brands (see also Blattberg and Wisniewski, 1989). These observations indicate both differential effectiveness of brands and asymmetries in market structures. The implication is that market response functions should satisfy the condition that the pairwise share ratios are allowed to be context dependent, that is, contingent on the presence of other choice alternatives. The market share shifts modeled in this way are not necessarily proportional and may represent privileged substitution effects between choice alternatives.

Leeflang and Wittink (1996) describe customer-focused assessments by estimating asymmetric market share response functions. Their model is calibrated with the same data set discussed in Section 11.1 for the estimation of competitive reaction functions (equation (11.15)). The structure of the market response functions is similar to that used for the competitive reactions. The criterion variable is the natural logarithm of the ratio of market shares in successive periods for brand $j = 1, \ldots, n$: $\ln(m_{jt}/m_{j,t-1})$ which is a function of the natural logarithm of the ratio of prices in successive periods and the first differences of four promotional variables (refunds, bonus activities, sampling, featuring) of all brands $r = 1, \ldots, n$:

Table 11.3 Statistically significant effects ^{a} in market share response functions.

Criterion variable	Relevant predictors for each brand						
Market share ^{b}	1	2	3	4	5	6	7
m_1	p, ft	ft		sa		sa	
m_2		p, bo, ft	ft	ft	p	p^*	
m_3			p		ft		
m_4		ft	ft^*	bo, ft			sa
m_5	p			bo^*	p, ft	sa, ft	
m_6	p	p, bo	sa			rf, sa	
m_7	ft	p				p^*	p
Maximum possible number of effects per cell ^{c}	2	4	3	5	4	5	5

^{a} The letters are used for predictor variables that have statistically significant effects in the multiple regression; p = price, sa = sampling, rf = refund, bo = bonus, ft = feature defined as in (11.15). If the sign of the coefficient for the predictor in the multiple regression is counter to expectations, the letter has the symbol $*$ next to it.
^{b} Market share: $\tilde{m}_j = \ln(m_{jt}/m_{j,t-1})$.
^{c} Own-brand effects are in the cells on the diagonal; cross-brand effects are in the off-diagonal cells.

Source: Leeflang, Wittink (1996, p.114).

$$\ln(m_{jt}/m_{j,t-1}) = \lambda_j + \sum_{r=1}^{n} \sum_{t^*=1}^{T^*+1} \gamma_{jrt^*} \ln(p_{r,t-t^*+1}/p_{r,t-t^*}) \qquad (11.16)$$

$$+ \sum_{r=1}^{n} \sum_{t^*=1}^{T^*+1} \sum_{x=1}^{4} \zeta_{xjrt^*}(x_{r,t-t^*+1} - x_{r,t-t^*}) + u_{jt}$$

where u_{jt} is a disturbance term and all other variables have been defined before.

We show in Table 11.3 the predictor variables with statistically significant effects for each brand's market share equation. In this study 13 own-brand effects are obtained, that is, in 13 cases when $j = r$, the marketing instrument of brand j has a statistically significant effect with the expected sign on the brand's own market share. Because each brand does not use all marketing instruments, the maximum possible number of own-brand effects varies between the brands (the maxima are shown in the last row). Across the brands the maximum number of own-brand effects is 28.

There are 18 cross-brand effects significant, with the expected sign, indicated as off-diagonal entries in Table 11.3. The maximum number of cross-brand effects equals 168. Thus, the proportion of significant cross-brand effects (18/168 or 11 percent) is much lower than the proportion of significant own-brand effects (13/28 or 46 percent). From Table 11.3 we can draw some conclusions about competition based on consumers' response function estimates. For example, brand 3's market share is affected only by feature advertising for brand 5. On the other hand, brand 7 only affects brands 4's market share with sampling.

11.3 Congruence between customer-focused and competitor-centered approaches

In the preceding sections we discussed two approaches to diagnose competition. We now consider whether the nature of competitive reaction effects is congruent with the nature of market responses. Congruence between market response and competitive reaction function results is indicated if, for example, brand j reacts to an action by brand r only if brand r's action negatively affects j's market share.

Empirical research suggests[11] that competitors react to each other more often or more intensely than they need to, based on market response. Possible reasons for excessive reactions include the following. Managers make judgments about which brands belong to a competitive set. Then, if the marketing activity is increased for any brand in this set, managers of the other brands tend to react. Importantly, the judgments about the set are rarely based on the effects of activities for one brand on other brands' sales or market shares. Under this condition it is in managers' interests to be aggressive. For example, it appears that the personal cost to a manager of not reacting to an effective marketing initiative for another brand (in the sense that the share of the manager's brand decreases) is higher than the cost of reacting to an ineffective marketing initiative. Of course, the absence of a complete understanding of consumers' sensitivities to marketing activities is likely to lead to excessive competitive reactions.

In this section we describe a framework that can be used to enhance the congruence between competitor-oriented and customer-focused decision making. The framework relates consumer response and competitive reaction effects, and it provides a basis for categorizing over- and underreactions by managers.[12] It is related to the framework introduced in Sections 9.3 and 11.1.

We consider a market to be "in equilibrium" if the market shares m_{jt} for brands $j = 1, \ldots, n$ are stable over time. That is, apart from perturbations, $m_{jt} = m_{j,t-1} \cong m_j$. Now suppose that brand j changes variable u_{hj}, i.e. the value of its h-th marketing instrument, which affects its own market share:

$$\frac{\delta m_j}{\delta u_{hj}} \neq 0. \tag{11.17}$$

---

11. See Chen, Smith, Grimm (1992), Brodie, Bonfrer, Cutler (1996), Leeflang, Wittink (1996). See also the discussions in Kreps, Wilson (1982), Deshpandé, Gatignon (1994), Armstrong, Collopy (1996) and Leeflang, Wittink (1996, 2000).

12. The framework is based on economic arguments. For a discussion of limitations of this frame and of other frames, see e.g. Johnson, Russo (1994).

If there is no competitive reaction, the market is in "disequilibrium". Since managers often strive to preserve market share, competitive reactions are common. The expression for the total effect on j's share of a change in u_{hj}, taking the competitive reaction effects $u_{\ell r}$, $\ell = 1, \ldots, L_r$ and $r = 1, \ldots, n$, $r \neq j$, and the corresponding cross-brand effects into account can be written as:

$$\frac{\delta m}{\delta u_{hj}} = \frac{\delta m_j}{\delta u_{hj}} + \sum_{\substack{r=1 \\ r \neq j}}^{n} \sum_{\ell=1}^{L_r} \frac{\delta m_j}{\delta u_{\ell r}} \frac{\delta u_{\ell r}}{\delta u_{hj}} \tag{11.18}$$

where $\delta m_j / \delta u_{hj}$ indicate the direct effects (compare equation (11.6)). The competitive reaction effects $\delta u_{\ell r} / \delta u_{hj}$ multiplied by the cross-brand market effects $\delta m_j / \delta u_{\ell r}$ are expected to result in the total effect being smaller than the direct effect shown in (11.17).

Competitive reaction effects *should* occur in the presence of nonzero cross-brand effects. That is, if a change in brand j's instrument h affects i's market share,

$$\frac{\delta m_i}{\delta u_{hj}} \neq 0 \tag{11.19}$$

then brand i must react to compensate for the market share loss. The total effect of brand j's change in marketing instrument h on i's market share is:[13, 14]

$$\frac{\delta m}{\delta u_{hj}} = \frac{\delta m_i}{\delta u_{hj}} + \sum_{\ell=1}^{L_i} \frac{\delta m_i}{\delta u_{\ell i}} \frac{\delta u_{\ell i}}{\delta u_{hj}}. \tag{11.20}$$

Thus, in the presence of a change in instrument h for brand j for which (11.20) holds, the market will return to equilibrium if:

$$\frac{\delta m}{\delta u_{hj}} = 0 \tag{11.21}$$

or

$$\frac{\delta m_i}{\delta u_{hj}} = -\sum_{\ell=1}^{L_i} \frac{\delta m_i}{\delta u_{\ell i}} \frac{\delta u_{\ell i}}{\delta u_{hj}}. \tag{11.22}$$

Expression (11.22) can be rewritten as

$$\frac{\delta m_i}{\delta u_{hj}} \frac{u_{hj}}{m_i} = -\sum_{\ell=1}^{L_i} \frac{\delta m_i}{\delta u_{\ell i}} \frac{u_{\ell i}}{m_i} \frac{\delta u_{\ell i}}{\delta u_{hj}} \frac{u_{hj}}{u_{\ell i}} \tag{11.23}$$

---

13. See also Metwally (1992) who uses a similar line of reasoning.
14. Note that (11.20) defines the total effect of a change in u_{hj} on the market share of brand i, while (11.18) defines the total effect of a change in u_{hj} on brand j's share.

or

$$\eta_{m_i,u_{hj}} = -\sum_{\ell=1}^{L_i} \eta_{m_i,u_{\ell i}} \cdot \rho_{u_{\ell i},u_{hj}} \qquad (11.24)$$

where

$\eta_{m_i,u_{hj}}$ = the cross-brand market share elasticity for brand i
with respect to brand j's instrument h,

$\eta_{m_i,u_{\ell i}}$ = the own-brand market share elasticity for brand i
with respect to instrument ℓ,

$\rho_{u_{\ell i},u_{hj}}$ = the reaction elasticity for brand i's
instrument ℓ with regard to brand j's instrument h.

In markets with stable long-run market shares, expression (11.24) should hold on average for all combinations of marketing instruments and all pairs of brands i and j. At the level of *individual* brands and instruments, however, deviations may occur partly due to uncertainty in the estimated effects. If (11.24) does not hold, and the (absolute) cross-brand market share elasticity systematically exceeds the (absolute) right-hand side in (11.24), we have *underreaction* for brand i when it defends its market share. The defending brand i shows *overreaction* to the attacking brand j in the opposite inequality case. If only one marketing instrument is used by i in reaction to a change in a marketing instrument for brand j, then the reaction elasticity for the preservation of market share must equal:

$$\rho_{u_{\ell i},u_{hj}} = -\frac{\eta_{m_i,u_{hj}}}{\eta_{m_i,u_{\ell i}}}. \qquad (11.25)$$

It follows from (11.25) that the reaction elasticity is linearly related to the cross-brand market share elasticity and is inversely related to the own-brand market share elasticity. Relation (11.25) is a relation between three kinds of elasticities. We use the partial derivatives of these elasticities in a framework to distinguish competitive situations. For simplification, the framework is restricted to the absence/presence of effects, i.e. the derivatives are either zero or not, which results in eight possible combinations, shown in Figure 11.1.

In cell A of Figure 11.1 all three effects are non-zero. This case is identified as "intense competition" under which brand i uses marketing instrument ℓ to restore its market share, which is affected by brand j's use of variable h.

In the presence of a cross-brand market share effect ($\eta_{m_i,u_{hj}} \neq 0$), brand j's loss of market share will not be recovered if:

- the own-brand market share effect is zero ($\eta_{m_i,u_{\ell i}} = 0$) as in cell B;
- there is no competitive reaction effect ($\rho_{u_{\ell i},u_{hj}} = 0$) as in cell C;
- there is neither a competitive reaction effect nor an own-brand market share effect as in cell D.

	Cross-brand market share effect[a]			
	YES $\dfrac{\delta m_i}{\delta u_{hj}} \neq 0$		NO $\dfrac{\delta m_i}{\delta u_{hj}} = 0$	
	Competitive reaction effect		Competitive reaction effect	
	YES $\dfrac{\delta u_{\ell i}}{\delta u_{hj}} \neq 0$	NO $\dfrac{\delta u_{\ell i}}{\delta u_{hj}} = 0$	YES $\dfrac{\delta u_{\ell i}}{\delta u_{hj}} \neq 0$	NO $\dfrac{\delta u_{\ell i}}{\delta u_{hj}} = 0$
Own-brand market share effect YES $\dfrac{\delta m_i}{\delta u_{\ell i}} \neq 0$	A Intense competition	C Underreaction Lost opportunity for defender[b]	E Defender's game	G No competition
NO $\dfrac{\delta m_i}{\delta u_{\ell i}} = 0$	B Spoiled arms for defender[b]	D Ineffective arms	F Overreaction Spoiled arms for defender[b]	H No competition

[a] i = Defender, j = Attacker
[b] Defender may lack information on own market share effects

Source: Leeflang, Wittink (1996, p. 106).

Figure 11.1 A categorization of combinations of cross market share-, competitive reaction-, and own market share effects.

Cell B involves the use of an ineffective instrument ("spoiled arms") chosen by i to react to j. The cases in cell C are identified as *underreactions*: brand i should defend its market share but does not react, even though instrument ℓ is effective. We define this to be a "lost opportunity" for defender i. If there are no reaction effects and the own-brand market share elasticities are equal to zero we speak about "ineffective arms" (cell D).

In case of a zero cross-brand market share effect, competitive reaction effects should be absent if preservation of market share is the objective. In the third column of Figure 11.1, we identify *overreactions*. In cell E ("defender's game") reaction occurs with an instrument that has an own-brand effect, although there is no cross-brand market share effect. Cell F involves (unnecessary) reaction with an instrument that is ineffective. We call this "spoiled arms for the defender". Finally, cells G and H are defined as "no competition" because of the absence of both a cross-brand market share effect and a competitive reaction effect.

This framework suggests that knowledge about *cross-brand* and *own-brand* market share effects allows managers to prepare themselves for competitors' activities in terms of whether or not and in what manner reactions are desirable. In this manner, a consumer-focused approach that captures consumer responses to marketing helps management to diagnose competition.

In their application, Leeflang and Wittink (1996) find that managers in a Dutch non-food product catagory tend to overreact. In a replication study, Brodie, Bonfrer and Cutler (1996) find that managers in one product catagory in New Zealand also tend to overreact.

11.4 Game-theoretic models of competition

In the previous sections we have essentially treated the marketing initiatives for individual brands as exogenous variables. Only the reactions were treated in Section 11.1 as endogenous variables. Yet in the marketplace managers consider not only what they believe to be the consumer response but also what they expect competitors will do when a marketing initiative is considered. These complexities make the choice of an action in a competitive situation seem intractable, because what is optimal for one brand depends on what other brands do. And what other brands do depends on what the first brand does, etc.[15] In the normative models discussed in Sections 8.3 and 8.4 we determine the optimal marketing mix for one brand assuming particular reaction patterns of competition. This implies that one does *not* derive a simultaneous optimum for all brands in the product class. Instead each brand manager treats the competitors' strategies as given and computes her own *best response*. Simultaneous solutions call for game-theoretic approaches, and some researchers have applied game theory in a marketing context. Most of the early game-theoretic models[16] are theoretical and lack empirical applications. Since the early eighties powerful advances in game theory have taken place, particularly in the area of dynamic games. As a result, the theory is now more applicable to the modeling of real-world competitive strategies.[17]

In this section we discuss a few game-theoretic models after we introduce some relevant concepts.[18] We restrict ourselves to game-theoretic models with a mathematical structure that corresponds to the structure of other models in this book.[19]

A distinction is made between cooperative and non-cooperative game theory. Cooperative game theory examines the behavior of colluding firms through the maximization of a weighted average of all firms' profits. If we have two firms with profits π_1, π_2 this means:

$$\max_{x_{\ell j}} \pi = \lambda \pi_1 + (1 - \lambda)\pi_2 \tag{11.26}$$

where

$$\lambda = \text{the weight for firm 1,}$$
$$x_{\ell j} = \text{marketing instrument } \ell \text{ of firm } j, j = 1, 2, \ell = 1, \ldots, L.$$

15. See Moorthy (1985).
16. Examples are Friedman (1958), Mills (1961), Shakun (1966), Baligh, Richartz (1967), Gupta, Krishnan (1967a, 1967b), Krishnan, Gupta (1967).
17. Moorthy (1993).
18. More complete treatments can be found in Hanssens et al. (1990, Chapter 8), Erickson (1991), Moorthy (1985, 1993).
19. Useful books on game theory include Luce, Raiffa (1957), van Damme (1987) and Friedman (1991).

In empirical studies this weight is determined by the data.

In the modern world, competition takes place among a few competitors whose interests are interdependent such that each competitor's actions affect the others.[20] This situation is characterized by strategic competition, for which non-cooperative game theory is used. Nash equilibrium (Nash, 1950) is the central concept of non-cooperative game theory. It is defined as a set of strategies, one for each competitor, defined such that no competitor wants unilaterally to change its strategy. In a Nash equilibrium, each strategy is a competitor's best option, given the best strategies of its rivals, where "best" is defined according to specified objectives. If the objective is profit, Nash equilibria are obtained for all ℓ and j:

$$\frac{\delta \pi_j}{\delta x_{\ell j}} = 0, \quad j = 1, \ldots, n, \quad \ell = 1, \ldots, L, \tag{11.27}$$

where

$$\pi_j = f(x_{\ell j}).$$

Most studies of non-cooperative games have involved a duopoly ($n = 2$) or triopoly ($n = 3$) (Teng, Thompson, 1983), although efforts have been made to extend the analysis to a larger number of competitors (Dockner, Jørgenson, 1991). And while early game theory applications emphasize *static* models, more recent models are *dynamic*. In the *differential games* models the critical state variables (sales, market share) are assumed to change with respect to time according to specified *differential equations*. In differential game models, two or more brands are optimizers ($n \geq 2$) (Deal, 1975).

Two types of Nash equilibria can be pursued: *open-loop*, in which $x_{\ell j}$ is a function of time, and *closed-loop* equilibria, which define the $x_{\ell j}$ to be a function not only of time but also of the current state of the system (Erickson, 1991, p. 11). More specifically, if Z represents the state variables, and t indicates time, $x_{\ell j}(t)$ indicates an open-loop strategy, while $x_{\ell j}(Z, t)$ is a closed-loop strategy. In an open-loop strategy, the time path of a marketing decision variable for each brand must be determined in advance for the entire planning horizon. In a closed-loop each brand's marketing instrument is determined as the competition unfolds, and the state variables Z take on values at each instant in time. Examples of state variables are market share and profit. For example, a firm may adjust its advertising expenditures over time as a function of the market share and/or profit to be realized. In this case a closed-loop strategy is followed. Although closed-loop strategies are realistic in that they take into account a brand's own performance and competitors' strategies, they are difficult to solve analytically. The academic literature, however increasingly favors the pursuit of closed-loop strategies.[21]

Non-cooperative game theory is a natural vehicle for models of oligopolistic competition (Moorthy, 1985, p. 268). Models that use game-theoretic principles date back

---

20. Moorthy (1993).

21. See, e.g., Erickson (1993, 1995), Chintagunta, Vilcassim (1994), Fruchter, Kalish (1997). Fruchter and Kalish (1997) also explain the relationship between open- and closed-loop strategies, using a new mathematical approach. Examples of game-theoretic models based on an open-loop strategy are Dockner, Jørgenson (1988), and Chintagunta, Rao (1996).

to Cournot (1838) and Bertrand (1883). Cournot argued for *quantity* (*q*) as the choice variable, whereas Bertrand argued for *price* (*p*) as the choice variable. In the Cournot model, competitors conjecture the quantities supplied by other firms, and they assume that other firms will do whatever necessary to sell the conjectured quantities. The resulting equilibrium is called a "Cournot-equilibrium". In the Bertrand model price is the decision variable. The resulting equilibrium is called a "Bertrand-equilibrium".

In single-firm decision-making under certainty, the choice, of either price or quantity as a decision variable, is moot. However if one solves for an equilibrium, it does matter that each firm's conjecture about the other firm's strategy variable is the correct one. For example, with two firms, and quantity and prices as decision variables, four kinds of equilibria can emerge: (price, price), (price, quantity), (quantity, price), (quantity, quantity). Specifically, the (price, quantity) equilibrium is the equilibrium that results if firm 1 chooses price while conjecturing that firm 2 sets quantity and firm 2 sets quantity, while conjecturing that firm 1 sets price.

The shift from theoretical, static game-theoretic models to empirical, dynamic models also shifts the attention from normative models to *descriptive game theory*. The latter involves the application of game-theoretic models to test whether marketplace data are consistent with one or another model specification. So, for example, Roy, Hanssens and Raju (1994) examined whether a leader-follower system or a mutually independent pricing rule (Nash) is most consistent with the pricing behavior in the mid-size sedan segment of the U.S. automobile market. Their results suggest that the leader-follower system is most consistent with the data.

As an example we discuss here a study by Gasmi, Laffont and Vuong (1992). They study the behavior of Coca Cola and Pepsi Cola, with quarterly data for the United States on quantity sold, price and advertising. They estimated various model specifications to allow for the possible existence of cooperative as well as non-cooperative strategic behavior in this industry. Their work proceeds with the specification of an objective function for each firm (a profit function) as well as demand and cost functions. Given these specifications, it is possible to obtain a system of simultaneous equations based on assumptions about the firm's behavior. Throughout it is assumed that there is a one-to-one relation between firm j and brand j, and the terms are used interchangeably. Gasmi et al. (1992) propose the following demand function for brand j:

$$q_j = \gamma_{j0} + \alpha_{jj}p_j + \alpha_{jr}p_r + \gamma_{jj}a_j^{1/2} + \gamma_{jr}a_r^{1/2}, \quad j \neq r, \quad j, r = 1, 2 \quad (11.28)$$

where

q_j = quantity demanded from brand j,

p_j = price per unit for brand j,

a_j = advertising expenditure for brand j.

We have omitted an error term and a subscript t for time periods from (11.28) for convenience. To illustrate the use of this model we assume the cost function is:

$$C_j(q_j) = c_j q_j, \quad (11.29)$$

where

$$c_j = \text{the constant variable cost per unit of brand } j.$$

The profit function can be written as:

$$\pi_j = p_j q_j - C_j(q_j) - a_j \tag{11.30}$$
$$= (p_j - c_j)(\gamma_{j0} + \alpha_{jj}p_j + \alpha_{jr}p_r + \gamma_{jj}a_j^{1/2} + \gamma_{jr}a_r^{1/2}) - a_j.$$

Gasmi et al. (1992) consider six games:

1. firms set prices and advertising expenditures simultaneously (naive static Nash behavior in price and advertising);
2. firm $j = 1$ is the leader in both price and advertising, and firm $r = 2$ is the follower;
3. firm $j = 1$ is the leader in price, but the two firms "behave Nash" in advertising;
4. total collusion, which amounts to maximizing (11.26), a weighted average of both firms' profits;
5. firms (first) collude on advertising, and compete (later) on prices;
6. firms collude on price knowing that they compete later on advertising expenditures.

The first three games are based on non-cooperative behavior whereas the last three games are based on "tacit" collusion.

To illustrate the specification of a system of simultaneous equations we consider the first game. The first-order conditions corresponding to a unique Nash equilibrium of the (one-stage) game are (expressed in terms of optimal reaction functions):

$$p_1^* = \frac{\alpha_{11}c_1 - \gamma_{10} - \alpha_{12}p_2^* - \gamma_{11}(a_1^*)^{1/2} - \gamma_{12}(a_2^*)^{1/2}}{2\alpha_{11}}$$

$$p_2^* = \frac{\alpha_{22}c_2 - \gamma_{20} - \alpha_{21}p_1^* - \gamma_{21}(a_1^*)^{1/2} - \gamma_{22}(a_2^*)^{1/2}}{2\alpha_{22}} \tag{11.31}$$

$$a_1^* = (1/2\,\gamma_{11}p_1^* - c_1)^2$$

$$a_2^* = (1/2\,\gamma_{22}p_2^* - c_2)^2.$$

If there is total collusion, as in the fourth game, a specific form of (11.26) is maximized:

$$\max_{p_1, p_2, a_1, a_2} \pi = \lambda\pi_1(p_1, p_2, a_1, a_2) + (1 - \lambda)\pi_2(p_1, p_2, a_1, a_2). \tag{11.32}$$

The first-order conditions of this maximization are:

$$\frac{\delta\pi}{\delta p_1} = \lambda\left[(p_1 - c_1)\alpha_{11} + \gamma_{10} + \alpha_{11}p_1 + \alpha_{12}p_2 + \gamma_{11}a_1^{1/2} + \gamma_{12}a_2^{1/2}\right] +$$
$$(1 - \lambda)(p_2 - c_2)\alpha_{21} = 0$$

$$\frac{\delta\pi}{\delta p_2} = \lambda(p_1 - c_1)\alpha_{12} + (1 - \lambda)\left[(p_2 - c_2)\alpha_{22} + \gamma_{20} + \alpha_{22}p_2 + \alpha_{21}p_1 + \right.$$

$$\gamma_{22}a_2^{1/2} + \gamma_{21}a_1^{1/2}] = 0 \tag{11.33}$$

$$\frac{\delta\pi}{\delta a_1} = \lambda\left[(p_1 - c_1)\tfrac{1}{2}\gamma_{11}a_1^{-1/2} - 1\right] + (1 - \lambda)\left[(p_2 - c_2)\tfrac{1}{2}\gamma_{21}a_1^{-1/2}\right] = 0$$

$$\frac{\delta\pi}{\delta a_2} = \lambda\left[(p_1 - c_1)\tfrac{1}{2}\gamma_{12}a_2^{-1/2}\right] + (1 - \lambda)\left[(p_2 - c_2)\tfrac{1}{2}\gamma_{22}a_2^{-1/2} - 1\right] = 0.$$

This system of four linear equations uniquely defines the four endogenous variables p_1, p_2, a_1 and a_2. The Hessian matrix of second-order conditions has to be negative semi-definite which imposes restrictions on the parameters.

Gasmi et al. (1992) include additional exogenous variables and specify functions for the demand intercepts (γ_{j0}) and for marginal costs (c_j) which makes the system identifiable. These functions together with the demand functions (11.28) can be estimated as a system of simultaneous equations. Gasmi et al. (1992) in fact derive a general model specification, and they use it to test the six games. The empirical results suggest that, for the period covered by the sample (1968-1986), some tacit collusive behavior in advertising between The Coca Cola Company and Pepsico, Inc. prevailed in the market for the cola drinks. Collusion on prices did not seem to be as well supported by the data. Thus the results favor the specification for game 5.

The study by Gasmi et al. (1992) deals with horizontal competition and collusion. Their model can be extended to consider vertical competition/collusion between competitors/partners in the marketing system as well.[22]

The demand equations (11.28) have a structure that is also used in other game-theoretic models, for example in studies by Kadiyali (1996) and Putsis, Dhar (1999).[23] Other demand equations that have been used were developed by Vidale and Wolfe (1957) and Lanchester.[24] More recently Chintagunta and Rao (1996) specify a logit model at the individual household level:

$$\pi_{jt} = \frac{\exp(\alpha_j + \beta_j\theta_{jt} + \gamma_j p_{jt})}{\sum_{r=1}^{2}\exp(\alpha_r + \beta_r\theta_{rt} + \gamma_r p_{rt})}, \quad j = 1, 2, \tag{11.34}$$

where

π_{jt} = the probability of purchase of brand j by an
individual consumer at t,

α_j = the intrinsic preference for brand j,

θ_{jt} = the component of brand j's preference that evolves
over time.

p_{jt} = the price of brand j at t.

---

22. Other game-theoretic models that deal with vertical competition/collusion can be found in Moorthy (1988), Chu, Desai (1995), Lal, Narasimhan (1996), Krishnan, Soni (1997), Gupta, Loulou (1998), Vilcassim, Kadiyali, Chintagunta (1999), Kim, Staelin (1999).
23. See also Putsis, Dhar (1998).
24. See Kimball (1957). For examples see Chintagunta, Vilcassim (1994), Erickson (1997).

This model accounts for preference accumulation to infer implications for dynamic pricing policies by firms in duopoly markets. Chintagunta and Rao make assumptions about the development of θ_{jt} over time. Preferences across consumers are aggregated to the segment level. Their results indicate that, given equal marginal costs for brands, in steady-state equilibrium the brand with the higher preference level charges a higher price.

CHAPTER 12

Stochastic consumer behavior models

Stochastic consumer behavior models can be characterized as follows:

'A stochastic model is a model in which the probability components are built in at the outset rather than being added ex post facto to accommodate discrepancies between predicted and actual results'

(Massy, Montgomery and Morrison, 1970, p. 4).

Thus, stochastic models take the probabilistic nature of consumers' behavior into account. By contrast, econometric models include an error component that may capture uncertainty due to model misspecification (omitted variables, functional form) or measurement error.

Much of the initial research on stochastic models focused on the specification of the distributional form. More recently attention has shifted toward including marketing decision variables in the models, and integrating the components of consumer behavior into a single framework. Stochastic models of consumer behavior are often classified according to the type of behavior they attempt to describe. The major categories are:

- purchase incidence (Section 12.1);
- purchase timing (Section 12.2);
- brand choice (Section 12.3);
- integrated models of incidence, timing and choice (Section 12.4).

Purchase incidence, purchase timing and brand choice are described by stochastic processes, i.e., families of random variables (X_t) indexed by t varying in an index set T $(t \in T)$ (Parzen, 1962, p. 22). A random or stochastic variable is a variable which can assume different values (or alternative value intervals) with some probability other than one. The values the random variable can take are defined in the state space which is the collection of possible outcomes of the stochastic process under study. For instance, if the process is the purchasing of a specific brand, the state space for one trial is Y(es), N(o), and for two trials it is (YY, YN, NY, NN). An event is defined as a single outcome of the stochastic process. For example, Y respectively YY are events of the process.

12.1 Purchase incidence

12.1.1 INTRODUCTION

Following Massy et al. (1970) purchase incidence models are models that specify *how many purchases will occur in a specified interval of time*. In purchase incidence models the probabilities that a purchase of a brand or product will occur in the time interval $(t, t + h)$ are considered: $P(P_u \in (t, t + h))$, where P_u is the purchase. Purchase incidence models are used to calculate other important quantities characterizing consumer behavior (Massy et al., 1970, Ehrenberg, 1988):

- the probability that the waiting time between one purchase and the next will be less or equal to some specified value;
- the probability that the number of purchases in a certain time interval (longer than h) will be equal to a given value;
- the penetration: the proportion of individuals who have bought the product/category at least once in a certain time interval;
- lost buyers, the proportion of individuals who purchased in period t, but not in period $t + 1$;
- new buyers, the proportion of individuals who did not purchase in period t, but did in period $t + 1$.

Models that deal with the first-mentioned probabilities are purchase timing models, which are intrinsically connected to purchase incidence of a specific form. A distribution for the interpurchase times defines the distribution of products bought in a given time period, and vice versa. Purchase incidence models describe the total number of units bought of a particular brand (brand sales) or product category (industry sales). Often they contain less behavioral detail than, for example, brand choice models.

12.1.2 THE POISSON PURCHASE INCIDENCE MODEL

Purchase incidence models were developed by Ehrenberg (1959, 1972, 1988) and Chatfield, Ehrenberg and Goodhardt (1966). These models are based on the Poisson process, which has the property that the distribution of the number of units purchased in any interval depends only on the length of that interval. The random variable (Y_{it}), denoting the number of units purchased by consumer i in a certain time period t, then follows a Poisson distribution with parameter λ:

$$P(Y_{it} = y_{it}) = f(y_{it} \mid \lambda, t) = \frac{e^{-\lambda t}(\lambda t)^{y_{it}}}{y_{it}!}, \tag{12.1}$$

$$i = 1, \ldots, I, \quad t = 1, \ldots, T.$$

The Poisson process has expectation: $E[Y_{it}] = \lambda t$, which shows that λ can be interpreted as the rate of the process. Its variance is equal to the mean. The probability of at least one purchase in the interval t, the penetration, which is of primary interest in purchase incidence models (Ehrenberg, 1988), is:

$$P(Y_{it} > 0) = 1 - e^{-\lambda t}. \tag{12.2}$$

The interpurchase times in the Poisson process follow an exponential distribution with mean $1/\lambda$:

$$f(t \mid \lambda) = \lambda e^{-\lambda t}. \tag{12.3}$$

An estimator for λ in the Poisson process[1] is simply the mean of the observed purchase frequencies: $\hat{\lambda} = \sum_{i=1}^{I} y_{it}/It$.

12.1.3   HETEROGENEITY AND THE NEGATIVE BINOMIAL (NBD) PURCHASE INCIDENCE MODEL

The assumptions underlying the Poisson process are quite restrictive in many marketing applications. For example, the assumption that all consumers have the same value of λ is unrealistic. Heterogeneity has been accommodated in several ways, most frequently by assuming that λ is a random variable that follows a gamma distribution across individuals:

$$f(\lambda \mid \beta, \alpha) = \frac{\alpha^{\beta} \lambda^{\beta-1} e^{-\alpha\lambda}}{\Gamma(\beta)} \tag{12.4}$$

with α and β being parameters of the gamma distribution and $\Gamma(\cdot)$ the gamma function. The gamma distribution is a very flexible distribution that can take on a variety of shapes. We note that if $\beta = 1, 2, 3, \ldots$, takes on integer values, then an Erlang distribution arises. From (12.1) and (12.4) the number of purchases for a (randomly selected) individual can be shown to follow a Negative Binomial Distribution (Ehrenberg, 1959, Morrison and Schmittlein, 1988, East, Hammond, 1996):

$$f(y_{it} \mid \beta, \alpha) = \binom{y_{it} + \beta - 1}{y_{it}} \left(\frac{\alpha}{\alpha + t}\right)^{\beta} \left(\frac{t}{\alpha + t}\right)^{y_{it}}. \tag{12.5}$$

The NBD has expectation: $E[Y_{it}] = \beta t/\alpha$, and its variance is: $Var[Y_{it}] = \beta t/\alpha + \beta t^2/\alpha^2$. Thus, the variance of the NBD exceeds that of the Poisson distribution, which equals the mean $\beta t/\alpha$. The probability of at least one purchase in the interval t, the penetration, is:

$$P(Y_{it} > 0) = 1 - \left(\frac{\alpha}{\alpha + t}\right)^{\beta}. \tag{12.6}$$

Estimators for α and β can be derived for example from the estimated mean $\bar{y}$ and variance σ^2 of the NBD: $\hat{\alpha} = (\bar{y}t)/(\hat{\sigma}^2 - \bar{y})$ and $\hat{\beta} = (\hat{\alpha}\bar{y})/t$. Morrison and Schmittlein (1988) derive conditions under which the NBD at the brand level leads to a NBD

---

1. An interesting procedure for estimating purchase frequency distributions based on incomplete data was provided by Golany, Kress and Philips (1986).

at the product class level. In empirical applications, the NBD seems to fit either well at both levels or at neither level.

Sichel (1982) has proposed the family of generalized inverse Gaussian distributions to describe heterogeneity in the purchase rate. A different category of models arises when the heterogeneity distribution is assumed to be discrete: the so-called finite mixture models. The finite mixture of Poissons has been applied to describe purchase incidence by a.o. Wedel, DeSarbo, Bult and Ramaswamy (1993). We describe that class of models in more detail in Section 17.2.

Apart from the pitfall that heterogeneity is not accounted for, another criticism of the Poisson process is that the exponential distribution of interpurchase times leads to highly irregular purchase behavior. Chatfield and Goodhart (1973) proposed to use the Erlang distribution, which leads to the Condensed NBD for purchase incidence. It describes a more regular pattern of purchase behavior. Such regular patterns of purchases have been confirmed empirically (Morrison, Schmittlein, 1988). Wheat and Morrison (1990) show how regularity can be estimated if we observe two interpurchase times.[2]

12.1.4 THE ZERO-INFLATED POISSON (ZIP) PURCHASE INCIDENCE MODEL

Yet another critique of the Poisson and NBD purchase incidence models is that they do not accommodate individuals who never buy. Both models predict that every individual will eventually buy the product, as t increases. Since for most products and categories there is a group of individuals who never buy,[3] these purchase incidence models tend to underestimate the percentage of zero purchases. One solution (Morrison and Schmittlein, 1988) is to add a component to the model that allows for an additional spike at zero, due to the class of non-buyers, with proportion π_0. The Zero-Inflated Poisson (ZIP) model is:

$$P(Y_{it} = y_{it}) = \pi_0 + (1 - \pi_0)\frac{e^{-\lambda t}(\lambda t)^{y_{it}}}{y_{it}!}. \tag{12.7}$$

The ZIP model has a mean: $E[Y_{it}] = \pi_0 + (1 - \pi_0)\lambda t$, and a variance: $Var[Y_{it}] = \lambda t(1 - \pi_0)(1 - \pi_0\lambda t)$. The penetration is:

$$P(Y_{it} > 0) = (1 - \pi_0)(1 - e^{-\lambda t}). \tag{12.8}$$

Estimates of π_0 and λ can be obtained from the equations for the mean $\bar{y} = (1 - \hat{\pi}_0)\hat{\lambda}t$, and the proportion of zeros: $P_0 = \hat{\pi}_0 + (1 - \hat{\pi}_0)e^{-\hat{\lambda}t}$. These equations need to be solved by iteration.

A straightforward extension accounts for both added zeros and heterogeneity, giving rise to the Zero-Inflated Negative Binomial Distribution (ZINBD). See Schmittlein, Cooper and Morrison (1993) for an application.

---

2. Other distributions that have been considered for interpurchase times are the inverse Gaussian, the lognormal and the Weibull distributions (Sikkel and Hoogendoorn, 1995).
3. The Poisson distribution is not defined for those subjects.

An extensive comparison of the Poisson, NBD, ZIP and ZINBD models, amongst others, to estimate the penetration of products was completed by Sikkel and Hoogendoorn (1995). They used panel data for 275 different food products, for 750 households. They found that ZIP and ZINBD have (small) biases in predicting penetration, although ZIP performed very well for small time intervals. They also encountered some problems with the above-mentioned estimators of the parameters, which did not always converge or were outside the possible domains.

12.1.5 ADDING MARKETING DECISION VARIABLES

Much research in purchase incidence modeling has focused on finding the appropriate distribution for purchase frequencies, and estimating important quantities from the data, including penetration, lost buyer percentages and so on. More recently, successful attempts have been made to include marketing decision variables as predictors into these models. The primary extension is that one parameterizes the mean of the distribution as a function of predictors. In such response types of purchase incidence models,[4] the effects of decision variables are measured by changes in the shapes and/or the parameters of the probability distributions.[5] Early attempts are Magee (1953) and Massy (1968). Magee's work, for example, is based on a "Poisson-type purchase model". The effects of promotional effort on sales are traced in this model, comparing the sales probability distributions of consumers exposed to promotional activity with the sales probability distributions of consumers who did not receive promotional attention.

We consider the simplest case, a Poisson distribution of purchase incidence of a particular product. Assume there are marketing decision variables x_ℓ, $\ell = 1, \ldots, L$, including for example the product's price, frequency of promotions, etc., but also consumer characteristics $z_{i\ell'}$, $\ell' = 1, \ldots, L'$. The idea is that the expected number of purchases by individual i in the period under consideration (μ_i), is related to those explanatory variables:

$$\mu_i = \exp\left(\sum_{\ell=1}^{L} \beta_\ell x_\ell + \sum_{\ell'=1}^{L'} \beta_{\ell'} z_{i\ell'} \right). \tag{12.9}$$

Model (12.9) accounts for variation in the purchase rate across the sample as a function of the explanatory variables. The mean of the purchase incidences is μ_i. The exponent in (12.9) guarantees that the predicted purchase rate is positive. With this formulation we can assess the effects of marketing variables on purchase incidence. The inclusion of consumer characteristics, such as demographic and socio-economic variables, is an alternative way to account for heterogeneity in the purchase rate across the sample.

Estimation of (12.9) in conjunction with (12.1) cannot be accomplished by solving closed-form expressions, but a likelihood funtion needs to be maximized nu-

---

4. For the terminology adopted here, see Leeflang (1974).
5. The developments here are based on the theory of generalized linear models: McCullagh and Nelder (1989).

merically,[6] where (12.9) is substituted for λ in equation (12.1). In a similar way, the estimation of a ZIP model with explanatory variables can be accomplished by substituting (12.9) in (12.7), formulating the likelihood and maximizing over the parameters. Estimation of a NBD with explanatory variables can be accomplished similarly. Formulation and estimation proceed in a similar way as in the Poisson case.

Several authors have used these Poisson and NBD regression models to describe purchase incidence. However, recently they are used primarily as building blocks in more complex models (Krishnamurthi and Raj, 1988, 1991, Tellis 1988a, Bucklin and Gupta, 1992, Wedel et al., 1993, Dillon and Gupta, 1996).

12.2 Purchase timing

Purchase timing models are intrinsically related to purchase incidence models in that the choice of a distribution for interpurchase times at the same time defines the distribution of purchase incidence. Some authors have preferred to work with purchase times rather than purchase incidence. A variety of statistical distributions can be assumed for the interpurchase times, such as the exponential, Erlang-2, gamma, Gompertz, Inverse Gaussian, log-normal and Weibull distributions (Sikkel and Hoogendoorn, 1995, Frenk, Zhang, 1997). The exponential and Erlang-2 distributions have been used most frequently (Chatfield, Goodhardt, 1973, Schmittlein, Morrison, Colombo, 1987, Morrison, Schmittlein, 1988). The models based on these distributions are parsimonious and usually fit the data well.

12.2.1 HAZARD MODELS

More recently, market researchers have used hazard models to describe interpurchase times (Gupta 1991, Jain and Vilcassim, 1991, Gönül and Srinivasan, 1993b, Helsen and Schmittlein, 1993, Wedel, Kamakura, DeSarbo, Ter Hofstede, 1995). The major advantage of this approach is that it accounts for so-called right-censoring. Right censoring occurs if a sample of consumers or households is observed for a time period of fixed length only, causing longer interpurchase times to have a larger probability of falling (partially) outside the observation period. If one does not account for right-censoring, we obtain biased estimates. The standard distributions that have been used for interpurchase times, such as the exponential and Erlang distributions, can also be formulated in a hazard framework.

In hazard models the probability of a purchase during a certain time interval, say t to $t + \Delta t$, given that is has not occurred before t, is formulated as:

$$P[t \leq T \leq t + \Delta t \mid T \geq t] \tag{12.10}$$

where T is the random interpurchase time variable.[7] Parametric methods for interpurchase times involve assumptions about their distribution. Two distinct classes of

---

6. See Section 16.6.
7. An extension of the formulation to multiple purchases is straightforward.

hazard models arise according to whether a discrete or a continuous distribution of the interpurchase times is assumed.

In *discrete-time* hazard models, the probability of a purchase in equation (12.10) is specified directly for given values of Δt:

$$P[t \leq T \leq t + \Delta t \mid T \geq t] = P[y \mid T \geq t] \tag{12.11}$$

where y is the number of *events* that has occurred during the interval $[t, t + \Delta t]$. An example of the expression for such a discrete time probability is provided by the Poisson distribution in (12.1). This illustrates the relationship between the hazard model and a purchase incidence model. The discrete-time formulation has the advantage that it leads to simple model formulations, which enables one to accommodate censoring and multiple events in a straightforward manner. Binomial models have also been used to model discrete durations in (12.11), but the Poisson distribution has the advantage of allowing for more than one event to occur in the discrete time interval.

In the *continuous-time* approach, Δt approaches zero in (12.10), to yield a continuous hazard rate $\lambda(t)$:

$$\lambda(t) = \lim_{\Delta t \downarrow 0} \frac{P[t \leq T \leq t + \Delta t \mid T \geq t]}{\Delta t}. \tag{12.12}$$

The hazard rate can be interpreted as the instantaneous rate of purchasing at time t. The distribution function of interpurchase times can then be derived:

$$f(t) = \lim_{\Delta t \downarrow 0} \frac{P[t \leq T \leq t + \Delta t]}{\Delta t} = \lambda(t) \exp\left[-\int_0^t \lambda(s)ds\right]. \tag{12.13}$$

Alternatively, (12.13) can be written as $f(t) = \lambda(t)S(t)$. Here, $S(t) = P(T > t)$ is the probability that a purchase has not yet occurred at t where $S(t)$ is the so-called survivor function. The advantage of this formulation becomes apparent in case of censoring, because $f(t)$ represents the density of any uncensored observation or completely observed interpurchase time. If, due to censoring, an interpurchase time is not completely observed, $S(t)$ provides the probability that the purchase has not yet occurred, since we only know that the interpurchase time is larger than t, the end of the observation period. The continuous-time approach appears to be the most commonly used approach in the marketing literature.[8] If the interpurchase times follow an exponential distribution (and the purchase incidence is Poisson), then the hazard rate and survivor functions are:

$$\lambda(t) = \lambda \tag{12.14}$$

and

$$S(t) = e^{-\lambda t}. \tag{12.15}$$

---

8. See, for example, Gupta (1991), Jain and Vilcassim (1991).

Thus, for the exponential distribution the hazard of a purchase is constant and independent of time. Also, purchases occur at random time periods, independent of past purchases. For other distributions the hazard rate and survivor functions can be formulated as well.

Flinn and Heckman (1983) proposed a very flexible (Box-Cox) formulation[9] for hazard functions. This is applied to brand switching problems by Vilcassim and Jain (1991). It includes many of the frequently used distribution functions as special cases, and the hazard rate is formulated as:

$$\lambda(t) = \exp\left[\gamma_0 + \sum_{\ell=1}^{L} \gamma_\ell \frac{t^{v_\ell} - 1}{v_\ell}\right]. \tag{12.16}$$

This formulation includes a variety of interpurchase time distributions as special cases. For example, if $\gamma_\ell = 0$ for all ℓ, then $\lambda(t) = \exp[\gamma_0]$ is constant, and the exponential distribution arises. If $\gamma_\ell = 0$ for $\ell > 2$, and $v_\ell = 1$, then $\lambda(t) = \exp[\gamma_0 - \gamma_1 + \gamma_1 t]$ which is the hazard rate of a Gompertz distribution.[10]

For all interpurchase time distributions except for the exponential, the hazard rate varies with time, so that those distributions account for nonstationarity of purchase timing and incidence. A decline in the event rate as a function of the elapsed time is often called inertia and is observed for interpurchase times (Helsen and Schmittlein, 1993). A hazard rate that increases with time is often called a snowballing phenomenon, observed in new-product adoption processes (Helsen and Schmittlein, 1993). Another useful way to accommodate nonstationarity is through the so-called piecewise exponential formulation. The piecewise exponential formulation assumes that the total observation period can be decomposed into, say, R shorter periods, in which the hazard is (approximately) constant. Thus, one considers, for example, R weekly or monthly purchase intervals, denoted by t_r, $r = 1, \ldots, R$, and $t_{r+1} = t_r + \Delta t$ where:

$$P[t_r \leq T \leq t_{r+1}] = \lambda_r. \tag{12.17}$$

Note that the hazard rate is constant within each period, but varies from period to period, thereby accounting for nonstationarity. This approach is quite flexible, because across time periods the hazard may take an arbitrary form. Since the hazard between t_r and t_{r+1} is constant for all r, the model assumes random purchase timing within each period.

Several hazard models have been compared empirically. Bayus and Mehta (1995) estimated gamma and Weibull distributions from replacement data on consumer durables, including color TV's, refrigerators, washing machines, vacuum cleaners and coffee makers. Many applications have dealt with household scanner panel data. Gupta (1991) applied exponential and Erlang-2 distributions to scanner data on ground coffee. Jain and Vilcassim (1991) estimated the exponential, Weibull, Gompertz, and

---

9. Box, Cox (1964). This specification is discussed in Sections 16.1.4 and 18.4.3.
10. For other special cases see Jain, Vilcassim (1991).

Erlang-2 distributions with scanner data on coffee, Vilcassim and Jain (1991) used the Weibull and Gompertz distributions on saltine crackers, Wedel et al. (1995) applied the piecewise exponential model to scanner data on ketchup, and Helsen and Schmitt-lein (1993) fitted a Weibull and a quadratic baseline hazard to saltine crackers scanner data. We note that Vilcassim and Jain (1991) and Wedel et al. (1995) explicitly deal with the timing of brand switching and repeat buying.

It is difficult to state general conclusions, except that the simple exponential model does not seem to describe interpurchase timing processes well. Each of the models used in the studies referred above, however, is more complex than the ones described here in that they accommodate heterogeneity of the hazard rate across subjects, and/or include marketing decision variables. We discuss these two topics in the next two sections.

12.2.2 HETEROGENEITY

The hazard modeling approach discussed here, assumes that consumers are homogeneous. Gupta (1991) handled heterogeneity in a way that is comparable to the approach described before in purchase incidence models. He assumed a parametric distribution of interpurchase times, specifically exponential or Erlang-2, and let heterogeneity be captured by a gamma distribution for the scale parameter β. The advantages of this approach are that it provides a natural extension of the NBD models discussed in Section 12.1.3, and that β can be directly interpreted as a measure of heterogeneity. The approach provides simple closed-form expressions that lead to analytically tractable estimation equations. Gupta (1991) applied the exponential-gamma and Erlang-gamma models to scanner panel data on coffee. The exponential distribution yielded $\hat{\lambda} = 0.38$ with a highly significant t-value, indicating a rate of purchase of slightly more than one pack in three weeks. The estimates for the exponential-gamma model were: $\hat{\alpha} = 13.26$, $\hat{\beta} = 5.00$ (both strongly significant), with an expectation of $\hat{\beta}/\hat{\alpha} = 0.38$. This result is indicative of heterogeneity in the sample with respect to the (exponential) hazard rate, but a modest amount as evidenced by the high value of $\hat{\alpha}$.

Various other approaches to accommodating heterogeneity were provided by Jain and Vilcassim (1991), Bayus and Mehta (1995) and Wedel et al. (1995). These authors used discrete mixing heterogeneity distributions, whereby a number of unobserved classes or segments are estimated along with the parameters of the hazard model. A discussion of those approaches is beyond the scope of this chapter. We refer to Section 17.2 for a general treatment of the mixture model approach. Gönül and Srinivasan (1993b) provide a comparison of continuous and discrete approaches to heterogeneity in hazard models for interpurchase times. Some heterogeneity can also be accommodated through the inclusion of consumer characteristics.

12.2.3 ADDING MARKETING DECISION VARIABLES

The inclusion of marketing decision variables in hazard models has received some attention. The basic idea for models that allows marketing decisions to influence purchase timing, is to reformulate the hazard function. An important case is presented by so-called proportional hazard models (Cox, 1975), for which:

$$\lambda(t \mid x(t)) = \lambda_0(t) \exp[x(t)'\beta] \qquad\qquad (12.18)$$

where

$$\lambda_0(t) = \text{the baseline hazard,}$$
$$x(t) = \text{a vector of explanatory variables at time } t,$$
$$\beta = \text{vector of parameters.}$$

Model (12.18) has two multiplicative components. The first term, the baseline hazard, captures the duration time dynamics as discussed in Section 12.2.1. The second term shifts the baseline hazard up or down proportionally dependent upon the effects of marketing decision variables and/or customer characteristics. Note that the exponent ensures that the effect of the covariates on the hazard is positive. In proportional hazard models the baseline hazard can take any of the discrete or continuous time specifications outlined above (compare (12.11) and (12.12)). Helsen and Schmittlein (1993) point out the advantages of such a proportional hazard model over a regression model of purchase times. For example, the regression model does not accommodate the appropriate distribution of purchase times, nor of censoring, leading to biased estimates of the effects of the covariates. The continuous-time proportional hazard specification was adopted in marketing research by, amongst others, Vilcassim and Jain (1991), Helsen and Schmittlein (1993), and Bayus and Mehta (1995), while Wedel et al. (1995) used a discrete-time specification of the proportional hazard model.

Wedel et al. (1995) analyzed weekly ketchup data on four brands with a hazard model estimated for two segments in the market, where for each segment repeat-buying and switching behavior is analyzed. A Box-Cox formulation of the baseline was used, involving linear (week) and log-linear (ln(week)) terms. Segment 1, constituting 45.6% of the sample, consists of mostly loyal Heinz buyers. The average interpurchase time of these consumers is about five weeks. Segment 2 constitutes 54.4% of the sample and has an average interpurchase time (seven weeks), which is about 30% longer than it is for consumers in segment 1. In segment 2 the market share of Heinz is half that in segment 1, whereas the shares of Del Monte, Hunt's and the other brands are three to four times as high. Almost 60% of all purchases in segment 2 consist of switches. We show the results in Table 12.1 where we see that the hazards of repeat buying and switching take different forms for the segments as indicated by the different coefficients for "Week" and "ln(week)" for repeating and switching between the two segments. Segment 1 is a segment of loyal buyers, where price is relatively more effective in inducing switching than repeating (see the price coefficients in Table 12.1), while segment 2 can be designated a segment of brand-

Table 12.1 Segment-level hazard model estimates for scanner ketchup data.

	Segment 1		Segment 2	
	Repeat	Switch	Repeat	Switch
Week	-0.01	-0.07[a]	0.03[a]	0.05[a]
ln(week)	1.30[a]	1.46[a]	0.56[a]	0.59[a]
Price	-0.76[a]	-1.02[a]	-1.16[a]	-0.92[a]

[a] Parameter estimates significant at the 1%-level

Source: Wedel et al. (1995, p. 460)

switchers for whom price is slightly more effective in inducing repeat buying (than switching).

Sinha and Chandrashekaran (1992) model the diffusion of an innovation, or rather the timing of the adoption of an innovation, using a hazard model. They explicitly account for the fact that a proportion of the subjects will never adopt the product. If the proportion of adopters is denoted by π_0, then the probability of observing a certain adoption time, given that the adoption occurs in the time period under study $(y = 1)$ is:

$$f(t \mid y = 1) = \pi_0 \lambda(t) S(t) \tag{12.19}$$

which is the probability of an adoption times the rate of purchase at time t multiplied by the probability of no purchase at time t. The probability of not adopting during the sample period $(y = 0)$ is:

$$f(t \mid y = 0) = (1 - \pi_0) + \pi_0 S(t) \tag{12.20}$$

which is the probability of never adopting plus the probability of eventual adoption after the sample period (i.e. censored in the particular sample). If the distribution of the adoption time is assumed to be exponential, so that the hazard rate and survivor function are provided by (12.14) and (12.15) respectively, this model is equivalent to the ZIP model for purchase incidence described in 12.1.4. Next to the exponential, Sinha and Chandrashekaran consider the Weibull and log-normal distributions for the adoption time.

12.3 Brand choice models

Brand choice models can be distinguished according to several criteria:

a. Assumptions about the stochastic process underlying the model. The brand choice behavior being constant in time (stationary) or not (non-stationary) yield, for example, Bernouilli, Markov, and learning models.

b. Whether brand choice behavior is assumed to be homogeneous or heterogeneous across consumers.
c. Whether or not the effects of marketing variables are accommodated.

We use these distinctions for the classification of brand choice models below.

12.3.1 MARKOV AND BERNOUILLI MODELS[11]

Markov processes can be classified according to the nature of the index set T (denoting time). When $T = \{0, 1, 2, \ldots, \}$ the stochastic process is said to be a discrete time process. When $T = \{t : -\infty < t < \infty\}$ or $T = \{t : t \geq 0\}$ the stochastic process is said to be a continuous time process. In addition to processes that evolve in discrete time, in modeling brand choice we consider processes with a discrete state space. Such discrete states will be denoted by $i, j, k, \ldots$.

Discrete time Markov brand choice models are based on Markov chains, in which one considers probabilities such as:

$$P(X_t = j \mid X_{t-1} = i, X_{t-2} = k, \ldots) \tag{12.21}$$

i.e. the probability that brand j is purchased at time t, given that brand i was purchased at $t-1$, brand k at $t-2$,.... These probabilities are called transition probabilities. A simple specification of the transition probability in (12.21) is obtained by assuming that the conditional probability at t depends only on the purchase at $t-1$. This was first studied by the Russian mathematician Markov, hence the name of the process. The Markov assumption implies that:

$$P(X_t = j \mid X_{t-1} = i, X_{t-2} = k, \ldots) = P(X_t = j \mid X_{t-1} = i). \tag{12.22}$$

If X_t satisfies (12.22), it is said to follow a Markov chain. Equation (12.21) presents a first-order Markov chain. In general, a stochastic process is said to be t'-order Markov if:

$$\begin{aligned} P(X_t = j \mid X_{t-1} = i, X_{t-2} = k, \ldots, X_{t-t'} = l, \ldots) \\ = P(X_t = j \mid X_{t-1} = i, X_{t-2} = k, \ldots, X_{t-t'} = l). \end{aligned} \tag{12.23}$$

In this chapter we concentrate on first-order ($t' = 1$) and zero-order ($t' = 0$) Markov models.

ZERO-ORDER MODELS

One refers to a zero-order (Markov) model, if the probability of purchasing a particular brand at t does not depend on purchasing behavior at $t-1, t-2$, etc. In other words, a zero-order model applies when current and future purchasing behavior does not

---

11. It is not our purpose to give a detailed study of brand choice models. For an extensive review, see, for example, Massy, Montgomery, Morrison (1970), Leeflang (1974, Chapters 3 and 7), Wierenga (1974). Introductory treatments are Montgomery and Urban (1969, pp. 53-93), Simon and Freimer (1970, Chapter 10).

depend on past purchase history (Massy, Montgomery and Morrison, 1970, Chapter 3). Thus (12.22) reduces to:

$$P(X_t = j \mid X_{t-1} = i, X_{t-2} = k, \ldots) = P(X_t = j). \tag{12.24}$$

If the random variable X takes one of only two values (representing two brands, or a purchase and non-purchase situation) $X = x = 1$, with probability π, and $X = x = 0$, with probability $1 - \pi$ we obtain the so-called Bernouilli model:[12]

$$P(X = x) = \pi^x (1 - \pi)^{1-x}. \tag{12.25a}$$

The expectation of the Bernouilli distribution is $E[X]=\pi$, and its variance is $Var[X]= \pi(1 - \pi)$. This is a distribution for an individual consumer. Let T be the number of purchase occasions for each consumer in the population. All have the same probability of purchasing a brand and $1 - \pi$ is the non-purchase probability. Then $\pi \cdot T = \eta$ is the expected number of purchases by a consumer. The probability that the number of times a purchase takes place, x is represented by a Binomial distribution:

$$P(X = x) = \binom{T}{x} \pi^x (1 - \pi)^{T-x}, \quad x = 0, 1, 2, \ldots, T \tag{12.25b}$$

In a multi-brand market, brands are denoted by $j = 1, \ldots, n$. Next, we assume that each consumer $i = 1, \ldots, I$ may purchase a brand j with probability $\pi_j, j = 1, \ldots, n$. We do not consider the situation of a non-purchase for convenience, and assume T purchase occasions. We observe x_j, the *number of times brand j is purchased*, for each j. Let $T = \sum_{j=1}^{n} x_j$ denote the total number of purchases observed. Now the multinomial model applies:

$$P(X_1, \ldots, X_n = x_1, \ldots, x_n) = \left(\frac{T!}{x_1!, \ldots, x_n!} \right) \prod_{j=1}^{n} \pi_j^{x_j}. \tag{12.26}$$

The multinomial model arises as the sum of T Bernouilli distributions (12.25a). The expectation of the multinomial random variable is: $E[X_j] = \pi_j T$, its variance is: $Var[X_j] = \pi_j(1 - \pi_j)T$, and the covariance is $Cov[X_j, X_k] = -\pi_j \pi_k T$. The binomial distribution results if $n = 2$. Thus, in the Bernouilli, binomial and multinomial models the market is described by a set of (stationary) probabilities, describing the purchase probabilities (or alternatively the market shares) of the brands.

The above models assume consumer homogeneity, i.e. all subjects have the same probability of purchasing a particular brand. Heterogeneity has been taken into account in the Binomial model by allowing π to follow a beta distribution across the population of consumers (Massy, Montgomery and Morrison, 1970, Chapter 3). The beta distribution is a flexible distribution that can take a variety of shapes:

$$f(\pi \mid \alpha_1, \alpha_2) = \frac{\Gamma(\alpha_1 + \alpha_2)\pi^{\alpha_1-1}(1 - \pi)^{\alpha_2-1}}{\Gamma(\alpha_1)\Gamma(\alpha_2)} \tag{12.27}$$

---

12. See Massy, Montgomery, Morrison (1970, Chapter 3), Wierenga (1974, p. 18).

with α_1 and α_2 as parameters. From (12.25b) and (12.27) the number of purchases (x) can be shown to follow a Beta-Binomial (BB) distribution:

$$f(x \mid \alpha_1, \alpha_2) = \binom{T}{x} \frac{\Gamma(\alpha_1 + \alpha_2)\Gamma(x + \alpha_1)\Gamma(T - x + \alpha_2)}{\Gamma(T + \alpha_1 + \alpha_2)\Gamma(\alpha_1)\Gamma(\alpha_2)} \tag{12.28}$$

with mean: $E[X] = \alpha_1 T/(\alpha_1 + \alpha_2)$.

In a similar way, heterogeneity can be accounted for in multinomial models describing multi-brand markets. Goodhardt, Ehrenberg and Chatfield (1984) proposed a Dirichlet distribution for the choice probabilities. The Dirichlet can be seen as a multivariate extension of the beta distribution. The Dirichlet distribution is defined as:

$$f(\pi_1, \ldots, \pi_n \mid \alpha_1, \ldots, \alpha_n) = \frac{\Gamma\left(\sum_{j=1}^{n} \alpha_j\right) \prod_{j=1}^{n} \pi_j^{\alpha_j - 1}}{\prod_{j=1}^{n} \Gamma(\alpha_j)}. \tag{12.29}$$

By compounding the multinomial and the Dirichlet one obtains the DirichletMultinomial (DM):

$$f(x_1, \ldots, x_n \mid \alpha_1, \ldots, \alpha_n) = \frac{T!\Gamma\left(\sum_{j=1}^{n} \alpha_j\right) \prod_{j=1}^{n} \Gamma(x_j + \alpha_j)}{\Gamma\left(\sum_{j=1}^{n} \alpha_j + T\right) \prod_{j=1}^{n} \Gamma(\alpha_j)x_j!} \tag{12.30}$$

with the mean of X_j: $E[X_j] = \alpha_j T/\left(\sum_{r=1}^{n}\alpha_r\right)$. The Beta-Binomial in equation (12.28) arises as a special case for a two-brand market ($n = 2$).

Strong empirical support for the DM is provided by Ehrenberg and coauthors in their work over the past 30 years (see for example Ehrenberg, 1988, Uncles, Ehrenberg and Hammond, 1995). They discuss many applications where the DM is a useful description of brand purchase behavior. Regularities based on the DM have been found in product markets for food and drink products, personal care products, gasoline, aviation fuel, and motor cars, OTC medicines, as well as in TV program and channel choice and shopping behavior (Uncles, Ehrenberg and Hammond, 1995). In many markets, the DM model does a good job of explaining observed regularities in purchase behavior, such as the percentage of consumers buying in a certain period, the number of purchases per buyer, the repeat purchases, the percentage of loyals, etc. In Table 12.2 we show some of the findings in Uncles, Ehrenberg and Hammond (1995). The results apply to the instant coffee item belonging to the Folgers brand. Table 12.2 shows that the Dirichlit-Multinomial (DM) model does quite well in predicting market characteristics in stationary markets (i.e. the second row contains predicted percentages that are close to the actual ones). The authors conclude that this constitutes one of the best-known empirical generalizations in marketing. However, criticisms have been raised, pertaining to the absence of marketing variables and the stationarity assumption.

Finally, we mention an alternative approach for the accommodation of heterogeneity in which a discrete instead of a continuous mixing distribution is used. Such

Table 12.2 *Performance of the DM model: Observed (O) and Predicted (P) values for Folgers instant coffee.*

	Buyers			Repeat	Loyal	% who also bought			
	% Wk[a]	% Yr	% once	%	%	MH[b]	TC	HP	SA
O	1	18	53	49	13	48	35	40	39
P	1	17	47	47	15	41	37	37	36

[a]%Wk denotes the percentage of people who bought in a week; %Yr in one year, and % once the percentage who bought only once.
[b]MH = Maxwell House, TC = Tasters Choice, HP = High Point, SA = Sanka.

Source: based on Uncles, Ehrenberg, Hammond (1995, p. G72).

models are the finite mixture models which offer the advantage that segmentation strategies can be developed. We discuss these in Section 17.2.

FIRST-ORDER MARKOV MODELS

A first-order Markov model applies if only the last purchase has an influence on the present one, i.e.,

$$P(X_t = j \mid X_{t-1} = i, X_{t-2} = k, \ldots) = P(X_t = j \mid X_{t-1} = i) = p_{ijt}. \quad (12.31)$$

Because the p_{ijt} are (conditional) probabilities, they must have the following properties:

$$0 \le p_{ijt} \le 1, \quad \text{for all } i, j = 1, \ldots, n, \quad t = 1, \ldots, T \quad (12.32)$$

$$\sum_{j=1}^{n} p_{ijt} = 1, \quad \text{for all } i = 1, \ldots, n, \quad t = 1, \ldots, T. \quad (12.33)$$

where n is the number of brands. We assume consumer homogeneity, i.e. consumers have the same p_{ijt} (compare Section 9.1). If one makes the additional, simplifying assumption that $p_{ijt} = p_{ij}$, for all i and j, i.e. the transition probabilities are independent of time, the resulting Markov chain is said to be stationary. The transition probabilities p_{ij} can be represented in a matrix. This transition probability matrix TP is represented as:[13]

$$TP = \begin{bmatrix} p_{11} & p_{12} & \cdots & p_{1n} \\ p_{21} & p_{22} & \cdots & p_{2n} \\ \cdot & \cdot & \cdots & \cdot \\ \cdot & \cdot & \cdots & \cdot \\ \cdot & \cdot & \cdots & \cdot \\ p_{n1} & p_{n2} & \cdots & p_{nn} \end{bmatrix}. \quad (12.34)$$

13. *TP* is a stochastic matrix that has the property of having at least one eigenvalue equal to one, which is caused by the constraint in (12.33).

Table 12.3 Market shares predicted with a first-order Markov Model.

Time period	Market share brand 1	Market share brand 2
0	0.5	0.5
1	0.55	0.45
2	0.575	0.425
3	0.5975	0.4025
.	.	.
.	.	.
∞	0.600	0.400

The diagonal elements $(p_{11}, p_{22}, \ldots, p_{nn})$ are the repeat purchase probabilities. The off-diagonal elements are the brand-switching probabilities.

If the market shares in period t are in the (row) vector $m_t = [m_{1t}, m_{2t}, \ldots, m_{nt}]$ one can use the transition probability matrix, TP, to predict market shares in future periods through the relation between the market shares at $t + 1$, $m_{t+1} = [m_{1,t+1}, \ldots, m_{n,t+1}]$ and market shares in period t, m_t, written in matrix formulation as:

$$m_{t+1} = m_t TP. \tag{12.35}$$

We illustrate this with an example of two brands. Consider the following transition probability matrix,

$$TP = \begin{bmatrix} 0.8 & 0.2 \\ 0.3 & 0.7 \end{bmatrix}$$

and assume that the current (period 0) market shares are $m_{10} = 0.50$, $m_{20} = 0.50$. In period $t = 1$, the predicted market shares are computed as the matrix product $m_t TP$:

$$\begin{aligned} \hat{m}_{11} &= m_{10} p_{11} + m_{20} p_{21} \\ &= 0.5 \times 0.8 + 0.5 \times 0.3 = 0.55 \end{aligned}$$

and

$$\begin{aligned} \hat{m}_{21} &= m_{10} p_{12} + m_{20} p_{22} \\ &= 0.5 \times 0.2 + 0.5 \times 0.7 = 0.45. \end{aligned}$$

Predicting further into the future, we use the relation:

$$m_t = m_0 TP^t \tag{12.36}$$

where $TP^2 = TP \cdot TP$, and $TP^3 = TP \cdot TP \cdot TP$, and so on. Using this relation, one obtains the market shares shown in Table 12.3. In equilibrium (steady state), the

Table 12.4 Estimated transition probabilities for US beer brands.

	Brand choice in $t + 1$			
Brand choice in t	1	2	3	4
1	0.81	0.01	0.18	0
2	0.14	0.75	0	0.11
3	0	0.25	0.74	0.01
4	0.20	0.12	0	0.68

predicted market shares are respectively 0.60 and 0.40. These steady state market shares collected in the vector m, (or shares) are independent of time, and satisfy:

$$m = m \cdot TP \leftrightarrow m(I - TP) = 0 \qquad (12.37)$$

which shows that m is a (left) eigenvector of TP corresponding to the eigenvalue 1. In the particular example above with two states:

$$m = \left(\frac{p_{21}}{p_{21} + p_{12}}, \frac{p_{12}}{p_{21} + p_{12}} \right). \qquad (12.38)$$

The stationary market shares in Table 12.3 can be directly computed from equation (12.38) as: $m_1 = 0.3/0.5$, and $m_2 = 0.2/0.5$. It can be shown that under suitable conditions the Markov chain reaches an equilibrium situation, in which $m_0 \to m$ as $t \to \infty$, regardless of the initial market shares m_0.

Horowitz (1970) estimated transition probabilities for a market consisting of four U.S. premium brewers. Twenty years of yearly market share data were available. The results are shown in Table 12.4.[14] The estimation of transition probabilities from market share data can provide useful descriptive information. For example, in Table 12.4 we see that brand 1 enjoys the highest repeat purchase probability. Brand 4 has the lowest market share (about 11 percent), and the results in Table 12.4 suggest that this is due to its relative inability to keep its current customers, $\hat{p}_{44} = 0.68$, but also due to its failure to attract many new customers.

It may be instructive to examine how market shares change over time if the transition probabilities are stationary. Current market shares are: $m_1 = 0.350$, $m_2 = 0.283$, $m_3 = 0.255$, $m_4 = 0.113$. With the transition probabilities of Table 12.4, the steady state market shares are: $m_1 = 0.340$, $m_2 = 0.306$, $m_3 = 0.241$, $m_4 = 0.113$. Thus, brand 2 would gain more than two share points at the cost of brands 1 and 3. Nevertheless, this market is relatively stable.

We emphasize that several assumptions underlie these results:

a. the transition probabilities are stationary;
b. all consumers make exactly one purchase in each period;

---

14. See also Telser (1962b, 1963).

c. consumers all have the same conditional and unconditional brand choice probabilities.

Assumption *a*, that the transition probabilities are stationary, may be unrealistic, for example if a firm takes corrective action for a brand that is losing market share. The literature contains several models that allow the transition probabilities to vary, such as Maffei (1960), Harary and Lipstein (1962), Howard (1963) Styan and Smith (1964), Ehrenberg (1965), Montgomery (1969) and Leeflang (1974).

Assumption *b* is related to the fact that time is divided into discrete intervals. This assumption is less restrictive the longer the time unit. However assumption *a* becomes more problematic as the time unit becomes longer. One way to alleviate assumption *b* is to assume a two-brand market ($j = 1, 2$) where $j = 1$ denotes a particular brand and $j = 2$ all other brands, including a no-purchase option. Another suggestion is to add a no-purchase option to the *n* existing brands (Harary, Lipstein, 1962, Telser, 1962a).

The fist two assumptions can also be addressed by a so-called "semi-Markov model". In such a model, the time between two purchases *i* and *j* is considered to be a random variable t_{ij}, with corresponding density function $f_{ij}(t)$, rather than a constant. The sequence of transitions in these models is Markovian, but it is not Markovian from one time period to another. For that reason it is called a semi-Markov process. This process is described not only by a transition probability matrix *TP*, but also by a "holding-time matrix" with elements $f_{ij}(t)$ (see Howard, 1963). Some early applications are given by Herniter (1971) and Wierenga (1974, pp. 215-216). More recently, such semi-Markov models have been formulated as hazard models of brand switching (Vilcassim and Jain, 1991, Wedel et al., 1995). Here the hazard of a switch from brand *i* to brand *j* is modeled as: $f_{ij}(t) = \lambda_{ij} S_{ij}(t)$ (compare equation (12.18)), where $S_{ij}(t)$ denotes the survivor function for a switch from *i* to *j*, i.e. the probability that *t* is larger than the censoring time. The hazard can be parameterized in various ways as shown in Section 12.2. A detailed discussion of these semi-Markov and hazard models for brand switching is beyond the scope of this book.

With respect to assumption *c*, we note that in many situations the conditional choice probabilities differ across individuals, i.e. the population is heterogeneous. We can accommodate heterogeneity by making assumptions about the distribution of the p_{ij} over the population of consumers. Morrison (1966) developed a heterogeneous aggregate Markov model where a particular transition probability was assumed to be beta distributed. More generally a vector of transition probabilities can be assumed to follow a multivariate beta distribution, see Jones (1973) and Leeflang (1974, p. 183). These developments are quite similar to those for the DM model in equations (12.29) and (12.30). However, this approach has received relatively little attention in the literature.

Yet another way to accommodate heterogeneity is through a discrete mixture distribution, giving rise to a finite mixture of Markov models. Such a model has been developed by Poulsen (1990). He modeled the purchases by new triers of a certain brand, and subsequent purchases of that and other brands by those triers in five subsequent waves. We give a brief description of that model here. It is assumed that there are $s = 1, \ldots, S$ unobserved segments, where each individual has probability θ_s to belong to segment s (for all s). Given a segment s, a sequence of buy/not buy decisions is described by a first-order Markov process. There are two possible outcomes, to buy (1) and not to buy (0) the product, at two consecutive occasions indexed by i and j. The probability of buying on the two occasions is denoted by $p_{ij|s}$, conditional on segment s. If we know to which segment an individual belongs, that probability can be written according to a first-order Markov model, as:

$$p_{ij|s} = \pi_{i|s}\pi_{j|is}.\tag{12.39}$$

Thus, the probability of choosing alternative i at occasion 1 and alternative j at occasion 2, respectively (given segment s), is equal to the probability of choosing i multiplied by the probability of choosing j given that i was chosen previously. The latter probabilities form the transition matrix which describes the probabilities of switching among the brands. Since the segment membership of individuals is unknown, the unconditional probability is the probability of being in a segment multiplied by the purchase probability, summed across all segments:

$$p_{ij} = \sum_{s=1}^{S} \theta_s\pi_{i|s}\pi_{j|is}.\tag{12.40}$$

We show in Table 12.5 results for the two segments Poulsen recovered. Segment 1 (19% of the sample) has a high initial probability of buying the brand (0.68) and a probability of 0.50 of switching into the brand at the next purchase. Segment 2 (81% of the sample) has a much lower probability of buying the brand (0.13) and a very low probability (0.06) of switching into it, if no purchase was made. Also, the probability of a repeat is much lower in segment 2 (0.21) than in segment 1 (0.71). From Poulsen's analyses it appears that the mixture of first-order Markov models provides a much better description of purchase behavior than the homogeneous first-order Markov model.

The results in Table 12.5 suggest that the Markovian assumptions (specifically point c above) may not hold in models of purchase behavior.[15] Researchers who applied the Markov model may not have been overly concerned with the restrictive nature of the underlying assumptions. They have used the model as a tool that captures some of the dynamics of markets. Generally speaking, the Markov model has often been applied because of its performance as a predictor of dynamic aggregate market behavior, not because it describes how individual consumers behave.

12.3.2 LEARNING MODELS

In learning models the entire purchase history is taken into account in each subsequent purchase. Well-known applications in marketing include those by Kuehn (1961,

---

15. See also Ehrenberg's (1965) pessimistic view about the applicability of Markov chains.

Table 12.5 Mixture of first-order Markov model estimates from purchase data.

Segment	s = 1				s = 2	
$\pi_{i|s}$	no buy	buy			no buy	buy
	(i = 0)	(i = 1)			(i = 0)	(i = 1)
	0.32	0.68			0.87	0.13
$\pi_{j|is}$	no buy	buy			no buy	buy
	(i = 0)	(i = 1)			(i = 0)	(i = 1)
no buy (j = 0)	0.50	0.50	no buy (j = 0)		0.94	0.06
buy (j = 1)	0.29	0.71	buy (j = 1)		0.79	0.21

Source: Poulsen (1990, p.13).

1962). Learning may have a positive effect in the sense that increased familiarity with the product increases the chance that it will be re-purchased in the future. The effect of learning may also be negative, for example due to satiation.

Applications of the linear learning model are provided by Carman (1966), McConnell (1968), Wierenga (1974, 1978), Lilien (1974a, 1974b) and Lawrence (1975). Wierenga found that the linear learning model produced better descriptions of brand choice behavior than homogeneous and heterogeneous zero-order and first-order Markov models did.

We do not provide details about linear learning models because these have received limited attention in recent years. These models have the following restrictions. First, they are only suited for two-brand markets, and are not easily extended. Second, only positive purchase feedback is accommodated. Third, there are technical problems associated with model estimation on micro- and macro-level data. These problems may have limited the applicability of the model, leading to a reduction in its popularity (Leeflang and Boonstra, 1982).

12.3.3 BRAND CHOICE MODELS WITH MARKETING DECISION VARIABLES

Choice modeling has grown to be a very substantial area in marketing research over the past few decades.[16] In this section we show how marketing instruments can be linked to the parameters in stochastic choice models. We start by adding variables to the zero-order binomial and multinomial models. Specifically, we discuss the most common of the zero-order models, the logit model, and then describe two important generalizations, the nested logit and the probit model.

---

16. We do not provide a complete overview of the literature in this quickly growing area. Instead, we describe the main principles. See for more information about this topic, for example, the Special Issues on Choice Models of *Marketing Letters*, vol. 8, number 3, 1997 and vol. 10, number 3, 1999.

THE MULTINOMIAL LOGIT MODEL

In a multinomial choice model an individual chooses between n alternatives. The binomial model is a special case for $n = 2$ alternatives. The assumption is that a consumer will choose the alternative that gives him maximal utility (see, for example, Luce, 1959). The utilities are assumed to have a fixed component and a random component. The $n \times 1$ vector of (unobserved) random utilities that the ith individual derives from the jth alternative, U_j, can be represented as:[17]

$$U_j = x'_j \beta + \varepsilon_j \tag{12.41}$$

where x'_j is a $(1 \times L)$ row-vector of marketing variables related to the j-th choice for the ith individual, β is a $(L \times 1)$ vector of unknown parameters, and ε_j is the error term or the random part of utility.[18] Each individual i chooses the brand with the maximal utility. Thus the observed choice variable y_j is defined as:

$$y_j = \begin{cases} 1 \text{ if } U_j > U_r \text{ for all } r \neq j, \quad r = 1, \ldots, n, \\ 0 \text{ otherwise.} \end{cases} \tag{12.42}$$

Define $\pi_j = P[y_j = 1]$. If the ε_j are independently and identically distributed with Weibull density functions, the multinomial logit model applies. The choice probability of an individual i for alternative j, given a multinomial logit model, can be expressed as:[19]

$$\pi_j = \frac{\exp(x'_j \beta)}{\sum_{r=1}^{n} \exp(x'_r \beta)}. \tag{12.43}$$

This leads to a multinomial distribution of the choice probabilities as in (12.26), with the choice probabilities dependent upon marketing variables as shown in (12.43). The multinomial logit model is perhaps the most frequently used choice model in marketing (as well as in other disciplines).[20] Important application areas include the analysis of household-level scanner data (Guadagni and Little, 1983) and conjoint choice experiments (Louvière and Woodworth, 1983).

The multinomial logit model, however, suffers from the *Independence of Irrelevant Alternatives* (IIA) property, which states that the odds of choosing one alternative over another is constant regardless of whichever other alternatives are present.[21] Formally if C and $D \subset C$ denote two sets of alternatives, then the IIA-assumption for two alternatives j and r (Luce, 1959) is:

$$\frac{P(j \mid C)}{P(r \mid C)} = \frac{P(j \mid D)}{P(r \mid D)}. \tag{12.44}$$

---

17. Although the utilities and probabilities refer to an individual i, we omit this index for convenience.
18. Note that this defines a linear compensatory utility formation rule (Fishbein, 1967).
19. See for a derivation, for example, McFadden (1974), Urban, Hauser, (1980, Chapter 11).
20. For marketing applications see, for example, Punj and Staelin (1978), Guadagni and Little (1983), Louvière and Hensher (1983), Carpenter and Lehmann (1985), Kamakura and Russell (1989), Chintagunta, Jain and Vilcassim (1991) and Erdem (1996). An overview of issues arising in logit model applications in marketing is provided by Malhotra (1984) and McFadden (1986).
21. See also Section 9.4 and the discussion on asymmetric models in Chapter 14.

In the multinomial logit model this property arises directly from the independence assumption of the error terms. It may not be realistic in many marketing applications, especially if some of the alternatives are close substitutes. On the positive side, if the IIA-assumption holds, future demand can simply be predicted with the closed-form expression (12.43) and the estimated values of the parameters (Urban, Hauser, 1980, Chapter 11). However, if similarities across alternatives are incorrectly assumed away, the estimated effects of marketing variables are incorrect.

McFadden (1986) shows how one can deal with problems that arise from the IIA-assumption, including statistical tests of IIA. If IIA does not hold, other models can be used, often at the cost of computational complexity. We discuss two such models, the Nested MultiNomial Logit model (NMNL) and the MultiNomial Probit (MNP) model.

One model that alleviates the independence of irrelevant alternatives assumption is the NMNL model (McFadden, 1981). In this model consumer choice may follow a hierarchy of differentiating characteristics. We consider an example from Kalwani and Morrison (1977, pp. 472-474), in which consumers consider products in the margarine market according to two main characteristics: the form and brand name. A consumer first chooses a form (cups or sticks), with probabilities $\pi_r (r = 1, 2)$, and then conditional upon a particular form, chooses a brand with conditional probability[22] $\pi_{j|r}$. If three brands are available as sticks and two brands are available as cups, we have the conditional probabilities $\pi_{j|r}$ $j = 1, 2, 3$ for $r = 1$ and $\pi_{j|r}$ $j = 1, 2$ for $r = 2$. For a graphical representation of this kind of hierarchy see Figure 14.1.

The assumption is that a consumer's utility can be separated into two components, one attributable to form (r) and the other to the brand name (j):

$$U_{jr} = U_r + U_{j|r} = V_r + V_{j|r} + \varepsilon_r + \varepsilon_{j|r} \tag{12.45}$$

where V_r is the deterministic part of the utility associated with the highest level of the hierarchy, etc. Using similar arguments as in (12.43), the choice probability at the *lowest* level of the hierarchy (brand choice given product form r) can be derived:

$$\pi_{j|r} = \frac{\exp(V_{j|r})}{\sum_{k=1}^{n} \exp(V_{k|r})}. \tag{12.46}$$

The choice at the highest level of the hierarchy (r) can be derived from utility maximization:

$$\pi_r = P[\max_j U_{jr} > \max_j U_{jr'} \text{ for all } r', \quad r' \neq r] \tag{12.47}$$

$$= P[U_r + \max_j U_{j|r} > U_{r'} + \max_j U_{j|r'} \text{ for all } r' = 1, \ldots, n', \quad r' \neq r].$$

An expression for $\max_j U_{j|r}$ can be obtained from the properties of the double exponential distribution, since the maximum of a set of double exponentially distributed

---

22. See also Roberts, Lilien (1993).

variables (with unit variance) also follows a double exponential distribution with expectation:

$$E[\max_j U_{j|r}] = \ln \left(\sum_{j'=1}^{n} e^{V_{j'|r}} \right).$$ (12.48)

Expression (12.48) is called the "inclusive value" of the utility for the brand name which is included in the utility for the form as shown in (12.49). From (12.47) and (12.48) the choice probabilities at the highest level of the hierarchy can be shown to be:

$$\pi_r = \frac{\exp \left(V_r + \ln \left(\sum_{j'=1}^{n} e^{V_{j'|r}} \right) \right)}{\sum_{r'=1}^{n'} \exp \left(V_{r'} + \ln \left(\sum_{j'=1}^{n} e^{V_{j'|r'}} \right) \right)}.$$ (12.49)

The unconditional choice probability of any alternative, jr, is simply $\pi_{jr} = \pi_{j|r} \cdot \pi_r$. In this model the brand utilities at the lowest (brand name) level of the hierarchy affect the utilities at the highest (form) level through the inclusive values. For a comprehensive treatment of the NMNL model see Ben-Akiva and Lerman (1985, Chapter 10), who include extensions to higher-order nestings and implications for the elasticity structure. The NMNL model has been used to model choices in product categories such as soft drinks (Moore and Lehmann, 1989), coffee (Kannan and Wright, 1991) and peanut butter (Kamakura, Kim and Lee, 1996). The latter authors apply the NMNL model as well as an extension to mixture formulation which allows for a partitioning of the market by different segments. For a specification of the NMNL model at the aggregate level, see Section 14.5.

In the MultiNomial Probit (MNP) model the disturbances of the random utility in (12.41) are assumed to follow a multivariate normal distribution ($\varepsilon_j \sim N(0, \Omega)$). This distribution allows the utilities of alternatives to be correlated, so that the IIA-assumption can be relaxed. However, a closed-form expression for the probability that individual i chooses alternative p_j cannot be derived, because it involves a multidimensional integral. Probabilities can be obtained by numerical methods if the number of choice alternatives is limited to 3 or 4. Early applications include those by Currim (1982) and Kamakura and Srivastava (1984, 1986). A comprehensive treatment of the MNP model is given by Daganzo (1979). McFadden (1989) developed a simulation method for calculating the probabilities that an individual chooses a particular alternative. Briefly, it is based on drawing repeated samples from the multivariate normal distribution for the error terms, and approximating the integral by summations over the repeated draws. This simulation method has stimulated interest in the MNP model, leading to applications in marketing by, amongst others, Chintagunta (1992a), Elrod and Keane (1995) and Haaijer, Wedel, Vriens and Wansbeek (1998).

MARKOV RESPONSE MODELS

In the Markov response models the transition probabilities, p_{ijt} with $i, j = 1, \ldots, n$, $t = 1, \ldots, T$ are related to decision variables. Early examples are found in Telser (1962a, 1962b), Hartung and Fisher (1965), Lee, Judge and Zellner (1970), Leeflang and Koerts (1974), and Horsky (1977b). To illustrate, we examine Hartung and Fisher's work in some detail. In their study the market is treated as a quasi-duopoly, i.e. $n = 2$. They assume that the transition probability matrix is non-stationary, and (12.35) can be written as:

$$m_{1t} = (p_{11t} - p_{21t})m_{1,t-1} + p_{21t}. \tag{12.50}$$

Hartung and Fisher relate transition probabilities to decision variables in the following way. Brand loyalty for brand 1 is,

$$p_{11t} = \gamma_1 \frac{d_{1t}}{d_{1t} + d_{2t}} \tag{12.51}$$

where

$$d_{1t} = \text{number of outlets where brand 1 is available,}$$
$$d_{2t} = \text{number of outlets where brand 2 is available,}$$
$$\gamma_1 = \text{a constant.}$$

Similarly, brand switching to brand 1 is defined as:

$$p_{21t} = \gamma_2 \frac{d_{1t}}{d_{1t} + d_{2t}}. \tag{12.52}$$

In this case, the values of the transition probabilities are not restricted to the range zero to one.

Hartung and Fisher obtained the following estimates: $\hat{\gamma}_1 = 4.44$, $\hat{\gamma}_2 = 0.64$. With these values, it follows that p_{11t} will become larger than one if the outlet share of brand 1 exceeds about 22.5 percent. Nevertheless, Hartung and Fisher found that, for their problem, equations (12.51) and (12.52) were sufficiently accurate. However, Naert and Bultez (1975) applied the same model to a brand of gasoline in Italy and obtained meaningless results. This led them to propose alternative formulations for the transition probability functions. One of these defines the transition probabilities as exponential functions of the relative number of outlets rather than as linear functions of outlet share. This modification produces more acceptable estimates.

A more recent approach to accommodate explanatory variables is provided by Givon and Horsky (1990). Their formulation is somewhat similar to the Hartung and Fisher approach, but they include price and lagged advertising effects into the conditional Markov probabilities. A quite general framework for including marketing variables into Markov models of brand switching is provided by Zufryden (1981, 1982, 1986) and Jones and Landwehr (1988). They demonstrate that the multinomial logit model framework described above can be used to estimate Markov response

Table 12.6 Markov logit model results for $n = 2$ market.

Predictor variable	Parameter estimate	t-value
Constant	-3.25	-25.08
Income	0.55	4.46
Price	0.21	2.01
Last brand	1.60	13.08

Source: Zufryden (1981, p.653).

models with explanatory variables. Their work thus rigorously extends the earlier work by Hartung and Fisher and others. Zufryden introduces a last-state specification vector z, for individual i, where $z = (z_1, z_2, \ldots, z_n)$ is a vector of zeros and ones indicating the state an individual was last in. For example, $z_1 = \ldots = z_{n-1} = 0, z_n = 1$ indicates that brand n was purchased last by individual i. This last-state specification vector is included among the explanatory variables in a logit specification for $\pi_{j|r}$ analogous to (12.43), resulting in:

$$\pi_{j|r} = \frac{\exp(z'\gamma_r + x'_j\beta)}{\sum_{r'=1}^{n} \exp(z'\gamma_{r'} + x'_{r'}\beta)}. \tag{12.53}$$

Thus, this model includes past purchases as a predictor in a logit model with a parameter vector γ_r indicating the effect of a previous brand purchase on the probability to choose j, $\pi_{j|r}$. Including $z'\gamma_r$ into the logit model (12.43) results in a specification of the conditional probability of choosing j, given a previous purchase of r, indicated by z.

The zero-order multinomial model (12.43) is a restricted version of the model (12.53). The first-order hypothesis is maintained if we do not reject the null hypothesis $\gamma_r = 0$ for all r. If the evidence favors (12.53), the implication is that if the values of the explanatory variables x_j change, the first-order Markov transition probabilities also change. We note that a more general formulation can be obtained if the impact of the explanatory variables is allowed to depend on the last brand purchased, which amounts to replacing β by β_r in equation (12.53).

Zufryden (1981) estimated his model on data covering one year for a two-brand market (brand A versus all others O). The explanatory variables were income and price (both at two levels, high and low). We show his estimation results in Table 12.6 which indicate that both low income and low price result in a significantly increased probability of choice. The significance of the coefficient for Last brand indicates that a zero-order model is strongly rejected for this market. Zufryden obtained first-order Markov probabilities from this model. These are shown in Table 12.7. Table 12.7 reveals that there are some marked differences in the switching probabilities especially between the income classes. The lower-income segment has higher loyalty and

Table 12.7 Estimated switching probabilities
among brand A and other brands (O)
for two income and price levels.

		Low income			High income	
Low price		A	O		A	O
	A	0.29	0.71	A	0.19	0.81
	O	0.08	0.92	O	0.05	0.95
High price		A	O		A	O
	A	0.25	0.75	A	0.16	0.84
	O	0.06	0.94	O	0.04	0.96

Source: Zufryden (1981, p.657).

switching to brand A, compared with the higher-income segment. For each income segment, a low price leads to greater loyalty than a high price does. We note that the model did not include interactive effects between income and price. Thus, the main effects are: an increase in the repeat purchase probability from high- to low-income of about 50 percent, and an increase in the same from high- to low-price of almost 20 percent.

12.4   Integrated models of incidence, timing and choice

In the previous sections we described models for the purchase incidence, purchase timing and brand choice (or brand switching) separately. Several authors have integrated such descriptions of separate consumer behavior processes into one single framework. Some of these models have also included components of market segmentation. The purpose of those models is to provide managers with insights about the possible sources of gains and losses of sales, about the consumer characteristics and marketing variables that affect sales, and about the causes of brand loyalty and brand switching. Many of the approaches compound the (Poisson- or NBD-) distributions for purchase frequency or distributions of purchase timing (exponential or Erlang) with (multinomial, Dirichlet-Multinomial, or Markov) models of brand choice. Early examples of this approach are Jeuland, Bass, and Wright (1980) and Goodhardt, Ehrenberg and Chatfield (1984). However the importance of this stream of research was recognized through the seminal work of Gupta (1988). The basic setup of these approaches is as follows:

1. Assume a Poisson distribution for purchase frequency, y: $P(y \mid \lambda)$.
2. Assume a gamma heterogeneity distribution for the purchase rate: $G(\lambda)$.

Table 12.8 Integrated models of purchase quantity choice and timing.

Author(s)	Choice	Timing	Quantity	x-var's	Segments
Zufryden (1978)	Linear learning	Erlang	CNBD[a]	No	No
Jeuland, Bass, Wright (1980)	Dirichlet-Multinomial	Gamma	NBD	No	No
Goodhardt, Ehrenberg, Chatfield (1984)	Dirichlet-Multinomial	Gamma	NBD	No	No
Zufryden (1981, 1982)	Markov	Exponential, gamma	Poisson, (C)NBD	Yes	No
Hauser, Wisniewski (1982)	Semi-Markov		-	Yes	No
Dalal, Lee, Sabavala (1984)[a]	Bernouilli	Poisson	-	No	No
Wagner, Taudes (1986)	Polya distribution	Exponential	Poisson	Yes	No
Gupta (1988)	Multinomial	Erlang 2	Multinomial	Yes	No
Krishnamurthi, Raj (1988)[b]	Multinomial	-	Normal	Yes	A-priori
Pedrick, Zufryden (1991)	Dirichlet-Multinomial	NBD	-	Yes	No
Vilcassim, Jain (1991)	Hazard modeling approach		-	Yes	No
Chiang (1991)	Utility maximization	Multinomial	Normal	Yes	No
Bucklin, Gupta (1992)	Multinomial (nested logit)	Binomial	-	Yes	Mixture
Chintagunta (1993)	Utility maximization	Multinomial	Normal	Yes	Random effects
Böckenholt (1993a, 1993b)	Dirichlet-Multinomial	Gamma	NBD	Yes	Mixture
Wedel et al. (1995)	Poisson	Piecewise exponential	Poisson	Yes	Mixture
Dillon, Gupta (1996)	Dirichlet-Multinomial	Gamma	NBD	Yes	Mixture

[a] CNBD = Constrained Negative Binomial Distribution.
[b] Do not assume choice/quantity/timing to be independent.

3. Obtain the unconditional distribution of y by integrating out the heterogeneity distribution. This leads to a NBD (see Section 12.1):
$NBD(y) = \int P(y \mid \lambda)G(\lambda)d\lambda$.
4. Assume a multinomial distribution for choice, x: $M(x \mid p)$.
5. Assume a Dirichlet heterogeneity distribution for the choice probabilities: $D(p)$.
6. Obtain the unconditional distribution of x by integrating out the heterogeneity

Table 12.9 The Böckenholt (1993a, 1993b) purchase incidence and brand
           choice model family.

Model	Purchase incidence rate	Brand selection probabilities
	Heterogeneity in:	
Dirichlet-gamma	Gamma	Dirichlet
Dirichlet-Poisson	None	Dirichlet
Multinomial-gamma	Gamma	None
Multinomial-Poisson	None	None

distribution. This leads to a Dirichlet-Multinomial (DM) distribution: $DM(x) = \int M(x \mid p)D(p)dp$.

7. In the final step, the joint distribution of purchase frequency and choice is obtained, assuming independence: $NBDM(y, x) = NBD(y) \cdot DM(x)$.

From this framework, important quantities such as market share, penetration, duplication, brand switching and repeat buying can be obtained. Most approaches in this field follow a similar format, but there are many variations. Table 12.8 provides an overview of selected approaches. Some of the models do not explicitly account for either timing or incidence, but a distribution for timing is implicitly defined through the assumption of a distribution for purchase incidence, or vice versa.

We briefly describe the models by Böckenholt (1993a, 1993b), of which a modified version was applied in marketing by Dillon and Gupta (1996). The data are contained in a subjects-by-brands purchase-frequency data matrix. The model (for each segment) follows the scheme outlined above. It is assumed that the overall purchase rate follows a Poisson distribution (conditional upon the segments) and that the parameter of the Poisson distribution (the expected purchase rate) follows a gamma distribution across respondents within each segment. By compounding these two distributions, the overall purchase incidence follows a negative binomial distribution, with the log-mean parameterized in terms of consumer purchase rate variables (see Section 12.1). Conditional upon the overall purchase incidence, the brand choice frequencies are assumed to follow a multinomial distribution. Heterogeneity is accounted for by letting the multinomial purchase probabilities follow a Dirichlet distribution. Compounding the Dirichlet and the multinomial results in a Dirichlet-Multinomial (DM) distribution of brand purchases. The choice probabilities of the DM model are re-parameterized in terms of explanatory (marketing mix, product attribute) variables (see Section 12.3.3). The purchase frequency and brand choice components are assumed to be independent in this model, so that the joint distribution is the product of the purchase frequency and brand choice distributions. The model is very general: it accounts for heterogeneity in both overall purchase incidence and brand choice in three ways:

1. Through the inclusion of the mixing distributions, a gamma for the Poisson parameter and a Dirichlet for the multinomial choice probabilities.

2. Through two types of explanatory variables, those related to the consumers and those related to brands. The first set of explanatory variables is included in the expectation of the negative binomial distributions. The second set is included in the linear predictor of the Dirichlet-Multinomial distributions;

3. Through segments, operationalized via a mixture model (see Section 17.2).

Several models arise as special cases, by assuming homogeneity in the brand selection probabilities and/or in the purchase incidence, by assuming the absence of segments or the effects of predictor variables. We show in Table 12.9 special cases of Böckenholt's model (1993a, 1993b).

Dillon and Gupta (1996) applied this framework to a survey of household purchases of paper towels. The model showed that less than 10% of the households are price sensitive. Also price sensitivity was higher for households with more children and for heavy purchasers. Five segments were used to characterize purchase behavior. Two of the largest switching segments were very price sensitive in both brand choice and category purchase. Dillon and Gupta (1996) showed that the modeling framework outperforms a variety of competing models, among which models without brand variables, without loyal, choice or any segments. In addition, the model outperformed the approaches by Colombo and Morisson (1989), Krishnamurthi and Raj (1991), Grover and Srinivasan (1992) as well as the Goodhardt, Ehrenberg and Chatfield (1984) type of models. Earlier Monte Carlo work by Böckenholt (1993a, 1993b) had also provided strong support for the validity of this general approach.

CHAPTER 13

Multiproduct models

For many firms it is critical to consider interdependencies between products offered in the marketplace. For example, Procter & Gamble offers several brands in the detergent product category. Each individual brand may at some time have been positioned to serve a specific consumer segment. However, if each brand manager maximizes the performance of a brand independently of other brands in the same category sold by the same firm, then the distinction in positioning may blur over time. It is conceivable that the intensity of competition between brands belonging to the same firm gradually resembles the intensity of competition between brands for different firms.

At Procter & Gamble this problem is addressed organizationally by having a category manager who coordinates the marketing activities of brand managers. Instead of having the brand managers maximize the performances of their brands independently, the objective is to maximize the joint performance at the category level. One possible consequence of this coordination is that the effects of brand-level marketing activities on other brands of the same firm are close to zero. Multiproduct models account for such interdependencies.

Multiproduct models should be developed for products that have something in common. The category management problem is essentially an example of a *product line* which consists of a group of products that are closely related, for example because they have similar functionality or because they are sold through similar outlets (see e.g. Kotler 1997, p. 436).

In this chapter we discuss different forms of interdependence and we illustrate modeling approaches for the treatment of interdependence in Section 13.1. In Section 13.2 we discuss a model designed to assist management with the allocation of resources to various product groups. In Section 13.3 we focus on product line pricing and include a brief discussion of product bundling. We end with two sections in which we refer to models specifically developed to assist retailers. In Section 13.4 we focus on shelf space allocation and in Section 13.5 we discuss the problem of allocating advertising expenditures across multiple products.

13.1 Interdependencies

In general, three types of interdependencies are considered:

- demand interdependencies;
- cost interdependencies;
- risk interdependencies.

In this chapter we focus attention mostly on *demand* interdependencies.

Cost interdependencies reflect purchasing, production, distribution and other marketing economies or diseconomies (Montgomery, Urban, 1969, p. 343). Many of the merger and acquisition activities in the 1990's, for example in the oil industry, appear to be motivated by an expectation of scale economies. In the retail sector some of the immediate benefits due to acquisitions obtained by retailers include an enhanced power vis à vis the manufacturers in the negotiation of prices. Apart from a reduction in variable costs, it is also possible that fixed financial and managerial resources can be spread over a larger number of units.

Risk interdependencies are probably less relevant. For public companies, investors can diversify their holdings so as to control their risks. However, managements may seek to maintain full-time jobs for all employees, and therefore seek to minimize demand fluctuations at the corporate level. Similarly, management of private companies may under some conditions reduce the expected return in exchange for a reduction in the variance in revenues or cash flow over time. Thus, management may have some interest in offering a portfolio of products for which both the mean and the variance of returns over time are controlled. Risk interdependencies are studied in portfolio analysis.

We now discuss the *demand* interdependencies in more detail below.

In the introduction we mentioned the need for firms such as Procter & Gamble to coordinate the activities of brand managers so that the performance of *brands* is maximized at the product category level. Similarly, the brand manager should engage in marketing activities for the different *varieties, package sizes*, etc. to maximize the joint performances of the *items* at the brand level (subject to product category coordination). As we argued above, these interdependencies tend to have negative consequences at the brand- and the category level. In other cases, coordination by management is desirable to exploit the opportunity to realize positive consequences. Well-known demand interdependencies are complementarity and substitution. Complementarity of products is a positive demand effect whereby an increase in demand for one item tends to lead to an increase in the other items. Or, the marketing activity for one item has a positive effect on its demand and also on the demand for the other item. By contrast, substitution occurs when these effects are negative (as in the examples of the brand manager coordinating marketing activities for items, and the category manager doing the same for multiple brands so as to minimize substitution effects).

To illustrate, consider the following equation used by Reibstein and Gatignon (1984):

$$q_{jt} = \exp(\beta_{0j}) \prod_{r=1}^{n} p_{rt}^{\beta_{rj}} \exp(u_{jt}) \qquad (13.1)$$

where

q_{jt} = the quantity demanded for brand j in period t,

p_{rt} = the price of brand r in period t,

u_{jt} = a disturbance term for brand j in period t,

n = the number of brands.

In this model, the own-brand price elasticity is captured by β_{rj} when $j = r$. This effect is expected to be negative, based on economic theory. For $j \neq r$, we consider the following possibilities:

1. $\beta_{rj} = 0$: products j and r are independent in the sense that the cross-price effect of brand r on the quantity demanded of brand j is zero;
2. $\beta_{rj} > 0$: products j and r are substitutes in the sense that a decrease in the price of brand r decreases the quantity demanded of brand j;
3. $\beta_{rj} < 0$: products j and r are complements in the sense that a decrease in the price of brand r increases the quantity demanded of brand j.

We note that if $\beta_{rj} = 0$ there is no need to include the price of brand r in the demand model for brand j. However, in practice we may include such brands to test a null hypothesis of independence. The structure of (13.1) is similar to that of demand models, such as the SCAN*PRO model in equation (9.19).

The formalization of actual models that can be used in practice is potentially very complex. If we assume the availability of weekly, store-level data for all items, a manufacturer may want to take the effects of tens or hundreds of items into account. Many of these items have separate marketing activities, and aggregation across items is justified only for items with identical marketing support over time and between stores (see Christen, Gupta, Porter, Staelin, Wittink, 1997). It is very easy for an analyst to encounter a problem with 1,000 or so predictor variables that may be relevant. There are, however, theoretical and conceptual arguments we can use to simplify the structure. For example, if a comparative advertising campaign is initiated for one brand, it is likely that the cross effects involving other brands mentioned will become stronger. In general, consumers evaluate the substitutability between different brands by comparing the product characteristics, the packages, the prices, etc. As the perceived similarity increases, the degree of substitution should increase. Thus, we can also use our own judgments about product similarities to categorize brands or items in terms of the expected magnitudes of cross effects, and use this categorization to place restrictions on the multitude of possible effects.[1]

---

1. See also the discussion about market boundaries in Section 14.3.

So far we have discussed demand-side interdependencies from the manufacturer's point of view, and we have argued that the substitutability is a function of the marketing mix. The nature and degree of competition between items is also influenced, however, by the layout of the stores in which the items are sold. For example, if all package sizes of Miller Lite beer are located next to each other, and similarly all package sizes of Bud Lite beer are placed together (but at some distance from the Miller Lite items), we expect stronger within-brand effects than would exist if the placement of all items is by package size. Of course one expects the retailer to use a layout that reflects the consumer decision-making process. Thus, this layout is consistent with a consumer who tends to choose the brand and variety before the package size is chosen.[2] Nevertheless, the layout used by the retailer facilitates some product comparisons more than other ones, and this layout can therefore affect the nature of competition captured by cross-item effects.

We can also consider the demand interdependencies from the retailer's perspective. Retailers employ category managers who have responsibility for the assortment, the layout and other aspects relevant to the demand side. As is the case for the category managers of a manufacturer, these category managers also have the objective to maximize the performance of their categories (subject to additional considerations between categories, discussed shortly). Empirical research results (e.g. Gupta, 1988, Bell, Chiang, Padmanabhan, 1997, 1999) suggest that, on average, more than 80 percent of sales increases due to temporary promotions of items is attributable to other items within the same product category.[3] Thus, much of the promotional activity employed by retailers (who often pass trade promotion expenditures offered by manufacturers through to consumers) is inconsequential at the category level. Competition between stores is, however, affected by "loss leaders" or "traffic builders", items that are believed to influence a consumer's choice of the store to visit for the purchase of a basket of goods in a given week.

Walters (1991) developed a conceptual framework for the analysis of retail promotional effects that includes brand substitution effects, store substitution effects, and the effects of promotions on complementary goods. We show an adapted version of Walter's conceptual model in Figure 13.1.

In this model, the primary focus is on the demand for product j in one of two stores. In each store, this demand is assumed to be a function of the promotional activities for the product itself, of promotions for complements and substitutes offered in the same store, of promotions for the same product in a second store and of promotions for the product's complements and substitutes in this second store. Only these six effects in store one are reflected in the arrows shown in Figure 13.1.

Walters used the following model to estimate intra- and inter-store effects of temporary price cuts:

---

2. See also Foekens, Leeflang, Wittink (1997) and Section 14.5.

3. van Heerde, Leeflang, Wittink (1999b) show that this percentage depends on the level of the promotional discount and the type of support (feature, display, feature and display) offered.

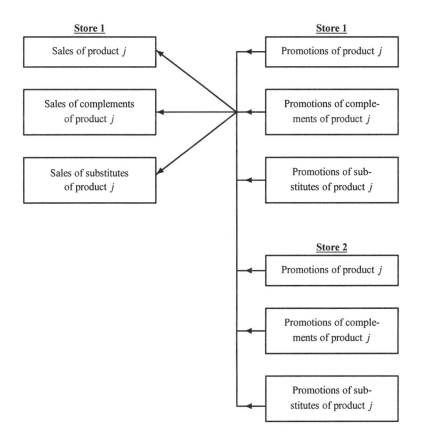

Source: based on Walters (1991, p.19).

Figure 13.1 Conceptual model of retail promotion effects.

$$q_{kjt} = \alpha_{0kj} + \sum_{k'=1}^{K} \sum_{r=1}^{n} \alpha_{k'r} p_{k'rt} + u_{kjt} \qquad (13.2)$$

where

q_{kjt} = unit sales of brand j in store k, week t,

$p_{k'rt}$ = the unit price of brand r in store k', week t,

K = the number of stores,

n = the number of brands,

u_{kjt} = a disturbance term.

To estimate the parameters in (13.2), Walters used store-level scanner data, covering 26 weeks, for four product categories. In one product category, cake mix, three brands were used as potential substitutes. The complementary product category was defined as cake frosting. His empirical results show that:

- own-brand price promotions significantly affect sales of the brand in the same store;
- virtually all of these sales increases emanate from other brands in the same category offered in the same store (i.e. intrastore, interbrand substitution effects);
- price promotions for one brand are often effective in stimulating sales of complementary products within the same store (i.e. intrastore, interbrand complementary effects);
- price promotions rarely create interstore effects.

We note that these results are consistent with the idea that the majority of product categories at the store level face inelastic category demand (Hoch, Kim, Montgomery, Rossi, 1995).

13.2 An example of a resource allocation model

Gijsbrechts and Naert (1984) specify a general form of a marketing resource allocation model. Their model is intended to help management with the allocation of a given marketing budget B over n product groups. The model accounts for:[4]

- the response of market share to marketing activities relevant to the different products;
- the relation between market share, sales and profit;
- a set of strategic constraints imposed by top management.

The general model is represented in equations (13.3)-(13.9) below:

$$\max_{b_j} \pi = \sum_{j=1}^{n}((p_j - c_j)q_j - b_j - FC_j) - FC \qquad (13.3)$$

subject to

$$q_j = m_j Q_j \qquad (13.4)$$
$$Q_j = Q'_j(b_1, O_1, \ldots, b_n, O_n, b_{1c}, O_{1c}, \ldots, b_{nc}, O_{nc}, ev) \qquad (13.5)$$
$$m_j = m'_j(b_1, O_1, \ldots, b_n, O_n, b_{1c}, O_{1c}, \ldots, b_{nc}, O_{nc}) \qquad (13.6)$$
$$\text{for } j = 1, \ldots, n$$
$$lo_j \le m_j \le up_j, \quad \text{for all } j = 1, \ldots, n \qquad (13.7)$$

$$\sum_{j=1}^{n} b_j \le B \qquad (13.8)$$

---

4. We closely follow Gijsbrechts, Naert (1984).

$$b_j \geq 0, \text{ for all } j = 1, \ldots, n \qquad\qquad (13.9)$$

where

$$
\begin{aligned}
\pi &= \text{total profit across } n \text{ product groups,} \\
p_j &= \text{the price per unit in product group } j, \; j = 1, \ldots, n, \\
c_j &= \text{the variable cost per unit in group } j \text{ excluding} \\
    &\quad \text{marketing effort,} \\
q_j &= \text{the number of units sold in product group } j, \\
b_j &= \text{the total marketing resources allocated to group } j, \\
FC_j &= \text{the fixed cost attributable to group } j, \\
FC &= \text{other fixed cost,} \\
m_j &= \text{total market share of the items in product group } j, \\
Q_j &= \text{product category sales group } j, \\
O_j &= \text{other marketing variables for group } j, \\
b_{jc} &= \text{marketing resources allocated to products of group } j \\
       &\quad \text{by competitors,} \\
O_{jc} &= \text{``other marketing variables'' of competitive brands in} \\
       &\quad \text{group } j, \\
ev &= \text{environmental variables, affecting product category} \\
   &\quad \text{sales,} \\
\ell o_j, \, up_j &= \text{lower, upper bounds on market share for group } j, \\
B &= \text{the total marketing budget,}
\end{aligned}
$$

and where time subscripts and disturbance terms are omitted for convenience.

Empirically, Gijsbrechts and Naert (1984) use the objective function to cover one period of one year. Equation (13.3) shows that profit is maximized with respect to "marketing resources", b_j. These marketing resources are aggregates of variables such as advertising, promotion, personal selling and distribution expenses. The simplifying assumption is that these marketing variables have homogeneous effects and that aggregation across these different activities does not distort the results.

The lower and upper limits on the market shares of the different groups (equation (13.7)) are imposed by corporate management. These limits may be based on strategic and other considerations that are outside the demand model. For example, the lower bounds on market share, ℓo_j, may be imposed for product groups in which top management wants to invest and maintain a minimum presence in the market with the expectation of future potential. Conversely, cash flow considerations may force the placement of upper limits, up_j, on market shares. One may view these limits as reflecting some risk interdependencies between the product groups. Cash flow and investment considerations show up in product portfolio analyses.[5]

The model is a multi-product group demand model. In principle, it allows for all cross effects at the product group level. Thus, both substitution- and complementary effects between product groups can be taken into account. However, the model does not contain cost functions. Thus, the cost variables are exogenous, and there is no allowance for interdependencies on the cost side.

Gijsbrechts and Naert calibrated the demand functions with subjective data (see also Section 16.9). The managers of product groups were asked to specify market shares they expected to have for various possible combinations of values for b_j, O_j, b_{jc} and O_{jc}, $j = 1, \ldots, n$. Given a budget B, and lower and upper bounds for market shares, a nonlinear optimization routine is applied to obtain the values for $b_1, \ldots, b_n$ that yield maximum profit for the next budget period.

13.3 Product line pricing

Due to demand- and cost interrelationships within a product line, and because there are usually several price-market targets, the product line pricing problem has been mentioned as one of the major challenges facing a marketing manager. Monroe and Della Bitta (1978, p. 417) argue that complementarity between items may show up through the prices of items in a product line even if the items are inherently substitutable. Thus, through the addition of new items or by changing some prices, a firm may increase the demand for the product line. Also, products that have functional complementarity present a challenging pricing problem. Examples are razors and razor blades, copiers and paper, computers and multiple software models, etc. In the razor example, consumers have no demand for the blades unless they have the razor with which the blades can be used. Given also the availability of other razors, the manufacturer has an interest in distributing the razor widely. If the manufacturer faces no competition on the blades, it is desirable to offer the razor at a very low price, and to derive profits from the blades. However, the common introduction of private-label blades reduces the manufacturer's price for the blades. The problem is to consider the demand- and cost functions jointly so that the dependencies are used in the determination of prices.

Other dependencies between items are considered in the bundling literature. In this literature three options are distinguished:

- pure bundling, a strategy in which only the bundle of products (or services) is offered;
- pure components, a strategy in which only the components are offered;
- mixed bundling, a strategy in which both the bundle and the components are offered.

---

5. See, for example, Wind, Mahajan, Swire (1983).

Much of the literature focuses on the optimal strategy and the optimal prices,[6] under a variety of scenarios.

The issue of product line pricing has been addressed by many researchers.[7] Game-theoretic analysis has focused on the pricing of related or substitute goods. This work often ignores channel structure issues, and is typically restricted to a small set of brands. An exception to the tendency by empirical researchers to ignore the role of channel pricing, is Zenor (1994), whose model we discuss at the end of this section. One of the early multiproduct models, in which interdependencies between brands belonging to a firm's product line are considered, was developed by Urban (1969b). Urban specifies demand- and cost functions for a firm offering brands in several product groups $h = 1, \ldots, H$. We modify Urban's model slightly for convenience. Sales of brand j, one of the brands of product group h, is modeled through the demand for product group h, with interdependencies between the product groups, and the market share of brand j in the product group, as follows:

$$q_{jht} = \alpha \cdot \bar{p}_{ht}^{\beta_{1h}} \left(\sum_{r=1}^{n} a_{rht} \right)^{\beta_{2h}} \left(\sum_{r=1}^{n} d_{rht} \right)^{\beta_{3h}} \tag{13.10}$$

$$\cdot \prod_{\substack{h'=1 \\ h' \neq h}}^{H} \bar{p}_{h't}^{\beta_{1h'}} \left(\sum_{r=1}^{n(h')} a_{rh't} \right)^{\beta_{2h'}} \left(\sum_{r=1}^{n(h')} d_{rh't} \right)^{\beta_{3h'}}$$

$$\cdot \frac{p_{jht}^{\gamma_{1jh}} \cdot a_{jht}^{\gamma_{2jh}} d_{jht}^{\gamma_{3jh}}}{\sum_{r=1}^{n} p_{rht}^{\gamma_{1rh}} a_{rht}^{\gamma_{2rh}} d_{rht}^{\gamma_{3rh}}}$$

where

q_{jht} = sales of brand j (of product group h) in period t,

$\bar{p}_{ht}$ = average price of product group h in period t,

a_{rht} = advertising expenditures of brand r (of product group h) in period t,

d_{rht} = percent of distribution outlets carrying brand r (of product group h) in period t,

p_{jht} = price of product j in product group h in period t,

n = the total number of brands in product group h,

$n(h')$ = the total number of brands in product group h'.

A disturbance term is omitted in (13.10) for convenience. By specifying this relation for all brands in a firm's product line, total revenue can be obtained by sum-

---

6. See, for example, Hanson, Martin (1990), Cready (1991), Rao (1993), Kaicker, Bearden (1995), Sirohi (1999).
7. Monroe, Della Bitta (1978), Moorthy (1984), Reibstein, Gatignon (1984), Rao (1984, 1993), Zenor (1994), Bultez, Gijsbrechts, Naert (1995), Kadiyali, Vilcassim, Chintagunta (1996).

ming the products of the brands' unit sales and prices. The cost function captures
interdependencies between the different brands as follows:

$$TVC_{jht} = AVC_{jht}q_{jht} \prod_{\substack{r'=1 \\ r'\neq j}}^{H'} q_{r'h't}^{\delta_{jr'}} \tag{13.11}$$

where

TVC_{jht} = total variable cost of producing brand j (of product
group h) in t,

AVC_{jht} = the average variable cost for brand j in h if produced
independently of other products (brands) of the firm,

$q_{r'h't}$ = the quantity of brand r' (of product group h') produced by the firm,

$\delta_{jr'}$ = cross variable cost elasticity of brand j with respect
to $r' = 1, \ldots, H', \quad r' \neq j$.

It is assumed that the firm produces one brand $r', r' = 1, \ldots, H'$ in each of the
H' product groups, where $H' \leq H$. Substracting TVC_{jt} and fixed production and
variable advertising and distribution costs from the total revenue yields total profit.
Optimization of the profit function is performed by an iterative search routine. The
application of the model identified significant product (brand) interdependencies.
Based on an empirical application, Urban recommended changes in the marketing
mix of the products in the line so that the interdependencies could be exploited for
additional profit.

More recently Zenor (1994) developed a category-level pricing model. He compared
the potential profits of a coordinated *"category level"* pricing strategy with an unco-
ordinated *"brand level"* pricing strategy. Zenor's model for optimization is a linear
demand function:[8]

$$q_j = \alpha_{0j} + \sum_{r=1}^{n} \alpha_{rj}p_r \tag{13.12}$$

where

q_j = sales of brand j,
p_r = price of brand r, and
n = total number of relevant brands.

For n brands the complete system of demand-price relationships used for optimization
is:

$$q = \alpha + Ap \tag{13.13}$$

8. Similar models were used by Bultez, Gijsbrechts, Naert, Vanden Abeele (1989) and Juhl, Kristensen (1989).

where

q = $n \times 1$ vector of sales for the n brands,

α = $n \times 1$ vector of constant terms,

A = an $n \times n$ matrix of own- and cross-demand sensitivities for all pairs of brands,

p = an $n \times 1$ vector of retail brand prices.

Gross brand profits can be expressed as:

$$\pi = (\operatorname{diag} q)'(p - c) \tag{13.14}$$

where

c = an $n \times 1$ vector of variable production costs associated with each brand.

Zenor (1994) introduces the coalition-brand matrix Z, with elements $z_{ij} = 1$ if brand j belongs to "coalition" i, $z_{ij} = 0$, if not. If a manager pursues category management, it creates a formal "coalition" between the brands in its product line. Thus if brands $j = 1, .., 4$ constitute a formal coalition under category manager $i = 1$, and brands $j = 5, 6$ are excluded, then $z_{11} = z_{12} = z_{13} = z_{14} = 1$, and $z_{15} = z_{16} = 0$. Equation (13.14) specifies the gross profits resulting from treating the brands independently. The "coalition" profits are obtained by pre-multiplying (13.14) by the coalition matrix Z:

$$\pi_c = Z(\operatorname{diag} q)'(p - c). \tag{13.15}$$

Zenor's empirical analysis shows the benefits of coordinated decision making: the implied profit increase is as high as 30 percent.

13.4 Shelf space allocation models

The marketing problem for a retailer is enormously complex. For example, many supermarkets offer tens of thousand of items. The retailer faces not only the question of which items to offer and in what manner (content and layout of the assortment)[9], but also what prices to charge, how to advertise the outlet and the items, and how to conduct promotions. If we treat items and product categories independently, then these problems can be analyzed separately for each of many components. However, the most intriguing question centers around dependencies. Thus, supermarket retailers use certain items (e.g. fruits such as bananas, soft drinks such as Coca Cola) to attract consumers to the store by offering these items at promoted prices. If this is a productive strategy, then the promotion of these items at low prices must have positive effects on the sales of other items. Relatively little is known about the effectiveness

---

9. See Rao and McLaughlin (1989) for an analysis of the retailer's new-product acceptance/rejection decision.

of alternative approaches used by retailers to affect total store sales. Thus, there is a great deal of uncertainty about the optimality of marketing decisions at the retail level.

According to Bultez and Naert (1988b), consultants to retailers essentially recommend shelf space allocations proportional to revenues or profits, potentially augmented by cost considerations such as handling costs and inventory control costs. By contrast, academic researchers have considered the sensitivity of demand to shelf space. It is easy to demonstrate that the optimal amount of space for a given item is a function of own- and cross-item demand sensitivities.

Bultez and Naert (1988b) have developed SH.A.R.P. (SHelf Allocation for Retailer's Profit) to capture demand interdependencies. In this sense shelf space allocation models constitute an important part of multiproduct models.[10] The objective is to maximize profit across n items:

$$\underset{sh_r}{\text{Max}} \left\{ \sum_{r=1}^{n} g_r q_r(sh_1, \ldots, sh_n) - \sum_{r=1}^{n} C_r \right\} \tag{13.16}$$

subject to

$$\sum_{r=1}^{n} sh_r \leq SH \tag{13.17}$$

and

$$sh_r \geq 0 \text{ for all } r = 1, \ldots, n \tag{13.18}$$

where

sh_r = space allocated to item r, with $r = 1, \ldots, n$,

g_r = gross profit margin or markup per unit of item r sold,

q_r = item r's unit sales volume as a function of $sh_1, \ldots, sh_n$,

C_r = replenishment cost functions due to carrying item r in the assortment,

SH = total shelf space available for the assortment.

In the model each item's sales volume q_r is a function of the space allocation,[11] i.e. the sh_r's. Since an increase in shelf space should increase sales, the expectation is that $\delta q_r / \delta sh_r \geq 0$, and hence $\eta_{rr} = (\delta q_r / \delta sh_r)(sh_r / q_r) \geq 0$ (i.e. the shelf space elasticity is expected to be positive).[12] The cross elasticities $\eta_{rj} = (\delta q_r / \delta sh_j)(sh_j / q_r)$ are either negative (substitutes), positive (complementary items) or zero. Importantly the interdependencies are captured through these cross effects.

---

10. For literature reviews see Corstjens, Doyle (1981), Bultez, Naert (1988b) and Bultez (1995).
11. We closely follow Bultez, Naert (1988b).
12. See also Curhan (1972).

On the cost side, the expectations are that: $\delta C_r / \delta q_r \geq 0$, i.e. higher sales volume implies extra replenishment operations, holding other aspects such as shelf space constant, and $(\delta C_r / \delta sh_r \mid dq_r = 0) \leq 0$, i.e., more shelf (storage) space reduces replenishment operations, when the demand stays constant.

The Lagrangian function for the nonlinear programming problem defined in (13.16)-(13.18) is:

$$\mathcal{L} = \left(\sum_{r=1}^{n} g_r q_r - \sum_{r=1}^{n} C_r \right) + \lambda \left(SH - \sum_{r=1}^{n} sh_r \right) \tag{13.19}$$

with

$$\lambda \geq 0$$

The optimal share of the total available space to be allocated to item r is:

$$sh_r^* = sh_r / SH = (\gamma_r c_r + \bar{\eta}_{.r}) / (\bar{G} + \bar{N}) \tag{13.20}$$

where

sh_r^* = optimal share of shelf space for item r,

γ_r = the percent decrease in handling cost resulting from a one percent increase in space $(\delta C_r / \delta sh_r)(sh_r / C_r)$,

c_r = C_r / π = product r's replenishment cost relative to the total assortment profitability π,

$\bar{\eta}_{.r}$ = $\sum_{j=1}^{n} w_j \eta_j$ = the weighted mean of all elasticities (own: $j = r$, and cross $j \neq r$) with respect to r's space share, where $w_j = \pi_j / \pi$, i.e. the relative profitability of item j,

$\bar{G}$ = $\sum_{r=1}^{n} \gamma_r c_r$, and

$\bar{N}$ = $\sum_{r=1}^{n} \bar{\eta}_{.r}$.

Equation (13.20) implies that priority in shelf space allocation should be given to those items for which shelf space contributes the most to reducing handling costs $(\gamma_r c_r)$ and to items whose shelf space contributes the most to sales of the most profitable items $\bar{\eta}_{.r}$.

Bultez and Naert (1988b) suggest a pragmatic hierarchical approach which first distributes the total shelf space SH across the various product classes (allocation along the width-axis of the assortment) and then allocates space to the items within the lot assigned to each product class (allocation along the depth-dimension). The model of

Corstjens and Doyle (1981) focuses on interactions between product classes, while SH.A.R.P. includes interactions between product classes and interactions between items within a product class. Bultez and Naert (1988b) use attraction models to estimate shelf space elasticities at both levels. In the empirical section they report that SH.A.R.P. was applied to multiple assortments in Belgian supermarket chains. Reallocations of shelf space resulted in increases in profit varying from about 7 percent to 34 percent.

The attractiveness of a product class depends on the attractiveness of the items within the product class and the shelf space allocated to these items. Hierarchical models offer good opportunities to relate these two levels of attractiveness. For a discussion of these models see Section 14.5. Bultez, Gijsbrechts, Naert and Vanden Abeele (1989) integrate another, asymmetric, attraction model in SH.A.R.P. We discuss this model, which relates the interactions at both levels, in Section 14.4.

13.5 Multiproduct advertising budgeting

In this section we present and discuss a model designed to optimize the allocation of advertising expenditures to individual product categories and media for a retailer. In the model, the sales in a given product category is assumed to be a function of advertising for that category, advertising for other categories, and general store campaigns.

Doyle and Saunders (1990) propose a multiproduct advertising budgeting model that can be used to allocate expenditures to different product categories and media. We first discuss the basic elements of their model and the attractive aspects with respect to specific synergies captured in their approach. We then suggest opportunities for additional research.

Doyle and Saunders introduce the problem of determining the optimal amount of advertising by arguing that for a single item the relevant factors are the item's margin and the sensitivity of demand with respect to advertising (holding other marketing activities constant). With multiple items, the retailer should also consider the cross-item advertising effects (and the effects of advertising individual items) on store traffic. Also, the support offered by the manufacturers plays a role.

In practice, advertising decisions are often made through what Doyle and Saunders call a bottom-up approach. Essentially, the optimal advertising decisions made in this approach ignore cross-item (cross-category) effects. Thus, possible complimentary and substitution effects across items are ignored. To illustrate, we consider the budgeting problem at the category level, consistent with Doyle and Saunders. In the bottom-up approach, we have:

$$q_{jt} = f_j(a_{jt}) + u_{jt}, \quad j = 1, \ldots, n \qquad (13.21)$$

where

q_{jt} = retail sales of category j in period t,

a_{jt} = advertising expenditure for category j in period t,

u_{jt} = a disturbance term.

By summing (13.21) across the categories, $j = 1, \ldots, n$, we obtain total retail sales.

For an empirical analysis Doyle and Saunders propose a semilog[13] specification and allow for lagged effects (which we ignore for convenience). The (simplified) model specification at the category level in the bottom-up approach is then:

$$q_{jt} = \beta_{0j} + \beta_{1j} \ln a_{jt} + u_{jt}. \tag{13.22}$$

Given a total advertising budget A, the allocation rule is:

$$a^*_{jt} = \frac{cm_j \beta_{1j}}{\sum_{r=1}^{n} cm_r \beta_{1r}} * A \tag{13.23}$$

where

$$cm_j = \text{the contribution margin of category } j.$$

Doyle and Saunders improve on this simple scheme by allowing for complementarity (and substitution) effects in advertising for specific product categories (top-down approach):

$$q_{jt} = \beta_{0j} + \sum_{r=1}^{n} \beta_{1jr} \ln a_{rt} + u_{jt}. \tag{13.24}$$

Given this ("top-down") approach the allocation rule is:

$$a^*_{jt} \approx \frac{\sum_{r=1}^{n} cm_r \beta_{1jr}}{\sum_{j=1}^{n} \sum_{r=1}^{n} cm_r \beta_{1jr}} * A. \tag{13.25}$$

In this more general, top-down, approach the allocation rule reflects the own- and cross-category effects. Thus, if the advertising for one category affects that category's sales as well as the sales of other categories, then all those effects multiplied by the corresponding contribution margins are taken into account. A practical difficulty is that if we want to allow all categories to have cross effects, and we want to allow for multi-period lagged effects, (13.24) is quickly saturated. And of course, the model excludes price and other variables which may bias the estimated parameters. To overcome these problems, Doyle and Saunders cross correlated sales and advertising (with leads and lags up to four periods) after filtering the data through transfer function analysis.[14] These cross correlations showed between four and ten predictor variables (including current- and lagged own-category, and cross-category variables) for the twelve categories of a European retailer with almost 1,000 stores, based on three years of weekly data.

A variation of equation (13.24) was estimated, with a restricted set of advertising variables (based on the significance of correlations between the filtered variables), plus some seasonal and cyclical terms. In all cases, advertising expenditures were defined separately for each of three media: catalogs, press and television. Seven of

---

13. To avoid the problem of taking logarithms of zero values, the value 1 is added to all advertising data (which we do not show).

14. See Section 17.3.

the twelve product categories had been heavily promoted, three in catalogs, six in the press, and three on television (one category was advertised in each of the media). Because of this, only the combination of media and product categories with nonzero budgets could be considered in the optimization process. However, the remaining five product categories were occasionally featured in general store campaigns or in general sales events. These five product categories' sales were potentially affected by these general advertising variables as well as by advertising for other categories.

The existing allocation had almost half the advertising budget assigned to the press, about 30 percent to the catalog and about 20 percent to television. The empirical results, however, showed that of 37 statistically significant advertising effects, 24 were for expenditures in the TV medium, 10 for the catalog medium, and three for the press. Roughly consistent with this, the *optimal* allocation suggested that 65 percent of the budget be allocated to TV, 30 percent to the catalog and about five percent to the press. Among the categories, the optimal allocation was to have 40 percent for candy (on TV), 20 percent for children's wear (in the catalog) and 10 percent for toys (on TV). Interestingly, candy also had the largest actual sales amount, and it accounted for more than 20 percent of total store sales. And the 40 percent recommended for candy was heavily influenced by the large frequency with which it achieved a significantly positive cross effect. Also, as expected, the TV medium had proportionally more current (fewer lagged) effects than the other two media.

The optimal amount of advertising for the store can be derived by summing the own- and cross-category effects multiplied by the corresponding profit contributions. This calculation suggested that the budget be quadrupled ($32 million recommended versus $8 million actual). Top management declined to accept this recommendation, but the existing budget was reallocated largely consistent with the suggested percentages. Doyle and Saunders report that both sales and profits improved, more than the industry sector averages, and close to model predictions.

This application shows quite nicely how the allocation of advertising to product categories and media can be improved, based on an analysis of available data. Importantly, the recommended relative allocations (but not the absolute ones) were adopted by management and the predicted results achieved.

Nevertheless, it is instructive to consider possible model enhancements. For example, although the *profit* equations included manufacturer support for advertising, this support should be allowed to influence the effectiveness of the retailer's advertising. Also, the model does not accommodate own- and cross effects of (category) prices. Both the content of advertising and the categories advertised may influence the price sensitivity (and the resulting margins used in the optimization procedure).

We also note that the allocation rule is based on the marginal effects of advertising on sales. If a given category has no significantly positive own- or cross effect, the implication is that it be allocated zero advertising expenditures. However, a zero marginal effect does not imply that advertising should be avoided altogether. In addition, given the dramatic change in allocation from previous practice, both to the media and to the categories that had received advertising support, it is desirable to allocate some funds to the five categories previously excluded.

CHAPTER 14

Model specification issues

In this chapter we discuss specification issues that transcend the intended use of a model (Chapter 8), the specific level of demand (Chapter 9), the amount of behavioral detail (Chapter 10) and the specific models discussed in Chapters 11-13.

We first discuss issues with regard to the aggregation level at which a model is specified, in terms of units and time periods (Section 14.1). The aggregation over time follows the material on modeling marketing dynamics in Chapter 6.

Aggregation differs from pooling observations. In pooling we maintain the disaggregate nature of the data, but use data on multiple units and multiple periods to estimate, often, a common set of parameters. The differences are introduced in Section 14.2. We consider pooling methods in more detail in Section 16.2.

Importantly, valid model specification depends critically on a proper definition of the relevant market or the market boundaries. This issue is discussed in Section 14.3.

Related to questions about market definition is the topic of asymmetries in competition (see also Chapters 9 and 12). We discuss non-hierarchical models that accommodate asymmetries in Section 14.4, and introduce hierarchical models in Section 14.5. We compare hierarchical and non-hierarchical models in Section 14.6.

14.1 Specifying models at different levels of aggregation

14.1.1 INTRODUCTION

In Chapter 9 we introduce the specification of models according to different levels of demand. The demand for "a product j" can be defined at the individual, household, store, chain and market level. Other demand levels are defined at the segment (Section 17.2) or at the regional level (Bass, Wittink, 1975, Wittink 1977, Leeflang, van Duijn, 1982a, 1982b).

The product j can also be defined at different levels such as the item, the stock-keeping unit (SKU), brand, product line, and firm level. Separate models may be developed to support the decisions made at these different levels. Thus models may differ in their model scope. Data can be aggregated along each of these dimensions, separately or jointly. We refer to these types of aggregation as entity aggregation.

Common sense, at least to the user of a model, suggests that a model should be specified at the same level of aggregation at which decisions are made. For example, if a manager wants to use model results for pricing or advertising decisions that apply to all households and all stores in a given market, the implication of this rule would be that the model should be estimated with market-level data. Interestingly, this seemingly sensible idea is not consistent with analytical and empirical research results. Even if differences between households and differences between stores are of no interest to the manager, it is helpful to use data that contain such differences.

To explore the pro's and con's of using data at alternative levels of aggregation, we specify a household-level model and derive a store-level model. We also consider the relation between store- and market-level models.

Data *aggregation* can occur over *units* and over *time* periods. Often, models are specified for arbitrarily chosen periods of time. For example, market research firms may decide to collect sales and associated data on a weekly basis. Here too the question is whether, or under what conditions, the substantive conclusions are invariant to aggregation over time.

14.1.2 ENTITY AGGREGATION

We start with a simple example of entity aggregation along the model scope dimension. Consider the following market share model:

$$m_{jt} = \beta_{0j} + \beta_{1j}\, as_{jt} + \beta_{2j}\, m_{j,t-1} + u_{jt}, \tag{14.1}$$
$$j = 1, \ldots, n, \ t = 1, \ldots, T$$

where

$$m_{jt} = \text{market share of brand } j \text{ in period } t,$$
$$as_{jt} = \text{advertising share of brand } j \text{ in } t,$$
$$u_{jt} = \text{a disturbance term, and}$$
$$n = \text{number of brands.}$$

This model has been calibrated by Reuyl (1982) and Leeflang, Reuyl (1986) for 14 ($n = 14$) individual brands and six leading firms of the German cigarette industry. The available data represent 28 bimonthly observations, thus $T = 28$. Lagged dependent variables are introduced in the response function to account for the fact that the market share does not adjust fully to changes in advertising share because of ignorance, inertia, cost of change, etc.

The market shares of the brands owned by one firm can be aggregated to firm shares. Similarly brand advertising shares can be aggregated to firm advertising shares. The fluctuations in firm shares can then be explained by the following firm share model:

$$fm_{jt} = \gamma_{0j} + \gamma_{1j}\, fas_{jt} + \gamma_{2j}\, fm_{j,t-1} + v_{jt}, \tag{14.2}$$
$$j = 1, \ldots, n', \ t = 1, \ldots, T$$

where

Table 14.1 *Parameter estimates and standard errors for market share and firm share equations (14.1) and (14.2).*

Brand	Advertising share		Lagged market share	
	$\hat{\beta}_{1j}$	$\hat{\sigma}_{\hat{\beta}_{1j}}$	$\hat{\beta}_{2j}$	$\hat{\sigma}_{\hat{\beta}_{2j}}$
1	0.02^a	0.01	0.69^a	0.14
2	0.04^a	0.01	0.34^a	0.18
3	0.04^a	0.01	0.64^a	0.18
4	0.01	0.08	0.95^a	0.06
Firm	Firm advertising share		Lagged firm share	
	$\hat{\gamma}_{1j}$	$\hat{\sigma}_{\hat{\gamma}_{1j}}$	$\hat{\gamma}_{2j}$	$\hat{\sigma}_{\hat{\gamma}_{2j}}$
A	0.03^a	0.02	0.64^a	0.16

^{a} Parameters statistically significant at the 5%-level.

Source: Reuyl (1982, p.130 and p. 139).

$$fm_{jt} = \text{market share of firm } j \text{ in period } t,$$
$$fas_{jt} = \text{advertising share of firm } j \text{ in } t,$$
$$v_{jt} = \text{a disturbance term},$$
$$n' = \text{number of firms } (n' = 6).$$

In Table 14.1 the parameter estimates and the corresponding estimated standard errors of the regression coefficients of (14.1) for four brands and the corresponding firm share equation (14.2) are given. The firm share equation refers to company A, which owns and markets all four brands. Thus:

$$fm_{jt} = \sum_{r=1}^{4} m_{rt} \quad \text{and} \quad fas_{jt} = \sum_{r=1}^{4} as_{rt}. \tag{14.3}$$

The differences between the estimated parameter-values of the four brands are substantial. We apply tests to see if these differences are statistically significant. To this end we pool the data of the four brands and test the hypothesis of equality of intercepts and slopes.[1] This hypothesis is rejected. Interestingly, the intercept and slope of the firm share equation appear to be close to the averages of the coefficients for the brand share equations. Nevertheless, the test result indicates that the brands differ in the effects of advertising share and lagged market share.

A large part of recent empirical research in marketing science has focused on models of brand choice specified at the household level (individual demand).[2] In

---

1. This so-called Chow-test is discussed in Section 16.2.
2. See, e.g. Chapter 12.

a number of such models, the effects of marketing variables on brand choice are determined conditional upon a purchase in the product category. One of the advantages of household-level models is that heterogeneity between households, in brand preferences and in sensitivities to marketing variables, can be explored. Understanding this household heterogeneity is critical to marketing managers for the successful development and implementation of market segmentation strategies. Mixture models have been developed that account for this heterogeneity (Section 17.2). Even if the model user does not want to exploit household heterogeneities in the use of marketing activities, it may still be necessary to accommodate such heterogeneities in a model intended only to produce the best *average* marketing effects.

If heterogeneity in the household-level model is ignored, it is possible to derive, in a fairly straightforward manner, a specification that produces identical parameter estimates at an aggregate level. Gupta, Chintagunta, Kaul and Wittink (1996) show how a store-level model can be obtained that necessarily gives the same parameter estimates as the household-level model does from which it is derived, as long as the aggregation is restricted to households' purchases occurring under homogeneous conditions. For example, actual brand choices occurring in a given store and a given time period can be aggregated to the store level as long as the marketing variables stay constant during the time period. Thus, if homogeneity in parameters across households can be assumed, and if homogeneity in marketing variables across the observations over which aggregation takes place is maintained, then an aggregate demand model that is analytically consistent with an individual demand model will produce identical results (Gupta et al., 1996).

A brand choice model is usually formulated by assuming that households consider n alternative brands that belong to a product category. Conditional upon a product category purchase, the criterion variable, for a given household and at a given time, takes on the value one for the brand chosen and zero for the remaining brands. We assume that households maximize their utility from a product category purchase:

$$U_j = x'_j \beta + e_j \tag{14.4}$$

where

$$U_j = \text{the utility associated with the purchase}$$
$$\text{(consumption) of brand } j,$$
$$x'_j = \text{the values of a set of variables associated with}$$
$$\text{brand } j \text{ at the time of purchase,}$$
$$e_j = \text{an error term.}$$

Compare also the discussion in Section 12.3.3 ((12.41)-(12.43)). With n alternatives, each household is expected to choose the brand that maximizes utility. The probability that alternative 1 (π_1) is preferred is:

$$\pi_1 = P[U_1 > U_2 \text{ and } U_1 > U_3 \text{ and } \dots \text{ and } U_1 > U_n] \tag{14.5}$$

where

$$P[U_1 > U_2] = P[(x_1' - x_2')\beta + e_1 - e_2] > 0$$

or

$$P[e_2 - e_1] < (x_1' - x_2')\beta.$$

If the error terms are i.i.d. with Weibull density functions, one obtains the multinomial logit model with brand choice probabilities:

$$\pi_j = \frac{\exp(x_j'\beta)}{\sum_{r=1}^{n} \exp(x_r'\beta)}. \tag{14.6}$$

Parameter estimation occurs with maximum likelihood methods (Section 16.6). The *likelihood function* (L), for an observed sample of purchases made by a household shopping in store k in week t, can be written as (Gupta et al., 1996, p. 387):

$$L = \prod_t \prod_k \prod_j \prod_{o_{jkt}} \pi_{jkt}^{\delta_{o_{jkt}}} \tag{14.7}$$

where

$$\delta_{o_{jkt}} = 1 \text{ if brand } j \text{ is purchased on occasion } o_{jkt},$$
$$= 0 \text{ otherwise.}$$

If aggregation across household purchases occurs *within* store and *within* week (such that the variables defined in x_j' are constant), then the same model structure applied to store data that express the number of units sold for each brand (per store, per week) produces identical parameter estimates. Thus, if the store data truly represent all household purchases, and parameter heterogeneity across households is ignored, we should be indifferent between the individual- and aggregate models.

In practice, only a sample of households participate in a purchase panel. Market research firms such as IRI and ACNielsen invite a probability sample of households to use plastic cards or wands so that the research firms obtain electronic records of (selected) purchases. In practice, some households refuse to participate, and the households who agree to participate may have omissions and errors in their purchase records (see also Chapter 15). Gupta et al. (1996) find statistical support for the statement that the panel household data are not representative of the store data. However, a comparison of *average* estimated price elasticities for data collected in small towns shows that the substantive difference between inferences from household- and store data is small if the household data are selected in a manner that is consistent with the model specification at the store level. Gupta et al. (1996) distinguish between *household- and purchase selection*, and show that "purchase selection", whereby only the purchases of brands selected for analysis are used for estimation, provides results that are much closer to store data results than "household selection". In the latter case only households that restrict their purchases to the subset of brands analyzed would be included for parameter estimation of the brand choice model.

Of course a primary attraction of household-level data is the opportunity to explore heterogeneity in purchase behavior and in responsiveness to marketing activities. And even if household heterogeneity is of no interest to the marketing manager, it may still be necessary to accommodate it in a household-level model in order to obtain the best *average* parameter estimates. The reason is that a heterogenous brand choice model typically obtains different results from a homogeneous specification because the homogeneous specification produces biased and inconsistent parameter estimates (Chintagunta, Jain and Vilcassim, 1991).

Different approaches are available for the accommodation of household heterogeneity in household-level data. However, in store-level data information on purchases made by individual households is lost, due to the aggregation of purchases over the households. To examine the comparability of results for a heterogeneous multinomial logit model (of household purchases) and a store-level model, Gupta et al. (1996) use an aggregate market share specification derived by Allenby and Rossi (1991a).[3]

The *market share* model that accommodates household *heterogeneity* produces estimated price elasticities that are uniformly smaller than the homogeneous multinomial logit model (Gupta et al. 1996, p. 392). This difference is due to two conflicting considerations:

1. The accommodation of heterogeneity tends to produce higher (in an absolute sense) average price elasticities (Jain, Vilcassim, Chintagunta, 1994). This is important because it implies that accommodation of heterogeneity is critical even if one is interested only in the average effects.
2. The use of market share reduces the price elasticities (relative to a model based on unit sales).

In this comparison the reduction in elasticities from unit sales to market share is apparently much greater than the increase in elasticities expected when household heterogeneity is accommodated.

Gupta et al. (1996) derived a multinomial store-level model that is based on the principle of utility maximization. They show how results can be obtained from store-level data consistent with multinomial brand choice model results. However, the commercial practice favors traditional and relatively straightforward demand models of store data. A popular market response function is the SCAN*PRO model (see equation (9.19)). A simplified version is:

$$q_{kjt} = \alpha_k \prod_{r=1}^{n} \left[\tilde{p}_{krt}^{\beta_{rj}} \prod_{\ell=1}^{L} \gamma_{\ell rj}^{D_{\ell krt}} \right] e^{u_{kjt}}, \tag{14.8}$$

3. Their specification accommodates heterogeneity through a Taylor series approximation. If this approximation is close enough, and product category unit sales is constant over time, then their market share model will produce similar results as the corresponding random-effects logit model. In such a model the parameters are assumed to follow a continuous distribution for the sample of households. For a different model that incorporates household heterogeneity in the analysis of store-level aggregate data, see Kim (1995).

$$k = 1, \ldots, K, \, t = 1, \ldots, T, \, j = 1, \ldots, n$$

where

q_{kjt} = unit sales for brand j in store k, week t,

$\tilde{p}_{krt}$ = unit price for brand r in store k, week t, relative to its regular price,

$D_{\ell krt}$ = an indicator variable for the ℓ-th store promotion activity (such as feature advertising and display) for brand r in store k, week t.

Importantly, this specification does *not* accommodate household heterogeneity. In addition, with data on multiple stores, it also does not allow the stores to differ in the effects of marketing variables. However, the equation omits variables that allow for seasonality in demand, which in practice are typically included. In addition, store indicator variables are omitted. With store dummies and the multiplicative specification, the model assumes that the stores have equal promotion effects in a proportional sense (i.e. relative to each store's base sales amount).

Although a similar specification is used frequently by IRI and ACNielsen, who both collect data from supermarkets and other stores equipped with scanners, it is of no use to managers and researchers who do not have access to the individual store data.[4] The question of interest is now the following. If the only data available for analysis are the same variables summed or averaged across the stores, and a similar model structure is used, are the parameter estimates comparable? Note that we do not ask whether the store data are representative of *market* data (the market data contain data from all stores on which data are available). Instead, the question is whether a nonlinear model applied to linearly aggregated (summed or aggregated) data can produce equivalent parameter estimates. Thus if a manager wants to make marketing decisions at the market level (jointly for all stores), will a market-level model be satisfactory?

To illustrate the problem, Christen, Gupta, Porter, Staelin and Wittink (1997) simplify the SCAN*PRO *store-level* model as follows:

$$q_k = \alpha_k \tilde{p}_k^\beta \gamma^{F_k} \tag{14.9}$$

where

F_k = the featuring of a brand in store k, measured by a dummy variable, $k = 1, \ldots, K$,

and the brand and week subscripts and the disturbance term have been dropped for convenience. The linear aggregation of data across the stores produces the following

---

4. IRI and ACNielsen offer model results based on propriety household- and/or store-data to clients. The same clients typically have to use data aggregated across stores if they want to do response modeling themselves.

averages:

$$\bar{q} = \frac{1}{K}\sum_{k=1}^{K} q_k, \quad \bar{p} = \frac{1}{K}\sum_{k=1}^{K} \tilde{p}_k \text{ and } \bar{F} = \frac{1}{K}\sum_{k=1}^{K} F_k \quad (14.10)$$

where

$\bar{F}$ = the fraction of stores engaging in a promotion
activity, here featuring.

A similar, nonlinear, model structure for the resulting *market-level* data is:

$$\bar{q} = \bar{\alpha}\,\bar{p}^{\beta'}\gamma'^{\bar{F}}. \quad (14.11)$$

In general, $\beta \neq \beta'$ and $\gamma \neq \gamma'$ since:

$$\frac{1}{K}\sum_{k=1}^{K} q_k = \frac{1}{K}\sum_{k=1}^{K} \alpha_k \tilde{p}_k^{\beta}\gamma^{F_k} \neq \bar{\alpha}\left(\frac{1}{K}\sum_{k=1}^{K} \tilde{p}_k\right)^{\beta} \gamma^{\frac{1}{K}\sum_{k=1}^{K} F_k} = \bar{\alpha}\,\bar{p}^{\beta}\gamma^{\bar{F}}. \quad (14.12)$$

On the other hand, if the market-level aggregates were to represent *geometric* means of unit sales and price, then parameter equivalence obtains since:

$$\left(\prod_{k=1}^{K} q_k\right)^{1/K} = \left(\prod_{k=1}^{K} \alpha_k \tilde{p}_k^{\beta}\gamma^{F_k}\right)^{1/K} \quad (14.13)$$

$$= \left(\prod_{k=1}^{K} \alpha_k\right)^{1/K}\left(\prod_{k=1}^{K} \tilde{p}_k\right)^{\beta/K}\gamma^{1/K\sum_{k=1}^{K} F_k}.$$

Thus, if the multiplicative store-level model is the desired specification, then the equivalent market-level model should be applied to data aggregated in a manner consistent with the (nonlinear) model specification. Unfortunately, the market-level data are produced primarily for tracking the market performance and the intensity of marketing activities for the brands at the retail level. In other words only arithmetic means are provided by the data suppliers.

To obtain analytical insight into the nature of a systematic difference in the parameters γ and γ' that is due to the linear aggregation of data belonging to a nonlinear model, Christen et al. (1997) use a simplified store model:

$$q_k = \gamma^{F_k}. \quad (14.14)$$

From (14.14) it is easy to examine the bias that occurs in the market model due to store heterogeneity in feature advertising.

The market model that corresponds to (14.14) is as follows (see also (14.11)):

$$\bar{q} = \gamma'^{\bar{F}} \quad (14.15)$$

from which the expression for γ' is:

$$\gamma' = \exp\left[\frac{\ln \bar{q}}{\bar{F}}\right].$$ (14.16)

From (14.14), given that F_k is either 0 or 1, the correct expression for $\bar{q}$ is:

$$\bar{q} = \bar{F}\gamma + (1 - \bar{F}).$$ (14.17)

Substituting this correct expression into the formula for γ', we obtain:

$$\gamma' = \exp\left[\frac{\ln(\bar{F}\gamma + 1 - \bar{F})}{\bar{F}}\right] = (\bar{F}\gamma + 1 - F)^{1/\bar{F}}, \quad 0 < \bar{F} \le 1.$$ (14.18)

The systematic difference between γ' and γ is:

$$(\gamma' - \gamma) = (\bar{F}\gamma + 1 - \bar{F})^{1/\bar{F}} - \gamma.$$ (14.19)

It is now possible to see that if $\gamma = 1$, there is no difference between γ' and γ. Also, if $\bar{F} = 1$, there is no difference. These two conditions indicate that if the promotion activity has no effect ($\gamma = 1$), or if all stores simultaneously promote ($\bar{F} = 1$), there is no bias due to linear aggregation. Otherwise $\gamma' \ne \gamma$, if aggregation occurs over stores that are heterogeneous in their marketing activities, which is unavoidable in case of aggregation over stores belonging to different chains.

By taking the derivative of the expression that shows the difference between γ' and γ ((14.19)) with respect to $\bar{F}$, we find that this difference (bias) increases as the proportion of stores promoting the brand decreases (except when $\bar{F} = 0$). The derivative with respect to γ shows that the bias increases with γ if $\gamma > 1$ but decreases with γ if $\gamma < 1$. The first result (how the bias depends on $\bar{F}$) is especially noteworthy, because it can create the following paradoxical situation.

Suppose that a multiplicative model (a variation of (14.11)) is estimated based on market-level data. If $\hat{\gamma}'$ is large enough, the brand manager may conclude that it should be profitable to stimulate more stores to engage in the promotional activity at a given time. If the strategy works, $\bar{F}$ will increase, for at least some time periods. Everything else being equal, if $\bar{F}$ becomes a larger proportion in periods when it is not zero, the next time γ' is estimated its expected value decreases (because the bias decreases when $\bar{F}$ increases). With the new estimate, the manager may decide that it is not profitable to stimulate such a large number of stores to promote the brand. But when $\bar{F}$ returns to its original value, the bias increases again, resulting in a higher γ' value, which persuades the manager to stimulate more stores to promote the brand, etc. Such a pattern of changing results may cause a critical manager to question the empirical findings. However, model builders and model users who do not understand that linear aggregation produces the bias are likely to conclude that the market response results suggest that *at any given time* the proportion of stores promoting should be small.

Christen et al. show that for models with *many variables*, as in the basic SCAN* PRO model (14.8) when analytical expressions of bias are very complex, the biases in estimated effects from market-level data can be very large. For example, for data on peanut butter brands, the market model produced a feature advertising multiplier (γ') of 4.26, while the store model showed $\hat{\gamma} = 1.36$ (in both cases averaged across three brands). Thus, the market model can generate a highly biased estimate of the increase in sales due to feature advertising of a brand, holding other things constant (more than 4 times the base amount of sales, if all stores feature the brand, in the market model versus substantially less than 2 times in the store model). For display, the market model had an average multiplier of 14.15, while the store model showed only 1.80 !

We conclude that for nonlinear market response models, a critical determinant of aggregation bias is heterogeneity in marketing activities across the units over which the data are summed or averaged. Thus, in case of linear aggregation of the data (the individual values are added or averaged, as is done for market status reports), the use of a *nonlinear* model will create biased parameter estimates if the marketing activities differ between the units across which the aggregation takes place. *Linear* models are not subject to this bias, because linear aggregation is consistent with the application of a linear model.

There is, however, another source of aggregation bias which is also applicable if the model is linear.[5] Krishnamurthi, Raj and Selvam (1990) show that if the units over which aggregation occurs are heterogeneous in both marketing activities and in the parameters representing the marketing effects, the requirement for no aggregation bias in a linear model is zero covariance between the marketing activities and the corresponding parameters. Is zero covariance a likely condition? We know that stores, especially those belonging to different chains, exhibit a high degree of heterogeneity in marketing activities. This heterogeneity may be based on positioning strategies. For example, chains differ in the kinds of households they target, and this positioning should result in different advertising, pricing and promotion campaigns for a variety of brands.[6] Differences in marketing campaigns between the chains lead to differences in chain patronage (while at the same time differences in chain positioning will be based on perceived differences between households). These arguments suggest that zero covariance across stores between the marketing activities for brands and the associated effects is a very unlikely condition. We summarize the various arguments in Table 14.2.

These results indicate that if the primary purpose of the use of a marketing model is to obtain valid estimates of the effects of marketing activities, it is important to use data at the most *disaggregate* level. However, this does not necessarily imply that disaggregate models will outperform aggregate models in *forecasting* aggregate-level results. We briefly consider this issue.

Sales forecasts at (say) the market level can be obtained from models estimated at different aggregation levels. One obvious possibility is a model based on market-level data. Alternatively one can use chain-level data to estimate a model with separate (or

---

5. We emphasize that it is usually impossible to justify the applicability of a linear model to real-world data.
6. The resulting heterogeneity in the execution of strategies across chains for a given brand may not be desirable to the brand manager. Thus, some coordination between manufacturer and retailer is desirable.

Table 14.2 Aggregation bias in paramater estimates for linear and nonlinear models.

Effects of marketing activities	Marketing activities	
	Homogeneous	Heterogeneous
Homogeneous	No bias	Bias, if nonlinear model (Christen et al., 1997)
Heterogeneous	Small bias, if any (Allenby and Rossi, 1991a)	Bias, if nonlinear model, plus another bias in case of non-zero covariance for all models (Krishnamurthi et al., 1990)

Source: Christen et al. (1997, p. 232).

equal) parameters per chain, and calculate market-level sales forecasts by aggregating the chain-level sales predictions. A third alternative would be to derive the model sales forecasts by aggregating individual store forecasts obtained from a store-level model, such as, for example, relation (14.8). Differences in forecasting accuracy of models defined at different levels of aggregation have been studied for a long time.[7] These studies suggest that *disaggregate models* tend to *outperform* an *aggregate model*.

Foekens, Leeflang and Wittink (1994) compared the forecasting accuracy at the aggregate chain and market levels for models defined at the store, retail chain and metropolitan market level. They used the loglinear SCAN*PRO model[8] to study the effects of temporary price cuts, displays and feature advertising on a brand's unit sales at the indicated levels. They found that substantive conclusions about the nature or magnitude of these effects tend to be more valid at the disaggregate levels. For example, store-level models have the highest relative number of statistically significant parameter estimates in the expected range of values, followed by chain models which outperform the market-level model. The *store models* with *homogeneous* (identical) parameters across chains, provide the highest proportion of statistically significant parameter estimates in the expected range of values. *Heterogeneous store* models provide the *best fit*, followed by heterogeneous chain models. The *heterogeneous store models* also provide the best *forecasting* accuracy results.

Aggregate models are more likely to be misspecified than comparable disaggregate models, for at least two reasons:

1. If the disaggregate model is non-linear, an aggregate model applied to linearly aggregated data in general cannot provide unbiased estimates, as we discussed before.
2. Only disaggregate models can accommodate parameter heterogeneity.

---

7. See Grunfeld, Griliches (1960), Edwards Orcutt (1969), Aigner, Goldfeld (1973, 1974), Blinkley, Nelson (1990).
8. See (14.8) and, for a more detailed description, Section 9.3.

Some models have been developed that combine disaggregate and aggregate data. For example, Russell and Kamakura (1994) use the substitution patterns observed in a micro-level (household) analysis to assist in the estimation of a market share model based on retail tracking data. The result is a market share model with a flexible pattern of brand competition that is linked to the pattern of preferences observed in the micro-level data.

Russell and Kamakura use the micro-level data to generate the total number of market segments (S), the estimated volume-weighted choice probabilities Θ_s, the estimated relative segment size RS_s for each segment s and the probability π_{hs} that household h belongs to segment s. This is done by latent class analysis (Section 17.2). The $\widehat{\Theta}_s$ and $\widehat{RS}_s$ for each segment s are used in the macro-analysis. For this purpose Russell and Kamakura (1994) define the intrinsic attraction of brand j within segment s (IA_{js}) as:

$$IA_{js} = \ln\left(\frac{\widehat{\Theta}_{js}}{\widehat{\Theta}_s}\right) \tag{14.20}$$

where

$\quad \widehat{\Theta}_s$ = the geometric mean of the purchase probabilities

$\qquad$ of brand j, $\widehat{\Theta}_{js}$, $\quad j = 1, \ldots, n$, in segment s.

The macro-model specification is:

$$m_{jt} = \sum_{s=1}^{S} \widehat{RS}_s\, m_{jst} \tag{14.21}$$

$$m_{jst} = \exp[\alpha_{jst}] \bigg/ \sum_{r=1}^{n} \exp[\alpha_{rst}] \tag{14.22}$$

$$\alpha_{jst} = \gamma_j + \widehat{IA}_{js} + \beta_{1j}\, p_{jt} + \beta_{2j} npp_{jt} \tag{14.23}$$

where

$\qquad m_{jt}$ = market share of brand j in t,

$\qquad m_{jst}$ = market share of brand j in segment s in t,

$\qquad \alpha_{jst}$ = the attraction of brand j in segment s in t,

$\qquad \gamma_j$ = a brand-specific intercept that reflects brand j's

$\qquad\qquad$ marketing activity, adjusted for price and promotion,

$\qquad p_{jt}$ = price of brand j in t,

$\qquad npp_{jt}$ = non-price promotion of brand j in t,

$\qquad \beta_{1j}, \beta_{2j}$ = brand-specific response parameters for brand j, and

$\qquad\qquad$ where the disturbance terms are omitted for convenience.

The $\widehat{IA}_{js}$ are obtained from (14.20). The macro-level data are used to estimate the parameters γ_j, β_{1j} and β_{2j}. Even though β_{1j} and β_{2j} are constant over the segments, the price and promotion elasticities are segment-specific because of the differences in the intrinsic brand attractions $\gamma_j + IA_{js}$ across segments.

14.1.3 TIME AGGREGATION

The arguments presented in 14.1.2 about entity aggregation also apply to aggregation over time. For example, for a nonlinear model, if only monthly or bimonthly observations are available, and the marketing activities differ between weeks, it is unavoidable that an aggregation bias occurs. However, in addition to such problems there is an issue that stems from the inclusion of lagged variables to estimate the duration of (manufacturer) advertising effects. Advertising effects on sales are not just immediate for reasons given in Section 6.1.

Clarke (1976) observed a systematic relation between the estimated duration of advertising effects and the time period of the data: the longer the time interval, the longer the estimated duration of the effect of advertising (in a linear model): see Table 6.1.

To show how this aggregation problem arises, we follow Leone (1995). A simplified linear model, constructed to estimate the current and lagged effects of advertising for one brand on its sales, is:

$$q_t = \alpha + \beta_1 a_t + \beta_2 a_{t-1} + \ldots + \beta_{s+1} a_{t-s} + u_t \tag{14.24}$$

where

q_t = unit sales in period t,

a_t = advertising expenditures in period t,

u_t = a disturbance term.

The estimation of separate parameters for $(s + 1)$ advertising variables is often problematic (due to multicollinearity and insufficient observations). For that reason it is convenient to assume a specific form in which the parameters are related. The Koyck formulation assumes that the effect decays geometrically, i.e.: $\beta_s = \lambda \beta_{s-1}$ for all $s > 1$. It is then possible to derive the following expression:

$$q_t = \alpha(1 - \lambda) + \beta a_t + \lambda q_{t-1} + u_t - \lambda u_{t-1} \tag{14.25}$$

(compare: (6.9)-(6.11)). By forcing the parameters to be constrained in this way, we obtain an equation that contains only two unknown slope parameters. The disadvantage is that the assumption of geometric decay may not be correct. In addition, the error term in (14.25) has an unusual structure that incorporates the same parameter associated with the lagged sales variable.

We now consider the issue that arises in aggregation over time. Specifically, assume that the time period t (e.g. t can represent days or weeks) is in fact the correct period for parameter estimation. For example, if most households make brand purchases every week, then it is conceivable that weekly data provide the best opportunity for estimation (if the marketing activities are also constant within weeks). But what if only quarterly data are available? Then we could estimate parameters from the following relation:

$$q_T = \alpha' + \beta' a_T + \lambda' q_{T-1} + u_T \tag{14.26}$$

where

$$q_T = \text{sales in quarter } T,$$
$$a_T = \text{advertising expenditures in quarter } T,$$
$$q_{T-1} = \text{lagged sales, i.e. sales in quarter } T - 1, \text{ and}$$
$$u_T = \text{disturbance term.}$$

However, if (14.25) is specified on weekly data, and we aggregate this equation to the quarterly time period, we obtain:

$$\sum_{t=1}^{13} q_t = \sum_{t=1}^{13} \alpha(1 - \lambda) + \beta \sum_{t=1}^{13} a_t + \lambda \sum_{t=1}^{13} q_{t-1} + w_t \tag{14.27}$$

where

$$w_t = \text{disturbance term} = \sum_{t=1}^{13}(u_t - \lambda u_{t-1}).$$

The lagged term in (14.27) represents the sales over 13 weeks but it is just one week removed from $\sum_{t=1}^{13} q_t$. This term would be the proper lagged variable. However, if only quarterly data are available, it is not observable. In (14.26) q_{T-1} is lagged sales for the previous quarter !

The proper specification at the quarterly time interval is:

$$q_T = (13)\alpha(1 - \lambda) + \beta a_T + \lambda q_T + \lambda X_T \tag{14.28}$$

where

$$X_T = \text{the difference between } sales \text{ in the last week}$$
$$\text{covered in } T \text{ and the last week before } T (= q_{13} - q_0).$$

Since X_T is also not observable, estimation of the equation requires approximations. Bass and Leone (1986) use a simple approximation (see Leone, 1995, p. G145), and find in empirical comparisons that the bias pertaining to (14.26) is reduced in (14.28) but not eliminated.

Of course, the fact that the time interval influences the estimated duration of advertising effects does not indicate what the correct time interval is. One perspective is to choose the data interval that corresponds as closely as possible to the average household interpurchase time for the brand or the product category (Hanssens, Parsons, Schultz, 1990, p. 70, Leone, 1995, p. G147). Another perspective is that the shorter it is the better, because shorter time intervals for the data provide more flexibility for the estimation of lagged effects.

Given that households differ in interpurchase time, having the shortest possible intervals makes it more likely that the actual lagged effects can be correctly captured. For additional treatments of this aggregation problem, see Kanetkar, Weinberg, Weiss (1986), Russell (1988), Srinivasan and Weir (1988), Vanhonacker (1988).

14.2 Pooling

Aggregation differs from pooling observations. In pooling we maintain the disaggregate nature of the data. However, we often use all the data to estimate a common set of parameters. In general, time-series data for each of several cross-sectional units, e.g. consumers, stores, chains, segments, regions, items, brands, etc. can be combined for parameter estimation. The existence of multiple observations within several cross sections gives rise to both opportunities and problems in the application of estimation methods. In this section we discuss some of these. Issues pertaining to the decision whether or not to pool the data for purposes of estimation and how to pool the data are discussed in Section 16.2.

Relative to aggregation, pooling offers the following advantages:

1. The number of observations available for parameter estimation is (much) greater; for example, with 52 weekly observations, pooling the data across 30 stores gives 1560 observations, compared to just 52 if the data are aggregated to the market level.
2. Pooling data avoids the bias identified in Section 14.1.2, that occurs when data are summed or averaged and a nonlinear model is used.
3. Pooling data offers the opportunity to exploit both cross-sectional (e.g. between stores) and time-series variation for parameter estimation; or, if only the time-series variation is considered relevant or appropriate, the model can be specified accordingly (or estimation methods can be employed that do the same; see Section 16.2).
4. Pooling data does not require an assumption of parameter homogeneity; it is possible to test this assumption, and heterogeneity can be accommodated in a variety of ways (see e.g. Bass and Wittink, 1975, Moriarty, 1975, Leeflang, van Duijn, 1982a, 1982b, and Section 16.2).

The difference between pooling and aggregation can be illustrated with the models introduced in Section 14.1.2. There we specified a firm share model (14.2), estimated from 27 observations:

$$f\hat{m}_{At} = \underset{(0.04)}{0.09} + \underset{(0.02)}{0.03} \, fas_{At} + \underset{(0.16)}{0.64} \, fm_{A,t-1}. \tag{14.29}$$

The equivalent pooled relation was estimated across the four brands with $4 \times 27 = 108$ observations, and resulted in:

$$\hat{m}_{At} = \underset{(0.00)}{-0.00} + \underset{(0.01)}{0.04} \, as_{At} + \underset{(0.01)}{0.99} \, \hat{m}_{A,t-1}. \tag{14.30}$$

The parameter estimates of the lagged endogenous variable, 0.64 in (14.29) and 0.99 (14.30), differ significantly. One possible reason for this is the contribution of cross-sectional variation in (14.30). For example, a brand with high market share in $t-1$ tends to have high market share in t. Note also that the estimated standard errors differ quite considerably. For example, the estimated effect of the lagged endogenous variable has a standard error of 0.16 in (14.29) but only 0.01 in (14.30). Thus, pooling data offers the possibility for greatly increasing the reliability of the estimates, provided that pooling is appropriate. Before a decision is made to pool, it is important to test the homogeneity hypothesis (see Section 16.2). For these four brands, the test result indicated that the homogeneity assumption is invalid (see Section 14.1.2).

14.3 Market boundaries

To define a brand's market share, it is necessary to know which other brands belong to the same market. Thus, while it is operationally simple to create a market or industry sales figure, the problem is to define the relevant market or the market boundaries. In some instances, the primary competitors are quite visible and easily identified. However, in differentiated product markets brands compete potentially in non-obvious ways. The definition of relevant market is also complex if the number of competing brands is large, or if there are product substitutes that formally belong to a different industry. And new entrants may not be easily characterized with respect to a market in which it primarily competes. The complexity of the problem increases further if more disaggregate units of analysis, such as stock-keeping units (SKU's) are used as the basic unit of analysis (Fader, Hardie, 1996).

We briefly consider an example to illustrate the problem. In a study of the cereal market Ghosh, Neslin and Schoemaker, (1984) mention that over 140 different brands of cereals were recorded by panel members.[9] To minimize the occurrence of zero values for advertising in an attraction model, data were aggregated to 29 brands. Consumers' consideration sets are likely to contain a very modest number of alternatives. Thus assuming that 29 brands directly compete with each other may not be realistic. It will also be useful to narrow the set of brands for managerial use. Thus, managerial use considerations and consumer aspects have to be weighted against what is desirable from a modeling perspective (especially with regard to biases that can result from improper aggregation, see Section 14.1).

Other relevant aspects include regional differences and distribution characteristics which can be used to obtain a reasoned way of aggregating brands. To keep the number of alternatives modest, researchers often do something like the following. Create a five-brand market: the brand, three major competitors, and a fifth item constituting the remaining items or the "competitive fringe" combined. Although it is inappropriate to assume that the brands combined into a competitive fringe are homogeneous, it is often better to include those brands in this manner than not to include them at all. A

---

9. See also Naert, Weverbergh (1985).

Table 14.3 Analytical methods for customer-oriented product market definitions.

Based on purchase behavior	Based on customer judgments
• cross-elasticity of demand	• decision-sequence analysis
• brand switching measures	• perceptual mapping
• consideration sets	• customer judgments of substitutability
• asymmetric non-hierarchial models	
• hierarchical models	

Source: based on Day, Shocker, Srivastava (1979, p. 11).

model based on such a five-brand market does retain the possibility of heterogeneous parameters for the three major competitors.[10]

In most industries, competitors are portrayed in terms of how intensively they compete. Aaker (1995, p. 66) distinguishes (1) very direct competitors, (2) others that compete less intensively, and (3) still others that compete indirectly but are still relevant.[11] Aaker provides an unequivocal market definition which depends on a few key variables. With respect to cola drinks, for example, key variables are cola/noncola, diet/nondiet and caffeine/noncaffeine.[12] The attributes may be either concrete, as in this example, or abstract.[13]

Day, Shocker and Srivastava (1979) propose the following market definition:

"the set of products judged to be substitutes within those usage segments in which similar patterns of benefits are sought and the <u>customers</u> for whom such usages are relevant"

(Day et al., 1979, p. 10).

They distinguish demand or customer-oriented approaches from approaches that take a supply perspective. A supply perspective might lead to definitions of products and markets by similarity of: manufacturing processes, raw materials, physical appearance, function or other such criteria. The customer-oriented approaches are classified according to the use of behavioral or judgmental data: see Table 14.3. We briefly discuss these methods, but focus more attention on the methods in the left-hand column of Table 14.3. The demand-based methods can be based on individual or aggregate demand data.

---

10. See for an example: Leeflang, Reuyl (1984a).
11. See also Plat, Leeflang (1988), who model direct and indirect competitors. How managers identify competitors in practice is described by Clark and Montgomery (1999).
12. Aaker (1995, p. 66).
13. See also Wedel, Vriens, Bijmolt, Krijnen, Leeflang (1998).

Approaches based on the *cross-elasticity of demand* are considered standard by most economists (see Section 11.2). The results in Table 11.3, for example, suggest that the demand for brand 1, is sensitive to some promotions for brands 2, 4 and 6. The demand for brand 6 on the other hand, is sensitive to some promotional activities for brands 1, 2 and 3, etc. Taken literally, the results in Table 11.3 indicate asymmetry in cross effects. These results are also consistent with the view that consumers form restricted subsets of alternatives.[14] Restricted subsets can be incorporated in attraction models, at least in principle.[15] For example, relation (9.25) can be modified into:

$$m_{jt} = \frac{A_{jt}}{\sum_{CS_j \subset \{1,\dots,n\}} A_{rt}} \tag{14.31}$$

where

$$
\begin{aligned}
m_{jt} &= \text{market share of brand } j \text{ in } t, \\
A_{jt} &= \text{attraction of brand } j \text{ in } t, \\
CS_j &= \text{the consideration set relevant to purchases of brand } j, \\
\{1,\dots,n\} &= \text{the set of alternative products (brands).}
\end{aligned}
$$

The results in Table 11.3 could be used to specify:

$$j = 1 : CS_1 = \text{brands } 1, 2, 4, 6$$

$$\vdots$$

$$j = 6 : CS_6 = \text{brands } 1, 2, 3, 6$$

where

$$\{1,\dots,n\} = \{1,\dots,7\}.$$

Cross elasticities defined at the store or chain level can also be used to define competition between *stores*. Using weekly scanner data representing 18 product categories, Hoch, Kim, Montgomery and Rossi (1995) estimated store-specific price elasticities. They related these elasticities to a comprehensive set of demographic and competitor variables that describe the trading areas of each of the stores. Hoch et al. find that customer demographic variables such as age, household size, income and the percentage of consumers who are ethnic, are much more influential than competitive variables on price sensitivity. This result is consistent with the idea that stores attract different types of customers who on average tend to be loyal to a primary store.

The (measured or estimated) *transition probabilities* (see Section 12.3) is a second method. This method is used to define the degree of brand switching. In a strict sense, transition probabilities that do not differ significantly from zero indicate that the relevant pairs of brand do not belong to the same market or market segment. Novak (1993) provides a survey of approaches for the analysis of market structure based on brand switching data.

---

14. See also Hauser, Wernerfelt (1990), Roberts, Lattin (1991).
15. For details, see Batsell and Polking (1985). See also Chintagunta (1998), Park, Hahn (1998).

A third approach to define market boundaries is based on the determination of "restricted choice sets". A choice set is defined as the final consideration set, i.e. the set of alternatives considered immediately prior to brand choice.[16] If individual purchase data are available, restricted choice sets can be incorporated into models of individual consumer choice behavior. For example, Siddarth, Bucklin and Morrison (1995) developed an approach to analyze choice sets on the basis of household scanner panel data, using a Bayesian (updating) procedure in conjunction with the multinomial logit model. They define choice set shares as the percentage of households for whom a given brand is a choice set member. An analysis of estimated choice sets across panelists reveals that market share does not coincide with choice set share. The results of Siddarth et al., (1995) also show that promotions can *expand* choice sets. Thus, the definition of a market is potentially sensitive to promotions and other marketing activities.

Chiang, Chib and Narasimhan (1999) use a Bayesian estimation procedure to determine choice sets at the individual level. Their findings are based on scanner panel data. The main findings are: ignoring consideration set heterogeneity understates the impact of marketing mix and overstates the impact of preferences and past purchase feedback.

It is relatively straightforward to apply the preceding methods to data sets with a restricted number of "items" (brands, stores, etc.). However, as the number of items in a product category expands it may be necessary to place prior restrictions on the nature of competition (see e.g. Ghosh et al., 1984). Such restrictions can emerge from the specification of asymmetric non-hierarchical models (Section 14.4) and hierarchical models (Section 14.5).

We discuss other approaches to structure markets and to define their boundaries in Section 17.2.

The analysis based upon customer judgments are complementary to the approaches based on purchase behavior.

Decision sequence analysis considers protocols of consumer decision making, which indicate the sequence in which various criteria are employed to reach a final choice. Households often use stage-wise processing of information (phased decision strategies) prior to purchase. For example, some alternatives may be excluded for failing to meet minimum requirements on specific attributes, and the remaining set of alternatives may be compared on the same or other attributes. The implication is that at least two stages are involved: one in which options are eliminated and another in which a choice is made from the remaining options.

In the consumer behavior literature a distinction is often made between processing by brand and processing by attribute (Engel, Blackwell, Miniard, 1995, pp. 191-192). This distinction is relevant, for example, to a determination of the order in which product-attribute information is acquired or processed by consumers.[17] The usual

---

16. Shocker, Ben-Akiva, Boccara and Nedungadi (1991).
17. See also the Elimination-by-Aspects (EBA) models of choice behavior (Tversky, 1972, Batsell, Polking, 1985).

procedure for a decision sequence analysis is to ask individuals to verbalize what is going on in their minds as they make purchase decisions in the course of a shopping trip. With these "protocols" one can generate a model of the way a subject makes decisions. Such a model specifies the attributes used to differentiate choice objects and the *sequence* and *method* by which information on these attributes is combined.

Perceptual mapping is a set of approaches used to represent the position of brands in geometric space. The brands that are closest together in such a space are expected to face the highest degree of competition. Thus, market definitions and boundaries can be inferred from groups of brands located close together. See, for example, Bijmolt (1996). Shugan (1987) and Waarts, Carree and Wierenga (1991), among others, show how such maps can be constructed from scanner data.

Customer judgments of substitutability may be obtained in a variety of ways.[18] One approach is to focus on customer choice. A buyer of brand j could be asked what brand would have been purchased if brand j had been out of stock. If the answer is brand i, $i \neq j$, one could ask what would be chosen if i were also out of stock, etc.

Another approach is the association of products with specific use contexts or applications. Product users are asked to identify a list of usage situations or product applications. For each use context one can then ask the users to name *all* the products/brands that are appropriate. Another group of respondents can also be asked to make judgments about the appropriateness of each product for each use context. The products would be *clustered* based on the similarity of their appropriate use contexts.

14.4 Modeling asymmetric competition

An important component in present-day modeling of marketing-mix effects is the accommodation of asymmetries in competition. Arguments in support of unequal competition between brands in a product category can be found in the literature on consumer behavior, brand positioning and competition.

Research on consideration sets suggests that an average household actively considers for purchase only two or three brands within a product category (Hauser, Wernerfelt, 1990). The size of the consideration set is what remains after options are eliminated, as discussed in Section 14.3.

The theory on brand positioning (e.g. Hooley and Saunders, 1993) suggests that (new) items in a product line should be positioned so as to avoid cannibalization. Thus, everything else being equal, the cross-market share effects for items produced by a given firm should minimize within-firm substitution. As a result there is much product differentiation designed to appeal to a multitude of segments in most product categories.

Based on aggregate data, empirical studies show unequal levels of competition between brands. For example, Blattberg and Wisniewski (1989) argue in favor of tiers of brands due to quality and price differences. Leeflang and Wittink (1994, 1996) report highly idiosyncratic estimated cross-market share effects for seven brands.

---

18. See Day, et al., (1979), Srivastava, Alpert, Shocker (1984), Aaker (1995, Chapter 4).

From a practical perspective, the existence of many items in a product category often requires that researchers place restrictions on the nature of competition in consumer response models. Thus, in a market with many items, the question is how, not whether, asymmetry in competition should be accommodated.

In our discussion of alternative methods for the accommodation of asymmetry in the market structure of a product category, we make a distinction between hierarchical and non-hierarchical models. The non-hierarchical models are discussed in this section, the hierarchical models are discussed in Section 14.5. The relation between the models discussed in this section and Section 14.5 is shown in Figure 14.2 in Section 14.6.

ATTRACTION MODELS[19]

Market share attraction models are examples of non-hierarchical models that can be used to accommodate asymmetric competition. An example, a non-robust model, is discussed in Section 11.2; see equation (11.16) and Table 11.3. In Section 9.4 (equations (9.33) and (9.34)) we discuss the Fully Extended Attraction model (FEA model) which can account for asymmetry. We modify equation (9.34) to focus on the item instead of the brand as the unit of analysis.

Suppose that a market consists of B brands, and that each brand is available in S package sizes. Let each item be indexed by its brand (b) and its size (s). Also, there are L marketing instruments. Then the FEA model has the following structure, with the item as the unit of analysis (ignoring the error term), for $s = 1, \ldots, S, b = 1, \ldots, B$:

$$m_{sb,t} = A_{sb,t} \left/ \sum_{j=1}^{B} \sum_{i=1}^{S} A_{ij,t}, \quad t = 1, \ldots, T \right. \tag{14.32}$$

where

$$A_{sb,t} = \exp \left[\beta_{0sb} + \sum_{\ell=1}^{L} \sum_{j=1}^{B} \sum_{i=1}^{S} x_{\ell ij,t} \beta_{\ell sbij} \right],$$

$m_{sb,t}$ = market share of item (s, b) in period t,

$A_{sb,t}$ = the attraction of item (s, b) in period t,

$x_{\ell ij,t}$ = value of the ℓ-th explanatory variable for item (i, j) in period t,

$\beta_{\ell sbij}$ = parameter representing the own- $((s, b) = (i, j))$ and the cross-effects $((i, j) \neq (s, b))$ of $x_{\ell ij}$ on A_{sb},

β_{0sb} = an intercept term.

In the fully extended attraction model, items are allowed to have unique own-effects and all possible cross-effects are accommodated. The cross-elasticities are defined as

---

19. This section is based on Foekens, Leeflang, Wittink (1997).

(ignoring time-subscript t):

$$e^{\ell}_{sb,ij} = \frac{\partial m_{sb} x_{\ell ij}}{\partial x_{\ell ij} m_{sb}} = \left(\beta_{\ell sbij} - \sum_{c=1}^{B} \sum_{r=1}^{S} m_{rc} \beta_{\ell rcij} \right) x_{\ell ij}, \quad (i, j) \neq (s, b). \quad (14.33)$$

Equation (14.33) indicates that the effect of marketing variable $x_{\ell ij}$ differs between the items (i, j) and (s, b). Thus, equation (14.32) allows for asymmetric competition between the items.

Even with a modest number of items the FEA model can easily pose estimation problems. For example, assume the number of items ($n \equiv B \times S$) is 20 and the number of explanatory variables (L) four. Then the number of parameters in the FEA model equals $n + Ln^2 = 1620$. For an estimation sample of one year of weekly observations for all 20 items there are $52 \times (20-1) = 988$ linearly independent observations. Since $988 < 1620$ restrictions on the nature of the competitive structure would be required. Among the possibilities are:

1. specification of a "Cluster-Asymmetry Attraction model" (henceforth CAA model);
2. the model developed by Carpenter, Cooper, Hanssens and Midgley (1988) (henceforth the CCHM model);
3. the specification of a hierarchical model (Section 14.5).

CLUSTER-ASYMMETRY ATTRACTION MODEL

In the CAA model (Vanden Abeele, Gijsbrechts, Vanhuele, 1990) it is assumed that the market can be structured as clusters of items. Criteria (e.g., brand name, package size, product form) are specified a priori such that the use of each criterion results in the identification of one or more clusters. If clustering is effective, competition between items within clusters is stronger than between items of different clusters. The approach allows clusters to be overlapping, i.e. items may belong to more than one cluster. Thus, the model allows multiple hierarchies to structure the market simultaneously.

The CAA model incorporates cross-effects which are related to a priori defined clusters of items by introducing one asymmetry parameter per clustering criterion. Thus, asymmetric competition is modeled parsimoniously and requires the estimation of only a small number of parameters.

We use brand name and package size as clustering criteria. A brand cluster consists of all items with a given brand name. Thus, for B names we can define B brand clusters. Similarly, for S package sizes we can define S size clusters. Note that an item can be a member of two (or more) clusters. The CAA model has the following specification:

$$m_{sb,t} = A_{sb,t} AB^{\theta_B}_{sb,t} AS^{\theta_S}_{sb,t} \left/ \sum_{j=1}^{B} \sum_{i=1}^{S} A_{ij,t} AB^{\theta_B}_{ij,t} AS^{\theta_S}_{ij,t}, \right. \quad (14.34)$$

$$s = 1, \ldots, S, b = 1, \ldots, B, t = 1, \ldots, T$$

where

$$A_{sb,t} = \exp\left[\beta_{0sb} + \sum_{\ell=1}^{L} x_{\ell sb,t} \beta_{\ell sbsb}\right],$$

$$AB_{sb,t} = \begin{cases} g(A_{i'b,t} \mid \forall i' \in V_b) & \text{if } s \in V_b \\ 1 & \text{otherwise} \end{cases}$$

$$AS_{sb,t} = \begin{cases} g(A_{sj',t} \mid \forall j' \in V_s) & \text{if } b \in V_s \\ 1 & \text{otherwise} \end{cases}$$

$m_{sb,t}$ = the market share of item (s, b) in period t,

$A_{sb,t}$ = the "context-free" attraction of item (s, b),

$x_{\ell sb,t}$ = the ℓth marketing variable of item (s, b),

$\ell = 1, \ldots, L,$

V_b = the set of items belonging to the bth brand cluster,

V_s = the set of items belonging to the sth package size cluster,

$AB_{sb,t}$ = a correction factor corresponding to the choice context of the brand cluster of item (s, b); this factor is a function of the attractions of all items of V_b,

$AS_{sb,t}$ = a correction factor corresponding to the choice context of the package size cluster of item (s, b), calculated from the attractions of all items of V_s, and

g = a non-negative monotone function.

$A_{sb,t}$ is called context-free because it is a function only of an item's own marketing variables, and does not depend on other choice alternatives in the choice set. The unknown parameters in the CAA model are β_{0sb}, $\beta_{\ell sbsb}$, θ_B and θ_S. The parameters $\beta_{\ell sbsb}$ are comparable to the own-effect parameters of the FEA model in (14.32). The parameters θ_B and θ_S are the asymmetry parameters. These parameters measure the degree of the competitive impact resulting from the corresponding cluster. If $\theta_B = 0$ there is no cross-competitive effect emanating from the brand clusters. In that case, competition is symmetric between the package sizes of a given brand. Likewise if $\theta_S = 0$ the attraction of item (s, b) does not depend on the choice context as defined by the package size cluster. As has been demonstrated by Vanden Abeele et al., the asymmetry parameters should lie in the $[-1, 0]$ interval.

Vanden Abeele et al. suggest a number of alternative definitions for the function g such as: (1) the "arithmetic total cluster attraction" (ATCA) specification: $g_1(A_{ib,t} \mid i \in V_b) \equiv \Sigma_{i \in V_b} A_{ib,t}$, and (2) the "geometric total cluster attraction" (GTCA) specification: $g_2(A_{ib,t} \mid i \in V_b) \equiv \Pi_{i \in V_b} A_{ib,t}$. The other specifications are: AACA and

GACA (see Vanden Abeele et al., 1990). The above definitions hold for brand clusters. Similar definitions can be provided for the size clusters.

The CAA model has been incorporated into the SH.A.R.P. model (Bultez and Naert, 1988b), which is discussed in Section 13.4. Incorporating the CAA model in SH.A.R.P. offers opportunities to integrate the diversity of substitution effects that may stem from brand loyalty, preference for a specific variety or package-size, and purchasing habits. The model that accounts for asymmetric cannibalization in retail assessments is described in Bultez, Gijsbrechts, Naert and Vanden Abeele (1989).

CCHM MODEL

In the model developed by Carpenter et al. (1988) no a priori clustering is assumed. The CCHM model is a restricted version of a fully extended attraction model that includes an empirically selected subset of all possible cross-competitive effects. The FEA model contains $L(n-1)$ *cross-effect* parameters *for each item* ($n=B \cdot S$). If no parameter restrictions are imposed this would allow complete flexibility in the nature of the cross-competitive effects of the items' marketing variables. However, it seems unrealistic to assume that in a market with many items all competitive effects are non-zero and unique. Carpenter et al. (1988) use a stagewise approach for the determination of relevant cross-effects. First, an extended attraction (EA) model is estimated. In an EA model all cross-effects or asymmetry parameters are zero. By cross-correlating the residuals for a given item with each marketing variable of every other item, potential cross-effects are identified based on the statistical significance of the simple correlations. The marketing instruments identified as potential sources of asymmetric competition for a given item are then added to the attraction model, and the resulting asymmetric model is reestimated (yielding new estimates for the own-effect parameters as well). This attraction component can formally be represented as:

$$
A_{sb,t} = \exp\left[\beta_{0sb} + \sum_{\ell=1}^{L} x_{\ell sb,t}\beta_{\ell sbsb} + \sum_{\substack{\ell(i,j)\in W_{(s,b)} \\ (i,j)\neq(s,b)}} x_{\ell ij,t}\beta_{\ell sbij} \right]
\qquad (14.35)
$$

where

$W_{(s,b)}$ = the set of variables with potential cross-effects on the market share of item (s, b) obtained from the residual analyses.

The estimation of the model in (14.35) tends to require a much smaller number of parameters than is required for the FEA model (14.32).

14.5 Hierarchical models

By hierarchical models we mean models which:

- are based on a hierarchical structure;
- include predictor variables defined at each choice level.

At the household level, these models are based on the assumption that consumers use stage-wise processing in choosing items. Consumers may differentiate items according to dimensions such as brand name, package size, product variety, and price. For example, consumers may first choose a brand name and, given that decision, choose a particular item (e.g. a package size for that brand). The number of possible hierarchies depends on the number of dimensions on which the items differ. Specifically, the number of unique hierarchical structures is equal to the number of orders in which the dimensions can be considered. For example, with three dimensions ($d = 3$) (e.g. brand, variety, package size), six alternative structures ($d! = 6$) can be distinguished under the assumption that there is no interaction between the dimensions.

In our example, competition is formulated in two stages: the brand level and the package size level. For a hierarchy of brand name followed by package size, the implication is that items which belong to the same brand compete directly, while items belonging to different brands compete indirectly through the brand level. We note that while it is possible to derive a hierarchical model at the aggregate level from a household model, we cannot claim that if a hierarchical model is preferred over other models at the aggregate level, households necessarily behave hierarchically.

In Figure 14.1 we show two possible hierarchical structures for the dimensions of brand name and package size. In structure "$S1$", the first dimension is brand name and the second dimension is package size. For structure "$S2$", package size is the first and brand name is the second dimension. We recognize that the competitive structure may be consumer-specific; see, for example, Vanden Abeele and Gijsbrechts (1991), Gönül and Srinivasan (1993a) or Siddarth, Bucklin and Morrison (1995). With aggregate data, we cannot account for heterogeneity across individuals.

In a hierarchical model each of the choice levels can be modeled by a separate market share model, applied to aggregate data, with explanatory variables defined at the corresponding choice level. Cross-competitive effects can be included in the models at each choice level.

In the remainder of this section we discuss the models for the hierarchical structure in which brand name is chosen before the package size ($S1$). The model formulation for $S2$ is analogous and is not shown. We note that the formulation for a structure with more than two dimensions is straightforward. We first discuss the most general structure of a hierarchical model, viz. the *"Fully Extended" Nested MultiNomial Logit* (FENMNL) model. We then discuss several alternative specifications which are nested in this general formulation.

We define:

$$q_{sb,t} = \text{unit sales (e.g. number of kilograms)}$$

Structure S1 (brand-size hierarchy)

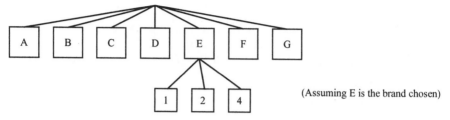

(Assuming E is the brand chosen)

Structure S2 (size-brand hierarchy)

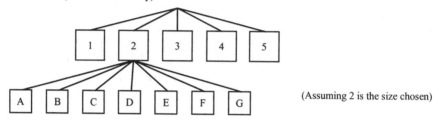

(Assuming 2 is the size chosen)

*Figure 14.1 Two alternative hierarchical structures with respect to the choice of brands (A, ...,
G) and package sizes (1, ..., 5).*

for size s, brand b in period t, $t = 1, \ldots, T$,

$$q_{.b,t} \equiv \sum_{s=1}^{S} q_{sb,t} = \text{unit sales for brand } b \text{ in period } t,$$

$$q_{...,t} \equiv \sum_{b=1}^{B} \sum_{s=1}^{S} q_{sb,t} = \text{unit sales for the product category in}$$
period t.

Then, the market share of an item (s, b) equals:

$$m_{sb,t} = m_{b,t} \times m_{s|b,t} = \frac{q_{.b,t}}{q_{...,t}} \times \frac{q_{sb,t}}{q_{.b,t}} = \frac{q_{sb,t}}{q_{...,t}} \tag{14.36}$$

where $m_{b,t}$ and $m_{s|b,t}$ are the market share for brand b, and the conditional market
share for size s, given brand b, respectively.

Let $C_{s|b}$ denote the set of package sizes which have marketing instruments with a
cross-effect on the share of size s (given brand b). Analogously, let C_b denote the set
of brands which have marketing instruments that have a cross-effect on the market
share of brand b. Then the FENMNL model can be formalized as follows:

$$m_{s|b,t} = A_{s|b,t} \bigg/ \sum_{i=1}^{S} A_{i|b,t} \tag{14.37}$$

where

$$A_{s|b,t} = \exp\left[\beta_{0sb} + X'_{sb,t}\beta_{sbsb} + \sum_{\substack{i \in C_{s|b} \\ i \neq s}} X'_{ib,t}\beta_{sbib}\right]$$

where

$X'_{ib,t}$ = a (row) vector of observed characteristics (with marketing variables ℓ, $\ell = 1, \ldots, L$, $x_{\ell ib,t}$) measured at package size/brand level (item level), $i \in C_{s|b}$ or $i = s$,

β_{sbib} = a (column) vector of unknown parameters reflecting the own ($i = s$) and cross ($i \neq s$) effects (given brand b) of the marketing instruments of size i on the (conditional) market share of size s, and

β_{0sb} = an intercept.

The market share of brand b can be written as:

$$m_{b,t} = A_{b,t} \bigg/ \sum_{j=1}^{B} A_{j,t} \tag{14.38}$$

where

$$A_{b,t} = \exp\left[\alpha_{0b} + Y'_{b,t}\alpha_{bb} + \sum_{\substack{c \in C_b \\ c \neq b}} Y'_{c,t}\alpha_{bc} + (1 - \sigma_b)IV_{b,t}\right],$$

$Y'_{b,t}$ = is a (row) vector of observed marketing variables of brand b defined at the brand level (that is, $Y_{b,t}$ is *aggregated* over $X'_{sb,t}$, $s = 1, \ldots, S$),

$Y'_{c,t}$ = defined in a similar way for brand c,

α_{bc} = a (column) vector of parameters, reflecting the own ($c = b$) and cross ($c \neq b$) effects of the marketing instruments of brand c on the market share of brand b,

α_{0b} = is an intercept, and

$IV_{b,t}$ = is the inclusive value variable for brand b defined as:

$$IV_{b,t} = \log\left(\sum_{s=1}^{S} \exp\left[\beta_{0sb} + X'_{sb,t}\beta_{sbsb} + \sum_{\substack{i \in C_{s|b} \\ i \neq s}} X'_{ib,t}\beta_{sbib}\right]\right). \tag{14.40}$$

(14.39)

The inclusive value variable is the log of the sum of the attractions of all package sizes belonging to brand b. The term involving the unknown parameter $(1 - \sigma_b)$ measures the effect of the total attractiveness of the set of package sizes of brand b on the brand's market share. In the FENMNL model the value of σ_b can vary between zero and one.

Several hierarchical models are nested in the FENMNL model, for example:

- the FEMNL model: the "Fully Extended" MultiNomial Logit model, for which the condition holds that $\sigma_b = 0$ for all b, i.e. the inclusive value variable has *full* impact;
- the FESQA model: the "Fully Extended" SQuared Attraction model, for which $\sigma_b = 1$ for all b, i.e. the inclusive value variable has *no* impact. In this model it is assumed that the share models for different stages are independent of each other. The FESQA can be interpreted as the product of two attraction models.

Like the FEA model, the ("fully extended") FENMNL model has its (more restrictive) "extended" counterpart: the ENMNL model. In this model the unique cross-competitive effects are eliminated. In that case the attractions have the following structures:

$$A_{s|b,t} = \exp[\beta_{0sb} + X'_{sb,t}\beta_{sbsb}] \tag{14.41}$$

$$A_{b,t} = \exp[\alpha_{0b} + Y'_{b,t}\alpha_{bb} + (1 - \sigma_b)IV_{b,t}] \tag{14.42}$$

where

$$IV_{b,t} = \log\left(\sum_{s=1}^{S} \exp[\beta_{0sb} + X'_{sb,t}\beta_{sbsb}]\right).$$

Several models are nested in the ENMNL model, viz.:

- the EMNL model: the "Extended" MultiNomial Logit model for which $\sigma_b = 0$ for all b;
- the ESQA model: the "Extended" SQuared Attraction model for which $\sigma_b = 1$ for all b.

The nonhierarchical FEA model is connected to the hierarchical models through a specific version of the "highest order" hierarchical model (the FENMNL model). This specific version is indicated as FEMNL* and is shown between the boxes for the hierarchical and nonhierarchical models in Figure 14.2.

14.6 A comparison of hierarchical and non-hierarchical asymmetric models

In Figure 14.2 we show the *relations* between the models discussed in the preceding two sections. The figure includes models not discussed in the preceding sections but which connect other models or are simplifications.[20]

In Table 14.4 we identify characteristics on which hierarchical, CCHM and cluster-asymmetry attraction (CAA) models differ. To facilitate the discussion of hierarchical model characteristics, we use the FENMNL model as its most general case. We compare FENMNL against the two other models that embody other forms of restrictions on the competitive structure in markets with many items. We identify differences in the a priori structuring of the market and the sources of asymmetry in the first two aspects shown in Table 14.4.

The third point of difference is the number of parameters in each model. The CCHM model potentially requires a very large number of parameters, while this number is small for the CAA model. The FENMNL model has an intermediate position in this respect. For example, for $B = 5$, $S = 4$ (hence $n = 20$) and $L = 4$, the maximum numbers of response parameters are: 1600 (CCHM), 420 (FENMNL) and 82 (CAA), respectively.

Importantly, the implementation of the CCHM model and the hierarchical models differs in the manner in which potential cross-effects are *identified*. In the CCHM model cross-effects are identified from an analysis of residuals from the EA model. A variable with a potential cross-effect is added if the share residuals of an item are significantly correlated with that variable. If there is only one relevant cross-effect (i.e. it is the only missing variable in the EA model) the resulting simple correlation coefficient between the variable and the residuals should be statistically significant. However, if two or more cross-effects exist, the simple correlation coefficients may not be a valid basis to identify the group of relevant predictor variables. For example, it is possible that the simple correlation between such a variable and the residuals is nonsignificant due to the omission of another relevant variable.

In the hierarchical (FENMNL) model we can incorporate all possible cross-effects (for the items included in that branch), as long as the number of items within a given branch is small. For branches with a large number of items, Foekens et al. (1997) use Haugh-Pierce bivariate causality-tests to identify potential cross-effects (see Pierce and Haugh, 1977).[21] That is, the relation is tested separately for each marketing variable of (say) item (i, b) and the (conditional) market share of item (s, b), $i \neq s$. As a consequence, the identified group of potential "causal" variables may also exclude some variables which in fact have a causal relationship with the dependent variable. However, the causality test is not always needed.

It should be clear from these comparisons and from the relations between all specific models shown in Figure 14.2 that there is no straightforward basis for pre-

---

20. See for more detail Foekens et al. (1997).
21. These tests are introduced in Section 18.4.4.

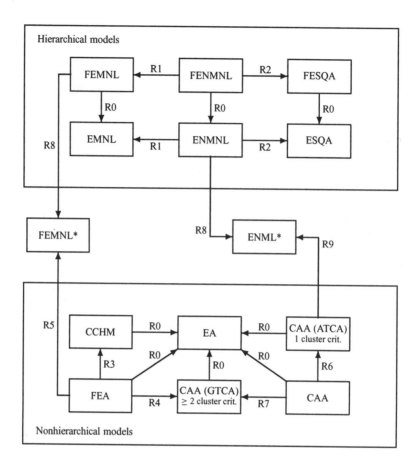

Models: FENMNL = Fully Extended Nested MultiNomial Logit; ENMNL = Extended Nested MultiNomial Logit; ENMNL* = a specific version of the ENMNL model which connects ENMNL with a specific version of CAA; FEMNL = Fully Extended MultiNomial Logit; FEMNL* = a specific version of the FEMNL model which connects FEA with FEMNL; EMNL = Extended MultiNomial Logit; FESQA = Fully Extended SQuared Attraction; ESQA = Extended SQuared Attraction; FEA = Fully Extended Attraction; EA = Extended Attraction; CCHM = FEA developed by Carpenter et al.; CAA = Cluster-Asymmetry market share Attraction; (ATCA) = (Arithmic Total Cluster Attraction: a specification of the CAA model); (GTCA) = (Geometric Total Cluster Attraction specification).

Model references: FENMNL; (14.37)-(14.39), ENMNL: (14.40)-(14.41); FEA: (14.32); CCHM: (14.35); CAA: (14.34).

Restrictions: R0: set all cross-effect or asymmetry parameters to zero; R1: set $\sigma_b = 0$ for all brands b; R2: set $\sigma_b = 1$ for all brands b; R3: use a subset of cross-effect parameters based on residual-analysis; R4: item's attraction includes cross-effect parameters which relate to the item's "cluster-members" only; R5: exclude all cross-effect parameters between items of different brands; R6: set $\theta_s = 0$, and use ATCA specifications; R7: use GTCA specification; R8: set all brand-level parametes to zero and let $\sigma_b = \sigma$ for all brands b; R9: set $\theta_B = -\sigma$.

Source: based on Foekens et al. (1997, p. 361).

Figure 14.2 The relations between alternative market share models.

Table 14.4 Characteristics of three asymmetric market share models.

Aspect	Hierarchical model (FENMNL)[a]	Extended attraction model with subset of cross-effects (CCHM model)[a]	Cluster-Asymmetry Attraction (CAA) model
A priori structuring of the market	Hierarchical structuring assumed	No structuring	Structuring by clusters
Sources of asymmetry	Marketing instruments	Marketing instruments	Clusters of items
Number of model response parameters[b]	Large, $\leq B^2 L + B S^2 L$	Very large, $\leq L n^2$	Small, $L n + 2$
Identification of potential cross-effects	Causality tests (bivariate testing)	Residual analysis	Through definition of clusters
Model estimation	Log-linear estimation technique, sequential procedure	Log-linear estimation technique, sequential procedure	Log-linear estimation technique, iterative

[a]FENMNL = Fully Extended Nested Multinomial Logit model.
CCHM = EA model with subset of cross-effects, developed by Carpenter et al. (1988).
[b]B = number of brands, S = number of package sizes; L = number of marketing instruments; $n \equiv B \times S$.

Source: Foekens et al. (1997, p. 368).

ferring one of these models in an empirical application. We could suggest that the CAA model is attractive for (large) markets in which: (1) multiple market structuring criteria are simultaneously active, and (2) the competition is dominated by one marketing instrument. With only one instrument there is no concern about the assumption that asymmetries are not instrument-dependent. Similarly, we expect that the attractiveness of hierarchical models increases with the number of items.[22]

---

22. A preliminary comparison of the different models based on data for one product category reveals that the ESQA-model has the best predictive validity and is second best on face validity. See Foekens et al. (1997).

PART THREE

Parameterization and validation

CHAPTER 15

Organizing data

As indicated in the discussion about the model-building process in Section 5.1, the step that logically follows model specification is parameterization. Model specification forces the decision maker to be explicit about which variables may influence other variables, and in what manner. In the specification stage, variables are categorized (e.g. criterion versus predictor) and operationalized. Also, plausible functional forms have to be considered. Sometimes data are available or can be obtained without much effort. In other cases it may be necessary to develop specific instruments for the measurement of variables.

Having "good" data is a prerequisite to meaningful, and hence implementable, model building. In Section 15.1 we discuss what is meant by "good" data. Recently marketing managers have experienced an explosion in the availability of data, especially scanner-based data. This explosion not only enriches the opportunity for managers to understand markets through numerically specified models but it also limits managers' abilities to track market changes in traditional ways. Essentially the data revolution requires that managers use decision-support systems. We introduce such systems briefly in Section 15.2.

We discuss well-known data sources, including scanner data, for the measurement of performance indicators and variables that influence performances in Section 15.3. We describe the process leading to the definition of the required set of data in Section 15.4. Data collection is the first step in parameterization. Another question involves the selection of a technique for the extraction of model parameter estimates from the data. The complexity of parameterization depends on appropriate estimation methodology which in turn depends on the types of data, variables and models. We discuss these issues in detail in Chapters 16 and 17.

15.1 "Good" data

Having "good" data is a prerequisite for meaningful model building. It is also essential for all decision making in marketing. "Good" data encompasses *availability, quality, variability* and *quantity*. These four elements determine the "goodness" of the data. Since the purpose of model building is to learn about relations between variables a critical question is whether the data allow for the estimation of inferences desired by management. The answer to this question determines the "goodness" of the data, and it depends on the *intended use* of a model. The parameterization of causal models used for description, conditional forecasting or prescription, requires the availability of data of all relevant predictor variables. However, the estimation of time-series models used, for example, for *unconditional forecasting*, is possible with nothing more than time-series data on the endogenous (criterion) variable.

AVAILABILITY

The first condition for data is their availability. It is common for an internal accounting department to have data on a firm's own actions and performance. Thus, data should be available on unit sales, revenues, prices of the firm's products, advertising expenditures, wholesale and retail margins, promotions and personal selling expenditures, and market coverage. The availability of such data does not imply that the data are directly usable. We return to this aspect when we discuss data quality.

Some data are more difficult to construct or to extract from company records than is true for other data. And usually marketing models need to incorporate information from other firms. For these reasons it is common for managers to purchase data, gathered regularly or incidentally, from market research firms. IRI and ACNielsen, two large research firms, provide market feedback reports on a large number of product categories gathered through scanner equipment in supermarkets, drugstores, etc. Even then the available data may be incomplete. Incompleteness in the form of missing predictors is a problem since the estimated effects of the available variables will be biased (if there is covariation between included and excluded predictor variables).

Dependent upon the precise purpose of the model-building effort it may be useful to gather additional data. For example, only about 40 percent of the gourmet coffee category was covered by scanners in the US in 1997. For a complete understanding of the gourmet coffee market the commercially available data would have to be supplemented, for example by surveys. It is now common for different data sources to be combined. For example, sales data collected through scanning at the household level may be combined with household level media coverage data. These data are sometimes available from a single source, but quite often not. If different market research agencies collect these different data types, techniques of data-fusion can be generally employed. Initially, ad hoc procedures were used to match households from two data bases on the basis of similarity in (often demographic) characteristics. Nowadays, statistical procedures are available that, based on multiple imputations of the missing data, yield fused data sets with known statistical properties (Kamakura, Wedel, 1997).

Generally speaking, data on industrial markets are harder to obtain than consumer data. Systematic records are rarely kept by individual firms. Although systematic data gathering by commercial market research agencies is growing, it is often limited to some large markets (such as electronic components). Customization in industrial markets complicates the problem: products, prices and services are often customer specific and usually not publically available, and the actions of competitors are often unknown (Brand, Leeflang, 1994). For more details on data sources see Section 15.3.

QUALITY

Here quality of data refers to the *validity* and *reliability* of data. A measure is valid if it measures what it is supposed to measure. Even if a measure is *valid* it will in many cases not be possible to measure it without error. The degree to which a measure is subject to random error is assessed by its *reliability*. Errors in the measurement of predictor variables can cause their estimated effects to be biased. It is in general quite difficult to define appropriate measures for variables such as "product quality" and "the value of a brand".[1] Much effort has been put into the development of appropriate measurement scales. Handbooks of validated scales are available that inform market research practice (Bearden, Netemeyer and Mobley, 1993). The validity of data used to measure the effectiveness of such variables on sales or profit is, generally speaking, not high. In addition, the validity of directly observable data available from, say, the accounting department, may also be low (see Section 5.1). Furthermore, data obtained from panels and surveys are subject to biases and sampling error.

VARIABILITY

If a variable shows no variation we cannot measure its impact on the criterion variable. Relation (8.8) is an example in which price was excluded because the price data did not show sufficient variability. The precision of an estimated effect for a predictor variable depends on the amount of sample variation. We use the word "precision" to describe the "estimated standard error" or (statistical) unreliability.

For models with multiple predictor variables, the "goodness" of the data also depends on the amount of *covariation* between the predictors. Thus the precision of the estimated effect of one predictor depends positively on its own variation and, usually negatively, on the amount of covariation with other predictors.

The variability of marketing mix variables may be less than what is needed for the estimation of their effects. For example, due to price competition the price range observed in a market may be low, or the range of variation in a product attribute such as package size is limited. In such cases the revealed preference data (choices) in the market place may be supplemented with other data. Experiments may be used in which desired variation in marketing mix elements is induced. A powerful technique is conjoint choice experimentation in which product profiles are experimentally designed, and choices among them are made by respondents (Louvière, Woodworth, 1983). Models are available to integrate such stated preference data with revealed preference data (Morikawa, 1989).

Sometimes there are multiple *sources of variation* that can be used to infer relations. Scanner data are obtainable at the household-, store-, chain- and market-level. Assume that for a given product category and a given metropolitan area one has access to, say, 52 weeks of data on 60 *stores*. A critical question then becomes whether both time-series (weeks) and cross-sectional (stores) variation are suitable for pa-

---

1. See, for example, Doyle (1989), Kamakura, Russell (1993), Keller (1993), Rangaswamy, Burke, Oliva (1993), Simon, Sullivan (1993), Sunde, Brodie (1993), Agarwal, Rao (1996).

rameterization. Our perspective is the following. If *retailers* use knowledge about the households shopping at their outlets, and about the competitive environment to determine marketing activities, then the cross-sectional variation cannot be used in a single equation model. Instead, the dependencies of the marketing activities on such factors would have to be explained simultaneously with the dependency of demand on marketing actions. Over time, *for a given store* the household characteristics and the competitive environment tend to be stable. Thus, the time-series variation in, for example, promotional activities can be used as long as changes in such activities occur "randomly".

If a *brand manager* wants to determine the effects of differences in variables across stores, such as size, composition and size of the assortment, and store environmental variables (e.g. customer and competitive characteristics) on brand sales, cross-sectional variation is essential. These types of consideration should influence how data that contain both time-series and cross-sectional variation are combined. We discuss methods for pooling time-series and cross-sectional data in Section 16.2. From these examples we conclude that the determination of "good" data depends on the *intended use* of a model *and* the *nature of the problem* faced by management.

QUANTITY

The final condition for "good" data is quantity. If a probability sample of observations is used to estimate a population mean, the sample size influences the precision of this estimate. However, if the interest focuses on the relation between variables, it is the amount of variation in a predictor (as well as covariation between predictors) that influences the precision of estimated effects.

The quantity of observations is, however, a critical factor for one's ability to estimate all model parameters. Specifically, the number of observations has to exceed the number of unknown model parameters. This requirement is simply a necessary condition that needs to be met for all parameters to be estimable in principle. Many researchers suggest that the quantity (number of observations) should be at least five times the number of parameters. The advisability of this rule of thumb depends, as we have argued above, on the amount of variation in and the amount of covariation between the predictor variables.

It is also useful to reserve some data for a validation exercise. Model building is an iterative process, and if one data set is used to estimate several alternative specifications before one specification is selected, then the usual statistical criteria are no longer valid. This type of estimation is often referred to as pretest estimation (Leamer, 1978). If the purpose of the model building is to test theories, the final specification should be validated on one or more new data sets. These other data sets could represent different product categories, different regions, different time periods, etc. If the model results are intended to be the basis for marketing decisions, an appropriate test is whether the model predictions, conditional upon specific marketing actions, outperform predictions from a manager (testing the model against managerial judgment). For more on validation, see Chapter 18.

If the initial quantity of data is inadequate for model estimation, the model builder can consider one or more constrained estimation methods. For example, suppose one wants to estimate the demand for one brand as a function of six marketing variables. If there are nine other brands that belong to the same product category, and it is desirable to have cross-brand effects for all brands and all variables, then the number of marketing variable parameters is 60. Obviously one year of weekly data is insufficient if the data are limited to time-series observations for one cross section. One solution to the problem is to obtain time-series data for other cross sections. In that case the issue of pooling cross-sectional and time-series variation has to be considered (see Sections 14.2 and 16.2). An alternative solution is to employ constrained estimation. For example, one could force some of the other brands to have zero cross effects by eliminating those brands' variables altogether. Or one could combine some brands and force parameters to be the same for brands belonging to common subsets. Note that all model-building efforts involve simplifications of reality. For example, the discussion above assumes that one desires to estimate all possible own- and cross-brand main effects. This starting position involves the implicit assumption that all interaction effects between the marketing predictors are zero.

15.2 Marketing management support systems

The use of electronic means to record purchases in supermarkets and other retail outlets has led to an exponential increase in the availability of data for modeling purposes. McCann and Gallagher (1990, p. 10) suggest that the change from bimonthly store audit data about brands to weekly scanner data (see Section 15.3) results in a 10,000 fold increase in available data (scanner data also measure more variables for a larger number of geographic areas at the UPC/SKU-level). Assume a brand group would normally spend five person-days analyzing one report based on bimonthly store audit data. Analyzing means here detecting important changes, explaining changes, discussing reasons for explanations, etc. This group would have to increase its size about 1,000 times or become 1,000 times more efficient (or some combination of these) in order to analyze weekly store-level scanner data in the same manner as the audit data.[2] To prevent this explosion in manpower, much of the analysis of more detailed and more frequently available scanner data has to become automated. One way to accomplish this is through the development and application of marketing management support systems. The following types of "computerized Marketing Management Support Systems (MMSS)" can be distinguished:[3]

- MarKeting Information System (MKIS);
- Marketing Decision Support System (MDSS);
- Marketing Knowledge-Based System (MKBS);
- Marketing Case-Based Reasoning system (MCBR);

---

2. See Mitchell, Russo, Wittink (1991).
3. van Bruggen (1993, pp. 4-5). See also van Bruggen, Smidts, Wierenga (1998), Wierenga, van Bruggen (2000).

- Marketing Neural Nets (MNN);
- Marketing Creativity-Enhancement Program (MCEP).

A MKIS harnesses marketing-related information to facilitate its use within the firm (Lilien, Rangaswamy, 1998, p. 315). A MKIS consists of a database (or databank[4]) with marketing data and statistical methods that can be used to analyze these data (statistical methods bank[4]). The statistical analyses are used to transform the data into information for marketing decisions.

A MDSS differs from a MKIS in that it contains a model base (modelbank[4]) in addition to a databank and a statistical methods bank. The purpose of a MDSS can be described as the collection, analysis, and presentation of information for immediate use in marketing decisions.[5]

A MKBS is a more advanced system than the previous two in the sense that theoretical knowledge and empirical generalizations are included. A restricted version of MKBS is an "expert system" which is related to the concept of "artificial intelligence" (AI). AI is concerned with the creation of computer programs that exhibit intelligent behavior.[6] The program solves problems by applying knowledge and reasoning that mimics human problem solving. The expert system approach is one of the earliest techniques for the creation of intelligent programs.

Typically, an expert system focuses on a detailed description (model) of the problem-solving behavior of experts in a specific area. The label *knowledge system* is more general because it encompasses and uses knowledge from experts but also other knowledge sources such as information available from books and articles, empirical results and experience. Nevertheless, the terms knowledge- and expert system are often used interchangeably.[7] Examples of such systems are:[8]

- PEP, a system designed to support the planning of consumer sales promotion campaigns (Bayer, Lawrence, Keon, 1988);
- ADCAD (ADvertising Communication Approach Design), a system to assist managers with the definition of marketing and advertising objectives, with advertising decisions regarding the positioning of a product/service, with the message, etc. (Burke, Rangaswamy, Wind, Eliashberg, 1990);
- ADDUCE, a system that predicts how consumers will respond to advertisements from a description of ad, audience, brand and market characteristics (Burke, 1991);
- BMA (Brand Manager's Assistant), a knowledge based system to assist brand management (McCann, Lahti, Hill, 1991);
- NEGOTEX (NEGOTiation EXpert), a system that provides guidelines to individuals or teams preparing for international marketing negotiations (Rangaswamy, Eliashberg, Burke, Wind, 1989).

---

4. See Montgomery, Urban (1969, 1970).
5. See Cox, Good (1967), Smith, Brien, Stafford (1968).
6. McCann, Gallagher (1990, p. 33).
7. McCann, Gallagher (1990, p. 34).
8. See also van Bruggen (1993) and the special issue on "expert systems in marketing" of the *International Journal of Research in Marketing*, vol. 8, nr. 1, 1991.

Expert systems have also been developed to generate management reports based on statistical analyses of frequently collected marketing data. Examples of systems that analyze scanner data are Cover Story (Schmitz, Armstrong, Little, 1990) and INFER (Rangaswamy, Harlam, Lodish, 1991).

Mitchell, Russo and Wittink (1991) discuss the distinguishing characteristics of human judgment, expert systems and statistical models for marketing decisions. They argue that ideally systems are developed to collaborate with managers. The most effective collaboration can be identified based on detailed knowledge of the advantages and disadvantages of the alternatives. For example, humans cannot, on average, beat models in repetitive decisions that require the integration of data on multiple variables, often expressed on noncomparable scales. On the other hand, humans have the intellectual capacity to construct theories and to provide arguments so critical for model specification. They note that the role of systems as collaborators in managerial tasks should be distinguished from the role of decision support systems. The role of the latter is to provide input to decision-making but not to draw inferences or make decisions. In a man-machine expert system, the system shares decision-making responsibility with the user. Management support systems are effective in solving problems that require serial processing, whereas the human mind is "designed" for parallel processing tasks.

Wierenga and van Bruggen (1997) discuss extensions of the marketing knowledge-based systems (MKBSs).[9] A marketing case-based reasoning system (MCBR) is based on the fact that analogical reasoning is a natural way to approach problems. The analogizing power of a decision maker can be strengthened by a MCBR, a system that stores historical cases with all the relevant data kept intact. The ADDUCE-system infers how consumers will react to a new advertisement by searching relevant past advertisements. Thus, it can be interpreted as a knowledge system with a case-based reasoning system as one of its components. This indicates that the different systems are not necessarily distinct. McIntyre, Achabal and Miller (1993) built a MCBR to forecast the retail sales for a given promotion based on historical analogs from a case base.

Neural networks can be used to model the way human beings attach meaning to a set of stimuli or signals. Artificial neural networks can be trained to make the same types of associations between inputs and outputs as human beings do. An important feature of a neural network is its ability to learn. Marketing neural nets (MNNs) may be useful for the recognition of new product opportunities and to learn to distinguish between successful and less successful sales promotion campaigns.

Marketing creativity-enhancement programs (MCEPs) are computer programs that stimulate and endorse the creativity of marketing decision makers. Because the MCBR, MNN and MCEP were developed only recently, their value for marketing management support cannot be evaluated yet.

---

9. We closely follow Wierenga and van Bruggen (1997). See also Wierenga, van Bruggen (2000).

The support tools discussed thus far are defined from the perspective of a *supply-side* approach. The descriptions emphasize features and capabilities rather than the conditions under which they are appropriate. By contrast, Wierenga and van Bruggen (1997) introduce the concept of marketing problem-solving mode (MPSM), a *demand-side* perspective to marketing support systems.

> *"An MPSM characterizes the problem-solving process of a marketer. Different marketing decision makers can use different MPSMs. And the same decision maker can use different modes at different times. The required type of support depends on the MPSM employed by a decision maker"*

(Wierenga, van Bruggen, 1997, p.21).

A classification of MPSMs is developed, based on different cognitive models of the way a marketing manager solves a problem. Four MPSMs are defined: *optimizing, reasoning, analogizing,* and *creating.*

A manager using the *optimizing* mode may be assisted either by "just" a marketing model or by a MKBS. Marketing models may provide the best quantitative solution, whereas a MKBS provides an optimal solution if the problem is described in terms of qualitative relations between the variables. In this way Wierenga and van Bruggen match the MPSM-classification with the MMSS-classification. Thus, given the above discussion it is obvious that a MNN or a MCBR provide support in cases where managers solve problems by *analogizing,* etc.

Both MDSS and MKBS require the collection and storage of (large amounts) of data. We discuss important data sources in Section 15.3.

15.3 Data sources

The sources of data for consumer durables, industrial goods and services are different from those for frequently bought consumer goods. Although the models discussed in this book are generalizable to all types of products and services, their actual use may require extra work to identify appropriate data. In this respect we refer to Brand and Leeflang (1994) regarding the research on modeling industrial markets and the special issue of *Management Science,* November 1995, regarding the use of (OR) models in service management. Here the use of judgmental or subjective data and subjective estimation methods is relevant as we discuss in Section 16.9. In what follows we discuss data for frequently bought consumer goods.

Data from the accounting department (internal data) and from independent marketing information services (external data) are important sources of information for marketing researchers and marketing executives. During the past few decades the use of data for decision-making purposes has become widespread. The introduction of

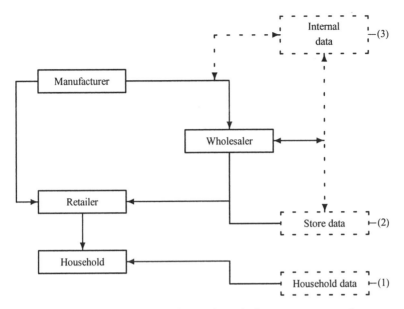

Figure 15.1 Points in the marketing channel where measures are taken.

mathematical marketing models may also have stimulated the demand for and the production of these data. In this section we discuss some well-known data sources.[10]

Revealed preference data reflecting choices, sales and shares and a (sub)set of causal variables can be measured at, at least, three levels in the marketing channel viz:

- at the household level, for example, through a household panel whose purchases are electronically recorded;
- at the retail level by means of a store audit or electronic (scanner-based) registration of activities;
- at the manufacturer level.

We show these levels in Figure 15.1. Data obtained as "ex-factory sales" are internally generated by the manufacturers. These can be corrected for changes in inventory at the wholesale and retail level, so as to measure sales (as opposed to production).

We next discuss information available at the three levels, starting with the household level. This is followed by a focus on data available through electronic (scanner-based) means, and a discussion of other sources of information on causal variables (causal data).

---

10. For a more extensive discussion see e.g. Malhotra (1996, Chapter 4).

HOUSEHOLD LEVEL

Traditionally, and in some countries this is still the standard, information from house-holds showing repeat purchase and brand switching behavior is obtained through diary panels.[11] Such a panel consists of families who use a preprinted diary in which they record their weekly purchases in specified product categories. Typically, the item (brand name, type of product, weight or quantity, kind of package), number of units and price along with store information are reported for each purchase. The families are geographically dispersed, while the panel is demographically balanced so the data can be projected to the national level in a given country. Families are recruited so that the composition of the panel mirrors the population as much as possible on specified characteristics. Panel members are compensated for their participation, often with gifts. Families are dropped from the panel at their request, if they fail to return their diaries, or if their records are unreliable. The diaries are returned weekly. Clients of diary panel services use the data to assess among other things: the size of the market for a product, the proportion of families buying over time, the amount purchased per household, brand share over time, the frequency of purchase and amount purchased per transaction, average price paid, etc. In some panels, the members are asked to record whether purchases are on promotion.

In the US household panel services are provided by, for example, NPD Research, Inc., Market Research Corporation of America (MRCA), Market Facts and National Family Opinion.[12] In Europe these services are available from, amongst others, GfK and Attwood.

STORE (RETAIL) LEVEL

For many decades, the ACNielsen Company dominated the industry consisting of systematic data gathering at the retail level for the purpose of tracking the perfor-mances of brands. The bimonthly audit data, still available in many countries all over the world, are based on national probability samples. Auditors visit the same stores, every two months. During the visit they take a complete inventory of all items covered (for the product categories for which manufacturers are clients), and they record all invoices since the previous visit. Total purchases by the retailer plus the reduction in inventory provide the revenue (based on the shelf price prevailing at the time of the audit) and unit sales information for each item per store. Other information collected includes out-of-stock conditions (at the time of the audit), and certain promotional activities such as premiums, bonus packs, sampling and featuring. A probability sample of store data, weighted by certain store characteristics and previous period results, produces highly accurate estimates of brand performance at the national level. However, as the coverage of purchases by electronic means increases in a country, the bimonthly audit service tends to disappear.

---

11. Other names for the consumer panel are diary panel (Malhotra, 1996, pp. 134-137) and mail consumer panel (Hanssens, Parsons, Schultz, 1990, p. 63).
12. Green, Tull, Albaum (1988, p. 117).

In Europe, GfK provides clients with sales, retail availability, prices, etc. of consumer durable products. For other product categories not covered by ACNielsen, Audits and Surveys' National Total Market Audit provides data in some countries.

MANUFACTURER LEVEL

The manufacturer's *internal accounting* system can provide "shipped sales" or "ex-factory sales". To measure household purchases, these data have to be corrected for changes in inventory at the wholesale and retail levels. Inventory changes at the retail level are obtained through store audits; inventory changes at the wholesale level are obtained from sales representatives who take on the role of intelligence gatherers or from wholesale audits. These corrections of the "ex-factory" sales are performed a couple of times per year. The ex-factory sales of a manufacturer's own brand can be combined with the corresponding figures of other brands in a given product category available from an independent institute. In that way, estimates of total industry sales, industry sales per segment and brands' market shares are obtained.

EVALUATION

The precision of the data from each of these sources is not guaranteed. Yet, if household survey- or store audit data are used for marketing decisions, a certain rigor must be imposed.[13] Problems in this realm have been identified by, for example, Assael (1967), Nenning, Topritzhofer, Wagner (1979), Shoemaker and Pringle (1980), Leeflang, Olivier (1980, 1982, 1985) and Plat (1988).

Leeflang and Olivier observed substantial differences for measures of sales, market share and price between the different levels in Figure 15.1. Nonresponse bias is a major reason for problems with *sample survey data*. For example, households who buy relatively inexpensive brands have a higher response rate than households who buy the more expensive brands. The nonresponse bias in *store audit data* results from the refusal of some retailers such as discounters, to cooperate. Leeflang and Olivier (1985) demonstrated that the data bias leads to large differences in marketing decisions between consumer panel data and store audit data.

SCANNER DATA

The availability of data for parameterization of marketing models has increased during the past decade through adoption of scanners by retailers.[14] In the early 1970s laser technology in conjunction with small computers first enabled retailers in the US to record electronically or "scan" the purchases made in their stores. Since then, after a period of slow growth, the adoption of scanning has increased rapidly, and scanner data have become available for decision support in marketing at many organizations. Although scanning was originally used by retailers simply as a labor- and cost-saving

---

13. See Frankel and Frankel (1977).
14. See also Leeflang, Plat (1988) and Foekens, Leeflang (1992).

Table 15.1 Development of scanning in food stores.

Country	December 1987		January 1990		January 1994
	Stores with scanners	% ACV[a]	Stores with scanners	% ACV	% ACV
North America					
USA	14,660	55	18,530	62	71
Canada	1,011	38	1,390	45	50
Europe					
Finland	306	15	1,252	45	80
Sweden	697	22	1,158	44	85
France	1,529	28	3,200	43	74
Great Britain	495	17	1,497	39	76
Denmark	220	15	850	37	83
Belgium	410	15	686	31	83
Germany	985	10	2,730	29	39
Norway	311	15	537	26	58
Netherlands	385	13	638	25	56
Ireland	15	4	70	19	39
Italy	650	7	2,300	17	56
Spain	475	7	850	14	57
Austria	153	5	302	10	53
Switzerland	52	1	160	3	10

[a] ACV=All Commodity Volume

Source: Nielsen (1988, p. 39) and information from ACNielsen (the Netherlands) BV.

device, the computerized accumulation of point-of-sale information puts a library of accurate and detailed purchase records at the disposal of many marketing researchers and marketing managers.

Several years after the first scanners were installed in the US, scanning was introduced in Europe. To coordinate the encoding of products and the exchange of data, several organizations in the European countries established clearing institutes to amalgamate the data of affiliated retailers. In addition, systems for automated transmission of transaction data were developed, and the possibilities for natural electronic funds transfer systems (EFTS) were studied. Table 15.1 illustrates the rapid development of scanning in the grocery industry.

In Table 15.1 the penetration of scanning devices (or scanners) among food stores is measured by the percentage of all commodity volume covered by scanning stores. Clearly large differences exist between the US and Europe, and between European countries. Today, in the US, Canada, and in most countries in Europe, scanning-based (store) samples have been developed that project with known sampling error to the national level and often to specified regions. The figures in Table 15.1, however, indicate that, at least in some European countries, the penetration of scanners in 1994 was too low for managers to rely solely on scanner data for marketing decisions. The use of these data will primarily be complementary to the traditional consumer panel and retail store audit data in those countries.

Although the original intent for scanner data collected by market research firms was to aid brand managers, retailers increasingly recognize opportunities too. For example, scanner data analysis can be the basis for space allocation of items in a product category to maximize store profits (Chapter 13). To be able to do this for as many stores equipped with scanners as possible, both ACNielsen and IRI have expanded the number of stores from which they obtain (purchase) data. And since the sales teams of the manufacturers want to maximize the space for the brands they have responsibility for, the manufacturers are also interested in having access to data on all scanner-based stores. Thus, the market research firms now favor having census of all scanner-equipped retailers. At the same time, manufacturers and retailers have an increasing need to obtain solutions that maximize their joint profits.

Scanning has many advantages for consumers, retailers, wholesalers and manufac-turers. Scanning-based samples have been constructed at the household level and at the retail level ("scanning-based store samples"). To provide a sense of the benefits of scanning, we assume the use of scanning-based *store* samples.[15] The following benefits can be distinguished:

- Greater accuracy, in the sense that much of the human element in recording prod-uct movements is eliminated. Also, more accurate price data may be obtained as variations in prices are known and can be related to the relevant quantities. This does not mean, however, that mistakes do not occur. For example, checkout clerks may skip items and computer records may be inaccurate (Foekens, Leeflang, 1992).
- Relatively low costs of data collection.
- Shorter data intervals. Since at the retail level it is rare for changes in prices on promotion to be made within a week, scanner data are normally recorded on a weekly basis. However, the data interval can be as short as a day, as it often is in Japan. The shorter data interval provides insight into short-term fluctuations, and it avoids summing or averaging across heterogeneous conditions (see Section 14.1.2).
- Exact data intervals. In the traditional store audits, the stores are visited on dif-ferent days, resulting in a rolling sample. As a consequence, the aggregated audit

---

15. See also Bloom (1980), Prasad, Casper, Schieffer (1984).

data can differ systematically from the true bimonthly measures. These differences are referred to as "instrument bias". This bias does not exist with scanning.
- Speed of reporting. Instead of four to eight weeks after the period of observation, reports are available within days after the scanned period.

In *scanner panels*, each household may use an ID-card similar to a credit card. Panel members are asked to present their card at the checkout counter each time they shop. This allows each panel member's ID-number to be recorded next to the set of items purchased by the member.[16] Such data from scanner panels are supplied by IRI to clients through its Infoscan Service. Behavior Scan (from IRI) is a household scanner panel designed to support controlled tests of new products or advertising campaigns.[17] An alternative to the ID card is to ask households to scan at home or at the store and to identify the store in which the purchases were made. This is done by ACNielsen and GfK (Consumerscan and Microscan) both of which supply each participating household with a wand.

The data from scanning-based store samples are known as "volume tracking data".[18] The data provide information on purchases by brand, size, flavor or formulation (Stock-Keeping Unit-level: SKU) and are based on sales data collected from the checkout scanner tapes. Volume tracking data are supplied through Infoscan (IRI), Scantrack (ACNielsen), Nabscan (The Newspaper Advertising Bureau) and TRIM (Tele-Research, Inc.). The following measures are reported:[19]

- volumes (at the SKU-level);
- revenues;
- actual prices;
- ACV = the All Commodity Volume of the store or store revenue;
- ACV Selling = the ACV for an item or group of items reported only in stores with some movement of that item;
- baseline sales: an estimate of unit sales under non-promoted conditions.

Also, regular prices are estimated to make a distinction between those prices and promotional prices which reflect temporary discounts.

These descriptions indicate how data on relevant decision variables are captured. In addition the promotional environment in a store is measured through the separate collection of information on displays and features. Merchandising is a generic name for promotional activity conducted by a store to increase sales (Little, 1998). The market research companies report four mutually exclusive types of "merchandising": (1) display only, (2) feature only, (3) display and feature together, and (4) unsupported price cuts. Several of these can be subdivided further, if desired, for example by type of display. Most of these non-price promotional variables are collected as zero-one measures. Measures of merchandising activity can also be defined analogously to those for distribution.

---

16. Malhotra (1996, p. 137).
17. Cooper, Nakanishi (1988, p.96). See also Abraham, Lodish (1992).
18. Malhotra (1996, p. 137).
19. See, for example, Cooper, Nakanishi (1988, pp. 93-95).

A more advanced system consists of the *combination* of scanner panel data with cable TV advertising exposure records. The combination of information in a single data set is referred to as single-source data. Single-source data provide integrated information on household purchases, media exposure, and other characteristics, along with information on marketing variables such as price, promotion and in-store marketing efforts.[20] We mentioned in Section 15.1 that data fusion is desirable if all data do not pertain to a single group of households.

CAUSAL DATA

Price-, promotion-, and distribution data are natural components [21] of the data collection methods just discussed; however, data on manufacturer advertising and product quality are not. There are, however, agencies that specialize in the collection of *advertising* expenditures, such as Leading National Advertisers (LNA) in the US. In many models predictor variables such as gross rating points (GRP's) on TV-ratings are used. These data are collected, for example, by Nielsen (Nielsen Television Index)[22] and Arbitron (Arbitron monitors local and regional radio and TV diary panels).[23]

Product quality is hard to define and to measure for use in a marketing model. Some authors have used proxy variables such as the number of items in an assortment.[24] Steenkamp (1989) provides an extensive overview of the measurement of product quality.

In most models discussed in this book, the fundamental unit of analysis is the brand. Given the wide range of assortments offered in many product categories, the brand is a product line comprising many Stock-Keeping Units (SKU's). Most SKU's can be described in terms of a few physical characteristics to distinguish the items. Examples are SKU-attributes such as brand name, package size, "formula", flavor, etc. Marketing research firms use several criteria[25] to determine what can be treated as an SKU-attribute: each attribute must be recognizable by consumers in an objective manner (i.e. physically distinguishable), the variation in each attribute across SKU's must be discrete, and each attribute must be applicable to every SKU. The analysis challenge is to define the smallest set of SKU-attributes that capture the relevant variability across all SKU's within a product category for possible inclusion in a model. The reason for minimizing the set is that the number of SKU-attributes and levels quickly explodes for a complex product category.

Fader and Hardie (1996) calibrated a multinomial logit model based on household data as follows. The deterministic part of their model has two components:

• a preference component which represents the household's base preference toward a SKU;

---

20. Malhotra (1996, p. 141). See for applications of single source data Deighton, Henderson, Neslin (1994), and Lodish et al. (1995a, 1995b).
21. Hanssens et al. (1990, p. 64).
22. See also Lodish et al. (1995a, 1995b).
23. See Danaher, Sharot (1994) for an application and an explanation.
24. See Telser (1962b), Leeflang, Koerts (1974), Leeflang (1977b).
25. We closely follow Fader, Hardie (1996).

- a marketing mix component to capture the effects of marketing variables on the household's choice behavior.

The preference component is decomposed into SKU-specific intercept terms that capture SKU-attribute effects. In Fader and Hardie's application the attributes describe SKU's in the product category of fabric softeners with ten levels on the brand attribute (brand name), four levels on a size attribute, four levels distinguishing form (sheets, concentrated, refill, liquid), and four levels for formula (regular, staingard, unscented, light). The specification of SKU-attributes, allows the preference component to be captured by 22 attribute levels. In principle, these four attributes can create $10 \cdot 4^3 = 640$ unique SKU's. Of these only 56 existed in the database. Importantly, while a traditional choice model would have a single preference component for each of the 56 SKU's, the attribute specification, with main effects only, is more parsimonious (has fewer parameters) and offers the model user attribute effects which can become the basis for forecasting sales for any of the 584 non-existent SKU's.

OTHER DATA INPUTS

Other data inputs refer to environmental variables such as size and age distribution of the population, temperature, and macroeconomic variables such as gross national product, per capita income and employment.[26] One can also use stated preferences and other subjective consumer judgments.

Measures of sales, "merchandising", distribution, etc. can be defined at different levels of aggregation with respect to (groups of) stores, regions, time periods, and products. Little (1998) emphasizes that to be most useful, these measures should have parallel and consistent meanings across the different levels. He also suggests a class of integrated measures that start with information routinely provided by data suppliers. The information is first decomposed and then aggregated analytically to refer to store groups, product lines, and multi-week periods.

15.4 Data collection through model development: A case study

The process of model development can help managers decide what information to collect and it can also improve the use of existing information.[27] This holds in particular for measurement problems and causal models estimated through LISREL (Section 17.1). In this section we illustrate how the development of a parsimonious model contributes to the collection, organization and use of data for decision making. The case study concerns the modeling of the sales performance of a Dutch detergent brand when scanner data are unavailable. In many non-US-markets and especially for industrial goods, services and some consumer durables this is a typical scenario.

---

26. For a survey of these secondary data services, see Malhotra (1996, Appendix 4a).
27. See indirect benefits 3 and 4 in Section 3.2.

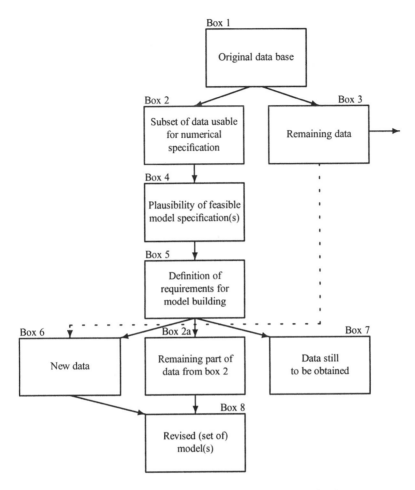

Figure 15.2 The process of data collection through model development.

We show a flow chart in Figure 15.2. Box 1 represents the original data base. The data base is separated into two subsets: Box 2 contains the data useful for estimation; Box 3 contains data not of immediate relevance for numerical specification.[28] The available data can be the basis for an initial model specification (see Box 4). In fact, the model builder is likely to face difficulties choosing just one specification, especially if the data are incomplete (e.g. missing variables, missing details on some variables). Thus, the initial effort may produce a set of alternative model specifications based on available data.

At this point the model builder may decide that the available data are inadequate. For example, if there are no data at all on a predictor variable that is believed to be

---

28. For example, the firm may collect data to monitor the performance of some brands in product categories in which it is not competing, but may enter in the future.

critical or the data on that variable are incomplete or of very poor quality, this is
a likely judgment. Alternatively, the model builder could estimate several specifications hoping that it is possible to obtain valid and reliable estimates of the effects of
available predictor variables. The same judgment of data inadequacy may occur if the
empirical results are unconvincing (e.g. the parameter estimates are implausible). In
practice this more often leads to respecification of the model than to the collection
of new data. Nevertheless, this initial modeling effort, both the model specifications
that can be estimated and the actual empirical results, can be instrumental in helping
the model builder identify the data that are required for successful completion of the
model building task.

The process leading to this definition of requirements for model building (Box 5)
is illustrated in Figure 15.2. Some of the data from Box 2 may be of use (Box 2a).
Often, however, new data are needed to supplement the original subset. Some of the
required data are obtainable on relatively short notice, for example, from market research agencies. The remaining data in Box 3 may also be more relevant than initially
thought. The result is a new data set (Box 6). Some of the desired data will not be
immediately available (Box 7). But the data in Box 6 and Box 2a lead to a revised set
of models (Box 8).

We now take the initial approach used by an analyst working on behalf of a brand
manager. The brand manager had expressed an interest in a numerically specified
equation showing the effects of marketing variables on brand sales. The analyst obtained access to a data base that led her to specify a linear market share- and a linear
product category sales model. Table 15.2 shows the subset (Box 2) from the original
data base pertinent to parameter estimation of the market share- (15.1) and product
category sales (15.2) equations. In the equations, bimonthly values for A_{t-1} and Inc_t,
are obtained through interpolation.

$$\hat{m}_{jt} = \underset{(1.8)}{5.1} + \underset{(3.2)}{7.9} \frac{a_{j,t-1}}{A_{t-1}} - \underset{(1.5)}{7.2} \frac{p_{jt}}{P_t} + \underset{(2.1)}{9.2} d_{jt} \qquad (15.1)$$

$$T = 29, \ R^2 = 0.56$$

$$\hat{Q}_t = \underset{(41)}{202} - \underset{(10.1)}{0.29} \frac{Inc_t}{CPI_t} - \underset{(11.7)}{29.5} \frac{P_t}{CPI_t} + \underset{(0.15)}{0.31} \frac{A_{t-1}}{CPI_t} - \underset{(0.47)}{0.29} t \qquad (15.2)$$

$$T = 32, \ R^2 = 0.47$$

where

$$
\begin{aligned}
m_{jt} &= 100 q_{jt}/Q_t, \\
n &= \text{the number of detergent brands (see Table 5.2),} \\
n^* &= \text{the number of brands in the market consisting of deter-} \\
&\qquad \text{gents and other cleaning products (see Table 5.2),}
\end{aligned}
$$

Table 15.2 Original data base for model specification and estimation (Box 2, Figure 15.2).

Symbol	Variable	Source[a]
q_{jt}	sales of brand j in (period) t in thousands of kilos[b]	Nielsen
Q_t	product category sales in t in thousands of kilos	Nielsen
a_{jt}	advertising expenditures of brand j in t in thousands of guilders[c]	B.B.C.
$A_{t'} = \sum_{t=1}^{3} \sum_{t=1}^{n^*} a_{rt}$	total advertising expenditures of n^* brands per half year t', in thousands of guilders[c]	B.B.C.[d]
p_{jt}	price per unit of brand j in t in guilders	Nielsen
$P_t = \frac{1}{n} \sum_{r=1}^{n} p_{rt}$	average price over n brands in t in guilders	Nielsen
d_{jt}	market coverage of brand j in t, measured as a fraction of the total number of shops where the product class is sold	Nielsen
$Inc_{t''} = \sum_{t=1}^{6} Inc_t$	national income in nominal terms per year t''	N.C.B.S.[e]
CPI_t	Consumer Price Index in t	N.C.B.S.

[a] Agency that supplied the data.
[b] Bimonthly data (t covers two-month periods).
[c] Data available only on a six-month basis.
[d] Bureau of Budget Control.
[e] The Netherlands Central Bureau of Statistics.

T = the number of observations,

t = time index $t = 1, \ldots, 32$, where t = bimonthly period, and

The figures in parentheses are estimated standard errors of the coefficients.

We can criticize the specifications with or without reference to the numerical estimates as follows. Both models assume that all effects are linear. This is undesirable and unrealistic, as we discussed in the section on robust models (7.2.5). In the estimated market share equation, if the advertising ratio is zero (no advertising for brand j in $t - 1$), if the relative price is two (the brand's price is twice the average detergent brand's price), and the market coverage is half, the predicted market share equals −4.7, clearly an impossibility. Even if this combination of values for the marketing variables is unlikely to occur, it implies that the linearity assumption is untenable. Similar arguments can be made against the linearity of effects in the product category sales equation. For example, detergent is a basic product that many households will not want to be without (i.e. low substitutability). Also, there is only modest opportunity to expand total product category sales. Under these conditions, product category unit sales is likely to experience decreasing increments for successive increases in advertising. Nonlinear effects are also likely for the income and price variables.

Despite these concerns, it is comforting that most slope coefficients in both equations have expected signs. For the time index variable there is not a strong expectation, although one may argue that if the population of households increases over time, a positive marginal effect might exist, to the extent that changes in the national income variable do not capture population changes.

The specification can also be criticized with regard to the following implicit assumptions. One, in the market share equations, the advertising share does not have a current effect. Two, advertising has no lagged effect beyond one period. Three, all interaction effects are assumed to be zero. Each of these assumptions can be said to be inconsistent with existing empirical evidence. For example, there is an extensive literature on the interaction between (manufacturer) advertising and price. In addition, one may argue that the influence of marketing variables for other brands (reflected in the category variables) should not be assumed to be homogeneous (see Foekens, Leeflang, Wittink, 1997). Of course, with only a small number of observations ($T = 29$ for the market share equation), the model builder has no choice but to ignore many relevant complexities.

Other aspects that deserve attention center around the measurement of variables. The advertising share variable is defined for a broader market than is true for market share and average price. It is desirable that total advertising be defined for the detergent product category instead of the broader market with cleaners. There are also inconsistencies in the time period in which variables are measured. The total advertising variable is defined for six-month periods while national income is defined annually. Interpolation is necessary to estimate data for these variables on a bimonthly basis. However, the resulting data contain measurement error that can bias the slope coefficients.

The lagged advertising share variable is subject to an additional source of measurement error. For example, the effect is arbitrarily specified to occur after one bimonth, the unit in which the time periods have been defined by ACNielsen. Yet the true effect may occur more quickly, for example after one month. Strictly speaking this could require that advertising be measured for a different bimonthly period, for example such that February and March advertising expenditures are used to explain sales in March and April, etc. For a discussion of this problem see Section 14.1.3.

The results show modest R^2 values (0.56 for the market share equation, and 0.47 for the product category sales equation). Although these values are large enough for the equations to have significant explanatory power (see Chapter 16), it is useful to consider possible reasons for the R^2 values to be relatively low. The (unadjusted) R^2 value is the amount of variation in the criterion variable accounted for by the predictor variables. This value can be low for the following reasons:

1. There are many relevant predictors, each of which has a modest amount of (marginal) explanatory power; if only a few predictors are used, the total explanatory power will be modest.

2. Most relevant predictors have nonlinear effects; if linear effects are assumed, the explanatory power will tend to be reduced.
3. The effects of many predictors depend on the level(s) of one or more other predictors (interaction effects); the omission of interaction effects tends to reduce the explanatory power.
4. Measurement error in one or more predictor variables tends to reduce the explanatory power (and can cause the estimated effect(s) to be biased toward zero).
5. One or more predictor variables can have little variation in the estimation sample; if all relevant predictors have no variation, it is not only impossible to estimate effects, but the amount of variation in the criterion variable will consist of random noise, such that the R^2 value will tend toward zero.

Based on the various arguments presented above, we can say that the estimated equations give rise to the following desiderata.

a. Make the *market definition*[29] for the total advertising variable consistent with the other variables. An effort needs to be made to define this variable for the detergent product category (to reduce measurement error).
b. *Obtain* bimonthly *data* for the total advertising variable and for national income. Having actual data avoids the interpolation that produces estimated values within the half year for total advertising and within the year for national income (to reduce measurement error).
c. *Expand the set of predictor variables.* For example, advertising expenditures can be broken down by media (television, radio, press). Also, the product category variables can be decomposed into separate variables for each other brand. Bultez and Naert (1973) show that a superior model specification obtains if each competing brand is treated uniquely. Also, the product category sales variable might depend on the stock of automatic washing machines. Thus, there are many potentially relevant predictor variables that can be added (to reduce omitted variable bias).
d. Accommodate plausible *interaction* effects. A logical candidate is the possible dependence of the market share effect of (relative) price on advertising (share). The price effect may also depend on market coverage and on national income. Thus, several interaction variables can be added (to reduce omitted variable bias).
e. *Increase the number of observations.* Obviously, many of these plausible model additions cannot be accommodated without more data. One way to accomplish this is to measure variables at a lower level of aggregation (e.g. stores, households), and a smaller time interval (e.g. weeks, days). A reduction in aggregation can avoid certain biases (Chapter 14). Both a lower aggregation level and a smaller time interval will increase the number of observations which may also increase the amount of variation in the predictor variables. In that manner, more predictor variables can be accommodated so that the specification can become more realistic.

---

29. See also the discussion on market boundaries in Section 14.3.

Modifications of relations (15.1) and (15.2), possible after new data became available, did not result in substantial improvements. One outcome of the critical examination was that a possible nonresponse bias of the store audit data became of interest. Inspection revealed that purchases in discount stores were not included in the audit. Since brand j was hardly sold in discount stores, this meant that brand j's market share of the national market was overstated. This nonresponse bias could be reduced through the use of consumer panel data. These data also supplied information about the stock of automatic washing machines and non-price promotions. A revised numerical specification of the product class sales model is given in equation (9.17).

The "new data" (Box 6), and the data from Box 2 that remained, were used to parameterize a revised set of market share- and product category sales equations (Box 8). The ratio of the explained variation over the total variation in the criterion variable increased substantially for both models.

For more discussion of (more extensive) models relevant to this product category based on weekly scanner data, see the discussion of hierarchical models in Section 14.5. The data used to parameterize these models constitute the last step of the data collection process described here.

CHAPTER 16

Estimation and testing

In this chapter we consider methods and procedures for the estimation of model parameters. In Section 16.1 we provide a treatment of a simple linear relation between one criterion variable and one predictor variable. Although such a specification lacks practical relevance, it is attractive for a careful treatment of model assumptions, and a conceptual explanation of the basis for the assumptions. And most of the principles that apply to the linear model remain relevant as long as nonlinear effects for the original variables can be accommodated by transforming variables (so that the transformed variables are linearly related). In Section 16.1 we discuss the estimation of the parameters of the linear model using either time-series data or cross-sectional data. Estimation methods for pooled time-series and cross-sectional data are discussed in Section 16.2. In Section 16.3 we introduce estimation methods that are suitable when one or more assumptions required for the simplest methods are violated.

While in both Sections 16.1 and 16.2 we assume one-way causality, we consider simultaneous causality in Section 16.4. In Section 16.5 we discuss situations in which the model is not linearizable. Such problems require nonlinear estimation methods. Specifically, we discuss maximum likelihood estimation in Section 16.6. This is followed in Section 16.7 by nonparametric estimation which in its purest form allows for complete flexibility in the nature of the effect of changes in a given predictor variable on the criterion variable. Thus, nonparametric estimation avoids the problem of selecting an appropriate functional form a priori. In addition, it accommodates interaction effects between the predictor variables in a flexible way.

In Section 16.8 we discuss issues relevant to the estimation of models with behavioral detail, and in Section 16.9 we review subjective estimation. Subjective estimation is attractive in the absence of data or when the quality of data is insufficient.

We note that our discussion is limited to standard procedures. More detailed treatments can be found in econometrics textbooks. Goldberger (1998) provides a very clear and lucid discussion. Berndt (1991) is quite accessible with attractive discussions about research issues in economics. Baltagi (1998), Gujarati (1995), Intriligator, Bodkin and Hsiao (1996), Johnston (1984), and Pindyck and Rubinfeld (1991) are standard texts that contain relatively easy-to-follow treatments. Greene (1997) and Judge, Griffiths, Hill, Lütkepohl and Lee (1985) are general state-of-the-art textbooks. Amemiya (1985), Davidson and McKinnon (1993) and Hamilton (1994) provide advanced descriptions.

16.1 The linear model

In econometrics a distinction is made between linear- and nonlinear models. A linear model is linear in the parameters which means that the original variables are linearly related or can be transformed such that the relation between the transformed variables is linear. Models for which no transformations can make the model linear in the parameters are (intrinsically) nonlinear models (Section 5.3.3).

16.1.1 THE TWO-VARIABLE CASE

We assume the following relation for n cross sections and T time-series observations per cross section:

$$y_{jt} = \alpha_j + \beta_j x_{jt} + u_{jt}, \quad j = 1, \ldots, n, \quad t = 1, \ldots, T \tag{16.1}$$

where

y_{jt} = the value of the criterion variable in observation jt,

x_{jt} = the value of the predictor variable in observation jt,

u_{jt} = the (unobservable) value of the disturbance term

in observation jt,

α_j = the unknown intercept for cross section j,

β_j = the unknown slope parameter for cross section j.

We assume in this model that each cross section has unique parameters, and that these parameters can be estimated from time-series data.

In (16.1), β_j is the systematic change in y_{jt} when x_{jt} increases by one unit, and α_j is the constant part of y_{jt} when x_{jt} equals zero.

Given sample data, $t = 1, \ldots, T$ for each cross section j, relevant to the problem for which a model is desired, the most common method for estimating the two unknown parameters is Ordinary Least Squares (OLS). The objective is to obtain parameter estimates, $\hat{\beta}_j$ and $\hat{\alpha}_j$, by minimizing:

$$\sum_{t=1}^{T} (y_{jt} - \hat{y}_{jt})^2 \quad \text{for each } j \tag{16.2}$$

where

$$\hat{y}_{jt} = \hat{\alpha}_j + \hat{\beta}_j x_{jt}, \quad t = 1, \ldots, T.$$

By taking partial derivatives of (16.2) with respect to $\hat{\beta}_j$ and $\hat{\alpha}_j$, and setting those equal to zero, we obtain:

$$\frac{\partial \sum_{t=1}^{T} (y_{jt} - \hat{y}_{jt})^2}{\partial \hat{\beta}_j} = -2 \sum_{t=1}^{T} x_{jt} (y_{jt} - \hat{\alpha}_j - \hat{\beta}_j x_{jt}) = 0 \tag{16.3}$$

$$\frac{\partial \sum_{t=1}^{T} (y_{jt} - \hat{y}_{jt})^2}{\partial \hat{\alpha}_j} = -2 \sum_{t=1}^{T} (y_{jt} - \hat{\alpha}_j - \hat{\beta}_j x_{jt}) = 0. \qquad (16.4)$$

From (16.4) we have:

$$\hat{\alpha}_j = \left(\frac{\sum_{t=1}^{T} y_{jt}}{T} \right) - \hat{\beta}_j \left(\frac{\sum_{t=1}^{T} x_{jt}}{T} \right) = \bar{y}_j - \hat{\beta}_j \bar{x}_j. \qquad (16.5)$$

By substituting (16.5) into (16.3) we obtain:

$$\hat{\beta}_j = \frac{\sum_{t=1}^{T} x_{jt} y_{jt} - \dfrac{\sum_{t=1}^{T} x_{jt} y_{jt}}{T}}{\sum_{t=1}^{T} x_{jt}^2 - \dfrac{\left(\sum_{t=1}^{T} x_{jt} \right)^2}{T}}. \qquad (16.6)$$

We could discuss error-term assumptions and derive estimators for this model. Since (16.1) is unrealistically simple we defer the discussion of error-term assumptions to section 16.1.3.

16.1.2 THE L-VARIABLE CASE

The basic model (16.1) can be written for the case of L predictor variables as:

$$y_{jt} = \beta_{1j} x_{1jt} + \beta_{2j} x_{2jt} + \ldots + \beta_{Lj} x_{Ljt} + u_{jt}, \qquad (16.7)$$
$$j = 1, \ldots, n, \quad t = 1, \ldots, T$$

where

$\quad y_{jt} \ = \ $ the value of the criterion variable in observation jt,
$\quad x_{\ell jt} \ = \ $ the value of the ℓ-th predictor variable, $\ell = 1, \ldots, L$, for observation jt,
$\quad \beta_{\ell j} \ = \ $ the unknown parameters, $\ell = 1, \ldots, L$, for cross section j,
$\quad u_{jt} \ = \ $ the value of the disturbance term in observation jt,
$\quad T \ = \ $ the number of observations per cross section.

For a model with an intercept term, we can specify $x_{1jt} = 1$ for all jt, in which case β_{1j} is the constant term. For a given cross section j, the relations can also be written as:

$$\begin{bmatrix} y_{j1} \\ y_{j2} \\ \vdots \\ y_{jT} \end{bmatrix} = \begin{bmatrix} x_{1j1} & x_{2j1} & \cdots & x_{Lj1} \\ x_{1j2} & x_{2j2} & \cdots & x_{Lj2} \\ \vdots & \vdots & & \vdots \\ x_{1jT} & x_{2jT} & \cdots & x_{LjT} \end{bmatrix} \begin{bmatrix} \beta_{1j} \\ \beta_{2j} \\ \vdots \\ \beta_{Lj} \end{bmatrix} + \begin{bmatrix} u_{j1} \\ u_{j2} \\ \vdots \\ u_{jT} \end{bmatrix} \qquad (16.8)$$

which in matrix notation becomes:

$$Y_j = X_j \beta_j + u_j \tag{16.9}$$

where

Y_j = a column vector of T values for the criterion variable,

X_j = a matrix of order $T \times L$ with values taken by the
    L predictor variables $x_{1j}, \ldots, x_{Lj}$,

β_j = a column vector of L unknown parameters, and

u_j = a column vector of T disturbance terms.

If observations on $x_{\ell jt}$, $\ell = 1, \ldots, L$ and y_{jt} are available over time for a given cross section, we speak about time-series data. Alternatively, (16.7) can also be specified for a given t with cross-sectional observations:

$$y_{jt} = \gamma_{1t} x_{1jt} + \gamma_{2t} x_{2jt} + \ldots + \gamma_{Lt} x_{Ljt} + u_{jt} . \tag{16.10}$$

Thus in (16.10) each time period has unique parameters which would be estimated from cross-sectional data.

Finally time-series and cross-sectional data can be used together which results in pooled time-series and cross-sectional data. We discussed this in Section 14.2, and we elaborate on it in Section 16.2.

Parameter estimates for (16.7) and (16.10) are obtained analogously to the process shown in (16.2)-(16.6). Thus, the least-squares estimates of the parameters $\beta_{1j}, \ldots, \beta_{Lj}$ in (16.7) are the values $\hat{\beta}_{1j}, \ldots, \hat{\beta}_{Lj}$ which minimize the sum of the squared values of the residuals $\hat{u}_{jt}$, $t = 1, \ldots, T$, for a given cross section j:

$$RSS_j = \sum_{t=1}^{T} \hat{u}_{jt}^2 = \sum_{t=1}^{T} \left(y_{jt} - \sum_{\ell=1}^{L} \hat{\beta}_{\ell j} x_{\ell jt} \right)^2 \tag{16.11}$$

where

RSS_j = residual sum of squares for cross section j.

In matrix notation (16.11) becomes:

$$RSS_j = \hat{u}_j' \hat{u}_j = (Y_j - X_j \hat{\beta}_j)'(Y_j - X_j \hat{\beta}_j) \tag{16.12}$$
$$= Y_j' Y_j - 2\hat{\beta}_j' X_j' Y_j + \hat{\beta}_j' X_j' X_j \hat{\beta}_j.$$

Differentiating RSS_j with respect to $\hat{\beta}_j$ and setting the derivatives equal to zero, we obtain:

$$-2X_j' Y_j + 2X_j' X_j \hat{\beta}_j = 0 \tag{16.13}$$

or

$$\hat{\beta}_j = (X_j' X_j)^{-1} X_j' Y_j. \tag{16.14}$$

This expression for the ordinary least squares estimation of β_j is similar to the corresponding expression of $\hat{\beta}_j$ in the two-variable case (16.6).[1]

For statistical interference about the parameters of the linear model we also need a specification of the probability distribution of the disturbance terms. We discuss such a specification and assumptions about the disturbances in 16.1.3.

16.1.3 ASSUMPTIONS ABOUT DISTURBANCES

To obtain the statistical precision of the OLS-parameter estimates (or of forecasted values based on the estimated equation) several assumptions about the disturbance terms in (16.1) or (16.7) need to be satisfied. These assumptions are:

1. $E(u_{jt}) = 0$ for all jt;
2. $Var(u_{jt}) = \sigma_j^2$ for jt;
3. $Cov(u_{jt}, u_{jt'}) = 0$ for $jt \neq jt'$;
4. u_{jt} is normally distributed.

Other assumptions are:

5. There is no relation between the predictors and u_{jt}, i.e. $Cov(x_{jt}, u_{jt}) = 0$ (one-variable case). In other words the x_{jt} are nonstochastic or "fixed". For the L-variable case this implies $Cov(X_j', u_j) = 0$, in which case we have $E(u_j \mid X_j) = E(u_j) = 0$,
6. For the L-variable case, the matrix of observations X_j has full rank, that is the vectors in X_j are linearly independent (see footnote 1).

Before we consider each of these assumptions, we provide a rationale for the assumptions by analogy to statistical inference about the mean value of a population estimated from a probability sample. We use the following model:

$$y_i = \mu + u_i, \quad i = 1, \ldots, I \tag{16.15}$$

where

$$\mu = \text{the unknown population mean.}$$

If we take a simple random sample of size N (such that all possible samples of size N have an equal chance of being selected) from the population of all observations, $i = 1, \ldots, I$, it follows that:

1. $E(u_i) = 0$ for all i;
2. $Var(u_i) = \sigma^2$ for all i;
3. $Cov(u_i, u_j) = 0$ for $i \neq j$.

The "least squares" estimate of μ in (16.15) is obtained by minimizing:

$$\sum_{i=1}^{N} (y_i - \hat{\mu})^2. \tag{16.16}$$

---

1. We assume that X_j has rank L (or $X_j' X_j$ is nonsingular), and therefore its inverse $(X_j' X_j)^{-1}$ exists.

The derivative of (16.16) with respect to $\hat{\mu}$, set equal to zero, gives:

$$\frac{d \sum_{i=1}^{N} (y_i - \hat{\mu})^2}{d\hat{\mu}} = -2 \sum_{i=1}^{N} (y_i - \hat{\mu}) = 0. \tag{16.17}$$

And

$$\hat{\mu} = \frac{\sum_{i=1}^{N} y_i}{N} = \bar{y}. \tag{16.18}$$

Thus, we have derived the sample mean as the least-squares estimator of the population mean. And, given random sampling, we can claim the following:

1. $E(\bar{y}) = \mu$, because $E(u_i) = 0$ for all i;
2. $Var(\bar{y}) = \sigma^2/N$, because $Var(u_i) = \sigma^2$ for all i, and $Cov(u_i, u_j) = 0$, for all $i \neq j$.

Both of these results follow directly from independent, random sampling. It turns out that the mean of a simple random sample is the Best Linear Unbiased Estimate (BLUE) of the unknown population mean. It is unbiased because the expected value of the sample mean equals the population mean. And it is the best of all linear unbiased estimates in the sense that its variance is the smallest. The latter property is often referred to as efficiency. Thus, the sample mean is an efficient (minimum variance), unbiased estimator. Finally, $\bar{y}$ is normally distributed if u_i is normally distributed.

The beauty of these implications is that we can use the normal distribution for hypothesis testing about population mean values and for the construction of confidence intervals around a sample mean. The statistical procedures are based on the result that, given simple random sampling and the normality assumption, $\bar{y}$ is normally distributed with mean μ and variance σ^2/N:

$$\bar{y} \sim Normal(\mu, \sigma^2/N).$$

We note that the formula (16.18) for the arithmetic mean of the sample, $\bar{y}$, was in fact obtained by requiring that $\hat{\mu}$ minimizes the sum of the squared deviations. Thus, the well-known arithmetic mean is also the "least squares" estimate of the unknown population mean.

For statistical inference about regression model parameters it is convenient to borrow the error-term *assumptions* that follow from simple random sampling conducted to estimate a population mean. Note however that in regression analysis we rarely use random sampling to collect observations. Even if we did, the error term would not necessarily satisfy the assumptions. We use the analogy to simple random sampling merely to show that the assumptions about the disturbance term in a regression model are analogous to the implications of simple random sampling for the estimated population mean. The difference is that in inferences about a population mean we "only" need to make sure that we employ probability sampling and that the normal distribution applies (for which we can usually make reference to the Central Limit Theorem), while in regression every assumption about the error term needs to be explicitly considered. With regard to these assumptions, we can show, relevant to (16.6), that:

1. $E(\hat{\beta}_j) = \beta_j$ $\qquad$ if $E(u_{jt}) = 0$ for all jt, $\qquad$ (16.19)

2. $Var(\hat{\beta}_j) = \sigma_j^2 / \sum_{t=1}^{T}(x_{jt} - \bar{x}_j)^2$ $\left\{\begin{array}{l} \text{if } Var(u_{jt}) = \sigma_j^2 \text{ for } jt, \\ \text{and } Cov(u_{jt}, u_{jt'}) = 0 \\ \text{for } jt \neq jt'. \end{array}\right.$ $\qquad$ (16.20)

And $\hat{\beta}_j$ is normally distributed if u_{jt} is normally distributed for each cross section j. We can also show that $\hat{\beta}_j$ is BLUE, i.e. it is the Best Linear Unbiased Estimator of the unknown value of the slope in (16.1), *if the error-term assumptions hold*. For the L-variable model (16.7)-(16.9), the assumptions about the *disturbance term* can be expressed as follows:

1. The vector u_j has expectation zero:

$$E(u_j) = 0 \text{ or } E(u_j \mid X_j) = 0. \qquad (16.21)$$

2. For each cross-sectional unit j, the disturbance term has the same variance:

$$Var(u_j) = \sigma_j^2 \text{ for all } t = 1, \ldots, T. \qquad (16.22)$$

3. The disturbance terms are uncorrelated over time (zero autocorrelation) within each cross section j:

$$Cov(u_{jt}, u_{jt'}) = 0 \text{ for all } t \neq t'. \qquad (16.23)$$

4. Each disturbance term $u_{j1}, u_{j2}, \ldots, u_{jT}$ is normally distributed.

Conditions (16.22) and (16.23) together imply that the variance-covariance matrix of the disturbance vector u_j has the following structure:

$$Cov(u_j, u'_j) = \sigma_j^2 I \qquad (16.24)$$

where

$$I = \text{a } T \times T \text{ identity matrix.}$$

The vector of estimated parameters is specified in (16.14) as:

$$\hat{\beta}_j = (X'_j X_j)^{-1} X'_j Y_j.$$

If Y_j is a function of a vector of *random* variables, u_j, for which $E(u_j) = 0$, then $E(\hat{\beta}_j)$ is:

$$\begin{aligned} E(\hat{\beta}_j) &= E[(X'_j X_j)^{-1} X'_j Y_j] = E[(X'_j X_j)^{-1} X'_j (X_j \beta_j + u_j)] \\ &= \beta_j + E[(X'_j X_j)^{-1} X'_j u_j] = \beta_j + (X'_j X_j)^{-1} X'_j E(u_j) = \beta_j. \end{aligned}$$

Thus:

$$E(\hat{\beta}_j) = \beta_j \tag{16.25}$$

under the assumption of zero expectation for the disturbance term *and* the assumption that X_j is a nonstochastic matrix ($X_j =$ "fixed").

The variance-covariance matrix of $\hat{\beta}_j$ in (16.14) is derived as follows:

$$
\begin{aligned}
E[(\hat{\beta}_j - \beta_j)(\hat{\beta}_j - \beta_j)'] &= E[\{(X_j'X_j)^{-1}X_j'(X_j\beta_j + u_j) - \beta_j\} \\
&\quad \{(X_j'X_j)^{-1}X_j'(X_j\beta_j + u_j) - \beta_j\}'] \\
&= E[\{(X_j'X_j)^{-1}X_j'u_j\}\{u_j'X_j(X_j'X_j)^{-1}\}]
\end{aligned}
$$

or

$$E[(\hat{\beta}_j - \beta_j)(\hat{\beta}_j - \beta_j)'] = \sigma_j^2(X_j'X_j)^{-1} \tag{16.26}$$

based on (16.24). Since σ_j^2 is unknown it is usually replaced by an unbiased estimator $\hat{\sigma}_j^2 = \sum_{t=1}^T \hat{u}_{jt}^2/(T - L)$.

Importantly, we have derived statistical properties for the least-squares estimator by *assuming* that the error-term behaves in the same manner as is implied by random sampling for the sample mean as an estimator of the population mean. However, if these assumptions are incorrect, the statistical inference is invalid. We therefore now discuss possible violations of the error-term assumptions (and associated remedies).

16.1.4 VIOLATIONS OF THE ASSUMPTIONS

In practice, researchers often pay insufficient attention to the validity of the assumptions about the disturbance term. Relatively little time is usually spent on model specification (see Chapters 5-14), especially with regard to the relevance, the measurement and the nature (functional form, interactions) of the effects of predictor variables. And it is convenient to *assume* that the disturbance term is "well behaved" for statistical inference. Thus, users of regression analysis often (implicitly) assume that predictor variables' effects are linear, that predictor variables do not interact, that predictor variables are truly exogenous and that all relevant variables are included in the specification and are measured without error.

Unfortunately, the reality is very different from this ideal set of circumstances. We rarely have access to all relevant predictor variables, it is common for variables to be subject to measurement error, and the assumption of one-way causality is often questionable. Of course data quality problems (see Chapter 15) may prevent the model builder from verifying preconceived notions about the nature of some effects. For example, if a given predictor variable has minimal variation in the sample data, we may not be able to demonstrate the (empirical) superiority of one functional form derived from theory over another. Thus, data quality limitations may prevent the model builder from exploiting marketing knowledge to the fullest extent. However, empirical researchers also lack an incentive to do sufficient testing. One reason is that most model *users* have incomplete knowledge about the role error-term assumptions play in statistical inference. Thus, the model builder needs a more critical user. Another reason is that the rejection of one or more error-term assumptions may make it difficult or impossible for the model builder to complete the task of model building. By not examining the assumptions critically, the model builder can pretend that the estimated equation is useful.

We note that an estimated equation can be evaluated in terms of usefulness by considering its implications under a variety of conditions. For example, we could reject a model that produces predictions that are inherently implausible (see Chapter 15). But if we criticize someone's estimated model for having implausible implications under extreme conditions, the counter argument is often that the result should not be used outside the range(s) of variation in the sample data. The difficulty with this counter argument is that such restrictions about a model's applicability are rarely made explicit. It seems prudent, therefore, to use a ("robust") model specification that allows for the widest possible applicability.

In Table 16.1 we show possible reasons for violations of each of the assumptions, the consequence of this violation for parameter estimates, how each violation can be detected, and the available remedies.

NONZERO EXPECTATION

Violation of the first assumption, i.e. $E(u_j \mid X_j) \neq 0$, is the most serious one. One of the principal desiderata of parameter estimates is unbiasedness (or consistency). By analogy, if we desire to estimate an unknown population mean value, any probability sample will guarantee that the sample mean is unbiased. In regression analysis the unbiasedness property obtains if the model is correctly specified. All relevant predictor variables should be included, the proper functional form of the partial relation with respect to each predictor must be accommodated, etc. Misspecification of the model causes the parameter estimates to be biased. For example, an omitted predictor variable causes the parameter estimates to be biased, unless the omitted variable is uncorrelated with the included predictor variables. The amount of the bias increases with the degree of (positive or negative) correlation.

Violations of the first assumption are rarely detectable from a plot of the residuals, $\hat{u}_{jt} = (y_{jt} - \hat{y}_{jt}), t = 1, \ldots, T$, against each predictor variable. However, if only the assumed functional form is incorrect, such a plot should show a systematic pattern in the residual values. On the other hand, this plot will not suggest that a relevant predictor has been omitted (unless one has information about the values of the omitted variable). Other reasons for violations of the assumption $E(u_j \mid X_j) = 0$ are measurement error in one or more predictor variables and endogeneity for a predictor. Random measurement error in a predictor biases the estimated least-squares parameter toward zero. Endogeneity makes the least-squares estimator biased and inconsistent (see equation (16.157) in Section 16.6.3 for a definition of consistency). We note that neither measurement error nor endogeneity is detectable from an inspec-

Table 16.1 Violations of the assumptions about the disturbance term: reasons, consequences, tests and remedies.

Violated assumption	Possible reasons	Consequence	Detection	Remedy
1. $E(u_{jt}) \neq 0$ or $E(u'_j \mid X_j) \neq 0$	- Incorrect functional form(s) - Omitted variable(s) - Varying parameter(s)	- Biased parameter estimate[a]	- Plot residuals against each predictor variable - Test explanatory power of predictor variable as polynomial to varying degrees (RESET-test) - White test	- Modify the model specification in terms of functional form - Add relevant predictors - Allow parameters to vary - Use Instrumental Variables
2. $Var(u_{jt}) \neq \sigma^2$	- Error proportional to values of a predictor	- Inefficient parameter estimate	- Plot residuals against each predictor variable - Use Goldfeld/Quandt or White test	- Modify the specification (e.g. per capita) - Use GLS or ML[b]
3. $Cov(u_{jt}, u_{jt'}) \neq 0$, $t \neq t'$	- See 1.	- See 1.	**To detect autocorrelation:** - Plot residuals against time - Durbin Watson test - Durbin's h-test **To detect cause:** - See 1.	- See 1.
4. Nonnormal errors	- See 1.	- See 1.	**To detect normality:** - Plot distribution of residuals - χ^2-test - Shapiro Wilk - Bera-Jarque **To detect cause:** - See 1.	- See 1. - Robust regression - Box-Cox-transformation
5. Stochastic predictor correlated with the disturbance term	- Measurement errors - Edogeneity of predictor variable(s)	- See 1.	- Diagnose specification	- Simultaneous equations - Instrumental Variables
6. Multicollinearity	- Relations between predictor variables	- See 1. - Unreliable parameter estimates	- Regression of $x_{\ell j}$ on x_{rj}, $r \neq \ell$ - Elimination of $x_{\ell j}$ and re-estimation, use VIF - Factoranalyze the correlation matrix R of predictor variables	- Reformulate model - Create new predictors - Obtain more data - Apply other estimation methods (such as Ridge regression or Equity estimation)

[a] The bias due to an omitted relevant predictor variable depends on the correlation between included and excluded variables. If this correlation is zero, there is no bias (but the estimates are subject to less precision).
[b] GLS = Generalized Least Squares (Section 16.3), ML = Maximum Likelihood (Section 16.6).

tion of the residuals in the original equation. Thus, the model builder must possess the substantive knowledge that is critical for meaningful model building. For example, if price and advertising are used as predictor variables in a demand equation, the model builder must know how price and advertising decisions are made, and whether this decision-making process needs to be represented in a system of equations (see also Section 16.4) to account for endogeneity in either of these variables.

To test for the possibility of omitted variables, the predictor variables can be specified as polynomials to varying degrees. The explanatory power of extra terms is then used as a basis for detecting the omission of relevant predictor variables. A formal statistical test for misspecification in this context is the RESET-test[2]. The null hypothesis of the test is (16.7) and the alternative hypothesis is $E(u_j \mid X_j) = \xi_j \neq 0$. The test is based on the estimation of an extended model:

$$y_{jt} = \beta_{1j} x_{1jt} + \ldots + \beta_{Lj} x_{Ljt} + \alpha_{1j} z_{1jt} \tag{16.27}$$
$$+ \ldots + \alpha_{mj} z_{mjt} + u_{jt}, \quad t = 1, \ldots, T$$

where

$z_{1jt}, \ldots, z_{mjt}$ = the additional variables chosen in such a way
                          as to explain the elements $\xi_{jt}, t = 1, \ldots T$ of ξ_j best.

If $E(u_j \mid X_j) = 0$ is true for (16.7) then in (16.27) $\alpha_{1j} = \ldots = \alpha_{mj} = 0$. The alternative hypothesis is accepted if $\alpha_{\ell j} \neq 0$ for at least one ℓ, $\ell = 1, \ldots, m$. For the additional variables $z_{1jt}, \ldots, z_{mjt}$, Ramsey (1969) recommends adding the powers of $\hat{y}_{jt}$ (i.e. $\hat{y}_{jt}^2, \hat{y}_{jt}^3, \hat{y}_{jt}^4, \ldots$) obtained from the (OLS-)estimation of the original regression (16.7). The justification for this is that the powers of $\hat{y}_{jt}$ are functions of the powers and cross products of the original regressors. A limitation is that each power of $\hat{y}_{jt}$ is a linear combination of the original predictor variables, the squared predictors and cross products along with the coefficients of the original regression. Alternatively, one can follow Thursby and Schmidt (1977) who suggest the addition of second, third, and fourth powers (but not necessarily all) of each of the *predictor* variables. The use of powers of the original predictors is likely to be advantageous relative to the implicit linear combination of predictor terms in Ramsey's procedure. Nevertheless, a potential disadvantage of Thursby and Schmidt's suggestion is that cross products are excluded.

The RESET-test is an F-test based on incremental R^2. We provide details about this test in Section 18.4.2, but mention a few caveats here. First, the test only considers powers (and cross products, based on Ramsey's suggestion) of the "original" predictor variables $x_{1jt}, \ldots, x_{Ljt}$. If the null hypothesis is rejected, the model builder will lack information about the identity of the "real" missing variables. Interestingly, and not surprisingly given the use of powers, the test turns out to be powerful for detecting nonlinearities. This weakens its attractiveness for detecting other specification problems, since rejection of a model may be due to an omitted explanatory

---

2. Ramsey (1969, 1974).

variable or a wrong functional form. The identification of missing variables is especially arduous. Second, we mentioned earlier that the bias in parameter estimates is a positive function of the degree of correlation (absolute value) between included and excluded predictors: the stronger the correlation, the greater the bias. However, if this correlation is strong, then the power of the test for omitted variables based on squared and higher-order terms of included predictors decreases. Third, the RESET-test is quite sensitive to autocorrelation (which we argue is likely to occur in the error term in case of model misspecification).

We discuss the White test below because it is also frequently used for functional misspecification.

In this discussion we emphasize the importance of proper specification of the predictors. One needs a substantial amount of knowledge about consumers, competitors, and markets in general (e.g. market structure) and the nature of possible effects of marketing instruments to justify a specific model formulation. This knowledge should be used to the fullest extent possible in the specification of a theoretically appropriate model. The model can then be tested against alternative specifications.

One remedy for a violation of the first assumption (i.e., if $E(u_j \mid X_j) \neq 0$) is to find *instrumental variables* Z such that $E(u_j \mid Z_j) = 0$, while the matrix Z_j is highly correlated with X_j, and the number of variables in Z_j is at least L. It is easy to demonstrate that the instrumental variable estimator is consistent since $E(u_j \mid Z_j) = 0$.

Specifically, suppose that only *one* predictor variable in the X_j matrix is correlated with the error term u_j, say $x_{\ell j}$. We then only need to find instrumental variables to obtain $\hat{x}_{\ell j}$ such that $\hat{x}_{\ell j}$ is uncorrelated with u_j but (highly) correlated with $x_{\ell j}$. In this regard note that the other predictors remain, since they are not correlated with u_j and are of course perfectly correlated with themselves. Thus for the other predictors we use $\widehat{X}_{j(\ell)} = X_{j(\ell)}$ (meaning for all predictors but ℓ), since the predictors themselves are uncorrelated with u_j and there are no other variables more highly correlated with $X_{j(\ell)}$.

We want to employ multiple instrumental variables, if possible, to create the highest possible correlation between $\hat{x}_{\ell j}$ and $x_{\ell j}$, subject to $E(\hat{x}_{\ell j} \mid u_j) = 0$. This can often be accomplished by using lagged values of the criterion and predictor variables. Thus, let

$$x_{\ell j} = Z_j \gamma_j + v_j \tag{16.28}$$

where

$\quad x_{\ell j} = $ the predictor variable that is correlated with the error term u_j,

$\quad Z_j = $ a matrix of instrumental variables, possibly consisting of all

$\qquad\qquad$ lagged y_j and X_j variables,

$\quad v_j = $ vector of disturbances.

Then $\hat{x}_{\ell j} = Z_j (Z_j' Z_j)^{-1} Z_j' x_{\ell j}$. We replace the values for $x_{\ell j}$ in the X_j-matrix with the values for $\hat{x}_{\ell j}$, and apply least squares (this is the Two-Stage Least Squares or

2SLS estimator). For further detail, see for example Greene (1997, pp. 288-295). See also Section 16.4.

HETEROSCEDASTICITY

The second assumption, that the error term is *homoscedastic* (i.e. it has the same variance for all possible values of a predictor variable), is not nearly as critical as the first. Its violation "merely" reduces the *efficiency* of (ordinary least squares) parameter estimates. Thus if only the homoscedasticity assumption is violated, the least-squares estimator is (usually) unbiased but does not have minimum variance. In addition, the covariance matrix of the parameter estimates provides incorrect values. In many cases the critical remedy is to use an appropriately adjusted formula for the variances and covariances of the parameter estimates.

The benefit of using an estimator that incorporates the heteroscedasticity may be in doubt. There are two relevant aspects to this. One is that the true source of heteroscedasticity is usually unknown. Thus, an expression has to be estimated from the data which introduces uncertainty. The other is that in this case the theoretically superior estimator is only asymptotically more efficient than the least-squares estimator. The benefit in practice, therefore, depends also on the sample size.

It is straightforward to encounter heteroscedasticity when the model is well specified. In practice, one can well imagine that the disturbance term in the model is, for example, proportional to the value of a predictor variable, when the model is otherwise properly specified. Experience in model building reveals that heteroscedasticity occurs especially if cross-sectional data are used for estimation. Thus, heteroscedastic disturbances have traditionally been accommodated in analyses of cross-sectional data. In the literature, fairly complex tests for homoscedastic disturbances exist. We restrict the discussion here to the basic phenomenon.

For heteroscedastic disturbance terms, consider a relation between the (squared) disturbance and a predictor variable such as income,[3,4] as shown in Figure 16.1. Income of family i, $i = 1, \ldots, 12$ is measured along the horizontal axis and the squared residual values occur along the vertical axis. The apparent dependence of the squared disturbance on income can be tested by estimating the following model:

$$\hat{u}_i^2 = \gamma_0 + \gamma_1 x_{1i} + \varepsilon_i \tag{16.29}$$

where

$$\varepsilon_i = \text{a disturbance term.}$$

If $H_0 : \gamma_1 = 0$ is rejected, then the assumption of homoscedasticity for u_i is rejected.

Perhaps the best-known test of heteroscedasticity is the Goldfeld-Quandt test. This test is applicable if the model builder has a preconceived notion about the nature of heteroscedasticity (i.e. the residuals are not used to infer the nature of a possible

---

3. For a similar example, see Theil (1971, p. 197).
4. See, for example, Prais and Houthakker (1955).

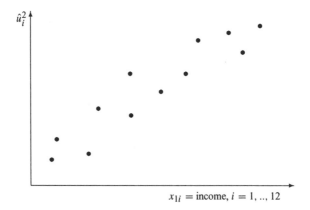

x_{1i} = income, $i = 1, .., 12$

Figure 16.1 A relation between the squared disturbance and income.

violation of the assumption). Goldfeld and Quandt considered the problem that the residuals obtained from estimating *one* set of parameters from a sample of data are not independent. Thus, if the 12 observations in the application involving income as a predictor can be categorized prior to data analysis according to the expected magnitude of the squared disturbance (i.e. let $E(u_1^2) \geq E(u_2^2) \geq E(u_3^2) \ldots$), the ratio $\sum_{i=1}^{6} \hat{u}_i^2 / \sum_{i=7}^{12} \hat{u}_i^2$ does *not* follow the F-distribution. This is because the numerator and denominator in the ratio can be shown to be dependent.

Goldfeld and Quandt (1965) proposed a ratio whose numerator and denominator are independent under the null hypothesis of homoscedasticity by partitioning the original data as follows (compare (16.9))

$$\begin{bmatrix} y_{jA} \\ y_{jB} \end{bmatrix} = \begin{bmatrix} X_{jA} & O \\ O & X_{jB} \end{bmatrix} \begin{bmatrix} \beta_{jA} \\ \beta_{jB} \end{bmatrix} + \begin{bmatrix} u_{jA} \\ u_{jB} \end{bmatrix} \tag{16.30}$$

where the vectors and matrices with subscript A refer to the first $\frac{1}{2}n$ observations and those with B subscripts to the last $\frac{1}{2}n$ (where the observations are still ranked according to the expected magnitude of the squared disturbance under the alternative hypothesis of heteroscedasticity). Importantly, the residuals $\hat{u}_i$, $i = 1, \ldots, n$ are obtained from fitting separate regressions to the first $\frac{1}{2}n$ and to the last $\frac{1}{2}n$ observations.[5] The ratio of the residual sums of squares from these regressions:

$$\frac{\hat{u}'_{jA} \hat{u}_{jA}}{\hat{u}'_{jB} \hat{u}_{jB}} \tag{16.31}$$

is F-distributed with $\frac{1}{2}n - k$ and $\frac{1}{2}n - k$ degrees of freedom under the null hypothesis.

A joint test for homoscedasticity and correct model specification is given by White (1980).[6] For this test, we refer to (16.10), which uses the cross-sectional observations

---

5. Goldfeld and Quandt (1965) also considered a modification of the test by omitting a middle group of observations.
6. See also Judge et al. (1985, p. 453).

$j = 1, \ldots, n$ for a given time period. Let $\hat{u}'_t = (\hat{u}_{1t}, \ldots, \hat{u}_{nt})'$ be a vector of least squares residuals for period t. The least squares variance estimator $\hat{\sigma}^2_t$ is:

$$\hat{\sigma}^2_t = \frac{1}{(n-L)}\hat{u}'_t\hat{u}_t = \frac{1}{(n-L)}RSS_t \qquad (16.32)$$

where

$$RSS_t = \text{residual sum of squares in period } t \, (= \sum_{i=1}^{n}\hat{u}^2_{it}).$$

Define:

$X'_t = $ a matrix of order $n \times L$ of cross-sectional observations for the L predictor variables $x_{1t}, \ldots, x_{Lt}$, in period t, where $x_{1t} = 1$,

$x'_{jt} = $ a row vector of predictor variables of the j-th cross-sectional observation in period t,

$$\widehat{V}_t = \frac{1}{n}\sum_{j=1}^{n}\hat{u}^2_{jt}x_{jt}x'_{jt}, \text{ and}$$

$$\widetilde{V}_t = \frac{1}{n}\hat{\sigma}^2_t X'_t X_t.$$

If homogeneity exists, $\widehat{V}_t$ and $\widetilde{V}_t$ will both be consistent estimators of the same matrix. Under heteroscedasticity these estimators will tend to diverge. The White test determines the significance of the difference $[\widehat{V}_t - \widetilde{V}_t]$. The test can be implemented through the estimation of auxiliary regressions on the residuals $\hat{u}_{jt}$ of (16.10) for each t:

$$\hat{u}^2_{jt} = \sum_{\ell=2}^{L}\alpha_{\ell t}x_{\ell jt} + \sum_{\ell=2}^{L}\sum_{\substack{\ell'=2\\ \ell'\geq\ell}}^{L}\alpha_{\ell\ell't}x_{\ell jt}x_{\ell' jt} + e_{jt}, \quad j = 1, \ldots, n \qquad (16.33)$$

where

$e_{jt} = $ a disturbance term.

The (unadjusted) value of the coefficient of determination R^2 (see Section 16.1.5) is computed for (16.33). The null hypothesis of the White test is:

$$H_0 : E(u^2_{jt}) = \sigma^2_t \qquad \text{for all } j = 1, \ldots, n$$
and the specification (16.10) is correct.

The alternative hypothesis is:

$$H_A : E(u^2_{jt}) \neq \sigma^2_t \qquad \text{for all } j = 1, \ldots, n$$
and/or (16.10) is not a correct specification.

Under the null hypothesis nR^2 has an asymptotic χ^2-distribution with degrees of freedom equal to the number of parameters in the auxiliary equation (16.33): $\frac{L(L+1)}{2} - 1$.

The White test is also a test for functional misspecification as indicated by the joint nature of the hypothesis. Thus, failure to reject the null hypothesis implies a lack of evidence for:

- the disturbances to be heteroscedastic, and
- the model specification to be incorrect.

If the null hypothesis is rejected, the model specification needs to be reconsidered. There are also tests that focus specifically on heteroscedasticity.[7]

We now examine the heteroscedasticity issue more closely by assuming it to exist in a prespecified form.[8] To simplify the exposition we consider the basic model (16.1) and suppose that:

$$
\begin{aligned}
1. \quad & E(u_{jt}) = 0 \\
2. \quad & Var(u_{jt}) = \sigma^2 x_{jt}^2.
\end{aligned}
\tag{16.34}
$$

This second assumption indicates that the error variance increases with the squared value of the predictor variable (somewhat analogous to the relation in Figure 16.1). For this specific form of heteroscedasticity we can use a transformation that results in the estimation of a different equation, where the new error term meets the homoscedasticity assumption and allows OLS estimation of the parameters of interest. If we multiply both sides of (16.1) by $1/x_{jt}$ we obtain:

$$
\frac{y_{jt}}{x_{jt}} = \frac{\alpha_j}{x_{jt}} + \beta_j + \frac{u_{jt}}{x_{jt}}.
\tag{16.35}
$$

In this form the error term u_{jt}/x_{jt} still has the expected value equal to zero, since $E(u_{jt}) = 0$ for a given value of x_{jt}. The variance of the error term in (16.35) is:

$$
Var\left(\frac{u_{jt}}{x_{jt}}\right) = \frac{1}{x_{jt}^2} Var(u_{jt}) = \frac{1}{x_{jt}^2} \cdot \sigma^2 x_{jt}^2 = \sigma^2.
\tag{16.36}
$$

In this case OLS is best, linear unbiased if it is applied to the new criterion variable y_{jt}/x_{jt} and the new predictor variable $1/x_{jt}$. This transformation involves *weighting* each observation by $1/x_{jt}$ so that as the value for x_{jt} increases, the weight declines. This estimation method is also known as *weighted* least squares (WLS), and it is a special case of the generalized least squares (GLS-) estimation methods. We discuss these methods in Section 16.3.

---

7. See, for example, Judge et al. (1985, pp. 447-448) for the Bartlett test of heteroscedasticity.
8. We closely follow Wittink (1988, pp. 181-182).

CORRELATED DISTURBANCES

In contrast to the first two assumptions, the implication of a violation of the third assumption is controversial. We return to the basic equation (16.1) which postulates the use of time series data for the estimation of parameters separately for cross section j:

$$y_{jt} = \alpha_j + \beta_j x_{jt} + u_{jt}, \quad t = 1, \ldots, T \tag{16.37}$$

Suppose we assume:

$$E(u_{jt}) = 0$$
$$u_{jt} = \rho_j u_{j,t-1} + \varepsilon_{jt}, \quad |\rho_j| < 1.$$

And also:

$$E(\varepsilon_{jt}) = 0 \tag{16.38}$$
$$Cov(\varepsilon_{jt}, \varepsilon_{jt'}) = 0, \quad t \neq t'.$$

In (16.37) the error terms are not independent but follow a first-order autoregressive process with parameter ρ_j. This feature is called autoregression, autocorrelation or serial correlation. The parameter ρ_j is known as the autocorrelation parameter or autocorrelation coefficient. Under these assumptions, it is possible to show mathematically that the parameter estimates α_j and β_j are unbiased. Indeed, virtually all econometric textbooks emphasize this point. For real-world problems, however, it is very difficult to claim that a model is correctly specified yet somehow the error terms are autocorrelated. Thus, we take the position that a violation of the third assumption results from model misspecification (e.g. incorrect functional form, omitted variable(s), varying parameters).

To detect a violation of the assumption that the disturbances for different observations have zero covariance, one can *plot* the residuals ($\hat{u}_{jt}$) against time. Figures 16.2 and 16.3 show cases of positive and negative autocorrelation, respectively. In Figure 16.2, a positive residual tends to be followed by another positive one, and a negative residual tends to be followed by a negative one. Positive autocorrelation means that the residual in t tends to have the same sign as the residual in $t-1$. On the other hand, in Figure 16.3 we see that the observations tend to have positive values followed by negative ones, and vice versa, which is a pattern of negative autocorrelation.

The best-known test statistic to detect (first-error) autocorrelation is the one developed by Durbin and Watson (1950, 1951). The Durbin-Watson test statistic is based on the variance of the difference between two successive disturbances:

$$E(u_{jt} - u_{j,t-1})^2 = E(u_{jt}^2) + E(u_{j,t-1}^2) - 2E(u_{jt}, u_{j,t-1}). \tag{16.39}$$

If successive disturbances are positively correlated (positive autocorrelation), the expected value of (16.39) is small, because of the negative sign of $-2E(u_{jt}, u_{j,t-1})$.

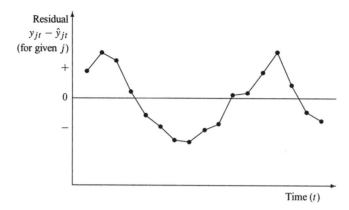

Figure 16.2 Positive autocorrelation.

Similarly, negative autocorrelation causes this last part of (16.39) to contribute to a high expected value for $E(u_{jt} - u_{j,t-1})^2$. To the extent that the residuals $\hat{u}_{jt}$ obtained by the ordinary least squares method are satisfactory approximations of the corresponding random disturbance terms u_{jt}, we have a similar result for $(\hat{u}_{jt} - \hat{u}_{j,t-1})^2$. These considerations lead to the Durbin-Watson test statistic (for a given cross section j):

$$D.W. = \frac{\sum_{t=2}^{n}(\hat{u}_{jt} - \hat{u}_{j,t-1})^2}{\sum_{t=1}^{n} \hat{u}_{jt}^2}. \tag{16.40}$$

The $D.W.$ statistic varies between zero and four. Small values indicate positive autocorrelation, large values negative autocorrelation.

Durbin and Watson (1950, 1951) formulated lower and upper bounds (d_L, d_U) for various significance levels,[9] and for specific sample sizes and numbers of parameters. The test statistic is used as follows:

1. Tests for positive autocorrelation:

   a. If $D.W. < d_L$, there is positive autocorrelation.
   b. If $d_L < D.W. < d_U$ the result is inconclusive.
   c. If $D.W. > d_U$, there is no positive autocorrelation.

2. Tests for negative autocorrelation:

   a. If $[4 - D.W.] < d_L$, there is negative autocorrelation.
   b. If $d_L < [4 - D.W.] < d_U$ the result is inconclusive.
   c. If $[4 - D.W.] > d_U$, there is no negative autocorrelation.

The Durbin-Watson test is not very powerful in the sense that the inconclusive range is quite large. Judge et al. (1985, p. 330) recommend that the upper critical bound

---

9. Tabulated values of d_L, d_U for different significance levels can be found in, for example: Theil (1971, pp. 721-725), Wittink (1988, pp. 306-307), Greene (1997, pp. 1016-1017).

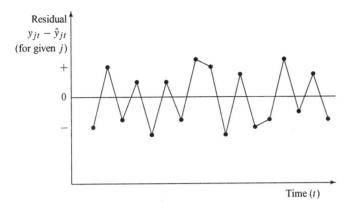

Figure 16.3 Negative autocorrelation.

(d_U) is used instead of the lower bound. Thus they essentially include the inclusive region as evidence of autocorrelation. We note that the Durbin-Watson statistic is a test for first-order autocorrelation, and does not consider higher-order autoregressive schemes.

In the presence of a lagged criterion variable among the predictor variables, the D.W. statistic is biased toward a finding of no autocorrelation. For such models Durbin (1970) proposed a statistic (D) defined as:

$$D = a \sqrt{\frac{T}{1 - T\hat{\sigma}_{\hat{\lambda}}^2}},$$

(16.41)

where, $a \simeq 1 - \frac{1}{2}(D.W.)$, T is the number of observations, and $\hat{\sigma}_{\hat{\lambda}}^2$ is the estimated variance of the slope coefficient for the lagged endogenous variable (in cross section j). Durbin (1970) shows that, asymptotically, D is a standard normal deviate. However for *small samples* the Durbin-Watson test is more powerful than the Durbin statistic in detecting $\rho_j \neq 0$ as demonstrated by Kenkel (1974).

Many software programs automatically compute and report the value of the Durbin-Watson statistic. We note that for cross-sectional observations the autocorrelation result is meaningless, since its value depends on the (arbitrary) ordering of cross-sectional observations. We also note that econometric textbooks suggest a remedy that essentially incorporates the systematic pattern in the residuals in the estimation method. We believe that this remedy should only be a last-resort approach. That is, the model builder should first do everything possible to have an acceptable model specification, etc. This is confirmed by, for example, Mizon (1995). If the model specification cannot be improved, one may treat autocorrelation similar to the approach used when the assumption about homoscedasticity is violated (compare (16.35)).

The procedure is the following. First the autocorrelation coefficient ρ_j is estimated from the residuals in cross section j:

$$\hat{\rho}_j = \frac{\sum_{t=2}^{T} \hat{u}_{jt}\hat{u}_{j,t-1}}{\sum_{t=2}^{T} \hat{u}_{j,t-1}^2}. \tag{16.42}$$

Next $\hat{\rho}_j$ is used to obtain the following transformed relation:

$$y_{jt} - \hat{\rho}_j y_{j,t-1} = \alpha_j(1 - \hat{\rho}_j) + \beta_j(x_{jt} - \hat{\rho}_j x_{j,t-1}) + \varepsilon_{jt} \tag{16.43}$$

where

$$\varepsilon_{jt} = u_{jt} - \hat{\rho}_j u_{j,t-1}, \text{ as defined in (16.38)},$$

and

$$\sqrt{1 - \hat{\rho}_j^2}\, y_{j1} = \alpha_j(1 - \hat{\rho}_j) + \beta_j\sqrt{1 - \hat{\rho}_j}\, x_{j1} + \varepsilon_{1t}.$$

In (16.43), if $\hat{\rho}_j = \rho_j$ the error term ε_{jt} would seem to satisfy the usual assumptions.

We note that (16.43) has considerable similarity to the use of first differences. Instead of using $(y_{jt} - y_{j,t-1})$ and $(x_{jt} - x_{j,t-1})$ as the variables, equation (16.43) substracts lagged values multiplied by the autocorrelation coefficient $\hat{\rho}_j$. The slope parameter for the transformed predictor variable is identical to the one in the original equation (16.1). Unfortunately, most researchers accept this treatment of autocorrelation as being acceptable to real-world problems. Thus, a common belief is that the parameter estimates are unbiased if the third assumption is violated. However, in practice, the reason for the violation tends to be a misspecification of the model. Therefore we propose as initial remedies the same ones for the violation of the first assumption (see Table 16.1).

Traditionally, the first-order autoregressive process (AR(1)) represented by (16.37) has been the primary autocorrelation process considered in econometrics (Judge et al., 1985, pp. 226-227). For annual data, the AR(1)-process is often sufficient for models with autocorrelated disturbances (with the caveat that it may mask other shortcomings in model specification). More recently, for models of frequently occurring data such as weekly scanner data and with the virtual elimination of computational constraints in estimation, other specifications have been considered. These include autoregressive processes of finite order greater than one.[10] An autoregressive process of order p, AR(p), has the following form (for the disturbance term):

$$u_{jt} = \rho_{1j}u_{j,t-1} + \rho_{2j}u_{j,t-2} + \ldots + \rho_{pj}u_{j,t-p} + \varepsilon_{jt} \tag{16.44}$$

where ε_{jt} satisfies (16.38).

---

10. For other stochastic processes such as moving average processes and combined autoregressive moving average processes, see, e.g., Judge et al. (1985, Chapter 8).

To accommodate seasonal processes, for quarterly data, p may be 4. Thomas and Wallis (1971) suggest that with quarterly data only the disturbances in corresponding quarters of successive years should be correlated. This leads to the specification of a *restricted* AR(4)-process:

$$u_{jt} = \rho_{4j} \cdot u_{j,t-4} + \varepsilon_{jt}. \tag{16.45}$$

For monthly data, $p = 12$ may be appropriate.

Lagrange Multiplier (LM) tests can be used to determine the choice of an auto-correlation process. For restricted AR(p)-processes, the LM-test statistic $T \hat{\rho}_{pj}^2$ has a $\chi^2_{(1)}$ distribution asymptotically, where $T = $ the total number of observations, and

$$\hat{\rho}_{pj} = \frac{\sum_{t=1}^{T-p} \hat{u}_{jt} \hat{u}_{j,t+p}}{\sum_{t=1}^{T} \hat{u}_{jt}^2} \tag{16.46}$$

where $\hat{u}_{jt}$, $\hat{u}_{j,t+p}$ are the OLS-residuals.

For the more general alternative (16.44), to test the null hypothesis $\rho_{1j} = \rho_{2j} = \ldots = \rho_{pj} = 0$ (i.e. for a given cross section j) the LM test statistic $T \sum_{r=1}^{P} \hat{\rho}_{rj}^2$ has a $\chi^2_{(1)}$ distribution, asymptotically.

In Section 16.3 we consider estimation with AR(1) errors. For the estimation of higher-order AR processes we refer to Judge et al. (1985, pp. 293-298).

NONNORMAL ERRORS

The fourth assumption, that the disturbances are normally distributed, may also be violated due to model misspecification. It makes sense, therefore, that this assumption not be examined until the model specification is reconsidered, if necessary. For the same reason it is efficient to examine the plausibility of the second and third assumptions before one checks the fourth. The disturbances need to be normally distributed for the standard test statistics for hypothesis testing and confidence intervals to be applicable. We can examine the validity of the fourth assumption indirectly through the residuals. If each error term separately satisfies all four assumptions, then the estimated error values (residuals) as a group will be normally distributed. Thus, if the residuals appear to be normally distributed, we cannot reject the hypothesis that each unobservable error term follows a normal distribution.

To examine whether the residuals are approximately normally distributed, we can categorize the residuals and construct a histogram. Such a histogram shows the relative frequency with which the (standardized)[11] residuals fall into defined classes. An inspection of the histogram may suggest deviations from normality in the form of

---

11. The residuals are standardized by dividing the observed values by the standard deviation of the residuals (the average residual equals zero under usual conditions).

skewness or kurtosis.

A relatively simple *test* for normality involves the chi-square distribution. This test compares the observed frequencies for a given set of categories with the frequencies expected under the null hypothesis of normally distributed error terms. The test is most powerful if the boundaries of the categories are determined in such a manner that each category has the same expected frequency. For instance, if we use five classes, we want to obtain boundaries[12] such that the expected relative frequencies under the null hypothesis of normality are 20 percent for each class. The larger the sample size, the larger the number of classes can be for maximum use of the data. The test involves the following statistic (for a given cross section j):

$$\chi^2 = \sum_{c=1}^{C} \frac{(O_c - E_c)^2}{E_c} \tag{16.47}$$

where

O_c = the observed frequency in category c,

E_c = the expected frequency in category c,

C = the number of categories.

A computed χ^2-value is compared with a tabulated value for a specified type I error probability and $(C - 1 - 1)$ degrees of freedom. The last degree of freedom is lost because the standard deviation is estimated from the residuals before the test is performed (assuming the regression equation contains an intercept, so that the mean residual is zero).

The literature on testing for normality is vast. Some commonly used tests are the Kolmogorov-Smirnov test, the likelihood ratio test and the Kuiper test. For a description and comparison of these tests, see, for example, Koerts and Abrahamse (1969, pp. 110-128). Other tests of the normality assumption are the Shapiro-Wilk W-test[13] and the Jarque-Bera test.[14] The Jarque-Bera test statistic for non-normality is also chi-square distributed (with 2 degrees of freedom):

$$\chi^2_{(2)} = \frac{(T - L)}{\hat{\sigma}^2} (\widehat{sk}^2 + \tfrac{1}{4}\widehat{ek}^2) \tag{16.48}$$

where

T = number of observations,

L = number of parameters,

$\hat{\sigma}$ = standard deviation of the residuals (for a given cross section j),

$\widehat{sk}$ = skewness of the distribution of the residuals (3rd moment)

---

12. Z-values, which represent standarized residual values under the null hypothesis.
13. See Shapiro, Wilk (1965).
14. See Bera, Jarque (1981, 1982), Stewart (1991, p. 162).

(for a given j),

$\widehat{ek}$ = excess kurtosis of the distribution of the residuals (4th moment) (for a given j).

Thus, this test determines whether the third and fourth moments of the residuals are consistent with the null hypothesis of normality. For additional tests of normality see Judge et al. (1985, pp. 826-827).

For some models the error term may not be normally distributed but there exists a transformation that produces normally distributed disturbances. Suppose that, if the effects of predictor variables are accounted for, y_{jt} is log-normally distributed. Then by taking the logs of y_{jt} we have criterion variable $\ln y_{jt}$ which is normally distributed (and hence we have normally distributed errors). This is a special case of a class of transformations considered by Box and Cox (1964). For this class they assume there exists a value λ such that

$$\frac{y_{jt}^{\lambda} - 1}{\lambda} = \beta_{1j}x_{1jt} + \ldots + \beta_{Lj}x_{Ljt} + \varepsilon_{jt}, \quad \lambda > 0 \qquad (16.49)$$

where the disturbance terms ε_{jt} are normally distributed (and homoscedastic). It can be shown that:

$$\lim_{\lambda \to 0} \frac{y_{jt}^{\lambda} - 1}{\lambda} = \ln y_{jt}. \qquad (16.50)$$

Apart from a difference in the intercept, $\lambda = 1$ yields the basic model for the L-variate case (16.7). In general, however, the Box-Cox transformation is applied primarily to let the data determine the most appropriate functional form. See Kristensen (1984) for a marketing application.

We note that with increases in sample sizes, it becomes easier to reject the null hypothesis of normally distributed errors. Thus, even minor deviations from normality can signify a violation of the assumption required for traditional statistical inference. If the model specification seems appropriate, it will be unappealing to follow strict rules with regard to such violations. To accommodate cases in which the normality assumption does not hold but the model specification is acceptable, researchers have developed robust regression methods. The interested reader is referred to Forsythe (1972), Huber (1973), Talwar (1974), Hinich and Talwar (1975) and Judge et al. (1985, pp. 828-839). For marketing applications, see Mahajan, Sharma and Wind (1984).

JOINT TESTS AND HYPOTHESES[15]

We reviewed diagnostic tests for individual assumptions about the disturbances of the classical linear model. Most of the tests apply to one specific assumption. However,

---

15. The following is based on Körösi, Mátyás and Székely (1992, Chapter 13).

the tests may require the acceptance of other assumptions. For example, the tests for autocorrelation assume that the disturbances are homoscedastic. In empirical applications, various assumptions may be jointly violated. This implies that the diagnostic value of individual test results is in doubt. An alternative approach is to apply joint tests for multiple assumptions. For example, the White test, discussed earlier, is a test for the joint investigation of homoscedasticity and correct model specification. We can also consider the RESET test a joint test. This test is based on the idea that various misspecifications can lead to a violation of the assumption that the expected value of the disturbances is zero. Possible misspecifications include omitted variables, the wrong functional form, dependence between the regressors and the disturbances, etc. In this sense, the RESET test is also a joint test.

Finally, we note that the Jarque-Bera test is a joint (LM) test for:

1. functional form;
2. heteroscedasticity;
3. autocorrelation, and
4. normality.

Based on the Jarque-Bera test, a whole family of LM tests can be derived, which can jointly test for two, three or all four assumptions.

Such joint tests are often used in empirical research. All these tests are available in the software program PCGIVE.[16]

THE PREDICTOR VARIABLES ARE STOCHASTIC

It is often convenient to consider the error-term assumptions under the condition that the predictor variables $x_{\ell j}$, $\ell = 1, \ldots, L$ are nonstochastic or "fixed". Essentially this means that we would take the observed values for the predictor variable(s) as given. However, if a predictor variable is in fact dependent upon other variables, the condition that $x_{\ell j}$ is "fixed" is untenable. We therefore use:

$$E(u_{jt} \mid x_{\ell jt}) = 0 \tag{16.51}$$

where

$x_{\ell jt}$ = a random variable.

See also (16.21). The assumption is violated (i.e. $E(u_{jt} \mid x_{\ell jt}) \neq 0$) if $x_{\ell jt}$ has measurement error or if $x_{\ell jt}$ in fact depends on y_{jt}. The consequence of a violation of this assumption is that the ordinary least squares parameter estimates are biased. The remedy lies in the use of simultaneous equation estimation methods (if $x_{\ell jt}$ depends on y_{jt}) or in the use of instrumental variables (if $x_{\ell jt}$ has measurement error). We return to these issues in Section 16.4.

---

16. See Hendry (1989).

MULTICOLLINEARITY

In model (16.9) we assume that the matrix of observations X_j has full rank,[17] or that the vectors in X_j are linearly independent. If this assumption is violated we encounter perfect collinearity. If X_j has a rank smaller than L, $X_j'X_j$ has a determinant with value zero. In that case $(X_j'X_j)^{-1}$ does not exist and the parameter estimates cannot be uniquely determined. Perfect collinearity is, however, unusual. If it happens, it is often due to a duplicate variable. The notion of "almost" linearly dependent vectors is, however, meaningful. This means $X_j'X_j$ does not have a zero determinant, but its value will be near zero. Hence $(X_j'X_j)^{-1}$ exists but its elements will be large. As a consequence the parameter estimates will have large variances and covariances, as shown in Section 16.1.5. Thus multicollinearity (almost linearly dependent vectors in the X_j-matrix) makes the parameter estimates unreliable.

Real-world data often show high degrees of correlation between predictors. Take, for example, the specification of a model to explain the demand for a product category at the household level. Variables such as household income and age of the head of the household may be relevant predictor variables. However, these variables tend to be correlated. In particular, income is partly a function of age. Also, while in this case it may be fine to assume that the variable "Age" is "fixed", it is more appropriate to let "Income" be a random variable. This dependency of income on age is unlikely to require novel estimation techniques (the collinearity should be modest). However, the interpretation of statistical results may become more complex. Specifically, one should consider both the direct effect of a change in "Age" and its indirect effect through "Income" on demand. The substantive interpretation of the estimated effects will then benefit from an explicit consideration of dependencies between predictor variables.

Collinearity between predictor variables can also result from decisions made by managers. Suppose, we argue that unit brand sales is a function of advertising and price. It seems inappropriate to assume that either variable is "fixed". Instead, a decision maker manipulates both variables, based on strategic considerations, marketplace conditions, cost considerations, etc. Only under restrictive assumptions can we assume that such predictors are truly exogenous. But the focus here is on a possible dependency between these variables. Imagine that consumers' price sensitivity depends on the amount of advertising.[18] A manager who manipulates both variables will then refrain from changing these variables independently. In that case, a real-world correlation between these marketing decision variables reflects, at least partly, the decision maker's belief about interactions between these variables. If her belief is very strong (i.e. price changes are strongly related to advertising changes), then it can become difficult or impossible to obtain reliable estimates of the separate main effects from marketplace data. And, verification of an interaction effect will then be especially difficult.

---

17. Compare footnote 1 and Section 16.1.3.
18. For a discussion of theoretical arguments and empirical generalizations, see Kaul and Wittink (1995).

Some of the procedures for detecting the presence of multicollinearity are (for a given cross section j):

1. The traditional approach to check for collinearity is to examine the correlation matrix R of the predictor variables. Highly positive or negative correlations are indications of potential difficulties in the estimation of reliable effects.
2. Do a factor analysis of the predictor variables to examine the structure of overlapping variation between the predictors. This is a more comprehensive examination of multicollinearity than the traditional approach which considers only the simple correlations.
3. Use multiple *regression* with $x_{\ell jt}$ as the *criterion variable* and the x_{rjt}, $r = 1, \ldots, L, r \neq \ell$ as the predictor variables, for all $\ell = 1, \ldots, L$. Each regression indicates how much one predictor is related to a linear combination of the other predictors.
4. Estimate the complete model with y_{jt} as a function of all L predictor variables. Next, *eliminate* one of the predictor variables $x_{\ell jt}$, and *re-estimate* the model. The parameter estimates that change the most are associated with predictor variables that are collinear with the deleted variable $x_{\ell jt}$. This can be done for each predictor variable in turn.

We discuss other procedures in Section 16.1.5. In that section we also discuss several approaches for the resolution of severe multicollinearity.

16.1.5 GOODNESS OF FIT AND RELIABILITY

If the error-term and other model assumptions are satisfied, we can evaluate the quality of the model, and identify substantive implications. In this section we discuss criteria pertaining to the model's goodness of fit and the (statistical) reliability of the coefficients. After that, we continue the discussion of the interrelations between the predictor variables.

GOODNESS OF FIT

A criterion by which we can measure a model's overall goodness of fit, that is, the degree to which fluctuations in the criterion variable are explained by the model, is the coefficient of determination or R^2.[19] It measures the proportion of total variance in the criterion variable "explained" by the model. With (16.7) as the model, let

$$\hat{y}_{jt} = \hat{\beta}_{1j} x_{1jt} + \ldots + \hat{\beta}_{Lj} x_{Ljt} \tag{16.52}$$

and

$$\hat{u}_{jt} = y_{jt} - \hat{y}_{jt}. \tag{16.53}$$

---

19. Also known as the squared multiple correlation coefficient.

R_j^2, the coefficient of determination for a given cross section, is defined as:[20]

$$R_j^2 = \frac{\sum_{t=1}^{T}(\hat{y}_{jt} - \bar{y}_j)^2}{\sum_{t=1}^{T}(y_{jt} - \bar{y}_j)^2} = \frac{\text{explained variation in } y_j}{\text{total variation in } y_j}. \tag{16.54}$$

The explained variation in y_j is also known as the regression sum of squares. The total sum of squares in y_j is referred to as the total variation in y_j. Expression (16.54) can also be written as:

$$R_j^2 = 1 - \frac{\sum_{t=1}^{T} \hat{u}_{jt}^2}{\sum_{t=1}^{T}(y_{jt} - \bar{y}_j)^2} = 1 - \frac{\text{unexplained variation in } y_j}{\text{total variation in } y_j}. \tag{16.55}$$

The unexplained variation is also called residual variation, error sum of squares, or residual sum of squares.

Expression (16.55) can be written in matrix notation as:

$$R_j^2 = 1 - \frac{\hat{u}_j' \hat{u}_j}{y_j^{*'} y_j^*} \tag{16.56}$$

where

$\hat{u}_j$ = a $T \times 1$ column vector of the T residuals,

y_j^* = a $T \times 1$ column vector of the observations of the criterion

variable in deviations from the mean. Thus,

$y_j^{*'} = (y_{1j} - \bar{y}_j, \ldots, y_{Tj} - \bar{y}_j)$.

We emphasize that R_j^2 is a relative measure. Its value depends on (see (16.55) or (16.56)):

1. how well the regression line fits the data as measured by variation in the residuals, and
2. the amount of dispersion in the values of the criterion variable.

It is tempting for researchers to regard estimated equations with high R^2 values favorably and low R^2 values unfavorably. Indeed, it is straightforward to agree with this notion if everything else remains the same. However, in practice, models that are structurally deficient (e.g. with implausible substantive implications) can have higher R^2 values than models with acceptable specifications. In addition, for some types of problems and data, all models necessarily have low R^2 values. Thus, low R^2 values should not be interpreted as indicating unacceptable or useless results nor should high R^2 values be interpreted to mean that the results are useful.

It is also worth noting that a high R^2 value may obtain at the cost of a high degree of positive autocorrelation.[21] In addition, the use of many predictor variables may

---

20. If the model does not contain a constant term it is not meaningful to express the observed values in deviations from the mean, in which case the denominator should read $\sum_{t=1}^{T} y_{jt}^2$ (Theil 1971, Chapter 4).
21. For an explanation of this phenomenon, see Koerts and Abrahamse (1969, Chapter 8).

result in artificially high R^2 values. Each predictor with a nonzero slope coefficient makes a contribution to R^2, with the actual contribution determined by the slope and the amount of variation for the predictor in the sample.[22] Also model comparisons based on R^2 values are not meaningful unless the comparisons are made on one set of data for the criterion variable (and the number of predictors is taken into account).[23]

The artificiality of R^2 is further illustrated by examples that indicate how researchers can manipulate the value of R^2 while the standard deviation of the residuals remains constant (see Wittink, 1988, pp. 209-213 for examples). The standard deviation of residuals is an absolute measure of lack of fit. It is measured in the same units as the criterion variable, and therefore it has substantive relevance.

If the criterion variable differs between two equations, either in terms of its definition or in terms of the data, comparisons based on R^2 values are meaningless. Models of the same criterion variable on the same data, that differ in the number of predictor variables, can be compared on R_a^2, the adjusted coefficient of determination. In this coefficient both the unexplained variation and the total variation are adjusted for degrees of freedom, $(T - L)$ and $(T - 1)$ respectively. The adjusted coefficient of determination for a given cross section j is defined as:

$$R_{a_j}^2 = 1 - \frac{\hat{u}_j' \hat{u}_j / (T - L)}{y_j^{*'} y_j^{*} / (T - 1)}. \tag{16.57}$$

From (16.56) and (16.57) we can show that R_j^2 and $R_{a_j}^2$ are related as follows:

$$R_{a_j}^2 = R_j^2 - \left[\frac{L - 1}{T - L} \right] (1 - R_j^2). \tag{16.58}$$

It follows that $R_{a_j}^2 < R_j^2$ (except for the irrelevant case of $L = 1$).

To summarize, the coefficient of determination for a given cross section j (R^2) is the percent of variation in the criterion variable, which exists in a *sample* of data, that is accounted for or explained by the estimated equation. It can be shown that this measure overestimates the true explanatory power of the model. A better estimate of the true explanatory power of this model is provided by the adjusted coefficient of determination R_a^2. In addition, for comparisons of alternative models, applied to the same criterion variable and the same data, R_a^2 is a more useful basis. Alternatively, statistical tests of the difference between alternative models are based on the difference in (unadjusted) R^2 values and the difference in degrees of freedom.

We also note that aggregation tends to produce "inflated" R^2 values. Thus, models of monthly scanner data typically have higher R^2 values than models of weekly scanner data. Similarly, models of purchases aggregated across households will have higher R^2 values than models of individual household purchase data. If high R^2 values are desired, the logical conclusion is to use aggregated data. However, aggregation almost always causes parameter estimates to be biased. Thus, even though

---

22. See Theil (1971, p. 167).
23. See also Koerts and Abrahamse (1969, p, 152, 1970).

R^2 values have some role to play in the model-building process, we need other criteria to determine the substantive usefulness of a model.

To illustrate the difficulty associated with the use of relative measures for substansive questions, we consider the following. As indicated, R^2 measures the percent of variation in the criterion variable explained by the model in the sample. A related measure determines the marginal contribution of each predictor variable to the model's explanatory power. In a simplified setting, imagine that the predictor variables in (16.7) are uncorrelated. In that case (for a given cross section j):

$$R^2 = \sum_{\ell=2}^{L} r_{y,x_\ell}^2 \tag{16.59}$$

where

r_{y,x_ℓ} = the simple correlation coefficient of y and x_ℓ.

For uncorrelated predictor variables, we can also show that:

$$r_{y,x_\ell}^2 = \hat{\beta}_\ell^2 \frac{s_{x_\ell}^2}{s_y^2} \tag{16.60}$$

where

s_{x_ℓ} = the standard deviation in the sample for x_ℓ,

s_y = the standard deviation in the sample for y.

Thus, (16.60) provides a measure of the contribution for each predictor variable to the model's explanatory power. Some software packages automatically provide *standardized* regression coefficients, defined as:

$$beta = \hat{\beta}_\ell \frac{s_{x_\ell}}{s_y}. \tag{16.61}$$

The interest in beta coefficients stems from the difficulty model users have in comparing slope coefficients. Each slope coefficient, $\hat{\beta}_\ell$, is interpretable only with respect to the unit in which predictor variable ℓ is measured. With different units of measurement for the predictor variables, the slope coefficients are not comparable. The beta coefficients are unitless, as are the correlation coefficients.

A comparison of (16.61) with (16.60) and (16.59) makes it clear that the beta coefficients have similar properties as R^2. Thus, the shortcomings associated with R^2 with respect to substantive interpretations also apply to the beta coefficients. In fact, if the model user wants to make pronouncements about the "relative importances" of predictor variables, based on the beta coefficients, several other conditions must be met. Since the amount of sample variation in x_ℓ plays a role in (16.61), this variation must be obtained through probabilistic processes. This means that the "importances" of predictor variables manipulated by managers, such as price and advertising, cannnot be meaningfully assessed in this manner.

To demonstrate the problem for predictor variables manipulated by managers,[24] consider the demand for a brand as a function of price and advertising. For these variables, the sample variances are determined by management based on, say, market characteristics. Suppose that two brand managers operate with similar products in two different geographic areas. Over time, one manager varies price a lot but keeps advertising at a fairly constant level. The other manager varies advertising a lot, but holds price approximately constant. Assume that in both cases, each variable varies sufficiently for the marginal effects of both predictor variables to be reliably estimable. But since the units of measurement differ between the predictors, one might be tempted to use beta coefficients. Since the standard deviation for the price variable will be large, but for the advertising variable small, the first manager is likely to conclude that price is "most important". Conversely, since the standard deviation for the advertising variable will be large but for the price variable small, the second manager may conclude that advertising is "most important". This example makes it clear why economists do not rely on beta coefficients for policy questions, and neither should marketing researchers.

On the other hand, household income, demographics, and attitudinal variables have acceptable properties for the use of relative measures. If the sample data have been generated via probability sampling then it is meaningful to use beta coefficients for substantive conclusions about the relative importances of such variables in explaining household behavior. Thus, only if all predictor variables have "natural" amounts of variation, and the data represent a probability sample, is it meaningful to use the beta coefficients to infer the relative importances of the predictor variables in a population. Even then, the correlation between predictor variables can complicate the interpretation of the beta coefficients. For example, collinearity makes it possible for the beta coefficients to fall outside the $[-1, +1]$ interval that pertains to correlation coefficients. Thus, if a beta coefficient falls outside this interval, multicollinearity needs to be considered. But this also means that differences in the collinearity between subsets of the predictor variables affect the magnitudes of the beta coefficients.[25]

RELIABILITY (STATISTICAL SIGNIFICANCE)

1. Test of the equation as a whole

As the number of predictor variables included in a model increases, the probability that at least one of the slope coefficients is statistically significant increases, even if none of the predictor variables *truly* relate to the criterion variable. For that reason, we should *first* determine whether the equation as a whole is better than what could be due to chance variation. The test statistic for this uses the explanatory power of the estimated equation. The null hypothesis is that the model lacks explanatory power.

24. The following is based on Wittink (1988, pp. 227-229).
25. Methods have been developed specifically to obtain reliable importance weights under conditions of multicollinearity; see Green, Carroll, DeSarbo (1978). For an in-depth discussion about this topic, see, for example, Goldberger, Manski (1995).

More specifically, all slope parameters are zero under the null hypothesis, i.e.:

Null hypothesis (H_0): $\beta_{2j} = \ldots = \beta_{\ell j} = \ldots = \beta_{Lj} = 0$ (16.62a)

Alternative hypothesis (H_A): at least one $\beta_{\ell j}$, $\ell = 2, \ldots, L$ (16.62b)

is different from zero.

If the error-term assumptions stated earlier hold, then under the null hypothesis the explained variance should be equal to the unexplained variance. The ratio of these two variances follows the F-distribution:

$$\frac{\sum_{t=1}^{T}(\hat{y}_{jt} - \bar{y}_j)^2/(L - 1)}{\sum_{t=1}^{T}(y_{jt} - \hat{y}_{jt})^2/(T - L)} = \frac{\text{Explained variance}}{\text{Unexplained variance}} \sim F_{(L-1),(T-L)}. \quad (16.63)$$

Since R_j^2 is the percent of variation explained for cross section j, and $(1 - R_j^2)$ is the percent unexplained, it is easy to show that an alternative expression for this F-ratio is:

$$\frac{R_j^2/(L - 1)}{(1 - R_j^2)/(T - L)} \sim F_{(L-1),(T-L)}. \quad (16.64)$$

In both expressions (16.63) and (16.64) the number of slope parameters in the model equals $(L - 1)$ which is also the number of degrees of freedom used to explain variation in the criterion variable. The number of degrees of freedom left for the unexplained variation is $(T - L)$, since one additional degree of freedom is used by the intercept. If the calculated F-value exceeds the critical value, we reject H_0. Only if the equation as a whole explains more than what could be due to chance does it make sense to determine the statistical reliability of individual slope coefficients.

Strictly speaking the F-test is valid only if all error-term assumptions are met. In practice, it is very difficult to specify a model that is complete and has no identifiable shortcomings. Typically, the residuals that remain after the model is first estimated will be reviewed and tested. Based on this residual analysis the model will be adjusted, and a second model will be estimated. This process often proceeds until the model builder has a specification that is theoretically acceptable and is consistent with the data. Such an iterative model-building process, while necessary, reduces the validity of statistical inferences. For this reason, and also for other reasons, it is important for the model builder to "test" the ultimate specification on a validation sample (see Chapter 18).

2. Tests of (individual) slope parameters
If the null hypothesis that all slope parameters are zero is rejected, we can conduct statistical tests of individual terms of the model. Assuming, again, that the four assumptions about the error term are valid (Section 16.1.3), we can evaluate the reliability of each of the estimates $\hat{\beta}_{\ell j}$, $\ell = 1, \ldots, L$. Under these conditions, for a model linear in the parameters and with normally distributed disturbance terms,

the OLS estimator $\hat{\beta}_{\ell j}$ of $\beta_{\ell j}$ also follows a normal distribution. It then follows that $(\hat{\beta}_{\ell j} - \beta_{\ell j})/\sigma_{\hat{\beta}_{\ell j}}$ is standard normally distributed. The standard deviation $\sigma_{\hat{\beta}_{\ell j}}$ is a function of σ_j, the standard deviation of the disturbance term. Since the latter has to be estimated from the residuals, we replace $\sigma_{\hat{\beta}_{\ell j}}$ by its estimate $\hat{\sigma}_{\hat{\beta}_{\ell j}}$, so that the test statistic:

$$\frac{\hat{\beta}_{\ell j} - \beta_{\ell j}}{\hat{\sigma}_{\hat{\beta}_{\ell j}}} \tag{16.65}$$

is t-distributed with $(T - L)$ degrees of freedom.[26] Usually the null hypothesis is formulated as follows:

$$H_0 \; : \; \beta_{\ell j} = 0$$

and H_0 is rejected if the calculated t-value for a given coefficient exceeds the tabulated value for the t-distribution. Most software programs provide p-values which, for a two-tailed test, show the probability of a type I error if the null hypothesis is rejected.

As the amount of empirical evidence with regard to demand sensitivity to specific marketing instruments accumulates, it seems inappropriate to continue the use of hypotheses of no effect. Farley, Lehmann and Sawyer (1995) argue that model builders should instead rely on average estimated effects from previous empirical analyses. Such average effects have been reported in various meta-analyses. New empirical results for problems studied earlier should then be tested against prevailing average effects.

Suppose that the current average effect for predictor variable $x_{\ell j}$ is c. Then the null hypothesis is:

$$H_0 \; : \; \beta_{\ell j} = c.$$

If we cannot reject this null hypothesis, the product/time/region for which data have been obtained is comparable to previous sources with regard to the average effect of variable ℓ. If we obtain an effect that is significantly different from the prevailing standard, we have an opportunity to consider the reason(s) for divergence. Farley et al., argue that this manner of testing will prove to be more informative than the traditional procedure.

To illustrate the traditional procedure, consider relation (15.1), for which $T = 29$, $L = 4$, $\hat{\beta}_2 = 7.9$ (the estimated effect of advertising share on market share) and $\hat{\sigma}_{\hat{\beta}_2} = 3.2$. Suppose we test whether $\hat{\beta}_2$ is significantly different from zero at the five percent level of significance. From (16.65) we obtain $\hat{\beta}_2/\hat{\sigma}_{\hat{\beta}_2} = 7.9/3.2 = 2.47$. The table of the t-distribution shows a critical t-value at the five percent level, for a one-tailed test (it is unlikely that more advertising reduces market share) with $29 - 4 = 25$ degrees

---

26. For more detail see introductory statistics and econometrics textbooks, such as Wonnacott and Wonnacott (1969, 1970), Wittink (1988), Greene (1997). Tables of the t-distribution are also reproduced in most of these textbooks.

of freedom, of 1.71. In this example we reject the null hypothesis that advertising share has *no* effect on market share.

In the context of an iterative model-building process, the result showing statistical significance for the advertising effect indicates that we want to retain the advertising variable in the model. If the slope had been insignificant, and we had expected the variable to be relevant, we would consider possible reasons for the nonsignificance in the sample. For example, the true functional form may differ from the one we assume. One might argue that this is not a likely explanation if we first examined and tested the residuals (and found no such evidence against the error-term assumptions). Thus, if the assumed functional form is incorrect the residuals should so inform us. However, residual tests are not conclusive. Specifically the power of any of the tests may be low. For that reason, we still consider the possibility that lack of statistical significance for an individual slope coefficient may be due to model misspecification.

In general, there are many possible reasons why the *t*-ratio for a given slope coefficient can be insignificant:

1. the predictor variable has an effect that is different from the functional form assumed (incorrect functional form);
2. the model excludes other relevant predictor variables (omitted variables);
3. the predictor variable is highly correlated with one or more other predictor variables included in the model (multicollinearity);
4. the sample data are insufficient (lack of power);
5. the predictor variable has no relation with the criterion variable (irrelevance).

Insignificance due to either of the first two reasons should stimulate us to investigate the existence of superior functional forms and/or additional predictor variables. The third reason requires the exploration of additional data sources, model reformulation, or alternative estimation procedures (as might be the case for the fourth reason). Only the fifth reason is proper justification for eliminating a predictor variable from the model. We must consider each of these possible reasons before we eliminate a predictor variable from the model.

We note that in a simple regression analysis (one predictor variable), the F-test statistic relevant to (16.62a) and the t-test statistic for (16.65) when $\beta_{\ell j} = 0$ provide the same conclusion.[27] Curiously, in a multiple regression analysis it is possible to reject the null hypothesis that all slope parameters are zero (16.62a) and at the same time find that none of the slope coefficients differ significantly from zero based on the t-test (16.65). This may occur if the predictor variables are highly intercorrelated. In this case the separate influences of $x_{\ell j}, \ell = 2, \ldots, L$ on y_j are unreliable (large estimated standard errors), while the model's explanatory power may be high.[28] Marketing data, especially at aggregate levels, often have a high degree of collinearity between the predictor variables. We pursue the issue of collinearity in more detail

---

27. This is true if both tests are conducted at the same level of significance and against the same alternative (i.e. a two-tailed *t*-test).
28. For an example, see Leeflang (1974, pp. 141-143).

Table 16.2 Multiple regression results (15.2).

	Predictor variable	Regression coefficient	Estimated standard error	Computed t-value
1.	(Intercept)	202	41	4.93
2.	Income (deflated by Price Index)	-0.29	10.1	0.03
3.	Average price (deflated by Price Index)	-29.5	11.7	2.52
4.	Total advertising expenditures (deflated by Price Index)	0.31	0.15	2.07
5.	Trend	- 0.29	0.47	0.61
	$T = 32, R^2 = 0.47.$			

after we introduce a test statistic for subgroups of slope parameters.

3. Joint test of subgroups of slope parameters

As we indicated in the previous discussion, it is possible for F- and t-test results to be in conflict. If the collinearity is concentrated in a subset of the predictor variables, then it is possible that two or more slope coefficients are insignificant based on individual t-tests but provide significant incremental explanatory power as a subgroup.

Tests of subgroups of variables are also of interest in case the model builder has arguments for the inclusion or exclusion of two or more predictor variables jointly. For example, with quarterly data one may propose seasonal effects. Three indicator variables may be used to allow the intercept to differ between the four quarters. A test of seasonal differences would then focus on the joint significance of all three parameters.

These joint tests are based on the incremental explanatory power of a group of at least two predictor variables. We use equation (15.2), the demand equation for the product class sales of detergents, to provide an illustration. We show the multiple regression results of (15.2) in Table 16.2.

The F-test of the model as a whole indicates that the null hypothesis $\beta_2 = \ldots = \beta_L = 0$ can be rejected. From tables of the t-distribution we find that the critical value of the five percent level of significance with $32 - 5 = 27$ degrees of freedom is 1.70 for a one-tailed test, and 2.05 for a two-tailed test. Thus, we cannot reject the null hypothesis that "Income" and "Trend" have no effect on the criterion variable, the demand for detergents at the product class level.

To test these two predictor variables' incremental explanatory power jointly, we estimate an alternative, *restricted*, model by eliminating Income and Trend. This restricted model has an R^2 of 0.43. The test of the null hypothesis that the parameters of Income (β_2) and Trend (β_5) are simultaneously equal to zero is performed using *an F-test based on incremental R^2*

$$H_0 \; : \; \beta_2 = \beta_5 = 0$$

is tested with the statistic:

$$F = \frac{(R_F^2 - R_R^2)/(DF_R - DF_F)}{(1 - R_F^2)/DF_F} \tag{16.66}$$

where

R_F^2 = the unadjusted R^2 for the full model,

R_R^2 = the unadjusted R^2 for the restricted model,

DF_R = the number of degrees of freedom left for the restricted model,

DF_F = the number of degrees of freedom left for the full model.

In this example:

$$F = \frac{(0.47 - 0.43)/(29 - 27)}{(0.53)/27} \approx 1.02.$$

At the five percent level, the critical F-value equals 3.35 ($F_{2,27}$). Thus we cannot reject the null hypothesis that parameters β_2 and β_5 are jointly zero. We conclude that the corresponding predictor variables are irrelevant (and that the insignificance of the individual t-tests is not due to collinearity between these two predictors).

The incremental R^2-test is one of the statistical tests that can be used for model selection. We discuss other statistical tests, for "nested models", in Section 18.4.2.

4. Multicollinearity

We mentioned four procedures for detecting the presence of multicollinearity in Section 16.1.4. We now discuss additional procedures and measures for the detection of multicollinearity.

a. *Comparing results for F-test and t-tests*
Multicollinearity may be regarded as acute, if the F-statistic shows significance and none of the t-statistics for the slope coefficients is significant.
b. *Estimated variances of the parameter estimates*
Multicollinearity inflates the estimated variances of the slope coefficients. Everything else being equal, the larger these estimates the greater the collinearity. However, large variances may also occur if the error variance is large or there is little sample variation in the predictor variable(s).
c. *Regressing each predictor variable on the other predictors*
This procedure reveals the amount of overlap between $x_{\ell j}$ and a linear combination of the other predictors x_{rj}, $r \neq j$. The $R_{\ell j}^2$ values that result from these

regressions, one at a time, can be used to quantify the overlap among any number of predictor variables.

A related measure is the variance inflation factor (VIF) computed as $(1 - R^2_{\ell j})^{-1}$. A VIF greater than 10 is often taken to signal that collinearity is a problem (Marquardt, 1970, Mason, Perreault, 1991).

d. *The correlation matrix*

Often empirical researchers examine the matrix of all bivariate correlation coefficients between the predictor variables. Based on some cutoff value a decision might be made about which pairs of predictors should not be included together. One problem with this procedure is that all bivariate correlations may be low and yet one predictor may be highly related to a linear combination of the remaining predictors (see the previous approach). Another problem is that the severity of a high bivariate correlation between two predictors depends on the sample size. For that reason statistical tests of multicollinearity[29] are meaningless. In this regard, Mason and Perreault (1991) demonstrated that the harmful effects of collinear predictions are often exaggerated and that collinearity cannot be viewed in isolation. They argue that the effects of a given level of collinearity must be evaluated in conjunction with the sample size, the R^2 value of the estimated equation, and the magnitudes of the slope coefficients. For example, bivariate correlations as high as 0.95 have little effect on the ability to recover the true parameters if the sample size is 250 and the R^2 is at least 0.75. By contrast, a bivariate correlation of 0.95 in conjunction with a sample size of 30 and an R^2 of 0.25 results in failure to detect the significance of individual predictors. Currently, the spectral decomposition of $X'_j X_j$ is advocated for the quantification of multicollinearity, based on one or more characteristic roots.[30]

Solutions to multicollinearity[31]

If any two predictors are perfectly correlated, the parameters of a regression equation cannot be estimated. Thus no solution to a multiple regression problem (other than combining the two predictors or deleting one) can be obtained if there is *extreme* multicollinearity. The approaches available for the resolution of non-extreme but severe multicollinearity include:

1. obtain more data relevant to the problem;
2. reformulate the model with the specific objective to decrease multicollinearity;
3. create new predictors;
4. apply estimation methods specifically developed for cases with severe multicollinearity;
5. eliminate a predictor variable with a t-ratio close to zero.

The last approach is simply that a predictor variable with a statistically insignificant t-ratio be eliminated. In general, an insignificant t-ratio indicates that the predictor

---

29. See Farrar, Glauber (1967), Kumar, (1975), Friedmann (1982).
30. See Belsley, Kuh, Welsh (1980), Judge et al. (1985, pp. 902-904), Belsley (1991).
31. We closely follow Wittink (1988, pp. 100-101).

variable is irrelevant or that it has an effect but we cannot obtain a reliable parameter estimate. The elimination of such a predictor variable from the model should be a last-resort option.

A better solution, of course, is to obtain more data. With more data, especially data with a reduced degree of multicollinearity, it is more likely that a significant effect can be obtained for any predictor variable. However, the opportunity to add data to the sample is often limited.

Another possible solution is to reformulate the model. In some sense, the elimination of one predictor variable amounts to a model reformulation. But we may also combine two predictor variables and in that manner resolve the problem. For example, this is appropriate if the two variables are substitute measures of the same underlying construct such as when the observations represent characteristics of individuals, and two of the predictors measure age and work experience. These two variables tend to be correlated, because both may measure individuals' learned skills for a certain job as well as their maturity. It may be sufficient to use one of these variables or to define a new variable that combines these two predictor variables.

If the source of multicollinearity is two or more predictor variables which capture different phenomena, such combinations are not appropriate. However, it may be possible to redefine the variables. Consider, for example, a demand model in which product category sales in t (Q_t) is explained by predictors such as total disposable income in t (Inc_t) and population size in t (N_t). These predictors are collinear because Inc_t is a function of the size of the population. However, by defining the variables on a per capita basis, such as Q_t/N_t and Inc_t/N_t, we create a simpler[32] model and eliminate the collinearity between Inc_t and N_t.

Other functional specifications of the model[33] can also reduce multicollinearity. For example, consider relation (16.7). The predictor variables $x_{2jt}, \ldots, x_{Ljt}$ vary over time,[34] and each of these variables may have a component that follows a common trend. In that case, bivariate correlation between the predictors will be high due to the common factor. The multicollinearity can be considerably reduced in the following manner.[35] First specify (16.7) for $t-1$:

$$y_{j,t-1} = \beta_{1j}x_{1j,t-1} + \beta_{2j}x_{2j,t-1} + \ldots + \beta_{Lj}x_{Lj,t-1} + u_{j,t-1}. \tag{16.67}$$

By subtracting (16.67) from (16.7), we state the model in terms of changes over time:

$$(y_{jt} - y_{j,t-1}) = \beta_{2j}(x_{2jt} - x_{2j,t-1}) + \ldots + \beta_{Lj}(x_{Ljt} - x_{Lj,t-1}) \tag{16.68}$$
$$+(u_{jt} - u_{j,t-1}).$$

Note that the reformulated model has no intercept. Apart from that, the model contains the same parameters. Importantly, this reformulation will not have the same degree of multicollinearity as the original model. Such opportunities for model reformulation are useful to consider when severe multicollinearity is encountered.

---

32. See also our discussion in Section 7.2.1.
33. Compare Chapter 5.
34. See also Rao, Wind, DeSarbo (1988).
35. We assume that x_{1jt} represents the constant term.

Some researchers advocate the creation of a matrix of orthogonal variables, constructed as linear combinations of the original predictor variables, based on principal components analysis or factor analysis.[36] If all components or factors are included in a subsequent multiple regression analysis, we can claim to have "solved" the collinearity problem in the sense that the components (factors) are uncorrelated. However, we are unlikely to have a useful substantive interpretation for the estimated effects. And if we transform these estimated effects based on the relations between the factors and the original predictors, we will derive exactly the same slope coefficients as if we had not first constructed the matrix of orthogonal variables. Only by deleting at least one orthogonal component (e.g. the one with the smallest explanatory power of y_j) do we have a chance of improved results. In this case we can also transform the effects back in terms of the original variables, in which case we have (slightly) biased effects with reduced statistical uncertainty.

The use of a subset of the principal components along with a transformation to the original variables is a simple example of alternative estimation procedures. More popular procedures are:

- ridge regression, and
- equity estimation.

The argument in favor of these alternative estimation methods is that we may accept a small amount of bias in the parameter estimates in order to gain efficiency, i.e. to reduce the variance of the slope coefficients. One procedure that does just that is *ridge regression*.[37] Marketing applications of ridge regression include Mahajan, Jain, Bergier (1977) and Erickson (1981).

The principle underlying *equity estimation*[38] is that recovery of the relative contribution of correlated predictor variables can be improved by first transforming the variables into their closest orthonormal counterparts. Rangaswamy and Krishnamurthi (1991) compared the performances of equity, ridge, OLS, and principal components estimators in estimating response functions. Overall, "equity" outperforms the three estimators on criteria such as estimated bias, variance and face validity of the estimates. Similar results were obtained in a simulation performed by the same researchers.[39]

Finally, we briefly consider the consequences of multicollinearity on understanding versus forecasting. If the purpose of the study is to develop a forecasting model, multicollinearity may not be an issue. For example, suppose x_{2j} is eliminated from the model because it is highly correlated with a linear combination of the other predictor variables. If x_{2j} is truly a relevant predictor, then the parameter estimates for the remaining predictors will be biased. Nevertheless, the forecasts produced by this

---

36. See, for example, Massy (1965) and Sharma (1996, Chapter 4).
37. For an introductory treatment see Hoerl, Kennard (1970), Marquardt (1970), Marquardt, Snee (1975), and Rangaswamy, Krishnamurthi (1991).
38. See Krishnamurthi, Rangaswamy (1987).
39. See also Rangaswamy, Krishnamurthi (1991, 1995) and Wildt (1993).

otherwise deficient model may still be accurate, since most of the explanatory power of x_{2j} is contained in one or more other predictor variables. As long as this correlation between x_{2j} and the other predictors *continues to exist*, the forecasts from this deficient model will *not* be systematically affected. On the other hand, if this correlation changes, the accuracy of the forecasts will be affected by the model's deficiency. (This happens especially when the predictor variables are controlled by a manager or a policy maker.) The reason is that the elimination of a relevant predictor variable biases the coefficients of the remaining predictor variables which affects the accuracy of conditional forecasts. The nature and magnitude of this bias depends, among other things, on the degree of multicollinearity. If the degree of multicollinearity changes from the estimation sample to new data, then the nature of the bias changes, thereby affecting the forecasting accuracy. Thus, for *conditional* forecasting multicollinearity is a serious problem, and the "solution" has to be similar to the situation when the primary objective of model building is to understand relationships.

If the objective is to understand or describe the relationship between a criterion variable and several predictor variables, it is critical that all relevant variables are included in the model. This is also true for normative decisions. The presence of multicollinearity may make it difficult or impossible to obtain the desired degree of reliability (i.e., low standard errors) for the coefficients. As a result the computed t-ratio for the slope coefficient of one or more predictor variables may be below the critical value. Yet for understanding it is not advisable to eliminate a (relevant) predictor. In this case, ridge regression or equity estimation should allow one to obtain slightly biased but reliable estimates for a fully specified model.

16.2 Pooling methods[40]

Section 16.1 focuses on estimation and testing issues relevant to models parameterized with either time-series data or cross-sectional data. For example, (16.7) is specified for time-series data while (16.10) is for cross-sectional data. In this section we discuss issues associated with the opportunity to pool time-series and cross-sectional data for estimation (use both sources of variation), and we discuss estimation methods for pooled data.

In matrix notation, we have considered the use of time-series data separately for each cross-sectional unit, such as for brand j, specified in (16.9):

$$Y_j = X_j \beta_j + u_j \quad \text{for each } j = 1, \ldots, n. \tag{16.69}$$

If we have T observations for each cross section, and pool the data, parameters are estimated from nT observations. Under the usual assumptions about the error terms, we can test the null hypothesis: $\beta_j = \beta_i$, $i, j = 1, \ldots, n$, $i \neq j$. This test is based on a comparison of the residual sum of squares when each cross section has unique parameters, as in (16.69), with the residual sum of squares when a single parameter

---

40. This section is based on Bass, Wittink (1975), Wittink (1977) and Leeflang, van Duijn (1982a, 1982b).

vector is estimated. The latter estimates are obtained from the pooled model:

$$
\begin{bmatrix} Y_1 \\ \vdots \\ Y_n \end{bmatrix} = \begin{bmatrix} X_1 \\ \vdots \\ X_n \end{bmatrix} \beta + \begin{bmatrix} u_1 \\ \vdots \\ u_n \end{bmatrix} \tag{16.70}
$$

or

$$
Y = X\beta + u \tag{16.71}
$$

where

Y = a $nT \times 1$ column vector of observations on the criterion variable,

X = a $nT \times L$ matrix of observations on the L predictor variables, and a first column of ones,

β = a $L \times 1$ column vector of (homogeneous) response parameters, and

u = a $nT \times 1$ column vector of disturbance terms.

We note that in the case where the cross sections represent brands, it is highly unlikely that (16.70) is preferred over (16.69). If the cross-sectional units refer to geographic regions or stores, it is plausible that parameters are equal (homogeneous) across the units.

Algebraically, (16.69) with a separate intercept term $x_{1jt} = 1$ for each $j = 1, \ldots, n$ can be stated as:

$$
y_{jt} = \beta_{1j} + \sum_{\ell=2}^{L} \beta_{\ell j} x_{\ell jt} + u_{jt}, \quad t = 1, \ldots, T, \quad j = 1, \ldots, n. \tag{16.72}
$$

Thus, (16.72) allows both the intercepts and the slope parameters to be unique for each cross section, as does (16.69).

Pooling offers certain advantages (see also the discussion in Section 14.2). However, if the homogeneity hypothesis is rejected then the estimates based on the pooled model (16.70) lack meaning (at best the homogeneous estimates are weighted averages). Nevertheless if the differences in parameters between the cross sections are small we may be willing to accept some bias in order to obtain reduced variances.[41] Even if the cross sections differ in parameter vectors, the statistical uncertainty about the separate estimates may "inflate" the differences considerably. Thus, the model builder faces the question how to trade bias (separate estimation minimizes the bias) off against variance (pooled estimation minimizes the variance).

---

41. To this end Wallace (1972) suggested weaker criteria. See also Brobst, Gates (1977).

Within the option to pool the data we distinguish four alternative estimation methods:

1. OLS (Ordinary Least Squares): we assume that all parameters are fixed and common for all cross-sectional units. This is pooling under complete homogeneity: see (16.70).

2. OLSDV (Ordinary Least Squares with Dummy Variables): we assume the slope parameters are fixed and common for all cross-sectional units, but the intercepts are unique for each cross section (contraining $\beta_{\ell 1} = \beta_{\ell 2} = \ldots = \beta_{\ell n}$, for $\ell = 2, \ldots, L$ in (16.72)):

$$y_{jt} = \beta_{1j} + \sum_{\ell=2}^{L} \beta_\ell x_{\ell jt} + u_{jt}, \quad t = 1, \ldots, T, \quad j = 1, \ldots, n. \quad (16.73)$$

3. VCP (Variance Components Pooling): under this method the slope parameters are fixed and common, but the intercepts vary randomly between the cross sections (see below).

4. RCR (Random Coefficient Regression): under this method the slope parameters as well as the intercepts are random variables, i.e. all parameters are random or unsystematic around a mean (Swamy, 1970, 1971).

An other option is to pool the data for some *variables* ("partial pooling": Bemmaor, Franses, Kippers, 1999) or over some *cross sections* which are "homogenous" ("fuzzy pooling": Ramaswamy, DeSarbo, Reibstein, Robinson, 1993).

There are only a few known applications of RCR in marketing.[42] An appealing extension is to expand RCR so that the cross sections can differ systematically and randomly in the parameters. In this manner Wittink (1977) allows for some parameter heterogeneity but to a much smaller extent than occurs if each cross section has unique and fixed parameters, as assumed in (16.72). However, the estimation is not always feasible.[43]

Variance components pooling (VCP) is essentially a compromise between the first two options: pooling with OLS under complete homogeneity, and pooling with OLSDV. For VCP we specify:

$$y_{jt} = \sum_{\ell=2}^{L} \beta_\ell x_{\ell jt} + \varepsilon_{jt}, \quad t = 1, \ldots, T, \quad j = 1, \ldots, n \quad (16.74)$$

where

$$\varepsilon_{jt} = v_j + w_{jt}. \quad (16.75)$$

The disturbance term ε_{jt} has two components: a random intercept pertaining to cross section j (v_j) and a component w_{jt} representing the random influence of cross

---

42. See Bass, Wittink (1975), Wittink (1977).
43. See Leeflang, van Duijn (1982b).

section j and time period t. Under the following assumptions (see Maddala, 1971):

$$E(\varepsilon_{jt}) = E(v_j) = E(w_{jt}) = 0$$
$$Cov(v_i, w_{jt}) = 0, \qquad \text{for all } i, j = 1, \ldots, n, \quad t = 1, \ldots, T$$
$$Cov(v_i, v_j) = 0, \qquad i \neq j$$
$$Cov(w_{it}, w_{jt'}) = 0, \qquad i \neq j, \text{ and/or } t \neq t' \qquad (16.76)$$
$$Var(v_j) = \sigma_v^2$$
$$Var(w_{jt}) = \sigma_w^2$$

we obtain $Var(\varepsilon_{jt}) = (\sigma_v^2 + \sigma_w^2)$. The variance-covariance matrix of the disturbance vectors $E(\varepsilon_j \cdot \varepsilon_j') = \Omega$ has the following structure:

$$\Omega = \sigma^2 \begin{bmatrix} A & O & \cdots & & O \\ O & A & \cdots & & O \\ & & \cdot & & \\ \cdot & \cdot & & & \cdot \\ & & \cdot & & \\ & & \cdot & & \\ O & O & \cdots & & A \end{bmatrix} \qquad (16.77)$$

where

$$A = \text{a matrix of order } T \times T,$$
$$O = \text{a } T \times T \text{ matrix of zeros.}$$

$$A = \begin{bmatrix} 1 & \dot{p} & \cdots & \dot{p} \\ \dot{p} & 1 & \cdots & \dot{p} \\ & \cdot & & \\ \cdot & \cdot & & \cdot \\ & \cdot & & \\ \dot{p} & \dot{p} & \cdots & 1 \end{bmatrix}$$

and $\dot{p} = \sigma_v^2 / (\sigma_v^2 + \sigma_w^2), 0 < \dot{p} < 1$.

Pooling under complete homogeneity, and assuming that the intercept is zero, results in a special case of VCP for which $\dot{p} = 0$ (i.e. $\sigma_v^2 = 0$). The estimates from this special case are known as "total estimates" (since both cross-sectional and time-series variation is used). If $\sigma_w^2 \to 0$, $\dot{p} \to 1$, we obtain the OLSDV estimates of the slope coefficients. OLSDV ignores the cross-sectional variation for parametric estimation, and the results are referred to as "within estimates". The VCP estimator attempts to strike a balance between these extreme approaches by allowing the data to determine the value of $\dot{p}$.

For the estimation of σ_v^2 and σ_w^2, Nerlove (1971) proposes a two-step procedure. The first step is based on the OLSDV-estimates:

$$\hat{\sigma}_v^2 = \sum_{j=1}^{n} \frac{\left(\hat{\beta}_{1j} - \sum_{j=1}^{n} \hat{\beta}_{1j}/n \right)^2}{n} \qquad (16.78)$$

$$\hat{\sigma}_w^2 = \frac{\sum_{j=1}^n \sum_{t=1}^T \hat{\varepsilon}_{jt}^2}{(nT - L)}. \tag{16.79}$$

These estimates result in $\hat{p} = \hat{\sigma}_v^2/(\hat{\sigma}_v^2 + \hat{\sigma}_w^2)$. After substituting these values in Ω, the variance components estimates can be obtained by Generalized Least Squares (see Section 16.3). For more detail, see Nerlove (1971), Maddala (1971), Bass and Wittink (1975), Leeflang and van Duijn (1982b).

We now return to the hypothesis of parameter homogeneity: $\beta_i = \beta_j$ for all $i \neq j$, where β_i, β_j are vectors of parameters as in (16.69). The classical test is often referred to as the Chow test.[44] The Chow-test, is an F-test with degrees of freedom v_1 and v_2:

$$F_{v_1, v_2} \sim \frac{(RSS_1 - RSS_2)/v_1}{RSS_2/v_2} \tag{16.80}$$

where

RSS_1 = residual sum of squares of the pooled regression (16.70),

RSS_2 = the sum of the residual sum of squares from the separate regressions (16.69),

v_1 = difference in degrees of freedom between the pooled regression and the separate regressions,

v_2 = total degrees of freedom unused from the separate regressions.

If the null hypothesis of homogeneity is not rejected, pooling the observations is statistically justified. For (16.80) the degrees of freedom are:

$$v_1 = (nT - L) - n(T - L) = (n - 1)L \tag{16.81}$$

and

$$v_2 = n(T - L). \tag{16.82}$$

If pooling all data and assuming homogeneity of all parameters is rejected, we may want to compare the estimation of separate parameter vectors (16.72) with OLSDV (16.73).

A comparison of OLSDV against the estimation of separate parameter vectors results in the following degrees of freedom for the numerator in (16.80):

$$v_1 = (nT - n - L + 1) - n(T - L) = (n - 1)(L - 1) \tag{16.83}$$

In this case, RSS_1 is the residual sum of squares of OLSDV (16.73).

---

44. Chow (1960), Fisher (1970).

Table 16.3 Parameter estimates for the model of regional lager beer purchases.

Region	Intercept	d	a	$\tilde{p}$	Inc	temp	R_a^2	D.W.	RSS
I	111.16	-6.18	0.08	-6.30	-2.72	-0.01	0.913	1.73	1.20
		$(2.89)^a$	(2.75)	(1.21)	(1.71)	(0.22)			
II	29.03	-0.58	0.13	-6.58	-0.69	0.05	0.906	2.56	0.76
		(1.03)	(4.10)	(1.55)	(0.49)	(2.80)			
III	0.19	-0.12	0.06	-0.89	0.75	0.07	0.744	2.66	1.92
		(0.10)	(2.38)	(0.19)	(0.22)	(2.80)			
IV	-58.59	1.56	0.07	-9.36	4.49	0.07	0.754	2.42	1.16
		(1.93)	(2.70)	(2.44)	(1.33)	(4.07)			
V	23.30	0.41	0.07	-14.40	-0.90	0.06	0.427	1.73	3.98
		(0.68)	(2.04)	(1.25)	(0.22)	(1.46)			

^{a} (absolute) t-values in parentheses.

Source: Leeflang, van Duijn (1982a, p. 5).

We show the application of pooling methods and tests on beer category data in the Netherlands.[45] The market consists of five regions. In each region, demand is a function of marketing instruments and environmental variables defined for the region. Importantly, there exist large differences in beer drinking behavior between the regions. The criterion variable is:

q_{jt} = liters (1 liter $\doteq$ 0.28 gallon) of lager beer purchased per capita (residents 15 years and older) $\times$ 10,000 in region j, period t.

The predictor variables are:

d_{jt} = number of retail outlets selling beer per capita $\times$ 10,000 in region j in period t,

a_{jt} = number of subscriptions per capita to magazines and newspapers with beer advertising, in region j and period t,

$\tilde{p}_{jt}$ = $\dfrac{p_{jt}}{PI_t}$ = average retail price per liter in region j in period t, deflated by the cost-of-living index in t (PI_t),

Inc_{jt} = real income per capita $\times$ 10,000 in region j and period t,

$temp_{jt}$ = average daytime temperature in region j in period t.[46]

We show OLS estimates for a model that is linear in the parameters and in the variables along with absolute values of the t-statistic for the slope coefficients, the ad-

45. See Leeflang, van Duijn (1982a, 1982b).
46. For more detail on variable definitions, see Leeflang, van Duijn (1982a).

Table 16.4 OLSDV slope coefficients for the model of regional lager beer purchases.

d	a	$\tilde{p}$	Inc	$temp$	R_a^2	RSS
0.68	0.06	-5.10	2.13	0.06	0.920	13.47
(5.23)	(5.40)	(2.27)	(5.44)	(5.32)		

Source: Leeflang, van Duijn (1982b, p. 68).

justed coefficients of determination R_a^2, values of the Durbin-Watson statistic (D.W.) and the residual sum of squares (RSS) in Table 16.3.

For each region the sample data consist of $T = 16$ quarterly observations. The results are poor. For example, the slope coefficient for d, distribution, often has the wrong sign (significant in region I). In all other regions, except perhaps region IV, distribution has a nonsignificant slope. This is largely due to the fact that the distribution variable has only a small amount of variation over time. Price and income are similarly rarely significant (and these variables also contain little variation over time). The only predictor variables that perform reasonably well are advertising and temperature. The advertising effect is always significant with the expected sign, while temperature only fails to show an effect in region I, and to a lesser extent, in region V. Since the cross-sectional variation is much greater than the time-series variation for many predictors, pooling will lead to statistically more reliable parameter estimates, derived from a wider space of variation.

To explore the insights obtainable from pooling the data, OLS, OLSDV and VCP were used on the combined data. The Chow test (16.80) is used to evaluate the null hypothesis of *homogeneity in all parameters, including the intercepts*. The calculated F-value is 8.76 which is highly significant. Thus, there is no justification to employ the parameter estimates obtained from OLS applied to (16.70).

We next use the Chow test to evaluate the null hypothesis of *equal slope parameters* for the five regions, but *different intercepts*. As in the previous statistic, the model, OLSDV in this case (16.73), is compared with the equivalent of five separate regressions (16.69). In this case the calculated F-value is 1.23 which is not significant. Based on this, we have statistical justification to rely on the OLSDV result. On the other hand, the test of the VCP model against the use of separate regressions for the regions shows a calculated F-value of 17.8 which is highly significant. Thus, the assumption of random intercepts as specified in the VCP model is also not justified.

Importantly, these tests lead to the conclusion that it is acceptable to assume homogeneity in the slope parameters. In other words, the five regions may be assumed to be alike in the sensitivity of beer purchases to distribution, advertising, price, income and weather. And although this result is based on pooling time-series data from five cross sections, the slope parameter estimates are based entirely on the time-series variation. This is because the indicator variables that allow for unique, fixed intercepts absorb the average differences in beer purchases between the regions. We show the

OLSDV result in Table 16.4.

We note that R_a^2 for the OLSDV model is higher than each of the R_a^2 values for the models estimated separately for each region. This is possible because the amount of variation in the criterion variable when the data are pooled is more than the sum of the corresponding regions. Specifically this amount of variation for the pooled model includes the average differences between the regions and these average differences are captured by the indicator variables for the regions. Importantly, we should not prefer the OLSDV model over the separate regressions merely because its R_a^2 value exceeds the value for each of the separate regression models. For example, in this application, the variance of the residuals for OLSDV is about the same as the average residual variance for the five separate regression results reported in Table 16.3.

Wittink (1977) allowed for systematic and random variation in parameters estimated for a market share model representing one brand. For region j the model is:

$$y_{jt} = \sum_{\ell=1}^{L} \beta_{\ell j} x_{\ell jt} + u_{jt}, \quad j = 1, \ldots, n, \quad t = 1, \ldots, T \tag{16.84}$$

where

$y_{jt} = $ the criterion variable for region j, time period t,

$x_{\ell jt} = $ the ℓ-th predictor variable for region j, time period t.

Systematic and random differences in the parameters are accommodated through the specification:

$$\beta_{\ell j} = \sum_{k=1}^{K} \gamma_k z_{\ell jk} + v_{\ell j}, \quad j = 1, \ldots, n, \quad \ell = 1, \ldots, L \tag{16.85}$$

where

$z_{\ell jk} = $ the (average) value for the k-th predictor variable in region j (to explain cross-sectional variation in parameter $\beta_{\ell j}$),

$v_{\ell j} = $ a disturbance term.

In an application, the differences between unique parameter estimates (from applying OLS separately to each region) and the corresponding estimates from (16.85) were quite large. One advantage of accommodating systematic differences through (16.85) is that it produces less variation in parameter estimates across the regions than exists in the separately estimated regressions. Another advantage is that one obtains a (possible) explanation for differences in parameters across the regions. For example, Wittink allowed the own-brand price elasticity to depend on advertising for the brand (specifically, the price elasticity was more negative in regions in which the brand had a higher advertising share).

16.3 Generalized Least Squares

OLS estimation is based on restrictive assumptions about the disturbance term. We discuss procedures, known as Generalized Least Squares-(GLS)-methods, that accommodate more general disturbance characteristics in this section. Specifically in GLS we relax at least one of the two assumptions specified in (16.22) and (16.23). Consider again the system of relations (16.71):

$$Y = X\beta + u$$

where all variables are defined as in Section 16.2. Thus we have $nT = M$ observations of time series and cross section data, and we assume that β is a vector of homogeneous response parameters. The variance-covariance matrix of the disturbances is now defined as:

$$E(uu') = \Omega \qquad (16.86)$$

where

$$\Omega = \begin{bmatrix} \omega_{11} & \cdots & \omega_{1M} \\ \vdots & & \\ \omega_{M1} & \cdots & \omega_{MM} \end{bmatrix} = \sigma^2 \Omega^*$$

which is a positive definite symmetric $M \times M$ matrix with full rank M, and where the ω_{ij} are the covariances of the disturbances. We can obtain an expression for the generalized least squares estimator of β in (16.71) as follows:

Let the matrix V be a nonsingular $nT \times nT = M \times M$ matrix, such that:[47]

$$V'V = \Omega^{*-1} \text{ or } (V'V)^{-1} = \Omega^*. \qquad (16.87)$$

We premultiply both sides of (16.71) by V:

$$Vy = VX\beta + Vu. \qquad (16.88)$$

The variance-covariance matrix of the disturbances (Vu) of (16.88) is:

$$E[(Vu)(Vu)'] = \sigma^2 V\Omega^* V'. \qquad (16.89)$$

Substituting (16.87) in (16.89) we obtain:

$$E[(Vu)(Vu)'] = \sigma^2 I. \qquad (16.90)$$

This shows that if we transform the variables by the V-matrix in (16.88), the disturbance terms satisfy the error-term assumptions contained in (16.22) and (16.23).

---

47. Since Ω, and thus Ω^*, is symmetric and positive definite, so are Ω^{-1} and Ω^{*-1}, and hence a matrix V satisfying (16.87) exists. See Theil (1971, p. 238).

Thus, the OLS-method could be applied to (16.88). The Generalized Least Squares estimator[48] is:

$$\hat{\beta} = (X'\Omega^{*-1}X)^{-1}X'\Omega^{*-1}Y \tag{16.91}$$

which can also be written as:

$$\hat{\beta} = (X'\Omega^{-1}X)^{-1}X'\Omega^{-1}Y \tag{16.92}$$

since $\Omega = \sigma^2\Omega^*$. This model and estimation method are "generalized" because other models can be obtained as special cases. The ordinary least squares estimator is one such special case in which $\Omega = \sigma^2 I$. We discuss other special cases below. The variance-covariance matrix of the GLS-estimator $\hat{\beta}$ is:

$$Var(\hat{\beta}) = (X'\Omega^{-1}X)^{-1} = \sigma^2(X'\Omega^{*-1}X)^{-1}. \tag{16.93}$$

If Ω is unknown, as it is in empirical work, we replace Ω by $\hat{\Omega}$ and use an Estimated Generalized Least Squares (EGLS) estimator (also called Feasible Generalized Least Squares (FGLS) estimator). This estimator is usually a two-stage estimator. In the first stage, the ordinary least squares estimates are used to define residuals, and these residuals are used to estimate Ω. This estimate of Ω is used in the second stage to obtain the EGLS estimator denoted by $\hat{\hat{\beta}}$.[49]

We now consider one special case in which the disturbances are *heteroscedastic*, often encountered when cross-sectional data are used. Assuming the heteroscedasticity is such that each cross section has a unique disturbance variance, we have:

$$E(uu') = \Omega = \begin{bmatrix} \sigma_1^2 I & O & \cdots & O \\ O & \sigma_2^2 I & \cdots & O \\ \vdots & & \ddots & \vdots \\ O & \cdots & & \sigma_n^2 I \end{bmatrix} \tag{16.94}$$

which is a diagonal matrix with σ_j^2, $j = 1, \ldots, n$ as diagonal elements. I is an identity matrix of order $T \times T$ and O is a $T \times T$ matrix with zeros. This special case of GLS is referred to as weighted least squares (WLS), because GLS can be interpreted as OLS applied to a transformed model (compare (16.35) in which the transformation involves a predictor variable) with variables:

$$\tilde{y}_{jt} = \frac{y_{jt}}{\sigma_j} \text{ and } \tilde{x}_{jt} = \frac{x_{jt}}{\sigma_j}. \tag{16.95}$$

The σ_j can be estimated by taking the square root of the unbiased estimator of the variance of the OLS-residuals:

$$\hat{\sigma}_j = \sqrt{\hat{\sigma}_j^2} = \sqrt{\sum_{t=1}^{T} \hat{u}_{jt}^2/(T-L)} \quad \text{for each } j = 1, \ldots, n. \tag{16.96}$$

---

48. First derived by Aitken (1935).
49. Judge et al. (1985, p. 171).

We note that in (16.94) and hence in (16.96) it is assumed that the variances are constant within each cross-sectional unit $j = 1, \ldots, n$.

We refer to (16.34) to emphasize that there are other opportunities for the accommodation of heteroscedasticity. In (16.34) the variance of the disturbance increases with the squared value of a predictor variable.[50] Prais and Houthakker (1955) suggested a variance proportional to the squared expected value of the criterion variable. To obtain estimated variances they divided the sample in m classes, and computed the squared average value of the criterion variable in each class.[51]

A second special case of GLS is typical for time-series data. In this case, the covariances, $Cov(u_{jt}, u_{jt'})$, $t \neq t'$ differ from zero (but we assume that the disturbances are homoscedastic). We consider the case that the disturbances are generated by a first-order autoregressive scheme, also called a first-order stationary (Markov) scheme (compare (16.37)):

$$u_{jt} = \rho_j u_{j,t-1} + \varepsilon_{jt}, \quad t = 1, \ldots, T, |\rho_j| < 1 \tag{16.97}$$

where the ε_{jt} are independent normally distributed random variables with mean zero, and variance equal to $\sigma_{\varepsilon_j}^2 = \sigma_\varepsilon^2$. We also assume ε_{jt} to be independent of $u_{j,t-1}$. For simplicity let $\rho_j = \rho$ (we relax this assumption below). By successive substitution for $u_{j,t-1}, u_{j,t-2}$ in (16.97) we obtain:

$$u_{jt} = \rho^s u_{j,t-s} + \rho^{s-1}\varepsilon_{j,t-s-1} + \ldots + \rho^2 \varepsilon_{j,t-2} + \rho\varepsilon_{j,t-1} + \varepsilon_{jt}. \tag{16.98}$$

After multiplying both sides of (16.98) by $u_{j,t-s}$ and taking expectations, we have:

$$\begin{aligned} E(u_{jt}, u_{j,t-s}) &= \rho^s E(u_{j,t-s}, u_{j,t-s}) + \rho^{s-1} E(\varepsilon_{j,t-s-1}, u_{j,t-s}) + \cdots \\ &\quad + \rho^2 E(\varepsilon_{j,t-2}, u_{j,t-s}) + \rho E(\varepsilon_{j,t-1}, u_{j,t-s}) + E(\varepsilon_{jt}, u_{j,t-s}) \\ &= \rho^s \sigma_u^2 \end{aligned} \tag{16.99}$$

since the ε_{jt} are independent of $u_{j,t-1}$ and u_{jt} has variance σ_u^2.[52] We also assume that $Cov(u_{jt}, u_{it'}) = 0$ for $j \neq i, i, j = 1, \ldots, n$.

The variance-covariance matrix Ω now has the following form:

$$E(uu') = \Omega = \sigma^2 \begin{bmatrix} P & O & \cdots & O \\ O & P & \cdots & O \\ \vdots & \vdots & & \vdots \\ O & O & \cdots & P \end{bmatrix} \tag{16.100}$$

---

50. See Judge et al. (1985, pp. 439-441) for a more general expression.
51. See Kmenta (1971, pp. 256-264) for other possibilities.
52. It can be shown that $\sigma_u^2 = \frac{\sigma_\varepsilon^2}{(1-\rho^2)}$.

where $P = $ a $T \times T$ matrix, $P = \begin{bmatrix} 1 & \rho & \rho^2 & \cdots & \rho^{T-1} \\ \rho & 1 & \rho & \cdots & \rho^{T-2} \\ \vdots & \vdots & \vdots & & \vdots \\ \rho^{T-1} & \rho^{T-2} & \rho^{T-3} & \cdots & 1 \end{bmatrix}$ and

O is a $T \times T$ matrix with zeros.

The elements of the matrix P can be estimated as follows:[53]

$$\hat{\rho} = \frac{\sum_{j=1}^{n} \sum_{t=2}^{T} \hat{u}_{jt} \hat{u}_{j,t-1}}{\sum_{j=1}^{n} \sum_{t=2}^{T} \hat{u}_{j,t-1}^2} \tag{16.101}$$

where the $\hat{u}_{jt}$ are the OLS-residuals. Then by substituting $\hat{\rho}$ for ρ in (16.100), we obtain $\widehat{P}$ and $\widehat{\Omega}$, and we use the EGLS estimator.

We now relax the assumption that ρ_j is ρ, since it is likely that the autocorrelation parameter differs over cross sectional units. Thus:

$$u_{jt} = \rho_j u_{j,t-s} + \varepsilon_{jt}, \quad t = 1, \ldots, T \text{ for each } j = 1, \ldots, n. \tag{16.102}$$

Given (16.102), the variance-covariance matrix is now:

$$E(uu') = \Omega = \sigma^2 \begin{bmatrix} P_1 & O & \cdots & O \\ O & P_2 & \cdots & O \\ \vdots & \vdots & & \vdots \\ O & O & \cdots & P_n \end{bmatrix} \tag{16.103}$$

where

$$P_j = \begin{bmatrix} 1 & \rho_j & \rho_j^2 & \cdots & \rho_j^{T-1} \\ \rho_j & 1 & \rho_j & \cdots & \rho_j^{T-2} \\ \vdots & \vdots & \vdots & & \vdots \\ \rho_j^{T-1} & \rho_j^{T-2} & \rho_j^{T-3} & \cdots & 1 \end{bmatrix}$$

and O is a $T \times T$ matrix of zeros.

The elements of P_j can now be estimated separately for each cross section:

$$\hat{\rho}_j = \frac{\sum_{t=2}^{T} \hat{u}_{jt} \hat{u}_{j,t-1}}{\sum_{t=2}^{T} \hat{u}_{j,t-1}^2} \quad \text{for each } j = 1, \ldots, n. \tag{16.104}$$

To demonstrate (again)[54] that one can also apply OLS to suitably transformed variables, in the presence of autocorrelation, we return to (16.7):

$$y_{jt} = \beta_{1j} x_{1jt} + \ldots + \beta_{Lj} x_{Ljt} + u_{jt}, \quad t = 1, \ldots, T, \quad j = 1, \ldots, n. \tag{16.105}$$

---

53. This is a least squares estimate of ρ. It differs slightly from the maximum likelihood estimator. See Judge et al. (1985, pp. 286-287) for other estimators.
54. See also equation (16.43).

By lagging this expression one period, and premultiplying by ρ_j, we obtain:

$$\rho_j y_{j,t-1} = \rho_j \beta_{1j} x_{1j,t-1} + \ldots + \rho_j \beta_{Lj} x_{Lj,t-1} + \rho_j u_{j,t-1}. \tag{16.106}$$

Subtracting (16.106) from (16.105) and using (16.97) we get:

$$y_{jt} - \rho_j y_{j,t-1} = \beta_{1j}(x_{1jt} - \rho_j x_{1j,t-1}) + \ldots + \beta_{Lj}(x_{Ljt} - \rho_j x_{Lj,t-1}) + \varepsilon_{jt}$$
$$\text{for } t = 2, \ldots, T \tag{16.107a}$$

and

$$\sqrt{1 - \rho_j^2}\, y_{j,1} = \beta_{1j}\sqrt{1 - \rho_j^2}\, x_{1j,1} + \ldots + \beta_{Lj}\sqrt{1 - \rho_j^2}\, x_{Lj,1} + \varepsilon_{j1}. \tag{16.107b}$$

If $\hat{\rho}_j$ is computed as in (16.104), where the residuals are obtained by applying OLS to (16.105), and $\hat{\rho}_j$ is substituted for ρ_j in (16.107), OLS can be applied to the transformed variables. We note that if x_{1jt} is a column of ones, for $j = 1, \ldots, n$, this procedure gives problems. One solution is to apply Nonlinear Least Squares (NLS) as proposed by Hildreth and Lu (1960).[55]

We now consider the model structure (16.71), but allow the disturbances to be simultaneously cross-sectionally heteroscedastic and time-wise autoregressive. We assume that $Cov(u_{jt}, u_{it}) = 0$, for $j \neq i$ and for all t (but relax this assumption below). The variance-covariance matrix can then be written as:

$$E(uu') = \Omega = \begin{bmatrix} \sigma_1^2 P_1 & O & \cdots & O \\ O & \sigma_2^2 P_2 & \cdots & O \\ \vdots & \vdots & & \vdots \\ O & O & \cdots & \sigma_n^2 P_n \end{bmatrix} \tag{16.108}$$

which is a $nT \times nT$ matrix, where P_j, $j = 1, \ldots, n$ is defined in (16.103) and O is a $T \times T$ matrix of zeros.

To obtain estimates of the parameters in (16.108), we proceed in several steps.[56] First OLS is applied to all nT observations in (16.71) from which residuals $\hat{u}_{jt}$ are obtained. We then estimate the autocorrelation parameters and incorporate these estimates in a manner such as outlined above. Next we estimate the model that now accounts for (first-order) autocorrelated disturbances, and estimate the error variance[57] for each cross section. In this case the relation between the estimated variance of the autocorrelated disturbance u_{jt} and the variance of the error term ε_{jt} (16.97) is:

$$\hat{\sigma}_{u_j}^2 = \frac{\sigma_{\varepsilon j}^2}{1 - \hat{\rho}_j^2}. \tag{16.109}$$

---

55. See also Cochrane and Orcutt (1949).
56. See, for example, Kmenta (1971, pp. 510-511).
57. See Theil and Schweitzer (1961) for an example.

Next we relax the assumption that the disturbances are independent between the cross sections, i.e. the assumption that $Cov(u_{jt}, u_{it}) = 0$ for $i \neq j$. We also allow the parameter vectors associated with the predictor variables to be heterogeneous:

$$Y_j = X_j\beta_j + u_j, \quad \text{for each } j = 1, \ldots, n.$$

The system of equations is:[58]

$$
\begin{bmatrix} Y_1 \\ Y_2 \\ \vdots \\ Y_n \end{bmatrix} = \begin{bmatrix} X_1 & O & \cdots & O \\ O & X_2 & \cdots & O \\ \vdots & \vdots & & \vdots \\ O & O & \cdots & X_n \end{bmatrix} \begin{bmatrix} \beta_1 \\ \beta_2 \\ \vdots \\ \beta_n \end{bmatrix} + \begin{bmatrix} u_1 \\ u_2 \\ \vdots \\ u_n \end{bmatrix} \quad \text{or}
\tag{16.110a}
$$

$$Y = Z\beta + u \tag{16.110b}$$

where

Y	$= \text{a } nT \times 1 \text{ vector,}$
Z	$= \text{a } nT \times Ln \text{ matrix,}$
β	$= \text{a } Ln \times 1 \text{ vector,}$
u	$= \text{a } nT \times 1 \text{ vector.}$

We assume

$$E(u_{jt}^2) = \sigma_j^2 \text{ for all } t, \tag{16.111}$$

$$Cov(u_{jt}, u_{is}) = 0 \text{ for all } t \neq s \text{ and all } i \text{ and } j, \tag{16.112}$$

(this assumption of no autocorrelation is relaxed shortly),

$$Cov(u_{jt}, u_{it}) = \sigma_{ji} \text{ for all } t \ (= \sigma_i^2 \text{ if } j = i) \tag{16.113}$$

which implies there is *contemporaneous* correlation between the disturbances for different cross sections. Using (16.111) through (16.113), we obtain:

$$
E(uu') = \Omega = \begin{bmatrix} \sigma_1^2 I & \sigma_{12}I & \cdots & \sigma_{1n}I \\ \sigma_{21}I & \sigma_2^2 I & \cdots & \sigma_{2n}I \\ \vdots & \vdots & & \vdots \\ \sigma_{n1}I & \sigma_{n2}I & \cdots & \sigma_n^2 I \end{bmatrix}
\tag{16.114}
$$

and

$$\hat{\beta} = (Z'\Omega^{-1}Z)^{-1}Z'\Omega^{-1}Y. \tag{16.115}$$

---

58. Because the n sets of equations in (16.110a) do not seem to be related, one refers to this structure as "seemingly unrelated regressions". See Zellner (1962).

Zellner (1962) proposed the following estimation procedure.[59] First estimate (16.110b) by OLS. Then estimate the elements of Ω from the OLS residuals:

$$\hat{\sigma}_{ji} = \frac{\sum_{t=1}^{T} \hat{u}_{jt}\hat{u}_{it}}{T - L} \text{ , for all } i \text{ and } j \tag{16.116}$$

where $\hat{\sigma}_{ii} = \hat{\sigma}_i^2$. Next, the EGLS estimator is created by substituting $\hat{\sigma}_{ji}$ for σ_{ji} in (16.114). By iterating this process it is possible to obtain better estimates of σ_{ji} (i.e. when the process converges).

We note that in one application, the $\hat{\sigma}_{ji}$ values were used to find explanations for the nature of competition between brands i and j.[60] This is conceptually akin to the idea that in empirical research the presence of autocorrelated (or contemporaneously correlated) residuals should often be interpreted as indicating that the model is misspecified. The use of Generalized Least Squares to accommodate such systematic patterns in the disturbances will not result in improved slope parameter estimates if the patterns are due to, for example, missing predictor variables or incorrect functional forms. We emphasize that model builders must be convinced that they have used the best possible model specification. And model builders should have a logical, substantively meaningful reason for the disturbances to be correlated when the model is otherwise assumed to be complete.

One example of a logical reason for contemporaneously correlated disturbances is provided by Wittink (1977). In equation (16.85) the parameters that are unique for each cross section are explained in part by other predictor variables which differ only cross sectionally. The estimation of this equation is based on estimated parameters as the criterion variable. Given that for each cross section a vector of parameters is obtained, it is natural to use the estimated variance-covariance matrix of these parameter estimates. If the estimated variances differ significantly cross sectionally for a given parameter, heteroscedasticity is accommodated. Similarly, the estimated covariances provide a reason why the disturbances are contemporaneously correlated across the equations for the parameters $\beta_{\ell j}, \ell = 1, \ldots, L$.

Finally, we show the structure of the variance-covariance matrix of the disturbances in case of contemporaneous correlation, heteroscedasticity and autocorrelation, assuming the autoregressive scheme described in (16.102). We then have:

$$E(uu') = \Omega = \begin{bmatrix} \sigma_1^2 P_{11} & \sigma_{12} P_{12} & \cdots & \sigma_{1n} P_{1n} \\ \sigma_{21} P_{21} & \sigma_2^2 P_{22} & \cdots & \sigma_{2n} P_{2n} \\ \vdots & \vdots & & \vdots \\ \sigma_{n1} P_{n1} & \sigma_{n2} P_{n2} & \cdots & \sigma_n^2 P_{nn} \end{bmatrix} \tag{16.117}$$

where

59. See Zellner (1962), Kmenta (1971, pp. 517-519). See also Leeflang (1974, pp. 124-127) and Leeflang (1977b).
60. See Clarke (1973). For an asymmetric, nonhierarchical market share model, Carpenter, Cooper, Hanssens and Midgley (1988) use the $\hat{\sigma}_{ji}$ values to identify potential cross-effects.

$$P_{ij} = \begin{bmatrix} 1 & \rho_j & \cdots & \rho_j^{T-1} \\ \rho_i & 1 & \cdots & \rho_j^{T-2} \\ \vdots & \vdots & & \vdots \\ \rho_i^{T-1} & \rho_i^{T-2} & \cdots & 1 \end{bmatrix} \qquad i, j = 1, \ldots, n.$$

In sum-constrained models $\sum_{j=1}^{n} \hat{u}_{jt} = 0$ for each $t = 1, 2, \ldots, T$. In that case there is by definition contemporaneous correlation of the disturbances in these models. As a consequence, however, the contemporaneous variance-covariance matrix (16.114) is singular, because the elements of each row total zero:

$$\sum_{i=1}^{n} \hat{\sigma}_{ji} = \frac{\sum_{i=1}^{n} \sum_{t=1}^{T} \hat{u}_{jt} \hat{u}_{it}}{T - L} = \frac{\sum_{t=1}^{T} \hat{u}_{jt} \sum_{i=1}^{n} \hat{u}_{it}}{T - L} = 0. \tag{16.118}$$

To avoid singularity, one equation is deleted. If the matrix Ω is *known*, the resulting parameter estimates are invariant to which equation (which cross-sectional unit) is deleted.[61] When the variance-covariance matrix is *unknown*, as usually is the case, the parameter estimates depend on which equation is deleted.[62] However, this problem can be resolved by imposing restrictions on the contemporaneous variance-covariance matrix.[63] We note that robustness may generally be lost if GLS estimation methods are used; see Leeflang, Reuyl (1979).

16.4 Simultaneous equations

Model building in marketing can involve:

- a single equation;
- multiple equations (such as in the case of multiple brands);
- simultaneous equations.

So far we have focused on single- and multiple-equation models. Simultaneous equations represent a special case of multiple equations. We use a system of simultaneous equations if more than one equation is needed to properly estimate relations. In such a system there are multiple *endogenous* variables which are the variables to be explained by the equations. The remaining variables are predetermined, consisting of *exogenous* and (potentially) lagged endogenous variables. Exogenous variables are taken as given, and are similar to the predictor variables used in a single-equation model.

   The concept of simultaneity refers to the idea that the endogenous variables are "explained" jointly and simultaneously by the predetermined variables and the disturbances. Importantly, an endogenous variable may be used both to explain other

---

61. See McGuire, Farley, Lucas, Ring (1968). See also Hanssens, Parsons, Schultz (1990, p. 89).
62. See Reuyl (1982), Leeflang, Reuyl (1983, 1984b) and Gaver, Horsky, Narasimhan (1988).
63. See McGuire et al. (1968), De Boer, Harkema (1983), Leeflang, Reuyl (1983), De Boer, Harkema, Soede (1996). See also Bultez, Naert (1973, 1975) and Nakanishi, Cooper (1974).

variables and to be explained, typically in different equations. As a result, such an endogenous variable cannot be stochastically independent of *all* disturbance terms. On the other hand, the predetermined variables may be assumed to be independent of the disturbances.

The need for special estimation methods for simultaneous equations derives especially from the violation of assumption 5 for the disturbances (Section 16.1.3) which states there is independence between the predictors $(x_{\ell jt})$ and the disturbances (u_{jt}). Thus, in essence the presence of an endogenous variable which has both an explanatory role and which is to be explained by the system is the reason for the violation of assumption 5.

We emphasize that there are other reasons why assumption 5 may be violated. For example, if a predictor variable is measured with error, we can analytically express the measured variable as a function of its true values and an error component. Having access only to the measured values for that variable for empirical analysis means that the measurement error gets included in the disturbance term in the equation. It is easy to demonstrate that under this condition the predictor variable is not independent of the disturbances. Thus, measurement error in a predictor variable also violates assumption 5.

We first illustrate the fundamental problem (a violation of assumption 5 with regard to the error term) caused by simultaneity in relationships. Consider a brand manager who faces a budget constraint that specifies a maximum of 10 percent of brand revenues in each period can be allocated to advertising expenditures for the brand (the manager faces some rebuke if more than 10 percent is spent). At the same time, the manager wants to spend the maximum amount possible because brand equity is assumed to be a positive function of advertising. Also, any positive difference between 10 percent and the actual percent is unavailable in future periods.

Under such conditions, the manager has strong incentives to allocate about 10 percent of expenditures to advertising every period. Due to various factors, both positive and negative deviations from exactly 10 percent can occur:

$$a_t = 0.1\, R_t + u_t \tag{16.119}$$

where

a_t = brand advertising expenditures in \$000,

R_t = brand revenues in \$000, and

u_t = an error term.

Simultaneously, the manager believes that advertising affects unit sales in the same period (we ignore for convenience the possibility of lagged effects). For simplicity of exposition, we assume a linear demand function:

$$q_t = \beta_0 + \beta_1 p_t + \beta_2 a_t + v_t \tag{16.120}$$

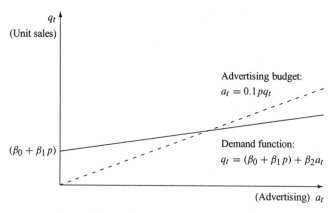

Figure 16.4 Relations between advertising and unit sales.

where

q_t = unit sales (in thousands of pounds),

p_t = price per unit in dollars, and

v_t = an error term.

We have two equations, and since $R_t = q_t \times p_t$, we also have two endogenous variables. One fundamental question is whether a_t is stochastically independent of v_t in (16.120). By substituting (16.120) into (16.119) we obtain:

$$a_t = 0.1(\beta_0 + \beta_1 p_t + \beta_2 a_t + v_t)p_t + u_t \qquad (16.121)$$
$$= 0.1\,\beta_0 p_t + 0.1\,\beta_1 p_t^2 + 0.1\,\beta_2 a_t\, p_t + 0.1\, v_t\, p_t + u_t.$$

It is clear from (16.121) that a_t depends on v_t. Thus, the error-term assumptions required for single-equation estimation of (16.120) cannot be justified.

If we further assume $p_t = p$ for all t, then the systematic parts of (16.119) and (16.120) can be graphically shown to be as follows (given our interest in estimating how unit sales depends on advertising). In Figure 16.4 the advertising budget line goes through the origin, and has a slope equal to $0.1\,p$. The demand function has an intercept equal to $(\beta_0 + \beta_1 p)$ which we assume to be positive. The slope of this demand function is β_2. At, and close to, the intersection of these two lines the actual observations for q_t and a_t will occur, leaving virtually no room to estimate the demand function.

If price changes over time, the demand function will shift in a parallel fashion. At the same time a different advertising budget (broken) line is created. As a result, each possible price value has its own demand function and its own advertising budget line: see Figure 16.5. In Figure 16.5 we have two intersections: each one between an advertising budget line (both lines going through the origin), and a demand function (these functions being parallel) for different values of the price variable (p_1, p_2). Importantly, if we know the advertising budget restriction, and if price varies over time, we can estimate the effect of advertising on demand. If OLS is used only on the

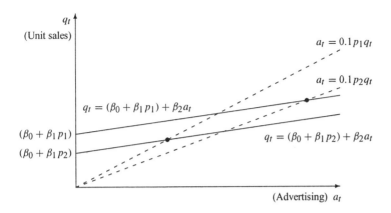

Figure 16.5 Relations between demand and advertising for different prices p_1 and p_2, where $p_2 > p_1$, $\beta_1 < 0$.

demand function, the estimated relation would be based on the intersections between the budget and demand equations. From Figure 16.5 we deduce that the estimated function would have a higher slope than the demand function based on advertising.

We note that in practice this set of equations will not exist. The advertising budget may well depend on revenue, but not in the restrictive sense posited here. And the demand function should accommodate nonlinear- and interactive effects for price and advertising.

In general we can specify a system of equations as follows:

$$Y\Gamma + XB = E \tag{16.122}$$

where

Y = a $T \times m$ matrix containing the endogenous variables,

Γ = a $m \times m$ matrix of parameters (and constraints),

X = a $T \times L$ matrix with exogenous variables and a column of ones,

B = a $L \times m$ matrix of parameters (and constraints),

E = a $T \times m$ matrix of disturbances.

In the example above, $m = 2$ and $L = 2$. This general description makes it possible to consider a variety of possible conditions. For example, if Γ is diagonal, then none of the endogenous variables depends on other endogenous variables. This reduces the problem to one for which it is possible to estimate each equation separately (or treat it as a multiple equation problem if the disturbances are correlated across equations).

If Γ is triangular (for example, any endogenous variable depends only on other endogenous variables that exist in equations specified earlier), we have essentially recursive equations. For example, we could imagine a brand manager with a demand equation such as (16.120) but an advertising budget that does not depend on current brand revenues. The adequacy of single-equation estimation procedures is then determined by the lack of correlation between the disturbances across these two equations.

When Γ is neither diagonal nor triangular (as is the case in the example above), we need to use special estimation methods. The simplest and perhaps most popular one is the two-stage least squares method 2SLS. This method is a special case of the method of *instrumental variables* (IV) introduced in Section 16.1.4. IV was developed around the following "estimation strategy" (Greene, 1997, p. 288). Suppose that in the classical model (16.7) the variables $x_{\ell jt}$, $\ell = 1, \ldots, L$, are correlated with u_{jt}. And imagine that there exists a set of variables $z_{\ell jt}$, $\ell = 1, \ldots, L'$, where $L' \geq L$,[64] such that the $z_{\ell jt}$ are correlated with $x_{\ell jt}$ but *not* with u_{jt}. Then we can construct a consistent estimator $\beta'_j = (\beta_{1j}, \ldots, \beta_{Lj})$ based on the assumed relationships among $x_{\ell jt}$, $z_{\ell jt}$ and u_{jt}. In this manner the set of original regressors is *replaced* by a new set of regressors, known as instrumental variables, which are correlated with the stochastic regressors but uncorrelated with the disturbances.

A simple example of an instrumental variable is the variable $\hat{q}_t$ which replaces q_t in (16.120). To show how $\hat{q}_t$ (and $\hat{a}_t$) can be obtained, we first change (16.119) as follows:

$$a_t = \alpha_0 + \alpha_1 q_t + u_t. \tag{16.123}$$

We can now express both q_t and a_t as a function of p_t by substituting (16.120) into (16.123):

$$a_t = \frac{\alpha_0 + \alpha_1 \beta_0}{1 - \alpha_1 \beta_2} + \frac{\alpha_1 \beta_1}{1 - \alpha_1 \beta_2} p_t + \frac{\alpha_1 v_t + u_t}{1 - \alpha_1 \beta_2}. \tag{16.124}$$

Similarly, we substitute (16.123) into (16.120):

$$q_t = \frac{\beta_0 + \beta_2 \alpha_0}{1 - \alpha_1 \beta_2} + \frac{\beta_1}{1 - \alpha_1 \beta_2} p_t + \frac{\beta_2 u_t + v_t}{1 - \alpha_1 \beta_2}. \tag{16.125}$$

These two equations show how, given the original equations (16.120) and (16.123), the endogenous variables can be expressed in terms of exogenous variables only. The resulting equations, (16.124) and (16.125), are reduced-form equations.

The IV method would use $\hat{a}_t$ and $\hat{q}_t$, obtained from the simple, linear regressions $a_t = f(p_t)$ and $q_t = g(p_t)$, and use these variables in (16.120) and (16.123) as follows:

$$q_t = \beta_0 + \beta_1 p_t + \beta_2 \hat{a}_t + v_t \tag{16.126}$$

$$a_t = \alpha_0 + \alpha_1 \hat{q}_t + u_t. \tag{16.127}$$

---

64. Often $L' = L$.

By assumption, i.e. if p_t is independent of v_t, it follows that $\hat{a}_t$ is independent of v_t. However, it should be obvious that p_t and $\hat{a}_t$ are perfectly correlated, since $\hat{a}_t$ is a linear function of p_t (see (16.124)). This means that the system of equations is underidentified: there are more parameters in (16.120) and (16.123) than independent estimates obtainable from the data.

This problem of underidentification is also evident if we attempt to use Indirect Least Squares (ILS). ILS does not use $\hat{a}_t$ and $\hat{q}_t$, generated by estimating (16.124) and (16.125), but focuses on the parameter estimates in these equations:

$$\hat{a}_t = a_1 + a_2 p_t \tag{16.128}$$

$$\hat{q}_t = b_1 + b_2 p_t. \tag{16.129}$$

It is easy to see that it is impossible to obtain five unique parameter estimates (α_0, α_1, β_0, β_1, β_2) from four coefficients (a_1, a_2, b_1, b_2). Interestingly, we can obtain $\hat{\alpha}_1 = a_2/b_2$. However, our primary interest is in obtaining good estimates of the demand equation, and the underidentification problem is located there. This problem is evident from the *order condition* for identifiability:

> *"the number of exogenous variables excluded from an equation must be at least equal to the number of endogenous variables included in the equation"*
> (Greene, 1997, p. 727).

For (16.120) there is one endogenous variable at the right-hand side, but the only exogenous variable in the system is included. Thus, given that no exogenous variable is excluded from that equation, the order condition is not satisfied, and (16.120) is not identifiable. On the other hand, for (16.123) the order condition is satisfied: there is one (right-hand side) endogenous variable (q_t), and one exogenous variable is excluded from that equation (p_t).

The order condition is necessary but not sufficient for identifiability. Sufficiency requires that the *rank condition* be satisfied. If there is exactly one solution for the parameters in (16.120) and (16.123) then the rank condition is satisfied.[65] From these conditions it should be clear that (16.123) needs an exogenous variable, and one different from p_t. Thus, to make (16.120) identifiable, we need to modify (16.123). Of course, this modification needs to be relevant to the problem. For example, if advertising is indeed only a function of demand in the same period, then there is no opportunity to obtain unique parameter estimates with desirable statistical properties for (16.120). On the other hand, if a_t partly depends on a_{t-1}, we can expand (16.123), and make (16.120) identifiable.[66] For examples of simultaneous-equation marketing models, estimated by 2SLS, see Farley, Leavitt (1968), Bass (1969a), Bass and Parsons (1969), Bass (1971), Cowling, Cubbin (1971), Parsons and Bass (1971),

---

65. See Greene (1997, pp. 727-730).
66. In that case we can employ IV, ILS and 2SLS as estimation methods. See Judge et al. (1985, pp. 595-596), Greene (1997, pp. 737-738).

Lambin, Naert and Bultez (1975), Lambin (1976), Albach (1979), Plat and Leeflang (1988).

We note that when model building in marketing was based on aggregated data, the simultaneity between sales and advertising was much more serious than it is today. For example, the advertising budget may be determined on an annual basis: as in (16.119) advertising expenditures may be restricted to 10 percent of revenues. However, if weekly data are available for the estimation of a demand equation, this restriction - the advertising budget equation - may have only a minor impact on the properties of the least-squares estimator for the demand equation. With the increasing availability of disaggregated data the advertising budget equation is virtually irrelevant. For example, scanner data allow model builders to estimate demand functions for individual items (such as a specific package size of a particular variety for a brand) from weekly data for individual stores. The advertising budget decision, instead, is often made at the brand level on an annual basis for a region covering many stores.

One of the assumptions of the 2SLS-method is that the disturbances of the different equations of the system are independent. We know from the discussion about seemingly unrelated regressions in Section 16.3 that parameter estimates of the system are inefficient if we do not account for contemporaneous correlations of the disturbances. An estimator that makes use of the cross-equation correlations of the disturbances is more efficient. The techniques that are generally used for joint estimation of the simultaneous system of relations include: three-stage least squares (3SLS), maximum likelihood (Section 16.6) and GMM (Generalized Method of Moments). Thus the 3SLS method includes the application of GLS to the system of structural relations.

Briefly, 3SLS works as follows. The estimator of the elements of the variance-covariance matrix of the disturbances Ω are obtained by first applying 2SLS on the set of simultaneous equations. The 2SLS residuals are then used to compute $\hat{\Omega}$ which allows 3SLS estimates to be obtained with $\hat{\Omega}$ and the "new regressors" $z_{1jt}, \ldots, z_{L'jt}$. It is also possible to iterate the 3SLS estimation method: I3SLS. For applications, see Schultz (1971), Houston (1977), Lancaster (1984), Carpenter (1987) and Tellis and Fornell (1988).[67] Carpenter studied competitive marketing strategies consisting of product quality levels, promotional expenditures and prices. Using a simultaneous equation model he examined the interrelations between these marketing instruments. For example he let prices and promotional spending be signals of product quality and allowed promotional spending to influence prices. A model of interrelations between marketing instruments requires the use of simultaneous equation estimation methods. Carpenter used 3SLS (and 2SLS) on a cross section of business-level PIMS data.[68] Tellis and Fornell (1988) used PIMS data to estimate the relation between advertising and product quality over the product life cycle.

I3SLS was employed by Lancaster (1984) to explore the relation between brand advertising and industry, brand and rival retail sales and market share. One might

---

67. See also Hanssens et al. (1990, p. 90).
68. See for information about the PIMS data base Buzzell, Gale (1987), Lilien, Kotler, Moorthy (1992, pp. 548-551).

wonder whether the use of simultaneous equation methods truly generates estimates that differ much from, say, OLS. Although there are examples of OLS estimates that are almost identical to the 2SLS/3SLS-ones,[69] the differences between estimates can be very large (Greene, 1997, p. 294, p. 760).

To conclude, we return to the IV method. We mentioned that the 2SLS- and 3SLS estimation methods are special cases of IV. To show this, we return to the system of relations (16.70):

$$Y = X\beta + u.$$

The IV method is used when the assumption $E(X'u) = 0$ is violated. The matrix X may be substituted by a matrix Z such that $E(Z'u) = 0$. Thus, every column of the new matrix Z is uncorrelated with u, and every linear combination of the columns of Z is uncorrelated with u. If Z has the same number of predictor variables as X, the IV estimator is:[70]

$$\hat{\beta} = (Z'X)^{-1}Z'Y. \tag{16.130}$$

Several options to choose an acceptable matrix Z can be found in the literature.[71] One approach is to choose L linear combinations of the columns of Z. Of all the different linear combinations of Z that we might choose, $\widehat{X}$ is the most efficient:

$$\widehat{X} = Z(Z'Z)^{-1}Z'X \tag{16.131}$$

which is a projection of the columns of X in the column space of Z. In this case Z can have (many) more variables than X. With this use of instrumental variables, $\widehat{X}$ derived from Z, we have

$$\begin{aligned}
\hat{\beta} &= (\widehat{X}'X)^{-1}\widehat{X}'Y \\
&= [X'Z(Z'Z)^{-1}Z'X]^{-1}X'Z(Z'Z)^{-1}Z'Y.
\end{aligned} \tag{16.132}$$

It can be shown[72] that this expression can also be written as:

$$\hat{\beta} = (\widehat{X}'\widehat{X})^{-1}\widehat{X}'Y. \tag{16.133}$$

Applications of IV methods can be found in empirical game theoretic models.[73] For example, the models of Gasmi, Laffont, Vuong (1992) and Kadiyali (1996) were estimated by IV methods. For further discussion about latent variables and errors-in-variables, relevant to simultaneous equation models, see Section 17.1.

16.5 Nonlinear estimation

In section 5.3.3 we show examples of intrinsically nonlinear models. We now discuss three approaches to estimate the parameters in these models; viz.:

---

69. See, for example, Schultz (1971).
70. See, for example, Greene (1997, p. 291).
71. See Greene (1997, Chapter 6), van der Ploeg (1997).
72. Greene (1997, p. 294).
73. See Section 11.4.

1. nonlinear least squares (NLS) (this section);
2. maximum likelihood (ML) (Section 16.6);
3. nonparametric and semi-parametric estimation (Section 16.7)

Maximum likelihood estimation also applies to linear models. Many of the OLS-based estimators discussed in the previous sections are ML estimators under the assumption of normality of the disturbance terms. We note that an equation may appear to be inherently nonlinear but on closer inspection may still be linearizable. For example, the attraction models in Section 9.4 were considered to be intrinsically nonlinear until log-centering methods made these models linear in the parameters.

We begin with a simple, non-robust, multiplicative model that can also be made linear in the parameters:

$$q_t = \beta_0 a_t^{\beta_1} e^{\varepsilon_t} \tag{16.134}$$

where

q_t = sales in units,

a_t = advertising expenditures in dollars,

ε_t = disturbance term.

For estimation this equation is made linear by a logarithmic transformation:

$$\ln q_t = \beta_0^1 + \beta_1 \ln a_t + \varepsilon_t \tag{16.135}$$

where

$$\beta_0^1 = \ln \beta_0.$$

One potential problem with this transformation is that a_t may be zero for some values of t. To avoid this, we could replace a_t by $(1 + a_t)$:

$$\ln q_t = \beta_0^1 + \beta_1 \ln(1 + a_t) + \varepsilon_t. \tag{16.136}$$

Adding a value of one is an arbitrary choice. The question is whether the results are sensitive to which value is added. To address this issue, Naert and Weverbergh (1977) added a parameter γ to a_t, obtaining:

$$\ln q_t = \beta_0^1 + \beta_1 \ln(\gamma + a_t) + \varepsilon_t. \tag{16.137}$$

Now (16.137) is intrinsically nonlinear in γ (but for a given value of γ it again becomes linear). One possibility is to apply a trial-and-error or *grid search* on γ.

For simplicity assume that for any value of γ, (16.137) is estimated by OLS, under the usual assumptions about the disturbance term. Then choose m values for γ, covering a plausibly wide range, and choose the value of γ for which the model's R^2 value is maximized. We illustrate the idea by showing a hypothetical plot of R^2 values associated with 8 different γ's (i.e. $m = 8$). In Figure 16.6 this plot shows that the maximum R^2 value[74] lies between the values γ_4 and γ_6, perhaps close to γ_5. For

---

74. The value of γ maximizing R^2 is a maximum likelihood estimate. See Goldfeld and Quandt (1972, pp. 57-58).

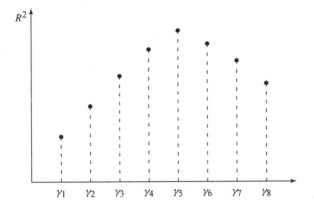

Figure 16.6 Coefficient of determination (R^2) as a function of γ (16.137).

greater accuracy, the grid search can be continued by choosing another set of values for γ between γ_4 and γ_6, until an acceptable level of accuracy is achieved.

Naert and Weverbergh (1977) faced such a problem with 24 observations. Advertising expenditures were measured in thousands of dollars, and two of the observations had zero entries. Based on a grid search, they obtained an optimal value of $\gamma = 114.75$ for which $R^2 = 0.771$, and $\hat{\beta}_1 = 0.60$. Interestingly, a very different result is obtained for $\gamma = 1$ at which value $R^2 = 0.49$ and $\hat{\beta}_1 = 0.12$. We show R^2 values for other values of γ in Table 16.5. This table shows that the model fit is extremely sensitive to the value of γ, especially to values below $\gamma = 50$. Of course, we cannot claim that the optimal value of γ, chosen through this grid search, provides the best estimate of the advertising elasticity. If we used a different specification, for example with additional predictor variables, the optimal value of γ may change, as may the sensitivity of R^2 to γ. We provide another example of a grid search in Section 17.4 where we discuss a varying parameter model.

The Box-Cox transformation, introduced in Section 16.1.4 is often used as a method of generalizing the linear model. This transformation is also used to linearize nonlinear relations by performing a grid search on transformations of the predictor variables (Greene, 1997, p. 480).

Grid search procedures are costly and inefficient, especially if a model is nonlinear in several of its parameters. Nonetheless relatively efficient methods have been devised. Fletcher (1980) and Quandt (1983) provide further details. An alternative procedure is *linearized regression*, [75] which consists of a sequence of linear approximations. Let:

$$Y_j = f(X_j, \beta_j) + u_j \tag{16.138}$$

---

75. Greene, (1997, p. 452).

Table 16.5 R^2 for selected values of γ.

γ	R^2
0.005	0.24
0.01	0.26
0.05	0.32
0.10	0.35
0.50	0.44
1	0.49
5	0.62
10	0.68
50	0.76
100	0.77
150	0.77
200	0.77

where Y_j, X_j, β_j and u_j are defined in (16.9) and f is a nonlinear function of X_j and β_j. First, initial values are given to the estimates $\hat{\beta}_j$, i.e. $\hat{\beta}_{j0}$.[76] Next $f(X_j, \beta_j)$ is approximated by a first-order Taylor expansion about $\hat{\beta}_{j0}$:

$$f(X_j, \beta_j) \simeq f(X_j, \hat{\beta}_{j0}) + \sum_{\ell=1}^{L} \left(\frac{\partial f}{\partial \beta_{\ell j}} \right)_{\beta_{\ell j} = \hat{\beta}_{\ell j0}} (\beta_{\ell j} - \hat{\beta}_{\ell j0}). \qquad (16.139)$$

Setting $\left(\dfrac{\partial f}{\partial \beta_{\ell j}} \right)_{\beta_{\ell j} = \hat{\beta}_{\ell j0}}$ equal to $\hat{f}_{\ell t}^0$, (16.138) can be written as:[77]

$$Y_j = f(X_j, \hat{\beta}_{j0}) + \sum_{\ell=1}^{L} \hat{f}_{\ell t}^0 (\beta_{\ell j} - \hat{\beta}_{\ell j0}) + u'_j \quad \text{or} \qquad (16.140)$$

$$Y_j - f(X_j, \hat{\beta}_{j0}) + \sum_{\ell=1}^{L} \hat{f}_{\ell t}^0 \hat{\beta}_{\ell j0} = \sum_{\ell=1}^{L} \hat{f}_{\ell t}^0 \beta_{\ell j} + u'_j. \qquad (16.141)$$

Letting

$$Y_{j0} = Y_j - f(X_j, \hat{\beta}_{j0}) + \sum_{\ell=1}^{L} \hat{f}_{\ell t}^0 \hat{\beta}_{\ell j0} \qquad (16.142)$$

---

76. For example, all parameters may be set equal to zero.
77. u'_j is not equal to u_j since the right-hand side of (16.139) is only approximately equal to $f(X_j, \beta)$.

we obtain:

$$Y_{j0} = \sum_{\ell=1}^{L} \hat{f}_{\ell t}^{0} \beta_{\ell j} + u'_{j} \tag{16.143}$$

an expression linear in $\beta_{\ell j}$ and thus amenable to estimation by OLS or other suitable estimation methods giving us a new vector of estimates $\hat{\beta}_{j} = \hat{\beta}_{j1}$. The procedure can now be repeated by considering a Taylor expansion about $\hat{\beta}_{j1}$. The process continues until two subsequent vectors of estimates $\hat{\beta}_{j,m}$ and $\hat{\beta}_{j,m+1}$ are equal, that is, until the process converges.

Other nonlinear estimation procedures derive from the formulation of a least squares objective function as a nonlinear programming problem. The objective is to minimize the sum of the squared residuals where $\hat{\beta}_{j}$ and $\hat{u}_{j}$ have to satisfy (16.138) for all elements of $\hat{\beta}_{j}$ and $\hat{u}_{j}$:

$$\text{minimize} \quad \hat{u}'_{j} \hat{u}_{j} \tag{16.144}$$

$$\text{subject to:} \quad Y_{j} - f(X_{j}, \hat{\beta}_{j}) - \hat{u}_{j} = 0.$$

For further reading and additional references see Fletcher, Powell (1963), Wilde, Beightler (1967), Amemiya (1985, Chapter 8), Judge et al. (1985, Appendix B, pp. 951-979), Greene (1997, Chapter 10, pp. 450-493).

Applications of nonlinear estimation methods appear in Naert, Bultez (1975), Gopalakrishna, Chatterjee (1992) and Parker (1992). We briefly discuss the communications response model of Gopalakrishna, Chatterjee (1992) who propose the following structure:

$$acs_{it} = \lambda acs_{i,t-1} + (1 - \lambda)c_{it}/(\delta + c_{it}) + u_{it} \tag{16.145}$$

where

$$acs_{it} = \text{the share of account } i\text{'s business potential}$$
$$\text{in period } t,$$
$$c_{it} = \text{the strength of communication with regard to}$$
$$\text{account } i \text{ in period } t \text{ (defined below)},$$
$$\delta = \text{an index of competitive communication strength,}$$
$$u_{it} = \text{a disturbance term.}$$

The communication strength is defined as:

$$c_{it} = \alpha_{1} a_{t} + \alpha_{2} p s_{it} + \alpha_{3}(a_{t} \times p s_{it}) \tag{16.146}$$

where

$$a_{t} = \text{advertising expenditures in dollars in period } t,$$
$$p s_{it} = \text{personal selling expenditures in dollars allocated}$$
$$\text{to account } i \text{ in period } t.$$

It is clear from (16.145) that λ is the (average) part of an account's share the firm under study carries over from the previous period. The other systematic part is attributable to the current period's communication strength relative to that of competitors. In the absence of information on competitors' communication efforts (see also Chapter 15), δ is used as a constant (over time and across accounts) index. The model formulation forces the relationship between the criterion variable and the relative amount of communication to be concave. That is, holding competitors' efforts constant, which is implicit in the constancy of δ, increases in c_{it} produce diminishing returns. We note that δ cannot be estimated independently of the parameters in (16.146). Therefore, δ is arbitrarily set equal to one.

The objective of the model is to help an *industrial* marketing manager assess the joint impact of advertising and personal selling effort on the share of account i's potential, i.e. the share of a given customer's business at the level of individual accounts. Although the parameters in (16.145) and (16.146) do not show this, Gopalakrishna and Chatterjee did allow for heterogeneity in the parameters λ, α_1, α_2, and α_3.

Data were available for a subset of the accounts at a firm selling electric cables, and covered 138 accounts for seven quarters. Of the accounts, 15 were classified as large (potential $\geq$ \$1 million), 68 small ($\leq$ \$100,000), and 55 medium. However, no statistical evidence obtained to support parameter heterogeneity between these three segments. Due to the intrinsic nonlinearity of effects in the proposed structure, a nonlinear least squares estimation procedure (SYSNLIN; see the SAS/ETS User's Guide, version 5, 1984) was used for parameter estimation. The lagged variable in (16.145) had an estimated effect of about 0.18 which suggests that the (average) carryover is modest. Both main effects and the interaction effect for advertising and personal selling were positive. Thus, there is a positive interaction between advertising and personal selling expenditures on the share of an account's business potential. However, due to the concavity in the effect of c_{it} on acs_{it}, the response curves for personal selling and advertising actually converge as advertising increases (see Figure 1 on p. 193 in Gopalakrishna and Chatterjee, 1992).

The authors also determine optimal communication plans for the firm. They do this separately for each segment (with segment-specific parameters, in the absence of statistical evidence to support this heterogeneity). Their optimization results suggest that profit can be increased by some 50 percent, if advertising is increased moderately (about 20 percent) and personal selling is increased dramatically for large accounts, strongly for medium accounts, and decreased to about zero for small accounts. In the single-period optimization, advertising expenditures would increase from about \$140,000 to about \$180,000. Sales force expenditures in total would increase from about \$80,000 to about \$200,000.

In this case, the optimal relative expenditures are about the same for advertising and sales force, which is consistent with the parameter estimates, $\hat{\alpha}_1 = 0.009$ and $\hat{\alpha}_2 = 1.28$. When advertising is adjusted on a per-account basis, i.e. 0.009×138 accounts $\doteq 1.28$. We note that the optimal results are obtained under the unrealistic assumption that competitors will not modify their communication expenditures.

16.6 Maximum Likelihood Estimation

16.6.1 MAXIMIZING THE LIKELIHOOD

There are different ways to obtain estimators. In the preceding sections we concentrated on the least squares method. In this section we discuss other methods to obtain estimators, viz. maximum likelihood *ML* methods. After an introduction of *ML* estimation methods, we discuss the large sample properties of the estimators. We then give some examples and applications. We end by summarizing some well-known statistical tests based on likelihoods.

In the social sciences, data are used to test hypotheses and to aid in theory construction. The principle of maximum likelihood, due to Fisher (1950), provides a statistical framework for assessing the information available in the data.[78] The principle of maximum likelihood is based on distributional assumptions about the data. Suppose that we have i random variables with observations y_i, $(i = 1, \ldots, N)$ such as purchase frequencies for a sample of N subjects. A probability density function for y_i is formulated, denoted here as: $f(y_i \mid \theta)$, where θ is a parameter characterizing the distribution (we assume θ to be a scalar for convenience). This formulation holds for both discrete (taking a countable number of values, possibly infinite) and continuous random variables (taking on an infinite number of values on the real line). Discrete random variables are for example 0/1 choices, or purchase frequencies, while market shares and some ratings on scales can be considered continuous random variables. Important characteristics of these random variables are their expectations and variances. In the purchase frequency example usually a (*discrete*) Poisson distribution is assumed (see Section 12.1):

$$f(y_i \mid \lambda) = \frac{e^{-\lambda}\lambda^{y_i}}{y_i!}. \tag{16.147}$$

The expectation of the Poisson variable in (16.147) can be shown to be $E(y_i) = \lambda$, and its variance is $\mathrm{Var}(y_i) = \lambda$.

One of the well-known *continuous* distributions is the exponential distribution:

$$f(y_i \mid \lambda) = \lambda e^{-\lambda y_i}. \tag{16.148}$$

The mean and variance of the exponential random variable in (16.148) are $E[y_i] = 1/\lambda$ and $\mathrm{Var}(y_i) = 1/\lambda^2$. This distribution is frequently used for interpurchase times.[79] The functions in (16.147) and (16.148) are known as the probability function (pf) and probability density function (pdf), respectively. Both the normal and the Poisson distributions are members of the exponential family, which is a general family of distributions that encompasses both discrete and continuous distributions. The exponential family is a very useful class of distributions. The common properties of the distributions in this class facilitate the simultaneous study of these distributions.

---

78. Eliason (1993, p.7).
79. Gupta (1991) and Chapter 12.

The maximum likelihood principle is an estimation principle that finds an estimate for one or more unknown parameters (say θ) such that it maximizes the likelihood of observing the data, $y_i, i = 1, \ldots, N$. The likelihood of a model (L) can be interpreted as the probability of the observed data y, given that model. A certain parameter value θ_1 is more likely than another, θ_2, in light of the observed data, so that $L(\theta_1 \mid y) > L(\theta_2 \mid y)$, if it makes those data more probable. The probability of observing y_i is provided by the pf or pdf : $f(y_i \mid \theta)$. Because the observations on the N subjects are assumed independent, the joint density function of all observations is the product of the densities over i:

$$L(\theta) = \prod_{i=1}^{N} f(y_i \mid \theta) \tag{16.149}$$

which is the likelihood. The likelihood is a function of the unknown parameter θ. The expression for the likelihood is considerably simplified if its natural logarithm is taken, in which case the product in (16.149) is replaced by a sum:

$$l(\theta) = \sum_{i=1}^{N} \ln f(y_i \mid \theta). \tag{16.150}$$

This expression is especially simple for members of the exponential family (Chapter 12). Since the natural logarithm is a monotone function, maximizing the log-likelihood (16.150) yields the same estimates as maximizing the likelihood (16.149).

In the Poisson example, the log-likelihood takes a simple form, the Poisson distribution being in the exponential family, and is:

$$l(\lambda) = \sum_{i=1}^{N} (-\lambda + y_i \ln(\lambda) - \ln(y_i!)). \tag{16.151}$$

The ML estimator of λ is obtained by setting the derivatives of the log-likelihood equal to zero:

$$\frac{\partial l(\lambda)}{\partial \lambda} = \frac{\partial \sum_{i=1}^{N} (-\lambda + y_i \ln(\lambda) - \ln(y_i!))}{\partial \lambda} = -N + \sum_{i=1}^{N} y_i \lambda^{-1} = 0. \tag{16.152}$$

Solving (16.152) provides the maximum likelihood estimator (MLE):

$$\hat{\lambda} = \sum_{i=1}^{N} \frac{y_i}{N} \tag{16.153}$$

which equals the sample mean.

Similarly, in the example of the exponential distribution, the log-likelihood is:

$$l(\lambda) = \sum_{i=1}^{N} (\ln(\lambda) - \lambda y_i). \tag{16.154}$$

Table 16.6 Data for the illustration of ML estimation.

Subject i	$y_i^{(1)}$	x_i	$y_i^{(2)}$
1	25	1	7
2	22	1	7
3	31	3	18
4	21	2	12
5	24	1	6
6	26	1	1
7	20	3	31
8	27	2	15
9	24	5	57
10	14	4	29

Taking the derivative of (16.154) with respect to λ yields the estimator:

$$\hat{\lambda} = \frac{N}{\sum_{i=1}^{N} y_i} \tag{16.155}$$

the inverse of the sample mean.

Gupta (1991) estimated the exponential model on interpurchase times from scanner data on regular coffee. In a sample of 100 households he obtained $\hat{\lambda} = 0.376$ (note that the situation is slightly more complicated because there are multiple interpurchase times for each subject, and $N=1526$). A graph of the Poisson and exponential log-likelihoods against λ yields a concave function, with a unique maximum, indicating that the *MLE* is unique. This property holds for all members of the exponential family.

16.6.2 EXAMPLE

To illustrate *ML* estimation, we use a small synthetic example. Assume we have data on yearly purchase frequencies for 10 subjects. The data, generated from a Poisson distribution with a mean of $\lambda = 25$ are shown in the second column of Table 16.6. Applying equation (16.153) we obtain a *ML* estimate of $\lambda = 23.4$, which is quite close to the true value of 25.

For more complex models, the likelihood equations do not yield closed-form expressions. Assume we have an explanatory variable, household size, x_i, with values shown in the third column in Table 16.6. Again, we generate the dependent variable, the number of sales through random draws from a Poisson distribution, with the mean parameterized as $\lambda_i = exp(1.5 + 0.5 * x_i)$, thus a Poisson regression model (see Section 12.1.5) with $\mu = 1.5$ and $\beta = 0.5$. Here we have an example of two parameters instead of a scalar. The data generated in this way are given in the last column of

Table 16.7 The iteration process from
Newton's algorithm.

r	μ	β	g	log-likelihood
1	0.00	0.00	0.00	-392.06
2	-0.81	0.88	0.10	-152.71
3	0.01	0.70	0.10	-108.10
4	1.35	0.53	0.45	-32.63
5	1.57	0.54	1.00	-29.12
6	1.55	0.54	1.00	-29.07

Table 16.6. In this case, there are no closed-form solutions for the two parameters. We therefore apply a numerical search procedure: Newton's algorithm, which maximizes the log-likelihood numerically[80]. Suppose we collect the parameters in the vector $\theta = (\mu, \beta)'$. Then given a set of starting values, in iteration r the parameter vector is found by:

$$\hat{\theta}_r = \hat{\theta}_{r-1} - gH(\hat{\theta}_{r-1})^{-1}S(\hat{\theta}_{r-1}) \qquad (16.156)$$

where

$$g = \text{the step length,}$$
$$H(\hat{\theta}_{r-1}) = \text{the matrix of second-order derivatives of the}$$
$$\text{log-likelihood evaluated at } \hat{\theta}_{r-1}, \text{ and}$$
$$S(\hat{\theta}_{r-1}) = \text{the vector of first-order derivatives of the}$$
$$\text{log-likelihood (as in 16.152) evaluated at } \hat{\theta}_{r-1}.$$

Both $H(\hat{\theta}_{r-1})$ and $S(\hat{\theta}_{r-1})$ are evaluated at the previous estimate $\hat{\theta}_{r-1}$. Table 16.7 shows the iteration process. The algorithm converged in $r = 6$ iterations; as a starting guess of the parameters we take the zero value. The algorithm is said to converge if the first derivative of the log-likelihood (16.152) changes less than 10^{-5}. Table 16.7 shows that the *ML* estimates are close to the true parameter values.

16.6.3 LARGE SAMPLE PROPERTIES OF THE ML-ESTIMATOR

The maximum likelihood approach derives much of its attractiveness from its large sample properties. Small sample properties of the *MLE* are usually not known, except when the criterion variable y_i, given the predictor variables' values, is normally distributed. These asymptotic properties are obtained if the sample size tends to infinity: $N \rightarrow \infty$. Under fairly general conditions, maximum likelihood estimators (*MLE*):

1. are consistent;

---

80. See Scales (1985), Eliason (1993)

2. have asymptotically minimum variance;
3. are asymptotically normal.

The first important property of the *MLE* is *consistency*. $\hat{\theta}$ is said to be consistent for θ if the probability that the estimate differs from the true value by less than any arbitrarily small number δ, approaches zero as $N \to \infty$:

$$\lim_{N\to\infty} P(|\hat{\theta} - \theta| > \delta) = 0. \qquad (16.157)$$

This property states that the *MLE* tends to the true value in probability for large samples.

Second, the *ML* approach yields asymptotically *efficient* estimators. An estimator is efficient if it has the lowest possible variance among all estimators in a particular class, and thus has the highest precision. The (asymptotic) variance of the estimator is defined as follows. First define the (matrix of) second derivatives of the log likelihood:

$$H(\theta) = -\frac{\partial^2 l(\theta)}{\partial \theta^2}. \qquad (16.158)$$

This is the Hessian, and is a measure of the amount of information supplied by the data on the parameter(s). Taking the expectation of the Hessian yields the expected information: the average information over all possible samples: $I(\theta) = E(H(\theta))$. This information measure is known as the (Fisher) information matrix. For the linear regression model with normally distributed errors: the expected and observed information matrices coincide and $H(\theta) = I(\theta) = X'X/\delta^2$. Inverting the *expected* information yields the asymptotic variance of the estimator: $AVar = I^{-1}(\theta)$. However, one may prefer to use the inverse of the observed information, $H^{-1}(\theta)$, since that is closer to the observations actually made.[81] The latter is particularly advantageous in smaller samples. Asymptotically the observed and expected value are the same. They are indentical for some parameterizations of distributions in the exponential family.

In the Poisson example above, the asymptotic variance *(AVar)* of the estimator can be computed by inverting the expectation of (16.158) and using (16.152):

$$AVar(\hat{\lambda}) = \left(-E\left(-\lambda^{-2}\sum_{i=1}^{N} y_i\right)\right)^{-1} = \left(\lambda^{-2}E\left(\sum_{i=1}^{N} y_i\right)\right)^{-1}. \qquad (16.159)$$

$$= \lambda/N$$

In this case the observed information is identical to (16.159), since

$$H^{-1}(\theta) = -(-\hat{\lambda}^{-2}\sum_{i=1}^{N} y_i)^{-1} = -(-\hat{\lambda}^{-2}N\hat{\lambda})^{-1} = \hat{\lambda}/N. \qquad (16.160)$$

---

81. See Lindsey (1996, p.305).

*Table 16.8 Estimation results of the
synthetic data example.*

Parameter	Estimate	*ASE*	*t*-value
μ	1.55	0.29	5.31
β	0.54	0.11	5.11

In this example we have a scalar parameter characterizing the Poisson or exponential processes. If we have a *vector* of parameters, the asymptotic variance-covariance matrix is obtained as the inverse of the Hessian matrix: $H^{-1}(\theta)$.

In the synthetic data example for the Poisson distribution provided in the previous section, we obtain the following Hessian matrix:

$$H = \begin{bmatrix} 17.90 & 47.50 \\ 47.50 & 134.93 \end{bmatrix}. \tag{16.161}$$

Inverting the Hessian, and taking the square root of the diagonal elements of the resulting matrix gives us the asymptotic standard errors *(ASE)* of the estimates. These are shown in Table 16.8. However, the conditions for the asymptotic approximations are unlikely to be valid in this example, since it is based on only 10 observations. It serves as a illustration of the computations.

A final important property of the *ML* estimator is that it is *asymptotically normal*. The proof of the asymptotic normality is obtained by a Taylor series expansion, yielding a quadratic approximation to the likelihood around θ, and applying the central limit theorem.[82] This property of the *ML* estimator allows statistical tests about the parameters, based on the normal distribution, to be conducted using an estimate of the variance in (16.158). Thus, asymptotically:

$$\hat{\theta} \sim N(\theta, H^{-1}(\theta)). \tag{16.162}$$

The above asymptotic properties of the likelihood hold under certain regularity conditions (Lindsey, 1996, p. 187). Although a full discussion of these regularity conditions is beyond the scope of this section, the following aspects may be useful in practice. The log-likelihood function is said to be regular if in an open neighborhood of the true parameter value, it can be approximated by a quadratic function. Such an approximation breaks down in situations where the true value lies on the boundary of the parameter space so that the quadratic approximation is inappropriate, or when the number of parameters to be estimated increases with the number of observations. The latter situation occurs if in our Poisson example a parameter exists for each individual i, i.e. λ_i for $i = 1 \ldots N$.

---

82. Compare Lindsey (1996, p. 199).

16.6.4 STATISTICAL TESTS

In this subsection we introduce some useful inferential tools for *ML* estimation. With the asymptotic distribution of $\hat{\theta}$ defined in (16.162), we have asymptotically:

$$z = \frac{\hat{\theta} - \theta}{\sqrt{AVar(\hat{\theta})}} \rightarrow N(0, 1) \tag{16.163}$$

which converges in distribution to a *standard* normal distribution. This is a very useful result that allows statistical tests for hypotheses formulated for θ, for example $H_0 : \theta = 0$, to be conducted using the z-test.

In Table 16.8 above, the t-values based on the asymptotic standard errors of the estimates are provided for the synthetic data example. The t-values show that the null hypotheses that the mean and regression parameters are zero is strongly rejected. Again, given the small sample size the asymptotic approximations will not be accurate in this example. However, since the data were actually generated with non-zero parameter values, the results of the t-tests are consistent with our knowledge about the structure of the data.

Equation (16.163) assumes a scalar parameter θ. If, however, θ is a $(L \times 1)$ vector of parameters, then tests on the entire parameter vector (or sub vectors) can be conducted using the Wald-test, say for $H_0 : \theta = \theta_0$:

$$W = (\hat{\theta} - \theta_0)' H(\hat{\theta})(\hat{\theta} - \theta_0) \tag{16.164}$$

which converges in distribution to a χ^2 variable with L degrees of freedom under the null hypothesis. The advantage of the Wald-test is that it allows for tests on several parameters of the model, without the need to re-estimate (a restricted version of) the model. In the Poisson regression example, the Wald test for jointly testing $\mu = 0$ and $\beta = 0$ yields a value of 161.87, with 2 degrees of freedom, which is highly significant.

Another frequently used test is the Likelihood Ratio *(LR)* test. A more detailed discussion of this test is given in Section 18.4.2. The *LR* test is used to investigate two models that are nested and chooses that model that has the highest likelihood of occurrence, given the observed data. The null hypothesis is again $H_0 : \theta = \theta_0$. Two models are estimated that yield log-likelihood values of $l(\hat{\theta})$ and $l(\hat{\theta}_0)$, respectively, where we assume the latter model to be more restricted, for example because one or more parameters are set to zero. Due to the fact that the two models are nested, minus twice the difference in their log-likelihood values is asymptotically distributed as χ^2 under the null hypothesis:

$$LR = -2(l(\hat{\theta}_0) - l(\hat{\theta})) \rightarrow \chi^2_{df} \tag{16.165}$$

where df is the difference in the number of parameters in θ and θ_0. The *LR* test necessitates the estimation of the two models, and is thus computationally more intensive than the Wald test. For the one parameter Poisson distribution example provided above, the *LR* test reduces to:

$$LR = -2N(\lambda - \lambda_0) - 2ln(\lambda_0/\lambda) \sum_{i=1}^{N} y_i. \tag{16.166}$$

If we re-estimate the model for the two-parameter Poisson regression synthetic data in Table 16.6, but restricting $\beta = 0$, we obtain a log-likelihood of $l(\theta_0) = -44.68$ (Newton's algorithm converged in 6 iterations to a parameter value of $\mu = 2.89$). Thus in this case the *LR* statistic for testing the models with and without (see Table 16.7) the restriction equals $LR = -2(-44.68 + 29.07) = 31.22$, which is highly significant at one degree of freedom (the difference in the number of parameter values for the two models). This is of course expected since these synthetic data were generated on the basis of a nonzero value of β. As a cautionary note we mention that the asymptotic χ^2-distribution for the Wald- and *LR* tests are unlikely to hold given the small sample size.

If the models to be compared are not nested, the *LR* test does not apply. Information criteria are then commonly used to identify the most appropriate model. These criteria such as Akaike's Information Criterion, AIC (Akaike 1974),the Schwartz Criterion (Schwartz, 1978), and the Consistent Akaike's Information Criterion, CAIC (Bozdogan, 1987) are discussed in Section 18.4.3.

16.7   Non- and semiparametric regression models

by Harald J. van Heerde

16.7.1   INTRODUCTION

The regression models discussed so far are parametric regression models. These models impose specific functional forms through which the criterion variable is explained by the predictor variables. If the functional forms are correctly specified, then the parameter estimates have desirable properties. A model builder is usually, however, uncertain about the shape of the relations. In that case, it is useful to consider more flexible approaches, such as nonparametric regression models and semiparametric regression models. Nonparametric regression models do not impose any functional relation between the criterion variable and the predictor variables (i.e., they lack parameters). Semiparametric regression models are partly parametric and partly nonparametric.

To provide a perspective on these alternative models, we first summarize the advantages and disadvantages of parametric regression models. Next, we do the same for nonparametric regression models, and we discuss two marketing applications. Finally, we introduce semiparametric regression models, and we motivate and discuss a marketing application of such a model as well.

We note that we discuss only non- and semiparametric *regression* models. This means that the criterion variable has at least interval-scale measurement. Thus, we do not present non- and semiparametric models with criterion variables that have binary or nominal scales, such as is the case in brand choice models.[83]

16.7.2 ADVANTAGES AND DISADVANTAGES OF THE PARAMETRIC REGRESSION
MODEL

In a parametric regression model, the model builder approximates reality by a mathematical function that is represented by parameters, such as (16.9). The effects of predictor variables on the criterion variable are quantified by parameters captured in the vector β. In general, parametric models have a parametric functional form and a parametric distribution of the error term. The error terms should have certain properties, as discussed under the assumptions, to justify statistical inference.

The advantages of parametric modeling lie in a number of optimality properties (Powell, 1994). If the assumed functional form is correct, the maximum likelihood estimators of the unknown parameters in the model are consistent, i.e., the estimates converge to the true values as the sample size increases to infinity. Also, the rate at which the estimates converge to the true values is maximal (i.e., the estimators are asymptotically efficient). This implies that there is not a better estimation procedure, if the error-term assumptions hold (which implies that the functional forms are correct).

The disadvantage of parametric modeling is its inflexibility. Our knowledge about functional forms is subject to a potentially high degree of uncertainty. That is, we are uncertain about the nature of the correct parametric specification of the response function. Incorrect specifications typically yield incorrect conclusions, i.e. the parameter estimates tend to be biased and/or inconsistent. One could try to solve this problem by considering alternative parametric specifications and performing standard specification tests. But this will not solve the problem if there is no guarantee that any of the parametric specifications considered is the true one. Indeed, it is possible that the true relationships do not belong to any parametric family (Briesch, Chintagunta and Matzkin, 1997). Thus, the cost of imposing the strong restrictions required for parametric estimation can be considerable (Härdle and Linton, 1994).

16.7.3 THE NONPARAMETRIC REGRESSION MODEL

In the nonparametric regression approach, one relates the criterion variable to predictor variables without reference to a specific form. We can represent nonparametric regression models as:

$$y_t = m(x_t) + u_t, \quad t = 1, \ldots, T \tag{16.167}$$

where

---

83. See, for example, the semiparametric brand choice model by Abe (1995) and the non- and semiparametric brand choice models by Briesch, Chintagunta, and Matzkin (1997).

$$y_t \ = \ \text{the value of the criterion variable in period } t,$$
$$m(x_t) \ = \ \text{a function of } L \text{ predictor variables } x \text{ measured in period } t,$$
$$u_t \ = \ \text{the disturbance term in period } t.$$

The function $m(x_t)$ contains no parameters. It has the L-dimensional vector x_t with predictors as its argument.

There are multiple nonparametric estimators for $m(x_t)$ in (16.167). The three major types are:[84]

1. kernel estimators;
2. k-nearest neighbor estimators; and
3. spline regression estimators.

Härdle (1990, p. 81) compares the three estimators in a simulation study and concludes that the kernel estimator, the k-nearest neighbor estimator and the spline regression estimator result in the same overall shape of the response function. We focus on the kernel estimator because it is a widely used nonparametric regression estimator. Before we discuss details of the kernel estimator, we provide a short introduction to the other two nonparametric estimators.

The *k-nearest neighbor estimator* uses "nearest neighbor" observations to estimate the criterion variable for given values of the predictor variables. Specifically, it creates an estimate of the criterion variable for specified values of the predictor variables (say: x_0) on the observations in the data set that are closest to x_0. Hence, the method searches among the observations $x_1, \ldots, x_T$ and identifies the k observations that have the shortest (Euclidian) distance to x_0. The value of the criterion variable given x_0 is estimated by taking the unweighted average of the y-values for these k observations.

The *spline regression estimator* represents $m(x_t)$ by connecting multiple cubic polynomials. The polynomials are connected at observation points x_i in such a way that the first two derivatives of $\hat{m}$ are continuous (Härdle 1990, p. 57). Kalyanam and Shively (1998) use a stochastic spline regression, which is a special variant of the spline regression estimator, for flexible estimation of the relation between sales and price. They approximate this response function by a piecewise linear function that has derivatives obtained by drawings from a normal distribution.

The intuition behind the *kernel method* (Nadaraya, 1964 and Watson, 1964) is that it computes a local weighted average of the criterion variable y given the values of the predictors x_0:

$$\hat{m}(x_0) = \sum_{t=1}^{T} w_t(x_0) y_t \tag{16.168}$$

---

84. Härdle (1990).

where $w_t(x_0)$ represents the weight assigned to the t-th observation y_t in the estimation of y for x_0. This weight depends on "the distance" of x_t from the point x_0, which is described by

$$w_t(x_0) = \frac{K\left(\dfrac{x_t - x_0}{h}\right)}{\sum_{t'=1}^{T} K\left(\dfrac{x_{t'} - x_0}{h}\right)} \qquad (16.169)$$

where $K(\cdot)$ is a "kernel function", and h the "bandwidth". By substituting (16.169) in (16.168) we obtain the kernel estimator

$$\hat{m}(x_0) = \frac{\sum_{t=1}^{T} K\left(\dfrac{x_t - x_0}{h}\right) y_t}{\sum_{t'=1}^{T} K\left(\dfrac{x_{t'} - x_0}{h}\right)}. \qquad (16.170)$$

To implement the kernel estimator, one has to choose the kernel function and the bandwidth parameter. Generally, the kernel function is a symmetric function around zero, it reaches its maximum at zero, and it integrates to one. A common choice for the kernel is the normal (Gaussian) kernel:

$$K\left(\frac{x_t - x_0}{h}\right) = \frac{1}{\sqrt{2\pi}} \exp\left(\frac{-(x_t - x_0)^2}{2h^2}\right). \qquad (16.171)$$

This kernel represents the density function of a normal distribution. The closer $\frac{x_t - x_0}{h}$ is to zero, the larger $K(.)$ is, i.e. the larger the weight for observation y_t in the computation of the estimate of y for x_0.

The bandwidth parameter selection is essential in kernel regression (and more critical than the choice of the kernel function). This parameter controls the peakedness of the kernel function. The smaller it is, the more peaked the kernel function is, and the more weight is put on the nearest observations. To illustrate, the bandwidth parameter in (16.171) can be interpreted as the standard deviation of a normal distribution. The smaller the standard deviation of a normal distribution, the smaller the width of the normal density function.

As the bandwidth decreases, the response curve is based on fewer observations at a given point. As a result, the response curve potentially becomes squigglier. This means that the bias in the shape of the curve is reduced at the cost of increased variance. A bandwidth parameter of (almost) zero leads to a response curve that connects the observations, resulting in zero bias but maximal variance. An infinite bandwidth parameter leads to a horizontal response curve: maximal bias and zero variance. Hence, the choice of the bandwidth parameter involves a trade-off between bias and variance. Most bandwidth selection techniques try to minimize some mean squared error criterion, i.e., the sum of squared bias and variance of the criterion variable.[85]

The advantage of nonparametric regression models relative to their parametric counterparts is their flexibility: a nonparametric approach does not project the observed data into a Procrustean bed[86] of a fixed parameterization (Härdle, 1990). Nonparametric modeling imposes few restrictions on the form of the joint distribution of the data, so that (functional form) misspecification is unlikely. Also the consistency of the estimator of the regression curve is established under much more general conditions than for parametric modeling. Rust (1988) introduced *nonparametric* regression models to marketing research. He emphasizes that nonlinearity, non-normal errors, and heteroscedasticity are automatically accommodated as inherent features of the method, without the use of special analyses requiring a high level of judgment and knowledge. However, it is, useful to remember that the primary substantive benefits consist of the relaxation of functional form constraints and the allowance for flexible interactions.

A disadvantage of the nonparametric approach is its convergence rate which is usually slower than it is for parametric estimators (Powell, 1994). Thus, precise estimation of the nonparametric multidimensional regression surface requires many observations.[87] In Table 16.9 we show the sample sizes suggested for given numbers of predictor variables (dimensionality) in a nonparametric regression model (for details see Silverman, 1986, p. 94)[88] to illustrate "the curse of dimensionality". For comparison purposes, we also show the sample sizes suggested for parametric regression models, based on the rule of thumb: "5 observations per parameter". From Table 16.9, we conclude that for a simple problem of a nonparametric brand sales model with three marketing instruments for each of three brands as predictor variables (i.e a total of nine own- and cross-brand variables), we would need almost 200,000 observations.

It is useful to provide some discussion of the numbers in Table 16.9. For the parametric model, the rule of thumb does not differentiate between main- and interaction effects. Thus, for each additional parameter we would need another five observations, no matter what kind of parameter it is. We know, however, that for most types of historical data, the degree of multicollinearity tends to increase as the number of predictors increases. As the multicollinearity increases we need a larger number of additional observations than the five proposed in the rule of thumb. And if the additional variables represent interaction effects, the increase in multicollinearity will be especially severe.

---

85. See Abe (1995) for a discussion on bandwidth selection techniques.
86. Procrustes is a figure in Greek mythology. He was a robber who took his victims home to cut or stretch them so that they fit in his bed.
87. For further discussion of parametric versus nonparametric regression models, see Härdle (1990, pp. 3-6) and Powell (1994, pp. 2444-2447).
88. Table 16.9 was derived in a nonparametric density estimation context and not in a nonparametric regression context. However, nonparametric regression is equivalent to estimating the density of the criterion variable given the predictor variables (Härdle, 1990, p. 21).

Table 16.9 Suggested sample sizes for nonparametric and parametric regression models.

Number of predictors	Suggested Sample sizes	
	Nonparametric model	Parametric model
1	4	5
2	19	10
3	67	15
4	223	20
5	768	25
6	2790	30
7	10700	35
8	43700	40
9	187000	45
10	842000	50

By contrast, the nonparametric model has sample size "requirements" that explode with the number of predictors. The reason is that in addition to accommodating functional forms flexibly, the nonparametric approach also allows completely flexible interaction effects. Thus, with two predictors we need to estimate a completely flexible three-dimensional response surface (see Figure 16.10). Importantly, with each additional predictor, the nature of possible interaction effects explodes and it is for this reason that the sample sizes imply a "curse of dimensionality".

The sample sizes shown in Table 16.9 for the nonparametric model should only be taken as suggestive. The critical determinants of the information required for sufficiently precisely estimated curves are the nature of variation for each predictor (ideally evenly distributed) and the nature of covariation between the predictors (ideally zero). On the other hand, in parametric regression, when the functional form is assumed to be known, the precision of parameter estimates depends on the amount of variation in each predictor (the greater the better), while the desired condition for covariation between the predictors is the same as for the nonparametric model.

Rust (1988) provides two nonparametric kernel regression applications. One is based on a study of the behavior of Hispanic consumers, and focuses on how Hispanic identification (x_1) and income (x_2) affect usage of Spanish media (y). A conventional regression analysis obtains an R^2 value of 0.13, while the nonparametric regression yields an R^2 of 0.36. Importantly, the relationship between the degree of Hispanic ethnic identification and the usage of Hispanic media is found to be nonlinear in a manner that is virtually impossible to anticipate, and difficult to specify parametrically. We show in Figure 16.7 that the use of Hispanic media increases when the Hispanic identification level goes from low to medium, then decreases a bit, after which it increases again with increasing identification levels. We note that the esti-

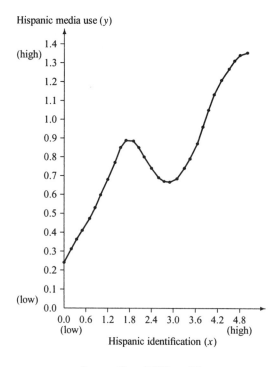

Source: Rust (1988, p. 15)

Figure 16.7 Use of Spanish language media as a function of Hispanic ethnic identification.

mated nonmonotonic relation needs further verification, since the unusual shape may also result from sparse data and from missing variables.

Rust's second application is an investigation of how profitability of a firm influences the compensation of its top marketing executives. In particular, cash salary (y) is taken to be a function of net profit (x). A parametric regression shows little explanatory power ($R^2 = .01$), but a nonparametric regression obtains $R^2 = 0.31$. The relation between executive salary and company profitability is nonlinear, with high salaries going to executives in companies with either large losses or large profits (Rust, 1988, Figure 10). Such unusual nonlinearities are difficult to anticipate. And with additional predictors, the problem of anticipating shapes becomes extremely complex given the infinite variety of possible interaction effects.

16.7.4 THE SEMIPARAMETRIC REGRESSION MODEL

Semiparametric regression models contain components of parametric and nonparametric regression models, and in some sense combine the advantages and disadvantages of parametric and nonparametric regression models. In case of an optimal combination of the two approaches, the semiparametric regression model has the efficiency (low variance) of parametric models and the flexibility (small bias) of nonparametric models. However, semiparametric models are not as flexible as non-

Table 16.10 Relative positions of three kinds of regression models.

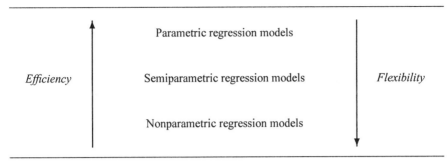

parametric models nor are they as efficient as parametric models. We show in Table 16.10 how semiparametric models are positioned between the parametric- and nonparametric ones.

We discuss two common examples of semiparametric regression models below: single-index models and semilinear models. The single-index model can be written as:

$$y_t = m(x_t'\beta) + u_t, \quad t = 1, \ldots, T. \tag{16.172}$$

This semiparametric model has a nonparametric component, the unknown function $m(.)$, and a parametric component, the parameter vector β. This model allows for some flexibility in the effect of x_t on y, but only through the nonparametric function $m(.)$ which operates on $x_t'\beta$. The dimensionality of the nonparametric function in this manner is reduced ($x_t'\beta$ is one-dimensional), and this facilitates estimation of $m(.)$. As a result, the curse of dimensionality that plagues fully nonparametric models does not apply. However, this nonparametric function tends to be difficult to interpret. For example, one may not be able to relate the characteristics of the nonparametric function to the original variables. We refer to Lee (1996, pp. 205-210) for estimators for the single-index model. The single-index model has not (yet) been applied in marketing.

The semilinear model (Robinson, 1988) can be written as:

$$y_t = m(x_t^{(1)}) + x_t^{(2)'}\beta + u_t, \quad t = 1, \ldots, T. \tag{16.173}$$

Here the vector of predictor variables x_t is split into two parts, $x_t^{(1)}$ and $x_t^{(2)}$. The effect of $x_t^{(1)}$ is modeled nonparametrically, while the effect of $x_t^{(2)}$ is modeled parametrically. Since $x_t^{(1)}$ contains fewer predictor variables than x_t, the nonparametric function $m(.)$ operates on a vector of lower dimensionality than the fully nonparametric model (16.167) does. In this way, the semilinear model reduces the curse of dimensionality. Robinson (1988) provides an estimation procedure for this model.

Van Heerde, Leeflang and Wittink (1999a) use a semilinear regression model for the estimation of the deal effect curve. The deal effect curve represents the relation between sales and price discounts. The marketing literature suggests several phenomena, such as threshold- and saturation effects, which may contribute to the shape of the deal effect curve.[89] These phenomena can produce severe nonlinearities in the curve, which may be best captured in a flexible manner. Van Heerde, Leeflang and Wittink model store-level sales as a nonparametric function of own- and cross-item price discounts, and a parametric function of other predictors (all indicator variables). Thus, flexible interaction effects between the price discount variables are accommodated as well.

The criterion variable of their semiparametric model is *log unit sales* of a given item or brand in a store-week. Taking log unit sales as the criterion variable, instead of unit sales, is desired because the parametric function is multiplicative. The multiplicative function assumes that the stores have homogeneous proportional effects.

The discount variables are *log price indices*. The price index is the ratio of actual price in a store-week to the regular price for an item in the store. Both actual and regular prices are available in the ACNielsen data sets. ACNielsen uses an algorithm to infer regular prices from actual prices and price promotion indicator variables. Price indices less than one represent temporary price cuts (deals).

For item j, $j = 1, \ldots, n$, the specification for the semiparametric model is:

$$\ln q_{kjt} = m(\ln(PI_{k1t}), \ln(PI_{k2t}), \ldots, \ln(PI_{knt})) + \sum_{\ell=1}^{L} \sum_{r=1}^{n} \gamma_{\ell rj} D_{\ell krt} +$$

$$\delta_{jt} X_t + \lambda_{kj} Z_k + u_{kjt}, \tag{16.174}$$

$$t = 1, \ldots, T \text{ and } k = 1, \ldots, K$$

where

$\quad q_{kjt} =$ unit sales (e.g., number of pounds) for item j in store k, in week t,

$\quad m(.) =$ a nonparametric function,

$\quad PI_{krt} =$ the price index (ratio of actual to regular price) of item r in store k in week t,

$\quad D_{1krt} =$ an indicator variable for feature advertising: 1 if item r is featured (but *not* displayed) by store k, in week t; 0 otherwise,

$\quad D_{2krt} =$ an indicator variable for display: 1 if item r is displayed (but *not* featured) by store k, in week t; 0 otherwise,

$\quad D_{3krt} =$ an indicator variable for the simultaneous use of feature and display; 1 if item r is featured *and* displayed by store k, in week t; 0 otherwise,

$\quad X_t =$ an indicator variable (proxy for missing variables

89. See, for example, Gupta and Cooper (1992).

and seasonal effects): 1 if the observation is in week t;
0 otherwise,

Z_k = an indicator variable for store k: 1 if the observation is
from store k; 0 otherwise,

γ_{1rj} = the own-item feature ad multiplier if $j = r$, or cross-feature
ad multiplier if $j \neq r$,

γ_{2rj} = the own-item display multiplier if $j = r$, or cross-feature
display multiplier if $j \neq r$,

γ_{3rj} = the own-item feature and display multiplier if $j = r$, or cross-
feature and display multiplier if $j \neq r$,

δ_{jt} = the seasonal multiplier for week t when the criterion variable
represents item j,

λ_{kj} = store k's regular (base) log unit sales for item j
when there are no price cuts nor promotion
activities for any of the items,

u_{kjt} = a disturbance term for item j in store k, week t,

n = the number of items used in the competitive set,

K = the number of stores in the sample, and

T = the number of weeks.

Equation (16.174) is a modification of the SCAN*PRO model (9.19). It is a fully flexible model as far as the main effects of the predictors are concerned, since all continuous predictors (price indices) are modeled nonparametrically. It also includes flexible
interaction effects between the price index variables of different items. However, it
does not allow for flexible interaction effects between the price index variables and
the indicator variables of the parametric part, nor between these indicator variables
themselves.

Van Heerde, Leeflang and Wittink (1999a) apply the model to three weekly store-
level scanner data sets, all from ACNielsen. We discuss the results from one American
data set for illustrative purposes. This data set comprises the three largest national
brands in the 6.5 oz. canned tuna fish product category. All brands have a substantial
amount of variation in the price discount levels. For example, more than 30 percent
of the observations for each item have a price promotion.

The data are pooled across stores of a given chain to obtain a sufficient number
of observations. The first half of the weekly observations in each data set is used for
estimation, leaving an equal number for validation. Data are available for 28 stores
of a supermarket chain in a metropolitan area. For each store there are 104 weeks
of data. Hence both the estimation and validation samples contain 1456 (28 × 52)
observations, which is much larger than the number suggested for a three-dimensional
nonparametric estimation problem (see Table 16.9).

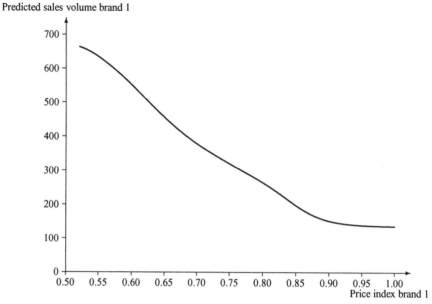

Predicted sales volume brand 1

Figure 16.8 Nonparametric own-brand deal effect curve for brand 1.

We show the own-item deal effect curve from the semiparametric model for brand 1 in Figure 16.8. The graph shows price index values on the x-axis and predicted incremental sales volumes on the y-axis. For the x-axis 1000 focal item price indices were generated, equally spaced between the lowest and highest price indices observed in the estimation sample. For this purpose, the other items' price indices were fixed at one. For each of these 1000 price indices we estimated the sales nonparametrically (for an average week and an average store). It is clear from this graph that there exists a threshold before the price index generates incremental volume. The minimal price discount that appears to be required before a sales increase occurs is about 10 percent, for this brand. There is, however, no evidence of a saturation effect.

The semiparametric model (16.174) also includes flexible cross-item price discount effects. We show one example of a cross-item deal effect curve in Figure 16.9. The curve shows the influence of price discounts for brand 3 on brand 1's sales. Interestingly, this curve also shows a threshold effect at approximately 10 percent. Thus, for discounts greater than 10 percent by brand 3, it appears that unit sales for brand 1 rapidly decrease. However this graph does show a saturation effect. Beyond a 30 percent discount, brand 1's sales appear to be immune to further discounts by brand 3.

The nonparametric part of equation (16.174) accommodates flexible interaction effects between price discounts of different brands, since $m(.)$ is a function of each brand's price index. To illustrate, we use the price indices for brands 1 and 2 to show a three-dimensional deal effect surface in Figure 16.10. Here, the vertical axis repre-

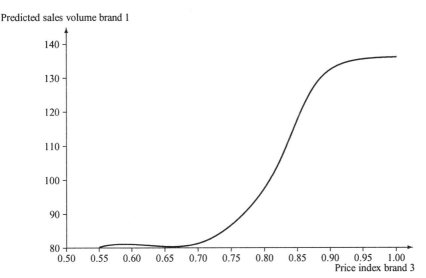

Predicted sales volume brand 1

Figure 16.9 Nonparametric cross-brand deal effect curve for brand 3's price index on brand 1's sales.

sents the predicted sales volume of brand 1. The other two axes represent the price indices of brand 1 and brand 2, respectively. The top part of the three-dimensional surface (the curve A-B) is brand 1's own-item deal effect, also shown in Figure 16.8, when the other two brands both have a price index of one. As one would expect, this curve tends to decrease in magnitude with a decrease in brand 2's price index (as is apparent when one moves forward from the curve A-B, along the axis of brand 2's price index). Importantly, the own-brand deal effect curve for brand 1 has a very different shape when brand 2's price index is, for example, at 0.55 compared to the index being at 1.0. Thus, the interaction effect is highly nonlinear which would be very difficult to model parametrically. Substantively, if brand 1 is promoted with a deep discount, brand 2 can reduce brand 1's sales gain considerably if it has a price discount of (at least) 25 percent.

Van Heerde, Leeflang and Wittink (1999a) also compare their semiparametric model to a parametric benchmark model. The parametric benchmark they use is ACNielsen's SCAN*PRO model for promotional effects (9.19). The comparison is performed by (a) contrasting the deal effect curve for the semiparametric- and parametric models, (b) comparing fit statistics in the estimation sample, and (c) comparing predictive results in the validation sample. As for (a), the authors conclude that "...the parametric model overstates the effects of the smallest and largest discounts and understates the effects of intermediate discounts". As for (b), they find that the flexible modeling of deal effects provides considerable gains in fit, and for (c) there are notable improvements in forecast accuracy. Decomposition of the prediction error shows that both the increased flexibility in nonlinear effects and in interaction effects contribute to improved performance for the semiparametric model. Separately, the proportional

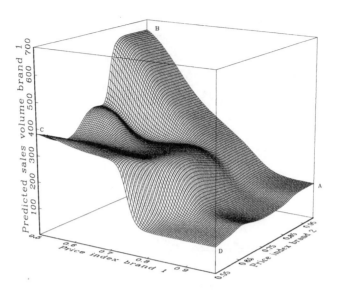

*Figure 16.10 Nonparametric deal effect surface for brand 1's sales with own-brand price index
effect and the cross-brand effect of brand 2's price index.*

improvement in bias is greater than the proportional improvement in variance, as one
would expect.

This semiparametric regression model should be applicable to other areas of marketing in which the functional form of main- and interaction effects is of crucial
interest. A promising area is the estimation of main effects of advertising on sales,
and interaction effects between, for example, price and advertising on sales. The
semiparametric approach offers opportunities to study selected effects flexibly while
the effects of other relevant predictors are modeled parametrically. It represents a
promising way to avoid the use of dimensionality that plagues fully nonparametric
models.

16.8   Illustration and discussion

In this section we discuss a few applications of the statistical tests introduced in Section 16.1. We also consider parameterization issues of models with behavioral detail.
We discuss estimation and testing of models with a substantial amount of behavioral
detail in Section 17.1.

To illustrate diagnostic test applications, we review studies of the influence of
tobacco advertising on smoking. This question has been the subject of official reviews in the United States (US DHHS, 1989), New Zealand (NZDH, 1989) and the
United Kingdom (Smee, Parsonage, Anderson and Duckworth, 1992). The UK study,
completed by the Economic and Operational Research Division of the Department
of Health in the UK, considers the evidence with respect to the effect of tobacco
advertising and the effect of advertising bans on tobacco consumption in selected

countries. One study included in Smee et al. (1992) is about the effectiveness of the Norwegian Tobacco Act. This Act was implemented in July 1975. Smee et al. obtained the following numerical specification:

$$\ln \tilde{q}_t = 0.105 + 0.862 \ln \tilde{q}_{t-1} - 0.022 \, TA_t \tag{16.175}$$

where

$\tilde{q}_t$ = sales of manufactured and roll-your-own tobacco
    per adult in year t,

TA_t = an indicator variable, $= 0$ through 1974, $= 1$ starting
    in 1975 (when the Act was implemented).

Equation (16.175) was estimated by OLS from annual data over the period 1964-1989. The original model specification included additional predictors such as the relative price of tobacco and real income, but the estimated effects for those variables were not statistically significant (the estimated effects in (16.175) are highly significant). Suitable data on advertising expenditures were not available. The indicator variable, TA_t, was used to estimate the influence of the Tobacco Act upon tobacco sales.

Diagnostic tests used by Smee et al. include the RESET test which is an F-test based on incremental R^2 (Section 16.1.5). With one additional predictor, Smee et al., obtained $F = 0.65$ which is not significant. Thus, this specific diagnostic test produced no evidence of misspecification. The power of this specific RESET test is probably very small, however.

Smee et al. used the Lagrange multiplier (LM) test for the null hypothesis $\rho_1 = \rho_2 = \rho_3 = 0$, where ρ_p, $p = 1, 2, 3$, are autocorrelation processes defined in (16.46). This test statistic has a $\chi^2_{(3)}$-distribution. Its calculated value is 1.41 which is not significant. Thus, there is no evidence of autocorrelated disturbances, specifically of order 1, 2 or 3.

Smee et al. (1992) used the White test to examine the assumption of homoscedasticity and to test the functional form. The χ^2-values of the White-test also provide no evidence of heteroscedasticity or misspecification. Finally, Smee et al. used the Jarque-Bera test to examine the normality assumption. This test is also chi-square distributed, and the null hypothesis of normality could also not be rejected. The power of this test is also minimal, however.

Smee et al. (1992) decided that since (16.175) withstood all tests for misspecification, they can conclude that the advertising ban in Norway reduced tobacco consumption by about 2 percent in the short run and $\dfrac{1}{1 - 0.862} \cdot 2\% \approx 14.5$ percent in the long run.

Although (16.175) could not be rejected based on the diagnostic checks, it can be criticized on the following aspects.[90]

---

90. See Leeflang, Reuyl (1995).

- Although suitable data on advertising were not available, the omission of advertising as a predictor variable may bias the estimated effect of the ban.
- The parameters were estimated from annual data, which leads to a data interval bias in the effects of lagged variables (see Section 6.1).
- The data cover a period of 25 years. It is implausible that the parameter of the lagged endogenous variable ($\tilde{q}_{t-1}$) is constant over such a long period. Thus, the use of the corresponding parameter estimate for the calculation of a long-term effect of the advertising ban is questionable. This long-run effect is very sensitive to the lagged variable parameter estimate.
- The effect of the indicator variable is estimated from a quasi-experimental design. One imagines that various forces in Norwegian society together produced the legislative climate for the Tobacco Act. This environment must also have produced other actions such as the introduction of health education programs, health warnings on tobacco packaging and restrictions on the sale of tobacco to young people. It is impossible to distinguish the effect of the Tobacco Act from the effects of such other initiatives that occurred at the same time.
- The criterion variable is product category sales of manufactured and roll-your-own cigarettes. Entity aggregation over the individual brands and over the different product categories can severely bias the parameter estimates, especially if the brands and categories compete against each other (see also Section 14.1.2).

We use this application to make several points. For example, it is important that we use diagnostic tests of the model specification, against the data. However, a lack of statistically significant results does not imply the model is acceptable. In this application all tests lack power so that we should rely on theoretical and conceptual arguments to critically evaluate the model specification. In this example there are serious shortcomings in the model specification, the variable definitions and the (aggregate) data.

We next consider the inclusion of behavioral detail at the aggregate level (see Chapter 12 for treatments at the individual level). We distinguish three kinds of flow models with behavioral detail at the aggregate level:

- models of intermediate market response;
- diffusion models;
- adoption models.

To estimate *models of intermediate market response*, we can use consumer panel data to calculate transition probabilities. Define $N_{ij,t+1}$ as the number of consumers in a sample who bought brand i in t and brand j in $t+1$ ($i,j = 1, \ldots, n$, $t = 1, \ldots, T$). Independent of whether the panel members all purchase the same number of units, we can compute switching from one brand to another on the basis of purchase sequences. The (maximum likelihood) estimates of, for example, the fraction of switching consumers ($p_{ij,t+1}$) can be obtained by the following expression:

$$p_{ij,t+1} = \frac{N_{ij,t+1}}{N_{it}}, \quad i,j = 1, \ldots, n, \quad t = 1, \ldots, T \tag{16.176}$$

where

N_{it} = the number of consumers who bought brand i
in period t.

In this manner, intermediate market response parameter estimates can be obtained from panel data in a straightforward fashion.

Now suppose that only the market shares of the different brands, $m_{jt}, j = 1, \ldots, n$, are available for several periods. To obtain transition probabilities, p_{ijt}, we assume that these probabilities are time independent, i.e. $p_{ijt} = p_{ij}$, and we define:

$$m_{j,t+1} = p_{1j}m_{1t} + p_{2j}m_{2t} + \ldots + p_{jj}m_{jt} + \ldots + p_{nj}m_{nt}, \qquad (16.177)$$
$$j = 1, \ldots, n \text{ and } t = 1, \ldots, T.$$

Given n brands, and one equation per brand, there are n^2 unknown parameters. However since:

$$\sum_{j=1}^{n} p_{ij} = 1, \quad \text{for } j = 1, 2, \ldots, n \qquad (16.178)$$

there are only $n(n-1)$ independent transition probabilities. There are nT observations, but since:

$$\sum_{j=1}^{n} m_{jt} = 1, \text{ for all } t \qquad (16.179)$$

only $(n-1)T$ are independent. In order to obtain reliable transition probability estimates $(n-1)T$ should be substantially larger than $n(n-1)$, or T should sufficiently exceed n. In addition, it is critical that the time period is closely linked to the purchase interval. Also, if the transition probabilities are not linked to marketing variables, we estimate probabilities from the aggregated data.

Telser (1963) shows how the p_{ij}-values can be estimated from the equations (16.177) after a disturbance term $u_{j,t+1}$ has been added.[91] In Section 12.3.3 we discuss a model in which the transition probabilities are related to decision variables. These probabilities and other parameters are estimated from aggregate data.[92]

The discussion of macro flow *adoption* models (Section 10.2) shows that these models require a substantial amount of (individual) data. These data have to satisfy various requirements, and as a consequence the data collection phase requires much effort.

The first piece of information needed is the definition and the *size of the target group* for the new product, for example the number of potential product users. If the new product is an acne remedy, the target group could be defined as the teenage population. More narrowly, we could limit the target group to those teenagers who

---

91. For a more rigorous derivation of this stochastic relation see Leeflang (1974, pp. 123-124).
92. For an extensive discussion of these models see Lee, Judge and Zellner (1970).

actually have an acne problem. What matters most is that all measures are consistent. For example, if the proportion trying the product in a given period is defined with respect to the total teenage population, then the target group should be defined likewise (or an appropriate adjustment should be made).

The definition of the *time units* is usually the smallest interpurchase time interval, e.g., a week. Many models are designed to estimate how many people will try the product over time. That is, we want to predict the number of people who will purchase the product the first week (assuming that one week is the time unit), the second week, and so on. The predictions are extrapolations to, say, the national level based on test market results. The selection of representative test markets is therefore crucial. But the selection of an appropriate test market is not enough. The following kinds of questions should be raised. Will product availability at the national level be the same as in the test market? Will the level of advertising be comparable? If not, we must adjust the trial rates accordingly. Such adjustments are not easy to make. For example, how does product availability depend on the deal offered to retailers? Without relevant data, an adjustment for changes is subjective, see equation (10.17).

As another example, suppose the intensity of advertising spending is very high in a test market, and higher than the company can comparably support in, say, a national introduction. How lower advertising spending affects the trial rates is, however, difficult to know if one has not considered the relation between the trial rate and advertising. It is therefore important to keep advertising spending in the test proportional to a national scale, in which case the relation between trial and advertising is not needed. However, in case of uncertainty about the proper level, it is useful to do some experimentation.

In new-product adoption models, the *trial rate* is a crucial variable. Some possible measures are:

1. Make regular shelf counts and inventory counts in the stores carrying the product to see how much is sold per unit of time. This is a superior measure (either in the test market or in the "real" market) to counting shipments from the factory, or from warehouses to retail stores, since the latter measures can distort sales because of "pipeline fillings"[93] and time lag effects. However, instead of regular counts in all stores it may be acceptable to use a representative sample of stores instead. The trial rate for the test market is then estimated by the trial rate in the sample stores.

2. The trial rate may be estimated from a panel of consumers. The adequacy of this measure depends on the size of the panel, its representativeness, and the product category purchase frequency. The use of scanner equipment in many stores makes it possible to obtain trial rates unobtrusively from household panels using plastic cards or wands (see Chapter 15).

3. A third method is to select a random sample of target market members and ask the selected individuals if they purchased the product and, if so, in what quantity.

---

93. Wholesalers and retailers have incentives to establish inventories of goods as part of the pipeline (the channel) from producers to final consumer (see also Section 15.3).

The manner in which repeat purchase information is obtained depends on the macro flow model. In the "SPRINTER"-type models a purchase-frequency distribution is defined for all consumers who "tried" the product. This distribution allows one to distinguish between, say, heavy and light users. Some triers are ready to make a new purchase the following period, others within two periods, yet others within three periods, and so on. However, it is difficult to obtain a valid/reliable distribution since by definition we have little information. Conceivably, this information is available for related products, for example, existing brands within the same product class. Alternatively, one could use a survey or study the purchase histories of consumers who participate in scanner-based household panels.

In the ASSESSOR model the repeat rate is estimated as the equilibrium share of a two-state Markov process: see equation (10.18). Here only *one* repeat rate was considered, although one might segment the market and determine a repeat rate for each segment.

In conclusion, we note that aggregate flow models pose more difficulties with regard to *data collection* than do aggregate response models without behavioral detail. Possible problem areas are: test market selection, control of marketing instruments, sampling of stores or consumers, and distribution of interpurchase times. Data collection has to be planned and carried out carefully, to ensure that the quality of information is high and the data characteristics match the intended use.

Estimation of the parameters of macro flow models closely follows the data collection efforts. The process appears to be easier than for models having no behavioral detail. For the latter models, we have to find an appropriate method, the selection of which depends on various diagnostic tests. In most aggregate flow models, initial parameter estimates, based on panels, store data or surveys, are in a sense "first stage" estimates. A comparison of *actual* (test) market results with predictions might then lead to adjustments in the parameter estimates. Such a process of gradually improving the fit by adapting parameter estimates is similar to the "updating"-step in the model-building process (Section 5.1). Often the adjustments require a lot of judgment. For more on this, see Section 18.6.

16.9 Subjective estimation

16.9.1 JUSTIFICATION

In the previous sections of this chapter we dealt with methods developed to extract parameter estimates from objective data, data that represent observed or observable quantities. If the estimated relations allow managers to be more effective decision makers than they would be otherwise, the question we address now is how we can generate similar quantifications in the absence of objective data.

To justify the use of alternative bases for the quantification of relations, we refer to the arguments we have made in favor of model building (see Section 3.2). For example, by formalizing relations between variables we give ourselves, and others, an opportunity to reflect on the quantified expressions. We can voice our opinions about what we believe to be incorrect aspects and we start an internal discussion about the relations in question. Perhaps most importantly, the model builders can document the performance of models. Such documentation provides us with an opportunity to determine a model's actual performance.

Without the formalization of predictions, conditional upon marketing activities, it is impossible to track the true quality of decisions made by managers. Thus, whether a model is estimated from objective or subjective data, an important advantage associated with model use is that managers will apply a systematic procedure to test the accuracy of model-based predictions. This can be done for a single model by itself, for multiple models or for models in alternative bases for predictions.

In the absence of models, decision makers (DM's) make judgments based on their own experiences, the experience of colleagues or the habits and beliefs that are part of an organizational culture. The judgments reflect implicit assumptions about response parameters. Rarely, however, do the implicit parameter values remain constant across conditions. It is especially for this reason that a "model of man" can outperform "man". That is, a *model* of repeated *judgments* made by one person can better predict the actual outcomes of those very *judgments*. There is a large body of research on the success of "models of man". For example, a regression model of an admission director's judgments of academic performance for MBA students (as a function of their GMAT scores, undergraduate GPA's, undergraduate institution qualities, etc.) predicts actual performances better than the very same judgments on which the model is estimated. The reason for this result is simple: the model is consistent. It gives exactly the same prediction today, tomorrow or any time given a set of values for the predictors. The admission director, however, makes judgments that are subject to noise (or to conditions that do not relate to the academic performance of the students). If the admission director's task were to admit the applicants who are expected to have the strongest academic performance, the model of the director's judgments will tend to generate predicted values with greater accuracy than the judgments.

Of course, we may argue that predictions from a model estimated with *objective data* can do even better. This should be true as long as the MBA program content and other aspects stay relatively constant over time. In that case data from students who have graduated can be used to obtain the parameter estimates that best explain their actual academic performance. The estimated model can then be used to predict the performance of future applicants. This model would of course also give exactly the same prediction any time it is used for a given set of values for the predictors. And this "model of outcomes" will outperform the "model of man" as long as the bases for actual performance remain the same.

We now want to restrict ourselves to cases in which there are no objective data or those data are insufficient. In the MBA application, past data may be insufficient if the students' characteristics change dramatically or the curriculum and/or the requirements for good performance are very different than in earlier times. In general, insufficiency of the data may also be due to a lack of variability in one or more predictors, excessive covariation between predictors or other severe problems. Also, the competitive environment for marketing decisions can change dramatically, for example, after a new brand enters the market. Thus, historical data sometimes do not provide insight into the relations that pertain to the new environment.[94] Most econometric models are "static" in the sense that both the structure and the parameters are fixed (we discuss an exception to this under varying parameter models in Section 17.4). Thus, subjective estimation may not just be attractive in the absence of objective data but also to overcome the limitations of historical data. Of course, if decision makers can identify changes in the market environment that invalidate an existing model, they should also be able to recognize the adaptation required in it. Possible adaptations include a more flexible model structure through, for example, the use of qualitative variables (such as indicator variables being "on" or "off", dependent upon the decision maker's assessment of market conditions) and varying parameters.

One benefit that we propose relevant to the use of models from subjective data is that it formalizes the process of predictions, and allows the decision maker to diagnose their accuracy. In addition, it forces decision makers to be explicit about how they believe variables under their control affect certain performance measures. And, when multiple experts provide judgments, the subjective estimation separately for each expert shows the nature and the extent of differences. If such differences get resolved before a decision is made, then the prevailing perspective gets disseminated. When experts cannot agree, future outcomes can serve as the basis for a determination of relative accuracy of alternative approaches.

The experts who supply subjective data are called assessors. The ultimate decision makers, internal and external consultants, and sales representatives are all potential assessors. Members of the sales force can be especially helpful when clues about future sales levels are gathered. The sales force members have contact with the customers, and this should allow them to provide relevant expertise. In addition if sales forecasts are used for the determination of sales quotas it is helpful to have sales force members involved in the process. For example, their participation will increase their confidence in the quotas being fair, and this will increase their motivation to achieve the quotas. Of course, there is also the possibility that they will try to "game" the system.[95]

Sometimes expertise is gathered from various stakeholders whose differences of opinion can be vast. A broad set of stakeholders may include company executives, dealers,

---

94. Marshall, Oliver (1995, p. 1), for example, suggest that decisions often depend on various subjective judgments about the future.
95. Compare Lilien, Rangaswamy (1998, pp. 130-131).

distributors, suppliers, consultants, forecast experts, etc. Some or all of these stake-holders may be asked to constitute a jury of executive opinion. When representatives of various groups of stakeholders get together, the purpose of the meeting is for the group to come as close as possible to a single judgment. A variation on this is the Delphi method in which experts write down their judgments in a first round. Each expert receives summary information about the independent judgments made, and this information can influence the expert's judgments in subsequent rounds.

In Section 16.9.2 we discuss methods of obtaining subjective point estimates, re-sponse functions and probability assessments. We consider how subjective judgments of multiple individuals can be combined in Section 16.9.3. The use of subjective data together with objective data receives attention in Section 16.9.4, and in Section 16.9.5 we provide an application.

16.9.2 OBTAINING SUBJECTIVE ESTIMATES

We consider three categories of subjective data obtainable from a *single* assessor:[96]

a. point estimation;
b. response functions;
c. probability assessments.

The subjective data consist of opinions (judgments) and intentions (Armstrong, 1985, Chapter 6). Intentions are indications individuals provide about their planned behav-ior or about the decisions they plan to make or the outcomes of those decisions. Opin-ions refer to forecasts about events whose outcomes are outside the assessors' control. Intention surveys are frequently used to forecast the demand for a new product (Mor-rison, 1979, Kalwani, Silk, 1982, Jamieson, Bass, 1989, Morwitz, Schmittlein, 1992). Other applications involve estimation of the impact of a possible entrant on a market (Alsem, Leeflang, 1994); see Section 16.9.5.

POINT ESTIMATION

Point estimation[97] provides partial information about the distribution of an unknown quantity. Suppose we ask an expert: "What is the probability that sales will be no more than one thousand units next month?" and it is seventy percent in the expert's judgment. The expert gives us information about the cumulative distribution function of next month's sales, but it is only partial in the sense that we do not know the prob-ability that sales will be no more than, for example, five hundred units. The expert's answer gives us one point (*A* in Figure 16.11) of a cumulative distribution function. Figure 16.11 shows two of the many possible functions that may pass through *A*. We note that the manner in which the question is formulated is important. It has, for example, no meaning for someone who is unfamiliar with the notion of probability.

---

96. Compare also Lilien, Kotler (1983, p. 130).
97. For an in-depth analysis see, for example, Lehmann (1983).

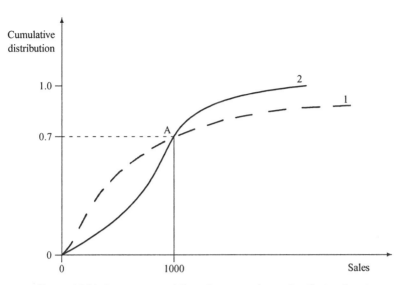

Figure 16.11 Point estimate (A) and two cumulative distribution functions.

We can provide some training, or we can change the descriptions, for example by using "chances" or "odds" which may be more familiar terms. If we only ask for a point estimate, we are often looking for a measure of central tendency. The answer may provide an estimate of the mode, the median, or mean, as illustrated below:

1. "What is your estimate of the most likely level of sales?" gives an estimate of the mode.
2. "What level of sales do you estimate you have an even chance of reaching?" provides an estimate of the median.
3. "What level of sales do you expect?" results in an estimate of the mean.

This type of questioning is appropriate if we desire to obtain estimates of such quantities as market share or sales. However, the assessor will by necessity give an estimate that is conditional upon an assumed level of various marketing instruments (for example, price, size of the sales force, etc.).

RESPONSE FUNCTIONS

A logical extension is to obtain a set of point estimates, one for each of a number of values of the marketing instruments, which generates a point estimate of a *response function*. At the same time, the construction of a subjective response curve enables us to estimate quantities that cannot normally be assessed directly, such as elasticities or response parameters. We consider an example[98] from the ADBUDG model:

---

98. This example is based on Little (1970); see also Lilien, Kotler (1983, pp. 131-134). Little's model is more complex than (16.180). For example, he considers long-run and short-run effects. In (16.180) we omit the brand index for convenience. ADBUDG's model structure is discussed in Section 5.3.3.

$$m_t = \alpha + (\beta - \alpha)\frac{a_t^\delta}{\gamma + a_t^\delta} \tag{16.180}$$

where

$$m_t = \text{market share of a brand in period } t,$$
$$a_t = \text{advertising expenditures of the brand in period } t, \text{ and}$$
$$\alpha, \beta, \gamma, \delta = \text{the parameters.}$$

Suppose we want to estimate the parameters of (16.180) subjectively. Specifically assume that the brand in question is a detergent with a sizeable market share. The obvious person to assist the model builder with parameter estimates is the brand manager. The brand manager has at least some knowledge of how the market operates, which competitors matter, and so on. Still, we cannot obtain the desired information if we simply ask: "what do you think α, β, γ and δ are?" Instead, we may ask: "what do you think market share will be in a few years, if all advertising is stopped from now on?" The answer is an estimate of α since for advertising equal to zero, market share is equal to α according to (16.180). Similarly we can ask the brand manager what will happen to market share if an unlimited amount is spent on advertising. The answer to this question is an estimate of β, since if advertising is very large, $a_t^\delta/(\gamma + a_t^\delta)$ approaches one, and thus m approaches $\alpha + (\beta - \alpha) = \beta$.

The next question is what market share obtains if advertising is left at its current level, say $a_t = c$ dollars. Let the answer be m_c. And we may ask what market share will occur if the advertising budget is increased by 50 percent. Let the corresponding share be m_{c+}. We then have the following two points of the market share function:

$$m_c = \alpha + (\beta - \alpha)\frac{c^\delta}{\gamma + c^\delta} \tag{16.181}$$

$$m_{c+} = \alpha + (\beta - \alpha)\frac{(1.5c)^\delta}{\gamma + (1.5c)^\delta}. \tag{16.182}$$

Since α and β are already "known" (16.181)-(16.182) is a system of two equations in two unknowns γ and δ. Solving this system yields estimates of the final two parameters.

To complete the process, suppose the brand manager estimates that without advertising, market share will drop to ten percent ($\alpha = 0.10$) and with saturation advertising it will reach seventy percent ($\beta = 0.70$). Suppose further that with the current budget ($\$810,000$), market share is expected to be 0.40, and with 50 percent higher advertising market share should become 0.415. Estimates for γ and δ are then found by solving:

$$0.40 = 0.10 + 0.60\frac{(810,000)^\delta}{\gamma + (810,000)^\delta}$$

$$0.415 = 0.10 + 0.60\frac{(1,215,000)^\delta}{\gamma + (1,215,000)^\delta}.$$

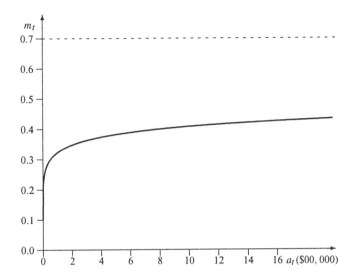

Figure 16.12 A brand manager's implicit market share function.

The estimated values are approximately: $\gamma = 30$ and $\delta = 0.25$. Figure 16.12 shows the brand manager's implicit market share function.

One may object that the four parameters in (16.181)-(16.182) are estimated from four observations. Hence the model fits the data perfectly. But there is, no guarantee that additional subjective judgments fit the market share function shown in Figure 16.12. Thus, we prefer to collect additional observations. For example, we may elicit market share estimates for advertising expenditures equal to the current budget plus 20 percent, plus 40 percent, ... minus 20 percent, minus 40 percent, and so on, thus providing a scatter of points through which a market share function can be fitted using (non-linear) estimation methods. In that case, deviations of the subjective estimates from the fitted curve allow us to check the consistency of a manager's estimates. In case of systematic deviations, we can consider an *alternative functional form*, in close cooperation with the manager.

The disadvantage of asking additional judgments is that it requires more time and effort from the manager. These judgments only capture the manager's expectations about market share, given values for one marketing instrument. However, extensions to multiple predictors are straightforward. Importantly, the judgments about market share given advertising are conditional on, for example, the brand's price and the marketing instruments for other brands.

To illustrate the approach for multiple predictors, we consider a market with two brands (j and c) which compete on price (p_{jt}, p_{ct}) and advertising (a_{jt}, a_{ct}). For simplicity, suppose there are two alternative price levels p_j^1, p_j^2 for brand j and two for brand c: p_c^1, p_c^2. Similarly, suppose a_j^1, a_j^2, a_c^1, a_c^2 are alternative levels of advertising expenditures. We now ask an assessor for a point estimate of brand j's

Table 16.11 Setup for subjective values of a brand's market share as a function of prices and advertising expenditures.

p_{jt}	p_{ct}	a_{jt}	a_{ct}	m_{jt}
p_j^1	p_c^1	a_j^1	a_c^1	m_j^1
p_j^1	p_c^1	a_j^1	a_c^2	m_j^2
p_j^1	p_c^1	a_j^2	a_c^1	m_j^3
$\vdots$	$\vdots$	$\vdots$	$\vdots$	$\vdots$
p_j^2	p_c^2	a_j^2	a_c^2	m_j^{16}

market share if $p_{jt} = p_j^1$, $p_{ct} = p_c^1$, $a_{jt} = a_j^1$, $a_{ct} = a_c^1$. Let this estimate be m_j^1. The assessor can then provide market share estimates for all sixteen combinations of p_{jt}, p_{ct}, a_{jt}, a_{ct} (see Table 16.11). These sixteen subjective observations could then be used, for example, to estimate a MCI-model:

$$m_{jt} = \frac{e^{\alpha_j} p_{jt}^{\beta_1} a_{jt}^{\beta_2}}{e^{\alpha_j} p_{jt}^{\beta_1} a_{jt}^{\beta_2} + e^{\alpha_c} p_{ct}^{\beta_1} a_{ct}^{\beta_2}} \cdot u_{jt} \qquad (16.183)$$

where

u_{jt} = a disturbance term.

Of course, if objective data were available (and of sufficient quality), we could estimate (16.183) also with such data. One advantage of using both objective and subjective data is that we can compare the estimated parameters. Systematic deviations could be attributable to misspecifications of the model as well as to the possible difficulty the assessor has contemplating how the brand's market share depends on the marketing variables. Thus, it is important to confront predictions from any model with actual results, and to make modifications where appropriate.

Most of the models developed for parameterization with subjective data date from the seventies. Examples are ADBUDG (Little, 1970), CALLPLAN (Lodish, 1971) and BRANDAID (Little, 1975a, 1975b). For more detail about these "decision models" based on subjective data see Rangaswamy (1993).[99] The judgmental assessment of market response to marketing variables is not without controversy. In laboratory research, Chakravarti, Mitchell and Staelin (1981) found that subjects who used the ADBUDG model made worse decisions than those who did not use it. Little and Lodish (1981) argue, however, that subjects in a laboratory experiment rarely have access to critical types of information, such as knowledge of the dynamics of a particular market. For example, in the laboratory studies in which judgments are compared with statistical models of those judgments, the information available to the DM is the same as that available to the model. Consequently, in the laboratory

---

99. See also Naert, Weverbergh (1981b).

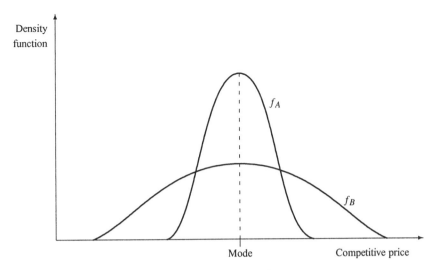

Figure 16.13 Subjective estimates of a competitive reaction.

the DM's cannot take advantage of any skills they may have with respect to other information not incorporated in the model (Blattberg, Hoch, 1990).[100]

PROBABILITY ASSESSMENT

We now consider the notion of probability assessment, that is assessment of a probability distribution. We start with a simple illustration to suggest the usefulness of eliciting an entire distribution. Suppose that a firm considers a price increase. The desirability of the increase depends on the subjective estimate from its sales manager of the likely price reaction of a major competitor. Assume that a modal value is used for an initial judgment. If the sales manager has much confidence in this estimate, implying a tight distribution such as f_A in Figure 16.13, then the modal value gives very precise information about the competitive price reaction and this modal value is a good basis for (partly) determining the optimal price increase, if any. On the other hand, if f_B in Figure 16.13 is the proper density function, then the modal value is a very uncertain estimate. If we know the prevailing density function we can conduct sensitivity analyses, i.e. determine how the optimal price increase depends on alternative competitive price reactions. And, in case the sensitivity is very high, it may be useful to determine whether the uncertainty about the price reaction can be reduced.

Benson, Curley and Smith (1995) identify two subprocesses in probability assessments viz: *belief assessment* and *response assessment*. Belief assessment includes the structuring and conditioning steps in which target propositions are identified and

100. See also McIntyre (1982), McIntyre, Currim (1982). Beach and Barnes (1987) review the vast literature on biases in judgment and decision making. For additional perspectives see Hogarth (1987), Philips (1987), Bunn and Wright (1991) and Gupta (1994).

defined, and relevant knowledge is evoked from the expert. Response assessment encompasses the steps in which numerical or verbal qualities are attached to the propositions. Belief assessment is dominated by reasoning, whereas response assessment is judgmental. The use of these subprocesses is relevant for the description of complex decision processes. Examples of models which can be parameterized in this way are the process models (Section 4.1) and the models that describe the decision process of an industrial buyer (Section 8.1). These models require skills of reasoning, making inference and deriving conclusions from data through the application of arguments.

To help managers with the construction of beliefs, decision analysts have developed structuring methods such as *graphical representations* and *direct questions*.

Graphical representations can be used to prompt relevant information from an individual decision maker and to structure that information in a visual form. Examples include hierarchical and non-hierarchical decision trees and knowledge maps. A knowledge map is an influence diagram without decision nodes i.e. containing only chance nodes, or

> *"a graphical representation which may cause the decision maker to consider information in the formal mental imagery"*
>
> (Browne, Curley, Benson, 1997, p. 11)

Knowledge maps can be used to obtain probabilities for individual factors, and to derive the best estimate of the probability for a critical event. We show an example of a knowledge map in Figure 16.14. This knowledge map relates to the probability of success for a new automatic product, called Electroglide. The product is designed to reduce fuel consumption through the substitution of electric power when a car cruises. Individual subjects were asked to predict the success of the new product by first evoking all the primary influences deemed relevant, then evoking secondary influences, etc. This process continued until each subject was satisfied with the resulting knowledge map (representing the subjects' beliefs). At the end, a probability qualifying their conclusion is elicited.

Directed questions are often used by decision analysts to elicit information based on checklists or questioning schemes. Although these methods can be useful for structuring knowledge, they have an important drawback. Subjects will consider aspects merely because of suggestions made by the decision analyst. This information, however, is not screened for relevance that is done naturally in decision-making tasks. This drawback is similar to potentially artificial elements in relation to the judgmental assessment of response.

The measurement of subjective probabilities relates to the philosophical view of probability which does not require that the probability of an event has a uniquely determinable value. In this subjective approach, probability expresses the beliefs of an individual based on personal knowledge and information. In that sense the subjective approach makes no attempt to specify what assessments are correct. However, not all assessments are admissible. For example, subjective probabilities should be

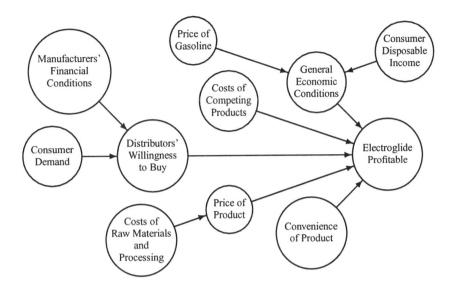

Source: Browne, Curley, Benson (1997, p. 17).

Figure 16.14 Illustration of a knowledge map.

coherent in the sense that there are no contradictions among them. Under this constraint it has been shown that subjective probabilities have properties of conventional probabilities.[101]

Although experiments reported in the literature show that individuals can provide appropriate subjective probabilities, it has been found that our ability to assess probabilities depends on:

a. *the assessment technique used,* and
b. *the assessor.*

It is also important that subjective probabilities are in accordance with the assessor's beliefs. Thus, the decision analyst may want to use methods that motivate to make this correspondence strong. This leads to a third point:

c. *the evaluation.*

We now discuss each of these three points in turn.

a. *The assessment technique*
Suppose that a DM is interested in a unit sales forecast for a new brand in period t : $\widehat{S}_t$. To this end the DM asks two sales representatives (assessors 1 and 2) the following questions:

101. See Savage (1954) and De Finetti (1964).

Table 16.12 Sales estimates and probabilities for two assessors.

	Assessor 1		Assessor 2	
	Estimates	Probabilities	Estimates	Probabilities
S_t^L	6 Million	0.1	4 Million	0.3
S_t^M	8 Million	0.8	7 Million	0.5
S_t^H	10 Million	0.1	10 Million	0.2
$E(S_t)$	8 Million		6.7 Million	
$Var(S_t)$	0.8 Million^2		4.41 Million^2	

- what is your lowest estimate of S_t: S_t^L;
- what is your most likely estimate of S_t: S_t^M;
- what is your highest estimate of S_t: S_t^H.

And, assuming that the three values are the only possible outcomes, each assessor also provides an indication of the probabilities of occurrence. We show the representatives' answers in Table 16.12. Assessor 1 is more optimistic about the new brand's sales than assessor 2, except for the highest estimate which is the same for the two assessors. Assessor 1 also has a much higher subjective probability for the most likely value of sales than assessor 2 does. As a result, the expected value for sales is higher while the variance is lower for assessor 1.

In the absence of knowledge about the shape of a subjective probability distribution, we can assess the uncertainty around the estimates by a variety of methods.[102] One method focuses on the fractions of the Cumulative Distribution Function (CDF).[103] Typically, five fractiles, 0.01, 0.25, 0.50, 0.75, and 0.99 are assessed. The first assessment is the 0.50 fractile which is the probability that sales in period t will be less than 0.50. $Q_{0.50}$ is obtained from the question: "Considering all possible levels of sales, what is the amount for which it is equally likely that sales will be more and that sales will be less than this value?" For assessor 2 in Table 16.12 the response would have been 7 Million, hence $Q_{0.50} = 7$ Million. We can obtain the 0.25 and 0.75 fractiles by asking: "If sales are, in fact, less than 7 Million, what amount of sales would divide the interval from 0 to 7 Million units into equally likely parts?" The resulting value is the 0.25 fractile, denoted as $Q_{0.25}$. The 0.75 fractile can be obtained from the question: "How would you divide the interval of sales over 7 Million units into equally likely parts?" Finally, the values for $Q_{0.01}$ and $Q_{0.99}$ can be obtained by asking: "What value of sales would you use such that the changes of sales being greater (less) than this value is only one in 100?" We can then construct a CDF-curve of sales by plotting the fractiles and corresponding sales values. We provide an example in Figure 16.15.

---

102. See Winkler (1967a), Smith (1967) and Hampton, Moore and Thomas (1977).
103. A similar example appears in Lilien and Kotler (1983, p. 135).

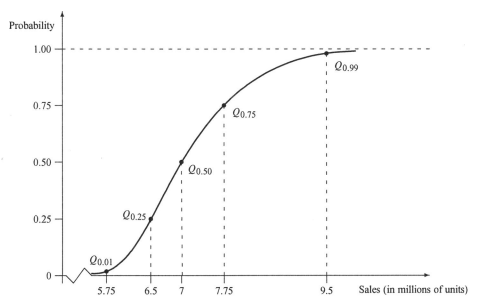

Figure 16.15 A cumulative subjective probability function for sales (assessor 2).

In some cases it is possible to specify the distribution *a priori*. It then suffices to obtain estimates of the parameters. We consider a few examples. Suppose the quantity we want to assess is, in the mind of the assessor, a random variable that is *normally* distributed. This distribution is then characterized by its two parameters, the mean μ, and the standard deviation σ. Since most people cannot provide direct estimates of the standard deviation, we may use two questions to estimate both μ and σ, for example:

1. "What is your estimate of sales such that there is a 2.5 percent chance that it will be higher?" (S_t^H).
2. "What is your estimate of sales such that there is a 2.5 percent chance that it will be below that level?" (S_t^L).

The mean is then estimated by taking the average of S_t^L and S_t^H:

$$\hat{\mu} = \frac{S_t^L + S_t^H}{2}. \tag{16.184}$$

Since 95 percent of the possible values of a normally distributed random variable lie within ± 1.96 standard deviations of the mean, the standard deviation is estimated by:

$$\hat{\sigma} = \frac{S_t^H - S_t^L}{3.92}. \tag{16.185}$$

For asymmetric distributions such as the beta distribution, low (S_t^L) high (S_t^H), and modal (S_t^M) estimates are necessary. The estimates of the mean and standard devia-

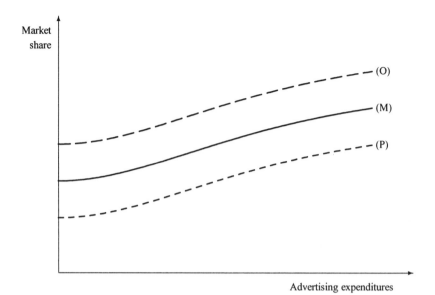

*Figure 16.16 Optimistic (O), modal (M) and pessimistic (P) market share-advertising response
functions (constant uncertainty).*

tion are then:

$$\hat{\mu} = \frac{S_t^L + 4S_t^M + S_t^H}{6} \tag{16.186}$$

$$\hat{\sigma} = \frac{S_t^H - S_t^L}{6}. \tag{16.187}$$

An assessor may find it useful to look at the shapes of alternative classical probability
distributions, as suggested, for example, by Grayson (1967). Distributions are shown,
for example, in the gallery of shapes investigated by Raiffa and Schlaifer (1961). If
the assessor finds a shape in the gallery that comes close to his thoughts, he can use
the corresponding probability distribution.

So far we have considered distributions of the values a random variable may take.
This idea can also be used for distributions of individual points on a response function.
For example, we could construct an optimistic, a pessimistic and a modal response
function. Figure 16.16 shows an example of a market share-advertising response
function for which the degree of uncertainty stays approximately constant over the
whole range of values of advertising. This is not the case in Figure 16.17, where the
uncertainty is modest for advertising expenditures within the interval RA, but large
outside that interval. This could result if the firm's advertising expenditure levels
have normally fallen within RA. Managers will be less confident about points on the
response curve that are outside their experience.

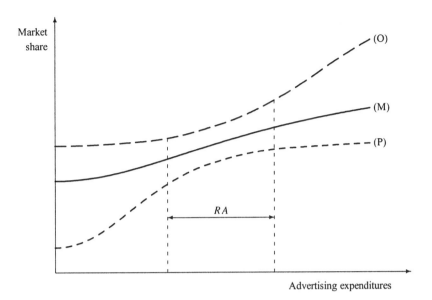

Figure 16.17 Optimistic (O), modal (M) and pessimistic (P) market share-advertising response functions (varying uncertainty).

b. *The assessor*

Winkler (1967a) showed that persons with previous training in quantitative methods, in particular in probability and statistics, are better in translating their judgments into probabilities than persons without such training. The elicitation of quality judgments also depends on managers' attitudes toward uncertainty and toward the process of measurement. Some people find it difficult to tolerate uncertainty. Others resist the quantification of their uncertainty, because they are skeptical about measurement of subjective states of mind.

c. *Evaluation*

An important question is whether the assessments correspond to the respondent's beliefs. Once the outcome is known it is possible to determine how close the expected value was to the actual value. Since we cannot evaluate the validity of subjective probabilities, we can only help the expert to make sure the probabilities are in accordance with her judgment.[104] The application of rules developed to make responses and beliefs correspond will, in fact, also contribute to the learning process. That is, these rules have the dual purpose of evaluating assessors and enabling them to become better experts, as shown by Winkler (1967c) in an experiment concerning the assessments of probabilities for outcomes of football games.

The two primary evaluation techniques are *actual bets* and *scoring rules*. Involving people in actual bets, with monetary rewards or penalties resulting from

---

104. See Winkler (1967b).

the quality of their responses, is one way to motivate people to report their personal assessments as accurately as possible. Monetary rewards, however, may not be sufficient to motivate the assessor to take the procedure seriously.

Scoring rules are used to determine a respondent's accuracy. The scores may be used to determine the weights in combined subjective estimates. For examples of scoring rules we refer to De Finetti (1965).

Other feedback methods are available if there are multiple assessors. We discuss the combination of judgments next.

16.9.3   COMBINING SUBJECTIVE ESTIMATES

If there are multiple experts who can provide subjective estimates, the challenge is how to combine the diversity of assessments. For example, lack of relevant information drives a DM to obtain expert opinions (Winkler, 1986) and it is likely that experts differ in the nature of their beliefs due to differences in their expertise. An average opinion can be obtained by a mathematical approach (see below). Alternatively, one may use a behavioral approach that aims to arrive at a consensus opinion.

The combination of subjective estimates generally leads to better results than one can obtain from a simple assessor, as demonstrated by Lawrence, Edmundson, O'Connor (1986), Mahmoud (1987) and Maines (1996). The accuracy of estimates improves because the random errors in individual estimates are "diversified away" (Ashton, Ashton, 1985). In this sense group estimates have the same advantage as the "model of man" which also removes the noise in subjective judgments.

Winkler (1968) presents mathematical approaches, which are (weighted) average methods. Let $f_i(\theta)$ be the subjective probability density function (continuous case) or the probability mass function (discrete case) of assessor i. The combined or pooled function $f(\theta)$ can then be written as:

$$f(\theta) = \sum_{i=1}^{I} w_i f_i(\theta) \tag{16.188}$$

where $w_i \geq 0$, and $\sum_{i=1}^{I} w_i = 1$, and where I is the number of assessors. In (16.188) w_i represents the weight given to the ith assessor's function . In order for $f(\theta)$ to be a proper density, the weights have to be restricted to *sum* to *one*. The same weighting schemes can also be applied to point estimates. Different weighting schemes correspond to different ways to determining the w_i. Winkler (1968, pp. B-63-B64) suggests the following methods.

1. Equal weights
If the decision maker has no reason to believe that one assessor is better than another, each assessor should have equal weight.

$$w_i = 1/I, \text{ for all } i. \tag{16.189}$$

2. Weights proportional to ranking
If the decision maker believes that the assessors can be ranked with respect to exper-

tise she may assign weights on the basis of these ranks. Each expert is given a rank from 1 (the worst) to I (the best). Given a rank ra_i, a simple way to assign the weight w_i is:

$$w_i = \frac{ra_i}{\sum_{i=1}^{I} ra_i} \qquad (16.190)$$

or

$$w_i = \frac{ra_i}{I(I+1)/2}. \qquad (16.191)$$

The drawback of this scheme is that the ratio of weights for the best and worst expert expands as the number of assessors increases. For example, with two assessors, the ratio of weights is 2 to 1. However, with six assessors, the ratio of weights for the best and worst assessors is 6 to 1. The dependency of this ratio on the number of assessors appears to be a severe drawback of this weighting scheme.

3. *Weights proportional to a self-rating*
According to this scheme each assessor is asked to rate his own expertise on a scale from 1 (the lowest) to, say, 10 (the highest). Let c_i be the rating assessor i assigns to himself. The weights are then obtained as follows:

$$w_i = \frac{c_i}{\sum_{i=1}^{I} c_i}. \qquad (16.192)$$

Although now the ratio of weights for, say, the best and worst assessors does not depend on the number of assessors, the weighting scheme does assume that the ratings have ratio-scaled properties. For example, an assessor rating his expertise equal to 10 would have twice the weight as an assessor with a rating of 5. And the assumption is also that the assessors have comparable interpretations of the scale values, a property that is rarely if ever applicable to rating scales.

4. *Weights based on scoring rules*
In Section 16.9.2 we mentioned that scoring rules can be used to evaluate an assessor's subjective judgments. Such scores can also be the basis for assigning weights to experts.

Winkler (1967a) has found by experimentation that applying scoring rules to such pooled estimates which he calls consensus scores, produces better results than simply averaging individual subject scores. An argument in favor of a scoring rule is that the score is based on performance accuracy. Nevertheless, one can also check whether the decision itself is sensitive to which weighting scheme is applied.

   A disadvantage of these methods is that the resulting $f(\theta)$ may be multimodal even if the constituting $f_i(\theta)$ are all unimodal. Winkler (1968) therefore proposed a

Table 16.13 Four sets of market share estimates, given advertising expenditures.

Assessor	Advertising Expenditures			
	0	$250,000	$500,000	$1,000,000
1	0.05	0.20	0.35	0.70
2	0.20	0.28	0.32	0.35
3	0.15	0.23	0.30	0.50
4	0.25	0.30	0.34	0.40

more complex pooling procedure based on the concept of (natural) conjugate distribution, originally developed to simplify Bayesian analysis.[105] This method has the advantage of providing a unimodal $f(\theta)$ if the underlying $f_i(\theta)$ are unimodal. A disadvantage, however, is that the method requires that each $f_i(\theta)$ be a member of the conjugate family, for example a *beta* distribution, which is reasonable only if each assessor feels that the particular distribution accurately reflects his judgments.

We now consider the pooling of response curves, with a hypothetical example of a set of market share-advertising response curves. Each curve is constructed by connecting a set of point estimates. The point estimates correspond to four levels of advertising expenditures: $0; $250,000; $500,000, and $1,000,000. Assume that four assessors have given the point estimates shown in Table 16.13 from which the response curves in Figure 16.18 are derived. The methods discussed above can be applied to the point estimates corresponding to each of the four levels of advertising.[106] For example with equal weights, pooled market share estimates of 0.1625, 0.2525, 0.3275, and 0.4875 are obtained. This pooled response curve is shown as *P* in Figure 16.18.

An obvious drawback of these individual response curves is that each one is not very different from being linear. As a result, the pooled curve also appears to be close to a linear one. Also, with zero advertising it is unlikely that market share can be much above zero in the long run.

Instead of averaging the individual responses to produce a pooled curve, one can consider the sixteen estimates in Table 16.13 as observations, and apply econometric analysis to arrive at a pooled response curve. This requires the specification of a functional relationship (Compare equation (16.183)).

The methods proposed above to arrive at a pooled response curve are purely mechanical. We can also use the data in Table 16.13 and Figure 16.18 and find out why assessor 1 believes that market share can be doubled by doubling advertising expenditures from $500,000 to $1,000,000, and why assessor 2 believes that this

---

105. A detailed treatment of (natural) conjugate distribution is given by Raiffa and Schlaifer (1961). See also Iversen (1984, pp. 64-66), Greene (1997, pp. 317-319), Lee (1997).
106. Combining natural conjugate distributions is not possible since the assessors have only been asked to supply point estimates and not entire distributions.

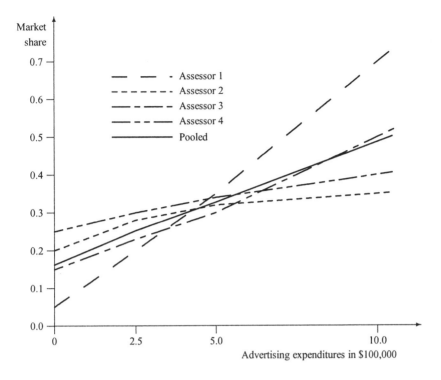

Figure 16.18 Four individual and one pooled response functions.

increase would only add three share points (from 0.32 to 0.35). Trying to find out why individuals have widely varying subjective estimates requires a *behavioral approach*.

The evaluation techniques, actual bets and scoring rules (Section 16.9.2) are known as *outcome feedback* evaluation methods. Another type of feedback is *cognitive feedback*.[107] Cognitive feedback provides assessors with information that allows them to compare relations between the individual judgments and the combined judgment. Some research indicates that outcome feedback is often ineffective (Balzer et al., 1992) while cognitive feedback has been found to be beneficial (Balzer et al., 1992, Gupta, 1994). We discuss below some approaches based on cognitive feedbacks, "group reassessment" and "feedback and reassessment".

Group reassessment
After experts have made individual assessments, they meet as a group to discuss each other's assessment and to arrive at a consensus point estimate (if each individual expert had made a point estimate), or a consensus distribution (if each expert had provided a subjectively estimated probability distribution). Such group discussions may not produce a true consensus, however. Once individuals have established their

---

107. See, for example, Balzer, Sulsky, Hammer and Sumner (1992), and the discussion in Gupta (1994).

own subjective judgments for others to see, they tend to defend their positions. At the same time, some individuals have a predisposition to be swayed by persuasively stated opinions of others. Also, dominating individuals and people with authority can have unusually strong influences. In addition, there is group pressure on an individual whose views are widely divergent from those held by many others to conform (Winkler, 1987). The impact of such psychological factors may be reduced by asking experts to reassess their own individual estimates, after a group result is obtained.

The potential pressures that may allow influence to dominate expertise in group discussions may be avoided with the use of recently developed group reassessment techniques: Nominal Group Techniques (NGT's) and Estimation-Talk-Estimation (ETE) meetings. A NGT-meeting starts by having individual experts write ideas and formulate their estimates independently. During the meeting, each individual in turn briefly presents one idea. All ideas are recorded on a flip chart, but no discussion takes place until all ideas are recorded. Following a discussion of all ideas, each expert records his or her evaluation of the ideas, by rank ordering or rating them. The scores are then *mathematically aggregated* to yield a group "consensus". This technique has been shown to be superior to the Delphi technique discussed below (Lock, 1987).

ETE-meetings are very similar to NGT. ETE requires "group estimation" before and after group discussions of the ideas. Rank ordering or rating does not necessarily take place (Parenté, Anderson-Parenté, 1987).

Feedback and reassessment
The objective of this class of methods is to avoid the problems associated with group (re)assessment while keeping the advantages. The best known among the feedback and reassessment techniques is the Delphi method, developed and extensively tested at the Rand Corporation.[108]

The Delphi method involves the repeated questioning (by interview or questionnaire) of a number of experts, while avoiding direct confrontations. In a first round experts report their individual assessments, and answer questions that are designed to bring out the experts' reasoning such as the factors relevant to the problem. For example, in assessing brand sales, an expert may make particular assumptions about the determinants of product class sales. Not only should the expert list the relevant factors but she should also discuss the assessment of these factors. Finally, the expert is asked to state what data would allow her to arrive at a better appraisal of the various factors, and consequently at a more confident answer.

In the second round each expert receives information about other experts' assessments, without, however, their identities. For example, the median and the interquartile range of point estimates provided by all experts may be communicated.[109] If entire distributions are estimated, the set of distributions may be reported. The feedback may include data previously requested by the experts, as well as factors and

---

108. See, for example, Dalkey and Helmer (1962), Helmer (1966), Jain (1993, pp. 331-337).
109. Brown, Helmer (1964).

considerations suggested by one or more experts. Based on the feedback, experts are asked to update their assessments, if necessary.

The results of the second round will, in general, have as many point estimates or distributions as assessors, but the spread is expected to be smaller. Feedback from the second round of estimates is also given to the assessors, who are once more asked to revise their assessments. It is expected that the individual estimates will show a tendency to converge as the collection of updated estimates continues. The process may continue until a sufficient degree of agreement is achieved, or until individual estimates remain unchanged between iterations. The rate of convergence tends to depend on the degree of divergence in the original estimates, on the reasons for differences, and on the evaluation of each expert's expertise relative to that of other experts.

Several studies suggest that the Delphi technique produces good results. An interesting application is by Larréché and Montgomery (1977) who asked for evaluations of marketing models with respect to their likelihood of acceptance by management. Lilien and Rangaswamy (1998, p. 131) discuss a Delphi study with 300 auto industry executives to forecast the sales of electric vehicles 10 years into the future.[110] The consensus favors hybrid (electric-combustion) engines, and the estimates are for roughly 150,000 of these vehicles to be on the road in the US in 2003.[111]

16.9.4 COMBINING SUBJECTIVE AND OBJECTIVE DATA

In practice, objective data may be available for some variables in a model, but not for all. Sometimes, subjective data can be generated to substitute for missing variables. However, we must then deal with the consequences for parameter estimation (for example, errors in the measurement of predictor variables cause ordinary least squares estimates to be biased and inconsistent). At other times, objective data may be available but not useful for analysis. For example, as we discussed in Section 8.3.1 historical price data may show insufficient variation to permit reliable estimation of price elasticity by econometric techniques. The econometric analysis can then be complemented by subjective methods.

Blattberg and Hoch (1990) suggest that model-based systems for decision making should be a hybrid system of 50 percent judgment (manager) and 50 percent model (customer). They find that this mix does better than either model or manager alone. A hybrid system may correct for the human's shortcomings in information processing while the human picks up on cues, patterns, and information not incorporated in the model (Bucklin, Lehmann, Little, 1998. p. 6).

---

110. This research was completed by the University of Michigan's Office for the Study of Automative Transportation.

111. For an extensive review of the application of Delphi see Gupta and Clarke (1996) A comparison of judgments obtained by a group consensus through a Delphi process and averaging individual judgments is made by Larréché and Moinpour (1983).

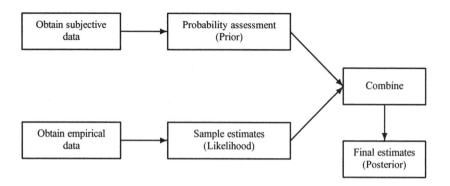

Source: Naert, Weverbergh (1981b, p. 107).

Figure 16.19 A general framework for Bayesian analysis.

Combining objective and subjective data and estimates can be accomplished by either formal or informal analysis, as we discuss below.

Formal analysis

Combining subjective and objective information in a formal way is achieved by Bayesian analysis. We show a general framework for Bayesian analysis in Figure 16.19. Suppose a firm wants to estimate the trial rate (θ) for a new product. Based on experience from launching other products in the same category, the trial rate is subjectively assessed. This subjective information is called prior information and may be available in the form of a prior distribution $f(\theta)$. The firm may also offer the product in a test market, thus obtaining sample information z. Let this sample evidence or objective information be available under the form of a sampling distribution $l(z \mid \theta)$. A decision to launch or not to launch would then be based on the posterior distribution $f(\theta \mid z)$ obtained from Bayes' Theorem:

$$f(\theta \mid z) = \frac{f(\theta)l(z \mid \theta)}{\int f(\theta)l(z \mid \theta)d\theta}. \tag{16.193}$$

Combining objective and prior information also applies to the estimation of response curves. Assume the following model:

$$y = X\beta + u \tag{16.194}$$

where β is a $L \times 1$ vector of unknown parameters. Without prior information β is estimated by, for example, ordinary least squares:

$$\hat{\beta} = (X'X)^{-1}X'y. \tag{16.195}$$

Suppose now that prior information is available on L' of the L parameters, i.e., a $L' \times 1$ vector of prior estimates $\hat{\beta}_p$. Prior information can be subjective, but also objective, such as estimates obtained from a meta-analysis (Section 3.3). So, for example, the prior value of a price elasticity can be set equal to -1.76, i.e. the average value found in a meta-analysis by Tellis (1988b). Assuming these prior estimates to be unbiased, we have:

$$E(\hat{\beta}_p) = \beta_p. \tag{16.196}$$

The prior estimates are subject to error:

$$\hat{\beta}_{p\ell} = \beta_{p\ell} + \mu_\ell, \quad \ell = 1, 2, \ldots, L' \tag{16.197}$$

where μ_ℓ is the error term for the ℓth estimate. Let the covariance matrix of the error term of the prior estimates be:

$$E(\mu\mu') = \Phi. \tag{16.198}$$

To formally combine objective and prior information, we write (16.197) in matrix form:

$$\hat{\beta}_p = A\beta + \mu, \text{ with} \tag{16.199}$$

$$A = (I \vdots O) \tag{16.200}$$

where I is an $L' \times L'$ identity matrix, and O is an $L' \times (L - L')$ matrix of zeros.[112] Combining (16.198) and (16.199) we obtain:

$$\begin{bmatrix} y \\ \hat{\beta}_p \end{bmatrix} = \begin{bmatrix} X \\ A \end{bmatrix} \beta + \begin{bmatrix} u \\ \mu \end{bmatrix} \tag{16.201}$$

or

$$Y = Z\beta + v$$

with

$$E(vv') = \begin{bmatrix} \sigma^2 I & O \\ O & \Phi \end{bmatrix}. \tag{16.202}$$

Thus, (16.201) can be estimated by generalized least squares.[113]

Informal analysis
Informal analyses can be used to adjust or update empirically determined coefficients. For example, parameter estimates from sample data can be adjusted by multiplying them by subjectively estimated indices whose reference value is one[114] (i.e. if the reference value is used no updating takes place). Alternatively, we can start with

---

112. We assume that prior information is available on the first L' estimators. The variables can be arranged such that this is the case.
113. For detailed discussions on Bayesian inference in econometrics see Schlaifer (1969), Zellner (1971), Iversen (1984), Lee (1997).
114. For an early application see Lambin (1972b).

judgmental parameters. Little (1975b) does this based on the idea that people tend to overinterpret patterns in historical data. Whatever form is used, we emphasize that combining subjective and objective elements generally leads to better parameterization, as found in many studies.[115]

We note that the empirical approach based on sample information is at the core of the analysis. Judgmental information is often not incorporated, and if it is, an ad hoc adjustment is more common than a formal one.

16.9.5 ILLUSTRATION

Qualitative and quantitative approaches are complementary. In Section 3.1, we introduced an example that is consistent with this idea. Objective and subjective data, qualitative and quantitative approaches, were used to study the following:

- the impact of an increase in the time available for commercials in the public broadcasting system in the Netherlands on the demand for advertising space in newspapers and magazines;
- the effect of the introduction of private broadcasting (planned for October 1989), supported in part by commercials, on the advertising volume in newspapers, magazines and public broadcasting in 1989 and 1990.

Alsem, Leeflang and Reuyl (1990) constructed an econometric model to answer the first question. This model, however, cannot be used to predict the effects of new entrants on the market. For this, the researchers employed an intention survey.

Intentions are most useful if the following conditions apply:[116]

1. the event to be predicted is important to survey participants;
2. the respondents have contemplated the event and know how they will act;
3. the respondents can execute the actions they are planning;
4. new information is unlikely to change the planned actions;
5. the respondents provide valid answers.

In this study data were collected about intentions of advertisers and advertising agencies, with respect to the size and allocation of their advertising budgets. In this case most of the conditions for an intention survey are satisfied. The introduction of private broadcasting is an important event to the respondents. The respondents are aware of the changes under consideration, and their media planning reflects the anticipated changes. If confidentiality is guaranteed, respondents are likely to give correct answers. The respondents not only can but also will fulfil their plans in nearly all cases.

However, condition (4) does not hold. If, for example, the audience figures of private broadcasting channels are lower than expected, advertisers will decrease the advertising budget for private broadcasting. To accommodate this, the study included a number of *scenarios* (Jain, 1993, p. 345, Schoemaker, 1995).

---

115. See also Lawrence, Edmundson and O'Connor (1986) and Makridakis (1989).
116. This subsection is based on Alsem, Leeflang (1994).

At the time the survey was held (August-September 1989; before the introduction of private broadcasting), two important aspects relevant to the future development of the broadcast media were uncertain:

1. the penetration of private broadcasting on the Dutch cable network;
2. the prices and constraints for advertising on the public broadcasting channels.

In the Netherlands, about 80 percent of the households are connected to a cable network. Private broadcasting (satellite television) is transmitted by cable. However, local authorities decide which channels are transmitted. Thus, the intentions would be subject to uncertainty about who would receive the new private channels. Scenarios were created to account for the (uncertain) degree of penetration.

It was also uncertain whether the (not very flexible) conditions and prices for advertising on the public channels would be changed, as a reaction to the entrance of a new competitor. The conditions include the extent of choice in the timing of advertising messages, whether restitution is given if the audience figures are lower than expected, how many days prior to broadcasting the commercials must be available to the channels, etc. The literature suggests that discrepancies between behavioral intentions and actual behavior can be partly explained by observable and measurable factors. In this application, a critical factor is the offer price of the commodity: the higher the offer price, the greater the discrepancy.[117] For this reason scenarios were created to accommodate the uncertainty in prices as well.

To obtain intentions from relevant decisions makers, a stratified random sample of 330 advertisers was drawn from 40 strata. The strata were defined by two characteristics, the product group (e.g. insurance, alcoholic drinks, automobiles, etc.) and the size of the advertising budget. There were twenty different product groups, and the population was divided into two groups of advertisers: advertisers with a relatively high budget, who spent at least one millon Dutch guilders in the preceding year, and advertisers who spent less than that amount. Hence, segments were used to obtain forecasts. Morwitz and Schmittlein (1992) suggest that the accuracy of forecasts based on intentions can be improved through the segmentation of panel members.[118]

Advertisers were asked to state the advertising budget and media allocation under different scenarios. They were also asked for permission to contact "their" advertising agencies about the same questions. Only 59 advertisers actually gave this permission. Advertisers and agencies were confronted with these scenarios *before* the entrance of private broadcasting companies on the Dutch advertising market in October 1989. At the time the survey was completed, it was clear whether private broadcasting would exist in 1990. The following scenarios and situations were used (see also Table 16.14):

1. the advertising budget and media allocation in 1988;
2. budget and media allocation in 1989, allowing for the use of private broadcasting;
3. budget and media allocation in 1990, assuming a (slow) penetration of private broadcasting channels up to 40% of the Dutch households;

---

117. Kealy, Dovidio, Rockel (1988), Kealy, Montgomery, Dovidio (1990).
118. A similar approach has been advocated by Weerahandi and Dalal (1992).

Table 16.14 Estimated advertising expenditures for 1989 and 1990 based on a sample of advertisers and advertising agencies[a,b].

Year	1988 (realization)	1989	1990	1990	1990
Scenario/situation	1	2	3	4	5
Penetration private broadcasting	-	-	40%	80%	80%
Conditions public broadcasting	-	Unchanged	Unchanged	Unchanged	Same as private broadcasting
Public broadcasting	450	476	474	347	400
Private broadcasting	-	57	244	391	343
Total television	450	533	718	738	743
Radio	72	82	93	92	88
Newspapers	709	665	694	690	690
Magazines	646	565	614	613	610
Total of these media	1,894	1,845	2,119	2,133	2,131

[a] In millions of Dutch Guilders. One guilder is approximately 0.5 US$.

[b] In the original study (Leeflang, Alsem, Reuyl, 1991), other media were also incorporated in the predictions, such as outdoor advertising, direct mail, sponsoring and sales promotions. In this table only media are reported of which the realized advertising expenditures of the respondents are known.

Source: Alsem, Leeflang (1994, p. 332).

4. budget and media allocation in 1990 with a penetration of 80%;
5. budget and media allocation in 1990 under the assumption that the conditions and prices of advertising on public broadcasting channels and on private broadcasting channels are the same. Penetration of private channels is 80%.

Using the intentions of the advertisers and their agencies, predictions for the entire market are calculated as follows:

$$\widehat{AE}_{j,t+1} = \frac{AE_{jt}}{AE'_{jt}} \cdot \widehat{AE}'_{j,t+1} \tag{16.203}$$

where

$\widehat{AE}_{j,t+1} = predicted$ advertising expenditures in medium j for the *entire market* in period $t + 1$ (1989),

$AE_{jt} =$ advertising expenditures of the *entire market* in medium j in t (1988),

$$AE'_{jt} = \text{advertising expenditures of the } \textit{sample} \text{ in medium}$$
$$j \text{ in } t \text{ (1988)},$$

$$\widehat{AE}'_{j,t+1} = \textit{intended} \text{ advertising expenditures of the } \textit{sample} \text{ in}$$
$$\text{medium } j \text{ in } t + 1 \text{ (1989)}.$$

Since intentions were also obtained for 1990, $\widehat{AE}_{j,t+2}$ can also be calculated:

$$\widehat{AE}_{j,t+2} = \frac{AE_{jt}}{AE'_{jt}} \cdot \widehat{AE}'_{j,t+2} \tag{16.204}$$

where $\widehat{AE}'_{j,t+2}$ are the intended advertising expenditures in $t + 2$ (1990).

Separate predictions were created for the advertisers and their advertising agencies. These predictions were then combined by computing an unweighted average. There are two reasons for using an unweighted average. First, from other questions in the survey it appeared that the allocation of the advertising budget over media was mostly a joint decision of advertisers and their agencies. Second, without prior knowledge of the accuracy of respondents forecasts, unweighted combinations generally provide the best predictions (Armstrong, 1985). We summarize the main results of the combined forecasts in Table 16.14. Because of the small sample size only large changes may indicate shifts in media market shares. The results in Table 16.14 suggest the following.

1. In 1989 television advertising expenditures would show a slight increase. The private broadcasting channel would have a share of television advertising expenditures of about 11%. Advertising expenditures in magazines would decrease.
2. In 1990 there would be fierce competition between private and public broadcasting. The degree of substitution between these two vehicles would depend on the penetration of private broadcasting, and on the prices and conditions for public broadcasting. If the conditions and prices would tend toward equality between public and private broadcasting, public broadcasting would not be as strongly affected by the new entrant. However, if the private broadcasting penetration is 80% and the conditions for public broadcasting are unchanged, the public broadcasting channels might lose their market leadership as early as in 1990.

In Section 18.7 we return to this example to discuss the validation of subjective estimates.

CHAPTER 17

Special topics in model specification and estimation

In this chapter we first discuss the specification and estimation of models with ob-served *and* unobserved variables based on LISREL. LISREL models are vehicles for bringing latent constructs and observational variables together. They encompass a wide variety of other models, such as simultaneous equation models (see also Section 16.4), seemingly unrelated regression models (see Section 16.3) and errors-in-variables models.

In Section 17.2 we discuss mixture regression models. Mixture regression models are models that assume the existence of heterogeneous groups of individuals in a population.

Next we focus on time-series models. Recall that in Section 4.4 we distinguish time-series (models) and causal models. Time-series models are uniquely suited to capture the time dependence of the criterion variable. In Section 17.3 we discuss the specification and estimation of ARMA and ARIMA models. We discuss the inclu-sion of seasonal effects and the inclusion of independent and explicitly formulated predictor variables through transfer functions.

There are reasons why it is important for models to accommodate changes in model structure and/or parameters. In Section 17.4 we discuss the specification and estimation of varying parameter models. In these models, the model parameters are allowed to vary.

17.1 Structural equation models with latent variables

17.1.1 OUTLINE OF THE MODEL AND PATH DIAGRAM

The foundations of structural equation models with latent variables come from Jöres-kog (1973, 1978). He developed LISREL, a computer program which has become almost synonymous with the models[1]. Structural equation models are models for the analysis of relationships among observed and unobserved variables. We use an

---

1. Many excellent texts on structural equation models have appeared, see for example Long (1983), Bollen (1989). For a comprehensive introduction to LISREL for marketing research, see Bagozzi (1994b), Diaman-topoulos (1994), Hair, Anderson, Tatham and Black (1995) and Sharma (1996).

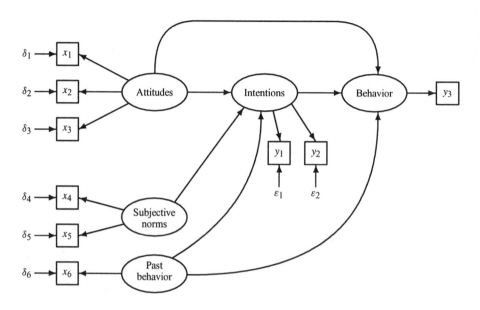

Source: based on Bagozzi (1994b, p. 366).

Figure 17.1 Example of a path diagram.

example of the effect of consumer attitudes and intentions on coupon usage, taken from Bagozzi (1994b, pp. 365-368), and introduced in Section 10.3. We partly repeat the discussion here. Figure 17.1 presents the path diagram (Figure 17.1 is identical to Figure 10.7). A path diagram is a graphical representation of a system of relations among observed and unobserved variables. The path diagram in the figure is based on the theory of reasoned action. It postulates that intentions influence behavior, while intentions are themselves affected by attitudes, subjective norms and past behavior. In addition, behavior is assumed to be directly affected by past behavior and attitudes. In the path diagram, circles indicate latent variables, in this application attitudes, subjective norms, intentions and (past) behavior. Square boxes indicate observed or "manifest" variables. Thus, in Figure 17.1 attitudes are measured by three items. Subjective norms and intentions are each measured by two, and behavior and past behavior each by one. The arrows between the circles indicate hypothesized (assumed) relations between latent variables, while the arrows between the circles and squares indicate measurement relations. Arrows pointing to the squares indicate measurement errors. Two types of observed variables are distinguished: indicators of exogenous and indicators of endogenous latent variables. The former are denoted by x, the latter by y. Indicators for endogenous variables in the example are measures of intentions (y_1 and y_2) and behavior (y_3), while exogenous indicators are the measures of attitudes (x_1, x_2 and x_3) , subjective norms (x_4 and x_5) and past behavior (x_6).

The relationships among the observed (or manifest) variables are reflected in the covariances among them. Those covariances form the basis for the estimation of a

Table 17.1 Covariance matrix for the variables in the coupon behavior study.

	y_1	y_2	y_3	x_1	x_2	x_3	x_4	x_5	x_6
Intentions y_1	4.39								
Intentions y_2	3.79	4.41							
Behavior y_3	1.94	1.86	2.39						
Attitudes x_1	1.45	1.45	0.99	1.91					
Attitudes x_2	1.09	1.31	0.84	0.96	1.48				
Attitudes x_3	1.62	1.70	1.18	1.28	1.22	1.97			
Subjective norms x_4	0.57	0.90	0.37	0.80	0.80	0.95	1.96		
Subjective norms x_5	1.06	1.26	0.77	0.93	1.13	1.19	1.09	1.72	
Past behavior x_6	2.21	2.50	1.48	1.20	1.01	1.42	0.90	1.13	2.50

Source: Bagozzi (1994b, p. 367).

structural equation model that describes the relations among variables according to a set of hypotheses. Importantly, structural equation methods focus on describing the covariances between the variables.[2] The population covariances among the variables are described in the matrix Σ. We show the sample covariance matrix for the application of attitudes and behavior for coupons, from a sample of 85 women, in Table 17.1. As expected, all covariances are positive in this study.

The structural equation model attempts to reproduce the covariances among the variables as accurately as possible with a set of parameters, θ, where the fundamental hypothesis is: $\Sigma = \Sigma(\theta)$. $\Sigma(\theta)$ is called the implied covariance matrix.

The structural equation model comprises two submodels. The first is called the *measurement model*, the second the *structural model*. The measurement model relates the observed indicators to a set of unobserved, or latent variables. This part of the model is also called a confirmatory factor model, if it is considered in isolation. The measurement models for the endogenous and exogenous indicator variables are formulated in a general form respectively as:

$$y = \Lambda_y \eta + \varepsilon \qquad (17.1)$$
$$x = \Lambda_x \xi + \delta \qquad (17.2)$$

where

$y = $ a $(p \times 1)$ vector of manifest endogenous variables,

$\eta = $ a $(m \times 1)$ vector containing the latent endogenous variables (i.e. the variables that are explained within the model),

$\Lambda_y = $ the $(p \times m)$ matrix of loadings, showing which manifest

---

2. More precisely they constitute the sufficient statistics for the model.

variable loads on which latent exogenous variable,

ε = a vector of error terms with expectation zero, and uncorrelated with η,

x = a $(q \times 1)$ vector of manifest exogenous variables,

ξ = a $(n \times 1)$ vector of latent exogenous variables (i.e. variables that explain the model),

Λ_x = the $(q \times n)$ matrix of loadings, showing which manifest variable loads on which latent exogenous variable, and

δ = a vector of error terms uncorrelated with ξ and expectation zero.

In this application to the theory of reasoned action, there are two latent endogenous variables: intention (η_1) and behavior (η_2). Intention (η_1) is measured by two indicators (manifest variables) $(y_1$ and $y_2)$, and behavior (η_2) by one (y_3). The *measurement model* for these *endogenous variables* is therefore:

$$
\begin{bmatrix} y_1 \\ y_2 \\ y_3 \end{bmatrix} = \begin{bmatrix} \lambda_{11}^y & 0 \\ \lambda_{21}^y & 0 \\ 0 & \lambda_{32}^y \end{bmatrix} \begin{bmatrix} \eta_1 \\ \eta_2 \end{bmatrix} + \begin{bmatrix} \varepsilon_1 \\ \varepsilon_2 \\ \varepsilon_3 \end{bmatrix}.
\tag{17.3}
$$

A similar set of equations determines the *measurement model* for the three latent *exogenous variables*, attitudes (ξ_1), subjective norms (ξ_2), and past behavior (ξ_3), from their indicators (respectively x_1 to x_3, x_4 to x_5, and x_6):

$$
\begin{bmatrix} x_1 \\ x_2 \\ x_3 \\ x_4 \\ x_5 \\ x_6 \end{bmatrix} = \begin{bmatrix} \lambda_{11}^x & 0 & 0 \\ \lambda_{21}^x & 0 & 0 \\ \lambda_{31}^x & 0 & 0 \\ 0 & \lambda_{42}^x & 0 \\ 0 & \lambda_{52}^x & 0 \\ 0 & 0 & \lambda_{63}^x \end{bmatrix} \begin{bmatrix} \xi_1 \\ \xi_2 \\ \xi_3 \end{bmatrix} + \begin{bmatrix} \delta_1 \\ \delta_2 \\ \delta_3 \\ \delta_4 \\ \delta_5 \\ \delta_6 \end{bmatrix}.
\tag{17.4}
$$

The error terms in both measurement models may be correlated. The respective covariance matrices of the vectors of error terms are denoted by Θ_ε and Θ_δ respectively. Φ denotes the covariance matrix of the latent exogenous variables ξ. Covariances of the endogenous variables are part of the structural component of the model described below. In order to make the measurement model identified, the latent variables must be assigned a scale. One way of doing that is to arbitrarily fix one of the loadings for each latent variable to one, so that the latent variable has the same scale as that indicator, for example $\lambda_{11}^y = 1$ and $\lambda_{32}^y = 1$ in (17.3). Another way to resolve that identification problem is to standardize the latent variables, which is accomplished by setting their variances equal to 1, so that Φ becomes a correlation matrix with diagonal values equal to one. See the structural equation modeling literature for details.

The structural part of the model captures the relationships between exogenous and endogenous (latent) variables:

$$
\eta = B\eta + \Gamma\xi + \zeta.
\tag{17.5}
$$

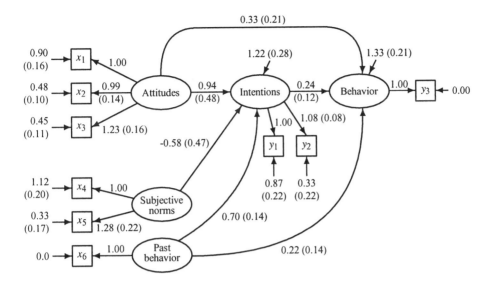

Source: based on Bagozzi (1994b, p. 366).

Figure 17.2 Estimated relations between coupon usage behavior, attitudes, subjective norms, intentions and past behavior.

The ($m \times m$) matrix B specifies the relationships among the m latent endogenous variables. Its diagonal equals zero (since the endogenous variables cannot affect themselves). If B is a lower triangular matrix, there are no reciprocal causal effects (e.g. η_1 influences η_2 but not vice versa), and the structural model is said to be recursive. The ($m \times n$) matrix Γ captures the effects of the exogenous variables on the endogenous variables, and ζ is a vector of disturbances with expectation zero and uncorrelated with the endogenous and exogenous latent variables. The error terms may be correlated and have a ($m \times m$) covariance matrix denoted by Ψ. In the example, there are three latent exogenous variables that according to the theory are hypothesized to affect the two endogenous variables of intentions and behavior. The equations of the *structural model* are therefore:

$$\begin{bmatrix} \eta_1 \\ \eta_2 \end{bmatrix} = \begin{bmatrix} 0 & 0 \\ \beta_{21} & 0 \end{bmatrix} \begin{bmatrix} \eta_1 \\ \eta_2 \end{bmatrix} + \begin{bmatrix} \gamma_{11} & \gamma_{12} & \gamma_{13} \\ \gamma_{21} & 0 & \gamma_{23} \end{bmatrix} \begin{bmatrix} \xi_1 \\ \xi_2 \\ \xi_3 \end{bmatrix} + \begin{bmatrix} \zeta_1 \\ \zeta_2 \end{bmatrix}. \tag{17.6}$$

The covariance matrices Θ_ε, Θ_δ, Φ and Ψ are specified to be diagonal. The estimation results are presented in Table 17.2 and in Figure 17.2. Attitudes and past behavior are found to significantly affect intentions while behavior is influenced by intentions only. The variance explained in intentions (R_I^2) is 65 percent and in behavior (R_B^2) 44 percent.

The significance of the *overall model fit* can be assessed by a χ^2-test. One can also use a number of goodness-of-fit indices[3].

---

3. See, for example, Sharma (1996, pp. 157-162).

Table 17.2 Parameter estimates of the coupon behavior study.

Measurement model			Structural model		
Parameter	Parameter estimate	Estimated standard deviation	Parameter	Parameter estimate	Estimated standard deviation
λ_{11}^{y}	1	-	γ_{11}	0.94^{a}	0.48
λ_{21}^{y}	1.08^{a}	0.08	γ_{12}	-0.58	0.47
λ_{32}^{y}	1	-	γ_{13}	0.70^{a}	0.14
λ_{11}^{x}	1	-	γ_{21}	0.33	0.21
λ_{21}^{x}	0.99^{a}	0.14	γ_{23}	0.22	0.14
λ_{31}^{x}	1.23	0.16	β_{21}	0.24^{a}	0.12
λ_{42}^{x}	1	-			
λ_{52}^{x}	1.28	0.22			
λ_{63}^{x}	1	-			

[a]Parameter estimates significant at the 5%-level.

The χ^2-statistic can be used to test the null hypothesis (H_0):

$$H_0 : \Sigma = \Sigma(\Theta). \tag{17.7}$$

In this statistic the sample covariance matrix S (see, for example, Table 17.1) is used as an estimate of Σ, and $\Sigma(\widehat{\Theta}) = \widehat{\Sigma}$ is the estimate of the covariance matrix $\Sigma(\Theta)$ obtained from the parameter estimates. Under the null hypothesis, we expect $S = \widehat{\Sigma}$ or $(S - \widehat{\Sigma}) = 0$. In this case, failure to reject the null hypothesis is desired, since this leads to the conclusion that statistically the hypothesized model fits the data. For example, a χ^2-value of zero results if $S - \widehat{\Sigma} = 0$. Here $\chi^2 = 41.21$. The relevant degrees of freedom (df) are $1/2(p + q)(p + q + 1) - L$, where L is the number of parameters estimated. In this example, $p + q$ is the number of manifest variables ($= 9$), and $L = 15$. Hence $df = 30$. With 30 degrees of freedom this is not significant at the 10-percent level, consistent with the hypothesis that the model fits the data.

The χ^2-value is sensitive to sample size. For a large sample size, even small differences in $(S - \widehat{\Sigma})$ will be statistically significant although the differences may not be practically meaningful. And with a small sample size it is difficult to reject a null hypothesis that is false. Hence other methods are frequently used to evaluate the fit of the model to the data.[4] Most of the fit indices are designed to provide a summary measure of the residual matrix $RES = S - \widehat{\Sigma}$. Three well-known measures are the Goodness-of-Fit Index (*GFI*), the *GFI* Adjusted for degrees of freedom (*AGFI*) and the Root Mean Squared Error (*RMSE*).[5]

---

4. See, for example, Marsh, Balla and McDonald (1988) and Bentler (1990) for a review of these statistics.
5. See also Section 18.5.

The goodness-of-fit index (*GFI*) is defined as follows:

$$GFI = 1 - \frac{tr[(\widehat{\Sigma}^{-1}S - I)^2]}{tr(\widehat{\Sigma}^{-1}S)^2} \tag{17.8}$$

where

$tr =$ trace of the matrix,

$I =$ the unity matrix.

GFI represents the amount of variances and covariances in S that are predicted by the model. It is analogous in interpretation to R^2 in multiple regression.[6] If $S = \widehat{\Sigma}$, $GFI = 1$. A rule of thumb is that *GFI* for good-fitting models should be greater than 0.90. In our example $GFI = 0.95$. Like R^2, *GFI* is affected by degrees of freedom. The *AGFI*, analogous to R_a^2 (equation (16.57)), is the *GFI* adjusted for degrees of freedom:

$$AGFI = 1 - \left[\frac{(p+q)(p+q+1)}{2df}\right][1 - GFI] \tag{17.9}$$

where

$p + q =$ number of indicators (in our example 9),

$df =$ number of degrees of freedom (30).

Researchers have used a value of $AGFI = 0.80$ as the cutoff value for good-fitting models. In our example, $AGFI = 0.91$.

The root mean squared error is the square root of the average of the squared residuals:

$$RMSE = \sqrt{\frac{\sum_{i=1}^{p+q}\sum_{j=1}^{i}(s_{ij} - \hat{\sigma}_{ij})^2}{(p+q)(p+q+1)/2}} \tag{17.10}$$

where

$s_{ij} =$ the i, j-th element of the sample covariance matrix,

$\hat{\sigma}_{ij} =$ the i, j-th element of the estimated covariance matrix.

The *RMSE* in our example is small: 0.049.

The statistical significance of each estimated parameter is assessed by its t-value (Table 17.2). If the parameter estimates are significant, the next question is whether the indicators are good measures for the latent constructs. To answer this we use the value of the *commonality* of the indicator. The commonality is the proportion of the variance of the manifest variable that is in common with the latent construct. The higher the commonality of an indicator the better or more reliable measure it is of the respective latent variable and vice versa. LISREL labels the commonality as *squared*

---

6. See section 16.1.5 (equations (16.54) and (16.55)).

*Table 17.3 Commonalities of the indicators
in the coupon behavior study.*

Latent variable	Commonalities
Intention	$y_1 = 0.80$
	$y_2 = 0.93$
Behavior	$y_3 = 1.00$
Attitude	$x_1 = 0.53$
	$x_2 = 0.68$
	$x_3 = 0.77$
Subjective norms	$x_4 = 0.43$
	$x_5 = 0.83$
Past behavior	$x_6 = 1.00$

multiple correlation. A rule of thumb is that commonalities should be at least 0.5, i.e. that an indicator has at least 50 of its variance in common with its construct. LISREL provides the commonalities for both endogenous and exogenous indicators (y- and x-variables): see Table 17.3. Note that x_4 fails to satisfy the desired commonality value. The *coefficient of determination* for the y- and x-variables indicates how well the manifest variables as a *group* serve as measure for the latent endogenous and exogenous variables. Commonalities and coefficients of determination indicate the fit of the measurement model.

Shifting attention to the structural model, the *squared multiple correlations for structural equations* indicate the amount of variance in each endogenous latent variable accounted for by the exogenous variables in the relevant structural equation. The *total coefficient of determination* shows the strength of the relationships for *all* structural relationships taken together.[7]

The LISREL formulation presented by equations (17.1) (17.2) and (17.5) is a very general one, and encompasses a wide variety of specific models. For example, simultaneous equation models arise as a special case when there are no latent variables, and each manifest variable is set identical to a corresponding latent variable (Section 17.1.4). Other well-known models that arise as special cases are seemingly unrelated regression models (Section 17.1.2), errors-in-variables models (Section 17.1.3), and confirmatory factor analysis (Section 17.1.5).

Structural equation models are frequently used in marketing. Including the early work (Bagozzi, 1977, 1980, Fornell, Larcker, 1981), structural equation models have been used, for example:

- in experimental research (Bagozzi, 1977);
- for theory development and theory testing (Phillips, Chang, Buzzell, 1983, Ailawadi, Farris, Parry, 1999);

---

7. See for these and other statistics Diamantopoulos (1994) and Sharma (1996, Chapter 6).

- for scale construction and testing (Section 17.1.5);
- to test the quality of data (Plat, 1988);
- to remove cross-cultural response baises in survey questionnaires (Steenkamp, Baumgartner, 1998).

17.1.2 SEEMINGLY UNRELATED REGRESSION MODELS

In estimating sales or market share models, it is possible that the errors of the equations for the different brands are correlated. For example, the model may overestimate the market share of some brands and underestimate the market shares for other brands. As a result the residuals tend to be negatively correlated across brands. These systems of relations are known as seemingly unrelated regressions. We introduced this situation in Section 16.3, see equation (16.110a), and we showed how models with contemporaneous error-term correlations can be estimated by GLS. Seemingly unrelated regressions can also be conveniently specified and estimated in a LISREL framework. For this purpose we can specify the structural equations as:

$$y = \eta \tag{17.11}$$
$$x = \xi \tag{17.12}$$
$$\eta = \Gamma\xi + \zeta \tag{17.13}$$

with a non-diagonal covariance matrix Ψ of the errors ζ.

17.1.3 ERRORS-IN-VARIABLES MODELS

It is well known that measurement errors in the predictor variables in regression equations can affect the parameter estimates. However, the consequences of such errors are hard to predict: parameter estimates may stay the same, increase or decrease in value.[8] LISREL provides a convenient framework for dealing with errors in variables.

Suppose we have measured a criterion variable y, and a set of predictor variables x which are potentially measured with error. Then the equations are:

$$y = \eta \tag{17.14}$$
$$x = \Lambda\xi + \delta \tag{17.15}$$
$$\eta = \Gamma\xi + \zeta. \tag{17.16}$$

Covariance in the measurement errors can be captured by specifying a non-diagonal covariance matrix of δ: Θ_δ. However, this model is not identified in general for $\Lambda_x = I$, i.e. the situation where there is one indicator per latent variable (or, a multivariate regression model with errors in the predictors). One solution is to have multiple measures for the same latent variable, ξ;[9] other solutions arise in certain overidentified models.[10]

---

8. See, for example, Vanden Abeele (1975), Ketellapper (1981, 1982), Amemiya (1985, Section 6.6).
9. See, for an application in marketing, Plat (1988, Chapter 3).
10. The reader is referred to Bollen (1989) for more details.

17.1.4 SIMULTANEOUS EQUATIONS

The classical econometric specification of simultaneous equations can be formulated in the LISREL framework as:

$$\eta = B\eta + \Gamma\xi + \zeta \tag{17.17}$$

where the interpretation of the parameter matrices B and Γ is as above. The measurement model for simultaneous equations with observed variables is: $y = \eta$ and $x = \xi$, i.e. each latent variable corresponds to one indicator so that (17.17) reduces to:

$$\eta = By + \Gamma x + \zeta. \tag{17.18}$$

Again, the error terms may have a covariance matrix denoted by Ψ, which allows them to be correlated. Thus, simultaneous equations can be seen as a special case, which can be estimated in the LISREL framework. For example, consider a model with two-way causality between sales (y_1) and advertising (y_2), both assumed to be measured without error. Price (x_1), in addition, influences sales. The structural equations (16.120)-(16.123) can be rewritten in the framework (17.18) as:

$$\begin{bmatrix} y_1 \\ y_2 \end{bmatrix} = \begin{bmatrix} 0 & \beta_1 \\ \beta_2 & 0 \end{bmatrix} \begin{bmatrix} y_1 \\ y_2 \end{bmatrix} + \begin{bmatrix} \gamma_1 \\ 0 \end{bmatrix} [x_1] + \begin{bmatrix} \zeta_1 \\ \zeta_2 \end{bmatrix}. \tag{17.19}$$

17.1.5 CONFIRMATORY FACTOR ANALYSIS

Confirmatory factor analysis involves the measurement of latent variables. Whereas in exploratory factor analysis the relations between latent factors and the measured set of variables are not specified beforehand but "identified" through the analysis (including rotations to aid in the interpretation), in confirmatory factor analysis these relations are specified a-priori in the model and the parameters relating latent constructs to their indicators are estimated. In the LISREL framework, this involves specifying the measurement model (17.2) (or equivalently the corresponding equation for the y's: (17.1)), where the covariance matrix of the error terms is Θ_δ, and Φ is the covariance matrix of the latent constructs. Specifying Φ to be non-diagonal allows for the latent constructs to be correlated. The measurement model links LISREL to classical test-theory.[11] Methods of assessing reliability and validity based on the LISREL approach are more general than traditional procedures based on correlations. An overview of how LISREL can be used to validate marketing constructs is provided by Steenkamp and van Trijp (1991). For example, they show that the unidimensionality of constructs

---

11. For details see Bollen (1989, pp. 219).

can be assessed by examining the fit of model (17.2) with $n = 1$ latent construct. The reliability of a latent construct can be assessed as:

$$
\rho(\xi) = \frac{\left(\sum_{i=1}^{q} \lambda_i^x\right)^2}{\left(\sum_{i=1}^{q} \lambda_i^x\right)^2 + \sum_{i=1}^{q} \delta_i}
\tag{17.20}
$$

which reduces to the Cronbach coefficient α if all loadings and error variances are equal.

17.2 Mixture regression models for market segmentation

17.2.1 INTRODUCTION

Heterogeneity has become a very important topic in the marketing literature. Marketing researchers have recognized the importance of the differences in behavior among consumers, and have developed models to accommodate such heterogeneity in marketing models. Marketing decisions depend critically on a correct understanding of heterogeneity. This heterogeneity also needs to be considered even if the model user cares only about average behavior. For example models of aggregate data may be sensitive to a variety of aggregation biases (see Section 14.1.2). Important insights into heterogeneity are obtained from the application of mixture models. Mixture models are models that assume the existence of a number of (unobserved) heterogeneous groups of individuals in a population. The theory of mixture models connects elegantly to market segmentation theory and it presents a statistical approach to a wide variety of segmentation problems.

In this section we review the application of mixture models to market segmentation problems. A major advance in segmentation methodology is due to the development of mixture models and mixture regression models (Wedel and Kamakura, 1998). The development of mixture models dates back to the nineteenth century (Newcomb, 1886). In finite mixture models, it is assumed that the observations of a sample arise from two or more unobserved segments, of unknown proportions, that are mixed. The purpose is to "unmix" the sample and to identify the underlying segments. Contrary to most of the traditional clustering procedures which merely present convenient heuristics for deriving data-based segments, mixture distributions present a model-based approach to segmentation. They allow for hypothesis testing and estimation within the framework of standard statistical theory.

The mixture model approach to segmentation presents an extremely flexible class of clustering algorithms that can be tailored to a very wide range of substantive marketing problems. Mixture models are statistical models which involve a specific form of the distribution function of the observations in each of the underlying populations (which is to be specified). The distribution function is used to describe the probabilities of occurrence of the observed values of the variable in question. The normal distribution is the most frequently used distribution for continuous variables, for example for preference ratings, that take values in the range of minus infinity to infinity. The binomial distribution describes the probabilities of occurrence of binary (0/1) brand choice-type data, and the Poisson distribution describes the probabilities of occurrence of purchase frequencies.

We specifically discuss recent developments in a particular area of mixture modeling: *mixture regression models*. These models extend the traditional mixture approach in that they *simultaneously* allow for the classification of a sample into groups, as well as for the estimation of a regression model within each of these groups. We provide a general framework for mixture regression models, based on Wedel and DeSarbo (1995). Within that general framework we review:

- mixture regression models;
- concomitant variable mixture regression models that allow for a simultaneous profiling of the underlying segments with background variables (comparable to variables in a cluster analysis), and
- latent Markov regression models that allow the probabilities of class membership to change over time and are therefore especially useful in the analysis of longitudinal data.

We start by describing the foundations of the general mixture model approach.[12]

17.2.2 GENERAL MIXTURE MODELS

In order to formulate the finite mixture model, assume that a sample of N subjects is drawn. For each subject, J variables $y_i = (y_{ij}, i = 1, \ldots, N, j = 1, \ldots, J)$ are measured. The subjects are assumed to arise from a population which is a mixture of S unobserved segments, in (unknown) proportions $\pi_1, \ldots, \pi_S$. It is not known in advance to which segment a particular subject belongs. The probabilities π_s satisfy the following constraints:

$$\sum_{s=1}^{S} \pi_s = 1, \quad \pi_s \geq 0, \quad s = 1, \ldots, S. \tag{17.21}$$

Given that y_{ij} comes from class s, the distribution function of the vector of measurements y_i is represented by the general form $f_s(y_i \mid \theta_s)$. Here θ_s denotes the vector of all unknown parameters for class s. For example, in the case that the y_{ij} within each segment are independent normally distributed, θ_s contains the means, μ_{js}, and variances, σ_{js}^2, of the normal distribution within each of the S segments. The basic idea behind mixture distributions is that the unconditional distribution is obtained from the conditional distributions as:

$$f(y_i, \phi) = \sum_{s=1}^{S} \pi_s f_s(y_i \mid \theta_s) \tag{17.22}$$

---

12. This discussion is based on Titterington, Smith, and Makov (1985) and McLachlan and Basford (1988).

where $\phi = (\pi, \theta)$ denotes all parameters of the model. This can easily be derived from the basic principles of probability theory: the unconditional probability is equal to the product of the conditional probability given s, times the probability of s, and this expression summed over all values of s.

The conditional density function, $f_s(y_i \mid \theta_s)$, can take many forms including the normal, Poisson and binomial distribution functions, as well as other well-known distribution functions such as the negative binomial, exponential, gamma, and inverse Gaussian that can be used to describe market phenomena. All of these more commonly used distributions present specific members of the so-called exponential family of distributions. This family is a general family of distributions that encompasses both discrete and continuous distributions. The exponential family is a very useful class of distributions. The common properties of the distributions in this class enables them to be studied simultaneously, rather than as a collection of unrelated cases. These distributions are characterized by their means μ_{js}, and possibly so-called dispersion parameters λ_{js}. In mixtures these parameters are typically assumed to be constant over observations within each segment s.

Often, the J repeated measurements on each subject are assumed to be independent. This occurs for example if a single subject provides evaluations of several (J) products or brands $j = 1, \ldots, J$. This implies that the joint distribution function for the J observations factors into the product of the marginal distributions:

$$f_s(y_i \mid \theta_s) = \prod_{j=1}^{J} f_s(y_{ij} \mid \theta_{sj}). \tag{17.23}$$

If, given the knowledge of the segments, the observations cannot be assumed to be independent, then one of the members of the multivariate exponential family may be appropriate. The two most important and most frequently used distributions in this family are the multinomial distribution, and the multivariate normal distribution. In the latter case, the distribution of y_i takes the well-known multivariate normal form, with μ_s the ($J \times 1$) vector of expectations, and Σ_s the ($J \times J$) covariance matrix of the vector y_i, given segment s.

17.2.3 MIXTURE REGRESSION MODELS

So far we described unconditional mixture models. Unconditional refers to the situation where there are *no* exogenous or explanatory variables to predict a *criterion* variable, y_i. For example, in the unconditional mixtures of normal distributions, the mean and variance of the underlying classes are estimated. In "conditional" mixture models the segment means are constrained in the form of regression models. These regression models relate a criterion variable to a set of predictor variables, for example preferences to perceived values of product attributes, or choices to marketing mix instruments. In this section, we describe a general framework for mixture regression models.[13]

---

13. The material in this section is based on Wedel and DeSarbo (1994, 1995) and Wedel and Kamakura (1998).

Generalized linear models (Nelder and Wedderburn, 1972) are regression models in which the criterion variable is assumed to be distributed according to one of the members of the exponential family. Generalized linear models deal with continuous variables that can be specified to follow a normal, gamma, or exponential distribution; for discrete variables the binomial, multinomial, Poisson or negative binomial distributions can be utilized. The expectation of the criterion variable is modeled as a function of a set of explanatory variables as in standard multiple regression models (which are a special case of generalized linear models). However, the estimation of a single aggregate regression equation across all consumers in a sample may be inadequate and potentially misleading if the consumers belong to a number of unknown classes (segments) in which the regression parameters differ. If the behavior of different consumers is studied, it is not difficult to find reasons for the existence of such heterogeneous classes. It is therefore no surprise that the application of the mixture regression approach has proven to be of great use in marketing.

We discuss the mixture regression framework by extending the unconditional mixture approach described above. We assume that the vector of observations (on the criterion variable) of subject i, y_i, arises from a population which is a mixture of S unknown segments in proportions $\pi_1, \ldots, \pi_S$. The distribution of y_i, given that y_i comes from segment s, $f_s(y_i \mid \theta_s)$ is assumed to be one of the distributions in the exponential family, or the multivariate exponential family. In addition to the criterion variable, a set of L non-stochastic explanatory variables $X_1, \ldots, X_L$, $(X_\ell = (x_{ij\ell})$, $j = 1, \ldots, J, \ell = 1, \ldots, L)$ is assumed to be available. A major difference from the mixture models discussed above is that the means of the observations in each class are to be predicted from a set of predictor variables. To this end, the mean of the distribution, μ_{isj}, is written as:

$$\mu_{isj} = g^{-1}(\eta_{isj}) \tag{17.24}$$

where $g(.)$ is some function, called a link-function, and η_{isj} is called the linear predictor. Convenient link-functions, called canonical links, are respectively the identity, log, logit, inverse and squared inverse functions for the normal, Poisson, binomial, gamma and inverse Gaussian distributions, respectively. The linear predictor for individual i in segment s is a linear combination of the L explanatory variables:

$$\eta_{isj} = \sum_{\ell=1}^{L} x_{\ell ij} \beta_{\ell s} \tag{17.25}$$

where

$\beta_{\ell s}$ = regression parameters to be estimated for each segment.

Thus for each segment a generalized linear model is formulated consisting of a specification of the distribution of the criterion variable within the exponential family, a linear predictor η_{isj}, and a function, $g(.)$, which links the linear predictor to the expectation of the distribution. For example, for the normal distribution the canonical link is the identity-link: $\eta_{isj} = \mu_{isj}$, so that by combining (17.24) and (17.25) a simple linear regression model for each segment arises. Note that the unconditional mixture of the previous section arises as a special case - the matrix X consists of one column with ones so that only an intercept β_s is estimated for each segment.

17.2.4 APPLICATION

We present an application of a mixture regression model provided by DeSarbo and Cron (1988). The model is based on a univariate normal density of the criterion variable within each class. The expectations of these densities are specified as linear functions of a set of explanatory variables. The model was used to analyze the factors that influence perceptions of trade show performance, and to investigate the presence of segments that differ in the importance attributed to these factors. This was done by evaluating trade show performance among 129 marketing executives. They were asked to rate their firm's trade show performance on eight performance factors, as well as on overall trade show performance. The performance factors included:

1. identifying new prospects;
2. servicing current customers;
3. introducing new products;
4. selling at the trade show;
5. enhancing corporate image;
6. testing of new products;
7. enhancing corporate moral, and
8. gathering competitive information.

Before presenting the results of the mixture regression analysis, we first report the results of a standard regression analysis. Table 17.4 presents the results of the OLS regression of overall performance on the eight performance factors. The table reveals that the factors "identifying new prospects" and "new product testing" were significantly related to overall trade show performance. The aggregate regression explained 37 percent of the variance in overall performance.

A mixture regression model applied to the same data reveals there exist two classes. The effects of the performance factors in the two classes are markedly different from those at the aggregate level, as shown in Table 17.4. Managers in segment 1 primarily evaluate trade shows in terms of *non-selling factors*, including "servicing current customers", and "enhancing corporate moral". Managers in segment 2 evaluate trade shows primarily on *selling factors*, including "identifying new prospects", "introducing new products", "selling at the shows", and "new product testing". Neither of the two segments considers "gathering competitive information" important. The percentages of explained variance in overall trade show performance in segments 1 and 2 were respectively 73 and 76 percent, a substantial improvement over the OLS results. The analysis shows that neglecting existing segments may lead to low explanatory power of models, to biased parameter estimates and incorrect managerial action.

Table 17.4 Aggregate and segment results of trade show performance.

Variable	Aggregate	Segment 1	Segment 2
Intercept	3.03	4.09^a	2.22^a
1. New prospects	0.15^a	0.13	0.24^a
2. New customer	-0.02	0.29^a	-0.16^a
3. Product introduction	0.09	-0.16^a	0.20^a
4. Selling	-0.04	-0.13^a	0.07^a
5. Enhancing image	0.09	0.13	0.07
6. New product testing	0.18^a	0.11^a	0.28^a
7. Enhancing moral	0.07	0.16^a	-0.03
8. Competitive information	0.04	-0.12	0.02
Size	100%	49%	51%

^{a}Parameter estimates significant at the 5%-level.

Source: based on DeSarbo, Cron (1988, p. 269, 273).

17.2.5 CONCOMITANT VARIABLE MIXTURE REGRESSION MODELS

In mixture models and mixture regression models, the segments identified are often described by background variables or concomitant variables (such as demographics) to obtain insights into the composition of the segments. Such profiling of segments is typically performed on the basis of a-posteriori class membership probabilities. These a-posteriori memberships, π_{is}, provide the probability that a particular subject i belongs to a certain class s (and have the properties that $0 \leq \pi_{is} \leq 1$, and $\sum_{s=1}^{S} \pi_{is} = 1$). The classes are frequently profiled in a second step of the analyses: a logit transformation of the posterior membership probabilities, $log(\pi_{is}/(1 - \pi_{is}))$, is regressed on designated external variables. The coefficient of a specific concomitant variable for a certain class represents the effect of that variable on the relative probabilities of subjects belonging to that class. However, the two-step procedure has several disadvantages. First, the logit-regression is performed independently from the estimation of the mixture model, and optimizes a different criterion - the sum of squared errors in the posterior probabilities rather than the likelihood. As a result, the classes derived in the first stage do not possess an "optimal" structure with respect to their profile on the concomitant variables. Secondly, this procedure does not take into account the estimation error of the posterior probabilities. Therefore, several authors have proposed models that simultaneously profile the derived segments with descriptor variables (Kamakura, Wedel, Agrawal, 1984, Wedel and Kamakura, 1998). These models are based on an earlier concomitant variable latent class model proposed by Dayton and MacReady (1988).

To develop the concomitant variable mixture regression model, let $\ell = 1, \ldots, L$

index concomitant variables, and $z_{\ell i}$ be the value of the ℓ-th concomitant variable for subject i, where the matrix $Z = ((z_{\ell i}))$. We again assume that the y_i are distributed according to some member of the exponential family, conditional upon unobserved classes as above. The starting point for the development of the model is the general mixture regression model defined by (17.22). The unconditional distribution for the concomitant variable mixture is formulated as:

$$f(y_i, \phi) = \sum_{s=1}^{S} \pi_{s|Z} f_s(y_i \mid \beta_s, \lambda_s). \tag{17.26}$$

Note that equation (17.26) is similar to equation (17.22), but the prior probabilities of class membership, π_s, have been replaced by $\pi_{s|Z}$. This is the core of the concomitant variable model approach: the prior probabilities of segment membership are explicitly reparameterized as functions of the concomitant variables. For this purpose the logistic formulation is often used:

$$\pi_{s|Z} = \frac{\exp \sum_{\ell=1}^{L} \gamma_{\ell s} z_{\ell i}}{\sum_{s=1}^{S} \exp \sum_{\ell=1}^{L} \gamma_{\ell s} z_{\ell i}}. \tag{17.27}$$

Equation (17.27) is called the submodel of the concomitant variable mixture, and it relates the prior probabilities to the concomitant variables. In order to include an intercept for each segment, $z_{1i} = 1$ is specified for all s. The parameter $\gamma_{\ell s}$ denotes the impact of the ℓ-th consumer characteristic on the prior probability for segment s. For example, a positive value of $\gamma_{\ell s}$ implies that a higher value of variable ℓ increases the prior probability that consumer i belongs to segment s. Another way of interpreting the concomitant variable model is based on the fact that the prior probabilities are equivalent to the segment sizes. Thus, this model allows the sizes of the segments to vary across demographic (and other) variables. The concomitant variable model designates what the segment sizes are according to each of an a-priori specified number of variables. Note that the mixture regression model arises as a special case if the matrix Z consists of one column of ones so that for each class, only a constant, γ_s, is specified in the submodel.

17.2.6 LATENT MARKOV MIXTURE REGRESSION MODELS

For longitudinal data, the assumptions underlying the mixture regression models described above may not be valid. In particular, the behavior of a specific subject and/or its membership to underlying segments may change over time. Mixture regression models applied to longitudinal data should potentially reflect such dynamics. There are several ways of dealing with time trends in mixture regression models. One approach, latent Markov mixture models, is described in some detail. For more details we refer to Wedel and Kamakura (1998, Chapter 7).

For ease of exposition, two time periods $t = 1$ and $t = 2$ are assumed. The segments at time $t = 1$ are denoted by $s = 1, \ldots, S$, and at time $t = 2$ by $u = 1, \ldots, U$. The criterion variable for subject i is $y_i = ((y_{ijt}))$, and the predictor variables $X_i =$

$((x_{ijt}))$ are defined accordingly. The extension to more than two periods is straight-forward.

The expected values of the criterion variable within classes is assumed to be provided by equations (17.24) and (17.25), i.e. we start from the mixture regression model. In the latent Markov model, subjects are assigned a simultaneous prior pro-bability of belonging to segment s at time $t = 1$ and to segment u at time $t = 2$: π_{su}. This simultaneous probability of segments s and u is specified as the product of the marginal probability of being in segment s at time t, and the conditional probability of being in segment u at time $t = 2$, given segment s at time $t = 1$:

$$\pi_{su} = \pi_s \pi_{u|s}. \tag{17.28}$$

Equation (17.28) presents the submodel of the latent Markov mixture regression model. The unconditional distribution of the data, analogous to equations (17.22) and (17.26) is:

$$f(y_i, \phi) = \sum_{s=1}^{S} \sum_{u=1}^{U} \pi_s f_s(y_i \mid \beta_s, \lambda_s) \pi_{u|s} f_u(y_i \mid \beta_u, \lambda_u). \tag{17.29}$$

The latent Markov mixture regression model can be used to investigate the effects of a set of predictor variables X on a criterion variable y in a number of unobserved classes, and at the same time the transitions of subjects among these segments over time.

17.3 Time-series models

17.3.1 INTRODUCTION

Marketing data for a brand often include measures on for example sales, repeated typically (at equally spaced intervals) over time. In Chapter 6 on marketing dynamics we dealt with lagged effects for predictor variables and distributed lags on the crite-rion variable, y, to capture such market dynamics. Time-series or ARIMA models are uniquely suited to capture the time dependence of a criterion variable. These models can describe patterns in data on a criterion variable as a function of its own past. Although the approach lacks foundations in marketing theory, it is attractive in the sense that the models can separate short-term from long-term marketing effects (when marketing variables are included).[14]

The shape of the market response function in time-series analyses is determined by a number of aspects, including prior theoretical knowledge, the objective of the model, and empirical analysis of the data. Most often, ARIMA models are identified from the data. Important statistics in building ARIMA models are the autocorrelation function(*ACF*) and partial autocorrelation function (*PACF*). To illustrate, let y_t be the

---

14. Comprehensive treatments of time series models are Pankratz (1991), Hanssens, Parsons and Schultz (1990, Chapter 4), Hanssens, Parsons (1993), Box, Jenkins and Reinsel (1994), Franses (1996, 1998).

sales of a brand in period t. The (ACF) at lag k is simply the correlation $\rho(y_t, y_{t-k})$. The ($PACF$) is the coefficient of y_{t-k} in the regression of y_t on all lagged values of y up to y_{t-k}. In general, the type of time series model to be fitted to the data is identified from plots of the ACF and $PACF$ against the lag k. Specific types of models correspond to specific autocorrelation functions, as explained below.

In our discussion of time-series models, we start with autoregressive models in which, say, sales are affected by sales levels in a previous period. We then describe moving average processes, in which it is assumed that random shocks in sales carry over to a subsequent period. This is followed by a discussion on ARMA models that combine the effects in the previous two models. We also discuss stationarity of time series, test of stationarity and integrated models that accommodate non-stationarity. We consider the inclusion of seasonal effects into time-series models, as well as time-series models that include the effect of predictor variables through so-called transfer function specifications. An extension of this is intervention analysis, where the effects of predictor variables take the form of steps or pulses.

17.3.2 AUTOREGRESSIVE PROCESSES

Let, y_t be the sales of a brand in period t. A common and fairly simple way to describe fluctuations in sales is with a first-order autoregressive process. In this process it is assumed that sales at $t - 1$ affect sales at t:

$$y_t = \mu + \phi_1 y_{t-1} + \varepsilon_t \tag{17.30}$$

where

μ = a constant,

ε_t = a disturbance term.

This model states that sales in period t are determined by sales in the previous period, $t - 1$. Depending on the value of ϕ_1 we distinguish three situations. If $\mid \phi_1 \mid < 0$, the effect of past sales diminishes. If $\mid \phi_1 \mid = 1$, the effect of sales in y_{t-1} has a permanent effect on sales. Sales will not revert to a historical level but will *evolve*. In the case where $\mid \phi_1 \mid > 1$, past sales become increasingly important; which appears to be unrealistic in marketing (Dekimpe, Hanssens, 1995a, p. 5). The process is stationary if $\mid \phi_1 \mid < 1$. In a stationary process the mean, variance and autocorrelation are constant in time. This model is indicated as AR(1). It can be identified from data using the AutoCorrelation Function (ACF) and Partial AutoCorrelation Function ($PACF$) calculated from sample data. The ACF and $PACF$ are statistics that can be used to identify the type of time series for a given data set. The ACF and $PACF$ of an AR(1) process are shown in Figure 17.3. Typically, the ACF decays exponentially and the $PACF$ shows a positive "spike" at lag 1 and equals zero thereafter, if ϕ_1 is positive. The ACF shows a damped wavelike pattern and the $PACF$ a negative spike at 1, if ϕ_1 is negative.

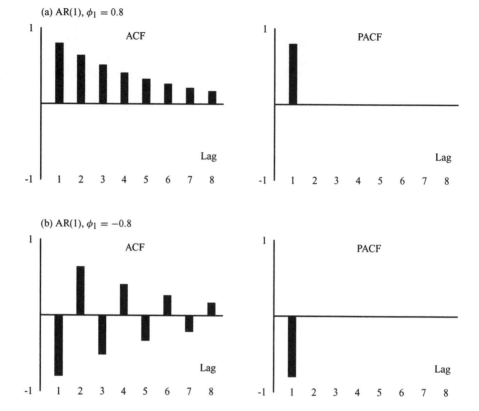

Source: Pankratz (1991, p. 40).

Figure 17.3 Two examples of theoretical ACF's and PACF's for AR(1) processes.

The order (p) of an AR(p) process is the highest lag of y_t that appears in the model. The general p-order AR process is written as:

$$\phi_p(B)y_t = \mu + \varepsilon_t \tag{17.31}$$

where

$$\phi_p(B) = (1 - \phi_1 - \phi_2 B^2 - \ldots - \phi_p B^p),$$

$$B = \text{the backshift operator defined by } B^k y_t = y_{t-k}.$$

For an AR(2) process $\phi_2(B) = (1-\phi_1 B-\phi_2 B^2)$ so that $(1-\phi_1 B-\phi_2 B^2)y_t = \mu+\varepsilon_t$ which leads to:

$$y_t = \mu + \phi_1 y_{t-1} + \phi_2 y_{t-2} + \varepsilon_t. \tag{17.32}$$

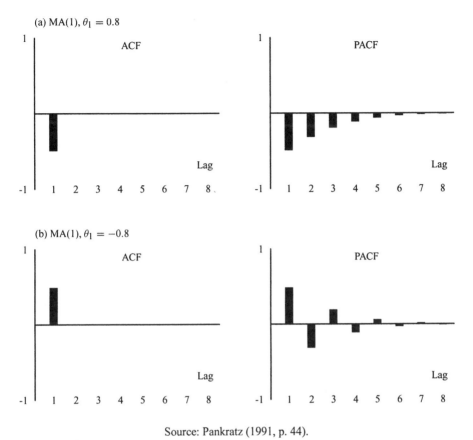

Source: Pankratz (1991, p. 44).

Figure 17.4 Two examples of theoretical ACF's and PACF's for MA(1) processes.

17.3.3 MOVING AVERAGE PROCESSES

A first-order moving average process assumes that a random shock at $t-1$ affects sales levels at time t:

$$y_t = \mu - \theta_1 \varepsilon_{t-1} + \varepsilon_t. \tag{17.33}$$

This model is indicated as MA(1). Note that the past random shock does not come from y_{t-1}, as in the AR(1) model, but it stems from the random component of y_{t-1}. The *ACF* and *PACF* for the MA(1) model are depicted in Figure 17.4. Here, the *ACF* shows a spike at lag 1, which is negative if $\theta_1 > 0$ and positive if $\theta_1 < 0$, while the *PACF* shows exponential decay in the former case, or a damped wavelike pattern in the latter.

Similar to the stationarity conditions for AR processes, MA processes need to satisfy conditions for invertibility. If the process is invertible, for example for an MA(1) process if $|\theta_1| < 1$, the order (q) of an MA(q) process is the highest lag of ε_t that appears in the model. Where $\mid \theta_1 \mid < 1$ the impact of past shocks diminishes, whereas $\mid \theta_1 \mid = 1$ implies that each random shock has a permanent effect on sales. The general q-order MA process is written as:

$$y_t = \mu + \theta_q(B)\varepsilon_t \tag{17.34}$$

where

$$\theta_q(B) = (1 - \theta_1 B - \theta_2 B^2 - \ldots - \theta_q B^q),$$
$$B = \text{the backshift operator defined as before.}$$

Specifically, for a MA(2) process, where $\theta_2(B) = (1 - \theta_1 B - \theta_2 B^2)$, leading to $y_t = \mu + (1 - \theta_1 B - \theta_2 B^2)\varepsilon_t$, we have:

$$y_t = \mu - \theta_1 \varepsilon_{t-1} - \theta_2 \varepsilon_{t-2} + \varepsilon_t. \tag{17.35}$$

17.3.4 ARMA PROCESSES

The AR and MA processes can be combined into a single model to reflect the idea that both past sales and past random shocks affect y_t. For example, the ARMA(1,1) process is:

$$y_t = \mu + \phi_1 y_{t-1} - \theta_1 \varepsilon_{t-1} + \varepsilon_t. \tag{17.36}$$

The *ACF* and *PACF* for an ARMA(1,1) model are depicted in Figure 17.5. Here, both the *ACF* and the *PACF* show exponential decay, or a damped wavelike pattern. The identification of mixed ARMA models from the *ACF* and *PACF* functions is not always straightforward, but in these cases an Extended *ACF* (*EACF*) is more useful in identifying the orders of mixed ARMA models.[15]

The mixed processes need to satisfy both stationarity and invertibility conditions. The orders (p, q) of an ARMA process are the highest lags of y_t and ε_t that appear in the model. For example, for an ARMA(1,1) process, $p = 1$ and $q = 1$. The general ARMA(p, q) process is formulated as follows:

$$\phi_p(B)y_t = \mu + \theta_q(B)\varepsilon_t \tag{17.37}$$

with $\phi_p(B)$ and $\theta_q(B)\varepsilon_t$ as defined above. As an example, for an ARMA(2,2) process, $\phi_2(B) = (1 - \phi_1 B - \phi_2 B^2)$ and $\theta_2(B) = (1 - \theta_1 B - \theta_2 B^2)$ so that:

$$y_t = \mu + \phi_1 y_{t-1} + \phi_2 y_{t-2} - \theta_1 \varepsilon_{t-1} - \theta_2 \varepsilon_{t-2} + \varepsilon_2. \tag{17.38}$$

Dekimpe and Hanssens (1995b) provide an overview of published univariate time series results in marketing. They identify 44 studies between 1987 and 1994 that

---

15. Details can be found in Tsay and Tiao (1984). The orders (p, q) of an ARMA process are quite often determined using information criteria: see Section 18.4.3.

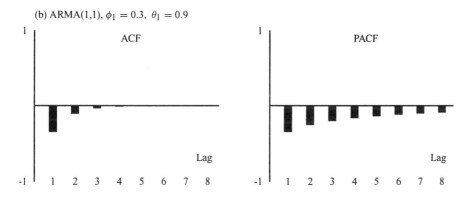

Source: Pankratz (1991, p. 46).

Figure 17.5 Example of theoretical ACF and PACF for ARMA(1,1) process.

have published results from such models, on a wide variety of durable (trucks, airplanes, furniture), nondurable food (cereal, catsup, beverages) and nonfood (detergents, toothpaste, cleaning aids) product categories and services (holidays, passenger transit, advertising).

17.3.5 STATIONARITY AND UNIT ROOT TESTING

We now define stationarity and invertibility formally. Stationarity requires that the roots of what are called the characteristic equations, $\phi_p(B) = 0$, "lie outside the unit circle". Similarly, invertability requires that the roots of $\theta_q(B)$ "lie outside the unit circle". For the AR(2) process this implies solving $(1 - \phi_1 B - \phi_2 B^2) = 0$ and for the MA(2) process solving $(1 - \theta_1 B - \theta_2 B^2) = 0$. In practice, a numerical routine can be used to solve these characteristic equations (if $p > 2$ or $q > 2$).

For example, for an AR(1) process $p = 1$. Then, $(1 - \phi_1 B) = 0$ is the characteristic equation. The root equals $1/\phi_1$, which is greater than one in absolute value if $\phi_1 < 1$. Thus, the null-hypothesis for testing nonstationarity is that $\phi_1 = 1$.[16] This test is called a unit root test. We redefine the AR(1)-model (17.30) as follows:

$$z_t = \mu + \gamma y_{t-1} + \varepsilon_t \tag{17.39}$$

where

$$z_t = y_t - y_{t-1}, \text{ and}$$
$$\gamma = \phi_1 - 1.$$

Then the unit root null hypothesis is $H_0: \gamma = 0$.

The reparameterized model (17.39) applied to data yields a t-statistic for $\hat{\gamma}$, which can be used to test H_0. This test is known as the Dickey-Fuller test. However, the t-statistic

---

16. Since most marketing series are positively correlated, we do not test $\phi_1 = -1$.

Table 17.5 Evolution and stationarity of 220 time series.

Model-type	Evolving		Stationary	
Sales	122	(68%)	58	(32%)
Market share	9	(22%)	31	(78%)
Total	131		89	

Source: Dekimpe and Hanssens (1995b, p. G114).

that is obtained cannot be evaluated with the regular tables of the t-distribution. Instead, special tables need to be used. The generalization of the Dickey-Fuller test to an AR(p) process yields the Augmented Dickey-Fuller test. This test is based on a reformulation of the AR(p) process as:

$$z_t = \mu + \gamma y_{t-1} + \delta_1 z_{t-1} + \delta_2 z_{t-2} + \ldots + \delta_p z_{t-p} + \varepsilon_t. \tag{17.40}$$

The Augmented Dickey-Fuller (*ADF*) test can be used to test the null hypothesis $\gamma = 0$. A large number of lagged first differences should be included in the *ADF* regression to ensure that the error is approximately white noise. In addition, depending on the assumptions of the underlying process, the test may be performed with or without μ in the model. Again, special tables are needed to assess the significance of the t-statistic.

An important application of unit root tests in marketing is provided by Dekimpe and Hanssens (1995a). They use the tests to determine whether sales are trending over time. If this is the case, they examine whether the trend can be related to marketing activity which implies multivariate persistence. Multivariate persistence is especially relevant for the design of marketing strategies that deliver sustainable, long-term marketing advantage.

In a second study, Dekimpe and Hanssens (1995b) apply unit root tests and other time-series methods to identify empirical generalizations about market evolution. Based on data from 400 published studies they conclude that evolution is the dominant characteristic in marketing series in general as well as in series with market performance measures as criterion variables. Although in many cases the necessary condition exists for making a long-run impact, market performance does not evolve over time in about 40 percent of all cases. The meta-analysis for performance measures is given in Table 17.5. The models are classified into sales models and market share models. The results show that evolution occurs in a majority of the brand sales models, and that a vast majority of the market share time-series models is stationary. This is consistent with arguments of Bass, Pilon (1980) and Ehrenberg (1994) that many markets are in a long-run equilibrium. The relative position of the brands is only temporarily affected by marketing activities.[17]

---

17. Other studies that assess the long-term impact of marketing instruments are, for example, Mela, Gupta, Lehmann (1997), Mela, Gupta, Jedidi (1998), Jedidi, Mela, Gupta (1999).

17.3.6 INTEGRATED PROCESSES

The ARMA processes described above are processes for series with a stationary mean. In these processes the mean value of y_t does not change over time. However, in marketing we often see that sales variables evolve (see Table 17.5) which implies nonstationarity. Nonstationary series can be formulated as ARMA processes for differenced series, $z_t = y_t - y_{t-1}$. The differencing operation removes a trend from the data. The corresponding model is called an ARIMA (Integrated ARMA) model.

As an example, consider an ARIMA(1,1,1) model:

$$z_t = \mu + \phi_1 z_{t-1} - \theta_1 \varepsilon_{t-1} + \varepsilon_t \tag{17.41}$$

where

$$z_t = y_t - y_{t-1}.$$

The *ACF* of a nonstationary process decays very slowly to zero. Therefore it is difficult to determine the AR and MA components from the *ACF* and *PACF*. However these functions for z_t (i.e. after differencing), display the typical patterns for ARMA processes, as illustrated above. In order to formulate the general ARIMA(p, d, q) process, integrated of order d, we define the differencing operator $\Delta^d = (1-B)^d$. For example, if $d = 1$ this amounts to taking $z_t = (1-B)y_t = y_t - By_t = y_t - y_{t-1}$. For $d = 2$ we have quadratic differencing $z_t^2 = (1-B)^2 y_t = (y_t - y_{t-1}) - (y_{t-1} - y_{t-2})$. Trends in marketing are often linear and sometimes quadratic, so that d in rarely greater than 2. The ARIMA(p, d, q) process can then be defined as:

$$\phi_p(B)\Delta^d y_t = \mu + \theta_q(B)\varepsilon_t. \tag{17.42}$$

17.3.7 SEASONAL PROCESSES

Many series of sales data in marketing display seasonal patterns, resulting from variation in weather and other factors. As a result sales fluctuate systematically around the mean level, such that some observations are expected to have values above and other observations below the mean. For example, sales of ice cream in Europe tend to be highest in the spring and summer and lowest in winter periods. The seasonal effects can be of the AR, the MA or the Integrated types, depending on whether sales levels or random shocks affect future sales, and on whether nonstationary seasonal patterns exist. Therefore a seasonal model may apply, with orders P, D, and Q respectively for the AR, I and MA components, denoted by ARIMA(P, D, Q)$_s$, with s the lag of the seasonal terms.

To illustrate, suppose there exists a seasonal pattern in monthly data, such that any month's value contains a component that resembles the previous year's value in the same month. Then a purely seasonal ARIMA(1,1,1)$_{12}$ model is written as:

$$z_t = \mu + \phi_{12} z_t{}^{12} - \theta_{12}\varepsilon_{t-12} + \varepsilon_t \tag{17.43}$$

where

$$z_t^{12} = \nabla^{12} y_t = y_t - B^{12} y_t = y_t - y_{t-12}, \text{ and}$$
$$\nabla^{12} = (1 - B^{12}).$$

The ARIMA$(0,1,1)_s$ is the most common seasonal model, and it provides an exponentially weighted moving average of the data. This simple model is written in two equivalent forms:

$$z_t = \mu + z_{t-s} - \theta_s \varepsilon_{t-s} + \varepsilon_t \tag{17.44}$$
$$\nabla^s z_t = \mu + (1 - \theta_s B^s)\varepsilon_t. \tag{17.45}$$

Seasonal processes can be identified from the *ACF* and *PACF* functions, similarly to the nonseasonal ARIMA processes above, except that the patterns occur at lags s, $2s$, $3s$, etc., instead of at lags 1,2,3, etc. Thus, for these purely seasonal processes:

- the *ACF* decays slowly at multiples of s in case of seasonal differencing of order s;
- the *ACF* decays at multiples of lag s and the *PACF* has spikes at multiples of lag s up to lag $P \times s$, after which it is zero, for seasonal *AR* processes;
- the *ACF* has spikes at multiples of lag s up to lag $Q \times s$, after which it is zero, and the *PACF* decays at multiples of lag s, for purely seasonal MA processes.

In practice, *seasonal* and *nonseasonal* processes occur together. However, an examination of *ACF* and *PACF* may suggest patterns in these functions at different lags. This general process is indicated as an ARIMA$(p, d, q)(P, D, Q)_s$ process:

$$\phi_P(B^s)\phi_p(B)\nabla^D \Delta^d y_t = \mu + \theta_Q(B^s)\theta_q(B)\varepsilon_t. \tag{17.46}$$

In (17.46) the seasonal and nonseasonal AR, MA and differencing operators are multiplied. In practice, the orders p,d,q, and P,D,Q, are small, ranging from 0 to 2 in most cases.

An application of an ARIMA model is provided by Blattberg and Neslin (1990, p.249). They model warehouse withdrawal sales data for a packaged good on 25 four-week periods in order to estimate incremental sales generated by a promotion. Examination of the series and the *ACF* and *PACF* functions yielded a ARIMA$(2,1,0)(0,1,0)_{13}$ model. That is, sales are affected by sales two (4-week) periods back, with linear trends in 1- and 13-period intervals. The estimated model is:

$$(1 + 0.83B + 0.58B^2)(1 - B)(1 - B^{13})y_t = -3686 + \varepsilon_t \tag{17.47}$$

or

$$y_t = 0.17y_{t-1} + 0.25y_{t-2} + 0.58y_{t-3} + y_{t-13} - 0.17y_{t-14} \tag{17.48}$$
$$-0.25y_{t-15} - 0.58y_{t-16} - 3686 + \varepsilon_t.$$

This application suggests that an ARIMA model can be quite useful for the estimation of complex time-series patterns. This model was used to estimate the incremental sales of a promotion.

17.3.8 TRANSFER FUNCTIONS

So far we have restricted the discussion to models of a criterion variable such as sales, as a function of past sales, random shocks and time. If we are insterested in estimating the effects of marketing variables, such as price and advertising, on sales when the latter variable is also subject to other complex patterns, we can include these variables in the model through a *transfer function*. To illustrate, assume there is just one explanatory variable, indicated by x_t. Often, the transfer function takes the form of a linear distributed lag function. Such a distributed lag function is a linear combination of current and past values of the explanatory variable $(x_t, x_{t-1}, \ldots)$. Thus, these models postulate that sales may respond to current and previous values of x, as is often the case for advertising. Suppose advertising affects sales as follows:

$$y_t = \mu + v_0 x_t + v_1 x_{t-1} + \varepsilon_t. \tag{17.49}$$

In this model sales in each period is affected by advertising in that period (x_t), and by advertising in the previous period (x_{t-1}). The general dynamic regression model formulation for one variable is:

$$y_t = \mu + v_k(B)x_t + \varepsilon_t \tag{17.50}$$

where

$$\mu = \text{a constant,}$$
$$v_k(B) = v_0 + v_1 B + v_2 B^2 + \ldots + v_k B^k, \text{ the transfer function,}$$
$$B = \text{the backshift operator, and}$$
$$k = \text{the order of the transfer function, which is to be determined.}$$

The transfer function, is also called the impulse response function, and the v-coefficients are called the impulse response weights. In the example, if sales do not react to advertising in period t, but only to lagged advertising, $v_0 = 0$. In that case, the model is said to have a "dead time" of one. In general, the dead time is the number of consecutive v's equal to zero, starting with v_0.

Before we discuss how the order of the impulse response function can be determined, we consider a well-known special case: the Koyck model. In this model, the impulse response weights are defined by $v_i = \alpha v_{i-1}$, for $i = 1, \ldots, \infty$. Thus, the response is a constant fraction of the response in the previous time period, and the weights decay exponentially. It can be shown that Koyck's model is equivalent to:

$$y_t = v_0 x_t + \alpha y_{t-1} + \varepsilon_t \tag{17.51}$$

or an AR(1) model with one explanatory variable of lag zero. Now, bringing the term involving the lagged criterion variable to the left-hand side of (17.51) results in:

$$(1 - \alpha B)y_t = v_0 x_t + \varepsilon_t \tag{17.52}$$

which can be rewritten as:

$$y_t = \frac{v_0}{(1 - \alpha B)}(x_t + \varepsilon_t). \tag{17.53}$$

This formulation is called the (rational) polynomial form of the Koyck model (see Section 6.1). In general, rational polynomial distributed lag models comprise a family of models, that are represented by substituting the following equation in (17.50):

$$v_{k,\ell}(B) = \frac{\omega_k(B)B^d}{\alpha_\ell(B)} \qquad (17.54)$$

where

$$\omega_k(B) = \omega_0 + \omega_1 B + \omega_2 B^2 + \ldots + \omega_k B^k, \text{ which contain}$$
the direct effects of changes in x on y over time,
$$\alpha_\ell(B) = \alpha_0 + \alpha_1 B + \alpha_2 B^2 + \ldots + \alpha_\ell B^\ell, \text{ which show}$$
the gradual adjustment of x to y over time, and
$$B^d = \text{the dead time (i.e. } d = 0 \text{ corresponds}$$
to dead time of $B^0 = 1$).

For the identification of dynamic regression models from data, two problems arise. The first is to find a parsimonious expression for the polynomial $v_{k,\ell}(B)$, and the second is to find an expression for the time structure of the error term, in the form of an ARIMA model. An important tool in the identification of transfer functions is the cross-correlation function (CCF), which is the correlation between x and y at lag k: $\rho(y_t, x_{t-k})$. The CCF extends the ACF for the situation of two or more series (those of x and of y), with similar interpretation: spikes denote MA parameters (in the numerator in (17.54)), and decaying patterns indicate AR parameters (in the denominator in (17.54)).

We note that the simultaneous identification of the transfer function and the ARIMA structure of the error in (17.50) is much more complex than it is for a single ARIMA process. An example that occurs frequently in marketing is one where the original sales series shows a seasonal pattern, for which an ARIMA$(1,0,1)(1,0,0)_{12}$ model is indicated. However, if temperature is included as an explanatory variable in the model, an ARIMA$(1,1,0)$ may suffice. Thus, the identification of the ARIMA error structure in (17.50) depends on the exogenous variables included in the model. Procedures that have been proposed for that purpose are the *LTF* (linear transfer function) method and the double prewhitening method. The core of these methods involves fitting univariate time series to the individual series, after which the estimated white noise residuals are used for multivariate analyses. This is called the prewhitening of variables.[18]

An alternative strategy that is useful especially with several input variables is the ARMAX procedure, which is an ARMA model for an endogenous variable with multiple exogenous variables. Franses (1991) applied this procedure to an analysis of

---

18. We refer to Hanssens, Parsons and Schultz (1990), Pankratz (1991) or Box, Jenkins and Reinsel (1994) for a description of these methods. Applications can be found in Bass and Pilon (1980), Leone (1983), and Doyle and Saunders (1985).

the primary demand for beer in the Netherlands. Based on 42 bimonthly observations from 1978 to 1984, using *ACF*'s and model tests, Franses obtained the following model:

$$\ln y_t = 0.17 y_{t-6} - 0.06\delta_1 + 2.30\delta_2 + 2.34\delta_3 + 2.51\delta_4 + 2.30\delta_5 +$$
$$2.37\delta_6 - 3.98\Delta^1 p_t + 2.27\Delta^1 p_{t+1} - 0.54\varepsilon_{t-1} + \varepsilon_t. \quad (17.55)$$

In this model, δ_1 to δ_6 are bimonthly seasonal dummies, p_t is the price, Δ^1 is a first-order differencing operator, and p_{t+1} is a price expectation variable that assumes perfect foresight. The model contains a lagged endogenous variable, a moving average component, seasonal effects (modeled through dummies rather then through differencing) and current price and future price effects. Substantively Franses concluded that tax changes may be effective if one wants to change the primary demand for beer, given the strong price effect. The positive effect of future prices suggests some forward buying by consumers. Advertising expenditures did not significantly influence the primary demand for beer.

In the transfer functions we consider the relations between criterion (y) and predictor variables (x).[19] The variables y and x may both be integrated of order d_y and d_x respectively, where $d_y \neq 0, d_x \neq 0$. We discuss the relevance of this below.

In the regression model:

$$y_t = \beta x_t + \varepsilon_t \quad (17.56)$$

there is a presumption that the ε_t are white noise series. However, this is unlikely to be true if $d_y \neq 0$ and/or $d_x \neq 0$. Generally, if two series are integrated of different order, i.e. $d_y \neq d_x$, linear combinations of them are integrated to the higher of the two orders $(max(d_x, d_y))$. If y_t and x_t are integrated to the *same* order $(d_y = d_x)$ then it is possible that there is a β such that:

$$\varepsilon_t = y_t - \beta x_t \quad (17.57)$$

is $I(0)$ (i.e. integrated to the order zero=white noise). Two series that satisfy this requirement are said to be *cointegrated*. Cointegration is a critical requirement for the modeling of time-series data to be meaningful in the sense that long-term effects can be predicted and long-term relations can be determined. In Section 17.3.5 we discussed the studies of Dekimpe and Hanssens (1995a, 1995b) in which long-term relations were established.

A useful tool to investigate whether the x and y series are cointegrated is the Engle-Granger cointegration test. A cointegration test involves the estimation of a cointegration regression between x and y and the application of a unit root test to the residuals from that regression. For further details see Engle and Granger (1987). Franses (1994) applied cointegration analysis to the analysis of new car sales, formulated in the framework of a Gompertz model for the growth process of sales.

---

19. See also, for example, Greene (1997, p. 852).

17.3.9 INTERVENTION ANALYSIS

Apart from traditional marketing variables such as price and advertising, we can accommodate discrete events in models of sales. Examples include a new government
regulation, the introduction of a competitive brand, a catastrophic event such as pois-
oning or disease relevant to food products, and so on. Intervention analysis extends
the transfer function approach described above for the estimation of the impact of
such events.[20] Intervention analysis in fact extends dummy-variable regression to a
dynamic context. The interventions may have two different effects: a pulse effect,
which is a temporary effect that disappears (gradually), or a step effect that is permanent once it has occurred. A strike could have a pulse effect on the production or
distribution of a product. The introduction of a new brand may permanently change
sales of an existing brand. The dummy variables for these two types of effects can be
represented as follows:

- pulse effect: $x_t^p = 1$ in the time periods of the intervention ($t = t'$), and $x_t^p = 0$
  in all other periods ($t \neq t'$);
- step effect: $x_t^s = 1$ in the time periods in which the event occurs and *all subsequent time periods* ($t \geq t'$), and $x_t^s = 0$ at all time periods before the event
  ($t < t'$),

where t' denotes the time of the intervention.

For intervention analysis the model defined by (17.50) and (17.54) applies, with the
x-variable defined as above. The form of (17.54) determines the nature of the *pulse*
interventions. If $v_p(B)x_t^p = \frac{\omega_0}{1-\alpha B}x_t^p$ then y_t shows a single spike at time t. In Figure
17.6 we show a number of pulse interventions.[21] In Figure 17.6a, y_t has a *stationary*
mean except for the effect of the pulse intervention at $t = t'$. During $t = t'$, y_t shifts
upward. Immediately after $t = t'$, the series returns to its previous level. For a series
with a *nonstationary* mean, a pulse intervention might appear as shown in Figure
17.6b. After $t = t'$, in which there is a downward shift, the series returns to the level
determined by its nonstationary character. The transfer function part is again $\omega_0 x_t^p$ as
in Figure 17.6a.

Figure 17.6c shows a pulse intervention at $t = t'$ and $t = t' + 1$, i.e., a multiperiod
temporary response. The transfer function part in $t = t'$ is $\omega_0 x_t^p$ and in $t = t' + 1$ it is
$\omega_1 B x_t^p$. Hence $v(B)x_t^p = (\omega_0 + \omega_1 B)x_t^p$. Notice that these effects are not cumulative;
the response of $\omega_0 x_t^p$ after $t = t'$ is zero, and the "secondary" response of $\omega_1 B x_t^p$ is
zero after $t = t' + 1$. If $v(B)x_t^p = \frac{\omega_0}{1-\alpha B}x_t^p$, the effect is a spike at $t = t'$, which decays
subsequently (if $| \alpha | < 1$). The series in Figure 17.6d shows a continuing dynamic
response following period t'. Each response after $t = t'$ is a constant fraction α of the
response during the previous period. The specification of $v(B)x_t^p$ is a Koyck model;
$\omega_0 x_t^p$ is the initial response of $t = t'$ and α is the retention rate (see equation (6.11)).

---

20. This approach was developed by Box and Tiao (1975).
21. We closely follow Pankratz (1991, pp. 254-264) who provides more details.

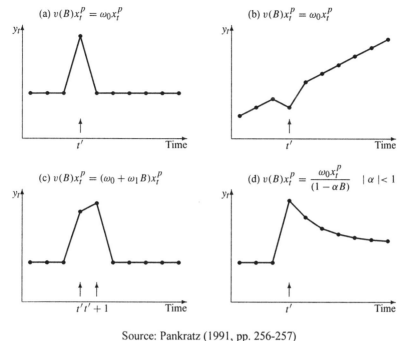

(a) $v(B)x_t^p = \omega_0 x_t^p$

(b) $v(B)x_t^p = \omega_0 x_t^p$

(c) $v(B)x_t^p = (\omega_0 + \omega_1 B)x_t^p$

(d) $v(B)x_t^p = \dfrac{\omega_0 x_t^p}{(1 - \alpha B)}$ $|\alpha| < 1$

Source: Pankratz (1991, pp. 256-257)

Figure 17.6 Examples of pulse interventions.

In Figure 17.7 we show some *step* interventions, i.e. *permanent* changes on y_t. Figure 17.7a shows a permanent effect that is immediate. Here $v(B)x_t^s = \omega_0 x_t^s$, $x_t^s = 0$ for $t < t'$ and $x_t^s = 1$ for $t \geq t'$. Figure 17.7b shows that a step intervention can be semi-permanent. Here $x_t^s = 1$ for $t = t', t' + 1, t' + 2$. Figure 17.7c illustrates a step intervention for a series with a nonstationary mean. A step intervention with dynamic effects is shown in Figure 17.7d. The transfer function of 17.7d is $(\omega_0 + \omega_1 B)x_t^s$, where $\omega_0 x_t^s$ captures the step during $t' - t' + 1$.

In the identification of intervention models, the linear transfer function approach (*LTF*) plays an important role.[22] In the discussion above, we have restricted our attention to the situation of a single regressor in the transfer function. The extension to multiple x-variables is straightforward, but the identification of the appropriate model becomes difficult.

We provide an application of intervention analysis to the analysis of sales for a fast-moving consumer good. The manufacturer of this product incurred two successive catastrophic events both of which affected the product's sales. We show a graph of the product's market share in Figure 17.8. The actual market share values and the time periods are disguised for reasons of confidentiality. Data were collected by a market

---

22. See, for example, Pankratz (1991, pp. 268-271).

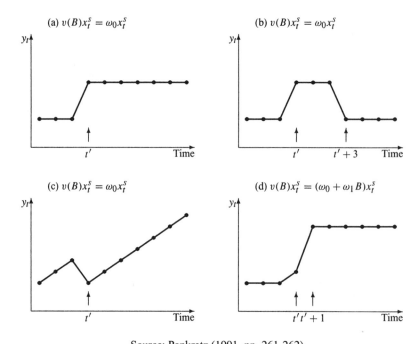

Source: Pankratz (1991, pp. 261-262)

Figure 17.7 Examples of step interventions.

research agency and are shown in periods of four weeks. The total length of the series is 52 (four-weekly) periods (4 years).

For this problem, no data on marketing variables were available, and the model was calibrated on market shares (y_t) only. The interventions occurred in periods 28 and 29. First, an ARIMA model was identified on the series up to the first intervention ($t \leq 27$). The *ACF* and *PACF* suggested an AR(1) model. There is no evidence of a seasonal pattern. The Dickey-Fuller unit root test indicated that the series is stationary. The estimates of the AR(1) model are presented below:

$$y_t = 27.20 + 0.36y_{t-1} + \varepsilon_t. \tag{17.58}$$

In this model, the AR(1) coefficient is highly significant. Subsequently, the interventions are modeled. Step functions were assumed for the two interventions based on an inspection of the data. Because the two interventions occur in two subsequent time periods, only a simple transfer function was estimated. The two intervention dummies are $x_{1t} = 0$ for $t = 1, \ldots, 27$ and $x_{1t} = 1$ for $t > 27$, and $x_{2t} = 0$ for $t = 1, \ldots, 28$ and $x_{2t} = 1$ for $t > 28$, respectively. The estimated intervention model is:

$$y_t = 27.18 + 0.44y_{t-1} - 5.83x_{1t} - 5.77x_{2t} + \varepsilon_t. \tag{17.59}$$

The R^2 of this model is 92.4 percent. The estimated standard error of each of the intervention effects is about 1.5, indicating that both effects are highly significant.

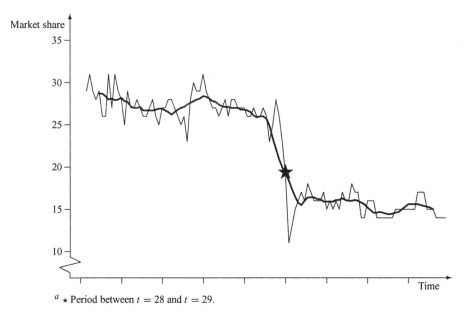

^{a} ⋆ Period between $t = 28$ and $t = 29$.

Figure 17.8 Market share of a brand subject to two catastrophic events.

The estimated standard error of the AR term is 0.1, so that this term is significant (as in 17.58). The model appears to fit the data quite well. The residuals do not show any remaining autocorrelation and are approximately normal. The step function specification of the interventions thus seems appropriate. The analysis suggests that both interventions have affected the share of the brand permanently over the time period considered in the study and it quantifies the magnitudes of the effects.

17.4 Varying parameter models[23]

In Section 7.2.4 we discussed why it is useful to adapt models. One possible adaptation is through the parameters. Model parameters can vary, even if the structure of the model stays the same. We refer to varying parameter models if the form of the model and the inclusion of variables are held constant but parameters vary over time and/or over cross-sections. In this section we briefly review models and techniques for parameter variation,[24] and discuss a specific application.

A simple approach is to separate time-series data into several periods and to estimate fixed parameters for a given model *(piecewise regression)*[25] to each period. This approach is attractive because of its simplicity. However, it is difficult to justify discrete changes in parameters. For example, if a new set of parameters is estimated each

23. This section is based on Foekens, Leeflang, Wittink (1999).
24. See also Judge, Griffiths, Hill, Lütkepohl and Lee (1985, Chapter 19).
25. See, e.g. McGee, Carleton (1970), Parsons (1975) and for an application Leeflang, Plat (1984).

calendar year, what is the argument in favor of fixed changes on January 1 and at the same time no changes at all during the rest of the year. It may also be impossible to anticipate in which direction the parameters will change prior to the beginning of a new calendar year. This would decrease the model's usefulness for decision-making purposes.

A *moving window regression*[26] allows the parameters to change slowly with each new data point. For example, a simple approach is to re-estimate all parameters by deleting the oldest observation and adding the newest to the sample. This method has the advantage that parameters change continuously, rather than discretely at arbitrary times. However, estimation is more time consuming although it can be done efficiently through recursive estimation (e.g. Reinmuth and Wittink, 1974). And systematic patterns may emerge which can suggest the nature of true dynamics.

Explicit approaches include those that model the parameters as a function of time[27] or model the parameters in a stochastic fashion.[28] A example is a two-stage sales-forecasting procedure developed by Smith, McIntyre and Achabal (1994). This procedure uses regression analysis in the first stage with data pooled across (similar) products. The second stage of the procedure updates selected parameters for each product on the basis of newly observed sales data.

Of greater substantive use are models in which marketing variables are allowed to interact. Gatignon and Hanssens (1987) define a class of models in which some variables explain variation in parameters associated with other variables. They demonstrate that these models are appropriate for accommodating interactions and are more useful than models in which the parameter variation is purely stochastic or depends only on time. Consider the following structure for a marketing interaction model:

$$y = f_1(X_1, \beta, u) \qquad (17.60)$$
$$\beta = f_2(X_2, \gamma, v) \qquad (17.61)$$

where

$y =$ a vector of product demand (e.g. brand sales),

$X_1 =$ a matrix of marketing and other variables,

$\beta =$ a vector of response parameters,

$X_2 =$ a (different) matrix of marketing and other variables which may affect one or more response parameters,

$\gamma =$ a vector of parameters explaining the response parameters, and

$u, v =$ are vectors of disturbance terms.

---

26. See Cleveland (1979), Mahajan, Bretschneider, Bradford (1980), Leeflang, Plat (1984), Eubank (1988) and Hastie, Tibshirani (1990).
27. See Parsons (1975).
28. See Wildt, Winer (1983), Blattberg, Kim, Ye (1994), Papatla, Krishnamurthi (1996).

Although the *demand* function (17.60) is usually estimated with time-series data, the *parameter* function (17.61) has been estimated both over time (e.g. Parsons and Vanden Abeele, 1981, Mela, Gupta, Lehmann, 1997) and over cross sections (e.g. Wittink, 1977).

We discuss a marketing interaction model developed for the estimation of dynamic promotion effects. Dynamic promotion effects exist because promotions such as temporary price cuts do not only increase sales at the time price is decreased but also displace future demand. Post-promotion dips in sales are expected to occur if consumers stockpile the promoted item, as is possible for frequently purchased non-perishable goods, or accelerate the purchase of a durable or nondurable product. However, models of promotional effects on brand sales often fail to detect significant post-promotion dips.[29] This failure may be due to a high degree of heterogeneity in consumer behavior, prior to, during, and subsequent to promotions. Ideally we accommodate this heterogeneity in models of household purchase behavior. However, there are many situations for which household data are unavailable or insufficient. Thus, it is important to use store-level data for maximum possible benefit. To fully understand promotion effects models must accommodate displacement of future demand.

We propose to estimate dynamic promotion effects with marketing interactions based on time-series and cross-sectional variation through a dynamic version of the SCAN*-PRO model. The static model is:

$$q_{kjt} = \left[\prod_{r=1}^{n} \left(\frac{p_{krt}}{\bar{p}_{kr}}\right)^{\beta_{rj}} \prod_{\ell=1}^{3} \gamma_{\ell rj}^{D_{\ell krt}}\right]\left[\prod_{t=1}^{T} \delta_{jt}^{X_t}\right]\left[\prod_{k=1}^{N} \lambda_{kj}^{Z_k}\right] e^{u_{kjt}}, \qquad (17.62)$$

$$j = 1, \ldots, n, \quad k = 1, \ldots, K, \quad t = 1, \ldots, T$$

where

q_{kjt} = unit sales for brand j in store k, in week t,

p_{krt} = unit price for brand r in store k, week t,

$\bar{p}_{kr}$ = the median *regular* unit price for brand r in store k,

$D_{\ell krt}$ = an indicator "variable" for non-price promotion ℓ equal
to 1 if brand r is promoted by store k in week
t, and 0 otherwise, where $\ell = 1$ "feature ad only", $\ell = 2$
"display only", and $\ell = 3$ "feature and display",

X_t = an indicator variable: 1 if the observation is in week t,
0 otherwise,

Z_k = an indicator variable for store k: 1 if the observation
is in store k; 0 otherwise,

---

29. See for a discussion Blattberg, Neslin (1990), Neslin, Schneider Stone (1996), Ailawadi, Neslin, (1998), van Heerde, Leeflang, Wittink (1999c).

u_{kjt} = a disturbance term,

$\quad n$ = the number of brands,

$\quad K$ = the number of stores, and

$\quad T$ = the number of weeks.

The arguments in favor of dynamics are as follows. Promotion frequency and depth of price discounts may influence consumers' price expectations. In turn, expectations of price and non-price promotional activities explain some consumer brand choice behavior (Kalwani, Yim, 1992). Thus consumers' stockpiling behavior of a brand (or product category) may also depend on the size and recency of temporary price discounts. If there exists substantial variation in these promotional activity components over time, we should find dynamic effects in models of promotion effects.

The β_{rj} are the price elasticities: the own-brand price elasticity if $r = j$ or a cross-brand elasticity if $r \neq j$. The $\gamma_{\ell rj}$ are the multipliers for promotion ℓ: own effects if $r = j$ or a cross-effect if $r \neq j$. The λ_{kj}'s are the store intercepts for brand j in store k, and δ_{jt} are the seasonal multipliers for week t for brand j. In (17.62), the own-brand price parameter $\beta_{rj}, r = j$ reflects the increase in brand j's sales in the presence of a temporary price cut for the brand. Reasons for this sales increase may include brand switching, consumption increase, stockpiling and purchase acceleration. With larger past discounts and with more recent price discounts, for both own- and other brands, this price parameter should move toward zero. Own-brand, feature- and display parameters may similarly decline with more recent promotions.

To create a dynamic version of (17.62), equations were specified for the price parameters, the promotion multipliers and the store intercept (λ_{kj}). To illustrate, we show the price parameter *process function* (17.63) for the own-brand price elasticity. In (17.63), the own-price elasticity depends on the *magnitude* and *time* since the previous price discount for own- and other brands. The expected signs are shown in parentheses below the equations.

$$\beta_{kjjt} = \beta_{0j} + \beta_{1j} \, Dsum_{kjt} + \beta_{2j} \, CDsum_{kjt} + \qquad (17.63)$$
$$\phantom{\beta_{kjjt} =} (-) \quad (+) \qquad\qquad (+)$$

$$\beta_{3j} \, d_\eta \left(\frac{1}{PTime_{kjt}} \right) + \beta_{4j} \, d_\eta \left(\frac{1}{CPTime_{kjt}} \right) + u_{kjjt}$$
$$\phantom{\beta_{3j} \, d_\eta} (+) \qquad\qquad\qquad (+)$$

where

$$Dsum_{kjt} = \sum_{s=1}^{\omega} \eta^{s-1} discount_{kj,t-s} \text{ for brand } j \text{ in store } k,$$

$\quad \eta$ = decline rate $(0 < \eta \leq 1)$,

$\quad \omega$ = number of weeks of history used for the explanatory

$\qquad$ variables in (17.63),

$$discount = \text{difference between regular and actual unit price,}$$

$$CDsum_{kjt} = \sum_{r \neq j}^{n} \sum_{s=1}^{\omega} \eta^{s-1} discount_{rj,t-s} \text{ for other brands } r \neq j,$$

$$d_\eta = \text{a dummy variable equal to 1 if } \eta = 1 \text{ and 0 if}$$
$$0 < \eta < 1,$$

$PTime_{kjt}$ = number of weeks since the last *own-price* promotion
(within last ω weeks preceding t) of brand j in store k,

$CPTime_{kjt}$ = number of weeks after the last *other-brand price* promotion
(within last ω weeks) of any brand $r \neq j$ in store k,

u_{kjjt} = a disturbance term.

In (17.63) the β's and η are the unknown parameters. In (17.63) there are separate discount magnitude and timing effects due to own brand and due to other brands. There are several reasons for this separation. For example the own-price elasticity may primarily reflect the purchase behavior of "loyal" consumers of brand j. These loyal consumers would adjust their stockpiling behavior based on the magnitude and timing of recent price promotions for brand j. However, competing brands may also entice brand switching if the promoted prices for those brands are sufficiently attractive. We expect, however, that consumers who prefer brand j will not adjust their purchase behavior to the same extent with identical variation in the magnitude and timing of recent price promotions for other brands. In addition, the activities for all other brands are aggregated.

The process function contains a decline rate parameter (η) in the definitions of *Dsum* and *CDsum* which allows more recent discounts to have a stronger effect on the own-brand price parameter, if $\eta < 1$. In that case $d_\eta = 0$ which eliminates the "price timing" variables from (17.63). For $\eta = 1$, the discounts in the preceding ω weeks are equally weighted. A grid search procedure is used for the determination of η.

We illustrate the measurement of the magnitude and timing variables in Table 17.6. In this example we use six weeks of history ($\omega = 6$) for the computation of *Dsum* and *PTime* in (17.63). Further, we assume a constant regular unit price of $\$1.00$. The discount measure is the difference between the regular and actual unit prices. By using $\omega = 6$, *Dsum* is undefined until period 7. In $t = 7$, *Dsum* = $.20 + .10$, due to discounts in $t = 2$ and $t = 4$, if $\eta = 1$. *PTime* is undefined until the period subsequent to the first discount for own brand. *CDsum* and *CPTime* are defined in analogous fashions.

The expected parameter signs in (17.63) show that we hypothesize that the own-brand price elasticity moves toward zero, the greater the magnitude of the most recent price promotion for own brand *(Dsum)* and for other brands *(CDsum)*, and the shorter the number of weeks since the previous price promotion for own brand *(PTime)* and for other brands *(CPTime)*. By substituting (17.63), and other process functions for the multipliers and the store/brand intercept (not specified here), in (17.62) we allow

Table 17.6 The measurement of magnitude and timing variables (decline rate $\eta = 1$).

	$t = 1$	$t = 2$	$t = 3$	$t = 4$	$t = 5$	$t = 6$	$t = 7$
actual p_{krt}	1.00	.80	1.00	.90	1.00	1.00	.75
$discount_{kjt}$	$.00^a$	.20	.00	.10	.00	.00	.25
$Dsum_{kjt}$	?	?	?	?	?	?	.30
$PTime_{kjt}$	?	?	1	2	1	2	3

^{a} Regular price $\bar{p}_{kj} = \$1.00$.

parameters to vary across stores and over time as a function of brand- and store-specific promotional activities.

Foekens et al. (1999) obtained various dynamic effects. In particular, baseline sales was found to be dynamic, consistent with expectations: an increase in sales due to a temporary price cut tends to reduce baseline sales (sales under nonpromoted conditions) in periods following the promotion. By allowing the store intercepts to vary based on the magnitude of a temporary price cut and on the time since a promotion, Foekens et al. (1999) also accommodated the illusive post-promotion dip.[30] They also obtained dynamic effects in the own-discount elasticity, specifically showing that the magnitude and time since a previous discount change this elasticity.[31]

---

30. This can also be accomplished by a model with lead and lagged effects. See van Heerde, Leeflang, Wittink (1999c).
31. This topic is also discussed by, for example, Krishna (1991) and Raju (1992).

CHAPTER 18

Validation

Two critical elements of model building are model specification and parameterization. Model specification depends on intended use, but should also be based on theoretical and experiential knowledge. Parameterization includes data collection, model estimation and model testing. In this chapter we consider an additional part of model building: validation[1] (also verification or evaluation).

In its broadest sense validation is an assessment of the quality of the model results. Validation criteria for model building can relate to:

- the model structure (specification);
- the data quality;
- the estimation method;
- the applicability of statistical tests (e.g. with regard to error-term assumptions);
- the correspondence of model results to theoretical and common-sense expectations;
- the model's (relative) performance, against alternative models;
- the relevance of model results to intended use.

We briefly review the different criteria in Section 18.1 and the relevance of statistical tests in Section 18.2. In Section 18.3 we discuss *face validity* criteria which are used to determine whether model results are in accordance with theoretical and/or common-sense expectations. (Literally, face validity refers to the extent to which one's face becomes red if one is questioned about the logic of the empirical results.) We introduce criteria for model selection in Section 18.4. The idea of model selection is that we often have alternative model specifications, and we use data to distinguish between the alternatives. The superiority of one model over another may depend on the product category and on competitive conditions but also on the quality of data. Even though theoretical arguments should inform the model specification, in marketing we want the empirical results to be not only consistent with what sound arguments dictate but also with how the marketplace behaves subsequent to model testing. With new data, the question is whether extant models apply, and with new models the question is whether the proposed specification outperforms prevailing benchmarks.

---

1. The meaning of validation varies across the sciences as well as within a discipline. For an in-depth discussion of this concept in a marketing context, see for example, Heeler, Ray (1972), Zaltman, Pinson, Angelmar (1973) and the special issue of the *Journal of Marketing Research,* vol. 16, February 1979.

If the model-building effort is intended to have descriptive validity (re: intended model use), we could restrict the validation effort to such aspects as model tests and face validity. However, in marketing, the empirical research almost always includes a measure of predictive validity. This is perhaps a reflection of the philosophy that for any model to be useful (even for descriptive purposes), it must have predictive validity. We introduce a framework, along with criteria, for predictive validity in Section 18.5. We illustrate the validation of models, with different degrees of behavioral detail, in Section 18.6, and end the chapter with a discussion of validation regarding subjective estimation in Section 18.7.

18.1 Validation criteria

We have argued that the success of a model depends on the likelihood of model acceptance. The aspects that contribute to the likelihood a model is implemented are:

- model-related dimensions;
- organization-related dimensions;
- implementation strategy dimensions.

In Chapter 7 we discussed implementation criteria with respect to model structure. Models that are simple, complete (on the critical issues), robust and adaptive are expected to be more successful than models that fail to satisfy these criteria. Other, more analytical, aspects with regard to model specification are covered in Chapter 14. The arguments we present in Chapter 14 often do not enter a model user's mind, but if a model generates wrong answers its use is likely to be short lived. Thus, the more that theoretical and analytical arguments are consistent with a given model specification, the higher its likelihood of success. Importantly, the data cannot sufficiently inform the user about the desired model specification. For example, the residuals of a poorly specified model may show that one or more error-term assumptions are violated. Yet, as we discuss in Chapter 16, the analysis of residuals does not suggest which remedy applies. We do claim that the closer the initial model specification is to being correct, the more diagnostically useful such a residual analysis can be. For example, if all relevant variables are included but the effect of just one predictor variable is not properly accommodated, it will be straightforward to identify the cause of the violation of an error-term assumption. This argument suggests that the model builder should spend a lot of time on the justification of the proposed model structure.

The probability of model implementation also depends on characteristics of the firm for which the model is developed. These characteristics include the model user, the interface between model builder and -user, and the way the firm is organized. We discuss these characteristics, and factors related to the implementation strategy for the model into the firm, in Chapter 19.

The success of a model also depends heavily on the "quality" of the data. The dimensions of availability, validity, reliability, variability and quality determine the "quality" of the data, as is discussed in Section 15.1. The quality of data, along with other considerations in turn influences the estimation method(s) covered in Chapter 16. Specifically in Section 16.1 we review the assumptions about the error term in the classical linear model, and we discuss the implications of violations of the error term assumptions. Importantly, a model's theoretical structure and the logic of empirical results need to be examined for issues such as:

- the direction of causality;
- the relevance of individual variables, in terms of both main- and interaction effects;
- the functional form of proposed relations;
- the constancy of parameters across sections, over time, or as a function of data characteristics;
- the constancy of the error variance;
- the independence of errors over time;
- the normality of errors;
- multicollinearity.

This portion of the validation exercise is called specification error analysis or "diagnostics".[2] If there is no evidence that the assumptions about the error term are violated, statistical tests can be applied to the model results. For example, we can test whether the model as a whole is statistically significant (with regard to its explanatory power), and whether individual parameter estimates are statistically significant.

Econometric analysis consists essentially of trying to explain variation in the criterion variable by fluctuations in the predictor variables. If a predictor does not vary in the sample data, it cannot explain variation in the criterion variable. Indeed, the amount of variation in, and covariation between, predictor variables influences the nature of statistical analysis. If the data are not amenable, other methods such as experimentation or subjective estimation should be considered. Thus the model builder needs to know what the data allow for.

The model-building process should end with "an acceptable, final model" as we discuss in Section 5.1. However, to arrive at a "final model" several models may have to be calibrated and tested. In marketing, the choice between alternative model specifications is often not straightforward, in part because relative performance depends on the measure(s). Over the years various criteria, search processes, empirical rules, and testing mechanisms have been proposed to guide model selection. With regard to statistical tests based on model fit, one approach is to specify a supermodel which "nests" all alternative models. Such a supermodel may not be of interest in itself but it can be useful to determine the adequacy of each alternative model. We discuss comparisons of nested models in Section 18.4. We list information criteria which can be used in model selection, and we mention how a choice can be made between competing nonnested models. We also introduce so-called causality tests which are used to dis-

---

2. See, for example, Wittink (1988, Chapter 7).

tinguish causality from association or to choose between *alternative* causal relations.

As we have mentioned, the primary purpose of a model can be descriptive, predictive or normative. Some validation criteria have greater relevance for one of these purposes than for another. For example, *face* validity is quite relevant if the model-building effort serves a *descriptive* purpose. If the primary use of the model is for prediction, then it is natural to focus especially on *predictive* validity. That is, while face validity is still relevant, especially for conditional forecasting,[3] the focus is likely to center around the performance of predictions. We regard the third purpose (normative) as the most demanding one. For a model to be used for normative decisions, model results should have face validity, should have predictive validity, and should have only a modest amount of statistical uncertainty.

We believe that the state of (predictive) validation in marketing is weak. Even if a model is proposed to demonstrate that the effects of interest have not been described properly in previous research it is common for researchers to use simple predictive validation schemes. For example, with time-series data, the sample is often split into two parts, an estimation and a validation sample. The estimation sample is used for parameter estimation, while the validation sample provides a basis for a determination of subsequent performance. Very little attention, however, is paid to the extent to which the validation sample has characteristics that differ from the estimation sample. Thus, such simple schemes may or may not allow for a proper determination of (conditional) predictive validity. We return to this topic in Section 18.5.

18.2 Statistical tests and validation criteria

We have argued, in Chapter 16, that the error-term assumptions in econometrics are needed for statistical inference. Of particular interest is the assumption that $E(u_i) = 0$ or $E(u_i \mid X_i) = 0$ for all i, $i = 1, \ldots, I$. If the predictor variables are "fixed", this first assumption about the error term is required for a claim that the parameter estimates are unbiased. To the extent possible, the data should be used to test this assumption. But a model builder who is interested in getting a model implemented may not have an incentive to complete an exhaustive search of all ways in which this most critical assumption can be falsified. For example, if we have exhausted the data for the measurement of relevant predictor variables, but nevertheless use statistical tests for omitted variables by adding polynomial expressions of the included predictor variables, we risk having to reject the model altogether as being invalid. Of course, in the long run, an incomplete model will be rejected. However, the model may have many attractive characteristics, and the model builder may want to believe that a long time will pass before it is found to be deficient.

---

3. Conditional forecasting is the term used to describe situations in which the model is used to obtain forecasts conditional upon certain decisions, such as a specific marketing mix (see Section 8.2). If the empirical results lack face validity, it is unlikely that one can obtain acceptable *conditional* forecast accuracy.

This dilemma suggests that if the model builder's rewards depend on model implementation, there is an implicit incentive to make only a partial attempt to falsify empirical results. The criteria for implementation by the model user should then include convincing results from the latest tests with the highest power to reject incorrect models.[4]

Statistical tests for the error term assumptions also have other limitations. Consider the third assumption, viz. $Cov(u_i, u_j) = 0, i \neq j$. For *time-series data,* econometric textbooks offer the following discussion when this assumption is violated (for convenience, we use a linear model with one predictor variable):

$$y_t = \alpha + \beta x_t + \varepsilon_t, \quad \text{for } t = 1, \ldots, T \tag{18.1}$$

where

$$\varepsilon_t = \rho \varepsilon_{t-1} + u_t \quad \text{and } E(u_t) = 0. \tag{18.2}$$

With these qualifications, it is possible to show that the OLS estimator is unbiased. Thus, the existence of a first-order autocorrelation in the error term does not have to detract from the validity of model specification (18.1). Unfortunately, the textbooks rarely discuss the source of a (first-order) autocorrelation, and the reader is not encouraged to be critical of the joint plausibility of (18.1) and (18.2). Instead, the common recommendation is to estimate the first-order autocorrelation, and to use Generalized Least Squares (GLS). With an estimated value for $\hat{\rho}$ in (18.2), the claim is made by many, including ourselves, that GLS provides asymptotically unbiased parameter estimates that are (asymptotically) more efficient than OLS.

The fact that it is possible to show analytically that autocorrelation does not have to lead to biases in the OLS estimates does, however, not provide support for the applicability of this particular perspective in practice. Since empirical model building is subject to severe limitations (e.g, incomplete model structure, missing variables), we expect that the existence of autocorrelated disturbances is virtually always due to misspecification. Therefore, we suggest the same remedy that applies in case of a violation of the first assumption ($E(u_i) = 0$) be applied for violations of the third assumption ($Cov(u_i, u_j) = 0$). The test for the presence of autocorrelated disturbances in time-series data is then merely a convenient way to explore the plausibility of the model. However, this recommendation is not much appreciated in empirical research. It is, after all, quite straightforward to use GLS with an estimated autocorrelation coefficient (this is the indicated solution if something equivalent to (18.1) and (18.2) is assumed). On the other hand, the search for a missing predictor variable can be interminable.

We believe that, in general, the proposed model is invalid if either one of these assumptions fails. As we mention in Chapter 16, in that case statistical inference cannot proceed, and substantive use of the results is not recommended.[5] Assumption

---

4. By the same token a researcher who wants a paper published in an academic journal may also lack the incentive to falsify a proposed model. Thus, reviewers of papers have to insist on the author's use of tests with the highest power to reject incorrect models.

5. Although we do not have specifics on the following argument, we can imagine having a model that fails a critical assumption but still provides guidance to managers, is better than the alternative of not having a model.

2, $(Var(u_i) = \sigma^2)$, however, can be violated when the model specification is correct. Especially with cross-sectional data it is common for the values of the criterion variable to vary in size, and for the error to be proportional to size. Thus, it can be quite logical to specify:

$$y_i = \alpha + \beta x_i + u_i, \quad i = 1, \ldots, I \tag{18.3}$$

where

$$E(u_i) = 0 \text{ and } Var(u_i) = \sigma^2 x_i^2. \tag{18.4}$$

Now one can use Weighted Least Squares (WLS), which is a specific form of GLS (see Chapter 16), dividing both sides of (18.3) by x_i. This will generate unbiased and efficient parameter estimates. In this sense, a finding that the second assumption is violated, does not invalidate the model specification.

The fourth assumption, normally distributed errors, we believe is also likely to be violated if the model specification is incorrect. If the error term captures the effects of a large number of omitted variables, each of which by itself has only a minor influence on the criterion variable, then it can be argued that this error term should be approximately normally distributed. A violation of the normality assumption could then indicate that there is an omitted variable with more than a minor impact. It is in this sense that the tests of three assumptions about the error term can invalidate a model specification. And, if there is no evidence that any of the assumptions is violated, based on rigorous testing, we can move on to other types of validation.

18.3 Face validity

Face validity relates to the believability of a model's structure and its output, or the validity at face value. Face validity is based on theoretical and common-sense expectations, and on broadly accepted previous empirical results. This *prior knowledge* can be put to work in various ways as indicated by Massy (1971, p. 6): in structuring the model, in selecting appropriate estimation methods and in benchmarking the results from new data.

The use of face validity as a criterion depends, of course, on the model builder's prior knowledge with regard to the phenomena under study. This knowledge should guide model specification (e.g. relevant variables, operationalization of measures, functional forms). The model structure that is ultimately subjected to estimation can therefore also be evaluated in terms of face validity. The bases for knowledge about marketing phenomena include theories developed in relevant disciplines, such as economics and psychology. Additional theoretical knowledge is generated within the field of marketing. And a large body of empirical results, much of it generated within the marketing field, can be used to determine the face validity of new empirical results. Of course, prior knowledge should not stifle the acceptance of surprising results. Current thinking about (marketing) problems is incomplete and sometimes incorrect.

One purpose of model building is to test the prevailing theories. Face validity, however, has a place when we believe our understanding of the nature of relationships is quite good.

Consider a model of (unit) sales for a brand, as a function of predictor variables such as own-brand price and own-brand advertising. Except for unusual cases, for example if price is interpreted by consumers as an indicator of quality, we expect price to have a negative effect on sales. Advertising, on the other hand is expected to have a positive effect on sales. Thus, ordinarily we are suspicious of empirical results that show "wrong" signs for the (partial) slope coefficients.[6]

Given a relatively large number of empirical studies in which price and advertising effects have been reported, and the meta-analyses completed on estimated effects (see Section 3.3), the argument has been made that today newly developed results should be tested against the average effects computed from published studies. The focus then shifts to a statistical test of the difference from the prevailing average effect, and the face validity of a significant difference in one direction. In this sense, the basis for face validity considerations about advertising effects can be the average advertising elasticity of 0.10 reported by Lambin, based on 38 cases (1976, p. 93) and also 0.10 based on 40 estimates analyzed by Leone and Schultz (1980). However, Assmus, Farley and Lehmann (1984) report an average short-term advertising elasticity estimate of 0.22, from 128 econometric model results. Assmus et al. (1984) also report an average carryover coefficient of 0.47, which implies a long-term sales impact of $1/(1 - 0.47) = 1.88$ times the short-term impact. Separately, Lodish et al. (1995b) report average long-term television advertising effects from 55 tests for a cross section of established brands of consumer packaged goods. One of their findings is that the first-year sales impact of (successful) advertising campaigns is approximately doubled when the lagged sales impact over the next two years is added. This long-term impact of about twice the short-term impact is more or less in line with the Assmus et al. result.

For price, Tellis (1988b) reports an average elasticity, based on 367 econometric studies, of -1.76. More recent estimates of price elasticity can be compared against this benchmark, and reasons for significant deviations in either direction should be explored. In this manner, the meta-analysis results can enrich the process of "face validation".

To illustrate the importance of allowing for surprises, we briefly review a study with strong interaction effects between advertising and price. Eskin (1975) reports on a field experiment for a new, inexpensive food snack, in which price and advertising are manipulated. If the experiment had not been conducted, management would have chosen either a combination of low price and low advertising or high price and high advertising. This is based on the idea that a low price generates a low margin which would not provide enough money for a large advertising campaign. Thus, a per-unit

---

6. The criticism will be muted if a coefficient with a sign opposite to expectations is not statistically significant. If the sign is "wrong" and the coefficient is significantly different from zero, we would suspect model misspecification.

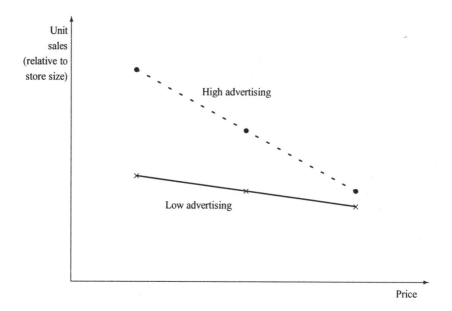

Figure 18.1 Relation between sales and price, separately for high- and for low advertising support.

cost argument would have been the basis for the joint advertising-price decisions. An alternative demand-based argument is that a higher amount of advertising enhances the strength of preference for the advertised product. Stronger preferences reduce consumers' price sensitivities, and this would also favor low-price with low-advertising and high-price with high-advertising combinations.

One advantage of experimental studies is that, with appropriate controls and randomization, there is less worry about omitted variables and other misspecification issues. In this case the model included certain control variables to minimize the confounds that occur in field experiments. Another advantage of experimentation is that the use of all possible combinations of alternative price levels and advertising amounts facilitates the estimation of interaction effects. In Eskin's model, the interactions were counter to expectations. At high levels of advertising, the aggregate price sensitivity was much higher than at low levels of advertising (see Figure 18.1). This suggests (in practice, one would determine the profit-maximizing combination) that the optimal mix would be either high advertising and low price, or low advertising and high price. Either of these demand-based combinations was inconsistent both with the supply-side argument and with the theory about how advertising for a brand affects an individual consumer's price sensitivity. Since an experimental-study result has more credibility than one based on non-experimental data, Eskin's explanation for the surprising result was easily accepted. The explanation was that higher amounts of advertising for a new brand attracts consumers who would ignore the product at lower advertising levels. These additional consumers have lower marginal utility for the product, and purchase it only if the price is low.

18.4 Model selection

18.4.1 INTRODUCTION

The face validation criteria discussed in the previous section may allow a model builder to reject some models. However, it is common for more than one model specification to produce plausible results. Thus, face validity considerations may not suffice when the desired result is to identify one "best" model. If neither theoretical arguments pertaining to model structure, nor the violation of error-term assumptions, nor face validity considerations allow the model builder to reject all but one of the alternative models, we use explicit model comparisons.

There are at least two ways in which explicit comparisons can be made between alternative models. In this section we discuss statistical methods that allow the model builder to test hypotheses regarding relative model performance in the estimation sample. We introduce nested model comparisons and applicable statistical tests in Section 18.4.2. In Section 18.4.3 we discuss nonnested model comparisons, which are especially relevant for tests of alternative functional forms.

In addition to the uncertainty faced by model builders in the selection of relevant predictor variables and functional forms, a less frequently confronted aspect concerns the causal direction. In marketing, most model builders assume that consumers' purchase behavior depends on marketing mix activities and ignore the possible reverse dependency. Notable exceptions are the simultaneous equations used to estimate the relation between sales and advertising (Bass, 1969a) and the relation between market share and distribution (Farris, Olver, de Kluyver, 1989). Statistical tests of causal direction ("causality tests") are rarely used in marketing. Exceptions are listed in Bult, Leeflang and Wittink (1997).

We discuss causality tests in Section 18.4.4. Such tests can be used to distinguish between alternative causal directions as well as between unidirectional- and multidirectional relations. Causality tests appear to be especially relevant when theoretical arguments and existing knowledge are insufficient. For example, if the model building is intended to quantify competitive reaction effects, it is virtually impossible to specify a priori who are the leaders and the followers. Also, leadership may depend on the marketing instrument. Thus, especially for relations such as those that capture competitive reaction effects, causality tests can be very helpful.

Bivariate causality tests have been used to reduce a large set of potentially relevant predictor variables. For example, in models of competitive reactions, the existence of seven competitors, each using five marketing variables, with the timing of reaction effects varying from a lag of one period to a lag of ten periods, one would need to accommodate 300 competitive predictor variables. To obtain a manageable set of predictors, Bult et al. (1997) used bivariate causality tests. They used these tests for a preliminary indication of causal relevance, and in the process made the competitive reaction equations identifiable.

18.4.2 NESTED MODELS

Nesting is a means of comparing alternative specifications where the parameters of the so-called lower-order equations are contained within the parameter space of higher-order ones. See Section 6.3, where we discuss model nesting in the context of dynamic models. We now use these models to illustrate the concept of "nesting".

We first show the structure of a higher-order model, viz. the Partial Adjustment Autoregressive model (PAA model). The model was calibrated by Leeflang, Mijatovich and Saunders (1992) with sales and promotion data for a pharmaceutical brand in the British market. The data stem from the "hypnotics and sedatives" segment of the pharmaceutical market. The marketing activity consisted of face-to-face communications (detailing) and impersonal media activity ("advertising"). Sales figures were based on the volume of drugs sold on prescription by pharmacists. The detailing variable measured the time spent by pharmaceutical sales representatives promoting the drugs. Magazine advertising was the cost of ads at the time of publication and direct mailing efforts based on the cost at the day of mailing. The data represented 36 monthly periods for the period January 1983 through December 1985.

In all models, the market share in period t (m_t) is related to shares of detailing effort (ds_t) and shares of journal and direct mail advertising (as_t). All variables were expressed in terms of deviations from the mean. As a consequence the models have zero intercepts. The PAA model has the following structure:

$$m_t = \beta_1 ds_t + \beta_2 as_t + \lambda m_{t-1} + u_t \tag{18.5}$$

where

$$u_t = \rho u_{t-1} + \varepsilon_t,$$
$$u_t = \text{a disturbance term,}$$
$$\rho = \text{the autocorrelation parameter, and}$$
$$\varepsilon_t = \text{an error term.}$$

Introducing the backward shift generator L, where $L(m_t) = m_{t-1}$ and substituting these generators in (18.5) we get:

$$m_t - \lambda L(m_t) = \beta_1 ds_t + \beta_2 as_t + \frac{\varepsilon_t}{1 - \rho L} \tag{18.6}$$

or

$$m_t = \frac{\beta_1 ds_t + \beta_2 as_t}{(1 - \lambda L)} + \frac{\varepsilon_t}{(1 - \lambda L)(1 - \rho L)}. \tag{18.7}$$

The following dynamic models are nested in (18.7):

1. Partial Adjustment model (PA) in which there is no autocorrelation, i.e.: $\rho = 0$ while $\lambda \neq 0$ (see:(6.30));
2. the Current-Effects Autoregressive model (CEA), in which $\lambda = 0$ but $\rho \neq 0$ (compare (6.27));

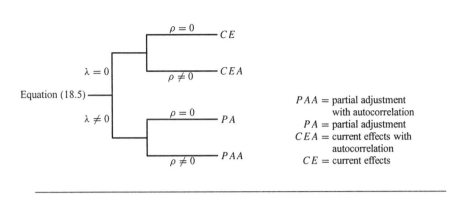

Figure 18.2 Nesting scheme.

3. the Current-Effects model (CE), in which $\rho = \lambda = 0$ (compare (6.24)).

We show the relations between the various models (CE, CEA, PA, and PAA) in a nesting scheme, in Figure 18.2.

We show in Table 18.1 the regression coefficients, t-statistics (in parentheses), the coefficients of determination (R^2), the Durbin-Watson statistics and Durbin's h-statistics. The coefficients in all four models are statistically significantly different from zero. The much stronger explanatory power (R^2 value) and the relevance of the lagged endogenous variable suggest that the partial adjustment (PA and PAA) models are better than the current effect models (CE and CEA). The estimated adjustment rates $\hat{\lambda}$, in the partial adjustment models, suggest the presence of delayed response effects.

It is interesting that between the two current effects models, the specification with autocorrelated errors (CEA) shows a substantial degree of first-order autocorrelation. Both models also have significant D.W. statistics. On the other hand, when the lagged endogenous variable is incorporated, the autocorrelation coefficient is very close to zero. Interestingly, the estimated current effects of both detailing and advertising are much smaller in the PA and PAA models, and the reduction in the detailing effect is especially large (both in an absolute and in a relative sense). However, the substantive conclusions differ greatly between, for example, the CEA and PA models.

We also note several other interesting aspects in Table 18.1. We have argued that the presence of first-order autocorrelation in the disturbance should rarely be treated through the addition of an autocorrelation parameter. If this were an appropriate remedy, then the Durbin-Watson (D.W.) statistic should be close to two in the CEA model. Since the D.W. statistic is not much different from its value in the CE model, it appears that the systematic pattern in the disturbances is not well captured by a first-order autocorrelated error structure.

The other aspect worth mentioning is that the R^2 value for CEA is lower than the

Table 18.1 Model estimates and test results.

Model	Detailing effort $\hat{\beta}_1$	Advertising effort $\hat{\beta}_2$	Lagged end.var. $\hat{\lambda}$	Auto- corr.coeff. $\hat{\rho}$	R^2	D.W. statistic	Durbin's h-statistic
CE	0.22 (4.75)	0.07 (2.84)	-	-	0.78	1.05	-
CEA	0.17 (3.62)	0.06 (2.96)	-	0.34	0.64	1.21	-
PA	0.07 (2.15)	0.04 (3.45)	0.68 (9.00)	-	0.94	2.01	-0.04
PAA	0.07 (2.22)	0.04 (3.51)	0.68 (9.27)	0.05	0.94	1.95	0.15

Source: Leeflang et al. (1992, p. 279).

value for CE. This may seem surprising given that the CEA model includes an additional parameter (for the autocorrelation). The reason for this "anomaly" is that OLS maximizes R^2. Thus, even if there are statistical arguments that favor the use of GLS over OLS, the fit of the model, expressed in terms of the *original* criterion variable, cannot improve.

Although the results in Table 18.1 clearly favor the PA model (the autocorrelation coefficient is irrelevant) we now formalize the nested model comparisons. Each pair of nested models can be tested with a likelihood ratio test (statistic):[7]

$$\eta = [\widehat{\Sigma}_0/\widehat{\Sigma}_1]^{-T/2} \tag{18.8}$$

where

$\widehat{\Sigma}_0$ = the residual sum of squares of a restricted model associated with the null hypothesis (H_0),

$\widehat{\Sigma}_1$ = the residual sum of squares of a less restricted model associated with the alternative hypothesis (H_1),

T = the number of observations.

The test statistic can be written as:

$$-2\ln\eta = T\ln\widehat{\Sigma}_0 - T\ln\widehat{\Sigma}_1 \tag{18.9}$$

which is asymptotically chi-squared distributed with ($p_1 - p_0$) degrees of freedom (Greene, 1997, p. 161) and where:

p_0 = number of parameters in the restricted model, and

p_1 = number of parameters in the "unrestricted" model.

---

7. This test was also used by Weiss and Windal (1980). See also Section 16.6.

Table 18.2 Likelihood ratio test statistics.

Restricted model (H_0)		Unrestricted model (H_1)		χ^2 test
Model	$-T \ln \widehat{\Sigma}_0$	Model	$-T \ln \widehat{\Sigma}_1$	$-2 \ln \eta$
CE	137.2	CEA	144.3	7.1[a]
CEA	144.3	PAA	181.5	37.2[a]
PA	181.4	PAA	181.5	0.1

[a] Statistically significant at the 1%-level

Source: Leeflang et al. (1992, p. 280).

Table 18.2 contains comparisons of the specifications.

Under classical hypothesis testing a more complex (less restricted) model is not chosen unless there is statistically significant evidence in its favor.[8] The first pair of models in Table 18.2 has the current-effects (CE) model as the restricted model (H_0) and the current-effects autocorrelation model (CEA) as the less restricted alternative (H_1). The associated chi-squared statistic is significant at the 1%-level, implying that the autoregressive current effects model is superior to the current effects model. By the same logic the second test result suggests that the autoregressive partial adjustment model (PAA) is superior to the autoregressive current-effect (CEA) model. However, the null hypothesis cannot be rejected based on the test of the partial adjustment model (PA) against its autoregressive counterpart (PAA). The partial adjustment model therefore emerges as the favored specification.

Other statistical tests for nested models include:

- the F-test of incremental explanatory power of an unrestricted model[9]
- the t-test (e.g. on λ, the lagged endogenous variable parameter in the PA model).

Both tests are appropriate if the predictor variables of the restricted model constitute a subset of the predictor variables of the unrestricted model (specifically one fewer in case of the t-test). If we apply this test on the model pair PA and CE, using the result in Table 18.1, we conclude that the PA model should be preferred over the CE model because $\hat{\lambda}$ is (highly) significant.

Nested models estimated by maximum likelihood can be tested applying the likelihood ratio test and the Wald test (see Section 16.6). Yet other selection tests are available.[10] Most tests are functions of the error sum of squares and thus are related. In addition, it is possible to perform (nested) model comparisons on information criteria. Since these criteria can also be used to distinguish between non-nested models

---

8. Compare Rust, Lee, Valente (1995).
9. See, for example, Foekens, Leeflang, Wittink (1999) and the discussion in Section 16.1.5.
10. See, for example, Hocking (1976), Greene (1997, Chapter 4).

(for example, if two specifications have the same predictor variables but differ in functional form), we discuss these criteria next.

18.4.3 NON-NESTED MODELS

Non-nested models may include the same predictor variables, or they may involve some variables that are unique to each model. Suppose we consider the following multiplicative model:

$$\ln m_t = \alpha_1 \ln ds_t + \alpha_2 \ln as_t + \alpha_3 \ln m_{t-1} + v_t \tag{18.10}$$

where

$$v_t = \text{a disturbance term, and}$$
all other variables are defined above.

Models (18.5) and (18.10) use the same variables[11] but have different functional forms. It is impossible to express model (18.10) as a constrained version of model (18.5), or vice versa, which renders the nested model tests inapplicable. For non-nested model comparisons and for models estimated with the method of maximum likelihood (Section 16.6), we can use information criteria such as the Akaike Information Criterion (AIC), the Schwarz criterion, Consistent AIC (CAIC), and a criterion developed by Allenby (1990). These criteria are full sample criteria (implying that there is no data splitting required as is often done for predictive validation as we discuss in Section 18.5). The information criteria seek to incorporate, in model selection, the divergent considerations of accuracy of estimation and the "best" approximation to reality. The statistics incorporate a measure of the precision of the estimate and a measure of parsimony in the parameterization of a model.

Akaike (1974) proposed a simple model comparison criterion, based on an information theoretic rationale. The precision of the estimated model is represented by the (natural) logarithm of the maximum likelihood ($\ln L$). A term, to penalize the $\ln L$ term for lack of parsimony, is subtracted from $\ln L$:

$$A = \ln L - \text{(number of parameters)} \tag{18.11}$$

where

$$A = \text{Akaike's criterion.}$$

An alternative expression that embodies the same principle is Akaike's Information Criterion.[12]

$$AIC = -2A. \tag{18.12}$$

As we mentioned earlier these criteria can also be used in nested models.

---

11. We use the same variable definitions as apply to (18.5). Note, however, that for the model that is linear in parameters, after transforming all variables logarithmically, the deviations are with respect to the mean of the logarithmic values for each variable.

12. Other reformulations are found in Akaike (1981).

Schwarz (1978) criticized Akaike's criterion as being asymptotically nonoptimal. He proposed a revised form of the penalty function as follows:

$$SC = \ln L - \left[\frac{\ln T}{2} \cdot (\text{number of parameters}) \right] \qquad (18.13)$$

where

$\qquad SC = $ Schwarz Criterion,

$\qquad T = $ the number of observations.

Allenby (1990) argued that both AIC and SC overemphasize parsimony, leading him to propose:

$$ALC = \ln L - \left[\frac{\ln 2}{2} \cdot (\text{number of parameters}) \right] \qquad (18.14)$$

where

$\qquad ALC = $ Allenby's criterion.

Bozdogan (1987) proposed a criterion which penalizes overparametarization more strongly then AIC. This Consistent AIC (CAIC) is computed as:

$$CAIC = -2 \ln L + (\text{number of parameters}) \cdot (\ln T + 1) \qquad (18.15)$$

where

$\qquad T = $ number of observations.

Rust, Simester, Brodie and Nilikant (1995) examined which of these and other model selection criteria perform best in selecting the current model based on simulated data. In their study the Schwarz criterion was the single best selection criterion. Due to the high correlation between the results for alternative model selection criteria they also suggest that the use of multiple model selection criteria may be unwarranted. However, as with all simulation studies, the generalizability of these results remains to be determined.

Another option for the selection of a functional form is the Box and Cox (1964) transformation, which includes linearity as a special case. The Box-Cox functional form can be written as:[13]

$$y_t^{(\lambda)} = \beta_0 + \beta_1 x_{1t}^{(\lambda)} + \beta_2 x_{2t}^{(\lambda)} + \ldots + \beta_L x_{Lt}^{(\lambda)} + e_t \qquad (18.16)$$

where

$$y_t^{(\lambda)} = \begin{cases} \dfrac{y_t^{\lambda} - 1}{\lambda} & \text{for } \lambda \neq 0 \\ \ln y_t & \text{for } \lambda = 0, \end{cases}$$

$\qquad x_{1t}^{(\lambda)}, \ldots, x_{Lt}^{(\lambda)} = $ predictor variables defined similarly,

$\qquad\qquad\qquad e_t = $ a disturbance term.

---

13. See also Section 16.1.4.

Relation (18.16) includes as special cases the models:

$$y_t = \beta_0^* + \beta_1 x_{1t} + \ldots + \beta_L x_{Lt} + e_t, \text{ for } \lambda = 1 \tag{18.17}$$

where

$$\beta_0^* = 1 + \beta_0 - \sum_{\ell=1}^{L} \beta_\ell$$

and

$$\ln y_t = \beta_0 + \beta_1 \ln x_{1t} + \ldots + \beta_L \ln x_{Lt} + e_t, \text{ for } \lambda = 0. \tag{18.18}$$

Although a family of functions is defined by (18.16), a conventional likelihood ratio hypothesis test of linearity involves the null hypothesis H_0: $\lambda = 1$ versus the alternative H_1: $\lambda \neq 1$.

In cases where the models are non-nested *and* differ in the set of variables, other tests are required. Examples are the J-test, the P-test, the P-E-test and a likelihood-ratio-based test developed by Vuong (1989).[14] The J, P and P-E-tests include the estimation of artificial compound models,[15] which we briefly describe here.

Consider the following non-nested regression models that also differ in the predictor variables:

$$y_i = f_i(X_i, \beta) + e_{Ni} \tag{18.19}$$
$$y_i = g_i(Z_i, \gamma) + e_{Ai} \tag{18.20}$$

where

$$y_i = \text{the } i\text{-th observation on the criterion variable,}$$
$$x_i, Z_i = \text{vectors of observations on predictor variables,}$$
$$\beta, \gamma = \text{parameter vectors, and}$$
$$e_{Ni}, e_{Ai} = \text{error terms.}$$

Let equation (18.19) represent the Null hypothesis, and let (18.20) be the Alternate hypothesis. Then the J- and P-tests are based on the following compound model:

$$y_i = (1 - \alpha_N) f_i(X_i, \beta) + \alpha_N g_i(Z_i, \gamma) + e_i \tag{18.21}$$

where

$$e_i = \text{the error term.}$$

In (18.21), if α_N is close to zero, the result favors the Null hypothesis (model 18.19), while if α_N is close to one, the Alternate hypothesis (model 18.20) is favored.[16]

---

14. Additional tests were developed by Rust and Schmittlein (1985). See also Fornell, Rust (1989), Oczkowski, Farrell (1998).

15. These tests have been applied in a marketing context by Balasubramanian and Jain (1994).

16. The J-test is appropriate when competing models are linear functions. The P-test is relevant if the models are nonlinear. If the alternative models differ in the transformations of the "original" criterion variable, the P-E-test is applicable. For more detail, see Davidson and MacKinnon (1981) or Balasubramanian and Jain (1994).

18.4.4 CAUSALITY TESTS[17]

Causality tests are used

- to distinguish between causal and noncausal relations or associations;
- to establish the direction of causality when variables are related;
- to reduce a large set of potential predictors so that multivariate models become identifiable (based on bivariate tests).

We distinguish bivariate and multivariate causality tests. Although multivariate tests are preferred for multivariate models, both bivariate- and multivariate tests can be used to identify causal relations and to distinguish causality from association. However, if the objective is to reduce the set of potential predictor variables (given insufficient degrees of freedom) only bivariate tests can be used. In this section we introduce several bivariate tests, and discuss an application. We then briefly mention multivariate tests.

Modern tests of causality are based on the following definition of causality proposed by Granger (1969):

A variable x is said to cause another variable y, with respect to a given information set containing x and y, if future y-values can be predicted better using past values of x and y than using the past of y alone.[18]

To formalize, suppose a marketing system is defined by the two-variable information set (x, y). The variable x is said to Granger cause y if the (one-step) expected quadratic forecasting error Q of using the bivariate model, is smaller than the Q of the univariate model, for at least one t (Judge et al., 1985, p. 667).

$$Q(y_{t+1} \mid y_1, \ldots, y_{t-K}, x_t, \ldots, x_{t-K*}) < Q(y_{t+1} \mid y_t, \ldots, y_{t-K}) \quad (18.22)$$

where K and K^* are positive integers, indicating the maximum memory length in x and y. If (18.22) is not true, y is not Granger caused by x. If x causes y and y causes x then (x, y) is a feedback system.

We now introduce five bivariate causality tests,[19] including two Granger tests and two Sims tests which are regression methods. The *Granger tests* are based on the following model:

$$y_t = \sum_{i=1}^{K} \pi_{11,i} y_{t-i} + \sum_{i=1}^{K} \pi_{12,i} x_{t-i} + u_t, \quad t = K + 1, \ldots, T \quad (18.23)$$

17. This section is based on Bult et al. (1997) . For an extensive discussion of causality tests see the special issues of the *Journal of Econometrics*, vol 39, (1-2). For overviews of causality tests applied in marketing see Hanssens et al. (1990, p. 168) and Bult et al. (1997, p. 452). We note that we use the concept of "causality" that can be tested with statistical methods. This concept is not based on cause and effect in a strict philosophical sense (see Judge, Griffiths, Hill, Lütkepohl and Lee, 1985, p. 667).

18. Other definitions of causality can be found in Zellner (1979) and in Hashemzadeh and Taylor (1988). Granger causality emphasizes the predictive properties of a model. Tests described here can be used for causal ordering with time-series data. The "causality" tests used on cross-sectional data are tests of associations.

19. Analytical arguments for these tests can be found in for example Chow (1983).

where

$$\pi_{11,i}, \pi_{12,i} \ = \ \text{parameters,}$$
$$u_t \ = \ \text{a serially independent random disturbance term}$$
$$\text{from a distribution with mean zero and covariance}$$
$$\text{matrix } \Sigma.$$

It is assumed that all polynomials have the same order K. If x_t does not cause y_t, $\pi_{12,i} = 0$ for $i = 1, \ldots, K$, or

$$y_t \ = \ \sum_{i=1}^{K} \pi_{11,i} y_{t-i} + u_t^* \tag{18.24}$$

where

$$u_t^* \ = \ \text{a random disturbance term.}$$

In both Granger tests (see below) the null hypothesis is that $\pi_{12,i} = 0, i = 1, \ldots, K$ in (18.23). Under the null hypothesis and the assumption that the disturbances are normally distributed with mean zero and variance σ^2, the statistic GS is distributed as an F-random variable with K and $(T - 2K)$ degrees of freedom. The *Granger-Sargent* test has the following form:

$$GS \ = \ \frac{(RRSS\text{-}URSS)/K}{URSS/(T - 2K)} \tag{18.25}$$

where

$$RRSS \ = \ \text{the residual sum of squares of the restricted relation}$$
$$(18.24),$$
$$URSS \ = \ \text{the residual sum of squares of the unrestricted relation}$$
$$(18.23).$$

The *Granger-Wald* test has an asymptotic χ_K^2 distribution under the null hypothesis (and is the asymptotic equivalent of the *Granger-Sargent F*-test):

$$GW \ = \ T \frac{\hat{\sigma}_{u_t^*}^2 - \hat{\sigma}_{u_t}^2}{\hat{\sigma}_{u_t}^2} \tag{18.26}$$

where

$$\hat{\sigma}_{u_t^*}^2 \ = \ \text{the estimate of } Var(u_t^*) \text{ in (18.24), and}$$
$$\hat{\sigma}_{u_t}^2 \ = \ \text{the estimate of } Var(u_t) \text{ in (18.23).}$$

The *Sims Methods* regress x_t on past, current and future y_t's. Sims (1972) showed that under the hypothesis of no causality from x to y, the regression parameters corresponding to future y_t's are equal to zero. The significance of the coefficients is tested using:

$$x_t = \sum_{i=-M}^{N} v_i y_{t-i} + \varepsilon_t, \quad t = N+1, \ldots, T-M \tag{18.27}$$

where

ε_t = a random disturbance term,

M, N = the maximum number of "future" and "past" y_t's.

The null hypothesis is $v_i = 0$, $i = -M, \ldots, -1$. Relation (18.27) is estimated in constrained ($v_i = 0$, $i = -M, \ldots, -1$) and unconstrained form. Under the null hypothesis and the usual assumptions the statistic SI is distributed as an F-random variable with M and $T - M - N - 1$ degrees of freedom:

$$SI = \frac{(RRSS\text{-}URSS)/M}{URSS/(T - M - N - 1)}. \tag{18.28}$$

One difficulty with the SI test is that the disturbance term ε_t in (18.27) is in general serially correlated, and consequently (18.28) does not have the claimed distribution if the null hypothesis is true (e.g. Geweke, Meese, Dent, 1983). To circumvent this problem a Modified Sims (MS) test was developed. In MS lagged values of x_t and y_t are included in the equations:

$$x_t = \sum_{i=1}^{P} \gamma_i x_{t-i} + \sum_{i=-M}^{N+P} v_i y_{t-i} + w_t, \tag{18.29}$$

$$t = N + P + 1, \ldots, T - M$$

where

w_t = a disturbance term.

Relation (18.29) is also estimated in constrained ($v_i = 0$, $i = -M, \ldots, -1$) and unconstrained form. The statistic MS is distributed under the null hypothesis as an F random variable with M and $(T - 2P - M - N - 1)$ degrees of freedom:

$$MS = \frac{(RRSS - URSS)/M}{URSS/(T - 2P - M - N - 1)}. \tag{18.30}$$

A fifth test is the double-prewhitening method or the *Haugh-Pierce* test (Haugh, 1976, Pierce, 1977, Pierce and Haugh, 1977). This test has been used in a marketing context by, for example, Hanssens (1980a, 1980b) and Leeflang, Wittink (1992). The direction of causality between y_t and x_t is established by cross correlating the residuals of the univariate models fitted to each. These residuals, say $\hat{u}_t$ and $\hat{v}_t$, are causally related in the same way as y and x. Therefore, causality can be detected by estimating the parameters in the regression of u_t on past, current and future v_t's in the same manner as would be done by regressing y_t on past, current and future x_t's.

The difference is that the residuals $\hat{u}_t$ and $\hat{v}_t$ are estimated by applying Box-Jenkins techniques to y_t and x_t. Under the null hypothesis that y and x are not causally related, $r_{uv}(k) = Corr(\hat{u}_{t-k}, \hat{v}_t)$ is asymptotically independently and normally distributed with mean zero and standard deviation $T^{-1/2}$, where $Corr$ is the correlation between the residuals $\hat{u}_{t-k}$ and $\hat{v}_t$. Using m correlations $r_{uv}(k)$, $(k = 1, \ldots, m)$, under the null hypothesis the test statistic HP is asymptotically chi-square distributed with m degrees of freedom:

$$HP = T \sum_{k=1}^{m} r_{uv}^2(k). \qquad (18.31)$$

There may be little consistency between the outcomes of the different causality tests, as is illustrated in the application that follows. Tests which are only asymptotically equivalent can give very different results in small samples. For one thing, the tests differ in the effective number of data points available for analyses. These consequences increase in severity the smaller the sample size.

Bult et al. (1997) applied these tests to both actual and simulated data for a study of the tests' power and alpha-values. In general, the best test is one with the highest power and the lowest alpha. Power is the probability of rejecting a false null hypothesis, and alpha is the probability of rejecting a true null hypothesis (for these two alternative states of nature, power and alpha do not have to be related). However, if bivariate causality tests are used to identify a multivariate model, one may be tolerant of a modest alpha value. Since a bivariate test may fail to uncover a causal relation that emerges only in the proper multivariate model, it may be prudent to simply choose the test with the highest power. This is consistent with the idea that excluding (potentially) relevant predictors is a more serious error than including irrelevant predictors in a multivariate model. For pure bivariate causality testing, Bult et al. (1997) recommend the Granger-Sargent test which is a relatively simple test, and has a *reasonable* amount of power and little bias in alpha. If the bivariate test is used only for identification purposes, the combination of high power and high alpha associated with the Granger-Wald test may be attractive, given the asymmetry in the cost of the two possible errors.

Section 11.1 includes a model with competitive reaction functions: see the equations (11.15). In these relations the potential number of predictor variables is so large that it exceeds the number of observations. Bivariate Haugh-Pierce causality test statistics were used to identify a subset of the potential predictors for multivariate modeling. We use a simplified version of model (11.15) to show how causality tests can be used to identify a (competitive reaction) function. We also show how much the conclusions about causal relations for a given data set may depend on the test statistic used.

Consider the following model in which the change in price of brand j in period t is a function of the changes in prices of competing brands r, for $j = 1, \ldots, n$:

$$\ln(p_{jt}/p_{j,t-1}) = \alpha_j + \sum_{\substack{r=1 \\ r \neq j}}^{n} \sum_{t^*=1}^{T^*+1} \beta_{jrt^*} \ln(p_{r,t-t^*+1}/p_{r,t-t^*}) + v_{jt}, \qquad (18.32)$$

$$t = T^* + 2, \ldots, T$$

where

p_{jt} = the price of brand j in period t,

v_{jt} = a disturbance term,

T^* = the maximum number of time lags, $T^* = 8$, [20]

T = the number of observations available, $T = 76$,

n = the number of brands, $n = 3$.

Relation (18.32) is a competitive reaction function with only "simple" competitive reactions: the price change for brand j is determined only by the price changes for competitive brand r, $r \neq j$, not by changes in other marketing variables. The changes are expressed as the logarithm of the ratio of prices in two successive periods. This reflects the idea that price changes for brands with different average price levels are more comparable on a percentage than on an absolute basis.

Aggregated weekly scanner data for a frequently purchased nondurable, nonfood, consumer product sold in The Netherlands covering a period of 76 weeks were used to calibrate (18.32). In this application, the prices of three brands are considered. The market research company ACNielsen (Nederland B.V.) collects and distributes these data in the Netherlands based on a sample of about 150 stores. Price changes primarily reflect temporary changes due to promotional activities. The number of parameters to be estimated per equation is $1 + (n - 1)(T^* + 1)$. Substituting $n = 3$ and $T^* = 8$, we find that even this strongly "simplified" model requires 19 parameters while there are $T - T^* - 1 = 67$ observations available for the estimation of (18.32). It is easy to see that in practice (with more brands, and more variables including lagged effects) the number of parameters can quickly exceed the sample size. This motivates the use of bivariate tests to select the potential predictors for the estimation of multivariate competitive reaction functions.

The question we address is whether the choice of a causality test has an impact on the composition of the set of predictor variables in the multivariate specification. We show a summary of the statistical significance results in Table 18.3. There is perfect agreement in test outcomes for the GW and HP tests. There is also perfect agreement between the two Sims tests, SI and MS, in the sense that both tests indicate no evidence of causality within the set of three price variables. Of the four cases of significance based on the GW test, two also show significance for GS. This is consistent with the result reported earlier, that the Granger-Sargent test has less power (and a smaller alpha) than the Granger-Wald test. Across all five tests however, the

---

20. In preliminary research we found that the maximum lag structure for the three brands is eight weeks. Thus the order of the polynomials also equals eight.

Table 18.3 Statistical significance results for five causality tests^a.

Source	Reaction (criterion)		
(predictor)	pr_1^b	pr_2	pr_3
pr_1	-	GW, HP	-
pr_2	GW, HP	-	GS, GW, HP
pr_3	GS, GW, HP	-	-

^{a} The entries indicate that the null hypothesis of no causality for the pair
of variables is rejected, based on the identified test statistic, $p < 0.05$.
^{b} $pr_j = \ln(p_{jt}/p_{j,t-1})$.

Source: Bult et al. (1997, p. 456).

results in Table 18.3 imply that conclusions about causality depend strongly on the
test used.

The outcomes in Table 18.3 indicate that changes in the present and/or past prices
of brand 1 may have causal effects on changes in the price of brand 2 (*GW, HP*),
but not on brand 3, etc. The tests also indicate (not shown) the most likely lags with
which causal effects occur.

One limitation of this study is that only bivariate causality tests were used and
compared for the identification of relevant predictors for the specification of a multivariate model. Multivariate causality tests, such as the VARMA-model (Judge et al.,
1985, p. 667), can be used to detect causality or to determine the direction of causality
in a fully specified model. For an application of the VARMA-model see Boudjellaba,
Dufour and Roy (1992). An alternative multivariate test was developed by Lütkepohl
(1989).

18.5 Predictive validity

We have argued that if a model is built primarily for descriptive purposes, it should
have face validity. If its primary purpose is for predictions, one might argue that
face validity is not required. It is well known, for example, that models lacking descriptive value can provide accurate forecasts. However, the marketing models that
are the topic in this book should be especially useful for *conditional* forecasting
purposes. Ideally, a model user specifies alternative marketing programs, and for each
possible program obtains an accurate, model-based forecast of consumers' purchase
behavior. This reflects the idea that a marketing manager's environment is to some
extent controllable. Marketing models should provide a basis for the manner in which
the manager can profitably shape that part of the marketplace in which his or her
brands operate. Thus, if the model builder wants to create a model that provides
information about the dependence of marketplace behavior on marketing activities, it
is critical that the predictive validation exercise is informative about the model's gen-

eralizability. Our view is that empirical research can identify regularities in the data but that observable systematic patterns in predicted values depend on marketplace characteristics.

In the marketing literature, it is very common for model builders to use some form of predictive validity as a statement of the model's usefulness. However, there is no established standard for the conduct of predictive validation. In this section we provide a perspective on this popular form of model validation.

If the marketplace, in which consumers react to the products and services offered to them, were a stable environment, research on marketing could concentrate on the generation and testing of laws that govern consumer purchase behavior. However, consumers are "fickle", technological advances influence consumers' needs and preferences, and firms make adaptations in their marketing programs. The question, then, is whether a result generated from data in one product category, representing one geographic area and one time period, generalizes to other conditions. Predictive validation can be used to address this question indirectly.

Another reason for predictive validation has to do with the fact that model builders use the sample data partly to guide model specification. If data collection and analysis were very expensive, model builders would work much harder on model specification, to generate one that is fully informed by the prevailing theoretical and empirical knowledge. Instead, initial model specifications tend to be poor and ill-informed. The more sample data are used to craft a model specification, the more the model fit to the same data will overstate the model's applicability to other data. Practices such as stepwise regression analysis reflect an inability or unwillingness by model builders to prepare well-informed initial model specifications. As a result, much of the effort that should be invested in model specification prior to data analysis is allocated to tinkering with the model based on the data. An iterative process may reduce the likelihood of biases in parameter estimates (e.g. biases due to model misspecification) but it also destroys the statistical properties of the estimators. The iterative process is often referred to as *pretesting*.

Suppose that we did complete the model specification stage, prior to data analysis, through an elaborate process which allows us to be very confident that:

1. we have properly defined the criterion variable;
2. we have identified all relevant predictor variables, and have chosen the most appropriate functional form for each predictor;
3. we have specified the relevant interaction effects to be accommodated;
4. we have reliable measures of all variables; etc.

Under these circumstances, there may be just one model specification to be subjected to estimation and testing. If there is no evidence of violations of error term assumptions, we use statistical tests to determine whether the model has (significant) explanatory power, and whether individual effects differ (significantly) from zero. These steps are especially relevant before we can claim descriptive validity for the model. But we may not conclude that the model is "best", unless we can rule out alternative specifications. Even then, the question remains to what extent the empirical results generalize to other product categories, to other regions, and to other time periods. To examine this, one could repeat the data collection and analysis and determine whether the proposed model "survives". One possible stringent test consists of a comparison of parameter estimates based on a null hypothesis of equal parameter values (across regions, over time, etc.).

But what if one wants to know the accuracy of forecasts? Econometricians have derived the statistical properties of model-based forecasts, given error-term assumptions. For example, if the simple, linear model applies:

$$y_i = \alpha + \beta x_i + u_i, \quad i = 1 \dots, I \tag{18.33}$$

we can use the estimated parameters and a specific predictor variable value, say x_0, to obtain the (conditional) forecast:

$$\hat{y}_0 = \hat{\alpha} + \hat{\beta} x_0. \tag{18.34}$$

If the error term assumptions hold, we can construct a confidence interval for the unknown value y_0, given x_0:[21]

$$\hat{y}_0 \pm t \, s_{\hat{y}_0} \tag{18.35}$$

where

$$s_{\hat{y}_0} = s \sqrt{1 + \frac{1}{I} + \frac{(x_0 - \bar{x})^2}{\sum_{i=1}^{I} (x_i - \bar{x})^2}},$$

t = the tabulated value of the t distribution, corresponding to the desired degree of confidence and the model's degrees of freedom, and

s = the estimated value of the standard deviation of y.

If the model is accurate, and generally applicable, then the confidence intervals so constructed should contain the actual y_0 values a specified percentage of the time (the percentage being equal to the degree of confidence).

In the absence of "pretesting" (the iterative process of model building) one can compute expected predictive validity measures. The formulas developed for this purpose[22] assume that the characteristics of predictor variables remain the same. Nevertheless, it is useful to employ these formulas, if the estimators have the assumed statistical properties, for at least two reasons. One has to do with managerial use. If a model is used for decision-making purposes, it is helpful to have a quantification of the expected error of model-based forecasts. The other is that the formulas can provide insight into the difference in expected predictive validity between alternative model specifications. For example, even if we reject a simplified version of a

---

21. See Wittink (1988, p. 47).
22. See e.g. Hagerty and Srinivasan (1991).

particular model (e.g. the preferred model includes an interaction term with a statistically significant effect, so that a model without the interaction term is statistically inferior), it is possible for the simplified version to outperform the preferred model in the accuracy of predictions. Simplified versions provide superior predictions if the disadvantage of a missing interaction term (which creates misspecification biases) is smaller than the advantage of estimating fewer parameters (which tends to reduce the estimated standard errors). We note, however, that misspecification biases will become more influential in relative performance comparisons of alternative model specifications if the characteristics of the predictor variables differ between estimation- and validation samples.

We now consider the more realistic setting in which "pretesting" is rampant. Strictly speaking, all statistical tests applied to the final model specification are invalid, but in both academic studies and in practical applications this problem is often ignored. Partly because of the many iterations through which model building tends to proceed, we insist on evidence of predictive validation. Here we have a potential conflict of interest. The individual who builds the model also tends to favor its use. Given that the model-building process is intensive and that the model builder has developed a personal preference for it, there is no incentive for him/her to engage in an exhaustive, potentially reductive, validation exercise. Since all models are incomplete by definition, any model subject to sufficient examination will eventually break down. This conflict of interest is one possible reason why the practice of predictive validation is poor, as we argue below.

If the model is estimated with *cross-sectional data*, it is common for model builders to split the data randomly into two samples. The first (analysis or estimation) sample is used to estimate parameters, to test the error term assumptions, etc. The second (holdout or validation) sample is used to quantify the predictive validity (we discuss predictive validity measures below). In this context, one advantage of using a validation sample is that in validation the model is penalized for each degree of freedom used to estimate an additional parameter. And this penalty is greater in validation measures than it is in measures that adjust for degrees of freedom in the estimation sample, such as adjusted R^2 and the standard deviation of residuals (see the formula for expected predictive validity). Also, the greater the number of data-based iterations the model builder goes through to arrive at the final model specification, the larger the expected deterioration in predictive validity relative to the fit in the estimation sample.

The question we pose is whether randomly splitting cross-sectional data into estimation and validation samples provides a true opportunity for the model builder to predictively validate the model. If we have built a model that is missing a critical variable so that one (or more) parameter estimates is (are) biased, will the predictive validity results be much poorer than the estimation results (e.g. will the predictive validity results suggest that the estimated model is inadequate)? Unfortunately, this is very unlikely in the case of random splitting. The reason is that estimation and validation samples are expected to have the same data characteristics. The bias in the effect of one or more included predictor variables will not reduce the model's predictive performance (relative to the model fit in estimation), if the correlation between included and excluded variables is the same in the estimation and validation samples. Thus, in case of randomly splitting the data there is no opportunity to *invalidate* the estimated model.

If the model builder uses *time-series data*, the situation is somewhat improved. Specifically, it is rare for model builders to split time-series randomly. There are several reasons for this. One is that the model may contain a lagged criterion variable in which case it is important to maintain the time sequence in the data. Another is that the time sequence in the data can be exploited in tests of autocorrelation in the error term. In addition, it is useful to examine a model's predictive validity to future time periods. Thus, if there are two years of, say, weekly data, the model builder may use the first year for estimation and the second year for validation. Time-series data can then provide an (implicit) opportunity to the model builder to check whether the results apply to a new time period. However, if the two years are very similar in data characteristics, for example if the market environment has not changed, then the validation exercise resembles the random splitting of cross-sectional data procedure. Thus, the larger the changes in the environment over time, the more powerful the validation exercise. At the same time, the larger the changes, the more likely it is that weaknesses in the model reduce the predictive validity. This suggests that model builders should at least report how the validation sample characteristics differ from the estimation sample.[23]

Time-series data also provide other useful options. For example, model users may insist on evidence that a proposed model outperforms some benchmark. Brodie and de Kluyver (1987), Alsem, Leeflang and Reuyl (1989) and Brodie, Danaher, Kumar and Leeflang (2000) compared the performance of marketing-mix models to that of a naive model, which predicts next period's value for the criterion variable to be this period's actual value. One might argue that little faith should be placed in the parameter estimates, if the proposed model does not outperform a (naive) model that lacks structural characteristics consistent with marketing traditions. As shown by Foekens et al. (1994), the relative performance also depends on the extent to which the *characteristics of the data change between estimation* and *validation samples*.

Foekens et al., (1994) argue the following:

• It is well known that the uncertainty of individual predictions is influenced by the distance between the *predictor variables' values* and the *sample means* (see equation (18.35)). For a new set of data this idea is captured by the change in average values in the predictor variables between estimation and validation sample data.
• Another way in which the structural similarity of estimation and validation data can be determined is by the correlation matrix for the predictor variables. For example, the forecasting accuracy of a misspecified model may not be reduced if

---

23. Foekens, Leeflang and Wittink (1994), for example, report the percent of stores involved in promotional activities, separately for estimation and validation samples (Table 3, p. 254).

the correlations remain the same. The greater the change in *correlations* the more likely it is to obtain poor predictive accuracy for misspecified models.

- One can determine the extent to which the same model, applied separately to estimation and validation data, produces different *parameter estimates*. Substantial differences may occur for several reasons. One is that the true parameters have changed. Another is that the estimated parameters differ because the model is misspecified, and this misspecification differentially affects the parameter estimates in the two samples.
- Additionally, the predictive validity will be affected by a difference in error variance between estimation and validation samples.

In Section 14.1 we present some of the findings of Christen, Gupta, Porter, Staelin and Wittink (1997) on aggregation bias in parameter estimates of loglinear models estimated with linearly aggregated data. Christen et al. show that this bias depends especially on the proportion of stores engaging in a promotion (i.e. on heterogeneity in promotional activities across the stores). Thus, at an aggregate level, such as the chain- or market level, changes in the proportion of stores engaged in a promotion may contribute to a deterioration in forecasting accuracy in validation relative to what might be expected based on model fit in estimation. In this way, an understanding of sources of biases in parameter estimates can provide direction to model builders for the purpose of diagnostic predictive validation.

Foekens et al. (1994) examined how each of the aforementioned factors contributed to the Mean Squared Error (*MSE*) in validation samples. They found that parameter instability (between estimation and validation samples) and a measure of the change in the correlations between the predictor variables have statistically significant effects on change in accuracy.

We now consider how available accuracy measures can provide some diagnostic value. The formula for the mean squared error in validation (see equation (18.43) below) shows that model performance depends on bias and variance. A more complete model should have a smaller bias but may have larger variance than a less complete model. If we desire to build a model that has the highest possible descriptive value, we should be especially interested in testing for *lack of bias* in the predicted values.

To formalize, suppose we have T observations in total, and use the first T^* observations for estimation, leaving $(T - T^*)$ for validation. Thus, the unknown parameters $\beta_1, \ldots, \beta_L$ in a multiple regression model are estimated using T^* observations. Substituting the estimates $\hat{\beta}_1, \ldots, \hat{\beta}_L$ and using the values of $x_{1t}, x_{2t}, \ldots, x_{Lt}$, for $t = T^* + 1, T^* + 2, \ldots, T$, the following predicted values of y_t are obtained:

$$\hat{y}_t = \hat{\beta}_1 x_{1t} + \hat{\beta}_2 x_{2t} + \hat{\beta}_3 x_{3t} + \ldots + \hat{\beta}_L x_{Lt}, \quad t = T^* + 1, \ldots, T. \qquad (18.36)$$

Comparing the predicted values $\hat{y}_t$ with the actual values of y_t, $t = T^* + 1, \ldots, T$, the predictive validity of the relation can be determined. To test for a lack of bias we can use the Average Prediction Error (APE):[24]

$$APE = \frac{\sum_{t=T^*+1}^{T}(y_t - \hat{y}_t)}{T - T^*}. \tag{18.37}$$

Note that the denominator in (18.37) is the number of observations in the validation sample. Also, positive and negative errors are allowed to offset each other. Thus, we can test the null hypothesis that the mean prediction error is zero, based on the t-test for the mean. Inability to reject the null hypothesis means that there is no evidence of *bias in the predictions.*

We note that this measure of bias is not as useful as one might think at first glance. For example, a result that $APE = 0$ means only that on average the actual and predicted values are the same. Nevertheless, it is quite possible for some or all predictions to be systematically away from the actual values. For example, a model with the wrong functional form will not produce a positive value for the APE as long as the positive and negative prediction errors in the validation sample offset each other. This will occur if the estimation- and validation sample data characteristics are the same!

To measure the predictive performance of the model, which depends on bias and variance, we can use the "Average Squared Predictor Error" ($ASPE$), also known as "Mean Squared Error" (MSE):

$$ASPE = \frac{\sum_{t=T^*+1}^{T}(y_t - \hat{y}_t)^2}{T - T^*}. \tag{18.38}$$

The use of squared terms means that large prediction errors are weighted more heavily than small errors. This measure is consistent with the least squares principle of regression analysis. However, it has the drawback that it summarizes the prediction errors in squared units. To obtain a value in the units of measurement for the criterion variable, we can use the Root of $ASPE$ viz. $RASPE$:

$$RASPE = \sqrt{\frac{\sum_{t=T^*+1}^{T}(y_t - \hat{y}_t)^2}{T - T^*}}. \tag{18.39}$$

The value for $RASPE$ can be compared to the standard deviation of residuals in the estimation sample. In general we expect the value of $RASPE$ to be greater than the standard deviation of the residuals, the actual difference being a function of the factors we have mentioned earlier. $RASPE$ is also known as the root mean squared error ($RMSE$) (Section 17.1).

A predictive validity measure that is dimensionless, easy to relate to, and potentially useful if one wants to make comparisons of forecast accuracy across different settings, is the Mean Absolute Percentage Error *(MAPE)*:

$$MAPE = \frac{1}{T - T^*} \sum_{t=T^*+1}^{T} \frac{|y_t - \hat{y}_t|}{y_t} \cdot 100. \tag{18.40}$$

---

24. See also Wittink (1988, pp. 268-269).

In this measure absolute, rather than squared, errors are computed, and each absolute error is expressed relative to the actual value, for observation t in the validation sample. If one believes that the magnitude of an error should be considered relative to the corresponding actual value, *MAPE* may be a suitable measure.

Other measures express the predictive performance of a given model relative to a benchmark model. As we have mentioned earlier, one naive (benchmark) model is to predict next period's value for the criterion variable with this period's actual value. The following Relative Absolute Error *(RAE)* measure incorporates this idea:

$$RAE = \frac{\sum_{t=T^*+1}^{T} |y_t - \hat{y}_t|}{\sum_{t=T^*+1}^{T} |y_t - y_{t-1}|} \tag{18.41}$$

where

$$y_t(\hat{y}_t) = \text{the actual (predicted) value in period } t.$$

If *RAE* is less than one, the model outperforms the benchmark represented by a naive model.

A measure that is conceptually similar to *RAE*, but uses squared prediction errors instead of absolute ones, is Theil's U-statistic:

$$U = \sqrt{\frac{\sum_{t=T^*+1}^{T}(y_t - \hat{y}_t)^2}{\sum_{t=T^*+1}^{T}(y_t - y_{t-1})^2}}. \tag{18.42}$$

As with the *RAE* measure, if Theil's U-statistic is less than one, the model generating $\hat{y}_t$ outperforms the naive model.

Theil (1965) shows how *ASPE*, the Average Squared Prediction Error in (18.38) can be decomposed:

$$ASPE = APE + (s_{\hat{y}} - rs_y)^2 + (1 - r^2)s_y^2 \tag{18.43}$$

where

APE = the Average Prediction Error (18.37),

$s_{\hat{y}}$ = the standard deviation of the predicted values,

s_y = the standard deviation of the actual values,

r = the correlation coefficient between actual and

predicted values.

The first term in (18.43) captures the squared bias, while the second and third terms together account for the prediction error due to unreliability (variance). For a model that is linear in the original variables, both the first- and the second term are zero in the *estimation* sample. The second term captures the difference in variability for the predicted values ($s_{\hat{y}}$) and the variability for the actual values (s_y) multiplied by the correlation between actual and predicted values. The third term is the proportion of the variance in the criterion variable in *validation* that is not attributable to the estimated relation.

The advantage of using such a decomposition of the prediction errors is that the model builder can diagnose the source(s) of the errors. It is, for example, very useful to distinguish between bias and variance. Consider a comparison of predictive validity between two models, one being the "preferred" model, the other being a simplified version. One would expect that the "preferred" model has less bias but potentially more variance. The decomposition allows the model builder to separate a difference in overall performance into differences due to bias and due to other components. Importantly, the more the validation data characteristics differ from the estimation data, the greater the expected contribution of the bias component to *ASPE*.

Once decompositions of prediction errors have been made, the natural question becomes to what extent the (validation) data provided an opportunity for the "preferred" model to show better performance than the benchmark model. For example, in a stable environment in which marketing activities show little variation, it may be difficult to beat a benchmark model that predicts next period's value to be this period's actual value. On the other hand, if there is a substantial amount of variation in marketing activities in the validation sample, it should be possible to "beat" the benchmark model. Another relevant aspect, as we mentioned earlier, is the extent to which validation sample characteristics differ from the estimation sample. The greater this difference, the stronger the opportunity to falsify a (wrong) model.

These considerations suggest that model builders should at least report central tendency and dispersion measures, for both estimation and validation samples, as practiced, for example, by Foekens et al. (1994). With access to this information a user can make a judgment about two relevant aspects:

- the extent to which the validation sample allows for model falsification (performance in validation- relative to estimation sample);
- the extent to which the validation sample allows the model to outperform a naive model.

Van Heerde, Leeflang, Wittink (1997) have used such considerations in quantifying what they call "diagnostic predictive validity". We discuss an application of this form of predictive validation in Section 18.6.

18.6 Illustrations

To illustrate the application of validation criteria, we first consider models with no behavioral detail. We also provide illustrations of models with some- and with a substantial amount of behavioral detail.

The SCAN*PRO model (Wittink, Addona, Hawkes, Porter, 1988) was originally estimated and tested on one year of weekly, store-level data separately for each of ten metropolitan areas (see Section 9.3). The estimated parameters were then used to predict the logarithmic sales indices in a second year of data. Conversion to the

Table 18.4 Theil's U-statistic for SCAN*PRO in year 1 (estimation) and year 2 (validation) in log sales index and sales index spaces.

| | log sales index | | sales index | | |
Market	year 1	year 2	year 1	year 2	sample size[a]
Boston	0.469	0.528	0.453	0.432	1833
Chicago	0.409	0.448	0.458	0.487	2636
Houston	0.547	0.604	0.525	0.850	2726
Indianapolis	0.693	0.674	0.649	0.650	1545
Jacksonville/Orlando	0.722	0.851	0.174	0.779	1483
Kansas City	0.577	0.624	0.707	0.637	1929
Los Angeles	0.667	0.727	0.633	0.693	3597
New York	0.549	0.664	0.421	0.487	1195
San Francisco	0.594	0.700	0.507	0.671	1638
Seattle	0.571	0.756	0.885	0.965	2219
Arithmetic average	0.580	0.658	0.541	0.665	
Median	0.574	0.669	0.516	0.660	

[a]The sample sizes are the number of store-week observations available in the second year

sales index space includes an adjustment based on the error variance to reduce the bias in predicted antilogarithmic values. We report the Theil's U-statistic results in Table 18.4. The arithmetic average Theil's U-value for the log sales index variables is 0.580 in estimation and 0.658 in validation. Thus, on average the SCAN*PRO model outperforms the benchmark incorporated in this statistic (18.42). In fact the results in Table 18.4 show that the model outperforms the *naive* specification in each of the ten metropolitan areas. This remains true when the logarithmic values are transformed to the original sales index.

Instead of expressing a model's performance relative to a naive model, as in Theil's U-statistic, it can be instructive to compute the absolute performance for each model separately. We show in Table 18.5 the mean absolute prediction error (in the sales index) for SCAN*PRO in the first column. This error varies from 23.52 in Jacksonville/Orlando to 72.91 in Seattle and is 37.12 on average. The SCAN*PRO model outperforms the naive model (column 3) in all metropolitan areas, consistent with the relative performance results in Table 18.4. The *naive* model error varies from 28.39 in Jacksonville/Orlando to 128.67 in Seattle, with an average of 62.47. These differences in absolute performance of the naive model suggest that the intensity of promotional activities is low in Jacksonville/Orlando and high in Seattle.

The second column in Table 18.5 shows the performance of a model that contains only weekly indicator variables. To the extent that the product is subject to seasonality and/or is promoted in the same weeks in year 2 as in year 1, such an alternative

Table 18.5 Mean absolute prediction error[a] for three models of year 2 in the sales index space.

Market	SCAN*PRO	weekly indicators	naive model
Boston	30.82	35.13	70.03
Chicago	31.52	47.99	79.26
Houston	36.11	65.46	63.42
Indianapolis	32.68	41.77	52.94
Jacksonville/Orlando	23.52	25.84	28.39
Kansas City	34.22	56.54	59.41
Los Angeles	43.02	32.81	48.16
New York	35.29	40.15	45.18
San Francisco	31.06	46.36	49.23
Seattle	72.91	109.02	128.67
Arithmetic Average	37.12	50.11	62.47
Median	33.45	44.06	56.17

[a]The magnitude of the error can be compared against the reference sales index of 100,   [-3pt] and actual values varying from 50 to 1.500.

naive model can perform well. Its actual performance is worse than the SCAN*PRO model's but better than the naive model's, with the exception of Houston and Los Angeles. In Houston the naive model outperforms the weekly indicators model, while in Los Angeles SCAN*PRO loses to the "weekly indicators". This validation exercise is also restrictive in the sense that we do not know how much of a difference exists in the predictor variables between the two years of data.

In today's market environment, managers have access to increasingly larger data bases. With an unlimited number of observations one can relax the restrictive assumptions inherent in traditional model specifications. Thus, instead of assuming a constant deal elasticity, as in SCAN*PRO, it is possible to let the elasticity vary with the deal magnitude. For example, consumers may be insensitive to temporary price cuts of less than ten percent. It is also conceivable that a saturation point is reached at discounts greater than, say fourty percent. Since it is difficult to anticipate the nature of the deal effect curve, a flexible, data-based approach may be attractive.

In Section 16.7 we introduced nonparametric and semiparametric estimation methods. We also discussed the semiparametric approach used by van Heerde, Leeflang and Wittink (1999a) to analyze the deal effect curve. With three national brands of tuna, they allow the own- and cross-deal effects to be flexible for each of the brands' sales. This approach also allows the own- and cross-brand deal effect curves to depend on the deal magnitudes of the other brands. Thus, both nonlinear- and interaction effects are derived from the data. In practice, the data requirements multiply as the

Table 18.6 MSE values in the validation sample for 3 tuna brands: semiparametric- versus parametric model.

Brand	Semi parametric	Parametric	Difference
1	0.50	0.57	-0.07
2	0.30	0.31	-0.01
3	0.37	0.36	0.01

Source: van Heerde, Leeflang, Wittink (1997).

number of predictor variables included in a nonparametric analysis increases. For that reason van Heerde et al. (1999a) accommodate the effects of all other predictor variables in the traditional (parametric) manner.

The validation results show that the semiparametric (combining nonparametric and parametric elements) model beats the parametric one for two of the three tuna brands. We show the *MSE* values in Table 18.6.

As we have argued, these results are difficult to interpret. For example, we do not know to what extent the validation data characteristics facilitate the emergence of a winning model, if the models behave differently. To alleviate this difficulty, van Heerde et al. (1997) introduce a concept called "diagnostic predictive validity". Specifically, they let the difference in (absolute) prediction error between the two models be a function of the validation data characteristics.

We illustrate the concept for brand 1:

$$
\begin{aligned}
Diff_{k1t} = {} & 3.36 - 2.94\, PI_{k1t} - 1.43\, PI_{k2t} - 3.41\, PI_{k3t} \\
& + 1.95\, PI^2_{k1t} + 0.55\, PI^2_{k2t} + 1.18\, PI^2_{k3t} \\
& - 0.60(PI_{k1t} * PI_{k2t}) + 0.50(PI_{k1t} * PI_{k3t}) + 0.90(PI_{k2t} * PI_{k3t})
\end{aligned}
\tag{18.44}
$$

where

$Diff_{k1t}$ = the difference in *absolute* prediction error between the parametric and the semiparametric model in store k, week t for brand 1,

PI_{kjt} = the price index (actual divided by regular price) for brand j in store k, week t.

In (18.44) all the estimated coefficients are statistically significant ($p < 0.05$). If all price indices are equal to 1.0, the predicted value of *Diff* equals 0.06 (the parametric model having a larger prediction error). This is twice the average value of 0.03 in the validation sample. Thus, the difference in performance is greater when there are no discounts at all than on average across the actual price index values. By taking the first derivative of (18.44) with respect to PI_{k1t}, and letting $PI_{k2t} = PI_{k3t} = 1.0$, we find that under these conditions the minimum value of *Diff* occurs at $PI_{k1t} = 0.78$ (the second derivative is positive). For this scenario the predicted value of *Diff* equals -0.03, meaning that at this discount for brand 1 the parametric model is predicted to have a smaller prediction error. As long as the price index for brand 1 is either above 0.92 or below 0.65 (holding the other price indices at 1.0), the semiparametric model will win in the validation sample, according to equation (18.44). Generally speaking, if either of the other brands' price indices is below 1, the semiparametric model's performance improves relative to the parametric one. Thus, whether the semiparametric model wins *on average* depends a great deal on the price index values in the validation sample. The benefits of this diagnostic predictive validity exercise are that:

- equation (18.44) shows under what conditions one model tends to outperform another, and
- the data characteristics should be taken into account when validation results are reported.

Alsem, Leeflang and Reuyl (1989) calibrated market share models for nine brands from three markets using bimonthly data. One of their models pertains to brand j in the dried soup market in the Netherlands:

$$m_{jt} = e^{\alpha_j} \left[\frac{p_{jt}}{p_{jt} + pc_t} \right]^{\beta_{1j}} \cdot \left[\frac{a_{j,t-1}}{a_{j,t-1} + ac_{t-1}} \right]^{\beta_{2j}} \cdot d_{jt}^{\beta_{3j}} \cdot u_{jt}, \qquad (18.45)$$

$$t = 1, \ldots, T$$

where

$\begin{aligned}
m_{jt} &= \text{market share of brand } j \text{ in period } t, \\
p_{jt} &= \text{price of brand } j \text{ in } t, \\
pc_t &= \text{mean competitive price, weighted by market shares,} \\
a_{jt} &= \text{advertising expenditures of brand } j \text{ in } t, \\
ac_t &= \text{advertising expenditures of brand } j\text{'s competitors,} \\
d_{jt} &= \text{effective store distribution of brand } j \text{ (measured as} \\
&\quad \text{ a fraction of all stores where the product is available),} \\
u_{jt} &= \text{a disturbance term, and} \\
T &= \text{total number of observations of the estimation sample.}
\end{aligned}$

We show the estimated parameters of (18.45) and some statistical test results in Table 18.7. One advantage of model (18.45) is that it has a simple structure. However, it is far from complete on important issues and it is not robust. For example, the model omits variables that represent the effective store distribution of competitive brands (d_{ct}). Also, temporary price discounts, displays and featuring are excluded. And while each brand has a (unique) number of varieties, the model is specified at the brand level. One might argue in favor of a hierarchical model (see Section 14.5), but the lack of available data makes its estimation unrealistic. On the other hand,

Table 18.7 Parameter estimates and statistical test results for (18.45).

Intercept	Relative price	Lagged advertising share	Effective store distri-bution			Durbin Watson statistic	Number of observa-tions
$\hat{\alpha}_j$	$\hat{\beta}_{1j}$	$\hat{\beta}_{2j}$	$\hat{\beta}_{3j}$	R^2	R_a^2	$D.W.$	T
-7.85	-1.45	0.08	1.23	0.85	0.81	1.27	17
$(-4.82)^a$	(-4.77)	(3.38)	(3.20)				

$^a t$-values in parentheses.

Source: Alsem et al. (1989, p. 189).

the model accommodates some interaction between the marketing instruments. For example, if d_{jt}, the number of sales outlets carrying brand j at t is equal to zero, then $m_{jt} = 0$, no matter the brand's advertising share. However, the same implication for advertising is less realistic, since zero advertising need not lead to zero market share.

The model was estimated on 17 bimonthly observations, covering a period of nearly three years. It is quite conceivable that model parameters change or that the model structure changes during such a long period. The number of observations however, is small. Six remaining bimonthly periods are used as a validation sample. An increase in the periodicity of the data implies some market instability which enhances the information content of the validation exercise.

As was observed earlier, the face validity of the model's structure is not high, for example equation (18.45) does not satisfy range and sum constraints. However, all parameter estimates are statistically significant ($p < 0.05$) and have the expected sign. Also, the magnitudes of the elasticities differ across the variables in a manner that corresponds to what one would expect. The value of the Durbin-Watson statistic is in the inconclusive region which indicates a possible concern about autocorrelation (and raises questions about the validity of other statistical tests). As indicated in Section 16.1, there are several possible reasons for the error term to be autocorrelated, such as omitted variables and structural changes. Other concerns include the definition of competition which is assumed to consist of the three largest brands. This definition was based on an earlier study of competitive reaction effects estimated from data for all brands.[25] The model may also suffer from the assumption of a quasiduopoly (brand j versus the other two brands treated jointly). Bultez and Naert (1973), for example, found that treating each competitor uniquely in an attraction model improved the outcome of the Durbin-Watson statistic.

Alsem et al. (1989) were especially interested in the use of predicted values for competing brands' variables. A brand manager can contemplate alternative values for own-brand marketing variables, and use the estimated parameters for those variables to produce market share predictions. However, along with each possible set of own-

---

25. See Leeflang, Reuyl (1985b).

Table 18.8 MAPE-values for relations (18.45) and (18.46).

	Relation (18.45)		Relation (18.46)
Estimated values of pc_t and ac_{t-1}		Actual values for pc_t and ac_{t-1}	Naive market share model
Competitive reaction functions as function of $p_{jt}, a_{j,t-1}, d_{jt}$	Naive models as function of pc_{t-1}, ac_{t-2}		
MAPE: 2.1	2.7	9.1	4.8

brand marketing activities, specific competing brands' actions have to be assumed. Alsem et al. used two models to generate predicted values for competitors:

- competitive reaction functions[26] showing how pc_t and ac_{t-1} in (18.45) are influenced by $p_{jt}, a_{j,t-1}$ and d_{jt};
- naive models relating pc_t and ac_{t-1} to these variables' past values.

The predicted values of competitive variables so generated were substituted in (18.45), along with actual values for p_{jt} and $a_{j,t-1}$ and the parameter estimates in Table 18.7, to obtain predicted market shares for brand j for the six bimonthly observations in the validation sample. They also used the actual values for pc_t and ac_{t-1} to create a third set of predicted market shares (in the unlikely case of perfect knowledge about competitors' activities). And they used a naive market share model as a benchmark:

$$m_{jt} = \delta_j + \gamma_j m_{j,t-1} + v_t \tag{18.46}$$

where

$\quad v_t = $ a disturbance term, and all other variables are
$\qquad$ defined as before.

We show *MAPE*-values for these four sets of predicted shares relative to the actual values in Table 18.8. Surprisingly, the results in Table 18.8 show that the use of actual values for pc_t and ac_{t-1} gives the highest *MAPE*, for equation (18.45). On the other hand, the competitive reaction functions provide estimated values of pc_t and ac_{t-1} which generate the smallest *MAPE*-value. It is unusual to have superior market share predictions from predicted competitors' activities than from actual values for those activities. One possible explanation is that the predicted values dampen the variability in the competitive variables in a manner that compensates for excessive variation in other model aspects. Nevertheless, these results suggest that the estimated competitive reaction functions provide an acceptable representation.

---

26. See Section 11.1.

Many models *with behavioral detail* use input from managers.[27] We use the SPRINTER new-product model, introduced in Section 10.2, to illustrate the idea of validating input from managers.

We assume that interaction between management and the model-building team has led to the structure shown in Figure 10.6. Validation starts with a critical evaluation of this structure and of the measurement of model inputs. We noted in Section 10.2, for example, that knowledge of total market sales may lead to adjustments. The distribution of frequency-of-purchase is based on survey data, and these data may indicate that the distribution figures should be adjusted. Similar validation checks should be made on individual inputs whenever possible. And, if one has reason to believe that some parameters are over- or underestimated, along with prior knowledge about the direction, then an adjustment is justified (and it should normally improve model performance).

Once all individual inputs have been evaluated, we still do not know how well the model actually describes the new-product purchase process. One possible test is to compare model predictions with test market data. The tracking of past results can lead to useful model updates.

In Section 10.2 we introduced the BASES model. If the supplier of BASES services tracks subsequent introductions of new products, BASES clients can learn the historical accuracy of predictions made (for products actually introduced). With each subsequent application, given to a new-product introduction, the predictive validity results can be updated. Note, however, that for BASES, ASSESSOR and other pretest-market models, the environment used for estimation is artificial (e.g. respondents are aware of the new product and they have access to it). Thus, the supplier should find out whether there are elements in the artificial environment that lead to biases in predictions to the real world. And there is an opportunity to determine whether the model performance depends on the product category, the type of consumers, etc.

One possible bias in the output of pretest market models derives from the judgments managers provide. For example, in ASSESSOR applications, consumer response is used to predict trial and repeat under the assumption that the product is known by and available to all target market members. To obtain market share predictions, ASSESSOR uses managerial judgments about the new brand's expected or planned consumer awareness and product distribution. The accuracy of the predictions is then determined not only by the validity of the model and the validity of consumer responses but also by the validity of the managerial judgments.

We show in Table 18.9 predicted and actual market shares for 24 new products evaluated with the ASSESSOR methodology. In the first column we have the initial predicted shares (i.e. based on managers' judgments about awareness and availability). On average, the predicted value is 7.9 percent. The second column shows the adjusted predicted shares. These are the predictions generated by ASSESSOR when the actual awareness and distribution data are used (which are measured after the new product is introduced). On average, the predicted adjusted value is 7.5 percent.

---

27. See also Naert (1975a, 1975b).

Table 18.9 Predicted versus actual market shares for ASSESSOR.

Product description	Predicted		Actual	Initial- Actual	Adjusted- Actual
	Initial	Adjusted			
Deodorant	13.3	11.0	10.4	2.9	0.6
Antacid	9.6	10.0	10.5	-0.9	-0.5
Shampoo	3.0	3.0	3.2	-0.2	-0.2
Shampoo	1.8	1.8	1.9	-0.1	-0.1
Cleaner	12.0	12.0	12.5	-0.5	-0.5
Pet Food	17.0	21.0	22.0	-5.0	-1.0
Analgesic	3.0	3.0	2.0	1.0	1.0
Cereal	8.0	4.3	4.2	3.8	0.1
Cereal	6.0	5.0	4.4	1.6	0.6
Shampoo	15.6	15.6	15.6	0.0	0.0
Juice Drink	4.9	4.9	5.0	-0.1	-0.1
Frozen Food	2.0	2.0	2.2	-0.2	-0.2
Cereal	9.0	7.9	7.2	1.8	0.7
Detergent	8.5	8.5	8.0	0.5	0.5
Cleaner	8.4	5.5	6.3	2.1	-0.8
Shampoo	0.8	2.3	2.5	-1.7	-0.2
Shampoo	7.1	7.9	7.6	-0.5	0.3
Dog Food	2.9	2.9	2.7	0.2	0.2
Cleaner	16.5	14.7	12.9	3.6	1.8
Shampoo	1.1	0.6	0.6	0.5	0.0
Frozen Food	2.6	2.0	2.2	0.4	-0.2
Lotion	27.1	27.1	28.7	-1.6	-1.6
Food	5.6	5.0	1.5	4.1	3.5
Shampoo	5.2	2.8	1.6	3.6	1.2
Average	7.9	7.5	7.3	0.6	0.2
Average Absolute Deviation	—	—	—	1.5	0.6

Source: Urban, Hauser (1980, p. 403).

This difference of 0.4 percentage points indicates that managers tend to overstate awareness and/or availability for a new product.

The third column shows the actual market shares achieved. Note that all of these columns are silent about the specific amount of time after introduction. Presumably each client has provided input and output values that represent an "equilibrium" or long-run result under normal market conditions. We mention this to make it clear that there is in fact uncertainty about the actual market share result.

The fourth and fifth columns in Table 18.9 show the prediction errors. On average, the prediction error is 0.6 for the initial predicted values and 0.2 for the adjusted predictions. Thus, the bias due to managers' overstatement of awareness/availability is reduced considerably (the difference of 0.4 percentage points mentioned above). Finally, the average absolute difference between predicted and actual shares is also reduced from 1.5 (column four) to 0.6 (column five).[28] This suggests that the largest part of the forecast error generated by the initial predictions is due to inaccuracy in managers' judgments. If the bias persists, the judgments themselves can be adjusted so that superior predictions are obtained prior to knowledge of the actual awareness and availability. Note that, unlike Alsem et al., here the use of actual instead of predicted values, improves model performance.

In Chapter 12 we introduced discrete (brand) choice models. These models are specified at the individual consumer level. We discuss in Section 17.2 heterogeneity in consumer response and how choice models can accommodate such heterogeneity. The performance of a discrete choice model can be compared with that of a naive model. One simple naive model[29] is to assume that each consumer chooses any brand with probability $1/n$ on every occasion. However, this benchmark is naive, in that it assumes that all n brands have the same market share $(1/n)$ and that all consumers have all brands in their consideration sets. A more useful benchmark is to assume that all consumers have chance probabilities equal to the brands' actual market shares. This benchmark still assumes that the consideration set is common across all consumers and that there is no variance in brand probabilities across consumers.

Other benchmark models represent heterogeneity in consumer choice behavior through the use of loyalty indices, etc. Kalwani, Meyer and Morrison (1994) propose the Dirichlet-Multinomial (DM) model as a benchmark. The DM-model's parameters are estimated from consumers' purchases in the estimation sample.

The foregoing discussion suggests that models with different degrees of behavioral detail and specified at different aggregation levels are best evaluated against uniquely specified benchmark models.

18.7 Validation of subjective estimates

In Section 16.9 we mention that scoring rules can be applied to evaluate the quality of an expert's subjective judgment. Such scores are part of the process to validate subjective estimates. Of course, the output of a subjectively estimated model can also be validated with the criteria presented in Sections 18.2-18.5. In this section we consider an approach that focuses explicitly on an expert's ability to make subjective judgments about output variables such as market share.[30]

For simplicity of exposition, we consider a mature market in which industry sales grow at the same rate as the population. There are two brands (j and c), which compete primarily through price and advertising. Suppose that market share response functions were considered for parameter estimation based on historical data, leading

---

28. For further details, see Urban and Katz (1983) and Urban and Hauser (1993, pp. 468-472).
29. We closely follow Kalwani, Meyer, Morrison (1994).
30. See also Naert (1975b).

Table 18.10 *Subjective values of market share for sixteen combinations of price*
levels and advertising expenditure values.

Combination	p_{jt}	p_{ct}	a_{jt}	a_{ct}	m^s_{jt}
1	p_j^1	p_c^1	a_j^1	a_c^1	m_j^1
2	p_j^1	p_c^1	a_j^1	a_c^2	m_j^2
3	p_j^1	p_c^1	a_j^2	a_c^1	m_j^3
$\vdots$	$\vdots$	$\vdots$	$\vdots$	$\vdots$	$\vdots$
16	p_j^2	p_c^2	a_j^2	a_c^2	m_j^{16}

to the following specification:

$$ m_{jt} = \alpha \left[\frac{p_{jt}}{p_{ct}} \right]^{\beta_p} \left[\frac{a_{jt}}{a_{ct}} \right]^{\beta_a} e^{u_{jt}} \tag{18.47} $$

where

m_{jt} = market share of brand j in period t,

p_{rt} = price brand r in period t, $r = j, c$,

a_{rt} = advertising expenditures of brand r in period
t, $r = j, c$,

u_{jt} = disturbance term, and

α, β_p, β_a = unknown parameters.

Suppose we now consider two alternative price levels for brand j: p_j^1, p_j^2, and for brand c: p_c^1, p_c^2. Similarly, a_j^1, a_j^2, a_c^1, a_c^2 are alternative levels of advertising expenditures. We now ask the manager of brand j what market share the manager expects if $p_{jt} = p_j^1$, $p_{ct} = p_c^1$, $a_{jt} = a_j^1$, and $a_{ct} = a_c^1$. Let the corresponding estimate be m_j^1. We repeat this for all sixteen combinations of p_{jt}, p_{ct}, a_{jt}, a_{ct}, as shown in Table 18.10 (this table is the same as Table 16.11). In this manner sixteen subjective market share observations are generated, which allow us to obtain another set of parameter estimates of (18.47) based on econometric methods.

We now have two sets of market share data: m_{jt} containing the historical data, and m^s_{jt} consisting of the subjective estimates. If we carry out two separate data analyses, we generate $\hat{\alpha}$, $\hat{\beta}_p$ and $\hat{\beta}_a$ from the historical data, and $\hat{\alpha}^s$, $\hat{\beta}_p^s$ and $\hat{\beta}_a^s$ from the sub-jective market share estimates. If these two sets of parameter estimates are "close", the evidence is consistent with the hypothesis that the manager provides subjective market share estimates close to marketplace observations. Assuming that the manager had never been exposed to the parameter estimates obtained from historical data, we can claim that the two sets of parameter estimates were generated independently.

Formally, "closeness" can be assessed in several ways. One possibility is to use a Chow test (see Section 16.2) of the null hypothesis that the parameters generating the

historical data are equal to the parameters that generate the subjective estimates. Another possibility is to use the historical data as a validation sample for the parameter
estimates obtained from the subjective market share estimates (see Section 18.5).

We note that when model complexity increases (e.g. as the number of relevant
predictor variables increases), it becomes virtually impossible for humans to learn the
marginal effects of the predictor variables by tracking historical data. The difficulty
humans face is that multiple predictor variables change at the same time, making it
likely that changes in a criterion variable are attributed incorrectly to specific predictor variables. On the other hand, econometric methods are specially suited to provide
the best possible estimate of a given predictor, holding other predictors constant.

In Sections 3.1 and 16.9 we discussed the use of intention surveys to obtain quantitative predictions of the effects of the introduction of private broadcasting on advertising expenditures in other media. The estimates of the advertising expenditures in
medium i for the entire market in period $t + 1$ ($\widehat{AE}_{i,t+1}$) are obtained as follows:

$$\widehat{AE}_{i,t+1} = \frac{AE_{it}}{AE'_{it}} \cdot \widehat{AE}'_{i,t+1} \tag{18.48}$$

where

$$AE_{it} = \text{advertising expenditures of the entire market}$$
$$\text{in medium } i \text{ in period } t,$$
$$AE'_{it} = \text{advertising expenditures of the } sample^{31} \text{ in}$$
$$\text{medium } i \text{ in } t,$$
$$\widehat{AE}'_{i,t+1} = intended \text{ advertising expenditures of the}$$
$$sample \text{ in medium } i \text{ in } t + 1.$$

The estimates $\widehat{AE}_{i,t+1}$ can be validated by comparing these predicted values with
the actual values, $AE_{i,t+1}$. The measure we use, is the percentage error of prediction
PEP:

$$PEP_{t+1} = \left[\frac{\widehat{AE}_{i,t+1}}{AE_{i,t+1}} - 1 \right] \times 100. \tag{18.49}$$

These prediction errors consist of two components. This is demonstrated by substituting (18.48) in (18.49) and rewriting this expression as:

$$PEP_{t+1} = \left[\left(\frac{\widehat{AE}'_{i,t+1}}{AE'_{i,t+1}} \right) \left(\frac{AE'_{i,t+1}}{AE_{i,t+1}} \right) \Big/ \left(\frac{AE'_{it}}{AE_{it}} \right) - 1 \right] \times 100. \tag{18.50}$$

---

31. The sampling procedure is described in more detail in Section 16.9.

Table 18.11 *Percentage error of prediction, decomposed into error due to behavior and sample, for advertising expenditures in the Netherlands, 1990.*

	PEP	PEB	PES
Public broadcasting	+19	+4	+14
Private broadcasting	+43	+49	-4
Total television	+26	+16	+9
Radio	-15	+11	-24
Daily newspapers	-14	+21	-29
Magazines	-26	+11	-33
Total of these media	-6	+17	-20

Source: Alsem, Leeflang (1994, p. 335).

The first component represents the *deviation* which occurs between *intended* and *actual behavior* within the sample in period $t + 1$. This can also be represented by the measure *PEB* (percentage error of actual behavior):

$$PEB_{t+1} = \left[\frac{\widehat{AE}'_{i,t+1}}{AE'_{i,t+1}} - 1 \right] \times 100 = \left[\frac{\widehat{AE}'_{i,t+1} - AE'_{i,t+1}}{AE'_{i,t+1}} \right] \times 100. \qquad (18.51)$$

The second component of (18.50) is the *sampling error*, which is defined as the percentage error of the sample (*PES*):

$$PES_{t+1} = \left[\left\{ \left(\frac{AE'_{i,t+1}}{AE_{i,t+1}} \right) - \left(\frac{AE'_{it}}{AE_{it}} \right) \right\} \bigg/ \frac{AE'_{it}}{AE_{it}} \right] \times 100. \qquad (18.52)$$

This component represents the (percentual) difference between the fraction of the advertising expenditures of the sample out of the total population in period $t + 1$ and the value of this fraction in period t. The larger the difference, the less representative the sample is in period $t + 1$.

The relation between *PEP*, *PEB* and *PES* (ignoring subscripts) can be written as:

$$(1 + PEP/100) = (1 + PEB/100) \times (1 + PES/100). \qquad (18.53)$$

Thus, the validation measure *PEP* can be decomposed into an error due to deviations between intentions and actual behavior and a sampling error. Such a decomposition can provide diagnostic value with respect to possible causes for prediction error. To illustrate, we use the outcomes of an intention survey to estimate the advertising expenditures of different media in the Netherlands in 1990, the year after the (possible) introduction of private broadcasting. In Table 18.11 we report the values of *PEP*, *PEB* and *PES*.

Table 18.11. shows that for the private broadcasting channel the model strongly overestimated (+43) advertising expenditures. The respondents represented the population well (a sample error of -4), so the prediction error was mainly attributable to a behavior intention error (+49). This intention error was partly due to reduced prices for commercial time on the private broadcasting channel. For the print media (daily newspapers and magazines), the respondents also overestimated their advertising expenditures (positive values of *PEB*), but the fraction of advertising expenditures in the population decreased (negative values of *PES*): other advertisers in the population increased their print advertising more than the advertisers in the sample. This sampling error is larger than the behavior error. Thus the positive intention/behavior error is overcompensated by the negative sampling error, resulting in a negative prediction error.

Still, the total advertising expenditures across all media are predicted quite well (*PEP* = −6%). However, this is in part because of opposite signs for errors in the two components. Thus, the high degree of accuracy in predicted total advertising expenditures is due to the fact that the component errors happen to offset. If these errors can be expected to show similar patterns in the future (i.e. if they are negatively correlated), then decreases in error in one component should be accompanied by increases in the other component's error.

PART FOUR

Use / Implementation

CHAPTER 19

Determinants of model implementation

We now examine the determinants of model implementation. We categorize the dimensions that contribute to the likelihood of implementation as follows:[1]

- model-related dimensions;
- organization-related dimensions;
- implementation-strategy dimensions.

The likelihood of implementation depends on the *model* itself. In Chapter 7, we formulated criteria that a model should satisfy: a model must be simple, complete, adaptive and robust. If a model satisfies these criteria it has a good chance of being implemented. However, such model structure "requirements" are necessary but not sufficient. The model parameters must be estimated reliably, an aspect we examined in detail in Chapters 16 and 17. Model acceptance will also be determined by any validation history, in the sense that successful validation experience will positively contribute to acceptance (Chapter 18). Model structure parameter estimation and model validation are all part of the technical validity component of the probability of success in implementation.[2] Another model-related dimension is the cost-benefit tradeoff. A model may do very well in the sense of being correct and complete and yet have no chance of being implemented if the model benefits do not exceed the costs. We elaborate on this in Chapter 20, where we expand on the discussion of model benefits in Chapter 3.

The probability of model implementation also depends on a number of contingencies related to the *organization* for which the model building project is carried out. Schultz and Slevin (1975) refer, in this respect, to organizational validity. Organizational validity comprises personal, interpersonal and organizational factors. Personal factors include the characteristics of the user, interpersonal factors relate to the interface between model user and model builder, and organizational factors consist of characteristics of the organization, and its environment. We discuss organizational validity in Section 19.1.

The basic strategy for implementation is the continuous model builder − model user interface, underlying a process view of model building as described in Section

---

1. See also Larréché, Montgomery (1975).
2. Schultz, Slevin (1975). Schultz and Henry (1981, p. 272) define a successful model as a model that adequately represents the phenomena being modeled *and* is used for the purpose for which it was designed.

5.1. Two aspects of the model-building process deserve further comment: model scope and the evolutionary nature of model building. We examine these aspects along with the model's ease of use, another element of *implementation strategy*, in Section 19.2.

19.1 Organizational validity

In this section we discuss the personal, interpersonal and organizational factors that are part of organizational validity. Research on model implementation and on computerized decision support systems (Section 15.2) has identified these factors as being influential.

19.1.1 PERSONAL FACTORS

Models should ideally be custom built, and developed in accordance with the *integrative complexity* of the model user. *Integrative complexity* is the ability of an individual to integrate information on multiple dimensions in a complex fashion.[3] Integratively more complex individuals can perform higher levels of information processing than integratively simple individuals. Thus, a model should be developed for a specific user in such a way that the model fits the manner in which the user makes decisions.

This focus on the model user's personal factors illustrates that it is important for a model builder to understand the alternative approaches the decision maker has access to and is comfortable with for making decisions. Thus, a model has to compete with whatever traditional approaches have been used in decision making. For example, a brand manager who has responsibility for, among other things, price and promotion decisions may have relied on weekly market status reports which provide brand performance measures (such as revenues, unit sales and market shares) along with marketing activities for a set of brands sold in specific distribution outlets. This manager would try to relate changes in the performance measures to changes in the marketing activities. Essentially the manager does the equivalent of a multiple regression analysis with a large number of (potential) predictor variables. We have argued elsewhere that models are (much) better at finding optimal information integration rules than humans are (Section 15.2). Purely from the perspective of efficiently integrating information on multiple variables expressed on disparate scales, humans will not beat models. However, humans have the capacity to recognize when a model is obsolete (for example, due to important changes in the environment). Thus, the objective of the model builder should be to recognize the strengths and weaknesses of the decision maker, and to identify to opportunity to melt the decision maker's strengths with the model's strengths.

For each individual, there is an optimum level of *"environmental complexity"* which maximizes the level of information processing. An integratively complex individual reaches this maximum at a higher level of environmental complexity than does

---

3. See Larréché (1974, 1975).

the integratively simple individual. Benbasat and Todd (1996) introduced the notion of *elementary information processes* (EIP's). EIP's are the basic building blocks of a decision strategy. These are low-level cognitive operations such as reading a value, combining two values, or storing a result in long-term memory. EIP's have been used to model a variety of decision processes.[4] To illustrate, the EIP's used in (preferential) choice strategies represent three classes of decision making effort:[5]

• the *processing effort* associated with calculations and comparisons within and among alternatives;
• the *recall efforts* associated with the retrieval of information;
• the *tracking effort*, associated with the storage and subsequent retrieval of information about alternatives.

A model builder can identify the EIP's in a specific decision-making situation to determine how a model can be designed which reduces these efforts for the model user. For an evaluation of model advantages with respect to effort, the model builder can consider both the *effort required of the decision maker to interact with the model* and the *effort required to process the information* generated by the model. The likelihood of implementation of the model partly depends on a comparison of efforts required for model use and efforts required in the traditional approach.

Successful implementation also depends on *"user involvement"* and *"personal stake".*[6] Not surprisingly, greater *user involvement* leads to higher implementation success rates.[7] User involvement is also central to the degree of interaction between developer (researcher) and user (manager). The more involvement between the two sides in terms of quantity and quality of interaction, the more likely it is that mutual confidence develops (see below).

Personal stake is the extent to which a model user's future performance depends on the model and its use. If the model can be shown to improve the quality of a manager's decision, and if improved decision making leads to better performance, then the model is more likely to be implemented.

The personal characteristics of the decision maker that affect implementation success[8] include general intelligence, work experience, length of time at the company and in the job, education, personality, decision style and attitude toward a model. The role of these factors in influencing model implementation is described by Zmud (1979). Zmund found that extroverted, perceptive individuals possess above-average positive attitudes toward models while older and less educated individuals were observed to exhibit less positive attitudes.

A distinction is often made between analytic and heuristic problem-solving styles. The analytic style is relatively formal and systematic in nature. Also, analytic decision

---

4. For example, see Johnson, Payne (1985) and Payne, Bettman, Johnson (1988).
5. We closely follow Benbasat and Todd (1996, pp. 245-246) but omit much detail.
6. Swanson (1974), Schultz, Ginzberg, Lucas (1984), Hanssens, Parsons, Schultz (1990, p. 327), Lucas, Ginzberg, Schultz (1990).
7. Schultz, Slevin (1983).
8. See also Wierenga, van Bruggen (1997).

makers have a fondness for data and analysis. The heuristic style is less formal and more ad hoc. The heuristic decision maker also places more value on intuition and experience. Experiments have shown that heuristic individuals are less likely to accept recommendations from model builders than analytic decision makers.[9]

19.1.2 INTERPERSONAL FACTORS: THE MODEL USER - MODEL BUILDER
         INTERFACE

Churchman and Schainblatt (1965) proposed the following matrix to represent four distinct *views* of the model user (MU) - model builder (MB) interface.

	MB understands MU	MB does not understand MU
MU understands MB	Mutual understanding	Communication
MU does not understand MB	Persuasion	Separate functions

"MU understands MB" means that the MU reacts to what the MB is trying to do in a manner that improves the manager's chances of succesfully exercising the duties assigned to the MU. We discuss distinct elements of these views below.

1. *Mutual understanding*
This position represents an ideal set of characteristics. The model user understands the pro's and con's of making decisions based on model output, and the model builder knows the various perspectives considered by the model user. The mutual understanding should lead to increased confidence about the outcome of the model-building process, and this will facilitate acceptance and use of the model.

2. *Communication*
In this view, the model user directs the model builder. Essentially, the user has decided that a model should improve the quality of decisions, and the user has identified at least conceptually the structure to be used by the model builder. However, the model builder will not have a complete understanding of the user's perspectives. Of course, it is critical that the user has a good understanding of elements from statistics, econometrics and operations research. The model builder depends on extensive and thorough communication of the model user's needs and expectations.

3. *Persuasion*
This view applies when the model user is uninformed about the role of models in decision making. The problem of model implementation is then one of the model builder selling the features of the model. Among the drawbacks of this position is that model advocates often promise more than can be delivered. This excess in promise

---

9. See Huysmans (1970a, 1970b), Doktor, Hamilton (1973) and Zmud (1979).

can show both in the model not fitting the decision making context and the model not performing at the promised level of accuracy.

The underlying rationale for this position is that model users (managers) are too busy to learn about models and do not have the patience to discuss details relevant to model development. It is then the task of the model builder to understand the manager well enough for the model to be accepted in principle and upon model completion based on the superiority of results. The persuasion task will require that the model builder understands the personality of the manager so that resistance to change can be overcome.

4. Separate functions

In this view the functions of model builder and model user are essentially separate and separable. The model builder has the responsibility of generating a workable model. This model may be intended for use in a large number of settings. Once the model is completed, its purpose, its function, and its results will be presented to managers who either accept or reject its use. A modest amount of customization may be provided, dependent upon the heterogeneity in user needs, data characteristics, etc.

Based on several studies,[10] it appears that the *mutual understanding* position is the most effective interface. This should be true especially if the entire model-building exercise takes place within an organization. The *communication* position may characterize situations in which managers oversee a group of individuals hired to provide model-building expertise. The last two positions represent cases where, for example, consultants or market researchers offer their services for a fee. Especially when the models are intended for widescale application, the supplier may work with leading users to make the model characteristics and model output fit their environments. Successful use in highly regarded or leading organizations then facilitates the diffusion of model use throughout an economy.

The first two positions, *mutual understanding* and *communication*, are also characterized by a relatively high degree of user involvement. In Section 19.1.1 we defined user involvement as the degree of interaction between user (manager) and builder (researcher). In the context of model building, user involvement depends on variables such as:[11]

- the user's understanding of model-building arguments and model characteristics;
- the user's evaluation of the quality of a model and its supporting mechanisms (people, hardware, data);
- the user's knowledge about approaches for conflict resolution (between participants in model development).

Factors that inhibit user involvement and prevent facile communication among the participants stem from fundamental differences between the personal and other char-

---

10. Dyckman (1967), Duncan (1974), Benbasat, Todd (1996).
11. See Hanssens et al. (1990, p. 327).

acteristics of model builders and model users. Hammond (1974) identified eight dimensions on which differences show. Managers and researchers differ in goal orientation, time horizon, comparative expertise, interpersonal style, decision style, problem definition, validation of analysis and degree of structure required. We briefly discuss these dimensions below.

1. *Goal orientation*
The model builder is motivated to pursue a goal of developing a model that produces valid and reliable results. In that regard, the model builder may want to impress model-building peers which can result in the model having a higher degree of sophistication than is desirable. By contrast, the manager (model user) will pursue personal goals that may be oriented towards obtaining a promotion. Thus, if the model allows the user to achieve superior performance in the short run, the manager should be favorably inclined. Hanssens et al. (1990, p. 327) mention that there is substantial evidence that the impact of a model on the user's job performance overshadows all other factors in predicting model acceptance.

2. *Time horizon*
The time horizon considered by managers for a model to assist in problem solving and decision making is generally shorter than the time horizon of a model builder.

3. *Comparative expertise*
A marketing manager is more familiar with the substantive aspects of marketing than the typical model builder is. The model builder is an expert on the methodology of model building. Although such differences in expertise may produce synergistic effects, these may also be counterproductive because of difficulties in communication. The jargon of the model builder may indeed be quite different from that of the manager.

4. *Interpersonal style*
Model builders are more likely to have a task-oriented interpersonal style. They will work together with others until the task is completed, whereas many managers have a more relationship-oriented style. Managers are interested in maintaining good relationships with peers and others, relatively independent of specific tasks.

5. *Decision style*
On an analytic-heuristic continuum, the model builder tends to be close to the analytic end, while the model user is close to the heuristic end of the scale. Even if the model user accepts the model builder's recommendations, the person with a heuristic problem-solving style is often disinclined to actually use the model results.

6. *Problem definition*
The typical model builder likes unambiguous and explicit problem definitions. Model builders also tend to limit themselves to those dimensions that are easily quantifiable.

The manager's problem definition is often vague and will include a number of qualitative considerations.

7. *Validation of analysis*

The model builder may be more interested in validating model structure and inputs, whereas the user is primarily interested in the output, i.e., how well the model performs. It is conceivable that the evaluation of model structure/inputs on the one hand, and model output on the other hand, converge. A short-run orientation on the part of the manager may, however, favor the use of a model just because the output appears promising. The longer-term orientation of the model builder requires that the model is structurally sound so that it can be expected to produce useful results in other time periods and under other conditions.

8. *Degree of structure required*

The manager views the environment as being relatively less structured than the model builder does. As a result, the manager may experience no frustration in making decisions with the aid of a model that relates only to one or a few of the dimensions of the problem. The model builder, on the other hand, prefers to take a comprehensive approach and feels uneasy if some components relevant to the decision cannot be accommodated in the model.

It should be clear that it is important for the model builder to be aware of such differentiating characteristics. These eight dimensions give operational meaning to the notion of "understanding" defined by Churchman and Schainblatt (1965). A thorough consideration of these differences should enable the model builder to develop an implementation strategy that reduces or eliminates these barriers. The ideal position of "mutual understanding" is one that may develop over time. Because of rapid increases in the nature and size of databases, managers can no longer operate in a traditional mode. Thus, managers must learn to interact competently and intelligently with model builders. By the same token, to be effective, model builders must understand the components of organizational decision making. Schultz and Henry (1981, p. 290) advocate the use of functionally related intermediaries to guide this process. If the model user and model builder cannot interact effectively, a market researcher may provide a useful interface.

Recent research affirms that the key issue for a model developer is the design of a system which demonstrably moves the decision maker toward an approach that is expected to provide more accurate outcomes.[12] Thus, the model builder will benefit from insights into the nature of information processing by the model user. A full understanding of the decision making context will suggest opportunities for the model builder to develop meaningful decision aids.

---

12. Todd, Benbasat (1994), Benbasat, Todd (1996).

19.1.3 ORGANIZATIONAL FACTORS

In Sections 19.1.1 and 19.1.2 we considered organizational validity in terms of the behavior of the *members* of the organization involved in a model-building project. In this section we discuss implementation issues related to organizational structure and to relations between members who work at different levels in an organizational hierarchy.

The primary organizational factors that contribute to the likelihood of model implementation are:

- top management support;
- a match between model structure and the decision making structure;
- the position of the model builders in the firm.

Top management support refers to (top or divisional) management support, or lack of resistance, for models.[13] Management support is essential before, during and after a model or a decision support system has been developed. According to Hanssens et al. (1990, p. 324):

> *"The evidence for the need of management support is so strong that any attempt to implement a system without it, and without the related conditions of commitment and authority to implement, will probably result in failure."*

Management support is in evidence if there is public support expressed by (top) management[14] and this support is reinforced through the authority and power of top managers.[15]

The importance of management support stems from the *resistance to change* which is nearly always present when a model is to be implemented. This resistance is not just due to technical aspects of the model or lack of understanding. Managers often believe that models present a threat to their job. Implementation of a model may indeed reduce a manager's flexibility. The manager may feel that the model imposes a rigid structure and multiple constraints on her decision-making authority. The model may be seen as a formal mechanism to control the manager's performance. Thus instead of relying solely on one's judgment, the manager now may start with model output.

To the extent that the model is incomplete, the manager should add subjective considerations reflecting missing model components so that superior decisions can be obtained. But the optimal manner of combining model output and subjective judgments is often difficult to determine. And the model user may feel that credit for positive outcomes will be given to the model while negative outcomes may be blamed on the subjective judgments. If such asymmetry is a serious issue, the manager will be tempted to rely on the model exclusively which may increase the chance of model

---

13. Hanssens et al. (1990, p. 324).
14. Schultz, Ginzberg, Lucas (1984).
15. Marcus (1983), Schultz, Slevin (1983), Robey (1984).

failure. Thus it is crucial that reward systems are properly aligned, and that the arguments in favor of combining subjective judgments with model output are spelled out.[16]

Resistance to change may be overcome through a program of education and preparation. This is what underlies Little's (1975b, p. 657) suggestion to start a model-building project by first having management attend an orientation seminar on the state-of-the-art of marketing models and model building. This should give managers a better understanding of what models can and cannot accomplish. It may also reduce their resistance to change.[17]

McCann and Gallagher (1990, pp. 217-219) describe several other impediments to the implementation of *expert systems*[18] in an organization. Expert systems that contain the marketing expertise of manager i may not be desired by manager j. For example, if manager j were to use the expert system and achieve favorable results, credit for these results may go to manager i.

An impediment to the *development* of an expert system is that if managers allow their knowledge to be placed into a computer, they are "selling" that knowledge to be used for an indefinite time period by the firm. Managers, however, are not paid for selling their knowledge but for "leasing" the knowledge for the duration of their employment. If managers place their expertise into a computer, the traditional employee/employer relationship breaks down. Also, the revelation of this expertise and knowledge, and the lack of knowledge, is a potential barrier to the codification of expertise. Top management has to provide incentives for managers to be partners in this area. Top management support is probably the most critical organizational factor for model implementation

The second organizational factor is the *match between model structure* and *organizational structure*. An often-voiced criticism is that models are partial representations of reality. For example, advertising budgeting models generally miss explicit consideration of media allocation, and media planning models often take the advertising budget as given. To see whether this is a serious pitfall, it is important to take the structure of the organization into account. If advertising budget decisions and media allocation decisions are made at different levels in the organizational hierarchy, then model implementation will be facilitated if the advertising budget model omits media allocation considerations. We elaborate on this point in Section 19.2.2.

The third organizational factor relates to the *position* of the *model builders* (or the information systems unit) *within the organization*. The following characteristics have been found to determine model acceptance: the size of the unit, its internal structure,

---

16. For an example of how model output and subjective judgments may be combined, see Blattberg and Hoch (1990), Gupta (1994) and Section 16.9.

17. See also a case study reported by Montgomery, Silk and Zaragoza (1971) concerning the introduction of their model DETAILER into a firm. Other examples can be found in Cooper, Nakanishi (1988, Chapter 7) and in McCann, Gallagher (1990, Chapter 13).

18. See Section 15.2.

the organizational and technical capabilities of the group, its reputation, the life cycle stage of the unit and the place of the unit in the organizational structure. We consider here only the last two points, the others being largely self-explanatory.

The marketing science (model-building) unit's life cycle stage affects implementation (Schultz, Henry, 1981, p. 289). In early stages, when strong organizational support is not yet present, implementation is more difficult than in later stages, when successful performance should create positive word-of-mouth and requests for other models from satisfied users.

In some firms marketing science projects are completed in the market research department. Alternatively, this department is responsible for the purchase of models from suppliers such as ACNielsen, IRI, GfK, Research International, etc. The latter situation pertains especially to smaller firms.[19] In those firms marketing science may be a one-person operation. A marketing scientist/model builder is likely to report to a product manager or marketing manager. Occasionally the model builder reports directly to the vice president for marketing. The involvement of higher levels in the organization occurs especially when models are developed on an ad-hoc basis to solve a specific problem. Examples are (possible) decisions to increase the price above a critical value (e.g. from below \$5 to about \$5), to change the advertising budget dramatically, to modify a loyalty program or to model the influence of a mishap on brand performance (see Section 17.3).

19.2 Implementation strategy dimensions

19.2.1 INTRODUCTION

An effective implementation strategy is one that reflects the arguments that increase the likelihood of model acceptance (Section 19.1). For example, a successful implementation strategy is more likely if it is based on the "mutual understanding" position than if it is based on one of the other three positions in the Churchman-Schainblatt framework (Section 19.1.2). And if we consider the model user to be the client of the model builder, marketing prowess dictates that the model builder has to understand the user's decision-making environment. The more the model builder knows about the user's way of thinking and the user's needs, the easier it will be to convince the client of model benefits. The "persuasion" position is, in this sense, second best. Educating the client is, of course, also much easier if one knows the client's situation. An educational effort must include time to provide management with at least partial knowledge of the process of model building and the pro's and con's of models.[20] We note that the learning aspects of management involvement in model building have been strongly advocated by various authors (Urban and Karash, 1971, Urban, 1972, 1974 and Little, 1975b). Their proposed implementation strategy

---

19. See Churchill (1995, p. 16).
20. See Section 19.1.3 where we suggest that the starting point for a project is an orientation seminar.

incorporates learning through evolutionary model building (see Section 19.2.2). We return to the topic of the relation between model structure and organization structure in Section 19.2.3 where we discuss issues dealing with *model scope*. We end this chapter by discussing how interactive computer systems can satisfy the *ease of use* requirement in Section 19.2.4.

19.2.2 EVOLUTIONARY MODEL BUILDING

In Section 7.2.2 evolutionary model building was introduced as a means to overcome inconsistency between the model structure criteria of simplicity and completeness. Simplicity is desired so that managers understand models. We note that understanding does not imply that the user must understand the mathematical, statistical, and technical aspects of the model. Rather the user must understand what the model does and does not do.

As an implementation strategy, evolutionary model building increases the likelihood of model acceptance for several reasons. First, evolutionary model building implies continuous user involvement, which should lead to reduced resistance to change. Second, it leads to a communication pattern that is more favorable to model acceptance. Since the user must understand the model's strengths and weaknesses at a conceptual level, evolutionary model building represents a model user - model builder interface that corresponds to the "persuasion" position in the Churchman-Schainblatt framework. Third, as we argue in Section 19.1.1, there exists an optimal match between the environmental complexity of a model and the integrative complexity of the user. By adopting an evolutionary model-building approach the user can and will ask that the model's environmental complexity is consistent with the user's integrative complexity. This should lead to an optimal or near-optimal match.

The adjective "evolutionary" further implies that there are dynamics involved. That is, a model seen by a user as adequately representing the environment at one point in time may not receive the same favorable evaluation after learning has taken place. Experience with the model may lead the model builder and the user to the realization that some aspects should be added, and that other aspects should be changed or even deleted. Thus, the optimal match between model and model user may change over time as a result of learning. Thus, an implementation strategy should allow for corrective action. Learning will also be operative in overcoming resistance to change. As such, evolutionary model building is more than just an adaptation to a user's wishes. As an implementation strategy it may also be instrumental in attitude change. For example, if the manager is closely involved in model development, the manager may become familiar with on-line computer systems. The increased familiarity with computer systems will eliminate a potentially important barrier to change.

The dynamics inherent in the evolutionary approach require the development of a series of successive model versions of increasing complexity.[21] Having a custom built model for each decision situation, and in addition, allowing for evolution in model complexity would be very inefficient if one had to start model development from

---

21. Urban and Karash (1971) propose such a sequence in the context of a new-product launching decision.

scratch each time a change occurs. Several authors, therefore, have argued for modular model building. Modularity means that a desired model is obtained by putting together a set of submodels. For example, Little's (1975a) BRANDAID marketing mix model consists of a set of modules, one for each marketing instrument. Thus, if the user does not want to include promotion variables, that module is simply not included in the model. If later on the manager decides to include promotion in the marketing mix, one does not have to start the whole model-building effort anew: the promotion module would be linked to the existing structure. Another example of a modular model is a marketing decision support system for retailers (Lodish, 1982)[22] where multiple marketing mix variables such as (national) advertising and retail mark up are part of the sales-response function.

In Section 19.1 we discussed the idea that models should ultimately reduce "the efforts" of the user. Benbasat and Todd (1996, p. 251) expect that if the effort is reduced through the use of decision aids (a model can be seen as a decision aid) or through other means such as training and experience, the model builder will also be more willing to formulate more complex models. In this way the model builder moves the decision maker toward a strategy which may provide increasingly accurate outcomes.

We discussed the SCAN*PRO model developed by Wittink, Addona, Hawkes and Porter (1988) in several sections. The original model is defined in Section 9.3, and we introduced a *simplified* version of the model in Section 14.1.2. More complex and more realistic SCAN*PRO-versions were developed by Foekens, Leeflang and Wittink (1994) as part of an evolutionary model building process. The changes involve relaxation of the homogeneous parameters assumption. Chain-specific (heterogeneous parameters) were shown to provide better fit and better forecasting accuracy (Section 14.1.2). In Section 16.7 we discussed a SCAN*PRO model estimated by a semiparametric method to avoid inappropriate constraints on functional forms. This evolution is appealing in the sense that a user may favor an initial version that is fully parametric because of its simplicity.

Other evolutionary versions of the SCAN*PRO model are:

- the varying parameters SCAN*PRO model discussed in Section 17.4;
- the dynamic SCAN*PRO model with leads and lags discussed briefly in Chapter 6.

The leads and lags are critical so that the expanded model allows sales effects from promotions to be decomposed into, for example, brand switching, stockpiling and other effects.[23] We summarize this evolutionary model-building process in Figure 19.1.

Not only the users, but also the model builders need training. Mutual understanding can be realized only if the model builders are also exposed to a formal treatment

---

22. See also Lodish (1981).
23. van Heerde, Leeflang, Wittink (1999b).

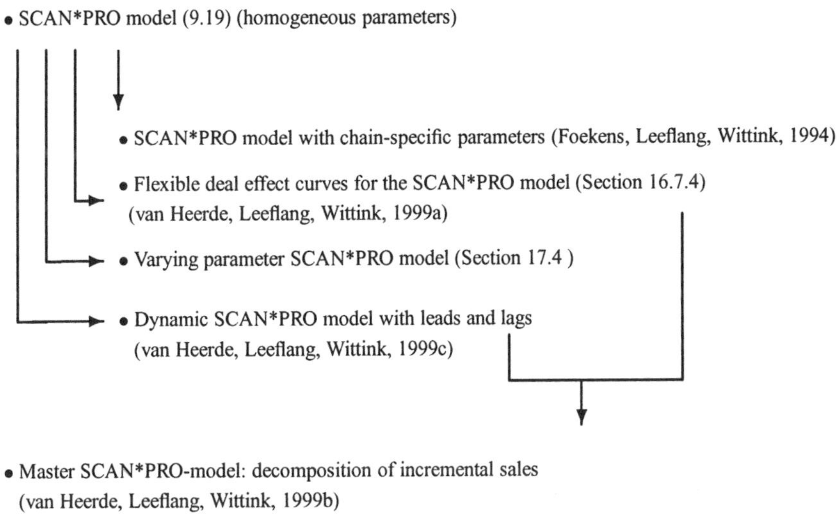

- SCAN*PRO model (9.19) (homogeneous parameters)

- SCAN*PRO model with chain-specific parameters (Foekens, Leeflang, Wittink, 1994)
- Flexible deal effect curves for the SCAN*PRO model (Section 16.7.4)
  (van Heerde, Leeflang, Wittink, 1999a)
- Varying parameter SCAN*PRO model (Section 17.4)
- Dynamic SCAN*PRO model with leads and lags
  (van Heerde, Leeflang, Wittink, 1999c)

- Master SCAN*PRO-model: decomposition of incremental sales
  (van Heerde, Leeflang, Wittink, 1999b)

Figure 19.1 Illustration of an evolutionary model-building process.

of the implementation problem (Schultz, Henry, 1981, p. 293). For example, model builders should learn about the behavioral and political realities of implementable model building. Thus, the model builders can learn from behavioral training, that is education aimed at increased awareness of individual and social actions. Schultz and Henry (1981) maintain that management scientists should know more about the art of management and behavior. They suggest that:

"a course focusing on implementation ought to be as important to the academic preparation of a management scientist as a course on programming"

(Schultz, Henry, 1981, p. 293).

Thus far, evolutionary model building has been proposed as a process of gradually moving from a relatively simple representation of a given problem to a more complex representation. There may, however, also be an evolution in the types of problems being modeled. Urban (1974, p. 9) found that evolutionary progress often means not only model changes, but also the identification of new model needs. Schultz and Slevin (1977, p. 16) mention that the chances of successful implementation are seriously impaired if the model building is very advanced and the user has little or no experience with models and model building. In that sense, early model-building efforts might concern well-structured problems, which are easy to systematize. After positive experience with such simple problems, the model building gradually evolves toward relatively unstructured problems. Examples are problems of a strategic nature.[24] The most serious problem with marketing strategy models is that such models

---

24. Surveys of strategy models are given by Wind (1981) and Wind, Lilien (1993). Other examples can be found in Zoltners (1982).

are rarely used by management (Wind, Lilien, 1993, p. 776). Most of the strategy models are *not* user-friendly, do *not* address key concerns of top managers, do *not* facilitate the process of making strategic choices and are more directed to brand strategies than to corporate strategy.

19.2.3 MODEL SCOPE

In this section we first examine the global versus local model-building controversy. We then discuss general versus detailed descriptions of marketing variables and hierarchical linking (the linking of different decision points).

Model scope is seen as an element of implementation strategy because it relates to the matching of model structure to organizational structure.

Global versus local models
Should one build models for the entire firm (global) or for parts of the company (local)? This problem has multiple aspects. First, successful model building often starts at the lower levels in an organization. A major reason is that structured problems are more likely to be found at the operational levels in the organization, and as indicated before, structured problems lend themselves more easily to modeling. Also the appropriate level of aggregation is more easily determined for structured than for unstructured problems. In that sense, one might argue that trying to model a firm as a whole is a risky undertaking, and that it is better to build and use local models, such as a media selection model, a marketing mix model, or a new product model. Global models can be obtained in three ways.

1. Develop a global model from the start
Most attempts to implement global models conceived as global from the start have failed. Considering the implementation criteria listed earlier, it should be clear why such global models are often doomed. For one thing, the enormous complexity makes them hard to understand. This complexity also makes close management involvement difficult, or at least, very expensive in management time. In addition, it is very hard to develop a global model from scratch that corresponds to the way the organization works. Heads of departments, for example, usually take into account a lot of detail in their decision making. This detail is, however, limited to the problems specific to the department. At higher levels in the organization a global view is desired, but this will automatically preclude taking a lot of detail into account. In that sense a global model that can also be used at individual levels of the organization seems almost like a *contradictio in terminis*.

2. Develop a global model from submodels
Instead of developing a global model from the start, one could first build a specific submodel (local models). Subsequently, one can implement a global model by establishing the links and feedbacks between the submodels. Difficulties with this approach are the following. First, there may be no room for formal links and feedback in the

organizational setup, and management may prefer to maintain the links informally. Second, even if the linking of local models into a global model were desirable, the model builder may face technical difficulties constructing the linkages.

3. *Integrating and linking local models over time*

If one starts with models of partial systems, the necessary links and feedbacks between the submodels can be developed over time as users sense the need for linkages. Links and feedbacks thus come into existence through a natural process rather than being forced onto an existing structure. We note, however, that performance of the total system may suffer if parts of the system are viewed incorrectly as independent units. In terms of optimization, the global optimum is often not equal to the sum of the optima for the submodels. Organizations, for example, get the behavior of the parts in line with overall objectives by imposing a set of heuristic constraints. For example, a brand manager might be told not to spend more than five percent of last year's sales revenue on advertising, or she might have to limit the number of promotions to a maximum of two during a specified time period. Such restrictions provide a simple mechanism to achieve coordination across organizational units.

Whether the firm takes "a global view" or wants to develop a model on a "stand-alone basis"[25] might depend on its orientation. Consider a firm that sells a frequently purchased consumer good and employs a marketing orientation. The product is edible and can therefore not be produced more than, say, two months prior to consumption. Now suppose that the firm holds on average over 30 percent of the market. Two or three times a year, the company offers a cents-off promotion. As a result, its (unit) market share may exceed 50 percent in promotion months. Let the timing and magnitude of promotions be determined by a marketing model (a local model). Assume that the objective is to maximize profit subject to the average share remaining at its current level. The promotional activities will then be terribly demanding on the production facilities of the firm. Since the goods cannot be produced much in advance of sales, production cannot be smoothed over the year, and will show substantial peaks. Although it might be important to have promotions for competitive reasons, it may be desirable financially to reduce the sales peak magnitudes (compare Section 17.4). Indeed a firm oriented toward operational efficiency favors smooth production and distribution which eliminates promotions altogether. Only with a global model can the production and marketing perspectives be effectively and optimally coordinated.

The business world has embraced the notion that the functional areas of the firm, such as marketing and production, should not act as independent units. Increasingly individual activities, nominally belonging to different functional areas, are coordinated and sometimes integrated.[26] Consider, for example, a consumer-goods firm that is contemplating an increase in promotional activities. If the marketing function acts independently, it would consider the effect of increased promotions on consumer de-

---

25. See Wind, Lilien (1993, p. 787).
26. See, for example, Webster (1992, 1994), Hausman, Montgomery (1997), Hoekstra, Leeflang, Wittink (1999).

mand. With appropriate data, one can estimate the gross effect and decompose it into sources of demand increases such as brand switching, stockpiling and consumption. Brand switching is often the largest component, but in a competitive market, one expects an increase in switching to one's own brand to be followed by an increase in switching to other brands (i.e. we expect competing brands to react, see Section 11.2). Thus, the net effect from brand switching may be very small. Also, the percent of the gross effect due to stockpiling tends to be ephemeral. Unless the stockpiling increases consumption (due to large inventories) or the stockpiling keeps consumers from considering alternative brands, this effect should also be very small. Still, it is conceivable that the marketing department concludes that promotions have beneficial effects on results exclusive of the impact on other operations.

If we jointly consider marketing and production, then we will also recognize the effects of promotions on the cost of production (and inventory, and distribution). The gross effect of a promotion on sales is often very large, which creates the illusion that favorable results are achieved. If we only consider the marketing aspects, we may conclude that the net effect is positive as well. But if we take production into account, we would also deduct the (extra) costs due to the additional variation in demand. Typically, it is harder to forecast demand in the presence of a promotional activity than in its absence. And distribution also becomes less efficient. When all these extra costs due to supply chain inefficiencies are subtracted, it may be unlikely that we can justify (increased) promotional activities.[27] Thus, decisions about marketing activities, based on global optimization may differ strongly from those based on optimization at the subunit level.

The logic of coordinating or integrating decisions across functional areas is also reflected in models that link marketing decisions to other functional areas. Eliashberg and Lilien (1993, p. 12) mention that they expect "interface modeling" (modeling that spans functional areas) to receive an increasing amount of attention.[28] Examples of research in which marketing is linked to at least one other function are listed in Table 19.1.

The area where most progress is made is the marketing-production interface. Examples include models of quality function deployment (relating customer-based preferences to internal engineering specifications[29]) and models for just-in-time (JIT) management and total-quality management (TQM).[30]

General versus detailed descriptors of marketing variables
For a market share model such as that described by equation (8.2), one might ask why the model does not include specific characteristics of advertising (such as the content of the advertising message, the quality of advertising copy, the media used, etc.) or specific descriptors of distribution (such as the types of distribution outlets, the store characteristics, the store locations, etc.). Instead of specifying the marketing

---

27. Abraham, Lodish (1989).
28. See also Lilien (1994).
29. See Hauser and Clausing (1988), Griffin (1992).
30. For additional examples, see Karmarkar (1996).

Table 19.1 Models that link marketing to other functional areas.

Other functional area	Reference
– Production	Eliashberg, Steinberg (1993), Karmarkar (1996), Dearden, Lilien, Yoon (1999)
– Strategic management	Wind (1981, 1982), Corstjens, Weinstein (1982), Larréché, Srinivasan (1981, 1982), Wind, Lilien (1993)
– Finance	Corstjens, Weinstein (1982), Mahajan, Wind, Bradford (1982), Abad (1987)
– Accounting	Dunne, Wolk (1977), Hulbert, Toy (1977)
– Research & Development	Griffin, Hauser (1993), Hauser, Simester, Wernerfelt (1996)

variables in *general* or broad terms (e.g. Gross Rating Points for advertising or percent of outlets in which the item is sold for distribution), one could decompose the variable into its constituent parts and use those components as separate predictor variables in the model.

There are two principal reasons why many models do not simultaneously contain both general and detailed measures of marketing variables. One reason is the complexity of modeling. The other reason has to do with the organizational structure.

1. The complexity of having both general and detailed measures of marketing variables in a model is illustrated by the multiproduct advertising budget model of Doyle and Saunders (1990) discussed in Chapter 13. An example of a model with greater complexity is Pedrick and Zufryden (1991). In this model the impact of advertising media plans and point-of-purchase marketing variables on consumer demand is estimated by integrating purchase incidence, brand choice and advertising exposure behavior.

   The complexity of models that include detailed measures along with general descriptors of marketing instruments can be reduced in part through modular model building. Examples of modular models are BRANDAID and ASSESSOR (Section 10.2). Modular model building is likely to be an important approach in the near future.[31]

2. Decisions about a general measure are often made before detailed decisions are formulated. Thus, a budget is usually determined before decisions are made on a campaign theme and the media. This sequence may reflect the organizational structure of the firm for which the model is developed. Thus, at one level in the firm (e.g. the director of marketing), decisions are made about the advertising budget for next year. At a lower level of the organization, the budget is an input (it is fixed) and a model may be used to allocate the budget to different media.

---

31. See also examples in Gupta (1988), and Chintagunta (1993a).

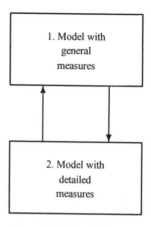

Figure 19.2 Model linkages.

If model development is intended to reflect the organizational structure of the client firm it is sensible, at least in the short run, to have a model focused on the general measure for use at higher levels, and a model with more specific or detailed measures for use at lower levels of the firm. However, to achieve global optimization of the marketing activities, it is critical that the modules are linked, as illustrated in Figure 19.2.

In Figure 19.2 a model with general measures is related to and linked with a corresponding model with detailed measures. For example, model 1 could specify unit sales as a function of variables such as price, Gross Rating Points and distribution coverage. Model 2 could then contain several equations, one indicating how Gross Rating Points are a function of advertising copy content, copy quality, the media, etc.

We show the nature of possible linkages in more detail in Figure 19.3. In this figure management starts with Marketing plan 1. This plan may result from discussions among managers with top financial, marketing and operations responsibilities. It may be based in part on output from model 1 in Figure 19.2. Thus, a model with general measures may be used to determine the GRP's, and the advertising expenditures, desired to achieve specific goals. The output from model 1 then becomes an input to model 2 which is used to relate GRP's to advertising campaign components. In this manner Marketing plan 1, in Figure 19.3, leads to Media plan 1. However, since Marketing plan 1 was produced independently of Media plan 1, it is desirable to see if there are opportunities to improve the profitability from Marketing plan 1. Thus, Media plan 1 can be used to specify Marketing plan 2, etc. This process of linking general measures to relevant components can be continued until it converges (i.e. until the differences between successive plans are very small). Of course, if possible, such linkages should be incorporated in the determination of the marketing plan from the start. Thus, if the management team has access to the model with general measures, and the evaluation of alternative marketing plans is based on the linkages to models with detailed measures, then there is no need for an iterative process.

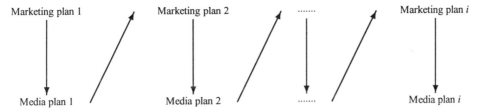

Figure 19.3 Sequence of outputs from and inputs into models with general and detailed measures.

We note that this type of iterative process links top-down and bottom-up approaches described in Section 13.5.

19.2.4 EASE OF USE

By ease of use we mean that the model is:

- easy to control, and
- easy to communicate with.

"Easy to control" means that the model should be constructed in such a way that it tends to behave as the manager would want it to. One interpretation of this is that ideally, if the manager believes that a price increase of ten percent will lead to a twenty percent decrease in sales, then the model should predict just that. If the model produces predictions that vary wildly from the manager's experience or judgment, it is likely that the manager will reject the model. It is critical that the model is tested so that it not only provides acceptable predictions from the model builder's perspective but especially from the user's perspective. Of course, some education of the user will be needed if the user's intuition is demonstrably wrong.

The "easy to communicate with" characteristic has many aspects. One is that model builders should be able to communicate their ideas in a manner that fits the model user. Thus, the model builder must have the user's perspective in mind to enhance the likelihood of successful model implementation.

Easy communication also means that it should be easy for the user to specify model inputs, and for the model to provide output quickly. The output should be constructed in a manner that suits the user. On-line conversational input-output and interactive computer systems are seen as being effective in bringing about ease of use. On-line computer systems:

- reduce barriers between model and user;
- aid the learning process by immediate response;
- make immediate availability of information possible;
- encourage the user to examine a large number of possible plans;
- can be made available to a number of different users.

The degree of interaction afforded by a decision aid is often an important precursor to usage. And active participation in model development, including the construction of a frame for output measures by the user, tends to lead to increased commitment, acceptance, support and use.[32]

---

32. See, for example, Huse (1980), Cats-Baril, Huber (1987), Barr, Sharda (1997).

CHAPTER 20

Cost-benefit considerations in model building and use

The development and use of models is justified if the (expected) benefits exceed the (expected) costs. For a firm that has adopted a model, this implies that profit with the model should be greater than without it. Of course this is not easily operationalized. *After model adoption*, we can quantify the benefits and make a comparison with the costs incurred. *Before implementation* of a model, both benefits and costs are based on potentially highly uncertain estimates.

In this chapter we start with a situation in which models are absent. In such a case we may use general arguments in favor of and against models, relative to the use of judgment for decisions (see Section 15.2). This ex-ante comparison includes the arguments that a model is consistent (a static model always provides the same output given the same input) and that it allows for inspection of the process used to generate output. By contrast, a manager's judgment tends to be sensitive to irrelevant variables and tends to overemphasize the most recent data. However, the manager can recognize that the market environment changes systematically, and adapt the decision-making process to reflect changing market conditions. Most models do not have this capability, although it is possible for model builders to incorporate dynamic elements in the models.[1]

Given that models should be adapted as our understanding of markets changes and as we gain access to more complete and more detailed data, it is important that we use a conceptual approach for the consideration of costs and benefits *before model development*. We do this in Section 20.1. In Section 20.2 we focus on cost components of model development and model use. We discuss how the benefits can be determined in Section 20.3. In Section 20.4 we present examples that illustrate how costs and benefits vary with the type of problem, the size of the firm, intended use of the model, and the amount of behavioral detail. We end with general observations of costs and benefits in Section 20.5.

---

1. See the discussion on varying parameter models in Section 17.4.

20.1 Tradeoffs

An ex-ante comparison between the use of a model and not using one is necessarily to a large extent conceptual. Mitchell, Russo and Wittink (1991) suggest that models beat human judgments, on average, in case of repetitive decisions that require the integration of data on multiple variables, often expressed in noncomparable scales (see also Section 15.2 and Section 16.9.1). This is largely because humans vary their judgments even if the objective data are identical. Even *a model* of a decision maker's *judgments* typically outperforms these very judgments! The reason is that the model uses only the systematic part in the decision maker's judgments (and eliminates the unsystematic or random part). However, to the extent that the decision maker's judgments are systematically wrong (e.g. overweighing some and underweighing other variables), a model based on actual outcomes will do even better.

An argument against any model of *actual* outcomes is that the model explains the past, but will not necessarily be applicable to the future. Model builders and model users must, therefore, assess the extent to which changing market conditions may reduce the validity of the model specification or the model parameters. Thus, one should compare the benefits that emanate, for example, from the model's consistency against the cost of missing dynamics. We note, however, that an evolutionary model-building process can reduce a model's shortcomings through the addition of appropriate extensions over time. The two most obvious extensions are:

1. allow model parameters to *depend* on market conditions (for example through varying parameter models), and
2. append a variable to the model that captures the decision maker's judgment.[2]

The first possible extension is attractive if there is a logical relation between the effects of marketing variables and measures of economic and other market conditions. The second option will work well if there are activities that are difficult to quantify but the decision maker has sound intuition about the influence of those activities.

Benbasat and Todd (1996) use a *cognitive cost-benefit approach* to examine how the selection of decision strategies depends on the interaction between tasks and decision aids. Decision aids are designed to reduce the effort required by the decision maker for the evaluation of alternative decision strategies.[3] Benbasat and Todd (1996) suggest that a decision maker, in choosing a strategy, weighs two major factors:

- the *benefits* to be derived from the strategy;
- the *cognitive effort* associated with:
  - *building* a model, and
  - *using* that model.

---

2. See Blattberg and Hoch (1990) for an application.
3. See also Todd, Benbasat (1994).

The costs of model utilization are important for the model builder and the model user. If the perceived or actual cost of using a proposed model is excessive, it may be advisable to formulate a simpler model. The model builder should focus closely on the effort required for model use, because barriers to model use will lead to rejection of the model. Counterproductive use may occur if the model is more complex than needed. Model complexity by itself, however, does not have to deter the user. Most users do not need to see the model details and they often do not want to see the complexities. Rather, they want a model that provides output they can understand and relate to. This output should be valid and reliable, and if the model allows the user to play relevant "what if" games, the user should not have to confront the model complexities.

20.2   The cost of building models

We consider the following cost components:[4]

a.   initial development costs;
b.   maintenance costs;
c.   costs inherent to model use;
d.   costs of marketing data.

a. *Initial development costs*
The cost of initial model development tends to be fixed. It is incurred once, when the project is first undertaken by the marketing science department or information system group within the firm. Alternatively, an outside consultant may be asked to develop and test a model for a fixed fee. If a model already exists, and can be rented from a consulting firm, then the entire cost becomes variable in that it depends on, for example, the frequency of use.

b. *Maintenance costs*
Model development is not a one-shot event. Maintenance costs relate to updating the model, such as, changing its structure, updating the parameter estimates, etc. These costs will be partly fixed, partly variable, in the sense that the frequency of structural change will depend on use intensity as well as dynamics in the marketplace.

c. *Costs inherent to model use*
Costs inherent to model use are:

- managerial *time;*
- the *effort* required of the decision maker to interact with the model,[5] and
- the *effort* required to process the information generated by the system.

---

4. See also Armstrong, Shapiro (1974).
5. Benbasat, Todd (1996).

The managerial time required for model development and model use needs to be considered as a cost. This time may be assessed in terms of the manager's salary. This time cost can be compared against the possible reduction in time that results from having the model do part of the job the manager used to do. For example, managers may spend less time on programmed and structured activities such as inventory management, media allocation, sales force management and control, and judging the consequences of alternative marketing programs. They will have more time available for unstructured activities such as the creation of entirely new marketing programs. This reallocation of time can result in important benefits.

The efforts required for interacting with the model and processing the output generated depend on the cognitive abilities and the experience of the user. However the model builder can facilitate the interaction by creating output in a user-friendly manner. Experience has shown that the user's efforts can be reduced through training and the availability of decision aids.

d. *Costs of marketing data*
The model builder has to specify a model that is theoretically appropriate and substantively meaningful. It also needs to be subjected to data. In order for the model to provide relevant output, the model builder needs data that fit the properties of the model. The data have to be collected or purchased. Alternatively, judgments can be used for the construction of a model that quantifies, for example, how experts believe product demand depends on marketing activities. Ultimately, the model becomes functional only if it is part of a larger marketing management support system (see Chapter 15).

20.3 Measuring benefits

In Section 3.2, we made a distinction between direct benefits and side benefits. Direct benefits are the improvements in decisions that result from model use. Side benefits are those generated from model use that were not intended or expected.

In this section we discuss the measurement of *direct* benefits. The quantification of benefits is difficult for a number of reasons.

a. Often the benefits of a model are determined on the same data used for model testing and parameter estimation. Such a comparison between situations in which the model is used versus not used would be biased in favor of the model as illustrated in the multiproduct advertising budgeting model of Doyle and Saunders (1990), discussed in Section 13.5.
b. For normative models it is possible to compare marketing decisions based on model output with the decisions that would have been made in the absence of a model. However, for descriptive models, including demand models, no optimal decisions are implied. One could propose to compare the estimated parameters with what managerial judgments would have generated, but such a comparison does not quantify the (possible) benefit from model use. If an estimated demand

model is used for decision making, then it should be possible to compare the quality of the decisions with what would have been done without the model. Obviously, these comparisons are not straightforward.

c. In all instances in which comparisons are made, the implicit assumption is that the model represents reality. In a limited way this is a testable proposition. The other way to think of it is that the benefits cannot be determined until after decisions have been made (or could have been made) based on the model. Indeed, we advocate that this be done repeatedly so that the model's limitations get clarified.

We illustrate these measurement problems, with a few examples.

1. A competitive bidding model

A setting in which benefits can be measured relatively easily is that of sealed competitive bidding, e.g. for a government contract. The bidding is sealed if each bidder is given one chance to make a price offer. The bidder with the lowest price offer wins.[6]

Let π = expected profit,

x = the bid price,

c = the cost of carrying out a contract, and

$P(x)$ = the probability of winning the contract at a price equal to x.

The actual cost c is unknown and is a random variable with expected value $\bar{c}$. Expected profit, $(\pi(x))$, for a price offer x is then:

$$\pi(x) = (x - \bar{c})P(x). \tag{20.1}$$

The general form of the expected profit function is shown in Figure 20.1. For low values of x, the probability of winning is high but expected profit is negative. For example, for $x = 0$, the probability of winning should be one, and expected profit would equal $-\bar{c}$. If $x = \bar{c}$, the expected profit is zero. As x increases, $P(x)$ decreases, and at some point, $(x = x_1$ in Figure 20.1), $P(x)$ and hence $\pi(x)$ is zero. The main problem in competitive bidding models is to estimate how $P(x)$ depends on x. Once $P(x)$ is specified, one can obtain the value of x, x^* in Figure 20.1, that maximizes expected profit.[7]

To evaluate the benefits derived from this model, we compare the performance of bids with and without the model. Edelman (1965) provides the data reproduced in Table 20.1. Results are shown for seven bid situations. The model was available to the team responsible for preparing the bid but it made no use of it for situations 1 through 6. Instead, the team applied traditional company procedures for bid preparation. The data in Table 20.1 show that the bid generated from the model was lower than the

---

6. Price is of course only one of the elements that affect the outcome of a bidding situation. For example, unreliable contractors may not be awarded the contract, even if their bids are the lowest. For a further discussion, see for example Haynes and Rothe (1974), Lilien, Kotler, Moorthy (1992, pp. 208-212).

7. While (20.1) is the bidding relation often used in the literature, it has an important shortcoming. It assumes that the probability of winning is not related to whether the calculated cost under- or overestimates the true cost.

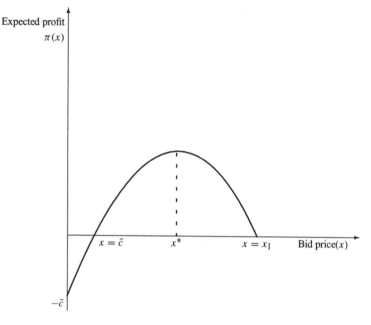

Figure 20.1 Expected profit as a function of bid price.

lowest competitive bid in 5 out of 6 cases. The actual bid made (bid without model) was lower than the lowest competitive bid in only 2 out of 6 cases. Thus, the model would have provided a much higher success rate.

The other relevant aspect is the difference from the lowest competitive bid, if the bid is successful. For the two cases in which the bid without model was successful, the bid with model would on average have been only 2.8% below the lowest competitive bid (versus 7.4% on average for the actual bids made). These results suggest clear benefits of the model.

For the seventh situation, there is unfortunately no bid price without the model. The team preparing the bid was favorably impressed with the model's performance, based on the first six situations, and had gained sufficient confidence in the model to abandon the traditional method. Although it is laudable that the model is accepted and used, given the favorable performance, it is unfortunate that the team does not continue to create competitive bids without the model so that the performance of the model can still be tracked relative to alternative methods. Such comparisons are useful for learning purposes. Management has the opportunity to gain further insight into the model's relative benefits. Also it is important to note that once one firm has become more successful in the bidding process, other firms either disappear or modify their bidding processes. One possibility is for competitors to simply subtract some amount from whatever bid is generated by their traditional processes. Another possibility is that they adopt a similar model. Such competitive reactions will modify the benefits of the bidding model and require adaptation.

Table 20.1 Competitive bidding model performance.

Situation	Bid without model	Bid with model	Lowest competitive bid	Bid without model: percent under (over) lowest competitive bid	Bid with model: percent under (over) lowest competitive bid
1	$44.53	$46.00	$46.49	4.2%	1.1%
2	47.36	43.68	42.93	(10.3)	(1.7)
3	62.73	59.04	60.76	(3.2)	2.8
4	47.72	51.05	53.38	10.6	4.4
5	50.18	42.80	44.16	(13.7)	3.1
6	60.39	54.61	55.10	(9.6)	0.9
7		39.73	40.47		1.8

Source: Edelman (1965).

2. New-product forecasting

The following example shows a somewhat different way of assessing the *value* of a model. It illustrates how validation can provide insight into how well a model represents reality.

In Section 10.2 we discuss the new-product forecasting model for durable consumer goods developed by Bass (1969b). The number of initial purchases at time t is a second degree equation in N_{t-1}, the cumulative number of initial purchases at time $t - 1$; see (10.18). The estimates of this relation are used to compute the total number of adopters ($\bar{N}$), the time of peak adoptions (t^*), the coefficients of innovation (p) and imitation (q), and the "peak sales" $N(t^*)$. We show actual and predicted sales in Figure 10.5.

One might conclude that the model provides accurate predictions. But in this example the sample data that were used to estimate model parameters include the time and magnitude of peak sales. The parameter estimates are then used to predict the time and magnitude of peak sales. Of course a model that accurately describes the phenomenon at hand should fit the observed data well. But a good fit to the same data used for parameter estimation is not a guarantee that the model will be valuable to the decision maker.

A real test is to examine whether the model predicts the time and magnitude of peak sales before these occur. Bass did this for color televisions. Based on sales of 0.7 (million) in 1963, 1.35 in 1964 and 2.50 in 1965, he predicted peak sales of 6.7 million in the U.S. in 1968. He found that these predictions of the time and magnitude of peak sales were quite accurate. Such predictions outside the sample data used for parameter estimation can provide true tests of a model's *value*.

3. *Optimal selection for direct mail*

An important issue for direct marketers is the selection of targets (households) for a direct mail campaign. Several methods have recently been advocated for the generation of more efficient selection procedures.[8] Bult and Wansbeek (1995) specify a profit function and, by setting marginal costs equal to marginal revenues, they determine which households should receive a mailing for the maximization of expected profit. They also show comparisons of their model with approaches such as CHi-square Automatic Interaction Detection (CH-AID)[9] and Gains Chart Analysis.

Historically, the most frequently used selection technique is a Recency, Frequency, and Monetary value (RFM) model. RFM-measures are used to classify households. Recency measures include the number of successive mailings since the previous response and the time since the previous response. Frequency measures include the number of purchases made in a certain time period. Monetary value is the amount of money spent during a specified period of time. The RFM-model allocates the values on each RFM-variable to distinct categories and assigns response probabilities to each category of each characteristic in accordance with observed *sample* behavior. Other households in the population who belong to the categories with the highest response probabilities are selected to receive a mailing.

CH-AID is an extension of the RFM model.[10] This method determines for every available characteristic the optimal split of the sample such that the within-group variance of the response is minimal. Given these splits, the method then selects the variable with the lowest within-group variance, and "the list" is subdivided according to this variable and its partition. The sublists so generated are analyzed in the same manner.

Gains chart analysis[11] is based on a three-stage procedure. First, the response in a target population to a previous test mailing is analyzed by means of multiple regression analysis. The household characteristics that predict response are identified and their impact is determined. In this first stage each member of the mailing list is given a propensity to respond to a future mailing. In the second stage, the population of households is ordered by this propensity. In the third stage, households are placed in groups of equal size, such that households with similar propensities are in the same group, and the average response per group is calculated. The graph that displays the relations between the ordered groups and the cumulative average response in these groups is the *gains chart*. The gains chart is used to determine the score level above which names are selected for the next mailing. This score level is known as the cutoff-level, the level at which one is indifferent between mailing and not mailing households.

Bult and Wansbeek (1995) advocate instead a profit maximization (PM) approach. They describe the relation between the response to a mailing and the fraction of

---

8. See, for example, Bult (1993a, 1993b), Wedel, DeSarbo, Bult, Ramaswamy (1993), Bult, Wansbeek (1995), Bult, Wittink (1996), Gönül, Shi (1998), van der Scheer (1998), Spring, Leeflang, Wansbeek (1999).
9. Kass (1976).
10. See Shepard (1990).
11. See Banslaben (1992).

Table 20.2 Net returns of three selection procedures.

| | Net returns | |
Procedure	Index	Profit (NLG)
CH-AID	81	95,025
Gains chart	100	117,761
PM	108	127,220

Source: Derived from Bult, Wansbeek (1995, p. 391).

people selected. Their approach is an improvement to the gains chart analysis because they analyze the response to a mailing and determine the optimal cutoff point at the *individual household* level. In their PM-approach the optimal cutoff point is obtained by equating marginal costs to marginal returns.

In an empirical application the CH-AID-approach, gains chart analysis and the PM-approach are compared in terms of net returns to a direct mail campaign. The sample data consist of 13,828 households targeted by a direct marketing company selling books, periodicals and music in the Netherlands. The criterion variable in this application is the response to a book offer. The data are divided in two parts of equal size: an analysis and a validation sample. The expected net returns for the total direct mail campaign, estimated by using the cutoff level of each of the three selection procedures, are given in Dutch guilders (NLG) and as an index, relative to the Gains chart, in Table 20.2.

The net returns are based on the validation sample and are projected to the total number of households in the "houselist" which is about 600,000. Table 20.2 shows that the PM-approach is expected to generate an extra profit of 9,459 Dutch guilders or an increase of 8 percent relative to the Gains chart analysis.

20.4 Some qualitative examples

The tradeoff between costs and benefits varies with a number of characteristics. We consider how the type of problem and the size of the firm, relative to the level of model detail may influence this tradeoff.

1. *The relation between the type of problem and the amount of behavioral detail*
First consider the problem of determining the marketing mix for an established product in a mature market. The models used for such problems typically do not have behavioral detail. Adding behavioral detail to these models may contribute little to the benefits. In fact the addition of detail might have a negative effect, because we are uncertain about the behavioral process that leads to a sale, and the input requirements are quite severe. Under some conditions it is conceivable that the positive difference

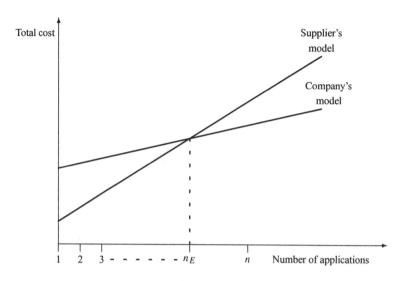

Figure 20.2 Total model cost as a function of the number of applications.

between benefits and costs is largest for models with no behavioral detail, for example models of aggregate data applicable to relatively homogeneous markets. Models of aggregate data require relatively modest costs. Yet their accuracy is high as long as the validity of conditional forecasts is not compromised. Since models of aggregate data cannot capture all relevant complexities of marketplace behavior, these models may show increasing discreprancies between forecasts and actual behavior as the marketing actions undertaken deviate more from the characteristics of sample data.

Now consider the development of an "early warning" system for a new product. In this case, the benefits from an aggregate response model are low because such models lack the detail and the dynamics relevant to a new-product situation. With more detail, the model should become more useful, up to a point. The ASSESSOR-model, a model with some behavioral detail, may be close to optimal from a cost-benefit point of view: it appears to provide accurate predictions and yet the model is not very complex nor excessively demanding for data collection. Importantly, an internet-based version of ASSESSOR, with three-dimensional displays of product displays can reduce the cost and increase the speed of data collection enormously.

2. The size of the firm and the amount of behavioral detail

Suppose the model under consideration is a new-product model. In the case of a single new product, fixed costs may be large if the firm builds the model and does not rent it. If the firm has multiple uses for a model, the total cost will rise less rapidly for a model built within the firm than for a model supplied from outside. We illustrate this idea in Figure 20.2. In this figure, if the number of model applications exceeds n_E, it pays for the firm to construct its own model. Multiple applications is typical for larger firms.

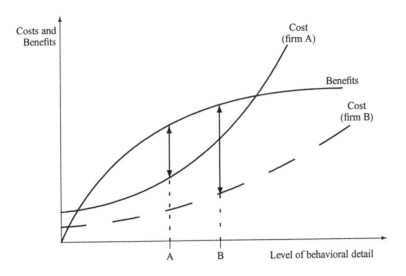

Figure 20.3 Costs and benefits for a large firm (firm B) and a small firm (firm A).

With regard to the amount of behavioral detail, consider two firms A and B. A is a small firm that introduces few new products per year (less than n_E in Figure 20.2). Company B is large and introduces more than n_E new products each year. For each product introduced, the cost curve for model use as a function of amount of behavioral detail should then be lower for B than for A, as illustrated in Figure 20.3. It follows that the optimal level of detail will be greater for large than for small firms. Similarly, for a firm with its own new-product model, the optimal level of detail increases as the number of model applications, i.e. the number of new-product introductions, increases.

Of course the decision whether to build or to rent a model also depends on other factors. While large firms can justify the cost of building a model much better than small firms can, it often is advantageous even for the largest firms to rent. The reason is that market research and consulting firms can apply a given model very frequently across a wide variety of conditions. Thus, the suppliers of new-product forecasting models can utilize this experience in any application. For example, the real-world successes of new products can be linked to predicted outcomes based on new-product model applications. The performance accuracy can be determined separately by type of product category, type of target market, etc. Only the outside suppliers of new-product services can generate the large databases that provide useful benchmarks. Thus, market research and consulting firms can validate a given model quickly and frequently. This opportunity also facilitates model adaptation both to characteristics that pertain to individual markets and to characteristics pertaining to a given market that change over time. In this manner model suppliers have an opportunity to understand contingencies and dependencies. In addition, since they have to convince many different audiences of the model's applicability, they also confront the model's strengths and weaknesses. Therefore even the largest firms tend to use outside suppliers for model-based forecasts of new-products.

For mature products, the models that provide estimates of promotional effects, such as SCAN*PRO (see Section 9.3) are also typically built by outside suppliers for similar reasons. However, there is an additional argument for models based on scanner data. The data collected from supermarkets, drugstores, mass merchandisers, etc. are purchased and controlled by a few market research suppliers. Since the market-level data used for tracking brand performance are less suitable for econometric modeling (Christen, Gupta, Porter, Staelin, Wittink, 1997), the modeling should be done on store or household-level data. However, these data are typically unavailable to manufacturers and retailers. Thus, the lack of suitable data makes it difficult or impossible for most firms to consider building a model inside the firm. Of course, larger firms should be able to obtain lower costs per application, in the form of quantity discounts.

20.5 General observations

The development of model building in marketing can be characterized as being in an era in which many models are actually implemented (4th era, see Section 1.1) with an increase in routinized model applications (5th era). Hence the diffusion process of model adoption appears to proceed successfully. Nevertheless, the implementation processes do not not always occur without resistance or fierce debate. The question of why models are *not* used in certain instances was addressed by Little (1970) as follows:[12]

- good models are hard to find;
- good parameterization is even harder;
- managers do not understand models;
- most models are incomplete.

Little's concept of a decision calculus, and his specification of criteria that a model must satisfy for it to be labelled a decision-calculus model, have contributed to the acceptance of models in marketing. In the past thirty years we have seen a high amount of productivity by model builders who develop models that tend to satisfy the implementation criteria. Still many problems remain, and model building in marketing has its limitations. Some consultants and managers also criticize marketing science for a lack of practical relevance. For example, Simon (1984, 1994) maintains that:

> "marketing science contributes virtually nothing to the important strategic issues of our era"
> (Simon, 1994, p. 41),

and

---

12. See also Section 1.1

"the practical significance of marketing science has remained very limited"
(Simon, 1994, p.40).

The premises underlying these criticisms are:

- market response functions are not regular;
- past data are not very useful for making practical marketing decisions, and
- marketing science does not use qualitative (judgmental) input.

Simon (1994, p.36) also maintains that there is a lack of closeness to the real world in the empirical studies. For example, he argues that the set of products in empirical studies is not representative of economic reality. Published empirical studies emphasize marketing mix effects relevant to frequently bought consumer goods such as coffee. In the face of this 'distortion' of reality, Simon (1994, p.36) talks about "coffee marketing science".

We discuss these limitations of marketing science below.[13]

Regularity

Despite being sensitive to unusual patterns of behavior, which may arise from a catastrophe experienced by a brand,[14] we find the marketplace surprisingly well behaved, at least from our perspective as builders of market response models. We do occasionally encounter irregularities but there are many possibilities to accommodate them.

Catastrophe theory models can capture complex behavior with nonlinear equations.[15] The same holds for the intervention models introduced in Section 17.3. Recently, contributions have been made to the modeling of structural breaks.[16] The tests and models to detect and specify breaks also offer opportunities to account for irregularities.

Other methods that can be used to estimate nonregular curves are:

1. splines and spline-transformations;[17]
2. maximum likelihood methods (Section 16.6);
3. nonparametric- and semiparametric estimation methods (Section 16.7).

Past Data

Most managers would agree that their marketing actions have consequences in periods
beyond the period in which they are taken. Consequently, time-series data, that is,

---

13. Our discussion is based on Parsons, Gijsbrechts, Leeflang, Wittink (1994) who commented on Simon's (1994) 'Marketing Science's Pilgrimage to the Ivory Tower'. Another comment is Little, Lodish, Hauser, Urban (1994).
14. See, for example, Section 17.3.
15. See Oliva, Oliver, MacMillan (1992).
16. See, for example, Bai, Perron (1998).
17. For an application in marketing, see Wedel, Leeflang (1998)

historical data, are *necessary* to identify marketing dynamics. Of course, we must be concerned about a model's applicability to future periods. Models must be adapted to changing circumstances. And we have to know whether a model only applies to the range of data observed in the past, or whether it is also applicable to operating values outside this observed range. A major disruption in the marketplace, such as the entry of a new competitor, may invalidate an estimated relation. Importantly, the application of marketing science to historical data provides managers with a reference point that forms an objective basis for adjustment. The idea that past data are not useful for making practical decisions is widespread. Lucas (1976) has forcefully argued that the parameters of an economic model may not remain constant in the face of policy changes in the presence of rational expectations. This proposition is known as the Lucas critique, and it has potentially devastating implications for the formulation of economic policy (and marketing policy) based on parameters estimated from past data.

Despite the appeal of the Lucas critique, a more pragmatic approach to the use of econometric relations for policy evaluation should still be valid. Sims (1980), for instance, argues that unless policy changes are major and wide-ranging, the effects of the Lucas critique may be limited, as the dynamics of the model will still in part be determined by nonpolicy parameters. Also, in some cases the direction in which changes in marketing policy are likely to alter parameter values can be addressed in advance.[18] In those cases, the parameters estimated from past data may provide upper and lower bounds around future levels. To the extent that parameters change systematically and predictably, models with varying parameters, such as those discussed in Section 17.4, will be useful. Entirely new modeling approaches are required, however, when consumers modify their behavior dramatically in response to policy changes.

Judgmental data
If market data are not available to estimate a model, marketing scientists may use managerial judgments. We discussed this issue in detail in Section 16.9. This approach may represent the best one can do given the lack of suitable marketplace data. However, this assumes that managers understand systematic patterns captured by marginal effects. Often, we prefer to use historical data to obtain a proper basis for an initial understanding of how the market works. If alternative scenarios under consideration involve substantial risks, and there is sufficient time, field experimentation may provide further support. If there is insufficient time or the maintenance of secrecy is paramount, the initial estimates can be updated with judgmental inputs. It is also possible for managers to use procedures analogous to those used in pretest market models such as ASSESSOR.

We conclude that:

1. market reponse functions are often regular;
2. past data are useful for making many practical marketing decisions;

---

18. Compare, for example, Assunção and Meyer (1993).

3. marketing science can and does use qualitative (judgmental) input.

Lack of closeness

Simon (1994) argues that the practical significance of marketing science is limited and that too many problems of minor practical relevance are treated with sophisticated methods in published papers. Also, only a small number of empirical studies represent the industrial and service sectors. Below we provide counter arguments, and we demonstrate the managerial relevance of marketing science.[19]

Marketing recipients of the Franz Edelman Award for Management Science Achievement convincingly demonstrate the managerial relevance and benefits of marketing science in *real-life applications*. The Edelman competition is sponsored by INFORMS and its College on the Practice of Management Science. With the award, the organization recognizes achievement in the practice of management science in the real world by focusing on work that has been implemented and has had significant impact on the target organization. The first prize in 1988 was awarded for a series of decision-calculus models developed for and implemented by Syntex Laboratories, a pharmaceutical company best known for its birth control pills. The models helped decide how large its sales force should be and how the members should be deployed (Lodish, Curtiss, Ness and Simpson, 1988). In part the work is based on CALLPLAN (Lodish, 1971), which was applied and refined over a 20-year period. The response functions of the model were estimated from subjective judgments provided by a team of knowledgeable managers and sales people.[20] These response functions were shown to give significantly better sales forecasts of each Syntex product for two years in the future than were the existing forecasts. The model and its output helped persuade Syntex management to greatly increase the size of its sales force and to redeploy it. The result of this change was a documented eight percent annual sales increase of 25 million dollars, which more than offset the incremental cost from increasing (and reorganizing) the sales force. The model was judged to have an important impact on the strategic direction of the firm by helping management to focus on marketing products with high potential.

A second-place winner in 1989 is a hybrid conjoint analysis and choice simulation for the design of a new hotel chain for the Marriott Corporation (Wind, Green, Shifflet, Scarbrough, 1989). The authors used a variety of other analyses, such as multidimensional scaling and cluster analysis, as well. They employed econometric techniques, such as dummy variable regression and ordinary and generalized least squares regression, at various stages to estimate model parameters. The study provided specific guidelines to Marriot for selecting target market segments, positioning services, and designing improved facilities in terms of physical layout and service characteristics. The result was Courtyard by Marriott. This new chain became the fastest growing moderately priced hotel chain in the United States with more than 100 hotels opened in about five years, and planned growth to 300 hotels in about ten

---

19. We closely follow Parsons et al. (1994).
20. See LaForge, Lamb, Cravens, Moncrief (1989).

years. The actual market share of Courtyard by Marriott was within four percent of the share predicted by the conjoint simulation.

The first-place winner in 1990 is a multiattribute choice model for determining product attributes desired by customers and for segmenting the market (Gensch, Aversa, Moore, 1990). ABB Electric was formed about 20 years ago, with capital from ASEA-AB Sweden and the RTE Corporation, to design and manufacture power transformers for the North American market. Just when this start-up was approaching the break-even point in its third year of existence, it was confronted with a 50 percent drop in total industry sales of electrical equipment. Consequently ABB's survival depended on taking customers away from established major competitors. In response, the firm developed a marketing information system based on multiattribute choice modeling that identified the current customers' perceptions of ABB's products versus various competitors' products. ABB used information on what customers want most from products to devise strategies for taking customers and market segments from competitors. The multinomial logit model's output enabled ABB to identify an opportunity to be the low-cost producer. The information also guided ABB in selecting new products that customers preferred and for which it had long-term cost advantages. ABB not only survived but it has grown to become the dominant firm in the industry with a dollar market share of 40 percent. In a statement at a 1988 board of directors meeting, ABB Electric's president said:

> *"Without the insights from our marketing models, it is unlikely we would have current sales of $25 million; in fact, without the use of these models, it is unlikely we would be here at all"*   (Gensch, Aversa and Moore, 1990, p. 18).

These perspectives were provided at a time when actual sales were more than $100 million.

Other practical examples of excellence in marketing science are described in the case histories of the winners of the Advertising Effectiveness Awards administered by the Institute of Practitioners in Advertising (IPA) (Broadbent, 1981, 1983, Channon, 1985, 1987, Feldwick, 1990, 1991). The objectives of these IPA Awards are:

- to demonstrate that advertising can be shown to work on measurable criteria, and to show that it is both a serious commercial investment and a contributor to profit;
- through this demonstration to improve understanding of the crucial role advertising plays in marketing generally as well as in specific applications;
- to achieve a closer analysis of advertising effectiveness and improved methods of evaluation.

Award categories include established consumer goods and services, new consumer goods and services, and small budgets. Marketing science - in particular econometrics - plays a key role in many IPA award-winning papers. While our previous examples relied heavily on subjective judgments or primary data collection, many of the IPA papers and the insights they provide are based on objective historical information on sales and advertising efforts. Examples of brands in the more recent IPA competition demonstrating advertising effectiveness by application of econometrics include

Karvo (decongestant capsules), Knorr Stock Cubes (soup stock), and PG Tips (tea) (Feldwick, 1991). Concerned that the awards may be too focused on short-run returns, the IPA created a new "broader and longer effects" category to highlight the longer term or indirect effects of advertising.

This book contains many other examples of models that demonstrate the managerial relevance of marketing science.

- We discuss ASSESSOR in Section 10.2. Urban and Katz report in 1983 that this pre-test-market evaluation model has been used to evaluate more than 200 products in more than 50 organizations.
- We discuss the SCAN*PRO model in various sections of this book. Commercial applications of this model focus on differences in effects between regions, retail outlets, and retail chains, and on asymmetries in own-brand effects and cross-brand effects (Blattberg, Wisniewski, 1989). Brand managers can use information about the effects of different promotional activities (such as display, feature advertisements, and temporary price cuts) to allocate trade promotion expenditures. Managers can use the estimated effects as a partial basis to reconsider direct retailer payments for display or feature activities or to modify off-invoice discounts that may be passed through by the retailer in the form of temporary price cuts. A conservative estimate is that SCAN*PRO has been used in 2,000 different commercial applications. It can be applied separately, for example, by geographic market (Nielsen distinguishes approximately 65 regions in the United States), by type of retail outlet (food stores, drug stores, food/drug combination stores, mass merchandise stores), and by retail chain. One extensive application involved data on 10 products for 2,670 stores and 104 weeks, or almost 3 million data points. SCAN*PRO applications tend to be issue driven. The client provides a description of well-defined managerial issues that can be addressed with an econometric model estimated from available data. The service is available in North America and in many European and Asian countries. SCAN*PRO results are reported to have had a substantial influence on the behavior of brand managers and sales-force personnel in terms of allocation of money, time, and effort to regions, outlets and marketing programs.
- PROMOTIONSCAN is an implemented model and automated system for measuring short-term incremental volume due to promotions by developing baselines or store-level "normal" sales using store-level scanner data (Abraham and Lodish, 1992). About 2,700 stores are in the data base. At least half of all major packaged goods marketers in the US have used PROMOTIONSCAN information. Abraham and Lodish discuss one case history, that of Conagra Corporation.

The SCAN*PRO and PROMOTIONSCAN models used by ACNielsen and IRI, and variations of those models, have made it clear that, in general, the temporary price cuts offered by retailers on selected items have very strong short-term sales effects. Detailed analyses of those effects have also shown that most of the time, the promotions are not profitable for the manufacturer. Thus, even if the potentially negative long-term effects (Mela, Gupta, Lehmann, 1997) are not explicitly taken into account, and even if the negative supply-chain effects are excluded, the passthrough of trade promotions by retailers does not generate sufficient incremental sales, on average, to make the promotion profitable. However, despite this finding, manufacturers are reluctant to decrease promotional spending. The primary reasons are:

1. retailers threaten to reduce shelf space, as Procter & Gamble learned when the firm decided to introduce an EDLP (Every Day Low Price) strategy, and
2. other manufacturers either increase or maintain promotional spending, as Procter & Gamble also learned.

On the other hand, when manufacturers found that coupons for mature brands typically are also unprofitable, they encountered a much more sympathetic distribution channel. Retailers find the coupons to be more of a nuisance than a profitable activity, so the desire by Procter & Gamble and other manufacturers to reduce coupon activity was met by very sympathetic retailers. Due to insights provided by scanner-based models, several manufacturers have reduced the distribution of coupons for mature brands by some fifty percent.

Other frequently used applications of marketing models are:

1. models developed for public policy purposes,[21] and
2. models for market structure analysis.

Market structure analysis has been used to guide marketing strategies.[22] Many commercial analyses have been performed for many different markets. Few examples are published however, because these and many other marketing science efforts are proprietary.

Econometric modeling is an important activity in the telecommunications industry. When the companies test personal communication services, video delivery services, and other services, they do econometric or statistical analyses of the trial data. Econometric models of the demand for telecommunication services and the resulting price elasticity estimates are key inputs for rate and new-product-introduction decisions. The companies use a variety of models including discrete choice models and time-series models. GTE Laboratories, for example, has an econometrician on staff who provides technical support on demand- and cost-modeling issues to GTE Laboratories Telephone Operations and GTE Directories, two of GTE Corporation's strategic business units. It is well known that GTE's competitors use similar models. Bolton has completed studies that link the demand for cellular service to customer satisfaction measures and internal company measures describing service attributes.[23] The telecommunication firms also find diffusion models to be valuable.

The public record of applied marketing science studies is scarce because, as Neslin (1992) notes, the econometrics needed for applications are often at an elementary

---

21. See, for example, Luik, Waterson (1996).
22. See Shocker, Stewart, Zahorik (1990).
23. See, for example, Bolton, Lemon (1999).

level which would not constitute a contribution to the literature. From an industry perspective, Broadbent (1983, p.4) argues:

"though we would welcome improved methods, in practice it is normally better to use tried and trusted methods."

Another reason for a lack of contribution to the published literature is that marketing managers have little time and usually have nothing to gain from writing about projects for external consumption. Thus, it is not surprising that most of the applications described in scientific journals illustrate methodological innovations and are written by academic scholars. Ideally, any such application should make a substantive contribution as well. In any event new techniques are tested over time, and the best become tried and trusted methods.

We conclude that:

- marketing science models are not restricted to frequently bought nondurable consumer goods;
- marketing science has impact on management decisions;
- marketing science contributes to the resolution of strategic planning issues, competitive strategy questions and public policy problems.

CHAPTER 21

Models for marketing decisions in the future

In this chapter we concentrate on developments that may influence the nature of model building and the use of models for marketing decisions in the future. In Section 21.1 we give examples of recent changes in the *practice of model building* and in the *nature of academic research*.

Then, in Section 21.2 we revisit the role of models in *marketing decisions* and suggest that empirical results should be communicated throughout the organization. We also discuss the benefits of continuous efforts to test model predictions, conditional upon marketing decisions, against real-world outcomes.

In Section 21.3 we provide a *broader framework* in which we propose that data collection start at the household level, includes relevant purchases in *all* outlets, unlike the prevailing situation in which data analysis and model building are often restricted to scanned purchases. Also model building will combine data on household needs, household purchases, household satisfaction levels (with the purchase and with the consumption) and household intent to repurchase as well as intent to communicate with others (word-of-mouth).

The customer will have a more pivotal role on future markets. This has consequences to the composition of the marketing mix and to model building in the future, as we discuss in Section 21.3.

21.1 Examples of recent developments in model building

The practice of model-based marketing decisions is heavily influenced by the research conducted at ACNielsen and IRI. To a large extent these two firms control the *data collected* at the household-and store-levels. Some clients obtain weekly tracking reports that show the performances and marketing activities for individual items *aggregated across stores*, but use other service providers for model building. Since stores tend to differ in marketing activities the use of aggregated market-level data not only covers up store differences (Hoch, Kim, Montgomery, Rossi, 1995) but can also distort the estimation of average marketing effects (Christen, Gupta, Porter, Staelin and Wittink, 1997).

The store-level data show similar performances and activities aggregated across the households visiting a given store. Here the aggregation is far less harmful for model building, because households visiting a given store are exposed to the same marketing activities within a given week. However, the typical store-level model does not accommodate heterogeneity in household preferences and in sensitivities to marketing instruments. Some current academic research includes attempts to not only accommodate but also to recover household heterogeneity from store-level data (e.g. Bodapati and Gupta, 1999). To the extent that household data are "representative"(see e.g. Leeflang, Olivier, 1985, Gupta, Chintagunta, Kaul, Wittink, 1996), these disaggregate data provide the best opportunities for managers to obtain a complete understanding of marketplace complexities in stores equipped with scanners. Of particular interest to managers are models that explain purchase incidence, brand choice and quantity decisions at the household level. For managers these models provide substantively meaningful results about, for example, the proportion of the increase in purchases of a given item due to promotions of the item that is attributable to brand switching, acceleration in purchase timing and increases in purchase quantities (e.g. Gupta, 1988, Bell, Chiang, Padmanabhan, 1997, 1999).

We believe that both household- and store-level data can provide meaningful insights about marketing phenomena. An important advantage associated with household data is that household heterogeneity can be fully exploited. On the other hand, for relatively infrequently purchased goods, household data are often insufficient due to sparseness. In addition, while the representativeness of household data appears to be acceptable for selected small cities in which a cooperating household uses the same plastic card in all supermarkets (Gupta, Chintagunta, Kaul, Wittink, 1996), there is considerable doubt about the representativeness in metropolitan areas. In those areas a system of plastic cards cannot cover all the outlets the households frequent, while a system of personal wands may or may not be appealing to households.[1]

These conflicting considerations suggests that managers will benefit most from models that *combine* household-and store data. Promising examples of joint usage of multiple data sources include Russell and Kamakura (1994). We discussed their model briefly in Section 14.1.2.

During the 1980's and 1990's, largely due to the adoption of scanner equipment by supermarkets, much of the academic research was focused on the effects of promotional activities. Guadagni and Little (1983)'s paper on the analysis of household purchase data is a classic. Little also advanced the use of models for the determination of incremental purchases and profitability resulting from (manufacturer) coupons, while Lodish has examined the profitability of trade promotions. The evidence appears to indicate quite strongly that most promotions for mature products are unprofitable. Mela and his associates have provided the initial results with regard to the long-term impact of promotions.[2] Their results suggest that households'

---

1. See also van Heerde (1999, p. 20).
2. See Mela, Gupta, Lehmann (1997), Mela, Gupta, Jedidi (1998), Jedidi, Mela, Gupta (1999). See also Dekimpe, Hanssens (1999), Dekimpe, Hanssens, Silva-Risso (1999), Franses, Kloek, Lucas (1999).

price sensitivities increase and brand equities erode, with increases in promotional expenditures.

These empirical findings should influence managers to rethink the allocation of marketing expenditures to various instruments. Indeed, we predict that the percent allocated to promotions will be reduced substantially, perhaps to the levels prevailing in the 1970's. Of course, there are other developments that also influence the budget allocation, as we discuss in Section 21.3.

The availability of scanner data has a tremendous effect on the opportunities for model *specification*. In the first three eras of model building in marketing (Section 1.1) the emphasis is on models for a single brand specified at the brand level. In the fourth and fifth era we see models specified at the SKU-level, covering multiple own- and other-brand items, where competition is defined at the product category level and sometimes covers multiple product categories. In the eighties we have seen an important shift in attention from just the demand to the demand function and the competitive reaction (Chapter 11). We now see an increasing attention for empirical game-theoretic models with an emphasis on horizontal competition (Section 11.4). Also there are studies on cooperation and vertical competition in the channel.[3] Examples of the latter are studies on the competition between marketing and retailing (Balasubramanian, 1998) guaranteed profit power (Krishnan, Soni, 1997) manufacturers' returns policies (Padmanabhan, Png, 1997), and manufacturer allowances and retailer-pass-through rates (Kim, Staelin, 1999). Many of these studies do not include (yet), empirical validations. Other studies consider satisfaction in marketing channel relationships (Geyskens, Steenkamp, Kumar, 1999) and interdependencies/relationships between channel partners (Kumar, Scheer, Steenkamp, 1995a, 1995b).

The phenomenon of shifts in power from manufacturers to retailers in many channels is the focus of much discussion and debate amongst marketing academicians and practitioners. This shift in power is also reflected in the construction of models specified at the retail chain- and individual store level where we also see models for *"micro marketing"* (Montgomery, 1997). We return to these developments in Section 21.3. We also expect other shifts in attention such as:

• from models for products toward the development of models for services;
• from models covering "metropolitan areas", regions and countries to models for international marketing activities;
• from tactical decisions to strategic decisions.

Models of scanner data have provided useful insights about, say, the average effectiveness of various marketing programs. Increasingly sophisticated models and estimation methods also allow managers to adjust the details of individual activities. For example, researchers have used *nonparametric* estimation methods to allow the *functional form* of the relation between variables to be completely determined by

---

3. See also Section 11.4.

the data. The curves so obtained often show dramatically different nonlinear effects than those implied by parametric estimation of models with transformed variables. Van Heerde, Leeflang and Wittink (1999a) find that the deal effect curve tends to be S-shaped. For many of the items analyzed, they find that temporary price discounts of less than 10 percent have little impact on sales (threshold effects). Above, say, 10 percent the impact increases rapidly and it levels off after perhaps 25 percent (saturation effects). While the data show that the percent discounts occur over this entire range, these results suggest that discounts of less than 10 percent and more than 25 percent are often not efficient.

To consider the profitability of temporary price discounts, it is also important for model builders to distinguish between the sources of sales increases. Broadly speaking, the primary sources are brand switching (e.g. households purchasing a promoted item when otherwise they would have chosen their regular brand), purchase acceleration (e.g. households purchasing larger quantities of an item or purchasing earlier than they would have in the absence of a promotion) and category expansion (e.g. households purchasing a promoted item in a product category from which they would otherwise not have purchased). These source(s) of sales increases differ in attractiveness to manufacturers and retailers. Thus, models of household- as well as of store-data should provide insight about the role of each possible source in purchase behavior. A model which provides answers to these questions, based on store data, has been developed by van Heerde, Leeflang and Wittink (1999b).

Household data are uniquely suitable for the identification of distinctions between households in terms of, for example, brand preferences, loyalty and switching behavior, incidence and brand choice sensitivities to marketing activities, etc. Indeed, it is clear that the 21st century is the century in which, largely through technological means, households will be increasingly exposed to individualized marketing programs. We discuss the role of models in this new environment in Section 21.3.

21.2 The role of models in management decisions

We discuss in Sections 15.2 and 16.9 the unique advantages of human judgment versus the advantages of models in (management) decisions. If all managers were familiar with these arguments and accepted the implications, we would see a much greater demand for model-building services. Managers are skeptical of models because:

1. they (may) believe that the use of models imposes constraints on their decision-making authority;
2. they believe that marketing is an art and that models provide inappropriately precise results; and/or
3. they have used a model once which promised far more than it could deliver.

Other arguments are discussed in Chapter 19.

Model acceptance will be facilitated if model builders can present convincing arguments why certain marketing decisions will improve with a model. In addition, having access to applications that demonstrate how other managers obtained substantial benefits will be critical to potential users. Even if the model builder is successful on these two aspects, it is important to show that the essence of certain, repetitive decisions can be captured effectively. Examples of marketing decisions appropriate for automation are assortment decisions, customized product offerings, coupon targeting, budget allocation, inventory decisions, etc.[4]. If the manager understands that statistical analyses of historical data can provide more valid insights than is possible from inspection of the data, then an additional argument is that the manager will have more time for creative and other tasks for which models are not suitable.

Resistance to model acceptance is likely to occur if the manager does not have at least a strong conceptual understanding of the model characteristics. Thus, the manager should know what a model does and does not cover with respect to the complex relations in the real world. Much of this understanding can be obtained from "what if" questions. That is, the manager should have the opportunity to use a computer, submit marketing program details, and find out what the model predicts will be the market behavior. The manager should find that all conditional predictions are reasonable. The model builder should be able to explain the logic of all results.

Once the model is completed, resistance to acceptance can be overcome if the manager is willing to play against the model. Each time a decision is made for which the outcome can be predicted by the model, the manager can record his/her forecast, and subsequently the accuracy of the manager's prediction can be compared against the model's. Obviously if this process is repeated, reliable comparisons can be made.

Once a model is in use, it is important to continue to check the accuracy of conditional predictions. These accuracies can be compared with what would be expected based on (initial) model estimation and testing. In addition, the forecast accuracies can be tracked over time against various conditions, etc. This tracking provides the model builder with an opportunity to identify the weakest aspects in the model.

In this sense, continuous tracking provides the model builder with a basis for deciding whether, for example, the model misses important components and needs to be respecified or whether, say, the parameters need to be updated periodically. In the former case the magnitudes of prediction errors may vary likely while in the latter case the magnitudes are likely to increase over time.

Assuming that confidentially issues are manageable, we believe it is useful for some model details to be communicated throughout the organization. Doing this will encourage others to consider opportunities for model building. In addition, it should provoke a broader discussion about the relevance of model components, about the nature of relations, and about the benefits to be obtained from marketing decisions. Importantly, when actual results turn out to be very different from the predictions, there will be a broader group of individuals who can provide "reasons why". And of

---

4. See Section 1.1 and Bucklin, Lehmann, Little (1998).

course if the marketing decisions are based on models that ignore how other parts of the organization are affected (such as the negative impact of promotional programs on production and logistics), the managers of those parts will be alerted. They can then argue for the inclusion of additional elements in a more inclusive model. We discuss the tendency to develop more "integrated", more "global", models in Chapter 19.[5]

21.3 A broader framework

There are major developments taking place in business as the end of the millennium approaches. For marketing the most critical one is the focus on (individual) customers. Computer hardware and software make it feasible for firms to examine the purchase behavior of individual households. Strategic consulting companies have reclaimed the 80/20 rule. For example, for many firms it appears that 20 percent of the customers account for 80 percent of the profits. The new element in the strategic frameworks used by consultants and managers is the customer (consumer).

Among recent empirical findings are that repeat purchase behavior is nonlinearly related to satisfaction. For example, when Xerox used a 5-point scale to measure customer satisfaction, respondents who gave Xerox a 5 (very satisfied) were six times more likely to repurchase than respondents who scored a 4 (satisfied). Separately, research results across various firms indicate that it is a lot cheaper to serve existing customers than it is to attract and serve new customers. In addition, loyal (existing) customers typically are less price sensitive than non-loyal customers. Although these results are not sufficient for management to decide how to distinguish between, say, loyals and switchers, this question is of great interest to both economists and marketing researchers.

Traditionally marketing has been about offering products and services communicated, distributed and priced in a manner that fits a target market's preferences and that allows a firm to maximize profits. However the shift in focus from products (and brand managers) to customers (and customer managers) implies that firms will now focus explicitly on the profitability of individual customers. Thus, a firm will select those customers for whom it can offer products and services better than other firms can, with whom it can develop long-term relations in such a way that each customer is expected to contribute to the firm's profits. These ideas are part of "new marketing frameworks". For example, Hoekstra, Leeflang and Wittink (1999) argue that (marketing) strategy should pursue the realization of superior customer values, and that business objectives should be stated in terms of the customer (e.g. customer satisfaction, customer retention). They call this "the customer concept".

We show a simple framework that reflects the critical role the customer plays in Figure 21.1. In this framework we assume the customer is a household, but it is straightforward to substitute any other consumption unit. We propose that a firm

---

5. See for an example, Hausman and Montgomery (1997). Their study refers to issues in "market-driven manufacturing".

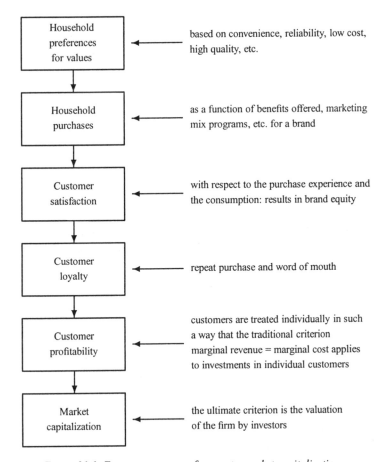

Figure 21.1 From consumer preference to market capitalization.

identifies meaningful customer values that it can satisfy better than other firms can (re: core competencies). The closer it can come to offering exactly what each individual household prefers (including where it can be obtained, how the benefits are perceived and what the price is), the more likely the household will be satisfied with the purchase and the consumption or use. High degrees of satisfaction will lead to customer loyalty, and as long as the financial considerations are appropriately considered, each customer is profitable (in an expected value sense). Of course, under certain conditions, some customers may contribute positively to profits only in the influence they have on other customers. Thus, in the same way that managers now focus on the profitability of goals at the category- instead of the brand- level, in the future the focus may shift from treating each customer independently to explicitly taking dependencies between customers into account. This requires a continuous, customer-oriented feedback system.[6] The monitoring system will concentrate on marketplace

6. We closely follow Hoekstra, Leeflang, Wittink (1999).

purchase behavior integrated with survey data. Customer managers should know not only what customers are purchasing (and why), but also how satisfied they are with the purchases made, with the interactions that occurred, and what unmet needs remain. In addition, customers should be categorized according to expected lifetime value. Ideally, the contact between the firm and the customer occurs continuously, in both directions, but in a manner that suits both parties.

A pitfall of current information systems about marketplace behavior in consumer goods markets is that the data emphasize the performance of own- and selected other brands. Consider the reporting systems designed by ACNielsen and IRI. Clients obtain on a regular basis (e.g. weekly) information about unit sales, dollar sales, average price, average promotion, average distribution, etc. for a subset of the items in a product category. Typically, client management chooses the subset of items on which information is made available. This subset is changed infrequently. Thus, client management observes marketplace behavior for a narrowly defined set of items that tends to be stable over time.

Such a reporting system provides highly reliable feedback from the marketplace. But it is product-oriented and it encourages the user to make direct comparisons against current competitors. Unit (or dollar) market shares also tend to be reported, consistent with an emphasis on relative measures. Such data may be acceptable if the objective of the firm is stated in terms of market share. It is clear, however, that existing purchase reporting system exclude activities that occur outside a narrowly defined set of items (re: the discussion about market boundaries in Section 14.3). Yet it appears that many firms have adopted information systems that encourage the user to engage in myopic behavior. Consider, for example, the advent of Starbuck's coffee. Not only did two highly regarded marketing firms, General Foods (GF) and Procter & Gamble (P&G), miss the new-product opportunity that Starbuck created, but the information system on the coffee market excluded the growth of Starbuck's and the behavior of its customers. Thus, GF and P&G may have emphasized their marketplace successes or failures relative to each other, due to an information system based on a priori defined market boundaries (the set of relevant competitors and the set of distribution channels), while Starbuck's pursued attractive options not covered by this system.

We propose, therefore, that the highly developed information systems that play a large role in consumer-goods industries be modified, so that consumer purchase behavior, consumer preferences and customer satisfaction become transparent. Currently, even if a firm does a substantial amount of consumer research, this consumer research is almost always ad hoc, and subject to both reliability and validity concerns. Thus, even if the total expenditures for such consumer research were equal to the expenditures for consumers' purchase data, we hypothesize that the impact of ad hoc research on marketing decisions is far less than proportional. A continuous, customer oriented feedback system that incorporates purchase behavior, customer satisfaction measurement and surveys of unmet needs, will allow soft data to have a greater influence, because of its continuity and regularity, as well as its known reliability and validity (and use in all organizational layers).

We imagine that firms select the target customers they want to serve, and the *information system* be *based* directly on data from these individual customers. With newly developed household-based technologies, it is possible for both ACNielsen and IRI to provide information at the household level. Of course, to the extent that the existing technology is restricted to a subset of channels, an expansion to a complete set e.g. through survey data is required. A system is needed that covers supermarkets, drugstores, mass merchandisers, etc. through convenient, relatively unobstrusive, plastic cards and/or wands. This system must also accommodate non-conventional outlets. For example in the case of coffee, purchases in cafes and restaurants, and consumption in businesses, institutions, airlines, etc., need to be included. It will then be possible to learn at the individual household level the share of category purchases accounted for by specific items (the "share of customer"). These household data can be aggregated in flexible ways, to obtain, for example, average household share by a variety of classifications. Importantly, such an information system will also facilitate the determination of net contribution per customer. In this manner the proposed system allows management to modify the set of customers to be served and to adapt marketing activities based on customers' actual or potential net contribution to profits.

It is a natural extension of this proposed system to not only provide the "score" at much more disaggregated levels than before (focused on the consumer rather than on the product), but also to provide "explanations" of the score and conditional forecasts of future "scores".

The adoption of a framework as Figure 21.1 implies, a.o., that many organizational functions need to receive relevant customer information. Managers responsible for marketing, production and other decisions need to know the "score" (e.g. share of customer expenditures) but also need to have access to the appropriate diagnostic information (e.g. *explanations* of purchase, satisfaction and preference data). Through direct clienting routines, employees can have real-time insight into customer profiles.

The last issue implies that firms may use approaches such as conjoint analysis (Green and Srinivasan, 1990, Wittink, Vriens and Burhenne, 1994) to quantify the tradeoffs households make between *alternative* benefits. However, the survey data collected for the quantification of household preferences will be collected on a regular basis (Wittink and Keil, 2000) and will be integrated with the purchase data. Currently, many firms only track household purchases (typically at aggregate levels), and to a lesser extent customer satisfaction data, on a regular basis.

By integrating these different data sources[7] managers will be in a much better position to consider new-product opportunities. Importantly, with the appropriate sets of models, managers can contemplate changes in the marketing mix at the individual household level that can be expected to enhance profitability and market capitalization. Thus, the challenge for model builders is to develop ways in which the appropriate relations can be developed at the individual level including profit implications.

---

7. See, for an example, Verhoef, Franses, Hoekstra (1999).

Adopting a pivotal role to the customers also has consequences for the *composition of the future marketing mix*. Marketing decisions will have to reflect, more then is currently the case, the interests of customers.[8] Consider how the joint efforts of manufacturers and grocery retailers have influenced how consumers are guided through the stores. Many aspects are arranged to entice the consumer to expend sums of money to the retailers' advantage. While it is possible for consumers to develop and maintain idiosyncratic choice rules, the manufacturer creates products, packages, package sizes and variations that can overwhelm the consumers' decision-making process. The retailer compounds the consumer's problem by, for example, giving preference in shelf-space management to items with favorable retailer margins. And both manufacturer and retailer offer a range of different kinds of promotions. For most consumers, the result is a myriad of aspects that together make it very difficult for each consumer to make optimal purchases, given consumer heterogeneity in utility functions.

Electronic home shopping should allow consumers to specify criteria (e.g. lowest unit price, selected ingredients) on which each consumer wants the selections to be made. Such an innovation will allow consumers to maximize their utility functions much more closely than ever before. Customized marketing programs can be created to help customers achieve utility maximization. For both manufacturers and retailers it will become critical to incorporate this new reality into future marketing decisions. We note that new communication media (e.g. the Internet) accelerate the diffusion of insights gained by individual consumers about the potential to realize gains in utility. Alternatively, new services will be created to help consumers maximize their objective functions. We now briefly discuss the consequences of adopting a more central role of the customer for the set of marketing instruments.

We imagine that customer-research-based new *product* or service development will be facilitated by the proposed information system. Management will have simultaneous access to consumer marketplace choice data and survey data. Diagnostic information will be available for "what if" questions, and the customer monitoring system includes actions by new competitors reflected in customer purchases from the very beginning. To accomplish this, supplemental information, for example through distribution outlets not commonly included in data collection, will have to be gathered.

New-product or service development will be a continuous process. Customers either volunteer new product ideas or respond to requests for information based on changes in customers' marketplace choices. Continuous customer-based new-product development is a natural consequence. A high-variety product line enables the customer to select the customized option he or she desires (Kahn, 1998). Under the customer concept decision making is pro-active not reactive.

Production may be on a just-in-time basis, and may not take place without an order. The customer defines quality. Customers buy benefits, not products. Therefore, services are added to the core product. Webster (1994) states that customer expectation revolve around the service aspects of the product offering, and that information

---

8. We follow Hoekstra, Leeflang, Wittink (1999).

can turn any product into a service and, thereby, build a customer relationship.

Full exploitation of consumer heterogeneity also allows for further distinction in *prices*, based on willingness to pay and based on differences in the service-enhanced product.

Just-in-time advertising and promotion define the *promotion* mix under the new marketing paradigm. Promotion and commercial messages will be tailored to specific needs. Messages will be "narrow-casted", and accessed by customers at the time of need.

Classical media may be used to invite interaction, but the focus will be on customer-initiated selection of information. There are always possibilities for the customer to contact the organization. Every message contains a telephone number, e-mail address, etc. to facilitate and stimulate two-way communication. Different messages and different media will be used for different customers and prospects. Communication emphasizes the maintenance of relations, while promotions are used to attract new customers.

The customer-based information system will also allow management to identify new *distribution* opportunities more easily. For example, under some conditions it may be desirable for consumer-goods manufacturers of frequently purchased branded items to engage in direct selling to households. Other consequences of the adoption of the customer concept are the use of direct *and* indirect distribution channels. Two-way communication and distribution is possible through media such as fax and the Internet. This offers opportunities for on-line product selection, virtual shopping and personal delivery. In the near future the simultaneous consideration of manufacturer and retailer perspectives will get more attention. Due to the increase in retailer power, it will be critical for manufacturers to offer marketing activities that have demonstrable benefits for cooperating retailers. Although the current projections for the use of the Internet for grocery purchases are quite modest, it is conceivable that a new venture such as Webvan will quickly achieve a similar amount of power currently attributed only to Walmart and will dramatically increase the use of the Internet for consumer goods.

Webvan will offer households the opportunity to do grocery shopping on-line. However, unlike Peapod which obtains goods from existing supermarkets, Webvan builds its own warehouse with more than 4 miles of conveyer belts. In this manner it avoids many of the traditional supermarket costs. If households place their orders a few days in advance (with appropriate incentives, this should be straightforward), Webvan could aggregate orders across households for each day, and have all suppliers provide the required amounts on an as-needed basis. Suppliers can provide goods either directly or via intermediaries if the daily supply of a given supplier is modest. Note that each warehouse is projected to cover the trading area of 20 supermarkets. Similar to the hub-and-spoke system used by Federal Express for express packages, Webvan can sort the goods received by households (as by destination for Federal Express), and prepare packages for home delivery by vans. In this manner, Webvan can eliminate virtually all spoilage of perishables and all inventories (projected to be about 3 percent of total revenues), eliminate many chores in the traditional retail outlets including (re)supplying store space and checkout, and deliver customized baskets of goods to subscribing households at no extra charge (for purchases above, say, $50) and at lower prices than any traditional supermarket can offer. The modeling of marketing-related phenomena can be done at the individual household level. Suggestions about potentially relevant items, based on the principles used by Amazon for suggestions to its customers about books and other items, can be based on a combination of purchase and survey data. Importantly, loyal customers can be rewarded in a new manner. Again, based on the purchase records, and survey responses, Webvan can add customized suprises to the customized basket of goods. The frequency and nature of these suprises would depend on the profitability of each household, and perhaps on the availability of new products, and the cooperation of manufacturers who want to offer trial amounts of new products through the retailer.

Such new ventures that come about through the Internet require that existing retailers as well as manufacturers adapt. To understand the impact of these new developments, existing firms have to understand how households will approach the new services. For example, existing retailers will have to interview their customers to understand how they should modify their operations to compete with the new operators. Preference-based models will allow the firms to determine the attractiveness of all strategic options available to them. However, the Internet-based operators have the advantage that they have continuous interaction with their customers which facilitates their collection and analysis of preferences for things not yet offered, satisfaction with the purchase and consumption of goods, and the relevance of marketing activities, including new products, on the loyalty, retention and profitability of individual customers. It appears therefore, that the Internet not only allows new firms to operate based on a much more complete understanding of individual customers, but their success will force the existing firms that have not yet adopted such an approach to follow the lead if they want to survive.

In summary, we offer the following perspective.

The modeling of marketing effects, such as promotions, price, advertising and distribution, has had strong impact on managerial decisions at the major consumer-goods manufacturers. Both ACNielsen and IRI report successful implementation of model results at firms in North America, Europe and Asia. The models appear to provide good insights into the short-term effects at the item or brand level. However, much more is needed to show long-term effects such as the possible reduction in brand equity due to promotional activities. On the other hand, managers appear to be quite confident that they have a good understanding of the long-term advertising effects based on the rule that the total effect is roughly twice the short-term effect.

Another aspect that requires more attention is the effect of marketing activities on profits at the level of the firm. It is now common for marketing managers to be asked for the profit implications of investments in marketing. To do this meaningfully, both short- and long-term profit implications should be considered. In addition, the use of, for example, promotions, has to be assessed not just in terms of the effects on sales and the attribution to different sources of sales gains, but also by considering the negation of benefits due to competitive reactions. Also, the effects on production, distribution and inventory management (supply chain) need to be included. Future model-building efforts will include a much more comprehensive examination of all these components.

We propose that future models provide managers with "what if" simulation capabilities so that both short-and long-run effects can be documented, likely competitive reactions can be taken into account, and profit implications for alternative marketing actions can be considered.

The developments we discussed in this chapter determine the demand for "new" *models* which can be used as an aid *for decision-making in marketing* in the future.

Bibliography

Aaker, D.A. (1995), *Strategic Market Management*, 4th ed., John Wiley & Sons, New York.

Abad, P.A. (1987), 'A Hierarchical Optimal Control Model for Co-ordination of Functional Decisions in a Firm', *European Journal of Operations Research*, vol. 32, pp. 62–75.

Abe, M. (1995), 'A Nonparametric Density Estimation Method for Brand Choice Using Scanner Data', *Marketing Science*, vol. 14, pp. 300–325.

Abelson, R.P. (1976), 'Script Processing in Attitude Formation and Decision Making' in Carral, J.D. and J. Payne (eds.), *Cognition and Social Behavior*, Lawrence Erlbaum, Hillsdale, NJ., pp. 33–45.

Abraham, M.M. and L.M. Lodish (1989), 'Fact-Based Strategies for Managing Advertising and Promotion Dollars: Lessons from Single Source Data', Working Paper # 89–006, Marketing Department, The Wharton School of the University of Pennsylvania.

Abraham, M.M. and L.M. Lodish (1992), 'An Implemented System for Improving Promotion Productivity Using Store Scanner Data', *Marketing Science*, vol. 12, pp. 248–269.

Agarwal, M.K. and V.R. Rao (1996), 'An Empirical Comparison of Consumer-Based Measures of Brand Equity', *Marketing Letters*, vol. 7, pp. 237–247.

Aigner, D.J. and S.M. Goldfeld (1973), 'Simulation and Aggregation: A Reconsideration', *The Review of Economics and Statistics*, vol. 44, pp. 114–118.

Aigner, D.J. and S.M. Goldfeld (1974), 'Estimation and Prediction from Aggregate Data when Aggregates are Measured more Accurately than their Components', *Econometrica*, vol. 42, pp. 113–134.

Ailawadi, K.L., P.W. Farris and M.E. Parry (1999), 'Market Share and ROI: Observing the Effect of Unobserved Variables', *International Journal of Research in Marketing*, vol. 16, pp. 17–33.

Ailawadi, K.L. and S.A. Neslin (1998), 'The Effect of Promotion on Consumption: Buying More and Consuming It Faster', *Journal of Marketing Research*, vol. 35, pp. 390–398.

Ainslie, A. and P.E. Rossi (1998), 'Similarities in Choice Behavior Across Product Categories', *Marketing Science*, vol. 17, pp. 91–106.

Aitken, A.C. (1935), 'On Least Squares and Linear Combination of Observations', *Proceedings of the Royal Society of Edinburgh*, vol. 55, pp. 42–48.

Ajzen, I. and M. Fishbein (1980), *Understanding Attitudes and Predicting Social Behavior*, Prentice-Hall, Englewood Cliffs, NJ.

Akaike, H. (1974), 'A New Look at Statistical Model Identification', *IEEE Transactions on Automatic Control*, vol. 19, pp. 716–723.

Akaike, H. (1981), 'Likelihood of a Model and Information Criteria', *Journal of Econometrics*, vol. 16, pp. 3–14.

Albach, H. (1979), 'Market Organization and Pricing Behavior of Oligopolistic Firms in the Ethical Drugs Industry', *Kyklos*, vol. 32, pp. 523–540.

Albers, S. (1998), 'A Framework for Analysis of Sources of Profit Contribution Variance between Actual and Plan', *International Journal of Research in Marketing*, vol. 15, pp. 109–122.

Allenby, G.M. (1990), 'Cross-Validation, The Bayes Theorem, and Small Sample Bias', *Journal of Business and Economic Statistics*, vol. 8, pp. 171–178.

Allenby, G.M., N. Arora and L. Ginter (1998), 'On the Heterogeneity of Demand', *Journal of Marketing Research*, vol. 35, pp. 384–389.

Allenby, G.M. and L. Ginter (1995), 'Using Extremes to Design Products and Segment Markets', *Journal of Marketing Research*, vol. 32, pp. 392–403.

Allenby, G.M. and P.E. Rossi (1991a), 'There is No Aggregation Bias: Why Macro Logit Models Work', *Journal of Business and Economic Statistics*, vol. 9, pp. 1–14.

Allenby, G.M. and P.E. Rossi (1991b), 'Quality Perceptions and Asymmetric Switching Between Brands', *Marketing Science*, vol. 10, pp. 185–204.

Allenby, G.M. and P.E. Rossi (1999), 'Marketing Models of Consumer Heterogeneity', *Journal of Econometrics*, vol 89, pp. 57–78.

Almon, S. (1965), 'The Distributed Lag Between Capital Appropriations and Expenditures', *Econometrica*, vol. 33, pp. 178–196.

Alsem, K.J. and P.S.H. Leeflang (1994), 'Predicting Advertising Expenditures Using Intention Surveys', *International Journal of Forecasting*, vol. 10, pp. 327–337.

Alsem, K.J., P.S.H. Leeflang and J.C. Reuyl (1989), 'The Forecasting Accuracy of Market Share Models Using Predicted Values of Competitive Marketing Behaviour', *International Journal of Research in Marketing*, vol. 6, pp. 183–198.

Alsem, K.J., P.S.H. Leeflang and J.C. Reuyl (1990), 'Diagnosing Competition in an Industrial Market', *EMAC/ESOMAR Symposium on 'New Ways in Marketing and Marketing Research'*, pp. 161–178.

Alsem, K.J., P.S.H. Leeflang and J.C. Reuyl (1991), 'The Expansion of Broadcast Media in the Netherlands: Effects on the Advertising Expenditures', *The Expansion of Broadcast Media: Does Research Meet the Challenges?*, ESOMAR, Madrid, pp. 65–79.

Amemiya, T. (1983), 'Nonlinear Regression Models' in Griliches, Z. and M.D. Intriligator (eds.), *Handbook of Economics*, North-Holland, Amsterdam, pp. 333–390.

Amemiya, T. (1985), *Advanced Econometrics*, Harvard University Press, Cambridge, Mass.

Amemiya, T. (1994), *Advanced Econometrics*, 6th pr., Harvard University Press, Cambridge, Mass.

Amstutz, A.E. (1967), *Computer Simulation of Competitive Market Response*, M.I.T. Press, Cambridge, Mass.

Amstutz, A.E. (1969), 'Development, Validation and Implementation of Computerized Micro Analytic Simulations of Market Behavior' in Aronofski, J.S. (ed.), *Progress in Operations Research*, John Wiley & Sons, New York, vol. 3, pp. 241–262.

Amstutz, A.E. (1970), 'Management, Computers and Market Simulation' in Montgomery D.B. and G.L. Urban (eds.), *Applications of Management Science in Marketing*, Prentice-Hall, Englewood Cliffs, NJ.

André, L. (1971), 'Short-Term Optimization of the Sales Force: The Case of an Industrial Product', CESAM Working Paper No. 16–0771, University of Louvain.

Armstrong, J.S. (1985), *Long-range Forecasting, from Cystral Ball to Computer*, 2nd ed., John Wiley & Sons, New York.

Armstrong, J.S., R.J. Brodie and S.H. McIntyre (1987), 'Forecasting Methods for Marketing, Review of Empirical Research', *International Journal of Forecasting*, vol. 3, pp. 355–376.

Armstrong, J.S. and F. Collopy (1996), 'Competitor Orientation: Effects of Objectives and Information on Managerial Decisions and Profitability', *Journal of Marketing Research*, vol. 33, pp. 188–199.

Armstrong, J.S. and A.C. Shapiro (1974), 'Analyzing Quantitative Models', *Journal of Marketing*, vol. 30, April, pp. 61–65.

Ashton, A.H. and R.H. Ashton (1985), 'Aggregating Subjective Forecasts: Some Empirical Results', *Management Science*, vol. 31, pp. 1499–1509.

Assael, H. (1967), 'Comparison of Brand Share Data by Three Reporting Systems', *Journal of Marketing Research*, vol. 4 , pp. 400–401.

Assmus, G., J.U. Farley and D.R. Lehmann (1984), 'How Advertising Affects Sales: Meta Analysis of Econometric Results', *Journal of Marketing Research*, vol. 7, pp. 153–158.

Assunção, J. and R.J. Meyer (1993), 'The Rational Effect of Price Uncertainty on Sales-Price Relationships', *Management Science*, vol. 39, pp. 517–535.

Bagozzi, R.P. (1977), 'Structural Equation Models in Experimental Research', *Journal of Marketing Research*, vol. 14, pp. 209–226.

Bagozzi, R.P. (1980), *Causal Models in Marketing*, John Wiley & Sons, New York.

Bagozzi, R.P. (ed.), (1994a), *Advanced Methods of Marketing Research*, Blackwell Publishers, Cambridge, Mass.

Bagozzi, R.P. (1994b), 'Structural Equation Models in Marketing Research: Basic Principles' in Bagozzi, R.P. (ed.), *Principles of Marketing Research*, Blackwell Publishers, Cambridge, Mass.

Bagozzi, R.P., H. Baumgartner and Y. Yi (1992), 'State versus Action Orientation and the Theory of Reasoned Action: An Application to Coupon Usage', *Journal of Consumer Research*, vol. 18, pp. 505–518.

Bagozzi, R.P. and A.J. Silk (1983), 'Recall, Recognition, and the Measurement of Memory for Print Advertisements', *Marketing Science*, vol. 2, pp. 95–134.

Bai, J. and P. Perron (1998), 'Estimating and Testing Linear Models with Multiple Structural Changes', *Econometrica*, vol. 66, pp. 47–78.

Balasubramanian, S. (1998), 'Mail versus Mall: A Strategic Analysis of Competition between Direct Marketers and Conventional Retailers', *Marketing Science*, vol. 17, pp. 181–195.

Balasubramanian, S.K. and A.K. Ghosh (1992), 'Classifying Early Product Life Cycle Forms via a Diffusion Model: Problems and Prospects', *International Journal of Research in Marketing*, vol. 9, pp. 345–352.

Balasubramanian, S.K. and D.C. Jain (1994), 'Simple Approaches to Evaluate Competing Non-Nested Models in Marketing', *International Journal of Research in Marketing*, vol. 11, pp. 53–72.

Balderston, F.E. and A.C. Hogatt (1962), *Simulation of Market Processes*, Institute of Business and Economic Research, University of California, Berkeley, California.

Baligh, H.H. and L.E. Richartz (1967), 'Variable-Sum Game Models of Marketing Problems', *Journal of Marketing Research*, vol. 4, pp. 173–183.

Baltagi, B.H. (1998), *Econometrics*, Springer Berlin.

Balzer, W.K., L.M. Sulsky, L.B. Hammer and K.E. Sumner (1992), 'Task Information, Cognitive Information or Functional Validity Information: Which Components of Cognitive Feedback Affects Performance?', *Organizational Behavior and Human Decision Processes*, vol. 53, pp. 35–54.

Banslaben, J. (1992), 'Predictive Modeling' in Nash, E.L. (ed.), *The Direct Marketing Handbook*, McGraw-Hill, New York.

Barnett, A.I. (1976), 'More on a Market Share Theorem', *Journal of Marketing Research*, vol. 13, pp. 104–109.

Barr, S.H. and R. Sharda (1997), 'Effectiveness of Decision Support Systems: Development or Reliance Effect?', *Decision Support Systems*, vol. 21, pp. 133–146.

Barten, A.P. (1977), 'The Systems of Consumer Demand Functions Approach: A Review', *Econometrica*, vol. 45, pp. 23–51.

Bass, F.M. (1969a), 'A Simultaneous Equation Regression Study of Advertising and Sales of Cigarettes', *Journal of Marketing Research*, vol. 6, pp. 291–300.

Bass, F.M. (1969b), 'A New Product Growth Model for Consumer Durables', *Management Science*, vol. 15, pp. 215–227.

Bass, F.M. (1971), 'Testing vs. Estimation in Simultaneous Equation Regression Models', *Journal of Marketing Research*, vol. 8, pp. 388–389.

Bass, F.M. (1986), 'The Adaption of a Marketing Model: Comments and Observations' in Mahajan, V. and Y. Wind (eds.), *Innovation Diffusion of New Product Acceptance*, Ballinger, Cambridge, MA, pp. 27–33.

Bass, F.M. (1995), 'Empirical Generalizations and Marketing Science: A Personal View', *Marketing Science*, vol. 14, pp. G6–G19.

Bass, F.M. and D.G. Clarke (1972), 'Testing Distributed Lag Models of Advertising Effect', *Journal of Marketing Research*, vol. 9, pp. 298–308.

Bass, F.M., T.V. Krishnan and D.C. Jain (1994), 'Why the Bass Model Fits without Decision Variables', *Marketing Science*, vol. 13, pp. 203–223.

Bass, F.M. and R.P. Leone (1986), 'Estimating Micro Relationships from Macro Data: A Comparative Study of Two Approximations of the Brand Loyal Model Under Temporal Aggregation', *Journal of Marketing Research*, vol. 23, pp. 291–297.

Bass, F.M. and L.J. Parsons (1969), 'A Simultaneous Equation Regression Analysis of Sales and Advertising', *Applied Economics*, vol. 1, pp. 103–124.

Bass, F.M. and T.L. Pilon (1980), 'A Stochastic Brand Choice Framework for Econometric Modeling of Time Series Market Share Behavior', *Journal of Marketing Research*, vol. 17, pp. 486–497.

Bass, F.M. and Y. Wind (1995), 'Introduction to the Special Issue: Empirical Generalizations in Marketing', *Marketing Science*, vol. 14, pp. G1–G5.

Bass, F.M. and D.R. Wittink (1975), 'Pooling Issues and Methods in Regression Analysis with Examples in Marketing Research', *Journal of Marketing Research*, vol. 12, pp. 51–58.

Basu, A.K., R. Lal, V. Srinivasan and R. Staelin (1985), 'Salesforce Compensation Plans: An Agency Theoretic Perspective', *Marketing Science*, vol. 4, pp. 267–291.

Basuroy, S. and D. Nguyen (1998), 'Multinomial Logit Market Share Models: Equilibrium Characteristics and Strategic Implications', *Management Science*, vol. 44, pp. 1396–1408.

Batra, R., J.G. Myers and D.A. Aaker (1996), '*Advertising Management*, 5th ed., Prentice-Hall, Upper Saddle River, NJ.

Batsell, R.R. and J.C. Polking (1985), 'A New Class of Market Share Models', *Marketing Science*, vol. 41, pp. 177–198.

Baumol, W.J. and T. Fabian (1964), 'Decomposition, Pricing for Decentralization and External Economics', *Management Science*, vol. 11, pp. 1–32.

Bayer, J., S. Lawrence and J.W. Keon (1988), 'PEP: An Expert System for Promotion Marketing' in Turban, E.

and P.R. Watkins (eds.), *Applied Expert Systems*, Elsevier Science Publishers, North-Holland, Amsterdam, pp. 121–141.

Bayus, B.L., S. Hong and R.P. Labe (1989), 'Developing and Using Forecasting Models of Consumer Durables, the Case of Color Television', *Journal of Product Innovation Management*, vol. 6, pp. 5–19.

Bayus, B.L. and R. Mehta (1995), 'A Segmentation Model for the Targeted Marketing of Consumer Durables', *Journal of Marketing Research*, vol. 32, pp. 463–469.

Beach, W.O. and V. Barnes (1987), 'Assessing Human Judgment: Has It Been Done, Can It Be Done, Should It Be Done?' in Wright, G. and P. Ayton (eds.), *Judgmental Forecasting*, pp. 49–62. John Wiley & Sons, New York.

Bearden, W.O., R.G. Netemeyer and M.F. Mobley (1993), *Handbook of Marketing Scales*, Sage, London.

Bearden, W.O. and J.E. Teel (1983), 'Selected Determinants of Consumer Satisfaction and Complaint Reports', *Journal of Marketing Research*, vol. 20, pp. 21–28.

Beckwith, N.E. (1972), 'Multivariate Analysis of Sales Responses of Competing Brands to Advertising', *Journal of Marketing Research*, vol. 9, pp. 168–176.

Bell, D.E., R.L. Keeney and J.D.C. Little (1975), 'A Market Share Theorem', *Journal of Marketing Research*, vol. 12, pp. 136–141.

Bell, D.R., J. Chiang and V. Padmanabhan (1997), The '84/14/2' Rule Revisited: What Drives Choice, Incidence and Quantity Elasticities?', Working Paper No. 277, John E. Anderson Graduate School of Management, UCLA.

Bell, D.R., J. Chiang and V. Padmanabhan (1999), 'The Decomposition of Promotional Response: An Empirical Generalization', *Marketing Science*, forthcoming.

Bell, D.R., T. Ho and C.S. Tang (1998), 'Determining Where to Shop: Fixed and Variable Costs of Shopping', *Journal of Marketing Research*, vol. 35, pp. 352–369.

Belsley, D.A. (1991), *Conditioning Diagnostics: Collinearity and Weak Data in Regression*, John Wiley & Sons, New York.

Belsley, D.A., E. Kuh and R.E. Welsh (1980), *Regression Diagnostics: Identifying Influential Data and Sources of Collinearity*, John Wiley & Sons, New York.

Bemmaor, A.C. (1984), 'Testing Alternative Econometric Models on the Existence of Advertising Threshold Effect', *Journal of Marketing Research*, vol. 21, pp. 298–308.

Bemmaor, A.C., Ph.H. Franses and J. Kippers (1999), 'Estimating the Impact of Displays and other Merchandising Support on Retail Brand Sales: Partial Pooling with Examples', *Marketing Letters*, vol. 10, pp. 87–100.

Bemmaor, A.C. and D. Mouchoux (1991), 'Measuring the Short Term Effect of In-store Promotion and Retail Advertising on Brand Sales: A Factorial Experiment', *Journal of Marketing Research*, vol. 28, pp. 202–214.

Ben-Akiva, M. and S.R. Lerman (1985), *Discrete Choice Analysis: Theory and Application to Travel Demand*, MIT Press, Cambridge, Mass.

Benbasat, I. and P. Todd (1996), 'The Effects of Decision Support and Task Contingencies on Model Formulation: A Cognitive Perspective', *Decision Support Systems*, vol. 17, pp. 241–252.

Benson, P.G., S.P. Curley and F.G. Smith (1995), 'Belief Assessment: An Underdeveloped Phase of Probability Elicitation', *Management Science*, vol. 41, pp. 1639–1653.

Bentler, P.M. (1990), 'Comparative Fit Indices in Structural Models', *Psychological Bulletin*, vol. 107, pp. 238–246.

Bera, A.K. and C.M. Jarque (1981), 'An Efficient Large-Sample Test for Normality of Observations and Regression Residuals', Australian National University Working Papers in Econometrics, No. 40, Canberra.

Bera, A.K. and C.M. Jarque (1982), 'Model Specification Tests: A Simultaneous Approach', *Journal of Econometrics*, vol. 20, pp. 59–82.

Berndt, E.R. (1991), *The Practice of Econometrics*, Addison-Wesley, Reading, MA.

Bertrand, J. (1883), 'Théorie Mathématique de la Richesse Sociale', *J. Savants*, pp. 499–508.

Bijmolt, T.H.A. (1996), *Multidimensional Scaling in Marketing: Towards Integrating Data Collection and Analysis*, Unpublished Ph.D. thesis, University of Groningen, the Netherlands

Blackburn, J.D. and K.J. Clancy (1980), 'LITMUS: A New Product Planning Model' in Leone, R.P. (ed.), *Proceedings: Market Measurement and Analysis*, The Institute of Management Sciences, Providence, RI, pp. 182–193.

Blattberg, R.C., R. Briesch and E.J. Fox (1995), 'How Promotions Work', *Marketing Science*, vol. 14, pp. G122–G132.

Blattberg, R.C. and S.J. Hoch (1990), 'Database Models and Managerial Intuition: 50% Model + 50% Manager', *Management Science*, vol. 36, pp. 887–899.

Blattberg, R.C., B. Kim and J. Ye (1994), 'Large-Scale Databases: The New Marketing Challenge' in Blattberg, R.C., R. Glazer and J.D.C. Little (eds.), The Marketing Information Revolution, *Harvard Business School Press*, Boston, Massachusetts, pp. 173–203.

Blattberg, R.C. and S.A. Neslin (1989), 'Sales Promotions: The Long and the Short of It', *Marketing Letters*, vol. 1, pp. 81–97.

Blattberg, R.C. and S.A. Neslin (1990), *Sales Promotions: Concepts, Methods and Strategies*, Prentice-Hall, Englewood Cliffs, NJ.

Blattberg, R.C. and S.A. Neslin (1993), 'Sales Promotions' in Eliashberg, J. and G.L. Lilien (eds.), *Handbooks in Operations, Research and Management Science, vol. 5, Marketing*, North-Holland, Amsterdam, pp. 553–609.

Blattberg, R.C. and K.J. Wisniewski (1989), 'Price-induced Patterns of Competition', *Marketing Science*, vol. 8, pp. 291–309.

Blinkley, J.K. and C.H. Nelson (1990), 'How Much Better is Aggregate Data?', *Economics Letters*, vol. 32, pp. 137–140.

Bloom, D. (1980), 'Point of Sale Scanners and their Implications for Market Research', *Journal of the Market Research Society*, vol. 22. pp. 221–238.

Böckenholt, U. (1993a), 'Estimating Latent Distributions in Recurrent Choice Data', *Psychometrica*, vol. 58, pp. 489–509.

Böckenholt, U. (1993b), 'A Latent Class Regression Approach for the Analysis of Recurrent Choice Data', *British Journal of Mathematical and Statistical Psychology*, vol. 46, pp. 95–118.

Bodapati, A.V. and S. Gupta (1999), 'Recovering Latent Class Segmentation Structure from Store Scanner Data', Research paper, Kellogg Graduate School of Management, Northwestern University, Evanston, Il.

Boer, P.M.C. de and R. Harkema (1983), 'Undersized Samples and Maximum Likelihood Estimation of Sum-Constrained Linear Models', Report 8331, The Econometric Institute, Erasmus University, Rotterdam.

Boer, P.M.C. de, R. Harkema and A.J. Soede (1996), 'Maximum Likelihood Estimation of Market Share Models with Large Numbers of Shares', *Applied Economics Letters*, vol. 3, pp. 45–48.

Boerkamp, E.J.C. (1995), *Assessing Professional Services Quality*, Unpublished Ph.D. thesis, University of Groningen, the Netherlands.

Bollen, K.A. (1989), *Structural Equations With Latent Variables*, John Wiley & Sons, New York.

Bolton, R.N. (1998), 'A Dynamic Model of the Duration of the Customer's Relationship with a Continuous Service Provider: The Role of Satisfaction', *Marketing Science*, vol. 17, pp. 45–65.

Bolton, R.N. and K.N. Lemon (1999), 'A Dynamic Model of Customers' Usage of Services: Usage as an Antecedent and Consequence of Satisfaction', *Journal of Marketing Research*, vol. 36, pp. 171–186.

Boudjellaba, H., J.M. Dufour and R. Roy (1992), 'Testing Causality Between Two Vectors in Multivariate Autoregressive Moving Average Model', *Journal of the American Statistical Association*, vol. 87, pp. 1082–1090.

Boulding, W., A. Kalra, R. Staelin and V.A. Zeithaml (1993), 'A Dynamic Process Model of Service Quality: From Expectations to Behavioral Intentions', *Journal of Marketing Research*, vol. 30, pp. 7–27.

Bowman, E.H. (1967), 'Consistency and Optimality in Managerial Decision Making' in Bowman, E.H. and R.B. Fetter (eds.), *Analysis for Production and Operations Management*, Richard D. Irwin, Homewood, Illinois.

Box, G.E.P. and D.R. Cox (1964), 'An Analysis of Transformations', *Journal of the Royal Statistical Society, Series B*, vol. 26, pp. 211–252.

Box, G.E.P., M. Jenkins and G.C. Reinsel (1994), *Time Series Analysis: Forecasting and Control*, Prentice-Hall, Englewood Cliffs, NJ.

Box, G.E.P. and G.C. Tiao (1975), 'Intervention Analysis with Applications to Economic and Environmental Problems', *Journal of the American Statistical Association*, vol. 70, March, pp. 70–79.

Boyd, H.W. and W.F. Massy (1972), *Marketing Management*, Harcourt, Brace, Jovanovich, New York.

Bozdogan, H. (1987), 'Model Selection and Akaike's Information Criterion (AIC): The General Theory and its Analytical Extensions', *Psychometrika*, vol. 52, pp. 345–370.

Brand, M.J. (1993), *Effectiveness of the Industrial Marketing Mix: An Assessment Through Simulation of the Organizational Buying Process*, Unpublished Ph.D. thesis, University of Groningen, the Netherlands.

Brand, M.J. and P.S.H. Leeflang (1994), 'Research on Modeling Industrial Markets' in Laurent, G., G.L. Lilien and B. Pras (eds.), *Research Traditions in Marketing*, Kluwer Publishers, Boston, pp. 231–261.

Briesch, R.A., P.K. Chintagunta and R.L. Matzkin (1997), 'Nonparametric and Semiparametric Models of Brand Choice Behavior', Working Paper, Department of Marketing, University of Texas, Austin.

Broadbent, S. (1981), *Advertising Works*, Holt, Rinehart, and Winston, London.

Broadbent, S. (1983), *Advertising Works 2*, Holt, Rinehart, and Winston, London.

Brobst, R. and R. Gates (1977), 'Comments on Pooling Issues and Methods in Regression Analysis', *Journal of Marketing Research*, vol. 14, pp. 598–606.

Brockhoff, K. (1967), 'A Test for the Product Life Cycle', *Econometrica*, vol. 35, pp. 472–484.

Brodie, R.J., A. Bonfrer and J. Cutler (1996), 'Do Managers Overreact To Each Others' Promotional Activity? Further Empirical Evidence', *International Journal of Research in Marketing*, vol. 13, pp. 379–387.

Brodie, R.J., P.J. Danaher, V. Kumar and P.S.H. Leeflang (2000), 'Principles to Guide the Forecasting of Market Share' in Armstrong, J.S. (ed.), *The Forecasting Principles Handbook*, forthcoming.

Brodie, R.J. and C.A. de Kluyver (1984), 'Attraction versus Linear and Multiplicative Market Share Models: An Empirical Evaluation', *Journal of Marketing Research*, vol. 21, pp. 194–201.

Brodie, R.J. and C.A. de Kluyver (1987), 'A Comparison of the Short-term Forecasting Accuracy of Econometric and Naive Extrapolation Models of Market Share', *International Journal of Forecasting*, vol. 3, pp. 423–437.

Bronnenberg, B.J. (1998), 'Advertising Frequency Decisions in a Discrete Markov Process Under a Budget Constraint', *Journal of Marketing Research*, vol. 35, pp. 399–406.

Bronnenberg, B.J. and L. Wathieu (1996), 'Asymmetric Promotion Effects and Brand Positioning', *Marketing Science*, vol. 15, pp. 379–394.

Brown, A. and A. Deaton (1972), 'Surveys in Applied Economics: Models of Consumer Behaviour', *The Economic Journal*, vol. 82, pp. 1145–1236.

Brown, A.A., F.L. Hulswit and J.D. Ketelle (1956), 'A Study of Sales Operations', *Operations Research*, vol. 4, pp. 296–308.

Brown, B. and O. Helmer (1964), *Improving the Reliability of Estimates Obtained from a Consensus of Experts*, P.2986, The Rand Corporation Santa Monica, California.

Brown, W.M. and W.T. Tucker (1961), 'Vanishing Shelf Space', *Atlanta Economic Review*, vol. 9, pp. 9–13.

Browne, G.J., S.P. Curley and P.G. Benson (1997), 'Evoking Information in Probability Assessment: Knowledge Maps and Reasoning-Based Directed Questions', *Management Science*, vol. 43, pp. 1–14.

Bruggen, G.H. van (1993) *The Effectiveness of Marketing Management Support Systems*, Unpublished Ph.D. thesis, Erasmus University, Rotterdam, the Netherlands.

Bruggen, G.H. van, A. Smidts and B. Wierenga (1998), 'Improving Decision Making by Means of a Marketing Decision Support System', *Management Science*, vol. 44, pp. 645–658.

Bucklin, R.E. and S. Gupta (1992), 'Brand Choice, Purchase Incidence and Segmentation: An Integrated Approach', *Journal of Marketing Research*, vol. 29, pp. 201–215.

Bucklin, R.E. and S. Gupta (2000), 'Commercial Use of UPC Scanner Data: Industry and Academic Perspectives', *Marketing Science*, vol. 19, forthcoming.

Bucklin, R.E. and J.M. Lattin (1991), 'A Two-State Model of Purchase Incidence and Brand Choice', *Marketing Science*, vol. 10, pp. 24–39.

Bucklin, R.E., D.R. Lehmann and J.D.C. Little (1998), From Decision Support to Decision Automation: A 2020 Vison, *Marketing Letters*, vol. 9, pp. 234–246.

Bult, J.R. (1993a), *Target Selection for Direct Marketing*, Unpublished Ph.D. thesis, University of Groningen, the Netherlands.

Bult, J.R. (1993b), 'Semiparametric Versus Parametric Classification Models: An Application to Direct Marketing, *Journal of Marketing Research*, vol. 30, pp. 380–390.

Bult, J.R., P.S.H. Leeflang and D.R. Wittink (1997), 'The Relative Performance of Bivariate Causality Tests in Small Samples', *European Journal of Operational Research*, vol. 97, pp. 450–464.

Bult, J.R. and T.J. Wansbeek (1995), 'Optimal Selection for Direct Mail', *Marketing Science*, vol. 14, pp. 378–394.

Bult, J.R. and D.R. Wittink (1996), 'Estimating and Validating Asymmetric Heterogeneous Loss Functions Applied to Health Care Fund Raising', *International Journal of Research in Marketing*, vol. 13, pp. 215–226.

Bultez, A.V. (1975), *Competitive Strategy for Interrelated Markets*, Unpublished Ph.D. thesis, Louvain University, Belgium.

Bultez, A.V. (ed.) (1995), Scientific Report 1992–1995, *CREER, Centre for Research on the Economic Efficiency of Retailing*, FUCAM, Facultés Universitaires Catholiques de Mons, Belgium.

Bultez, A.V., E. Gijsbrechts and P.A. Naert (1995), 'A Theorem on the Optimal Margin Mix', *Zeitschrift für Betriebswirtschaft*, EH 4, December, pp. 151–174.

Bultez, A.V., E. Gijsbrechts, P.A. Naert and P. Vanden Abeele (1989), 'Asymmetric Cannibalism in Retail Assortments', *Journal of Retailing*, vol. 65, pp. 153–192.

Bultez, A.V. and P.A. Naert (1973), 'Estimating Gravitational Marketing Share Models', Working Paper No. 73–36, European Institute for Advanced Studies in Management, Brussels, Belgium.

Bultez, A.V. and P.A. Naert (1975), 'Consistent Sum-Constrained Models', *Journal of the American Statistical Association*, vol. 70, pp. 529–535.

Bultez, A.V. and P.A. Naert (1979), 'Does Lag Structure Really Matter in Optimizing Advertising Expenditures?', *Management Science*, vol. 25, pp. 454–465.

Bultez, A.V. and P.A. Naert (1988a), 'When Does Lag Structure Really Matter... Indeed?', *Management Science*, vol. 34, pp. 909–916.

Bultez, A.V. and P.A. Naert (1988b), 'SH.A.R.P: Shelf Allocation for Retailers' Profit', *Marketing Science*, vol. 7, pp. 211–231.

Bunn, D. and G. Wright (1991), 'Interaction of Judgment and Statistical Forecasting Methods: Issues and Analysis', *Management Science*, vol. 37, pp. 501–518.

Burke, R.R. (1991), 'Reasoning with Empirical Marketing Knowledge', *International Journal of Research in Marketing*, vol. 8, pp. 75–90.

Burke, R.R., A. Rangaswamy, Y. Wind and J. Eliashberg (1990), 'A Knowledge Based System for Advertising Design', *Marketing Science*, vol. 9, pp. 212–229.

Buzzell, R.D. (1964), *Mathematical Models and Marketing Management*, Division of Research, Graduate School of Business Administration, Harvard University, Boston.

Buzzell, R.D. and B.T. Gale (1987), *The PIMS-Principles*, The Free Press, New York.

Capon, N. and J. Hulbert (1975), 'Decision Systems Analysis in Industrial Marketing', *Industrial Marketing Management*, vol. 4, pp. 143–160.

Carman, J.M. (1966), 'Brand Switching and Linear Learning Models', *Journal of Advertising Research*, vol. 6, pp. 23–31.

Carpenter, G.S. (1987), 'Modeling Competitive Marketing Strategies: The Impact of Marketing-Mix Relationships and Industry Structure', *Marketing Science*, vol. 6, pp. 208–221.

Carpenter, G.S., L.G. Cooper, D.M. Hanssens and D.F. Midgley (1988), 'Modelling Asymmetric Competition', *Marketing Science*, vol. 7, pp. 393–412.

Carpenter, G.S. and D.R. Lehmann (1985), 'A Model of Marketing Mix, Brand Switching and Competition', *Journal of Marketing Research*, vol. 22, pp. 318–329.

Cats-Baril, W.L. and G.P. Huber (1987), 'Decision Support Systems for Ill-structured Problems: An Empirical Study', *Decision Sciences*, vol. 18. pp. 350–372.

Chakravarti, D., A. Mitchell and R. Staelin (1981), 'Judgment Based Marketing Decision Models: Problems and Possible Solutions,' *Journal of Marketing*, vol. 45, Fall, pp. 13–23.

Channon, C. (1985), *Advertising Works 3*, Holt, Rinehart, and Winston, London.

Channon, C. (1987), *Advertising Works 4*, Cassell Educational Limited, London.

Chatfield, C., A.S.C. Ehrenberg and G.J. Goodhardt (1966), 'Progress on a Simplified Model of Stationary Purchasing Behavior', *Journal of Royal Statistical Society*, Series A, vol. 79, pp. 317–367.

Chatfield, C. and G.J. Goodhardt (1973), 'A Consumer Purchasing Model with Erlang Interpurchase Times', *Journal of the American Statistical Association*, vol. 68, pp. 828–835.

Chatterjee, R. and J. Eliashberg (1990), 'The Innovation Diffusion Process in a Heterogeneous Population: A Micromodelling Approach', *Management Science*, vol. 36, pp. 1057–1079.

Chen, Y., V. Kanetkar and D.L. Weiss (1994), 'Forecasting Market Share with Disaggregate or Pooled Data: A Comparison of Attraction Models', *International Journal of Forecasting*, vol. 10, pp. 263–276.

Chen, M.J., K.G. Smith and C.M. Grimm (1992), 'Action Characteristics as Predictors of Competitive Response', *Management Science*, vol. 38, pp. 439–455.

Chiang, J. (1991), 'A Simultaneous Approach to the Whether, What and How Much to Buy Questions', *Marketing Science*, vol.10, pp. 297–315.

Chiang, J., S. Chib and C. Narasimhan (1999), 'Markov Chain Monte Carlo and Models of Consideration Set and Parameter Heterogeneity', *Journal of Econometrics*, vol. 89, pp. 223–248.

Chintagunta, P.K. (1992a), 'Estimating a Multinomial Probit Model of Brand Choice Using the Method of Simulated Moments', *Marketing Science*, vol. 11, pp. 386–407.

Chintagunta, P.K. (1992b), 'Heterogeneity in Nested Logit Models: An Estimation Approach and Empirical Results', *International Journal of Research in Marketing*, vol. 9, pp. 161–175.

Chintagunta, P.K. (1993a), 'Investigating Purchase Incidence, Brand Choice and Purchase Quantity Decisions of Households', *Marketing Science*, vol. 12, pp. 184–208.

Chintagunta, P.K. (1993b), 'Investigating the Sensitivity of Equilibrium Profits to Advertising Dynamics and Competitive Effects', *Management Science*, vol. 39, pp. 1146–1162.

Chintagunta, P.K. (1998), 'Inertia and Variety Seeking in a Model of Brand-Purchase Timing', *Marketing Science*, vol. 17, pp. 253–270.

Chintagunta, P.K. (1999), 'Variety Seeking, Purchase Timing and the 'Lighting Bolt' Brand Choice Model', *Management Science*, vol. 45, pp. 486–498.

Chintagunta, P.K., D.C. Jain and N.J. Vilcassim (1991), 'Investigating Heterogeneity in Brand Preferences in Logit Models for Panel Data', *Journal of Marketing Research*, vol. 28, pp. 417–428.

Chintagunta, P.K. and V.R. Rao (1996), 'Pricing Strategies in a Dynamic Duopoly: A Differential Game Model', *Management Science*, vol. 42, pp. 1501–1514.

Chintagunta, P.K. and N.J. Vilcassim (1994), 'Marketing Investment Decisions in a Dynamic Duopoly: A Model and Empirical Analysis', *International Journal of Research in Marketing*, vol. 11, pp. 287–306.

Chow, G.C. (1960), 'Tests of Equality between Sets of Coefficients in Two Linear Regressions', *Econometrica*, vol. 28, pp. 591–605.

Chow, G.C. (1983), *Econometrics*, McGraw-Hill, New York.

Christen, M., Sachin Gupta, J.C. Porter, R. Staelin and D.R. Wittink (1997), 'Using Market-Level Data to Understand Promotion Effects in a Nonlinear Model', *Journal of Marketing Research*, vol. 34, pp. 322–334.

Chu, W. and P.S. Desai (1995), 'Channel Coordination Mechanisms for Customer Satisfaction', *Marketing Science*, vol. 14, pp. 343–359.

Churchill, G.A. (1995), *Marketing Research, Methodological Foundations*, 6th. ed., The Dryden Press, Fort Worth.

Churchman, C.W. and A. Schainblatt (1965), 'The Researcher and the Manager: A Dialectic of Implementation', *Management Science*, vol. 11, pp. B69–B87.

Clark, B.H. and D.B. Montgomery (1999), 'Managerial Identification of Competitors', *Journal of Marketing*, vol. 63, July, pp. 67–83.

Clarke, D. (1983), 'SYNTEX Laboratories (A)', Harvard Business School, Case number 9-584-033.

Clarke, D.G. (1973), 'Sales-Advertising Cross-Elasticities and Advertising Competition', *Journal of Marketing Research*, vol. 10, pp. 250–261.

Clarke, D.G. (1976), 'Econometric Measurement of the Duration of Advertising Effect on Sales', *Journal of Marketing Research*, vol. 13, pp. 345–357.

Clements, K.W. and E.A. Selvanathan (1988), 'The Rotterdam Model and its Applications to Marketing', *Marketing Science*, vol. 7, pp. 60–75.

Cleveland, W.S. (1979), 'Robust Locally Weighted Regression and Smoothing Scatterplots', *Journal of the American Statistical Association*, vol. 74, pp. 829–836.

Cochrane, D. and G.H. Orcutt (1949), 'Applications of Least Squares Regression Relationships containing Autocorrelated Error Terms', *Journal of the American Statistical Association*, vol. 44, pp. 32–61.

Colombo, R.A. and D.G. Morisson (1989), 'A Brand Switching Model with Implications for Marketing Strategies', *Marketing Science*, vol. 8, pp. 89–99.

Conamor, W.S. and T.A. Wilson (1974), *Advertising and Market Power*, Harvard University Press, Cambridge.

Cooil, B. and J.M. Devinney (1992), 'The Return to Advertising Expenditure', *Marketing Letters*, vol. 3, pp. 137–145.

Cooper, L.G. (1993), 'Market-Share Models' in Eliashberg, J. and G.L. Lilien (eds.), *Handbooks on Operations Research and Management Science, vol. 5, Marketing*, North-Holland, Amsterdam, pp. 259–314.

Cooper, L.G., D. Klapper and A. Inoue (1996), 'Competitive Component Analysis: A New Approach to Calibrating Asymmetric Market-Share Models', *Journal of Marketing Research*, vol. 33, pp. 224–238.

Cooper, L.G. and M. Nakanishi (1988), *Market-Share Analysis: Evaluating Competitive Marketing Effectiveness*, Kluwer Academic Publishers, Boston.

Corstjens, M. and P. Doyle (1981), 'A Model for Optimizing Retail Space Allocations', *Management Science*, vol. 27, pp. 822–833.

Corstjens, M and D. Weinstein (1982), 'Optimal Strategic Business Units Portfolio Analysis' in Zoltners, A.A. (ed.), *Marketing Planning Models*, North-Holland Publishing Company, Amsterdam, pp. 141–160.

Cotterill, R.W., W.P. Putsis and R. Dhar (1998), 'Assessing the Competitive Interaction Between Private Labels and National Brands', paper University of Connecticut / London Business School / Yale School of Management.

Cournot, A. (1838), *Recherches sur les Principes Mathématiques de la Théorie des Richesses*, Paris.

Cowling, K. and J. Cubbin (1971), 'Price, Quality and Advertising Competition: An Econometric Investigation of the United Kingdom Car Market', *Economica*, vol. 38, pp. 378–394.

Cox, D.E. and R.E. Good (1967), 'How to Build a Marketing Information System', *Harvard Business Review*, vol. 45, May-June, pp. 145–154.

Cox, D.R. (1975), 'Partial Likelihood', *Biometrika*, vol. 62, pp. 269–276.

Cox, Jr, E. (1967), 'Product Life Cycles as Marketing Models', *Journal of Marketing*, vol. 57, October, pp. 47–59.

Cready, W.M. (1991), 'Premium Bundling', *Economic Inquiry*, vol. 29, pp. 173–179.

Crow, L.E., R.W. Olshavsky and J.O. Summers (1980), 'Industrial Buyers' Choice Strategies: A Protocol Analysis', *Journal of Marketing Research*, vol. 17, pp. 34–44.

Curhan, R.C. (1972), 'The Relationship between Shelf Space and Unit Sales in Supermarkets', *Journal of Marketing Research*, vol. 9, pp. 406–412.

Currim, I.S. (1982), 'Predictive Testing of Consumer Choice Models Not Subject to Independence of Irrelevant Alternatives', *Journal of Marketing Research*, vol. 19, pp. 208–222.

Currim, I.S., C.B. Weinberg and D.R. Wittink (1981), 'Design of Subscription Programs for a Performing Arts Series', *Journal of Consumer Research*, vol. 8, pp. 67–75.

Cyert, R.M. and J.G. March (1963), *A Behavioral Theory of the Firm*, Englewood Cliffs, N.J., Prentice-Hall, Inc.

Daganzo, C. (1979), *Multinomial Probit*, Academic Press, New York.

Dalkey, N.C. and O. Helmer (1962), 'An Experimental Application of the Delphi Method to the Use of Experts', *Management Science*, vol. 9, pp. 458–467.

Damme, E. van (1987), *Stability and Perfection of Nash Equilibria*, Springer-Verlag, Berlin.

Danaher, P.J. (1994), 'Comparing Naive with Econometric Market Share Models, where Competitor's Actions are Forecast', *International Journal of Forecasting*, vol. 10, pp. 287–294.

Danaher, P.J. and R.J. Brodie (1992), 'Predictive Accuracy of Simple Versus Complex Econometric Market Share Models. Theoretical and Empirical Results', *International Journal of Forecasting*, vol. 8, pp. 613–626.

Danaher, P.J. and T. Sharot (1994), 'Cover Analysis: A New Tool for Monitoring Peoplemeter Panels', *Journal of the Market Research Society*, vol. 36, pp. 133–138.

Davidson, R. and J.G. MacKinnon (1981), 'Several Tests for Model Specification in the Presence of Alternative Hypotheses', *Econometrica*, vol 49, pp. 781–793.

Davidson, R. and J.G. MacKinnon (1993), *Estimation and Inference in Econometrics*, Oxford University Press, New York.

Day, G.S., A.D. Shocker and R.K. Srivastava (1979), 'Customer-Oriented Approaches to Identifying Product Markets', *Journal of Marketing*, vol. 43, Fall, pp. 8–19.

Day, G.S. en R. Wensley (1988), 'Assessing Advantage: A Framework for Diagnosing Competitive Strategy', *Journal of Marketing*, vol. 52, Spring, pp. 1–20.

Dayton, M.C. and G.B. MacReady (1988), 'Concomitant Variable Latent Class Models', *Journal of the American Statistical Association*, vol. 83, pp. 173–179.

Deal, K.R. (1975), 'A Differential Games Solution to the Problem of Determining the Optimal Timing of Advertising Expenditures', Unpublished Ph.D Dissertation, State University of New York at Buffalo.

Dearden, J.A., G.L. Lilien and E. Yoon (1999), 'Marketing and Production Capacity for Non-differentiated Products: Winning and Losing at the Capacity Cycle Game', *International Journal of Research in Marketing*, vol. 16, pp. 57–74.

Debreu, G. (1960), 'Review of R.D. Luce's Individual Choice Behavior: A Theoretical Analysis,' *American Economic Review*, vol. 50, pp. 186–188.

Deighton, J., C.M. Henderson and S.A. Neslin (1994), 'The Effects of Advertising on Brand Switching and Repeat Purchasing', *Journal of Marketing Research*, vol. 31, pp. 28–43.

De Finetti, B. (1964), 'Foresight: Its Logical Laws, Its Subjective Sources' in Kyburg, H.E., jr. and H.L. Smoker (eds.), *Studies in Subjective Probability*, John Wiley & Sons, New York, pp. 93–158.

De Finetti, B. (1965), 'Methods for Discriminating Levels of Partial Knowledge Concerning a Test Item', *The British Journal of Mathematical and Statistical Psychology*, vol. 18, pp. 87–123.

Dekimpe, M.G., P. François, S. Gopalakrishna, G.L. Lilien and C. Vanden Bulte (1997), 'Generalizing about

Trade Show Effectiveness: A Cross-National Comparison', *Journal of Marketing*, vol. 61, October, pp. 55–64.

Dekimpe, M.G. and D.M. Hanssens (1995a), 'The Persistence of Marketing Effects on Sales', *Marketing Science*, vol. 14, pp. 1–21.

Dekimpe, M.G. and D.M. Hanssens (1995b), 'Empirical Generalizations About Market Evolution and Stationarity', *Marketing Science*, vol. 14, pp. G109–G121.

Dekimpe, M.G. and D.M. Hanssens (1999), 'Sustained Spending and Persistent Response: A New Look at Long-Term Marketing Profitability, *Journal of Marketing Research*, forthcoming.

Dekimpe, M.G., D.M. Hanssens and J.M. Silva-Risso (1999), 'Long-Run Effects of Price Promotions in Scanner Markets', *Journal of Econometrics*, vol. 89, pp. 269–291.

DeSarbo, W.S. and W.L. Cron (1988), 'A Maximum Likelihood Methodology for Clusterwise Linear Regression', *Journal of Classification*, vol. 5, pp. 249–282.

Deshpandé, R. and H. Gatignon (1994), 'Competitive Analysis', *Marketing Letters*, vol. 5, pp. 271–287.

Dhar, S.K., D.G. Morrison and J.S. Raju (1996), 'The Effect of Package Coupons on Brand Choice: An Epilogue on Profits', *Marketing Science*, vol. 15, pp. 192–203.

Dhrymes, P.J. (1981), *Distributed Lags*, 2nd ed., North-Holland Publishing Company, Amsterdam.

Diamantopoulos, A. (1994), 'Modeling with LISREL: A Guide for the Uninitiated', *Journal of Marketing Management*, vol. 10, pp. 105–136.

Dillon, W.R. and S. Gupta (1996), 'A Segment Level Model of Category Volume and Brand Choice', *Marketing Science*, vol. 15, pp. 38–59.

Dockner, E. and S. Jørgenson (1988), 'Optimal Pricing Strategies for New Products in Dynamic Oligopolies', *Marketing Science*, vol. 7, pp. 315–334.

Doktor, R.H. and W.F. Hamilton (1973), 'Cognitive Style and the Acceptance of Management Science Recommendations', *Management Science*, vol. 19, pp. 884–894.

Dorfman, R. and P.O. Steiner (1954), 'Optimal Advertising and Optimal Quality', *The American Economic Review*, vol. 44, pp. 826–836.

Doyle, P. (1989), 'Building Successful Brands: The Strategic Options', *Journal of Marketing Management*, vol. 5, pp. 77–95.

Doyle, P. and J. Saunders (1985), 'The Lead Effect of Marketing Decisions', *Journal of Marketing Research*, vol. 22, pp. 54–65.

Doyle, P. and J. Saunders (1990), 'Multiproduct Advertising Budgeting', *Marketing Science*, vol. 9, pp. 97–113.

Duesenberry, J.S. (1949), *Income, Saving and the Theory of Consumer Behavior*, Harvard University Press, Cambridge, Mass.

Duffy, M. (1996), 'Econometric Studies of Advertising, Advertising Restrictions and Cigarette Demand: A Survey', *International Journal of Advertising*, vol. 15, pp. 1–23.

Duncan, W.J. (1974), 'The Researcher and the Manager: A Comparative View of the Need for Mutual Understanding', *Management Science*, vol. 20, pp. 1157–1163.

Dunne, P.M. and H.I. Wolk (1977), 'Marketing Cost Analysis: A Modularized Contribution Approach', *Journal of Marketing*, vol. 41, July, pp. 83–94.

Durbin, J. (1970), 'Testing for Serial Correlation in Least-Squares Regression when Some of the Regressors are Lagged Dependent Variables', *Econometrica*, vol. 38, pp. 410–429.

Durbin, J. and C.S. Watson (1950), 'Testing for Serial Correlation in Least Squares Regression, I', *Biometrika*, vol. 37, pp. 409–428.

Durbin, J. and C.S. Watson (1951), 'Testing for Serial Correlation in Least Squares Regression, II', *Biometrika*, vol. 38, pp. 159–178.

Dyckman, Th. (1967), 'Management Implementation of Scientific Research: An Attitudinal Study', *Management Science*, vol. 13, pp. B612–B619.

Easingwood, C.J. (1987), 'Early Product Life Cycle Forms for Infrequently Purchased Major Products', *International Journal of Research in Marketing*, vol. 4, pp. 3–9.

East, R. and K. Hammond (1996), 'The Erosion of Repeat-Purchase Loyalty', *Marketing Letters*, vol. 7, pp. 163–171.

Edelman, F. (1965), 'Art and Science of Competitive Bidding', *Harvard Business Review*, vol. 23, July-August, pp. 52–66.

Edwards, J.B. and G.H. Orcutt (1969), 'Should Estimation Prior to Aggregation be the Rule?', *The Review of Economics and Statistics*, vol. 51, pp. 409–420.

Ehrenberg, A.S.C. (1959), 'The Pattern of Consumer Purchases', *Applied Statistics*, vol. 8, pp. 26–41.

Ehrenberg, A.S.C. (1965), 'An Appraisal of Markov Brand Switching Models', *Journal of Marketing Research*, vol. 2, pp. 347–363.

Ehrenberg, A.S.C. (1970), 'Models of Fact: Examples from Marketing', *Management Science*, vol. 16, pp. 435–445.

Ehrenberg, A.S.C. (1972), *Repeat Buying, Theory and Applications*, North-Holland Publishing Company, Amsterdam.

Ehrenberg, A.S.C. (1988), *Repeat-buying: Facts, Theory and Data*, Oxford University Press, New York.

Ehrenberg, A.S.C. (1990), 'A Hope for the Future of Statistics: MSoD', *The American Statistician*, vol. 44, pp. 195–196.

Ehrenberg, A.S.C. (1994), 'Theory or Well-based Results: Which Comes First?' in Laurent, G., G.L. Lilien and B. Pras (eds.), *Research Traditions in Marketing*, Kluwer Academic Publishers, Boston, pp. 79–108.

Ehrenberg, A.S.C. (1995), 'Empirical Generalizations, Theory and Method', *Marketing Science*, vol. 14, pp. G.20–G.28.

Eliashberg, J. and G.L. Lilien (1993), 'Mathematical Marketing Models: Some Historical Perspectives and Future Projections' in Eliashberg, J. and G.L. Lilien (eds.), *Handbooks in Operations Research and Management Science, vol. 5, Marketing*, North-Holland, Amsterdam, pp. 3–23.

Eliashberg, J. and R. Steinberg (1993), 'Marketing-Production Joint Decision Making' in Eliashberg, J. and G.L. Lilien (eds.), *Handbooks in Operations Research and Management Science, vol. 5, Marketing*, North-Holland, Amsterdam, pp. 827–880.

Eliason, S.R. (1993), *Maximum Liklihood Estimation, Logic and Practice*, Sage Publications, Newbury Park, London.

Ellis, D.M. (1966), 'Building up a Sequence of Optimum Media Schedules', *Operational Research Quarterly*, vol. 17, pp. 413–424.

Elrod, T. and M.P. Keane (1995), 'A Factor Analytic Probit Model for Representing the Market Structure in Panel Data', *Journal of Marketing Research*, vol. 32, pp. 1–16.

Engel, J.F., R.D. Blackwell and P.W. Miniard (1995), *Consumer Behavior*, 8th ed., The Dryden Press, FortWorth, Texas.

Engle, R.F. and C.W.J. Granger (1987), 'Cointegration and Error Correction: Representation, Estimation and Testing', *Econometrica*, vol. 55, pp. 251–276.

Erdem, T. (1996), 'A Dynamic Analysis of Market Structure Based on Panel Data', *Marketing Science*, vol. 15, pp. 359–378.

Erickson, G.M. (1981), 'Using Ridge Regression to Estimate Directly Lagged Effects in Marketing', *Journal of the American Statistical Association*, vol. 76, pp. 766–773.

Erickson, G.M. (1991), *Dynamic Models of Advertising Competition*, Kluwer Academic Publishers, Boston.

Erickson, G.M. (1993), 'Offensive and Defensive Marketing: Closed-Loop Duopoly Strategies', *Marketing Letters*, vol. 4, pp. 285–295.

Erickson, G.M. (1995), 'Advertising Strategies in a Dynamic Oligopoly', *Journal of Marketing Research*, vol. 32, pp 233–237.

Erickson, G.M. (1997), 'Dynamic Conjectural Variations in a Lanchester Oligopoly', *Management Science*, vol. 43, pp. 1603–1608.

Eskin, G.J. (1975), 'A Case for Test Market Experiments', *Journal of Advertising Research*, vol. 15, April, pp. 27–33.

Eubank, R.L. (1988), *Spline Smoothing and Nonparametric Regression*, Marcel Dekker, New York.

Fader, P.S. and B.G.S. Hardie (1996), 'Modeling Consumer Choice Among SKUs', *Journal of Marketing Research*, vol. 33, pp. 442–452.

Fader, P.S. and J.M. Lattin (1993), 'Accounting for Heterogeneity and Nonstationary in a Cross-Sectional Model of Consumer Purchase Behaviour', *Marketing Science*, vol. 12, pp. 304–317.

Fader, P.S. and D.C. Schmittlein (1993), 'Excess Behavioral Loyalty for High Share Brands: Deviations from The Dirichlet Model for Repeat Purchasing', *Journal of Marketing Research*, vol. 30, pp. 478–493.

Farley, J.U. and H.J. Leavitt (1968), 'A Model of the Distribution of Branded Personal Products in Jamaica', *Journal of Marketing Research*, vol. 5, pp. 362–368.

Farley, J.U., D.R. Lehmann and A. Sawyer (1995), 'Empirical Marketing Generalization Using Meta-Analysis', *Marketing Science*, vol. 14, pp. G36–G46.

Farley, J.U. and L.W. Ring (1970), 'An Empirical Test of the Howard-Sheth Model of Buyer Behaviour', *Journal of Marketing Research*, vol. 7 pp. 427–438.

Farrar, D.E. and R.R. Glauber (1967), 'Multicollinearity in Regression Analysis: The Problem Revisited', *Review of Economics and Statistics*, vol. 49, pp. 92–107.

Farris, P.W., J. Olver and C.A. de Kluyver (1989), 'The Relationship between Distribution and Market Share', *Marketing Science*, vol. 8, pp. 107–128.

Farris, P.W., M.E. Parry and K.L. Ailawadi (1992), 'Structural Analysis of Models with Composite Dependent Variables', *Marketing Science*, vol. 11, pp. 76–94.

Feichtinger, G., R.F. Hartl and S.P. Sethi (1994), 'Dynamic Optimal Control Models in Advertising: Recent Developments', *Management Science*, vol. 40, pp. 195–226.

Feinberg, F.M. (1992), 'Pulsing Policies for Aggregate Advertising Models', *Marketing Science*, vol. 11, pp. 221–234.

Feldwick, P. (1990), *Advertising Works 5*, Cassell Educational Limited, London.

Feldwick, P. (1991), *Advertising Works 6*, NTC Publications, Henley-on-Thames.

Fiacco, A.V. and G.P. McCormick (1968), *Nonlinear Programming: Sequential Unconstrained Minimization Techniques*, John Wiley & Sons, New York.

Fishbein, M. (1967), *Attitude and the Prediction of Behavior: A Behavioral Theory Approach to the Relation between Beliefs about an Object and the Attitude Towards the Object. Readings in Attitude Theory and Measurement*, John Wiley & Sons, New York.

Fishbein, M. and I. Ajzen (1976), *Beliefs, Attitude, Intention and Behavior, An Introduction to Theory and Research*, Addison-Wesley Publishing Company, Reading, Mass.

Fisher, F.M. (1970), 'Test of Equality Between Sets of Coefficients in Two Linear Regressions: An Expository Note', *Econometrica*, vol. 38, pp. 361–366.

Fisher, R.A. (1950), *Contributions to Mathematical Statistics*, John Wiley & Sons, New York.

Fitzroy, P.T. (1976), *Analytical Methods for Marketing Management*, McGraw-Hill Book Company, London.

Fletcher, R. (1980), *Practical Methods of Optimization*, John Wiley & Sons, New York.

Fletcher, R. and M.J.D. Powell (1963), 'A Rapidly Convergent Descent Method for Minimization', *Computation Journal*, vol. 6, pp. 163–168.

Flinn, C. and J. Heckman (1983), 'The Likelihood Function for the Multi-State Multi-Episode Model' in *Advances in Econometrics vol. 2*, JAI–Press, Greenwich, pp. 225–231.

Foekens, E.W. (1995), *Scanner Data Based Marketing Modelling: Empirical Applications*, Unpublished Ph.D. thesis, University of Groningen, the Netherlands.

Foekens, E.W. and P.S.H. Leeflang (1992), 'Comparing Scanner Data with Traditional Store Audit Data', *Scandinavian Business Review*, vol. 1, pp. 71–85.

Foekens, E.W., P.S.H. Leeflang and D.R. Wittink (1994), 'A Comparison and an Exploration of the Forecasting Accuracy of a Loglinear Model at Different Levels of Aggregation', *International Journal of Forecasting*, vol. 10, pp. 245–261.

Foekens, E.W., P.S.H. Leeflang and D.R. Wittink (1997), 'Hierarchical versus Other Market Share Models for Markets with Many Items', *International Journal of Research in Marketing*, vol. 14, pp. 359–378.

Foekens, E.W., P.S.H. Leeflang and D.R. Wittink (1999), 'Varying Parameter Models to Accommodate Dynamic Promotion Effects', *Journal of Econometrics*, vol. 89, pp. 249–268.

Fornell, C. and D.F. Larcker (1981), 'Evaluating Structural Equation Models with Unobservable Variables and Measurement Error', *Journal of Marketing Research*, vol. 18, pp. 39–50.

Fornell, C. and R.T. Rust (1989), 'Incorporating Prior Theory in Covariance Structure Analysis: A Bayesian Approach', *Psychometrika*, vol. 54, pp. 249–259.

Forrester, J.W. (1961), *Industrial Dynamics*, M.I.T. Press, Cambridge, Mass.

Forsythe, A.B. (1972), 'Robust Estimation of Straight Line Regression Coefficients by Minimizing p-th Power Deviations', *Technometrics*, vol. 14, pp. 159–166.

Fourt, L.A. and J.W. Woodlock (1960), 'Early Predictions of Market Succes for New Grocery Products', *Journal of Marketing*, vol. 24, October, pp. 31–38.

Frankel, M.R. and L.R. Frankel (1977), 'Some Recent Developments in Sample Survey Design', *Journal of Marketing Research*, vol. 14, pp. 280–293.

Franses, Ph.H. (1991), 'Primary Demand for Beer in the Netherlands: An Application of ARMAX Model Specification', *Journal of Marketing Research*, vol. 28, pp. 240–245.

Franses, Ph.H. (1994), 'Modeling New Product Sales: An Application of Cointegration Analysis', *International Journal for Research in Marketing*, vol. 11, pp. 491–502.

Franses, Ph.H. (1996), *Periodicity and Stochastic Trends in Economic Time Series*, Oxford University Press.

Franses, Ph.H. (1998), *Time Series Models for Business and Economic Forecasting*, Cambridge University Press.

Franses, Ph.H., T. Kloek and A. Lucas (1999), 'Outlier Robust Analysis of Long-run Marketing Effects for Weekly Scanning Data', *Journal of Econometrics*, vol. 89, pp. 293–315.

Frenk, J.B.G. and S. Zhang (1997), ' On Purchase Timing Models in Marketing', Report 9720/A, Econometric Institute, Erasmus University, Rotterdam, the Netherlands.

Friedman, J.W. (1991), *Game Theory with Applications to Economics*, Oxford University Press, New York.

Friedman, L. (1958), 'Game Theory Models in the Allocation of Advertising Expenditures', *Operations Research*, vol. 6, pp. 699–709.

Friedman, M. (1953), *Essays in Positive Economics*, University of Chicago Press, Chicago.

Friedman, R. (1982), 'Multicollinearity and Ridge Regression', *Allgemeines Statistisches Archiv*, vol. 66, pp. 120–128.

Fruchter, G.E. and S. Kalish (1997), 'Closed-Loop Advertising Strategies in a Duopoly', *Management Science*, vol. 43, pp. 54–63.

Gasmi, F., J.J. Laffont and Q. Vuong (1992), 'Econometric Analysis of Collusive Behavior in a Soft-Drink Market', *Journal of Economics and Management Strategy*, vol. 1, pp. 277–311.

Gatignon, H. (1984), 'Competition as a Moderator of the Effect of Advertising on Sales', *Journal of Marketing Research*, vol. 21, pp. 387–398.

Gatignon, H. (1993), 'Marketing-Mix Models' in Eliashberg, J. and G.L. Lilien (eds.), *Handbooks in Operations Research and Management Science, vol. 5, Marketing*, North-Holland, Amsterdam, pp. 697–732.

Gatignon, H., E. Anderson and K. Helsen (1989), 'Competitive Reactions to Market Entry: Explaining Interfirm Differences', *Journal of Marketing Research*, vol. 26, pp. 44–45.

Gatignon, H. and D.M. Hanssens (1987), 'Modeling Marketing Interactions with Application to Salesforce Effectiveness', *Journal of Marketing Research*, vol. 24, pp. 247–257.

Gatignon, H., T.S. Robertson and A.J. Fein (1997), 'Incumbent Defense Strategies Against New Product Entry', *International Journal of Research in Marketing*, vol. 14, pp. 163–176.

Gaver, K.M., D. Horsky and C. Narasimhan (1988), 'Invariant Estimators for Market Share Systems and Their Finite Sample Behavior', *Marketing Science*, vol. 7, pp. 169–186.

Gensch, D.H., N. Aversa and S.P. Moore (1990), 'A Choice-Modeling Market Information System that Enabled ABB Electric to Expand its Market Share', *Interfaces*, vol. 20, pp. 6–25.

Geweke, J., R. Meese and W. Dent (1983), 'Comparing Alternative Tests of Causality in Temporal Systems', *Journal of Econometrics*, vol. 21, pp. 161–194.

Geyskens, I., J.B.E.M. Steenkamp and N. Kumar (1999), 'A Meta-Analysis of Satisfaction in Marketing Channel Relationships', *Journal of Marketing Research*, vol. 36, pp. 223–238.

Ghosh, A., S.A. Neslin and R.W. Shoemaker (1984), 'A Comparison of Market Share Models and Estimation Procedures', *Journal of Marketing Research*, vol. 21, pp. 202–210.

Gijsbrechts, E. and P.A. Naert (1984), 'Towards Hierarchical Linking of Marketing Resource Allocation to Market Areas and Product Groups', *International Journal of Research in Marketing*, vol. 1, pp. 97–116.

Givon, M. and D. Horsky (1990), 'Untangling the Effects of Purchase Reinforcement and Advertising Carryover', *Marketing Science*, vol. 9, pp. 171–187.

Golany, B., M. Kress and F.Y. Phillips (1986), 'Estimating Purchase Frequency Distributions with Incomplete Data', *International Journal of Research in Marketing*, vol. 3, pp. 169–179.

Goldberger, A.S. (1998), *Introductory Econometrics*, Harvard University Press, Cambridge, MA.

Goldberger, A.S. and C.F. Manski (1995), 'Review Article: *The Bell Curve* by Herrnstein and Muray', *Journal of Economic Literature*, vol. 23, pp. 762–776.

Goldfeld, S.M. and R.E. Quandt (1965), 'Some Tests for Homoscedasticity', *Journal of the American Statistical Association*, vol. 60, pp. 539–547.

Goldfeld, S.M. and R.E. Quandt (1972), *Nonlinear Methods in Econometrics*, North-Holland Publishing Company, Amsterdam.

Goldfeld, S.M. and R.E. Quandt (eds.) (1976), *Studies in Nonlinear Estimation*, Ballinger Publishing Company, Cambridge, Mass.

Gönül, F. and M.Z. Shi (1998), 'Optimal Mailing of Catalogs: A New Methodology Using Estimable Structural Dynamic Programming Models', *Management Science*, vol. 44, pp. 1249–1262.

Gönül, F. and K. Srinivasan (1993a), 'Modeling Multiple Sources of Heterogeneity in Multinomial Logit Models: Methodological and Managerial Issues', *Marketing Science*, vol. 12, pp. 213–229.

Gönül, F. and K. Srinivasan (1993b), 'Consumer Purchase Behaviour in a Frequently Bought Product Category: Estimation Issues and Managerial Insights From a Hazard Function Model with Heterogeneity',

Journal of the American Statistical Association, vol. 88, pp. 1219–1227.

Goodhardt, G.J., A.S.C. Ehrenberg and C. Chatfield (1984), 'The Dirichlet: A Comprehensive Model of Buying Behavior', *Journal of the Royal Statistical Society A*, vol. 147, pp. 621–655.

Gopalakrishna, S. and R. Chatterjee (1992), 'A Communications Response Model for a Mature Industrial Product: Applications and Implications', *Journal of Marketing Research*, vol. 29, pp. 189–200.

Granger, C.W.J. (1969), 'Investigating Causal Relations by Econometric Models and Cross Spectral Methods', *Econometrica*, vol. 37, pp. 424–438.

Grayson, C.J. (1967), 'The Use of Statistical Techniques in Capital Budgetting' in Robichek, A.A. (ed.), *Financial Research and Management Decisions*, John Wiley & Sons, New York.

Green, P.E., J.D. Carroll and W.S. DeSarbo (1978), 'A New Measure of Predictor Variable Importance in Multiple Regression', *Journal of Marketing Research*, vol. 15, pp. 356–360.

Green, P.E. and V. Srinivasan (1990), 'Conjoint Analysis in Marketing: New Developments with Implications for Research and Practice', *Journal of Marketing*, vol. 54, October, pp. 3–19.

Green, P.E., D.S. Tull and G. Albaum (1988), *Research for Marketing Decisions*, 5th ed., Prentice-Hall, Englewood Cliffs, NJ.

Greene, W.H. (1997), *Econometric Analysis*, 3rd ed., Prentice-Hall, Upper Saddle River, NJ.

Griffin, A. (1992), 'Evaluating QFD's Use in US Firms As a Process for Developing Products', *Journal of Product Innovation Management*, vol. 9, pp. 165–264.

Griffin, A. and J.R. Hauser (1993), 'The Voice of the Customer', *Marketing Science*, vol. 12, pp. 1–27.

Griliches, Z. (1967), 'Distributed Lags: A Survey', *Econometrica*, vol 35, pp. 16–49.

Grover, R. and V. Srinivasan (1992), 'Evaluating the Multiple Effects of Retail Promotions on Brand Loyal and Brand Switching Segments', *Journal of Marketing Research*, vol. 29, pp. 76–89.

Grunfeld, Y. and Z. Griliches (1960), 'Is Aggregation Necessarily Bad?', *The Review of Economics and Statistics*, vol. 42, pp. 1–13.

Guadagni, P.M. and J.D.C. Little (1983), 'A Logit Model of Brand Choice Calibrated on Scanner Data', *Marketing Science*, vol. 2, pp. 203–238.

Gujarati, D.N. (1995), *Basic Econometrics*, McGraw-Hill, New York.

Gupta, S. (1988), 'Impact of Sales Promotions on When, What and How Much to Buy', *Journal of Marketing Research*, vol. 25, pp. 342–355.

Gupta, S. (1991), 'Stochastic Models of Interpurchase Time with Time Dependent Covariates', *Journal of Marketing Research*, vol. 28, pp. 1–15.

Gupta, S. and L.G. Cooper (1992), 'The Discounting of Discounts and Promotion Thresholds', *Journal of Consumer Research*, vol. 19, December, pp. 401–411.

Gupta, S. and R. Loulou (1998), 'Process Innovation, Product Differentiation, and Channel Structure: Strategic Incentives in a Duopoly', *Marketing Science*, vol. 17, pp. 301–316.

Gupta, Sachin and P.K. Chintagunta (1994), 'On Using Demographic Variables to Determine Segment Membership in Logit Mixture Models', *Journal of Marketing Research*, vol. 31, pp. 128–136.

Gupta, Sachin, P.K. Chintagunta, A. Kaul and D.R. Wittink (1996), 'Do Household Scanner Data Provide Representative Inferences From Brand Choices: A Comparison with Store Data', *Journal of Marketing Research*, vol. 33, pp. 383–398.

Gupta, Sunil (1994), 'Managerial Judgment and Forecast Combination: An Experimental Study', *Marketing Letters*, vol. 5, pp. 5–17.

Gupta, S.K. and K.S. Krishnan (1967a), 'Differential Equation Approach to Marketing', *Operations Research*, vol. 15, pp. 1030–1039.

Gupta, S.K. and K.S. Krishnan (1967b), 'Mathematical Models in Marketing', *Operations Research*, vol. 15, pp. 1040–1050.

Gupta, U.G. and R.E. Clarke (1996), 'Theory and Applications of the Delphi Technique: A Bibliography (1975–1994)', *Technological Forecasting and Social Change*, vol. 53, pp. 185–212.

Haaijer, R., M. Wedel, M. Vriens and T.J. Wansbeek (1998), 'Utility Covariances and Context Effects in Conjoint MNP Models', *Marketing Science*, vol. 17, pp. 236–252.

Hagerty, M.R. and V. Srinivasan (1991), 'Comparing the Predictive Powers of Alternative Multiple Regression Models', *Psychometrika*, vol. 56, March, pp. 77–85.

Hahn, M. and J.S. Hyun (1991), 'Advertising Cost Interactions and the Optimality of Pulsing', *Management Science*, vol. 37, pp. 157–169.

Hair, J.E., R.E. Anderson, R.L. Tatham and W.C. Black (1995), *Multivariate Data Analysis with Readings,* Prentice-Hall, London.

Hamilton, J.D. (1994), *Time Series Analysis*, Princeton University Press, Princeton, NJ.

Hammond, J.S. (1974), 'The Roles of the Manager and Management Scientist in Successful Implementation', *Sloan Management Review*, vol. 16. pp. 1–24.

Hampton, J.M., P.G. Moore and H. Thomas (1973), 'Subjective Probability and Its Measurement', Memeographic Notes, London Graduate School of Business Studies.

Hanson, W. and R.K. Martin (1990), 'Optimal Price Bundling', *Management Science*, vol. 36, pp. 155–174.

Hanssens, D.M. (1980a), 'Bivariate Time Series Analysis of the Relationship between Advertising and Sales', *Applied Economics*, vol. 12, pp. 329–340.

Hanssens, D.M. (1980b), 'Market Response, Competitive Behavior and Time Series Analysis', *Journal of Marketing Research*, vol. 17, pp. 470–485.

Hanssens, D.M. and L.J. Parsons (1993), 'Econometric and Time-Series Market Response Models' in Eliashberg, J. and G.L. Lilien (eds.), *Handbooks in Operations Research and Management Science, vol. 5, Marketing*, North-Holland, Amsterdam, pp. 409–464.

Hanssens, D.M., L.J. Parsons and R.L. Schultz (1990), *Market Response Models: Econometric and Time Series Analysis*, Kluwer Academic Publishers, Boston.

Harary, F. and B. Lipstein (1962), 'The Dynamics of Brand Loyalty: a Markovian Approach', *Operations Research*, vol. 10, pp. 19–40.

Härdle, W. (1990), *Applied Nonparametric Regression*, Econometrics Society Monographs, vol. 19, Cambridge University Press, Cambridge.

Härdle, W. and O. Linton (1994), 'Applied Nonparametric Methods' in Engle, R.F. and D.L. McFadden (eds.), *Handbook of Econometrics*, vol. 4, Elsevier Science B.V., Amsterdam.

Hastie, T.J. and R.J. Tibshirani (1990), *Generalized Additive Models*, Chapman and Hall, London.

Hartung, P.H. and J.L. Fisher (1965) 'Brand Switching and Mathematical Programming in Market Expansion', *Management Science*, vol. 11, pp. 231–243.

Hashemzadeh, N. and P. Taylor (1988), 'Stock Prices, Money Supply, and Interest Rates, the Question of Causality', *Applied Economics*, vol. 20, pp. 1603–1611.

Haugh, L.D. (1976), 'Checking the Independence of Two Covariance Stationary Time Series: A Univariate Residual Cross Correlation Approach', *Journal of the American Statistical Association*, vol. 71, pp. 378–385.

Hauser, J.R. and D. Clausing (1988), 'The House of Quality', *Harvard Business Review*, vol. 66, May/June, pp. 63–73.

Hauser, J.R., D.I. Simester and B. Wernerfelt (1996), 'Internal Customers and Internal Suppliers', *Journal of Marketing Research*, vol. 33, pp. 268–280.

Hauser, J.R. and B. Wernerfelt (1990), 'An Evaluation Cost Model of Consideration Sets', *Journal of Consumer Research*, vol. 17, pp. 393–408.

Hausman, W.H. and D.B. Montgomery (1997), 'Market Driven Manufacturing', *Journal of Market Focused Management*, vol. 2, pp. 27–47.

Haynes, B. and J.T. Rothe (1974), 'Competitive Bidding for Marketing Research Services: Fact or Fiction', *Journal of Marketing*, vol. 38, July, pp. 69–71.

Heeler, R.M. and M.L. Ray (1972), 'Measure Validation in Marketing', *Journal of Marketing Research*, vol. 9, pp. 361–370.

Heerde, H.J. van (1999), *Models for Sales Promotion Effects Based on Store-level Scanner Data*, Unpublished Ph.D. thesis, Universtiy of Groningen, the Netherlands.

Heerde, H.J. van, P.S.H. Leeflang and D.R. Wittink (1997), 'Semiparametric Analysis of the Deal Effect Curve', Working paper, first version, Faculty of Economics, University of Groningen, the Netherlands.

Heerde, H.J. van, P.S.H. Leeflang and D.R. Wittink (1999a), 'Semiparametric Analysis of the Deal Effect Curve', Working paper, Faculty of Economics, University of Groningen, the Netherlands.

Heerde, H.J. van, P.S.H. Leeflang and D.R. Wittink (1999b), 'Decomposing the Sales Effect of Promotions with Store-Level Scanner Data', Working paper, Faculty of Economics, University of Groningen, the Netherlands.

Heerde, H.J. van, P.S.H. Leeflang and D.R. Wittink (1999c), 'The Estimation of Pre- and Postpromotion Dips with Store-Level Scanner Data', *Journal of Marketing Research*, forthcoming.

Helmer, O. (1966), *Social Technology*, Basic Books, New York.

Helsen, K. and D.C. Schmittlein (1993), 'Analysing Duration Times in Marketing: Evidence for the Effectiveness of Hazard Models', *Marketing Science*, vol. 11, pp. 395–414.

Hendry, D.F. (1989), *PG-GIVE: An Interactive Econometric Modeling System*, University of Oxford, Oxford.

Herniter, J.D. (1971), 'A Probabilistic Market Model of Purchasing Timing and Brand Selection', *Management Science*, vol. 18, pp. 102–113.

Herniter, J.D. and R.A. Howard (1964), 'Stochastic Marketing Models' in Hertz, D.B. and R.T. Eddison (eds.), *Progress in Operations Research*, John Wiley & Sons, New York, vol. 2, pp. 33–96.

Hess, J.E. (1968), 'Transfer Pricing in a Decentralized Firm', *Management Science*, pp. B310–B331

Hildreth, C. and J.Y. Lu (1960), 'Demand Relations with Autocorrelated Disturbances', Michigan State University, Agricultural Experiment Station, Technical Bulletin 276, East Lansing, Mich.

Hinich, M.J. and P.P. Talwar (1975), 'A Simple Method for Robust Regression', *Journal of the American Statistical Association*, vol. 70, pp. 113–119.

Hoch, S.J., B. Kim, A.L. Montgomery and P.E. Rossi (1995), 'Determinants of Store-Level Price Elasticity', *Journal of Marketing Research*, vol. 32, pp. 17–29.

Hocking, R.R. (1976), 'The Analysis and Selection of Variables in Linear Regression', *Biometrics*, vol. 32, pp. 1–49.

Hoekstra, J.C. (1987), *Handelen van Heroinegebruikers: Effecten van Beleidsmaatregelen*, Unpublished Ph.D. thesis, University of Groningen, the Netherlands.

Hoekstra, J.C., P.S.H. Leeflang and D.R. Wittink (1999), 'The Customer Concept', *Journal of Market Focussed Management*, vol. 4, pp. 43–75.

Hoerl, A.E. and R.W. Kennard (1970), 'Ridge Regression: Applications to Nonorthogonal Problems', *Technometrics*, vol. 12, pp. 69–82.

Hofstede, F. ter, J.B.E.M. Steenkamp and M. Wedel (1999), 'International Market Segmentation Based on Consumer-Product Relations', *Journal of Marketing Research*, vol. 36, pp. 1–17.

Hogarth, R. (1987), *Judgment and Choice* 2nd ed., John Wiley & Sons, New York.

Hooley, G.J. and J. Saunders (1993), *Competitive Positioning*, Prentice-Hall, New York.

Horowitz, I. (1970), *Decision Making and the Theory of the Firm*, New York, Holt, Rinehart and Winston, Inc.

Horsky, D. (1977a), 'Market Share Response to Advertising: An Example of Theory Testing', *Journal of Marketing Research*, vol. 14, pp. 10–21.

Horsky, D. (1977b), 'An Empirical Analysis of the Optimal Advertising Policy', *Management Science*, vol. 23, pp. 1037–1049.

Horsky, D. and L.S. Simon (1983), 'Advertising and the Diffusion of New Products', *Marketing Science*, vol. 2, pp. 1–10.

Houston, F.S. (1977), 'An Econometric Analysis of Positioning', *Journal of Business Administration*, vol. 9, pp. 1–12.

Houston, F.S. and D.L. Weiss (1974), 'An Analysis of Competitive Market Behavior', *Journal of Marketing Research*, vol. 11, pp. 151–155.

Howard, J.A. and W.M. Morgenroth (1968), 'Information Processing Model of Executive Decisions', *Management Science*, vol 14, pp. 416–428.

Howard, J.A. and J.N. Sheth (1969), *The Theory of Buyer Behavior*, John Wiley & Sons, New York.

Howard, R.A. (1963), 'Stochastic Process Models of Consumer Behavior', *Journal of Advertising Research*, vol. 3, pp. 35–42.

Huber, P.J. (1973), 'Robust Regression: Asymptotics, Conjectures and Monte Carlo', *The Annals of Statistics*, vol. 1, pp. 799–821.

Hughes, G.D. (1973), *Demand Analysis for Marketing Decisions*, Homewood, Ill., Richard D. Irwin, Inc.

Hulbert, J.M. and M.E. Toy (1977), 'A Strategic Framework for Marketing Control', *Journal of Marketing*, vol. 41, April, pp. 12–20.

Huse, E. (1980), *Organizational Development and Change*, West Publishing, New York.

Huysmans, J.H. (1970a), 'The Effectiveness of the Cognitive Style Constraint in Implementing Operations Research Proposals', *Management Science*, vol. 17, pp. 92–104.

Huysmans, J.H. (1970b), *The Implementation of Operations Research*, Wiley-Interscience, New York.

Intriligator, M.D., R.G. Bodkin and C. Hsiao (1996), *Econometric Models, Techniques and Applications*, Prentice Hall, Upper Saddle River, NJ.

Iversen, G.R. (1984), *Bayesian Statistical Inference*, Sage Publications, London.

Iyer, G. (1998), 'Coordinating Channels Under Price and Nonprice Competion', *Marketing Science*, vol. 17, pp. 338–355.

Jain, D.C. and N.J. Vilcassim (1991), 'Investigating Household Purchase Timing Decisions: A Conditional Hazard Function Approach', *Marketing Science*, vol. 10, pp. 1–23.

Jain, D.C., N.J. Vilcassim and P.K. Chintagunta (1994), 'A Random-Coefficients Logit Brand-Choice Model Applied to Panel Data', *Journal of Business and Economic Statistics*, vol. 12, pp. 317–328.

Jain, S.C. (1993), *Marketing Planning & Strategy*, 4th ed., South-Western Publishing Co., Cincinnati, Ohio.

Jamieson, L. and F.M. Bass (1989), 'Adjusted Stated Intention Measures to Predict Trial Purchase of New Products: A Comparison of Models and Methods', *Journal of Marketing Research*, vol. 26, pp. 336–345.

Jedidi, K., C.F. Mela and S. Gupta (1999), 'Managing Advertising and Promotions for Long-Run Profitability', *Marketing Science*, vol. 18, pp. 1–22.

Jeuland, A.P., F.M. Bass and G.P. Wright (1980), 'A Multibrand Stochastic Model Compounding Heterogeneous Erlang Timing and Multinomial Choice Process', *Operations Research*, vol. 28, pp. 255–277.

Johansson, J.K. (1973), 'A Generalized Logistic Function with an Application to the Effect of Advertising', *Journal of the American Statistical Association*, vol. 68, pp. 824–827.

Johansson, J.K. (1979), 'Advertising and the S-curve: A New Approach', *Journal of Marketing Research*, vol. 16, pp. 346–354.

Johnson, E.J. and J. Payne (1985), 'Effort and Accuracy in Choice', *Management Science*, April, vol. 31,4, pp. 395–415.

Johnson, E.J. and J.E. Russo (1994), 'Competitive Decision Making: Two and a Half Frames', *Marketing Letters*, vol. 4, pp. 289–302.

Johnston, J. (1984), *Econometric Methods*, McGraw-Hill, New York.

Jones, J. (1986), *What's in a Name?*, Gower, Aldershot.

Jones, J.M. (1973), 'A Composite Heterogeneous Model for Brand Choice Behavior', *Management Science*, vol. 19, pp. 499–509.

Jones, J.M. and J.T. Landwehr (1988), 'Removing Heterogeneity Bias from Logit Model Estimation', *Marketing Science*, vol. 7, pp. 41–59.

Jöreskog, K.G. (1973), 'A General Method for Estimating a Linear Structural Equation System' in Goldberger, A.S. and O.D. Duncan (eds.), *Structural Equation Models in Mathematical Psychology*, vol. 2, New York: Seminar, pp. 85–112.

Jöreskog, K.G. (1978), 'Statistical Analysis of Covariance and Correlation Matrices', *Psychometrica*, vol. 43, pp 443–477.

Jöreskog, K.G. and D. Sörbom (1989), *LISREL 7: A Guide to the Program and Applications*, 2nd ed., SPSS, Chicago.

Judge, G.G., W.E. Griffiths, R.C. Hill, H. Lütkepohl and T.C. Lee (1985), *The Theory and Practice of Econometrics*, 2nd ed., John Wiley & Sons, New York.

Juhl, H.J. and K. Kristensen (1989), 'Multiproduct Pricing: A Microeconomic Simplification', *International Journal of Research in Marketing*, vol. 6, pp. 175–182.

Kadiyali, V. (1996), 'Entry, its Deterrence, and its Accommodation: A Study of the U.S. Photographic Film Industry', *Rand Journal of Economics*, vol. 27, pp. 452–478.

Kadiyali, V., N.J. Vilcassim and P.K. Chintagunta (1996), 'Empirical Analysis of Competitive Product Line Pricing Decisions: Lead, Follow or More Together?', *Journal of Business*, vol. 69, pp. 459–488.

Kadiyali, V., N.J. Vilcassim and P.K. Chintagunta (1999), 'Product Line Extensions and Competive Market Interactions: An Empirical Analysis', *Journal of Econometrics*, vol. 89, pp. 339–363.

Kahn, B.E. (1998), 'Dynamic Relationships With Customers: High-Variety Strategies', *Journal of the Acadamy of Marketing Science*, vol. 26, No. 1, pp. 45–53.

Kaicker, A. and W.O. Bearden (1995), 'Component versus Bundle Pricing', *Journal of Business Research*, vol. 33, pp. 231–240.

Kalra, A., S. Rajiv and K. Srinivasan (1998), 'Response to Competitive Entry: A Rationale for Delayed Defensive Reaction', *Marketing Science*, vol. 17, pp. 380–405.

Kalwani, M.U., R.J. Meyer and D.G. Morrison (1994), 'Benchmarks for Discrete Choice Models', *Journal of Marketing Research*, vol. 31, pp. 65–75.

Kalwani, M.U. and D.G. Morrison (1977), 'A Parsimonious Description of the Hendry System', *Management Science*, vol. 23, pp. 467–477.

Kalwani, M.U. and A.J. Silk (1982), 'On the Reliability Validity of Purchase Intention Measures', *Marketing Science*, vol. 1, pp. 243–286.

Kalwani, M.U. and C.K. Yim (1992), 'Consumer Price and Promotion Expectations: An Experimental Study', *Journal of Marketing Research*, vol. 29, pp. 90–100.

Kalyanam, K. and T.S. Shively (1998), 'Estimating Irregular Pricing Effects: A Stochastic Spline Regression Approach', *Journal of Marketing Research*, vol. 35, pp. 16–29.

Kamakura, W.A. and S.K. Balasubramanian (1988), 'Long-term View of the Diffusion of Durables', *International Journal of Research in Marketing*, vol. 5, pp. 1–13.

Kamakura, W.A., B. Kim and J. Lee (1996), 'Modelling Preference and Structural Heterogeneity in Consumer Choice', *Marketing Science*, vol. 15, pp. 152–172.

Kamakura, W.A. and G.J. Russell (1989), 'A Probabilistic Choice Model for Market Segmentation and Elasticity Structure', *Journal of Marketing Research*, vol. 26, pp. 379–390.

Kamakura, W.A. and G.J. Russell (1993), 'Measuring Brand Value with Scanner Data', *International Journal of Research in Marketing*, vol. 10, pp. 9–22.

Kamakura, W.A. and R.K. Srivastava (1984), 'Predicting Choice Shares Under Conditions of Brand Interdependence', *Journal of Marketing Research*, vol. 21, pp. 420–434.

Kamakura, W.A. and R.K. Srivastava (1986), 'An Ideal Point Probabilistic Choice Model for Heterogeneous Preferences', *Marketing Science*, vol. 5, pp. 199–218.

Kamakura, W.A. and M. Wedel (1997), 'Statistical Data Fusion for Cross-Tabulation', *Journal of Marketing Research*, vol. 34, pp. 485–498.

Kamakura, W.A., M. Wedel and J. Agrawal (1994), 'Concomitant Variable Latent Class Models for Conjoint Analysis', *International Journal of Research in Marketing*, vol. 11, pp. 451–464.

Kanetkar, V., C.B. Weinberg and D.L. Weiss (1986), 'Estimating Parameters of the Autocorrelated Current Effects Model from Temporally Aggregated Data', *Journal of Marketing Research*, vol. 23, pp. 379–386.

Kanetkar, V., C.B. Weinberg and D.L. Weiss (1992), 'Price Sensitivity and Television Advertising Exposures: Some Empirical Findings', *Marketing Science*, vol. 11, pp. 359–371.

Kannan, P.K. and G.P. Wright (1991), 'Modelling and Testing Structured Markets: A Nested Logit Approach', *Marketing Science*, vol. 10, pp. 58–82.

Kapteyn, A., S. van de Geer, H. van de Stadt and T.J. Wansbeek (1997), 'Interdependent Preferences: An Econometric Analysis', *Journal of Applied Econometrics*, vol. 12, pp. 665–686.

Kapteyn, A., T.J. Wansbeek and J. Buyze (1980), 'The Dynamics of Preference Formation', *Journal of Economic Behavior and Organization*, vol. 1, pp. 123–157.

Karmarkar, K.S. (1996), 'Integrative Research in Marketing and Operations Management', *Journal of Marketing Research*, vol. 33, pp. 125–133.

Kass, G.V. (1976), *Significance Testing in, and Some Extensions of, Automatic Interaction Detection*, Doctoral Dissertation, University of Witwatersrand, Johannesburg, South Africa.

Kaul, A. and D.R. Wittink (1995), 'Empirical Generalizations about the Impact of Advertising on Price Sensitivity and Price', *Marketing Science*, vol. 14, pp. G151–G160.

Kealy, M.J., J.F. Dovidio and M.L. Rockel (1988), 'Accuracy in Valuation is a Matter of Degree', *Land Economics*, vol. 64, pp. 158–171.

Kealy, M.J., M. Montgomery and J.F. Dovidio (1990), 'Reliability and Predictive Validity of Contingent Values: Does the Nature of the Good Matter?', *Journal of Environmental Economics and Management*, vol. 19, pp. 244–263.

Keller, K.L. (1993), 'Conceptualizing Measuring and Managing Customer-Based Brand Equity', *Journal of Marketing*, vol. 57, January, pp. 1–22.

Kenkel, J.L. (1974), 'Some Small Sample Properties of Durbin's Test for Serial Correlation in Regression Models Containing Lagged Dependent Variables', *Econometrica*, vol. 42, pp. 763–769.

Ketellapper, R.H. (1981), 'On Estimating a Consumption Function when Incomes are Subject to Measurement Errors', *Economics Letters*, vol. 7, pp. 343–348.

Ketellapper, R.H. (1982), *The Impact of Observational Errors on Parameter Estimation in Econometrics*, Unpublished Ph.D. thesis, University of Groningen, the Netherlands.

Kim, B. (1995), 'Incorporating Heterogeneity with Store-Level Aggregate Data', *Marketing Letters*, vol. 6, pp. 159–169.

Kim, N., E. Bridges and R.K. Srivastava (1999), 'A Simultaneous Model for Innovative Product Category Sales Diffusion and Competitive Dynamics', *International Journal of Research in Marketing*, vol. 16 pp. 95–111.

Kim, S.Y. and R. Staelin (1999), 'Manufacturer Allowances and Retailer Pass-Through Rates in a Competitive Evironment', *Marketing Science*, vol. 18, pp. 59–76.

Kimball, G.E. (1957), 'Some Industrial Applications of Military Operations Research Methods', *Operations Research*, vol. 5, pp. 201–204.

King, W.R. (1967), *Quantitative Analysis for Marketing Management*, McGraw-Hill Book Company, New York.

Klein, L.R. (1962), *An Introduction to Econometrics*, Prentice-Hall, Englewood Cliffs, NJ.

Klein, L.R. and Lansing, J.B. (1955), 'Decisions to Purchase Consumer Durable Goods', *Journal of Marketing*, vol. 20, pp. 109–132.

Kmenta, J. (1971), *Elements of Econometrics*, Macmillan Publishing Co., New York.

Koerts, J. and A.P.J. Abrahamse (1969), *On the Theory and Application of the General Linear Model*, Rotterdam University Press, Rotterdam.

Körösi, G., L. Mátyás and I.P. Székely (1992), *Practical Econometrics*, Avebury, Aldershot, England.

Kotler, Ph. (1971), *Marketing Decision Making: A Model Building Approach*, Holt, Rinehart and Winston, New York.

Kotler, Ph. (1997), *Marketing Management: Analysis, Planning, Implementation, and Control*, 9th edition, Prentice Hall, Upper Saddle River, NJ.

Koyck, L.M. (1954), *Distributed Lags and Investment Analysis*, North-Holland Publishing Company, Amsterdam.

Kreps, D.M. and R. Wilson (1982), 'Reputation and Imperfect Information', *Journal of Economic Theory*, vol. 27, pp. 253–279.

Krishna, A. (1991), 'Effect of Dealing Patterns on Consumer Perceptions of Deal Frequency and Willingness to Pay', *Journal of Marketing Research*, vol. 28, pp. 441–451.

Krishna, A. (1992), 'The Normative Impact of Consumer Price Expectations for Multiple Brands on Consumer Purchase Behavior', *Marketing Science*, vol. 11, pp. 266–286.

Krishna, A. (1994), 'The Impact of Dealing Patterns on Purchase Behavior', *Marketing Science*, vol. 13, pp. 351–373.

Krishnamurthi, L. and S.P. Raj (1985), 'The Effect of Advertising on Consumer Price Sensitivity', *Journal of Marketing Research*, vol. 22, pp. 119–129.

Krishnamurthi, L. and S.P. Raj (1988), 'A Model of Brand Choice and Purchase Quantity Price Sensitivities', *Marketing Science*, vol. 7, pp. 1–20.

Krishnamurthi, L. and S.P. Raj (1991), 'An Empirical Analysis of the Relationship Between Brand Loyalty and Consumer Price Elasticity', *Marketing Science*, vol. 10, pp. 172–183.

Krishnamurthi, L., S.P. Raj and R. Selvam (1990), 'Statistical and Managerial Issues in Cross-Sectional Aggregation', Working paper, Northwestern University.

Krishnamurthi, L. and A. Rangaswamy (1987), 'The Equity Estimator for Marketing Research', *Marketing Science*, vol. 6, pp. 336–357.

Krishnan, K.S. and S.K. Gupta (1967), 'Mathematical Models for a Duopolistic Market', *Management Science*, vol. 13, pp. 568–583.

Krishnan, T.V. and H. Soni (1997), 'Guaranteed Profit Margins: A Demonstration of Retailer Power', *International Journal of Research in Marketing*, vol. 14, pp. 35–56.

Kristensen, K. (1984), 'Hedonic Theory, Marketing Research, and the Analysis of Complex Goods', *International Journal of Research in Marketing*, vol. 1, pp. 17–36.

Kuehn, A.A. (1961), 'A Model for Budgeting Advertising' in Bass, F.M. and R.D. Buzzell (eds.), *Mathematical Models and Methods in Marketing*, Homewood, Ill., Richard D. Irwin, Inc., pp. 315–348.

Kuehn, A.A. (1962), 'Consumer Brand Choice as a Learning Process', *Journal of Advertising Research*, vol. 2, pp. 10–17.

Kuehn, A.A. and M.J. Hamburger (1963), 'A Heuristic Program for Locating Warehouses', *Management Science*, vol. 9, pp. 643–666.

Kumar, N., L.K. Scheer and J.B.E.M. Steenkamp (1995a), 'The Effects of Supplier Fairness on Vulnerable Resellers', *Journal of Marketing Research*, vol. 32, pp. 54–65.

Kumar, N., L.K. Scheer and J.B.E.M. Steenkamp (1995b), 'The Effects of Percieved Interdependence on Dealer Attitudes', *Journal of Marketing Research*, vol. 32, pp. 348–356.

Kumar, T.K. (1975), 'Multicollinearity in Regression Analysis', *The Review of Economics and Statistics*, vol. 57, pp. 365–366.

Kumar, V. (1994), 'Forecasting Performance of Market Share Models: An Assessment, Additional Insights, and Guidelines', *International Journal of Forecasting*, vol.10, pp. 295–312.

LaForge, R.W. and D.W. Cravens (1985), 'Empirical and Judgement-based Salesforce Decision Models: A Comparative Analysis', *Decision Sciences*, vol. 16, pp. 177–195.

LaForge, R.W., C.W. Lamb jr., D.W. Cravens and W.C. Moncrief III (1989), 'Improving Judgement-Based

Salesforce Decision Model Applications', *Journal of the Academy of Marketing Science*, vol. 17, pp. 167–177.

Lal, R. and C. Narasimhan (1996), 'The Inverse Relationship Between Manufacturer and Retailer Margins: A Theory', *Marketing Science*, vol. 15, pp. 113–131.

Lal, R. and R. Staelin (1986), 'Salesforce Compensation Plans in Environments with Asymmetric Information', *Marketing Science*, vol. 5, pp. 179–198.

Lal, R. and J.M. Villas-Boas (1998), 'Price Promotions and Trade Deals with Multiproduct Retailers', *Management Science*, vol. 44, pp. 935–949.

Lambin, J.J. (1969), 'Measuring the Profitability of Advertising: An Empirical Study', *Journal of Industrial Economics*, vol. 17, pp. 86–103.

Lambin, J.J. (1970), *Modèles et Programmes de Marketing*, Presses Universitaires de France, Paris.

Lambin, J.J. (1972a), 'Is Gasoline Advertising Justified?', *Journal of Business*, vol. 45, pp. 585–619.

Lambin, J.J. (1972b), 'A Computer On-Line Marketing Mix Model', *Journal of Marketing Research*, vol. 9, pp. 119–126.

Lambin, J.J. (1976), *Advertising, Competition and Market Conduct in Oligopoly over Time*, North-Holland Publishing Company, Amsterdam.

Lambin, J.J., P.A. Naert and A.V. Bultez (1975), 'Optimal Marketing Behavior in Oligopoly' *European Economic Review*, vol. 6, pp. 105–128.

Lancaster, K.M. (1984), 'Brand Advertising Competition and Industry Demand', *Journal of Advertising*, vol. 13 (4), pp. 19–24.

Larréché, J.C. (1974), *Marketing Managers and Models: A Search for a Better Match*, Unpublished Ph.D. thesis, Stanford University.

Larréché, J.C. (1975), 'Marketing Managers and Models: A Search for a Better Match', Research Paper Series, No. 157, INSEAD, Fontainebleau.

Larréché, J.C. and R. Moinpour (1983), 'Managerial Judgement in Marketing: The Concept of Expertise', *Journal of Marketing Research*, vol 20, pp. 110–121.

Larréché, J.C. and D.B. Montgomery (1977), 'A Framework for the Comparison of Marketing Models: A Delphi Study', *Journal of Marketing Research*, vol. 14, pp. 487–498.

Larréché, J.C. and V. Srinivasan (1981), 'STRATPORT: A Decision Support System for Strategic Planning', *Journal of Marketing*, vol. 45, nr. 4, pp. 39–52.

Larréché, J.C. and V. Srinivasan (1982), 'STRATPORT: A Model for the Evaluation and Formulation of Business Portfolio Strategies', *Management Science*, vol. 28, pp. 979–1001.

Lawrence, M.J., R.H. Edmundson and M.J. O'Connor (1986), 'The Accuracy of Combining Judgmental and Statistical Forecasts', *Management Science*, vol. 32. pp. 1521–1532.

Lawrence, R.J. (1975), 'Consumer Brand Choice - A Random Walk?', *Journal of Marketing Research*, vol. 12, pp. 314–324.

Leamer, E.E. (1978), *Specification Searches: Ad Hoc Inference with Nonexperimental Data*, John Wiley & Sons, New York.

Lee, A.M. (1962), 'Decision Rules for Media Scheduling: Static Campaigns', *Operational Research Quarterly*, vol. 13, pp. 229–241.

Lee, A.M. (1963), 'Decision Rules for Media Scheduling: Dynamic Campaigns', *Operational Research Quarterly*, vol. 14, pp. 113–122.

Lee, A.M. and A.J. Burkart (1960), 'Some Optimization Problems in Advertising Media', *Operations Research Quarterly*, vol. 11, pp. 113–122.

Lee, M. (1996), *Methods of Moments and Semiparametric Econometrics for Limited Dependent Variable Models*, Springer-Verlag, New York.

Lee, P.M. (1997), *Bayesian Statistics*, John Wiley & Sons, New York.

Lee, T.C., G.G. Judge and A. Zellner (1970), *Estimating the Parameters of the Markov Probability Model from Aggregate Time Series Data*, North-Holland Publishing Company, Amsterdam.

Leeflang, P.S.H. (1974), *Mathematical Models in Marketing, a Survey, the Stage of Development, Some Extensions and Applications*, H.E. Stenfert Kroese, Leiden.

Leeflang, P.S.H. (1975), 'The Allocation of Shelf Space over Article Groups: A Portfolio Problem', *Proceedings ESOMAR-seminar of Product Range Policy in Retailing and Co-operation with Manufacturers*, Breukelen, The Netherlands, pp. 37–73.

Leeflang, P.S.H. (1976), 'Marktonderzoek en Marketingmodellen', *Marktonderzoek en Consumentengedrag, Jaarboek Nederlandse Vereniging van Marktonderzoekers*, vol. 2, pp. 217–252.

Leeflang, P.S.H. (1977a), 'Organising Market Data for Decision Making through the Development of

Mathematical Marketing Models', *Proceedings ESOMAR-seminar on Marketing Management Information Systems: Organising Market Data for Decision Making*, Brussels, Belgium, pp. 29–54.

Leeflang, P.S.H. (1977b), 'A Comparison of Alternative Specifications of Market Share Models' in Van Bochove, C.A., C.J. van Eyk, J.C. Siebrand, A.S.W. de Vries and A. Van der Zwan (eds.), *Modeling for Government and Business, Essays in Honor of Professor Dr. P.J. Verdoorn*, Martinus Nijhoff Social Sciences Division, Leiden, pp. 247–281.

Leeflang, P.S.H. (1995), 'Modelling Markets' in M.J. Baker (ed.), *Marketing Theory and Practice*, 3rd ed., MacMillan Business, London, pp. 125–159.

Leeflang, P.S.H., K.J. Alsem and J.C. Reuyl (1991), 'Diagnosing Competition for Public Policy Purposes', Working Paper No. 207, Marketing Studies Center, John E. Anderson Graduate School of Management, UCLA.

Leeflang, P.S.H. and A. Boonstra (1982), 'Some Comments on the Development and Application of Linear Learning Models', *Management Science*, vol. 26, pp. 1233–1246.

Leeflang, P.S.H. and J.J. van Duyn (1982a), 'The Use of Regional Data in Marketing Models: The Demand for Beer in the Netherlands, Part 1: Regional Models', *European Research*, vol. 10, pp. 2–9.

Leeflang, P.S.H. and J.J. van Duyn (1982b), 'The Use of Regional Data in Marketing Models: The Demand for Beer in the Netherlands, Part 2: Pooling Regional Data', *European Research*, vol. 10, pp. 64–71.

Leeflang, P.S.H. and J. Koerts (1973), 'Modeling and Marketing, Two Important Concepts and the Connection Between Them', *European Journal of Marketing*, vol. 7, pp. 203–217.

Leeflang, P.S.H. and J. Koerts (1974), 'Some Applications of Mathematical Response Models in Marketing based on Markovian Consumer Behaviour Models', *Proceedings ESOMAR-seminar for Forecasting in Marketing*, Amsterdam, pp. 287–319.

Leeflang, P.S.H. and J. Koerts (1975), 'A Concise Survey of Mathematical Models in Marketing' in Elliot, K. (ed.), *Management Bibliographies and Reviews*, vol. 1, MCB Books, Bradford, pp. 101–124.

Leeflang, P.S.H. and G.M. Mijatovic (1988), 'The Geometric Dual Lag Model', Research Memorandum no. 260, Insitute of Economic Research, Groningen University, The Netherlands.

Leeflang, P.S.H., G.M. Mijatovic and J. Saunders (1992), 'Identification and Estimation of Complex Multivariate Lag Structures: A Nesting Approach', *Applied Economics*, vol. 24, pp. 273–283.

Leeflang, P.S.H. and A.J. Olivier (1980), 'What's Wrong with the Audit Data We Use for Decision Making in Marketing', *Proceedings 33rd ESOMAR Congress*, Monte Carlo, pp. 219–239.

Leeflang, P.S.H. and A.J. Olivier (1982), 'Facing Panel Non-response, Consequences and Solution', *Proceedings 35th ESOMAR Congress*, Vienna, pp. 417–440.

Leeflang, P.S.H. and A.J. Olivier (1985), 'Bias in Consumer Panel and Store Audit Data', *International Journal of Research in Marketing*, vol. 2, pp. 27–41.

Leeflang, P.S.H. and F.W. Plat (1984), 'Consumer Response in an Era of Stagflation', *Proceedings EMAC/ESOMAR Symposium on Methodological Advances in Marketing Research in Theory and Practice*, Copenhagen, pp. 195–227.

Leeflang, P.S.H. and F.W. Plat (1988), 'Scanning Scanning Opportunities', *Proceedings 41st ESOMAR Conference*, Lissabon, pp. 471–484.

Leeflang, P.S.H. and J.C. Reuyl (1979), 'On the Application of Generalized Least Squares Methods to Logical Consistent Market Share Models', Onderzoeksmemorandum nr. 56, Institute of Economic Research, Faculty of Economics, University of Groningen.

Leeflang, P.S.H. and J.C. Reuyl (1983), 'On the Application of a New Estimator of the Disturbances in Logically Consistent Market Share Models', *Proceedings of the XII-th Annual Conference of the European Marketing Academy*, Grenoble, pp. 163–184.

Leeflang, P.S.H. and J.C. Reuyl (1984a),'On the Predictive Power of Market Share Attraction Models', *Journal of Marketing Research*, vol. 11, pp. 211–215.

Leeflang, P.S.H. and J.C. Reuyl (1984b), 'Estimators of the Disturbances in Consistent Sum-Constrained Market Share Models', paper presented at the ORSA-TIMS Marketing Science Congress, Chicago.

Leeflang, P.S.H. and J.C. Reuyl (1985a), 'Advertising and Industry Sales: An Empirical Study of the West German Cigarette Market', *Journal of Marketing*, vol. 49, pp. 92–98.

Leeflang, P.S.H. and J.C. Reuyl (1985b), 'Competitive Analysis Using Market Response Functions' in Lusch, R.F. et al. (eds.), *Educators' Proceedings*, American Marketing Association, Chicago, pp. 388–395.

Leeflang, P.S.H. and J.C. Reuyl (1986), 'Estimating the Parameters of Market Share Models at Different Levels of Aggregation with Examples from the West German Cigarette Market', *European Journal of Operational Research*, vol. 23, pp. 14–24.

Leeflang, P.S.H. and J.C. Reuyl (1995), 'Effects of Tobacco Advertising on Tobacco Consumption', *International Business Review*, vol. 4, pp. 39–54.

Leeflang, P.S.H. and M. Wedel (1993), 'Information Based Decision Making in Pricing', *Proceedings ESOMAR/EMAC/AFM Symposium on Information Based Decision Making in Marketing*, Paris, 17th-19th November 1993.

Leeflang, P.S.H. and D.R. Wittink (1992), 'Diagnosing Competitive Reactions Using (Aggregated) Scanner Data', *International Journal of Research in Marketing*, vol. 9, pp. 39–57.

Leeflang, P.S.H. and D.R. Wittink (1994), 'Diagnosing Competition: Developments and Findings' in Laurent, G., G.L. Lilien and B. Pras (eds.), *Research Traditions in Marketing*, Kluwer Academic Publishers, Boston, pp. 133–156.

Leeflang, P.S.H. and D.R. Wittink (1996), 'Competitive Reaction Versus Consumer Response: Do Managers Overreact?', *International Journal of Research in Marketing*, vol. 13, pp. 103–119.

Leeflang, P.S.H. and D.R. Wittink (2000), 'Explaining Competitive Reaction Effects', Research Report, SOM, Research Institute Systems, Organizations and Management, University of Groningen, the Netherlands, forthcoming.

Lehmann, E.L. (1983), *Theory of Point Estimation*, John Wiley & Sons, New York.

Leigh, T.W. and A.J. Rethans (1984), 'A Script-theoretic Analysis of Industrial Purchasing Behavior', *Journal of Marketing*, vol. 48, Fall, pp. 22–32.

Leone, R.P. (1983), 'Modeling Sales-Advertising Relationships: An Integrated Time-Series-Econometric Approach', *Journal of Marketing Research*, vol. 20, pp. 291–295.

Leone, R.P. (1995), 'Generalizing What is Known About Temporal Aggregation and Advertising Carryover', *Marketing Science*, vol. 14, pp. G141–G150.

Leone, R.P. and R.L. Schultz (1980), 'A Study of Marketing Generalizations', *Journal of Marketing*, vol. 44, January, pp. 10–18.

Lilien, G.L. (1974a), 'A Modified Linear Learning Model of Buyer Behavior', *Management Science*, vol. 20, pp. 1027–1036.

Lilien, G.L. (1974b), 'Application of a Modified Linear Learning Model of Buyer Behavior', *Journal of Marketing Research*, vol. 11, pp. 279–285.

Lilien, G.L. (1975), 'Model Relativism: A Situational Approach to Model Building', *Interfaces*, vol. 5, pp. 11–18.

Lilien, G.L. (1979), 'Advisor 2: Modelling the Marketing Mix Decision for Industrial Products', *Management Science*, vol. 25, pp. 191–204.

Lilien, G.L. (1994), 'Marketing Models: Past, Present and Future' in Laurent, G., G.L. Lilien and B. Pras (eds.), *Research Traditions in Marketing*, Kluwer Academic Publishers, Boston, pp. 1–20.

Lilien, G.L. and Ph. Kotler (1983), *Marketing Decision Making: A Model-Building Approach*, Harper and Row, London.

Lilien, G.L., Ph. Kotler and K.S. Moorthy (1992), *Marketing Models*, Prentice-Hall, Englewood Cliffs, NJ.

Lilien, G.L. and A. Rangaswamy (1998), *Marketing Engineering*, Addison-Wesley, Reading, Mass.

Lindsey, J.K. (1996), *Parametric Statistical Inference*, Clarendon Press, Oxford.

Little, J.D.C. (1966), 'A Model of Adaptive Control of Promotional Spending', *Operations Research*, vol. 17, pp. 1–35.

Little, J.D.C. (1970), 'Models and Managers: The Concept of a Decision Calculus', *Management Science*, vol. 16, pp. B466–B485.

Little, J.D.C. (1975a), 'BRANDAID: A Marketing-Mix Model, Part I: Structure', *Operations Research*, vol. 23, pp. 628–655.

Little, J.D.C. (1975b), 'BRANDAID: A Marketing-Mix Model, Part 2: Implementation, Calibration, and Case Study', *Operations Research*, vol. 23, pp. 656–673.

Little, J.D.C. (1979), 'Aggregate Advertising Models: The State of the Art', *Operations Research*, vol. 27, pp. 629–667.

Little, J.D.C. (1998), 'Integrated Measures of Sales, Merchandising and Distributions', *International Journal of Research in Marketing*, vol. 15, pp. 475-485.

Little, J.D.C. and L.M. Lodish (1969), 'A Media Planning Calculus', *Operations Research*, vol. 17, pp. 1–35.

Little, J.D.C. and L.M. Lodish (1981), 'Commentary on Judgment Based Marketing Decision Models', *Journal of Marketing*, vol. 45, Fall, pp. 24–29.

Little, J.D.C., L.M. Lodish, J.R. Hauser and G.L. Urban (1994), 'Commentary' (on Hermann Simon's 'Marketing Science's Pilgrimage to the Ivory Tower') in Laurent, G., G.L. Lilien and B. Pras, *Research Traditions in Marketing*, Kluwer Academic Publishers, Boston, pp. 44–51.

Lock, A. (1987), 'Integrating Group Judgments in Subjective Forecasts' in Wright, G. and P. Ayton (eds.), *Judgmental Forecasting*, John Wiley & Sons, Great Britain, pp. 109–127.

Lodish, L.M. (1971), 'CALLPLAN: An Interactive Salesman's Call Planning System', *Management Science*, vol. 18, pp. B25–B40.

Lodish, L.M. (1981), 'Experience with Decision Calculus Models and Decision Support Systems' in Schultz, R.L. and A.A. Zoltners (eds.), *Marketing Decision Models*, North-Holland, New York, pp. 165–182.

Lodish, L.M. (1982), 'A Marketing Decision Support System for Retailers', *Marketing Science*, vol. 1, pp. 31–56.

Lodish, L.M., M.M. Abraham, S. Kalmenson, J. Livelsberger, B. Lubetkin, B. Richardson and M.E. Stevens (1995a), 'How T.V. Advertising Works: A Meta Analysis of 389 Real World Split Cable T.V. Advertising Experiments', *Journal of Marketing Research*, vol. 32, pp. 125–139.

Lodish, L.M., M.M. Abraham, J. Livelsberger, B. Lubetkin, B. Richardson and M.E. Stevens (1995b), 'A Summary of Fifty-five In-market Experimental Estimates of the Long-Term Effect of T.V. Advertising', *Marketing Science*, vol. 14, pp. G133–G140.

Lodish, L.M., E. Curtis, M. Ness and M.K. Simpson (1988), 'Sales Force Sizing and Deployment Using a Decision Calculus Model at Syntex Laboratories', *Interfaces*, vol. 18, pp. 5–20.

Lodish, L.M., D.B. Montgomery and F.E. Webster (1968), 'A Dynamic Sales Call Policy Model', Working Paper 329-68, Sloan School of Management, M.I.T. Cambridge.

Logman, M. (1995), *Intrafirm Marketing-Mix Relationships: Analysis of their Sources and Modeling Implications*, Unpublished Ph.D. thesis, University of Antwerp (UFSIA), Belgium.

Long, S. (1983), *Covariance Structure Models, An Introduction to LISREL*, Sage University Press, London.

Louvière, J.J. and D.A. Hensher (1983), 'Forecasting Consumer Demand for a Unique Cultural Event: An Approach Based on an Integration of Probabilistic Discrete Choice Models and Experimental Design Data', *Journal of Consumer Research*, vol. 10, pp. 348–361.

Louvière, J.J. and G. Woodworth (1983), 'Design and Analysis of Simulated Consumer Choice or Allocation Experiments: An Approach Based on Aggregate Data', *Journal of Marketing Research*, vol. 20, pp. 350–367.

Lucas, H.C., M.J. Ginzberg and R.L. Schultz (1990), *Information Systems Implementation: Testing a Structural Model*, Ablex, Norwood, NJ.

Lucas, R.E. (1976), 'Econometric Policy Evaluation: A Critique' in Brunner, K. and A.H. Metzler (eds.), *The Phillips Curve and Labor Markets*, North-Holland, Amsterdam.

Luce, R.D. (1959), *Individual Choice Behavior: A Theoretical Analysis*, John Wiley & Sons, New York.

Luce, R.D. and H. Raiffa (1957), *Games and Decisions*, John Wiley & Sons, New York.

Luik, J.C. and M.J. Waterson (eds.), (1996), *Advertising & Markets*, NTC Publications, Oxfordshire, U.K.

Lütkepohl, H. (1989), 'Testing for Causation Between two Variables in Higher Dimensional Var Models', Working paper, University of Kiel, Germany.

MacLachlan, D.L. (1972), 'A Model of Intermediate Market Response', *Journal of Marketing Research*, vol. 9, pp. 378–384.

Maddala, G.S. (1971), 'The Use of Variance Components Models in Pooling Cross Section and Time Series Data', *Econometrica*, vol. 39, pp, 341–358.

Maffei, R.B. (1960), 'Brand Preferences and Simple Markov Processes', *Operations Research*, vol. 8, pp. 210–218.

Magat, W.A., J.M. McCann and R.C. Morey (1986), 'When Does Lag Structure Really Matter in Optimizing Advertising Expenditures?', *Management Science*, vol. 32, pp. 182–193.

Magee, J.F. (1953), 'The Effect of Promotional Effort on Sales', *Journal of the Operations Research Society of America*, vol. 1, pp. 64–74.

Magrath, A.J. (1988), *Marketing Smarts*, John Wiley & Sons, Chichester.

Mahajan, V., S.I. Bretschneider and J.W. Bradford (1980), 'Feedback Approaches to Modeling Structural Shifts in Market Response', *Journal of Marketing*, vol. 44, Winter, pp. 71–80.

Mahajan, V., P.E. Green and S.M. Goldberg (1982), 'A Conjoint Model for Measuring Self- and Cross-Price Demand Relationships', *Journal of Marketing Research*, vol. 19, pp. 334–342.

Mahajan, V., A.K. Jain and M. Bergier (1977), 'Parameter Estimation in Marketing Models in the Presence of Multicollinearity', *Journal of Marketing Research*, vol. 14, pp. 586–591.

Mahajan, V. and E. Muller (1986), 'Advertising Pulsing Policies for Generating Awareness for New Products', *Marketing Science*, vol. 5, pp. 89–106.

Mahajan, V. and E. Muller (1998), 'When Is It Worthwhile Targeting the Majority Instead of the Innovators in a New Product Launch?', *Journal of Marketing Research*, vol. 35, pp. 488–495.

Mahajan, V., E. Muller and F.M. Bass (1990), 'New Product Diffusion Models in Marketing: A Review and Directions for Research', *Journal of Marketing*, vol. 54, January, pp. 1–26.

Mahajan, V., E. Muller and F.M. Bass (1993), 'New Product Diffusion Models' in Eliashberg, J. and G.L. Lilien (eds.), *Handbooks in Operation Research and Management Science, vol. 5, Marketing*, North-Holland, Amsterdam, pp. 349–408.

Mahajan, V., E. Muller and S. Sharma (1983), 'An Approach to Repeat-Purchase Diffusion Analysis' in Murphy, P.E. et al. (eds.), *Educator's Conference Proceedings*, American Marketing Association, Chicago.

Mahajan, V. and R.A. Peterson (1985), *Models for Innovation Diffusion*, Sage Publications, Beverly Hills.

Mahajan, V., S. Sharma and Y. Wind (1984), 'Parameter Estimation in Marketing Models in the Presence of Influential Response Data: Robust Regression and Applications', *Journal of Marketing Research*, vol. 21, pp. 268–277.

Mahajan, V. and Y. Wind (1986), *Innovation Diffusion Models of New Product Acceptance*, Ballinger Publishing Company, Cambridge, MA.

Mahajan, V. and Y. Wind (1988), 'New Product Forecasting Models: Directions for Research and Implementation', *International Journal of Forecasting*, vol. 4, pp. 341–358.

Mahajan, V., Y. Wind and J.W. Bradford (1982), 'Stochastic Dominance Rules for Product Portfolio Analysis' in Zoltners, A.A. (ed.), *Marketing Planning Models*, North-Holland Publishing Company, Amsterdam, pp. 161–183.

Mahmoud, E. (1987), 'The Evaluation of Forecasts' in Makridakis, S. and S.C. Wheelwright (eds.), *The Handbook of Forecasting*, John Wiley & Sons, New York, pp. 504–522.

Maines, L. (1996), 'An Experimental Examination of Subjective Forecast Combination', *International Journal of Forecasting*, vol. 12, pp. 223–233.

Makridakis, S. (1989), 'Why Combining Works?', *International Journal of Forecasting*, vol. 5, pp. 601–603.

Malhotra, N.K. (1984), 'The Use of Linear Logit Models in Marketing Research', *Journal of Marketing Research*, vol. 21, pp. 20–31.

Malhotra, N.K. (1996), *Marketing Research*, 2nd ed., Prentice-Hall International Editions, Upper Saddle River, NJ.

Mann, D.H. (1975), 'Optimal Theoretic Advertising Stock Models: A Generalization Incorporating the Effects of Delayed Response from Promotion Expenditures', *Management Science*, vol. 21, pp. 823–832.

Marcus, M.L. (1983), 'Power, Politics and MIS Implementation', *Communications of the ACM*, vol. 26, pp. 430–444.

Marquardt, D.W. (1970), 'Generalized Inverses, Ridge Regression, Biased Linear Estimation', *Technometrics*, vol. 12, pp. 591–612.

Marquardt, D.W. and R.D. Snee (1975), 'Ridge Regression in Practice', *The American Statistician*, vol. 29, pp. 3–19.

Marsh, H.W., J.R. Balla and R. McDonald (1988), 'Goodness-of-Fit Indexes in Confirmatory Factor Analysis: The Effects of Sample Size', *Psychological Bulletin*, vol. 103, pp. 391–410.

Marshall, K.T. and R.M. Oliver (1995), *Decision Making and Forecasting*, McGraw-Hill.

Mason, Ch.H. and W.D. Perreault jr. (1991), 'Collinearity, Power and Interpretation of Multiple Regression Analysis', *Journal of Marketing Research*, vol. 28, pp. 268–280.

Massy, W.F. (1965), 'Principal Component Regression in Exploratory Statistical Research', *Journal of the American Statistical Association*, vol. 60, pp. 234–256.

Massy, W.F. (1968), 'Stochastic Models for Monitoring New-Product Introductions' in Bass, F.M., C.W. King and E.A. Pessemier (eds.), *Applications of the Sciences in Marketing Management*, John Wiley & Sons, Inc., New York, pp. 85–111.

Massy, W.F. (1971), 'Statistical Analysis of Relations between Variables' in Aaker, D.A. (ed.), *Multivariate Analysis in Marketing: Theory and Application*, Wadsworth Publishing Company, Belmont, Cal.

Massy, W.F., D.B. Montgomery and D.G. Morrison (1970), *Stochastic Models of Buying Behavior*, M.I.T. Press., Cambridge, Mass.

McCann, J.M. and J.P. Gallagher (1990), *Expert Systems for Scanner Data Environments*, Kluwer Academic Publishers, Boston.

McCann, J.M., W.G. Lahti and J. Hill (1991), 'The Brand Managers Assistant: A Knowlegde-based System Approach to Brand Management', *International Journal of Research in Marketing*, vol. 8, pp. 51–73.

McConnel, D. (1968), 'Repeat-Purchase Estimation and the Linear Learning Model', *Journal of Marketing Research*, vol. 5, pp. 304–306.

McCullagh, P. and J.A. Nelder (1989), *Generalized Linear Models*, Chapman and Hall, New York.

McFadden, D. (1974), 'Conditional Logit Analysis of Qualitative Choice Behavior' in Zarembarka, P. (ed.), *Frontiers in Econometrics*, Academic Press, New York.

McFadden, D. (1981), 'Econometric Models of Probabilistic Choice' in Manski, C.F. and D. McFadden (eds.), *Structural Analysis of Discrete Data with Econometric Applications*, MIT Press., Cambridge, Mass.

McFadden, D. (1986), 'The Choice Theory Approach to Market Research', *Marketing Science*, vol. 5, pp. 275–297.

McFadden, D. (1989), 'A Method of Simulated Moments for the Estimation of Discrete Response Models Without Numerical Integration', *Econometrica*, vol. 57, pp. 995–1026.

McFadden, D. and F. Reid (1975), 'Aggregate Travel Demand Forecasting from Disaggregated Behavioral Models', *Transportation Research Record*, 534, pp. 24–37.

McGee, V.E. and W.T. Carleton (1970), 'Piecewise-Regression', *Journal of the American Statistical Association*, vol. 65, pp. 1109–1124.

McGuire, T.W., J.U. Farley, R.E. Lucas jr. and W.L. Ring (1968), 'Estimation and Inference for Linear Models in which Subsets of the Dependent Variable are Constrained', *Journal of the American Statistical Association*, vol. 63, pp. 1201–1213.

McGuire, T.W. and D.L. Weiss (1976), 'Logically Consistent Market Share Models II', *Journal of Marketing Research*, vol. 13, pp. 296–302.

McGuire, W.J. (1969), 'The Nature of Attitudes and Attitude Change' in Lindzey G. and E. Aronson (eds.), *The Handbook of Social Psychology*, 2nd ed., Addison-Wesley Publishing Company, Reading, Mass., pp. 136–313.

McIntyre, S.H. (1982), 'An Experimental Study of the Impact of Judgment-Based Marketing Models', *Management Science*, vol. 28, pp. 17–33.

McIntyre, S.H., D.D. Achabal and C.M. Miller (1993), 'Applying Case-Based Reasoning to Forecasting Retail Sales', *Journal of Retailing*, vol. 69, pp. 372–398.

McIntyre, S.H. and I.S. Currim (1982), 'Evaluation Judgment-Based Marketing Models: Multiple Measures Comparisons and Findings' in Zoltners, A.A. (ed.), *Marketing Planning Models*, vol. 18, North-Holland, New York, pp. 185–207.

McLachlan, G.J. and K.E. Basford (1988), *Mixture Models: Inference and Applications to Clustering*, Marcel Dekker, New York.

Mela, C.F., S. Gupta and D.R. Lehmann (1997), 'The Long-Term Impact of Promotion and Advertising on Consumer Brand Choice', *Journal of Marketing Research*, vol. 34, pp. 248–261.

Mela, C.F., S. Gupta and K. Jedidi (1998), 'Assessing Long-term Promotional Influences on Market Structure', *International Journal of Research in Marketing*, vol. 15, pp. 89–107.

Mesak, H.I. (1992), 'An Aggregate Advertising Pulsing Model with Wearout Effects', *Marketing Science*, vol. 11, pp. 310–326.

Metwally, M.M. (1980), 'Sales Response to Advertising of Eight Australian Products', *Journal of Advertising Research*, vol. 20, pp. 59–64.

Metwally, M.M. (1992), 'Escalation Tendencies of Advertising', *Oxford Bulletin of Economics and Statistics*, vol. 40, pp. 153–163.

Mills, H.D. (1961), 'A Study of Promotional Competition' in Bass, F.M. and R.D. Buzzell (eds.), *Mathematical Models and Methods in Marketing*, Richard D. Irwin, Homewood, Ill., pp. 271–288.

Mitchell, A.A., J.E. Russo and D.R. Wittink (1991), 'Issues in the Development and Use of Expert Systems for Marketing Decisions', *International Journal of Research in Marketing*, vol. 8, pp. 41–50.

Mizon, G.E. (1995), 'A Simple Message for Autocorrelation Correctors: Don't', *Journal of Econometrics*, vol. 69, pp. 267–288.

Monroe, K.B. and A.J. Della Bitta (1978), 'Models for Pricing Decisions', *Journal of Marketing Research*, vol. 15, pp. 413–428.

Montgomery, A.L. (1997), 'Creating Micro-Marketing Pricing Strategies Using Supermarket Scanner Data', *Marketing Science*, vol. 16, pp. 315–337.

Montgomery, D.B. (1969), 'A Stochastic Response Model with Application to Brand Choice', *Management Science*, vol. 15, pp.323–337.

Montgomery, D.B. (1973), 'The Outlook for M.I.S.', *Journal of Advertising Research*, vol. 13, pp. 5-11.

Montgomery, D.B. and A.J. Silk (1972), 'Estimating Dynamic Effects of Market Communications Expenditures', *Management Science*, vol. 18, pp. B485–B501.

Montgomery, D.B., A.J. Silk and C.E. Zaragoza (1971), 'A Multiple-Product Sales Force Allocation Model', *Management Science*, vol. 18, Part II, pp. P3–P24.

Montgomery, D.B. and G.L. Urban (1969), *Management Science in Marketing*, Prentice-Hall, Englewood Cliffs, NJ.

Montgomery, D.B. and G.L. Urban (1970), 'Marketing Decision Information Systems: An Emerging View', *Journal of Marketing Research*, vol. 7, pp. 226–234.

Moore, H.L. (1914), *Economic Cycles: Their Law and Cause*, MacMillan, New York.

Moore, W.L. and D.R. Lehmann (1989), 'A Paired Comparison Nested Logit Model of Individual Preference Structure', *Journal of Marketing Research*, vol. 30, pp. 171–182.

Moorthy, K.S. (1984), 'Market Segmentation, Self Selection and Product Line Design', *Marketing Science*, vol. 3, pp. 288–307.

Moorthy, K.S. (1985), 'Using Game Theory to Model Competition', *Journal of Marketing Research*, vol. 12, pp. 262–282.

Moorthy, K.S. (1988), 'Strategic Decentralization in Channels', *Marketing Science*, vol. 7, pp. 335–355.

Moorthy, K.S. (1993), 'Competitive Marketing Strategies: Game-Theoretic Models' in Eliashberg, J. and G.L. Lilien (eds.), *Handbooks in Operations Research and Management Science, vol. 5, Marketing*, North-Holland, Amsterdam, pp. 143–192.

Moriarty, M. (1975), 'Cross-Sectional, Time-Series Issues in the Analysis of Marketing Decision Variables', *Journal of Marketing Research*, vol. 12, pp. 142–150.

Morikawa, T. (1989), *Incorporating Stated Preference Data in Travel Demand Analysis*, Ph.D. thesis, Department of Civil Engineering, MIT.

Morrison, D.G. (1966), 'Testing Brand Switching Models', *Journal of Marketing Research*, vol. 3, pp. 401–409.

Morrison, D.G. (1979), 'Purchase Intentions and Purchase Behavior', *Journal of Marketing*, vol. 43, pp. 65–74.

Morrison, D.G. and D.C. Schmittlein (1988), 'Generalizing the NBD Model for Customer Purchases: What Are the Implications and is it Worth the Effort?, *Journal of Business and Economic Statistics*, vol. 6, pp. 145–159.

Morwitz, V.G. and D.C. Schmittlein (1992), 'Using Segmentation to Improve Sales Forecasts Based on Purchase Intent: Which 'Intenders' Actually Buy?, *Journal of Marketing Research*, vol. 29, pp. 391–405.

Nadaraya, E.A. (1964), 'On Estimating Regression', *Theory Probability Applications*, vol. 9, pp. 141–142.

Naert, P.A. (1972), 'Observations on Applying Marginal Analysis in Marketing: Part I', *Journal of Business Administration*, vol. 4, Winter, pp. 49–67.

Naert, P.A. (1973), 'Observations on Applying Marginal Analysis in Marketing: Part II', *Journal of Business Administration*, vol. 4, Spring, pp. 3–14.

Naert, P.A. (1974), 'Should Marketing Models be Robust?', paper presented at IBM Conference on the Implementation of Marketing Models, Ottignies, Belgium.

Naert, P.A. (1975a), 'The Validation of Macro Models', *Proceedings ESOMAR Seminar on Market Modeling (Part II)*, Noordwijk aan-Zee, The Netherlands, pp. 17–30.

Naert, P.A. (1975b), 'Parameterization of Marketing Models' in Elliot, K. (ed.), *Management Bibliographies & Reviews*, vol. 1, MCB Books, Bradford, pp. 125–149.

Naert, P.A. (1977), 'Some Cost-Benefit Considerations in Marketing Model Building' in Topritzhofer, E. (ed.), *Marketing-Neue Ergebnisse aus Forschung and Praxis*, Gabler-Verlag, Wiesbaden, Germany.

Naert, P.A. and A.V. Bultez (1973), 'Logically Consistent Market Share Models', *Journal of Marketing Research*, vol. 10, pp. 334–340.

Naert, P.A. and A.V. Bultez (1975), 'A Model of a Distribution Network Aggregate Performance', *Management Science*, vol. 21, pp. 1102–1112.

Naert, P.A. and P.S.H. Leeflang (1978), *Building Implementable Marketing Models*, Martinus Nijhoff, Leiden.

Naert, P.A. and M. Weverbergh (1977), 'Multiplicative Models with Zero Entries in the Explanatory Variables', Working Paper 76-22, Centre for Managerial Economics and Econometrics, UFSIA, University of Antwerp.

Naert, P.A. and M. Weverbergh (1981a), 'On the Prediction Power of Market Share Attraction Models', *Journal of Marketing Research*, vol. 18, pp. 146–153.

Naert, P.A. and M. Weverbergh (1981b), 'Subjective Versus Empirical Decision Models' in Schultz, R.L. and A.A. Zoltners (eds.), *Marketing Decision Models*, North Holland, New York, pp. 99–123.

Naert, P.A. and M. Weverbergh (1985), 'Market Share Specification, Estimation and Validation: Toward Reconciling Seemingly Divergent Views', *Journal of Marketing Research*, vol. 22, pp. 453–461.

Naik, P.A., M.K. Mantrala and A.G. Sawyer (1998), 'Planning Media Schedules in the Presence of Dynamic Advertising Quality', *Marketing Science*, vol. 17, pp. 214–235.

Nakanishi, M. (1972), 'Measurement of Sales Promotion Effect at the Retail Level: A New Approach', Working Paper, Graduate School of Management, UCLA.

Nakanishi, M. and L.G. Cooper (1974), 'Parameter Estimation for a Multiplicative Competitive Interaction Model – Least Squares Approach', *Journal of Marketing Research*, vol. 11, pp. 303–311.

Nakanishi, M. and L.G. Cooper (1982), 'Simplified Estimation Procedures for MCI Models', *Marketing Science*, vol. 1, pp. 314–322.

Narasimhan, C. (1988), 'Competitive Promotional Stratagies', *Journal of Business*, vol. 61, pp. 427–449.

Narasimhan, C. and S.K. Sen (1983), 'New Product Models for Test Marketing Data', *Journal of Marketing*, vol. 47, Winter, pp. 11–24.

Nash, J. (1950), 'Equilibrium Points in n-person Games', *Proceedings of the National Academy of Sciences*, vol. 36, pp. 48–49.

Nelder, J.A. and R.W.M. Wedderburn (1972), 'Generalized Linear Models', *Journal of the Royal Statistical Society*, A135, pp. 370–384.

Nenning, M., E. Topritzhofer and U. Wagner (1979), 'Zur Kompatibilität alternativer kommerziell verfügbarer Datenquellen für die Marktreaktionsmodellierung: Die Verwendung von Prewhitening-Filtern und Kreuzspektanalyse sowie ihre Konsequenzen für die Analyse betriebswirtschaftlicher Daten', *Zeitschrift für Betriebswirtschaft*, vol. 49, pp. 281–297.

Nerlove, M. (1971), 'Further Evidence on the Estimation of Dynamic Economic Relations from a Time Series of Cross Sections', *Econometrica*, vol. 39, pp. 359–382.

Neslin, S.A., S.G. Powell and L.G. Schneider Stone (1995), 'The Effects of Retailer and Consumer Response on Optimal Manufacturer Advertising and Trade Promotion Strategies', *Management Science*, vol. 41, pp. 749–766.

Neslin, S.A. and L.G. Schneider Stone (1996), 'Consumer Inventory Sensitivity and the Postpromotion Dip', *Marketing Letters*, vol. 7, pp. 77–94.

Neslin, S.A. and R.W. Shoemaker (1983), 'A Model for Evaluating the Profitability of Coupon Promotions', *Marketing Science*, vol. 2, pp. 361–388.

Newcomb, S. (1886), 'A Generalized Theory of the Combination of Observations so as to Obtain the Best Result', *American Journal of Mathematics*, vol. 8, pp. 343–366.

Newell, A. and H.A. Simon (1972), *Human Problem Solving*, Prentice-Hall, Englewood Cliffs, NJ.

Nielsen Marketing Research (1988), *Met het Oog op de Toekomst*, ACNielsen (Nederland) B.V., Diemen.

Nillesen, J.P.H. (1992), *Services and Advertising Effectivenes*, Unpublished Ph.D thesis, Groningen, the Netherlands.

Nijkamp, W.G. (1993), *New Product Macroflow Models – Specification and Analysis*, Unpublished Ph.D. thesis, University of Groningen, the Netherlands.

Nooteboom, B. (1989), 'Diffusion, Uncertainty and Firm Size', *International Journal of Research in Marketing*, vol. 6, pp. 109–128.

Nordin, J.A. (1943), 'Spatial Allocation of Selling Expenses', *Journal of Marketing*, vol. 7, pp. 210–219.

Novak, T.P. (1993), 'Log-Linear Trees: Models of Market Structure in Brand Switching Data', *Journal of Marketing Research*, vol. 30, pp. 267–287.

NZDH, New Zealand Department of Health, Tonic Substances Board (TSB) (1989), *Health or Tobacco: an End to Tobacco Advertising and Promotion*.

Oczkowski, E. and M.A. Farrell (1998), 'Discriminating between Measurement Scales Using Non-Nested Tests and Two-Stage Least Squares Estimators: The Case of Market Orientation', *International Journal of Research in Marketing*, vol. 15, pp. 349–366.

Oliva, T.A., R.L. Oliver and I.C. MacMillan (1992), 'A Catastrophe Model for Developing Service Satisfaction Strategies', *Journal of Marketing*, vol. 56, July, pp. 83–95.

Oliver, R.L. and W.S. DeSarbo (1988), 'Response Determinants in Satisfaction Judgments', *Journal of Consumer Research*, vol. 14, pp. 495–507.

Padmanabhan, V. and I.P.L. Png (1997), 'Manufacturer's Returns Policies and Retail Competition', *Marketing Science*, vol. 16, pp. 81–94.

Paich, M. and J.D. Sterman (1993), 'Boom, Bust and Failures to Learn in Experimental Markets', *Marketing Science*, vol. 39, pp. 1439–1458.

Palda, K.S. (1964), *The Measurement of Cumulative Advertising Effects*, Prentice-Hall, Englewood Cliffs, NJ.

Pankratz, A. (1991), *Forecasting with Dynamic Regression Models*, John Wiley & Sons, New York.

Papatla, P. and L. Krishnamurthi (1996), 'Measuring the Dynamic Effects of Promotions on Brand Choice', *Journal of Marketing Research*, vol. 33, pp. 20–35.

Parasuraman, A. and R.L. Day (1977), 'A Management-Oriented Model for Allocating Sales Effort', *Journal of Marketing Research*, vol. 14, pp. 22–32.

Parenté, F.J. and J.K. Anderson-Parenté (1987), 'Delphi Inquiry Systems' in Wright, G. and P. Ayton (eds.), *Judgmental Forecasting*, John Wiley & Sons, New York, pp. 129–156.

Parfitt, J.H. and B.J.K. Collins (1968), 'Use of Consumer Panels for Brand-Share Prediction', *Journal of Marketing Research*, vol. 5, pp. 131–145.

Park, S. and M. Hahn (1998), 'Direct Estimation of Batsell and Polking's Model', *Marketing Science*, vol. 17, pp. 170–178.

Parker, P. (1992), 'Price Elasticity Dynamics over the Adoption Lifecycle', *Journal of Marketing Research*, vol. 29, pp. 358–367.

Parsons, L.J. (1975), 'The Product Life Cycle and Time-Varying Advertising Elasticities', *Journal of Marketing Research*, vol. 12, pp. 476–480.

Parsons, L.J. and F.M. Bass (1971), 'Optimal Advertising Expenditure Implications of a Simultaneous Equation Regression Analysis', *Operations Research*, vol. 19, pp. 822–831.

Parsons, L.J., E. Gijsbrechts, P.S.H. Leeflang and D.R. Wittink (1994), 'Marketing Science, Econometrics, and Managerial Contributions' in Laurent, G., G.L. Lilien and B. Pras (eds.), *Research Traditions in Marketing*, Kluwer, Academic Publisher, Boston, pp. 52-78.

Parsons, L.J. and R.L. Schultz (1976), *Marketing Models and Econometric Research*, North-Holland Publishing Company, Amsterdam.

Parsons, L.J. and P. Vanden Abeele (1981), 'Analysis of Sales Call Effectiveness', *Journal of Marketing Research*, vol. 18, pp. 107–113.

Parzen, E. (1962), *Stochastic Processes*, San Francisco, Holden-Day, Inc.

Payne, J.W., J. Bettman and E.J. Johnson (1988), 'Adaptive Strategy Selection in Decision Making', *Journal of Experimental Psychology: Human Learning, Memory and Cognition*, vol. 14, July, pp. 534-552.

Pedrick, J.H. and F.S. Zufryden (1991), 'Evaluating the Impact of Advertising Media Plans: A Model of Consumer Purchase Dynamics Using Single Source Data', *Marketing Science*, vol. 10, pp. 111–130.

Peterson, H. (1965), 'The Wizard Who Oversimplified: A Fable', *The Quarterly Journal of Econometrics*, May, pp. 209–211.

Petty, R.E. and J.T. Cacioppo (1986), 'The Elaboration Likelihood Model of Persuasion' in Berkowitz, L. (ed.), *Advances in Experimental Social Psychology*, vol. 19, Academic Press, New York, pp. 123–205.

Pham, M.T. and G.V. Johar (1996), 'Where's the Deal?: A Process Model of Source Identification in Promotional Settings', Paper, Columbia University.

Philips, L.D. (1987), 'On the Adequacy of Judgmental Forecasts' in Wright G. and P. Ayton (eds.), *Judgmental Forecasting*, John Wiley & Sons, New York, pp. 11–30.

Phillips, L.W., D.R. Chang and R.D. Buzzell (1983), 'Product Quality, Cost Postion and Business Performance: A Test of Some Key Hypotheses', *Journal of Marketing*, vol. 47, Spring, pp. 26–43.

Pierce, D.A. (1977), 'Relationships – and the Lack Thereof – between Economic Time Series, with Special References to Money and Interest Rates', *Journal of the American Statistical Association*, vol. 72, pp. 11–22.

Pierce, D.A. and L.D. Haugh (1977), 'Causality in Temporal Systems', *Journal of Econometrics*, vol. 5, pp. 265–293.

Pindyck, R.S. and D.L. Rubinfeld (1991), *Econometric Models & Economic Forecasts*, McGraw-Hill, New York.

Plat, F.W. (1988), *Modelling for Markets: Applications of Advanced Models and Methods for Data Analysis*, Unpublished Ph.D. thesis, University of Groningen, the Netherlands.

Plat, F.W. and P.S.H. Leeflang (1988), 'Decomposing Sales Elasticities on Segmented Markets', *International Journal of Research in Marketing*, vol. 5, pp. 303–315.

Ploeg, J. van der (1997), *Instrumental Variable Estimation and Group-Asymptotics*, SOM Theses on Systems, Organisations and Management, Groningen, the Netherlands.

Popkowski Leszczyc, P.T.L. and R.C. Rao (1989), 'An Empirical Analysis of National and Local Advertising Effects on Price Elasticity', *Marketing Letters*, vol. 1, pp. 149–160.

Popkowski Leszczyc, P.T.L. and H.J.P. Timmermans (1997), 'Store-Switching Behavior', *Marketing Letters*, vol. 8, pp. 193–204.

Poulsen, C.S. (1990), 'Mixed Markov and Latent Markov Modeling Applied to Brand Choice Behavior', *International Journal of Research in Marketing*, vol. 7, pp. 5–19.

Powell, J.L. (1994), 'Estimation of Semiparametric Models' in Engle, R.F. and D.L. McFadden (eds.), *Handbook of Econometrics*, vol. 4, Elsevier Science B.V., Amsterdam.

Prais, S.J. and H.S. Houthakker (1955), *The Analysis of Family Budgets*, Cambridge University Press, Cambridge.

Prasad, V.K., W.R. Casper and R.J. Schieffer (1984), 'Alternatives to the Traditional Retail Store Audit: A Field Study', *Journal of Marketing*, vol. 48, pp. 54–61.

Prasad, V.K. and L.W. Ring (1976), 'Measuring Sales Effects of some Marketing-Mix Variables and their Interactions', *Journal of Marketing Research*, vol. 13, pp. 391–396.

Pringle, G.L., R.D. Wilson and E.I. Brody (1982), 'NEWS: A Decision-Oriented Model for New Product Analysis and Forecasting', *Marketing Science*, vol. 1, pp. 1–29.

Punj, G.H. and R. Staelin (1978), 'The Choice Process for Graduate Business Schools', *Journal of Marketing Research*, vol. 15, pp. 588–598.

Putsis, W.P., S.K. Balasubramanian, E.H. Kaplan and S.K. Sen (1997), 'Mixing Behavior in Cross-Country Diffusion', *Marketing Science*, vol. 16, pp. 354–369.

Putsis, W.P. and R. Dhar (1998), 'The Many Faces of Competition', *Marketing Letters*, vol. 9, pp. 269–284.

Putsis, W.P. and R. Dhar (1999), 'Category Expenditure, Promotion and Competitive Market Interactions: Can Promotions Really Expand the Pie?', Paper London Business School / Yale School of Management.

Putsis, W.P. and S.K. Sen (1999), 'Should NFL Blackouts be Banned', *Applied Economics*, forthcoming.

Quandt, R.E. (1983), 'Computational Problems and Methods' in Griliches, Z. and M. Intriligator (eds.), *Handbook of Econometrics*, vol. 1, North-Holland, Amsterdam.

Raiffa, H. and R. Schlaifer (1961), *Applied Statistical Decision Theory*, Colonial Press, Boston.

Raju, J.S. (1992), 'The Effect of Price Promotions on Variability in Product Category Sales', *Marketing Science*, vol. 11, pp. 207–220.

Ramaswamy, V., W.S. DeSarbo, D.J. Reibstein and W.T. Robinson (1993), 'An Empirical Pooling Approach For Estimating Marketing Mix Elasticies with PIMS Data', *Marketing Science*, vol. 12, pp. 103–124.

Ramsey, J.B. (1969), 'Tests for Specification Errors in Classical Linear Least Squares Regression Analysis', *Journal of the Royal Statistical Society, Series B*, pp. 350–371.

Ramsey, J.B. (1974), 'Classical Model Selection Through Specification Tests' in Zarembka, P. (ed.), *Frontiers in Econometrics*, Academic Press, New York, pp. 13–47.

Rangan, V.K. (1987), 'The Channel Design Decision: A Model and an Application', *Marketing Science*, vol. 6, pp. 156–174.

Rangaswamy, A. (1993), 'Marketing Decision Models: From Linear Programs to Knowledge Based Systems' in Eliashberg, J. and G.L. Lilien (eds.), *Handbooks on Operations Research and Management Science, vol. 5, Marketing*, North-Holland, Amsterdam, pp. 733–771.

Rangaswamy, A., R.R. Burke and T.A. Oliva (1993), 'Brand Equity and the Extendibility of Brand Names', *International Journal of Research in Marketing*, vol. 10, pp. 61–75.

Rangaswamy, A., J. Eliashberg, R.R. Burke and Y. Wind (1989), 'Developing Marketing Expert Systems: An Application to International Negotiations', *Journal of Marketing*, vol. 53, October, pp. 24–39.

Rangaswamy, A., B.A. Harlam and L.M. Lodish (1991), 'INFER: An Expert System for Automatic Analysis of Scanner Data', *International Journal of Research in Marketing*, vol. 8, pp. 29–40.

Rangaswamy, A. and L. Krishnamurthi (1991), 'Response Function Estimation Using the Equity Estimator', *Journal of Marketing Research*, vol. 28, pp. 72–83.

Rangaswamy, A. and L. Krishnamurthi (1995), 'Equity Estimation and Assessing Market Response: A Rejoinder', *Journal of Marketing Research*, vol. 32, pp. 480–485.

Rangaswamy, A., P. Sinha and A.A. Zoltners (1990), 'An Integrated Model-based Approach to Sales Force Structuring', *Marketing Science*, vol. 9, pp. 279–298.

Rao, V.R. (1984), 'Pricing Research in Marketing: The State of the Art', *Journal of Business*, vol. 57, pp. S39–S60.

Rao, V.R. (1993), 'Pricing Models in Marketing' in Eliashberg, J. and G.L. Lilien (eds.), *Handbooks in Operations Research and Management Science, vol. 5, Marketing*, North-Holland, Amsterdam, pp. 517–552.

Rao, V.R. and E.W. McLaughlin (1989), 'Modeling the Decision to Add New Products by Channel Intermediaries', *Journal of Marketing*, vol. 53, pp. 80–88.

Rao, V.R. and L.J. Thomas (1973), 'Dynamic Models for Sales Promotion Policies', *Operational Research Quarterly*, vol. 24, pp. 403–417.

Rao, V.R., Y. Wind and W.S. DeSarbo (1988), 'A Customized Market Response Model: Development, Estimation and Empirical Testing', *Journal of the Academy of Marketing Science*, vol. 16, pp. 128–140.

Reddy, S.K., J.E. Aronson and A. Stam (1998), 'SPOT: Scheduling Programs Optimally for Television', *Management Science*, vol. 44, pp. 83–102.

Reibstein, D.J. and H. Gatignon (1984), 'Optimal Product Line Pricing: The Influence of Elasticities and Cross Elasticities', *Journal of Marketing Research*, vol. 21, pp. 259–267.

Reinmuth, J.E. and D.R. Wittink (1974), 'Recursive Models for Forecasting Seasonal Processes', *Journal of Financial and Quantitative Analysis*, September 1974, pp. 659–684.

Reuyl, J.C. (1982), *On the Determination of Advertising Effectiveness: An Empirical Study of the German Cigarette Market*, H.E. Stenfert Kroese, Leiden.

Roberts, J.H. and J.M. Lattin (1991), 'Development and Testing of a Model of Consideration Set Composition', *Journal of Marketing Research*, vol. 28, pp. 429–441.

Roberts, J.H. and G.L. Lilien (1993), 'Explanatory and Predictive Models of Consumer Behaviour' in Eliashberg, J. and G.L. Lilien (eds.), *Handbooks in Operations Research and Management Science, vol. 5, Marketing*, North-Holland, Amsterdam pp. 27–82.

Robey, D. (1984), 'Conflict Models in Implementation Research' in Schultz, R.L. and M.J. Ginzberg (eds.), *Management Science Implementation*, JAI Press, pp. 89–105.

Robinson, W.T. (1988), 'Marketing Mix Reactions to Entry', *Marketing Science*, vol. 7, pp. 368–385.

Rogers, R. (1962), *Diffusion of Innovations*, The Free Press, New York.

Rossi, P.E. and G.M. Allenby (1994), 'A Bayesian Approach to Estimating Household Parameters', *Journal of Marketing Research*, vol. 30, pp. 171–182.

Rossi, P.E., R.E. McCulloch and G.M. Allenby (1996), 'The Value of Purchase History Data in Target Marketing', *Marketing Science*, vol. 15, pp. 321–340.

Roy, A., D.M. Hanssens and J.S. Raju (1994), 'Competitive Pricing by a Price Leader', *Management Science*, vol. 40, pp. 809–823.

Roy, R., P.K. Chintagunta and S. Haldar (1996), 'A Framework for Investigating Habits, 'The Hand of the Past', and Heterogeneity in Dynamic Brand Choice', *Marketing Science*, vol. 15, pp. 280–299.

Russell, G.J. (1988), 'Recovering Measures of Advertising Carryover from Aggregate Data: The Role of the Firm's Decision Behavior', *Marketing Science*, vol. 7, pp. 252–270.

Russell, G.J. and W.A. Kamakura (1994), 'Understanding Brand Competition Using Micro and Macro Scanner Data', *Journal of Marketing Research*, vol. 31, pp. 289–303.

Rust, R.T. (1988), 'Flexible Regression', *Journal of Marketing Research*, vol. 25, pp. 10–24.

Rust, R.T., C. Lee and E. Valente, jr. (1995), 'Comparing Covariance Structure Models: A General Methodology', *International Journal of Research in Marketing*, vol. 12, pp. 279–291.

Rust, R.T. and D.C. Schmittlein (1985), 'A Bayesian Cross-Validated Likelihood Method for Comparing Alternative Specifications of Quantitative Models', *Marketing Science*, vol. 4, pp. 20–45.

Rust, R.T., D. Simester, R.J. Brodie and V. Nilikant (1995), 'Model Selection Criteria: An Investigation of Relative Accuracy, Posterior Probabilities, and Combinations of Criteria', *Management Science*, vol. 41, pp. 322–333.

Savage, L.J. (1954), *The Foundations of Statistics*, John Wiley & Sons, New York.

Scales, L.E. (1985), *Introduction to Non-linear Optimization*, MacMillan, London.

Scheer van der, H.R. (1998), *Quantitative Approaches for Profit Maximization in Direct Marketing*, Unpublished Ph.D. thesis, University of Groningen, the Netherlands.

Scheer van der, H.R. and P.S.H. Leeflang (1997), 'Determining the Optimal Frequency of Direct Marketing Activities for Frequently Purchased Consumer Goods', Research Report 97B45, SOM, Research Institute Systems, Organisations and Management, University of Groningen, the Netherlands.

Schlaifer, R. (1969), *Analysis of Decisions under Uncertainty*, McGraw-Hill, New York.

Schmalensee, R.L. (1972), *The Economics of Advertising*, North-Holland Publishing Company, Amsterdam.

Schmittlein, D.C., L.C. Cooper and D.G. Morrison (1993), 'Truth in Concentration in the Land of (80/70) Laws', *Marketing Science*, vol. 12, pp. 167–183.

Schmittlein, D.C., D.G. Morrison and R. Colombo (1987), 'Counting Your Customers: Who Are They and What Will They Do Next?', *Management Science*, vol. 33, pp. 1–24.

Schmitz, J.D., G.D. Armstrong and J.D.C. Little (1990), 'Cover Story: Automated News Finding in Marketing' in: Bolino, L. (ed.), *DSS Transactions*, TIMS College on Information Systems, Rhode Island, Prov., pp.

46–54.

Schoemaker, P.J.H. (1995), 'Scenario Planning: A Tool for Strategic Thinking', *Sloan Management Review*, vol. 36, pp. 25–40.

Schultz, H. (1938), *The Theory and Measurement of Demand*, University of Chicago Press, Chicago.

Schultz, R.L. (1971), 'Market Measurement and Planning with a Simultaneous Equation Model', *Journal of Marketing Research*, vol. 8, pp. 153–164.

Schultz, R.L., M.J. Ginzberg and H.C. Lucas (1984), 'A Structural Model of Implementation' in Schultz, R.L. and M.J. Ginzberg (eds.), *Management Science Implementation*, GT:JAI Press, Greenwich, pp. 55–87.

Schultz, R.L. and M.D. Henry (1981), 'Implementing Decision Models' in Schultz, R.L. and A.A. Zoltners (eds.), *Marketing Decision Models*, North-Holland, New York, pp. 275–296.

Schultz, R.L. and D.P. Slevin (1975), 'A Program of Research on Implementation' in Schultz, R.L. and D.P. Slevin (eds.), *Implementing Operations Research/Management Science*, American Elsevier Publishing Company, New York, pp. 31–51.

Schultz, R.L. and D.P. Slevin (1977), 'An Innovation Process Perspective of Implementation', Paper No. 601, Krannert Graduate School of Management, Purdue University.

Schultz, R.L. and D.P. Slevin (1983), 'The Implementation Profile', *Interfaces*, vol. 13, pp. 87–92.

Schultz, R.L. and D.R. Wittink (1976), 'The Measurements of Industry Advertising Effects', *Journal of Marketing Research*, vol. 13, pp. 71–75.

Schultz, R.L. and A.A. Zoltners (eds.) (1981), *Marketing Decision Models*, North-Holland, New York.

Schwartz, G. (1978), 'Estimating the Dimension of a Model', *Annals of Statistics*, vol. 6, pp. 461–464.

Sethi, S.P. (1977), 'Dynamic Optimal Control Models in Advertising: A Survey', *SIAM Review*, vol. 19, pp. 685–725.

Sethuraman, R., V. Srinivasan and D. Kim (1999), 'Asymmetric and Neighborhood Cross-Price Effects: Some Emprirical Generalizations', *Marketing Science*, vol. 18, pp. 23–42.

Shakun, M.F. (1966), 'A Dynamic Model for Competitive Marketing in Coupled Markets', *Management Science*, vol. 12, pp. 525–530.

Shankar, V. (1997), 'Pioneers' Marketing Mix Reactions to Entry in Different Competitive Game Structures: Theoretical Analysis and Empirical Illustration', *Marketing Science*, vol.16, pp. 271–293.

Shapiro, S.S. and M.B. Wilk (1965), 'An Analysis of Variance Test for Normality', *Biometrika*, vol. 52, pp. 591–611.

Sharma, S. (1996), *Applied Multivariate Techniques*, John Wiley & Sons,, New York.

Shepard, D. (1990), *The New Direct Marketing: How to Implement a Profit-driven Database Marketing Strategy*, Business One: Irwin, Homewood, Ill.

Shocker, A.D., M. Ben-Akiva, B. Boccara and P. Nedungadi (1991), 'Consideration Set Influences on Consumer Decision Making and Choice: Issues, Models and Suggestions', *Marketing Letters*, vol. 2, pp. 181–198.

Shocker, A.D. and W.G. Hall (1986), 'Pretest Market Models: A Critical Evaluation', *Journal of Product Innovation Management*, vol. 15, pp. 171–191.

Shocker, A.D., D.W. Stewart and A.J. Zahorik (1990), 'Market Structure Analysis: Practice Problems, and Promise' in Day G., B. Weitz and R. Wensley (eds.), *The Interface of Marketing and Strategy*, JAI Press, Greenwich, CT, pp. 9–56.

Shoemaker, R.W. and L.G. Pringle (1980), 'Possible Biases in Parameter Estimation with Store Audit Data', *Journal of Marketing Research*, vol. 17, pp. 91–96.

Shugan, S.M. (1987), 'Estimating Brand Positioning Maps Using Scanning Data', *Journal of Marketing Research*, vol. 24, pp. 1–18.

Sichel, H.S. (1982), 'Repeat Buying and the Generalized Inverse Gaussian-Poisson Distribution', *Applied Statistics*, vol. 31, pp. 193–204.

Siddarth, S., R.E. Bucklin and D.G. Morrison (1995), 'Making the Cut: Modeling and Analyzing Choice Set Restriction in Scanner Panel Data', *Journal of Marketing Research*, vol. 32, pp. 255–266.

Sikkel, D. and A.W. Hoogendoorn (1995), 'Models for Monthly Penetrations with Incomplete Panel Data', *Statistica Neerlandica*, vol. 49, pp. 378–391.

Silk, A.J. and G.L. Urban (1978), 'Pre-Test-Market Evaluation of New Packaged Goods: A Model and Measurement Methodology', *Journal of Marketing Research*, vol. 15, pp. 171–191.

Silverman, B.W. (1986), *Density Estimation for Statistics and Data Analysis*, Monographs on Statistics and Applied Probability, vol. 26, Chapman & Hall, London.

Simon, C.J. and M.W. Sullivan (1993), 'The Measurement and Determinants of Brand Equity: A Financial Approach', *Marketing Science*, vol. 12, pp. 28–52.

Simon, H. (1984), 'Challanges and New Research Avenues in Marketing Science', *International Journal of Research in Marketing*, vol. 1, pp. 249–261.

Simon, H. (1994), 'Marketing Science's Pilgrimage to the Ivory Tower' in Laurent, G., G.L. Lilien and B. Pras (eds.), *Research Traditions in Marketing*, Kluwer Academic Publishers, Boston, pp. 27–43.

Simon, L.S. and M. Freimer (1970), *Analytical Marketing*, Harcourt, Brace & World, New York.

Sims, C.A. (1972), 'Money, Income and Causality', *American Economic Review*, vol. 62, pp. 540–552.

Sims, C.A. (1980), 'Microeconomics and Reality', *Econometrica*, vol. 48, pp. 1–48.

Sinha, R.K. and M. Chandrashekaran (1992), 'A Split Hazard Model for Analysing the Diffusion of Innovations', *Journal of Marketing Research*, vol. 24, pp. 116–127.

Sirohi, N. (1999), *Essays on Bundling*, Unpublished Ph.D. thesis, Cornell University.

Sirohi, N., E.W. McLaughlin and D.R. Wittink (1998), 'A Model of Consumer Perceptions and Store Loyalty Intentions for a Supermarket Retailer', *Journal of Retailing*, vol. 74, pp. 223–245.

Skiera, B. and S. Albers (1998), 'COSTA: Contribution Optimizing Sales Territory Alignment', *Marketing Science*, vol. 17, pp. 196–213.

Smee, C., M. Parsonage, R. Anderson and S. Duckworth (1992), *Effect of Tobacco Advertising on Tobacco Consumption: A Discussion Document Reviewing the Evidence*, Economics & Operational Research Division Department of Health, London.

Smith, L.H. (1967), 'Ranking Procedures and Subjective Probability Distribution', *Management Science*, vol. 14, pp. B236–B249.

Smith, S.A., S.H. McIntyre and D.D. Achabal (1994), 'A Two-stage Sales Forecasting Procedure Using Discounted Least Squares', *Journal of Marketing Research*, vol. 31, pp. 44–65.

Smith, S.V., R.H. Brien and J.E. Stafford (1968), 'Marketing Information Systems: An Introductory Overview' in Smith, S.V., R.H. Brien and J.E. Stafford (eds.), *Readings in Marketing Information Systems*, Houghton Mifflin Company, Boston, pp. 1–14.

Solow, R.M. (1960), 'On a Family of Lag Distributions', *Econometrica*, vol. 28, pp. 393–406.

Spring, P., P.S.H. Leeflang and T.J. Wansbeek (1999), 'Simultaneous Target Selection and Offer Segmentation: A Modeling Approach', *Journal of Market-Focussed Management*, vol 4, pp. 187–203.

Srinivasan, V. (1976), 'Decomposition of a Multi-Period Media Scheduling Model in Terms of Single Period Equivalents', *Management Science*, vol. 23, pp. 349–360.

Srinivasan, V. and H.A. Weir (1988), 'A Direct Approach for Inferring Micro-Parameters of the Koyck Advertising-Sales Relationship from Macro Data', *Journal of Marketing Research*, vol. 25, pp. 145–156.

Srivastava, R.K., M.I. Alpert and A.D. Shocker (1984), 'A Customer-oriented Approach for Determining Market Structures', *Journal of Marketing*, vol. 48, 2, pp. 32–45.

Steenkamp, J.B.E.M. (1989), *Product Quality*, Van Gorcum, Assen.

Steenkamp, J.B.E.M. and H. Baumgartner (1998), 'Assessing Measurement Invariance in Cross-National Cunsumer Research', *Journal of Consumer Research*, vol. 25, pp. 78–90.

Steenkamp, J.B.E.M. and M.G. Dekimpe (1997), 'The Power of Store Brands: Intrinsic Loyalty and Conquesting Power', Onderzoeksrapport nr. 9706, Departement Toegepaste Economische Wetenschappen, Katholieke Universiteit Leuven, België.

Steenkamp, J.B.E.M. and H.C.M. van Trijp (1991), 'The Use of LISREL in Validating Marketing Constructs', *International Journal for Research in Marketing*, vol. 8, pp. 283–300.

Stewart, J. (1991), *Econometrics*, Philip Allan, Hemel Hemstead.

Styan, G.P.H. and H. Smith jr. (1964), 'Markov Chains Applied to Marketing', *Journal of Marketing Research*, vol. 1, pp. 50–55.

Sunde, L. and R.J. Brodie (1993), 'Consumer Evaluations of Brand Extensions: Further Empirical Results', *International Journal of Research in Marketing*, vol. 10, pp. 47–53.

Swamy, P.A.V.B. (1970), 'Efficient Inference in a Random Coefficient Regression Model', *Econometrica*, vol. 38, pp. 311–323.

Swamy, P.A.V.B. (1971), *Statistical Inference in Random Coefficient Regression Models*, Springer-Verlag, New York.

Swanson, E.B. (1974), 'Management Information Systems: Appreciation and Involvement', *Management Science*, vol. 21, pp. 178–188.

Talwar, P. (1974), 'Robust Estimation of Regression Parameters', Unpublished Ph.D. thesis, Carnegie-Mellon University.

Taylor, C.J. (1963), 'Some Developments in the Theory and Application of Media Scheduling Methods', *Operations Research Quarterly*, vol. 14, pp. 291–305.

Tellis, G.J. (1988a), 'Advertising Exposure, Brand Loyalty and Brand Purchase: A Two-Stage Model of Choice', *Journal of Marketing Research*, vol. 25, pp. 134–144.

Tellis, G.J. (1988b), 'The Price Elasticity of Selective Demand: A Meta-Analysis of Econometric Models of Sales', *Journal of Marketing Research*, vol. 25, pp. 331–341.

Tellis, G.J. and C.M. Crawford (1981), 'An Evolutionary Approach to Product Growth Theory', *Journal of Marketing*, vol. 45, October, pp. 125–132.

Tellis, G.J. and C. Fornell (1988), 'The Relationship between Advertising and Product Quality over the Product Life Cycle: A Contingency Theory', *Journal of Marketing Research*, vol. 25, pp. 64–71.

Tellis, G.J. and F.S. Zufryden (1995), 'Tackling the Retailer Decision Maze: Which Brands to Discount, How Much, When and Why?', *Marketing Science*, vol.14, pp 271–299.

Telser, L.G. (1962a), 'The Demand for Branded Goods as Estimated from Consumer Panel Data', *Review of Economics and Statistics*, vol. 44, pp. 300–324.

Telser, L.G. (1962b), 'Advertising and Cigarettes', *Journal of Political Economy*, vol. 70, pp. 471–499.

Telser, L.G. (1963), 'Least Squares Estimates of Transition Probabilities', in *Measurement of Economics*, Stanford, Stanford University Press, pp. 270–292.

Teng, J.T. and G.L. Thompson (1983), 'Oligopoly Models for Optimal Advertising when Production Costs Obey a Learning Curve', *Management Science*, vol. 29, pp. 1087–1101.

Theil, H. (1965a), 'The Analysis of Disturbances in Regression Analysis', *Journal of the American Statistical Association*, vol. 60, pp. 1067–1079.

Theil, H. (1965b), *Economic Forecasts and Policy*, North-Holland Publishing Company, Amsterdam.

Theil, H. (1969), 'A Multinomial Extension of the Linear Logit Model', *International Economic Review*, vol. 10, pp. 251–259.

Theil, H. (1971), *Principles of Econometrics*, John Wiley & Sons, New York.

Theil, H. (1975), *Theory and Measurement of Consumer Demand*, vol. 1, North-Holland Publishing Company, Amsterdam.

Theil, H. (1976), *Theory and Measurement of Consumer Demand*, vol. 2, North-Holland Publishing Company, Amsterdam.

Theil, H. and A. Schweitzer (1961), 'The Best Quadratic Estimator of the Residual Variance in Regression Analysis', *Statistica Neerlandica*, vol. 15, pp. 19–23.

Thomas, J.J. and K.F. Wallis (1971), 'Seasonal Variation in Regression Analysis', *Journal of the Royal Statistical Society, Series A*, vol. 134, pp. 67–72.

Thursby, J.G. and P. Schmidt (1977), 'Some Properties of Tests for Specification Error in a Linear Regression Model', *Journal of the American Statistical Association*, vol. 63, pp. 558–582.

Tinbergen, J. (1966), *Economic Policy: Principles and Design*, North-Holland Publishing Company.

Titterington, D.M., A.F.M. Smith and U.E. Makov (1985), *Statistical Analysis of Finite Mixture Distributions*, John Wiley & Sons, New York.

Todd, P. and I. Benbasat (1994), 'The Influence of Decision Aids on Choice Strategies: An Experimental Analysis of the Role of Cognitive Effort', *Organizational Behavior and Human Decision Processes*, vol. 60, pp. 36–74.

Torgerson, W. (1959), *Theory and Methods of Measurement*, John Wiley & Sons, New York.

Tsay, R.S. and G.C. Tiao (1984), 'Consistent Estimates of Autoregressive Parameters and Extended Sample Autocorrelation Function for Stationary and Nonstationary ARMA Models', *Journal of the American Statistical Association*, vol. 79, pp. 84–96.

Tversky, A. (1972), 'Elimination by Aspects: A Theory of Choice', *Psychological Review*, vol. 79, pp. 281–299.

Uncles, M., A.S.C. Ehrenberg and K. Hammond (1995), 'Patterns of Buyer Behavior: Regularities, Models and Extensions', *Marketing Science*, vol. 14, pp. G71–G78.

Urban, G.L. (1968), 'A New Product Analysis and Decision Model', *Management Science*, vol. 14, pp. 490–517.

Urban, G.L. (1969a), 'SPRINTER Mod. II: Basic New Product Analysis Model' in Morin, B.A. (ed.), *Proceedings of the National Conference of the American Marketing Association*, pp. 139–150.

Urban, G.L. (1969b), 'A Mathematical Modeling Approach to Product Line Decisions', *Journal of Marketing Research*, vol. 6, pp. 40–47.

Urban, G.L. (1970), 'SPRINTER Mod. III: A Model for the Analysis of New Frequently Purchased Consumer Products', *Operations Research*, vol. 18, pp. 805–854.

Urban, G.L. (1971), 'Advertising Budgeting and Geographical Allocation: A Decision Calculus Approach', Working Paper 532-71 (revised), Alfred P. Sloan School Management, M.I.T.

Urban, G.L. (1972), 'An Emerging Process of Building Models for Management Decision Makers', Working Paper No. 591-72, Alfred P. Sloan School of Management, M.I.T.

Urban, G.L. (1974), 'Building Models for Decision Makers', *Interfaces*, vol. 4, pp. 1–11.

Urban, G.L. (1993), 'Pretest Market Forecasting' in Eliashberg, J. and G.L. Lilien (eds.), *Handbooks in Operations Research and Management Science, vol. 5, Marketing*, North-Holland, Amsterdam, pp. 315–348.

Urban, G.L. and J.R. Hauser (1980), *Design and Marketing of New Products*, Englewood Cliffs, Prentice-Hall, NJ.

Urban, G.L. and J.R. Hauser (1993), *Design and Marketing New Products*, 2nd ed., Prentice-Hall, Englewood Cliffs, NJ.

Urban, G.L., J.R. Hauser and J.H. Roberts (1990), 'Prelaunch Forecasting of New Automobiles: Models and Implementation', *Management Science*, vol. 36, pp. 401–421.

Urban, G.L. and R. Karash (1971), 'Evolutionary Model Building', *Journal of Marketing Research*, vol. 8, pp. 62–66.

Urban, G.L. and M. Katz (1983), 'Pre-test-markets Models: Validation and Managerial Implications', *Journal of Marketing Research*, vol. 20, pp. 221–234.

US DHHS, US Department of Health and Human Services (1989), *Reducing the Health Consequences of Smoking: Twenty-five Years of Progress*, a Report of the US Surgeon General, DHHS Publication (CDC), 89-8411.

Vanden Abeele, P. (1975), *An Investigation of Errors in the Variables on the Estimation of Linear Models in a Marketing Context*, Unpublished Ph.D. thesis, Stanford University.

Vanden Abeele, P. and E. Gijsbrechts (1991), 'Modeling Aggregate Outcomes of Heterogeneous non-IIA Choice', *EMAC 1991 Annual Conference Proceedings*, Michael Smurfit Graduate Business School, University College, Dublin, pp. 484–508.

Vanden Abeele, P., E. Gijsbrechts and M. Vanhuele (1990), 'Specification and Empirical Evaluation of a Cluster-Asymmetry Market Share Model', *International Journal of Research in Marketing*, vol. 7, pp. 223–247.

Vanden Bulte, C. and G. L. Lilien (1997), 'Bias and Systematic Change in the Parameter Estimates of Macro-Level Diffusion Models', *Marketing Science*, vol. 16, pp. 338–353.

Van der Werf, P.A. and J.F. Mahan (1997), 'Meta Analysis of the Impact of Research Methods on Findings of First-Mover Advantage', *Management Science*, vol. 43, pp. 1510–1519.

Vanhonacker, W.R. (1988), 'Estimating an Autoregressive Current Effects Model of Sales Response when Observations are Aggregated over Time: Least Squares versus Maximum Likelihood', *Journal of Marketing Research*, vol. 15, pp. 301–307.

Verhoef, P.C., Franses, P.H. and J.C. Hoekstra (2000), 'The Impact of Satisfaction on the Breadth of the Relationship with a Multi-Service Provider', Working Paper, Rotterdam Institute of Business Economic Studies (RIBES).

Verhulp, J. (1982), *The Commercial Optimum, Theory and Application*, Unpublished Ph.D. thesis, Erasmus University, Rotterdam.

Vidale, H.L. and H.B. Wolfe (1957), 'An Operations-Research Study of Sales Response to Advertising', *Operations Research*, vol. 5, pp. 370–381.

Vilcassim, N.J. (1989), 'Extending the Rotterdam Model to Test Hierarchical Market Structures', *Marketing Science*, vol. 8, pp. 181–190.

Vilcassim, N.J. and D.C. Jain (1991), 'Modeling Purchase-Timing and Brand-Switching Behavior Incorporating Explanatory Variables and Unobserved Heterogeneity', *Journal of Marketing Research*, vol. 28, pp. 29–41.

Vilcassim, N.J., V. Kadiyali and P.K. Chintagunta (1999), 'Investigating Dynamic Multifirm Market Interactions in Price and Advertising', *Management Science*, vol. 45, pp. 499–518.

Vuong, Q.H. (1989), 'Likelihood Ratio Tests for Model Selection and Non-Nested Hypotheses', *Econometrica*, vol. 57, pp. 307–333.

Vyas, N. and A.G. Woodside (1984), 'An Inductive Model of Industrial Supplier Choice Processes', *Journal of Marketing*, vol. 48, Winter, pp. 30–45.

Waarts, E., M. Carree and B. Wierenga (1991), 'Full-information Maximum Likelihood Estimation of Brand

Positioning Maps Using Supermarkt Scanning Data', *Journal of Marketing Research*, vol. 28, pp. 483–490.

Wallace, T.D. (1972), 'Weaker Criteria and Tests for Linear Restrictions in Regression', *Econometrica*, vol. 40, pp. 689–698.

Walters , R.G. (1991), 'Assessing the Impact of Retail Price Promotions on Product Substitution, Complementary Purchase, and Interstore Sales Displacement', *Journal of Marketing*, vol. 55, April, pp. 17–28.

Wansbeek, T.W. and M. Wedel (1999), 'Marketing and Economics: Editor's Introduction', *Journal of Econometrics*, vol. 189, pp. 1–14.

Watson, G.S. (1964), 'Smooth Regression Analysis', *Sankhyā Ser.*, vol. A 26, pp. 359–372.

Webster, F.E. (1992), 'The Changing Role of Marketing in the Corporation', *Journal of Marketing*, vol. 56, October, pp. 1–17.

Webster, F.E. (1994), *Market Driven Management*, John Wiley & Sons, New York.

Wedel, M. and W.S. DeSarbo (1994), 'A Review of Latent Class Regression Models and Their Applications' in Bagozzi, R.P. (ed.), *Advanced Methods for Marketing Research*, Blackwell, Cambridge, pp. 353–388.

Wedel, M. and W.S. DeSarbo (1995), 'A Mixture Likelihood Approach for Generalized Linear Models', *Journal of Classification*, vol. 12, pp. 1–35.

Wedel, M.. W.S. DeSarbo, J.R. Bult and V. Ramaswamy (1993), 'A Latent Class Poisson Regression Model for Heterogeneous Count Data', *Journal of Applied Econometrics*, vol. 8, pp. 397–411.

Wedel, M. and W.A. Kamakura (1998), *Market Segmentation: Conceptual and Methodological Foundations*, Kluwer Academic Publishers, Boston.

Wedel, M., W.A. Kamakura, N. Arora, A.C. Bemmaor, J. Chiang, T. Elrod, R. Johnson, P. Lenk, S.A. Neslin and C.S. Poulsen (1999), 'Discrete and Continuous Representations of Unobserved Heterogeneity in Choice Modeling', *Marketing Letters*, vol. 10, pp. 219–232.

Wedel, M., W.A. Kamakura, W.S. DeSarbo and F. Ter Hofstede (1995), 'Implications for Asymmetry, Nonproportionality, and Heterogeneity in Brand Switching from Piece-wise Exponential Mixture Hazard Models', *Journal of Marketing Research*, vol. 32, pp. 457–463.

Wedel, M. and P.S.H. Leeflang (1998), 'A Model for the Effects of Psychological Pricing in Gabor-Granger Price Studies', *Journal of Economic Psychology*, vol. 19, pp. 237–260.

Wedel, M., M. Vriens, T.H.A. Bijmolt, W. Krijnen and P.S.H. Leeflang (1998), 'Assessing the Effects of Abstract Attributes and Brand Familiarity in Conjoint Choice Experiments', *International Journal of Research in Marketing*, vol. 15, pp. 71–78.

Weerahandi, S. and S.R. Dalal (1992), 'A Choice Based Approach to the Diffusion of a Service: Forecasting Fax Penetration by Market Segments', *Marketing Science*, vol. 11, pp. 39–53.

Weiss, P.L. and P.M. Windal (1980), 'Testing Cumulative Advertising Effects: A Comment on Methodology', *Journal of Marketing Research*, vol. 17, pp. 371–378.

Weverbergh, M. (1976), 'Restrictions on Linear Sum-Constrained Models: A Generalization', Working Paper No. 76–17, Centre for Managerial Economics and Econometrics, UFSIA, University of Antwerp.

Weverbergh, M. (1977), *Competitive Bidding: Games, Decisions, and Cost Uncertainty*, Unpublished Ph.D. thesis, UFSIA, University of Antwerp, Belgium.

Weverbergh, M., Ph.A. Naert and A. Bultez (1977), 'Logically Consistent Market Share Models: A Further Clarification', Working Paper No. 77-5, European Institute for Advanced Studies in Management, Brussels, Belgium.

Wheat, R.D. and D.G. Morrisson (1990), 'Estimating Purchase Regularity with Two Interpurchase Times', *Journal of Marketing Research*, vol. 27, pp. 87–93.

White, H. (1980), 'A Heteroscedasticity-Consistent Covariance Matrix Estimator and a Direct Test for Heteroscedasticity', *Econometrica*, vol. 48, pp. 817–838.

Wierenga, B. (1974), *An Investigation of Brand Choice Processes*, Rotterdam, Rotterdam University Press.

Wierenga, B. (1978), 'A Least Squares Estimation Method for the Linear Learning Model', *Journal of Marketing Research*, vol. 15, pp. 145-153.

Wierenga, B. and G.H. van Bruggen (1997), 'The Integration of Marketing Problem Solving Modes and Marketing Management Support Systems', *Journal of Marketing*, vol. 6, July, pp. 21–37.

Wierenga, B. and G.H. van Bruggen (2000), *Marketing Management Support Systems: Principles, Tools, and Implementation*, Kluwer Academic Publishers, Boston.

Wilde, D.J. and C.S. Beightler (1967), *Foundations of Optimization*, Prentice-Hall, Englewood Cliffs, NJ.

Wildt, A.R. (1993), 'Equity Estimation and Assessing Market Response', *Journal of Marketing Research*, vol. 30, pp. 437–451.

Wildt, A.R. and R.S. Winer (1983), 'Modeling and Estimation in Changing Market Environments', *Journal of Business*, vol. 56, pp. 365–388.

Wind, Y. (1981), 'Marketing Oriented Strategic Planning Models' in Schultz, R.L. and A.A. Zoltners (eds.), *Marketing Decision Models*, North-Holland, New York, pp. 207–250.

Wind, Y. (1982), *Product Policy: Concepts, Methods, and Strategy*, Addison-Wesley Publishing Company, Reading, Massachusetts.

Wind, Y., P.E. Green, D. Shifflet and M. Scarbrough (1989), 'Courtyard by Marriott: Designing a Hotel Facility with Consumer-Based Marketing Models', *Interfaces*, vol. 19, pp. 25–47.

Wind, Y. and G.L. Lilien (1993), 'Marketing Strategy Models' in Eliashberg, J. and G.L. Lilien (eds.), *Handbooks in Operations Research and Management Science, vol. 5, Marketing*, North-Holland, Amsterdam, pp. 773–826.

Wind, Y., V. Mahajan and D.J. Swire (1983), 'An Empirical Comparison of Standardized Portfolio Models', *Journal of Marketing*, vol. 47, no. 2, pp. 89–99.

Winkler, R.L. (1967a), 'The Assessment of Prior Distributions in Bayesian Analysis', *Journal of the American Statistical Association*, vol. 62, pp. 776–800.

Winkler, R.L. (1967b), 'The Quantification of Judgment: Some Methodological Suggestions', *Journal of the American Statistical Association*, vol. 62, pp. 1105–1120.

Winkler, R.L. (1967c), 'The Quantification of Judgment: Some Experimental Results', *Proceedings of the American Statistical Association*, pp. 386–395.

Winkler, R.L. (1968), 'The Consensus of Subjective Probability Distributions', *Management Science*, vol. 15, pp. B61–B75.

Winkler, R.L. (1986), 'Expert Resolution', *Management Science*, vol. 32, pp. 298–303.

Winkler, R.L. (1987), 'Judgmental and Bayesian Forecasting' in Makridakis, S. and S.C. Wheelwright (eds.), *The Handbook of Forecasting*, John Wiley & Sons, New York, pp. 248–265.

Wittink, D.R. (1977), 'Explaining Territorial Differences in the Relationship Between Marketing Variables', *Journal of Marketing Research*, vol. 14, pp. 145–155.

Wittink, D.R. (1987), 'Causal Market Share Models in Marketing: Neither Forecasting nor Understanding?', *International Journal of Forecasting*, vol. 3, pp. 445–448.

Wittink, D.R. (1988), *The Application of Regression Analysis*, Allyn and Bacon, Boston.

Wittink, D.R., M.J. Addona, W.J. Hawkes and J.C. Porter (1988), 'SCAN*PRO: The Estimation, Validation and Use of Promotional Effects Based on Scanner Data', Internal paper, Cornell University.

Wittink, D.R. and S.K. Keil (2000), 'Continuous Conjoint Analysis' in Gustafsson, A., A. Herrman and F. Huber (eds.), *Conjoint Measurement: Methods and Applications*, Prentice-Hall, Europe, forthcoming.

Wittink, D.R., M. Vriens and W. Burhenne (1994), 'Commercial Use of Conjoint Analysis in Europe: Results and Critical Reflections', *International Journal of Research in Marketing*, vol. 11, pp. 41–52.

Wold, F.M. (1986), *Meta Analysis: Quantitative Methods for Research Synthesis*, California Sage Press, Newburg Park.

Wonnacott, R.J. and T.H. Wonnacott (1970), *Econometrics*, John Wiley & Sons, New York.

Wonnacott, T.H. and R.J. Wonnacott (1969), *Introductory Statistics*, John Wiley and Sons, New York.

Yi, Y. (1989), 'An Investigation of the Structure of Expectancy-Value Attitude and its Implications', *International Journal of Research in Marketing*, vol. 6, pp. 71–84.

Yon, B. (1976), *Le Comportement Marketing de l'Entreprise: Une Approche Econométrique*, Dunod, Paris.

Zaltman, G., C.R.A. Pinson and R. Angelmar (1973), *Metatheory and Consumer Research*, Holt, Rinehart and Winston, New York.

Zellner, A. (1962), 'An Efficient Method of Estimating Seemingly Unrelated Regressions and Tests for Aggregation Bias', *Journal of the American Statistical Association*, vol. 57, pp. 348–368.

Zellner, A. (1971), *An Introduction to Bayesian Inference in Econometrics*, John Wiley & Sons, New York.

Zellner, A. (1979), 'Causality and Econometrics' in Brunner, K. and A.H. Meltzer (eds.), *Three Aspects of Policy and Policy-making: Knowledge, Data and Institutions*, North-Holland, Amsterdam, pp. 9–54.

Zellner, A. and M.M. Geisel (1970), 'Analysis of Distributed Lag Models with Applications to Consumption Function Estimation', *Econometrica*, vol. 38, pp. 865–888.

Zenor, M.J. (1994), 'The Profit Benefits of Category Management', *Journal of Marketing Research*, vol. 94, pp. 202–213.

Zentler, A.P. and D. Ryde (1956), 'An Optimum Geographical Distribution of Publicity Expenditure in a Private Organisation', *Management Science*, vol. 2, pp. 337–352.

Zmud, R.W. (1979), 'Individual Differences and MIS Success: A Review of the Empirical Literature', *Management Science*, vol. 25, pp. 966–979.

Zoltners, A.A. (1976), 'Integer Programming Models for Sales Territory Alignment to Maximize Profit', *Journal of Marketing Research*, vol. 13, pp. 426–430.

Zoltners, A.A. (1981), 'Normative Marketing Models' in Schultz, R.L. and A.A. Zoltners (eds.), *Marketing Decision Models*, North-Holland, New York, pp. 55–76.

Zoltners, A.A. (1982), *Marketing Planning Models*, North-Holland Publishing Company, Amsterdam.

Zoltners, A.A. and P. Sinha (1983), 'Sales Territory Alignment: A Review and Model', *Management Science*, vol. 29, pp. 1237–1256.

Zufryden, F.S. (1981), 'A Logit-Markovian Model of Consumer Purchase Behaviour Based on Explanatory Variables: Empirical Evaluation and Implications for Decision Making', *Decision Sciences*, vol. 12, pp. 645–660.

Zufryden, F.S. (1982), 'A General Model for Assessing New Product Marketing Decisions and Market Performance', *TIMS/Studies in the Management Sciences*, vol. 18, pp. 63–82.

Zufryden, F.S. (1986), 'Multibrand Transition Probabilities as a Function of Explanatory Variables: Estimation by a Least Squares Approach', *Journal of Marketing Research*, vol. 23, pp. 177–183.

Zwart, P.S. (1983), *Beslissingsprocessen van Detaillisten een Toepassing in de Drogistenbranche*, Unpublished Ph.D. thesis, Universtiy of Groningen, the Netherlands.

Author Index

Bagozzi, R.P., H. Baumgartner and Y. Yi (1992), 196

Bagozzi, R.P. and A.J. Silk (1983), 198

Bai, J. and P. Perron (1998), 557

Balasubramanian, S. (1998), 567

Balasubramanian, S.K. and A.K. Ghosh (1992), 131

Balasubramanian, S.K. and D.C. Jain (1994), 494

Balderston, F.E. and A.C. Hogatt (1962), 195

Baligh, H.H. and L.E. Richartz (1967), 215

Baltagi, B.H. (1998), 323

Balzer, W.K., L.M. Sulsky, L.B. Hammer and K.E. Sumner (1992), 431

Banslaben, J. (1992), 552

Barnett, A.I. (1976), 172

Barr, S.H. and R. Sharda (1997), 544

Barten, A.P. (1977), 167

Bass, F.M. (1969a), 203, 381, 487

Bass, F.M. (1969b), 184, 188, 551

Bass, F.M. (1971), 381

Bass, F.M. (1986), 187

Bass, F.M. (1995), 30, 31

Bass, F.M. and D.G. Clarke (1972), 91, 96, 98

Bass, F.M., T.V. Krishnan and D.C. Jain (1994), 187

Bass, F.M. and R.P. Leone (1986), 280

Bass, F.M. and L.J. Parsons (1969), 381

Bass, F.M. and T.L. Pilon (1980), 464, 468

Bass, F.M. and Y. Wind (1995), 32

Bass, F.M. and D.R. Wittink (1975), 267, 281, 361, 363, 365

Basu, A.K., R. Lal, V. Srinivasan and R. Staelin (1985), 150

Basuroy, S. and D. Nguyen (1998), 172

Batra, R., J.G. Myers and D.A. Aaker (1996), 15

Batsell, R.R. and J.C. Polking (1985), 284, 285

Baumol, W. J. and T. Fabian (1964), 107

Bayer, J., S. Lawrence and J.W. Keon (1988), 306

Bayus, B.L., S. Hong and R.P. Labe (1989), 181

Bayus, B.L. and R. Mehta (1995), 228–230

Beach, W.O. and V. Barnes (1987), 421

Bearden, W.O., R.G. Netemeyer and M.F. Mobley (1993), 303

Bearden, W.O. and J.E. Teel (1983), 198

Beckwith, N.E. (1972), 167

Bell, D.E., R.L. Keeney and J.D.C. Little (1975), 171

Bell, D.R., J. Chiang and V. Padmanabhan (1997), 254, 566

Bell, D.R., J. Chiang and V. Padmanabhan (1999), 254, 566

Bell, D.R., T. Ho and C.S. Tang (1998), 9

Belsley, D.A. (1991), 358

Belsley, D.A., E. Kuh and R.E. Welsh (1980), 358

Bemmaor, A.C. (1984), 73

Bemmaor, A.C., Ph.H. Franses and J. Kippers (1999), 363

Bemmaor, A.C. and D. Mouchoux (1991), 25

Ben-Akiva, M. and S.R. Lerman (1985), 161, 162, 175, 243

Benbasat, I. and P. Todd (1996), 527, 529, 531, 536, 546, 547

Benson, P.G., S.P. Curley and F.G. Smith (1995), 421

Bentler, P.M. (1990), 446

Bera, A.K. and C.M. Jarque (1981), 344

Bera, A.K. and C.M. Jarque (1982), 344

Berndt, E.R. (1991), 323

Bertrand, J. (1883), 217

Bijmolt, T.H.A. (1996), 286

Leeflang, P.S.H. and J.C. Reuyl (1984a), 112, 113, 119, 283

Leeflang, P.S.H. and J.C. Reuyl (1984b), 376

Leeflang, P.S.H. and J.C. Reuyl (1985a), 90, 166

Leeflang, P.S.H. and J.C. Reuyl (1985b), 155, 204, 513

Leeflang, P.S.H. and J.C. Reuyl (1986), 268

Leeflang, P.S.H. and J.C. Reuyl (1995), 166, 409

Leeflang, P.S.H. and M. Wedel (1993), 106

Leeflang, P.S.H. and D.R. Wittink (1992), 201, 206–209, 497

Leeflang, P.S.H. and D.R. Wittink (1994), 201, 286

Leeflang, P.S.H. and D.R. Wittink (1996), 201, 209–211, 214, 215, 286

Leeflang, P.S.H. and D.R. Wittink (2000), 211

Lehmann, E.L. (1983), 416

Leigh, T.W. and A.J. Rethans (1984), 127

Leone, R.P. (1983), 468

Leone, R.P. (1995), 31, 90, 279, 280

Leone, R.P. and R.L. Schultz (1980), 31, 166, 485

Lilien, G.L. (1974a), 240

Lilien, G.L. (1974b), 240

Lilien, G.L. (1975), 11

Lilien, G.L. (1979), 126

Lilien, G.L. (1994), 540

Lilien, G.L. and P. Kotler (1983), 3, 86, 416, 417, 424

Lilien, G.L., P. Kotler and K.S. Moorthy (1992), 3, 15, 25, 38, 126, 157–159, 382, 549

Lilien, G.L. and A. Rangaswamy (1998), 11, 184–186, 193, 306, 415, 433

Lindsey, J.K. (1996), 393, 394

Little, J.D.C. (1966), 108

Little, J.D.C. (1970), 5, 53, 81, 101, 104, 108, 120, 417, 420, 556

Little, J.D.C. (1975a), 5, 101, 108, 420, 536

Little, J.D.C. (1975b), 5, 27, 79, 108, 420, 436, 533, 534

Little, J.D.C. (1979), 66

Little, J.D.C. (1998), 314, 316

Little, J.D.C. and L.M. Lodish (1969), 80, 152

Little, J.D.C. and L.M. Lodish (1981), 420

Little, J.D.C., L.M. Lodish, J.R. Hauser and G.L. Urban (1994), 557

Lock, A. (1987), 432

Lodish, L.M. (1971), 22, 150, 153, 420, 559

Lodish, L.M. (1981), 536

Lodish, L.M. (1982), 536

Lodish, L.M., M.M. Abraham, S. Kalmenson, J. Livelsberger, B. Lubetkin, B. Richardson and M.E. Stevens (1995a), 31, 315

Lodish, L.M., M.M. Abraham, J. Livelsberger, B. Lubetkin, B. Richardson and M.E. Stevens (1995b), 31, 90, 315, 485

Lodish, L.M., E. Curtis, M. Ness and M.K. Simpson (1988), 150, 559

Lodish, L.M., D.B. Montgomery and F.E. Webster (1968), 80

Logman, M. (1995), 75

Long, S. (1983), 441

Louvière, J.J. and D.A. Hensher (1983), 241

Louvière, J.J. and G. Woodworth (1983), 241, 303

Lucas, H.C., M.J. Ginzberg and R.L. Schultz (1990), 527

Lucas, R.E. (1976), 558

Luce, R.D. (1959), 175, 241

Luce, R.D. and H. Raiffa (1957), 215

Luik, J.C. and M.J. Waterson (1996), 166, 562

Subject Index